THE BIOGRAPHY OF A CATHEDRAL

Saint Louis Carries the Crown of Thorns
into the Cathedral

The Biography of a Cathedral

The Living Story of Man's Most Beautiful
Creation, with Glimpses, through the Centuries, of the Pageant that Led to Notre Dame

by

ROBERT GORDON ANDERSON

LONGMANS, GREEN AND CO.

NEW YORK   TORONTO

1945

Contents

v

To

MARION ANDERSON

JULIE KERNAN

GEORGE BYE

with the deep gratitude of the author for their invaluable counsel, unwavering support, and heart-warming faith.

R. G. A.

THE BIOGRAPHY OF A CATHEDRAL

Proscenium

HE CATHEDRAL WAS A MAGNIFICENT GESTURE, THE NOBLEST, perhaps, ever made by man, upflung in pride in himself, entreaty to the Unknown, in fear and delight, then arrested forever against the sky.

The Cathedral too was a dream of what Heaven might be, made visible with stone forest-aisle and sunset pane. And within, by its altar, Heaven's own drama for eight hundred years has been played, with chant, bright robes and candles, the bread, the wine, and believing souls. About Man's relationship to the Unknown, his reunion with God, it is the greatest drama, the most sacred mystery in the world. And to house it, he built this, the loftiest shrine yet, and the most glorious ever, before or since, seen in this world.

In its heart is relived the great mystery. And its body is a beautiful miracle. But it is more than a noble gesture and miracle. It is also a sublimely concrete fact. No building, pyramid, Greek temple, Roman Pantheon, castle, skyscraper, community center ever so completely blended art and engineering and functionalism with the aspiration and the dream. Each lovely part has a practical or morally strategic purpose; the very adornments in flowering stone often being actual integers in the vast sum of weight and thrust. Though built of apparently unyielding stone and metal, the whole is a beautifully articulated and elastic organism. The infinite complexities of vault, course, buttress, of altar, bay, gargoyle, are united in service. Design of a superb competence and magnificent daring dominates and harmonizes all into an amazing unit. And the whole is ennobled by one of the greatest group aspirations of the race in one of those high tides of creative energy that rise only at rare intervals out of the ocean of time.

So it takes little straining of the fancy to humanize the Cathedral. Nor does its personalization even begin to affront common sense. Men poured life enough into it long ago.

And these tall glorious shrines, which are the most magnificent of man's monuments, and yet are no cold monuments, because they are still so glowingly alive, have the most vivid of biographies. They took part in so many of their creators' lives; in countless births and christenings of the illustrious, the humble, in committing innumerable throngs to the dust. They sent out men on crusades and voyages that changed the frontiers of the world and the mind. From them others went forth to discover whole new whirling

1

worlds in little retorts. Their bells have clanged out warnings, alarums; have sounded the death knell of old orders, the tocsin to the new. The confessionals have heard royal unburdenings of guilt, the transepts thieves' whispers. Their altars have been stained with blood.

The Cathedral was designed as a meeting-place of God with man and man with God. It was not only a place of worship apart, for no community center ever served so well God, and race, and state. It was holy of holies, council chamber, chief monument, symbol of race pride, university for the wise and library for the unlettered where they might hear fine music and look into picture books of coloured glass and stone. And, too, it was the cradle of parliaments and trade unions, parade ground for cardinals and generals and kings.

And far, far back should its biography go, further than any consecration or cornerstone-laying. For no life begins with its actual birth or ends with its death, but is with its ancestors and descendants part of a continuing life sequence. The Cathedral's biography has to do with the dawn of the world. The men who walked the earth and painted caves and chipped flint, built those great dolmen-roofed tombs, and threw into them their messages to the Unknown, their letters to the dead. So generations unnumbered tried, with groping fingers, to tear aside the curtain that hides the Unknown, developed creeds out of successive hypotheses of that other life to which all the Cathedral's ancestors—the dolmen, Druid altar, Roman temple, Christian basilica, and the Cathedral itself—were, in turn, the accredited portals.

But a mass or composite biography of the Cathedral would be too great. From the overwhelming whole one must fall back to one particular story, to one chronicle of one great cathedral—the fairest of these bright sacred theatres of God—and the story, implicit in it, of the actors who have played in its immortal drama. So shall the story of all be told.

Rheims, Amiens, Chartres, Canterbury, York, Cologne, Burgos, Milan—like the stars they are in number. Still, the choice should not take long. There is one excelling at more points than any other, more deeply drenched in history, and which, even for those who have seen them all, wears best of all. And in that long chain of religion and race, this one shows not one missing link. The dolmen stones of history's dawn were used as Druid altars. The Romans appropriated them for Jupiter. In turn, all these great dolmen roofs and altar stones and the building blocks of the pagan temple went into old Saint Etienne on Paris Isle which preceded the earliest, the first Notre Dame. Then, when these two old churches came down, these stones went into the Cathedral of Notre Dame we see and touch today.

With these physical emblems, the thoughts, gropings, aspirations of the men who chiselled these stones into basins for blood, burned flesh on them, or worked them into the great Christ cross that is the Cathedral, went into the Cathedral's making. They are as much a part of its exhibit as the coronation robe of Napoleon or the pieces of the True Cross and Crown of Thorns so jealously guarded there.

And the Cathedral's chronicle keeps step, most of the way, with the onward march of the race. It was man who built the Cathedral's ancestors, who received the message of light from the Unknown, and with it built up the faith that blossomed into the Cathedral.

An especially bright section of the long parade of man's progress, the pageant of his history, both sacred and profane, marched by our particular Cathedral. For it was built at a particularly auspicious time, during the confluence of the old Roman with the Gothic, and on an unusually favourable spot, on an island by a famous river, in the world's brightest capital, at the crossroads of the world.

By this famous river it stands, on an equally historic square. It was in the East that Our Lady bore Her Son. Therefore must all altars lie to the East and our Cathedral, in Paris, fronts the east side of the square; way across it, on the west side, rises the great police barracks, imposing enough. On the north border lie the grey hospital walls of the old Hôtel Dieu, whose cool vaulted wards and green gardens are faintly glimpsed through its great windows. On the fourth, the south side, are the two bridgeheads, a great high-riding bronze Charlemagne in a strip of green lawn, and the vine-clad quays that box in the old river. It is well that we have that river and square. They make a way for Our Lady out of the crowding roofs of Paris and though they cannot give it more altitude, they set the Cathedral apart, so that it appears to be built on a hill.

It is a good distance across the square; which, too, is a good thing. For if the pilgrim, in times of peace, after the tourist car sets him down before the three great arched, deeply-recessed, stone-folk-laden doors, walks away from them, clear across the square, to the barrack walls, he will get more clearly the impression which should be his first and last, lifting his soul up as do lovely hills seen from afar.

It is the superb effect of unity arising out of infinite variety, that noble integrity that makes the Paris Cathedral the great Gothic exemplar, that places it first in the great quartette: Paris, Rheims, Amiens, Chartres. And this effect of the magnificent façade would not be a whit decreased were you omnipresent and able to see façade, walls, apse, roof, towers, nave, aisles, all in one view. Indeed, architecturally speaking, the builders were omnipresent and never, for one second, through the centuries of building, lost that view. So this impression of unity never decreases but increases almost in ratio to the multiplication of structural details. Nowhere, in all that vast pile, do they crowd, jostle, blur. They meet in perfect accord, like an infinite number of notes all pointing up the central theme. From the gardens where old men play chess and women nurse their babies; from the Archbishop's Bridge; from Abelard's quay where the fishermen group; from tugs in the river below; from all these points you can see that full upsweep, that noble gesture of man written for all to see, from plain, river and hills, engraved forever on the Paris sky.

But it is not always so that one comes upon it, upflung there against the blue. It has different aspects—in the morning, the sun, the night, the mists. In the moonless dark, for instance, when one comes upon it, it looms over one like a ship coming into her pier— a dream or ghost ship, with crew and passenger list of illustrious phantoms, coming down that old river, out of the mists of the past, to anchor to the island and the present.

There are other times when we see it in the brilliant illuminations which Paris turns on in festival seasons. When these upflood on that ghost ship, it is no ship at all, but a great high carved mountain with lofty niche and arch and cliff colonnade cut out of hoar frost. Again the light rays play, mixing trick with truth, and that façade is something else again—a mountain-high valentine to Our Lady with tiers of lace and angels between. A change of lights and it is a cameo, with every detail delicately carved in miniature, only to be magnified to giant stature and set up there against the stars. Then all at once not the façade alone but the whole pile becomes alive as more lights upwell from garden and riverside. To dormer, shrine, pinnacle, spire, they give line and form while retaining the dream texture. One long beam brings, out of the dark, great troops of flying buttresses; another peoples the high moonlit steeps with prophet, saint, angel, and devil.

So startling is the effect in the spell of the lights—the crowding ghosts, the piled-up history—that it seems as though all the still folk up there, the very structural parts of the Cathedral, were shouting down to us in the square: "We are no effigies, no phantoms, no things inanimate; we are real!" The twenty-eight kings (of Israel, not France) across the façade proclaim, "We have much of Wisdom to give"; "We, Beauty and Splendour," the great rainbow wheels above; "Order, Harmony, Grace," the white colonnades; "And countless fascinating Parables and Tales," the thousand saints climbing within and without, all over the pile.

And now other Cathedral members add their message: Evil, the crouching gargoyles. . . . Human Vanity, the Gallic cock on the top of the flèche, who, in the morning, will be all gold. . . . Purity and Pity, the blue-canopied, gold-lilied Our Lady down under the roof. . . . Tragedy, the cross embroidered in iron high on the apse. . . . Aspiration, the arches pulling everything up toward the light and Heaven. . . . Truth and Abiding Faith, the twin towers. And theirs would seem the last word and the perfect summing up, coming from those towers on which the seven spires the first architects long ago planned never went up, since they in themselves were so noble a summation for the Cathedral.

Still, it is not the last word, for now there comes a vast shoving and pushing from around front, from the tympanum over the central portal, the great Last Judgement Door, where the sculptured dead struggle to thrust up and off their stone coffin lids. So they shout, louder now than all the rest,—"We cry you a question you cannot answer at all."

Nor is this riotous fancy, for they say those things when the lights flood up and sometimes, for those who have ears to hear, eyes to see, when there is no light at all. And now the still Christ, with his Judgement scales poised above, for the time answers nothing at all. The lights go off and once more the Cathedral is plunged into the darkness and the dream.

But this is no candlelight cathedral. Next morning will not show it haggard. Towers, frost-lace façade, gold cock, flying buttress dragons will still be there. Of course, with dawn, all that high population will seem still, brooding in niche, stopped in their promenade of the aerial galleries or on lovely ladders up near the flèche. But clear, as though cut out of the bright morning they will appear, like so many facts, all witnessing to the great fact—the greater truth—that is the Cathedral.

And at once another phase of that superb unity of the structure asserts itself, a unity which goes far beyond that of art and engineering. For it takes the symbolism—the Red Door, for instance, the wound in Christ's side, the apse for halo, chevet for thorns, the whole place itself for the cross with Christ stretched upon it—and blends all with the structure itself, so that you cannot tell where body of structure leaves off and spirit of symbolism begins. So adroitly, so implicitly has it all been done that not once does that symbolism seem extraneous, any more than true art can seem something extraneous. No more superimposed is it than flesh and tendons are on the bones of a hand, or upper current on lower in that old river out there. Both, being one and the same, flow on with, and in, the same motion. Knit into them, of them, the symbolism went in, and went up *with* vault and pillar and pier.

Until you recognize this beautiful harmony and identicalness, you cannot enter, with understanding, into Notre Dame. And without this realization you cannot, in fancy, rebuild the Cathedral with the earnest mediaeval builders, bringing back, as one would like to do, the joyous sounds of the industry and the spirited planning and contagious camaraderie. But for bishop architects and most of the masons, carpenters, leadsmiths, stonecutters and carters, the main event was not, proud as they were of it, the building of Notre Dame, but what was to go on within it. They had the grandly unique objective for which people all over the Ile de France were bending their backs, shouldering burdens and levies and digging into their savings, all with a dynamic piety such as the world has never since seen, not only to thrust those mighty and majestic structures nearer Heaven, but to make them worthy of the matchless story that would be told within them and of the sacrifice to be made on their altars. The greatest of all dramas, far removed from spectacle, but drama in its highest and purest sense, would be relived through the ages in the lovely sanctuary those humble workers, with such infinite pains and love and art, were preparing for it. That is core and heart and soul of Notre Dame.

Our Lady, in whose name the Cathedral was built, is the compassionate Mother who, every toiler there was sure, would plead for him too, since he felt himself unworthy even to approach the blessed feet of her Son. And yet, first and last, the whole pile is Christ, His body stretched out on transept cross-arms and nave upright. This belief is not something passive but a kinetic emotion that must be recognized as motive and mainspring by all who would enter into the soul of the Cathedral. Both divine drama and architecture must be read in its pure light, for scepticism did not build that miracle or bloom into its loveliness. And that faith, that light, that fire that gave it being was not something merely poetic. It was practical, as every stone attests, as did a long line of illustrious believers who knelt on these stones—Saint Louis, Loyola, Bossuet, Pascal, Saint Vincent de Paul, Verdier and a host of others, pragmatic mystics all, whose faith flowered not in roses but in practical deeds.

Who is responsible for this unity, this mortizing and dovetailing of symbolism and stone, faith and metal and glass, and beauty in all, no one will ever know. And does it matter whether it was Archbishop de Sulli who drew, with crozier, his first design in the earth, or de Chelles who, alone of the architects, had the sense to autograph his name in the stone—or a number of men? No one brain could be responsible. Hosts of masters-of-works, masons, monk designers, lay architects—all striving upward for elasticity, grace, and light—rejected this, accepted that, moulded here, modeled there. A composite father, then, the race, sired this creation in the womb of time. It took, say the records, seventy-two years to raise it from foundation piles to tower tops, and longer for chapels and portals. Yet to look at it, it does not seem as if it took any time at all, rather as though the Architect who designed the earth and set the stars' courses, had said, "Let there be a cathedral," and at once the infinite number of parts moved into their appointed places as inspired notes in a symphony score.

How blind was Raphael not to see it all! Raphael, the suave, the sweet, the perfect draughtsman. "Gothic," he called it, this style which, having flowered in the Ile de France, had been known as the "French style." And ponderous, blundering, barbaric, he meant. But then, Raphael liked cherubs. He could not detect—in the stone lace-work of Rheims, or the stone-picture book of Amiens, or the stone-framed sunsets of Chartres, in the union of all here in Paris—something greater even than the perfect but limited Greek temple, which could not stand more than one story. This something is the very summation of race, mass, composite art and yet is greater than all art. But how the word turned on Raphael! The term of reproach became one of glory, summoning, with its very mention, visions of that heaven clothed in glass and stone and of nobler men and more spacious eras.

More spacious this Gothic era certainly was, and in a broader sense, than ever was the so-called one of English Elizabeth. Kings, moved by some inner compulsion that was more than vanity, halved their treasuries to complete choirs. Queens wove tapestries and pawned their jewels for altars. Miser-bankers melted down their gold for pinnacle and spire. Carpenters, saddlers and armourers, gave their all to carve for it screens or *misereres*. There was no haggling about it; all was joyous, generous, exuberant for most of a grand seventy years here in Paris—for twice that span, in fact, if you take in all of Notre Dame's sisters. Quarrymen, with song, dug out stone at Montrouge and from the quarries under the Rue Saint Jacques. Singing wagoners brought in stone from all over the plain. Boatmen floated it down from Pontoise. Stained-glass workers came through the city gates with their portable crucibles and pitched their tents by the rising walls. And with cheers and lovely old hymns like "Fairest Lord Jesus" and "Star of the Sea," butchers, bakers, candle-stickmakers, literally, with nobles, chimney-sweeps, prostitutes, yoked themselves to carts, to hurry the material in.

That is why in building here, man did something more than build. As that mysterious coordination and organization which we call life was given to the chemicals—the bone, tissue, cells of the Cathedral's creator—so by his very conception and nurture of his creation, he transmitted to the cold chemicals—to the stone, metal, glass—warmth and life.

And what a succession of secular scenes the saints, through the centuries, have since looked down on from niche and window: The son of Henry the Second of England being buried, a stranger in a strange land, under the high altar. Saint Louis bringing in, with a glittering procession, he himself humbly barefoot, his relic of the Crown of Thorns and the True Cross. Philip the Fair with iron hoofbeat riding down that nave to send his armour crashing down before Our Lady. The excited chattering as the first parliament convened. Scottish Mary petitioning the Mary in whose name the Cathedral was built, for love and life, and, too, a revival of the sacred drama, which meant so much to her storm-tossed heart, in the dour churches of her own Edinburgh. Napoleon, heels a-click, bursting in from the Archbishop's Palace to be crowned. Revolutionary and Commune mobs racing through, with their pikes, their cries savage above the death rattle of the Old Order. The martyr priest praying for forgiveness for his murderers, as had his King and the Saint Stephen by whose doorway he lay on stones as red as the deepest crimsons in the great rose above. No more articulate are the professional guides, the news-vendors outside, no more vocal the gorgeously chasubled priests, the singing choirboys, the rolling organ up in the violet dusk of the west loft, than these history-drenched stones themselves. For him who has ears, they will unlock their tongues.

But they will not speak to all the unthinking pilgrims who (by their very presence giving Raphael the lie) step down from the tourist cars in that traffic of the quick which the *agent de police* directs before the Last Judgement portal and the traffic there of the dead. Quite alike they are, all these pilgrims of today, from Waterloo Station, Prague, Melbourne, Cairo, Lima, Ohio, and those in that portal trying so hard to get out from under their stone coffin lids. As alike, in fact, as peas in a pod, with only the clothes pod, with the centuries, changed.

We speak of the tourists, but it is only in times of peace that they will be there, not in times of war. Then the Cathedral is banked many feet deep in sandbags and the rose window eyes are blank and dead, their bright glass irises having been stored away. For invaders come and inevitably invaders go. Four times they have been here in a hundred and forty years, for France falls and rises again. Through two thousand, eight hundred years, a longer span than that of any other race, she has known the identity of race consciousness, and much of that time, of nationality. More often than any other land, she has been in the vanguard of the struggle for civilization, liberalism, and liberty. Into the troughs of defeat she has gone down, but time after time, she has risen to crest after crest of consummate glory.

These things are not beside the point even though this is to be the story of the Cathedral and of man's relationship to God through his altars. For the story of France can never be entirely dissociated from that of the Cathedral, it being a part of the very heart of France. Because they covet that France, the invaders have come with hard, not understanding minds, into the square before the Cathedral. In the First World War they aimed their Big Bertha shells at it. Fortunately only one bomb, which was not very effective, landed on Notre Dame. All the shells curved over the lovely pile or fell short of it, though many a shattering one landed near it; one on Saint Gervais, just over the stream, to kill seventy-five and wound ninety worshippers, just as the poignant Last Word of Christ echoed under the arches at the Good Friday services.

And in the very middle of our century, the enemy's brazen regimented trumpeters have stood, blaring out their blasphemous and bloody *Horst Wessel* song under the lovely west rose, and the gentle Mother and Child. So trumpeting, goose-stepping invaders come; and feet dragging, crying for mercy, invaders go.

So travellers are kept from the Cathedral they love until the foe vanishes east over the horizon. Then again the pilgrims throng by, the nuns with their little accordion-pleated alms cups, the postcard vendors outside, and the companies of saints and devils flanking the portals. Unceasing is that march. Over the stones, around the pillars, through the aerial galleries outside, up the three hundred and ninety-five steps to the towers, among the bats and pigeons and arrow-slits, goes on that endless patter, so like that of rain, the shuffle, so like the wind's whisper, of feet from all the corners of the world. Past a colourfully chasubled priest intoning noble old Gregorian phrase; child in long lace in the Baptism Chapel; bride in the next, poor but with a touch of Paris magic in her homemade hat; mothers praying for slain soldier sons at the tricolour altar; canon invoking, over the candle-ringed form in Saint Pierre's Chapel, the age-old *Requiescat*, the restless feet of the pilgrims wander.

Many pause reverently before these little human dramas in the ring of chapels. Others watch idly these supreme moments in others' lives. And they scarcely realize even the significance of the divine drama, glimpses of which they catch through the sanctuary grille, as they wander through the ambulatory. Yet sometimes there flashes even on these unheeding ones—for the Cathedral has a welcome for all—a gleam of light from the altar.

Often, scientists from the colleges, hospitals, and laboratories that crowd the immemorial Paris hills, wander in too. They are seeking the link between animal and man. Some are aware—though not all—of the greater story, the profounder logic of the link between the human and the Divine. But the greatest of them all, Pasteur, who came here to pray, recognized it; also that in the Cross and the Resurrection was the solution to life the scientists could not find. When they think up a truer logic, a better solution, why, they can tear the Cathedral down—only it wouldn't come.

So, on forever, goes that eternal march, that started with the first processional of Archbishop de Sulli. Even when all the lights are out, that is all but those over the tabernacle and the chapel of Our Lady, charwomen shuffle their dragging feet as they did when they mopped up after the old dusty pilgrims and crusaders sweating under their heavy armour. And with book or candle or cushion, sacristans are forever puttering about. Then, when those on guard nod in the night watches, out come the ghosts, from Sainte Geneviève, who saved Paris and the father church of the Cathedral, fifteen hundred years ago; Philippe Auguste marching with his serried ranks in blood-sprinkled mail to the altar; robed Richelieu; Villon lurking behind the pillars; the murdered archbishop buried here; the brides, the forlorn little dauphins here baptized; the Sun King; the organist who fell dead across the west organ keys; down through the long years to Pasteur, here but yesterday, praying for his magnificent victories over death.

And so they patter on still, those ghostly footsteps, all night, a shadowy procession without end, until the sun comes up beyond the upstream bridges and shines, through the lovely coloured eyes of the apse, on the altar, and the patter of immortal feet ceases, to be taken up by the mortal again.

Sometimes it may happen—though rarely—that the beauty of Notre Dame, of those forest aisles and the glowing panes and the snowy-summited towers, is a little overwhelming. But in those moments, when the sublimely great fact seems about to turn to unsubstantial dream, there is reaffirmation. For up there on the façade are strange marks, the most convincing testimony, which passersby rarely note. If they do, they consider the marks but roosting places for pigeons, although there are enough dormers and little belfries to serve all that fluttering host. Besides, the marks are too regularly placed and seem to come in pairs. On the façade, on the north, the old cloister side, back by the gardens, up over Saint Etienne's door south, those little square crevices, five or six inches across, climbing up toward the upper galleries, are almost lost to the eye in the wealth of sculptured detail, the whole glory of the ensemble. They are the holes for the scaffolding timbers, or putlogs, which were thrust in these holes and then bound to one another to make the scaffolding skeleton. Some of these holes have been sealed up with plaster, as was originally intended, but more have been left open. They were used by the masons and hodcarriers of Archbishop de Sulli and Architect de Chelles, Saint Louis' glass-workers and plumbers, and as late almost as yesterday by Viollet-le-Duc when he put all the kings' heads back.

And those scaffold timbers, those putlog holes, are structural and real. When the pageant of history, the weight of the years, and the significance of the drama within at times bewilder us, we turn to these masonry holes. As Doubting Thomas put his hands in the wound and the nail prints of Christ, so we thrust our fingers in the nail prints of the miracle that is Notre Dame, and know again that it is real.

The doors are open now and one can see down that long nave to the altar. The aisle is like a long forest path under arched trees, with the little shining house of safety at the end. But one can see, if one will, a longer distance than down that nave, a longer distance than up that river outside, through the years. . . .

I

The Island in the Seine. . . . The Stones of the Old Altars that will go into the Cathedral. . . . The First Burning of Paris, the Battle of Montparnasse, the Long-nosed Caesar, and the Death of a True Hero.

52 B.C.

IT WAS THE YEAR 52—NOT AS THE GAULS, LIKE ALL ANCIENT people counted it, a year to a moon, but as we reckon time— fifty-two years before a very simple event, the birth of a babe in a stable, split Time itself in two. And if it is hard to conceive of a day when there were no crosses and churchbells, still harder is it to think oneself back into an age when that Child was not in the consciousness of all, even negatively at least, of those who profess to have little to do with Him.

Quite impossible, too, it would be to tear out that universal background, to unravel the entire pattern of thought woven by that Child—to wash out, from the very warp and woof of existence, the red dye of His tragedy; to erase from history and memory all the crusades, the hospital and social services undertaken in His name; to blot out all the words, allusions, connotations; quench all the bright customs, the fêtes, saints' days, pageants, the very Christmas ways, all of which spring out from that life, like rays from His own gold monstrance over the Cathedral altar. So very surely did those tiny hands, wielding Destiny's sword, split time and man's history in twain. So completely did they sunder the thousands of years that marked man's emergence out of the slime from the almost two thousand since that have seen his further groping.

Almost out of that long and dark older dispensation and yet not quite in the new, was this crowd of Parisians who, on a bright spring morning of that year 52, angrily gesticulated around an open-air altar at the upstream end of an island in the Seine.

That they had groped their way quite far up out of the slime and were far ahead of the men who, in these valleys, ages before, had spent their time learning how to roast flesh, chip flint, and paint caves, was evident from the fine resonant periods of the priest as he took up the golden knife; from the very carving on

it, too, and the coral and the gold enamel on the warriors' shields
and the beautiful workmanship of the crests on their bright
helmets.

The glittering knife was for the mistletoe in the sacred oaks
which cast a wavering fishnet of sun-gold and leaf-shadow on
the altar; also for the bull, with horns highly polished, that stood
by it. The officiating priest was robed in white, and had a long
beard. He was very old. The oaks, of course, were much older,
and still more ancient was the altar. It was made of dolmen stones,
weighing many tons, which had served as roofs and lintels of
houses of the dead of past ages and really had framed the first
of God's theatres. For into the graves these stones had roofed, men
had thrown their letters to the dead, the first messages to the
Infinite. As for the river that embraced the island, its sugarloaf
huts, and the altar, it was older than the sum of all the ages of
the priests and greybeards in existence. It flowed out of the East
and time immemorial, to lose itself, under the Gauls' bright heaven
of the West, in the immemorial sea.

Its course then was the same as it is today; its gentle, serene flow
being split in two by the island then known as "Lutetia," "the
White City," and to become famous as Paris—very properly too,
since the island was shaped like a boat ("*par*" meant boat), and
these Parisii were the prize boatmen of the Seine. And they owed
much to the river. It was not only their great larder, but since
that "time immemorial" it had been for them "the road that
walked." Down it they went in their huge flat-bottomed barges—
like those now anchored below the wooden bridge, with their great
leather sails drying—to trade their wine casks and crimson cloth
down the Seine, to take in exchange bright amber and pastel for
tattooing which they would trade over the Channel for British
mastiffs and Cornish tin. They would mate these mastiffs with
the Paris wolves to breed their war-dogs.

Altogether, it was no wonder that the little island city, as soon
as it should grow big enough to have a coat-of-arms, should place
on it a ship with the motto, "It may rock but it never sinks,"
which it has kept down to today. But now for the first time in the
lives of the Parisii, that friendly river might turn out to be a
menace. If for them it was "the road that walked," their foemen
the Romans in barges could come down it too.

There were several boatmen in the circle that watched, fascinated, the priest's golden knife. They were brown and naked to
the waist. So, too, were the smutted smiths beside them, from the
island forges. But the horsemen from the remudas across the
river wore cloaks pinned with cunningly worked brooches and
looped over their shoulders. They and the warriors wore the long

trousers with which the inventive Parisians were setting the fashion centuries ahead. It was not, of course, to be adopted all at once, but the world was to go, not the way of the Roman toga, but of the Gallic breeches.

Even the pitchers and urns the women set down, as they paused to listen to the chant, had unique designs, in terra cotta with black triangles, that were quite modern in spirit. The large bronze ones, some with exquisitely carved grapes and even little wild horses climbing the handles, showed smart lines and artistic flares at the handles, like those of the helmets all about them, which boulevard hat designers would copy in the years to come. It is a pity, perhaps, that they did not copy also the warriors' tartan cloaks. For these were striped a brilliant red-and-white with dyes so fast that not for centuries would they fade. We have nothing now half as picturesque.

They made an unforgettable picture with all these things and their armlets, the thin beaten gold of the crown of the *vergobret,* their leader, the mighty gold serpent entwining his arm, the shields of all inlaid with gold and coral or silver enamel, and their helmets crested with bird and beast and burnished to a brightness like that of their own fair hair. That is, as bright as the hair of most of them who, with many rinsings of limewater and soap (the very first soap, too, in all the world), succeeded in living up to the Gauls' reputation for blondeness—just as they were, that very minute, living up to their renown for quick indignations and vivacious oratory.

Their indignation was over something as old as the altar around which they stood: the desire of other gentlemen to take from them their Paris. Some, from across the Rhine, had been trying it ever since they had crawled up, quite a long time after the Gauls, out of the slime—and would not succeed in getting there for just eighteen hundred and sixty-five years, until the fall of a man named Napoleon. Rome had tried it once already. The very autumn before, Caesar had ridden over that crude bridge, his long nose sniffing at the swaying of the wood trestles, for he was very particular about his bridges. But no sooner had the ice in the river melted, the spring wheat showed its first green, than the Parisii wanted their city back again. That is why, summoned by couriers, they were here. And to see just what was the appearance of this city, which was already so desirable and which would stay so through the ages, one must look through the wrong, the two-thousand-year, end of the telescope.

The shape of the island, though it was a trifle smaller, and the rise of hills, like the course of the river, were the same as they are today. But there were then no stone quays to box that river in, only strands of sand and gravel, and no row of majestic bridges to belt it, only two crude ones of thong-jointed wood. Instead of today's massing spires, pinnacles and chimneys, one saw a few wood towers, rough earthworks on the island's rim, with a considerable cluster of sugarloaf huts, two or three larger houses with silver slabs in their sides, and from the eaves the heads of foemen, pickled in resin, hanging; also a wattled compound with smoking forges and brightly emblazoned war chariots, leather sails on the beach, and everywhere those wild wolf-mastiff wardogs running loose. In place of the sea of mansards that now crowd up the surrounding hills, were grazing strings of horses by the river, sentinelled by silent, cloaked riders; and several score half-naked farmers ploughing brown patches out of the primeval green.

There are other important changes to make in fancy: from the three million inhabitants walking now the boulevard and *banlieu* pavements to the two thousand bright helmets gesticulating around the altar, more riding over the hills or rowing to Paris from up and down the river, and (for Caesar's figures are not to be trusted, as he always augmented his victories by doubling or trebling his opposition) seven or eight thousand more in the whole region for fifty miles around. And then, at the upstream end of the boat-shaped island, where now flying buttresses spread their mighty angles, and copper angels raise their trumpets in mid-air, stood this altar of old grave roofs chiselled into basins to catch the dripping blood. But the eternal question asked there of the skies has not changed. All—dolmen stones, Druid altar, and Cathedral—signalled from groping man to the Power he now leans upon, again shrinks from. All symbolized his quest for a "source of things" far harder to find than that of the longest river or of Heaven's winds.

But this morning, while those men with bright helmets argued, Our Lady, like the Child, was not, neither she herself nor her Cathedral. It would be thirty years more before she would come into the world at all, far overseas into a little kingdom called Judah. And it would have surprised the congregation around the altar into murdering you for a wizard, had you told them that under their browned loins were imprisoned a whole race who would build for an oriental lady a great house of stone, arched like the forests, of glass coloured like the sunsets.

Of course, some in that circle had a good education. The Druids, who had come into Gaul before the Gauls, had seen to that. Their "pope," as he was known, elected each year at a settlement later called Chartres after the tribe of the place, the Carnutes, was a power. He made signs over their armies when they went into battle, excommunicated whole villages when he chose, and ruled a well-organized see. The Druids ranged from the curates, or assistants, who strung lyres, sang epics by the Seine and the other rivers, to the more venerable who officiated at sacrifices, practiced divining powers, and taught the youth of the first families of an otherwise democratic country. These families, in Paris, were the ones that lived in the island's centre, in the larger houses with the silver sides. Where the dwellers in the beehive huts or the caves of the hill had only rude trestles and benches with heaps of dried leaves to sleep on, these aristocrats had carved chests, fine quality wolfskins, coffers filled with shining coins, and real wool mattresses. These people, the first in the world to use soap and coaches and giant scythes and coultered ploughs and reapers, had also astonished the great general from Rome into writing home, "Why, they even have contrived ingenious wheeled and horse-drawn troughs that have been equipped with teeth which, as the horses move down the rows, cut off the ears of corn!"

The original builders of the larger island mansions slept now in much snugger houses of stone. Between chariot wheels, set upright in the sandy flooring of caves, they lay, their swords and shields beside them, also bowls of bread and meat, for the longest of journeys. But before they had gone they had also taught their sons to throttle wolves, spear fish, and hew with the broadsword, and never, while there remained alive a comrade that could be saved, to desert a burning house or sinking ship.

The smiths over by the smoking compound had shown them how to forge those swords, the metal-workers the way to engrave them, also to chase the headstalls for their favourite horses in the remudas across the river, and how, with sharp tools, to trace and etch deep the designs in bracelets and shields, then the right method of working in the gold leaf and silver thread and pink coral. Of course, being aristocrats, they had not stayed long at these delicate tasks, but hand and foot and eye had been well trained. And the Druids had taught them the way of the clouds, that night came before day—as indeed the Great Night did—also astrology and a very vivid sort of oratory, an accomplishment some of them were displaying by that altar now.

They knew, too, the smartest of them, the Greek letters in which the Druids wrote down the minutes of their corporation meetings, and had solved many old Euclid and Pythagoras theorems propounded by trading Greeks coming up from Marseilles. But though these traders had brought many fine things in their packs, they had left out a very important thing—a simple law of computation. The young Gallic chiefs knew, of course, that if they mated with the young girls with the beautiful pitchers, they would, in the usual way of life, have large families. But they never guessed how one's seed might multiply through the ages. Such thoughts were more in the heads of people in that land to the East where Our Lady was to appear. They always thought a great deal about their seed.

No, none of these Gauls, these early Parisians in the red-and-white cloaks, saw themselves as worlds of cell-cities which their descendants in colleges to come in Paris, would proclaim them to be. They were unaware of those whirling microcosms called *genes* in themselves which would hand on through the centuries the Gallic love of the soil, of a good speech, a finely-carved tool, of their ability to drive a good bargain one minute, to die for an ideal the next. Indeed, being far behind not only their descendants but the contemporary Hindus and Greeks in physiology, though ahead in other things, all that these Gauls knew of themselves was that they possessed a few organs, a heart principally, and four flowing "humours"—blood, phlegm, and two other liquids which were supposed to produce melancholy and irritation or anger. This simplicity saved expense and trouble, all the thyroid tablets of their descendants, for instance. All they needed was an occasional splint or poultice—of soap mixed with herbs, very sweet-smelling and soothing—a ligature or neat job of trepanning, which the Druids could perform very creditably.

As for their race strain, much nonsense has been written about Gaul and Celt by the Rand McNally of the day, Geographer Strabo, who visited but a tenth of the lands he charted, and by Julius Caesar, who was coming up from the south on his way to quell the revolt. All the city historians of Athens and Rome had lumped all peoples in the north—Gauls, Goths, Germans, Burgundians, Britons, Bretons, whatnot—under the designation Celts. They declared them all blondes, too, a reputation to which the Parisians tried hard to live up with their patriotic shampoos. But modern ethnographers have not been too sure, either. Apparently, out of the region north and east of the Rhine, the great breeding-place of the fair-haired races the ancients grouped as Celts, one people detached itself, crossed the Rhine and possessed north France. They were, in the main, bright of hair, had long heads and blue eyes; they called themselves Celts and have since been accepted as truly such. These were our inventive, valourous French-ancestor Gauls.

Another human river called Celtic, some say of the North, others, from Asia, came to the Danube. This one, full of round-heads medium brunette, had very soon spilled over into central and south Gaul, already alive with Iberian, Ligurian, Massilian, Phoenician, Basque, Phocan Greek full brunettes. This confluence met, head-on, the river of the blonde north Celts, or Gauls, coming down. Small wonder then that Caesar and the scholars could not tell precisely what was a Celt. And it was a great miracle that the blonde percentage in Gaul and Paris kept so high. But we should at once disabuse our minds of any idea that the composite Frenchman is wholly or even half Latin. He is Ligurio-Iberian, Gallic, or Celtic, Frank, Latin, Norman—about in that order of preponderance—with a slight touch of Asia-Minorian, Semitic, Basque, and Greek.

But so far, here in Paris, he was only a Celtic Gaul. And as the warriors, horsemen, and smiths ranged around the altar, a very good stock it appeared to be, with sinewy bodies, yet chests finely deep for the forge, the fish-strike, the war cry, or the sword-stroke, and legs, when planted, sturdy and far enough apart as a good Frenchman's should be, for the saddle, the straight furrow, or the slanting deck. And their eyes could dart quickly enough, right or left, at signs of the trail or the foe. "The Gauls," said the Roman satirists, lazily lounging in their villas back home, "are so defiant that they shoot arrows into the lightning to scare it." But hard, bedrock Caesar, though he slaughtered them, knew better. "Open and frank are they," he wrote down in his tent at night. "They win battles, not by stratagem, but by valour alone." He had good reason to know how discouragingly audacious and shining their eyes could be in the face of danger or the arch-enemy Death.

In short, they were smoothly-articulated, swift-acting organisms, at one, in the youth of the world, with Life's poetry. In this they had the advantage over their smart descendants, who would strive so hard to retain all their science and recapture that poetry, and would make a pretty bad job of it, as do we all. To those old Gauls, natural objects were no mere chemical combinations, but things friendly, to be relied on. The stars were still warm torches to guide them, the river a father to lean upon, to lave them, to bear them when their time came down to the sea and the Gauls' bright Heaven of the West.

Of this the Druids had taught them too. Over and over they had stressed this most important truth in their curriculum—that the soul is immortal. It was a great help, with wolves all about, the Germans refusing to stay on their side of the great silver fence called the Rhine, and Caesar fast moving up. For with this belief of the Gauls, Death did not matter, which made them more likely ancestors than the men of the Rhine or Rome. For only from a race who thought more often of bright far-off heavens than of other men's acres, could spring such wholly French ideas as the Crusades and the Gothic, and such spirits as the only girl-warrior-saint or saint-king of very great fame in the calendar of any country.

The old human sacrifices, high on Montmartre, in which they ripped open human backs and prophesied from the entrails while they still quivered, were fast being outmoded. This morning, when the younger curate had come down from the sacred oak with the mistletoe, and had wrapped it, according to rite, in the white coverlet, the Druid pope raised the gold knife above the bull. Its whirring lightnings cut sharply across the smutted chests of the smiths and the women—many with fists that could fell a man—as gracefully full at bosom and hip as their pitchers; the warriors in gay red-and-white cloaks, wild beast and bird crests and bright helmets; and the black snouts and gleaming eyes of the wolf-mastiff wardogs, whose pink tongues, as their hearts pounded from baying or running in and out, added barbaric accents to the picturesque circle.

With one swift stroke, beautiful in its precision, the pope slit the bull's throat in a perfect semicircle from which the torrent of blood gushed into the chiselled basin. Then, after a second sure stroke had laid bare the entrails, he bent over, reading them. "I see," he said, "Caesar and his hobnailed legions marching."

And then the Druid, not only because he had here an audience which no Gaul with his flair for oratory could ignore, but also from a truly patriotic fervour, broke out into the expected speech. Every now and then he would pause to listen to the echoes coming from the hills and up the river, as though he too found his own words good. Every once in a while too, the heads under the bright helmets nodded with childlike pleasure at his compliments to their race.

But first he looked toward Montmartre, the Butte, Montparnasse, Valerien, and even Meudon and the Saint Cloud heights southwest —all the hills which looked down as they still look down on the island city. And up to them he stretched his hands as though he would take from them, as from the shelves of the gods, old chronicles. Then he told them, with vivid and rapid figures, of their fathers who had come into this fair valley:

"Parisians, know that just as there were lakes and rivers of water left after the Great Ice, so there are pools and rivers of men. Sometimes the pools stay quiet; but often the rivers spill over their banks to inundate other men's fields, as do"—he spat this out with disgust—"those Romans, those Germans! That is why the gods did not choose to show to them the good red iron. They saved that for whom? Why, for the bravest, the swiftest, and brightest of all the rivers of men, the fair-haired Gauls."

So pleased were they with their priest and themselves that the bright-helmeted warriors sent up through the grove a mighty shout, joyously augmenting it with the clashing of their shields and the banging of their weapons, the war hounds excitedly joining in with bloodcurdling baying.

If the wily old politician had flattered them a little, he had been reasonably accurate in his history drawn from old Druid traditions. That very moment it was being documented for their descendants, in the three great volumes of the Book of the Earth. Centuries later, scholars would find here—in the first volume, the lowest stratum of buried pine, the old stone weapons, the bronze in the oak volume above, and in the topmost layer of beech forest remains —accoutrements like those now on their own excited persons. He was right too about the good red iron. They and their Danubian Celtic cousins had found it smelted by Nature herself, ahead of all the rest of Europe.

He drew himself up like the fine figurehead of state he looked.

"With this iron we conquered Europe from the Euxine to the world's edge." And this was good history too, for as it would be with Rome, Spain, Britain, France, Germany, it was the comparative superiority of their arms as well as their valour and wit that gave the Gauls their great day in the sun. "There were no roads that knew not our tread, no rivers unfurrowed by our keels, no races that have not felt our swords." Since he was speaking of Europe and the Near East, he was not idly boasting here either. "And often in the night we went over the Alps to descend on the Seven Hills from which this upstart, the long-nosed Caesar, now has the effrontery to come.

"Now, other rivers of men we welcomed, particularly the Greeks. They brought us their mathematics and letters, their olive trees and bright coins. But this Caesar, who has risen by bribery and loot, tricks the Gauls scorn to use, what"—bitterly he rasped this out—"had he to offer? He copies all the things we have used before the rest of the world—our coultered ploughs, our fertilizing with manure and marl, our big-bellied casks, our high-wheeled carts. He covets our cunning locks, our wine made of hops, those gold serpents twined on your arms, your gold-and-coral shields, and"—all disgust now—"he even envies us our cleanliness and steals our soap. But it cannot wash out Caesar's stain or sweeten the world of his great stench!"

Just as the crowd was starting up again that terrifying clangour of banging weapons, war cries, and baying hounds, there came a shout from across the river, just above the old wood bridge. Boatmen were swiftly rowing there, horsemen galloping from the meadows, toward a man on a horse covered with lather. He was gesticulating now, and dramatically pointing up the river. Then he galloped toward them, with the dulled thunder of hooves on the planks, and the Druid pope's audience broke for the strand. Flinging himself from his horse, the rider poured out a report so swiftly and with such gutturalness that it sounded like a river of words tumbling over rocks in his throat.

"Caesar," he cried, "has been defeated at Gergovia." Then, at their shout, "Wait! He escaped, marched his hobnails north, and he camps now on the Saône. He has sent Labienus, his best commander, to take Paris!"

The Druid pope brushed him aside, and then down by the leather sails and little forest of masts he took up his interrupted speech in that vanished tongue of which French still retains but a dozen or so words.

"Hard are the legion's hobnails; harder is Caesar; and hardest of all are the harsh Roman gods. But they are not true gods. They allow images to be made of themselves, and the gods of Gaul do not like to be made in the likeness of men. No reverence has Rome. And reverence and humility in the face of the great mysteries we have shown ever since our fathers threw into the darkness of the tombs their letters to the unknown.

"And what would proud Caesar give for all our culture of the spirit? Battering rams, catapults, walking towers. Fire, murder, loot. He has sacked our cities by the score, murdered our children by the thousands, taken our maidens for bedfellows, our youths for perverted slaves."

On high the old man carried the torch of his speech and from it the Parisians took fire. Louder than ever now rang the tumult of voice and of arms. With this crescendo, came his final appeal:

"Ye sons of Gaul"—here, centuries ahead sounded the prelude to the Marseillaise—"restore your vanished glory, drive this Caesar out! It is the wish of the gods of Gaul who dwell in the bright Heaven of the West!"

They lost no time. At a signal, the horsemen across the river gathered the remudas of horses and they galloped across the bridge. Great slabs of beef, bags of meal, casks of wine and beer were piled on carts. The wooden tongues of the great wagons were raised, and the yokes were adjusted. Horses were hitched to these and the war chariots. Then came a vast embracing all around, a great splashing of oars, a thunder of hoofs. For the Gauls did many things splendidly, and most of them noisily. At their worst, they were vainglorious, disputatious; at their best, nobly united in their willingness to die for an idea.

So the citizens of Paris started out to defend their Paris and their altars, embryo of our Lady's Cathedral. It was getting to be a habit. This spring it was Rome that was doing the invading. Tomorrow it would be the Germans under some tribal alias or other. Strangely enough the Romans resented this. "The Germans have three reasons for invading you," they told the Gauls, "restlessness, greed, and the fertility of your acres. Also, they would love to be your masters."

The Parisian commander, old Camulogenus, rounding up his red-and-white cloaked warriors on the Left Bank—where now is the Jardin des Plantes—could remember six invasions during his lifetime: in B.C. 113, 109, 105, and three in the 70's. It would always be that way. Despite sacking Brennus and Louis and Napoleon, nine out of ten enemy generals, nine out of ten times, when they ordered a charge against the French, were ordering it *on French soil*. Even Clovis and the Sun King were to fight their battles chiefly to bring France up to what any disinterested cartographer would testify are her nature-designed borders—the Alps, Pyrenees, the two seas, and the Rhine.

Though he could make fine speeches all about glory, and leap to the charge, the Frenchman was a farmer or an artisan at heart, when he wasn't a scholar or artist; in short, considerable of a stay-at-home. Perhaps the fact that his acres are a little richer, fairer, and better watered than his neighbours' may lessen by a little his seeming restraint and excuse by just so much his neighbours' covetousness.

Anyway, in the continuance of an age-old habit, a goodly lot of veterans and recruits were going out from Paris this afternoon, to die for those acres and—though this they did not know—for a house not yet built for a Lady not yet born. And they made a fine show as the bright helmets, the chanting bards, the painted war chariots, and red-mouthed war dogs passed up the river road.

It had been a wonderful parade, but it was as nothing compared with the one that came back two days later. Not often does Paris have the chance of seeing two rival armies marching in parallel columns, one on the Left Bank, the other on the Right. From the wood palisade, the gravel strand, and the crude wooden bridge, the waiting women saw them: the Gallic long swords and rounder shields of gold and coral, the chariots and war dogs and famous helmets, on the site of the Jardin des Plantes and by the mouth of the Brook Bièvre; the squarer helmets, shorter swords and oblong shields, and the handsaws, picks, axes, and shovels of the Romans, where now stands the Arsenal. Both armies, though tired from the long forced march from Melun, were speeding at the double-quick in the hope of being the first to reach Paris.

The keen-witted Gauls had been outwitted. They had found the Romans, had seen their trenches and had heard their evening bugles over the marshes, forty miles up the Seine, by Melun. From around their campfires, their great slabs of beef and their casks of wine and beer, they had flung jibes at the Romans because of their very short swords which they, the Gauls, called "silly," and, in particular, because of those handsaws and picks and shovels and axes with which the foe was forever felling trees and cutting trenches. The Gauls scorned these as they did the enemy's breastplates; baring the breast to the foe was with the Gaul a matter of honour. No set protection should their hearts have, only a shield manoeuvred by the skill of the wearer. "Let the Roman fool," they said, "dig himself in." Ever heedless of terrain, they themselves encamped wherever the whim struck them; their camp wagons and war chariots, in a huddle, were their only barriers and these at their backs! If the strategy of the Gauls had only equalled their valour and if half the time they spent in enamelling and etching their arms had been devoted to the study of tactics, there would have been no Caesar's *Commentaries* for schoolboys to curse. And the Gallic campaigns would have been over in a fortnight—or else never begun. But while the Gauls slept, the Romans had stolen the barges of the people of Melun and by dawn were on the other shore.

But now, seeing that the Gauls, with all their lumbering chariots, had out-marched them, the Romans went up Montmartre hill and there encamped for the night. Peacefully, for several hours, their watch-fires glimmered upon the hill where one day would be the Moulin Rouge and the windmills of Galette. Then, in the third watch, while the camp-tenders were replenishing the watch-fires, it was the Romans' turn to be dumbfounded. For suddenly a great light spread over the sky—a false dawn at midnight. Burning clots from the sugar-loaf houses were riding the great billows of smoke. Over the wooden bridge the Gauls were carrying their household goods. When the last man had crossed, old Camulogenus deliberately fired the north bridge, then the south.

Here on the Left Bank, all the citizenry of Paris milled with the cattle. The horses, their distended nostrils smarting from the smoke, and frightened by the unreal light, stampeded. Each sugar-loaf house was now a crackling torch. A haymow, it seems, could not have burned quicker. The bridges were red roads of light. Little gold fringes ran up the sacred oaks and masts. The leather sails sloughed off in great flakes. The sky above the hills—a sulphur saffron from the reflection—was turned to pulsing vermilion as the fire leaped upon some fresh object in its path. In later years opera houses would burn, and palaces, but never would Paris be devoured so completely. To save her, her citizens had destroyed her.

The women and children bedded down in the caves and groves on the hill of the Left Bank, the Gallic warriors, too, slumbered on their arms. Weary from the forced march and the labour of firing the city, they slept all too soundly. Faults they may have had, but excessive caution was not one of them. And now too few outposts were flung out. Besides, between them and the Roman camp on Montmartre lay the island of embers and the concealing curtain of smoke. So they did not see the tables again being turned; the Romans on the mainland north of the island stealing down to the shore and there silencing the thole-pins of the larger barges stolen from the people of Melun. Meanwhile, the smaller boats, unmuffled and skeleton-manned, were sent up the Seine as though for Melun. The tremendous tumult the crews made should have aroused suspicion, and some of the Gauls did wake. But they took this retreat for real, and thought the whole Roman army was in flight. Old General Camulogenus sent some detachments he could ill spare to keep pace on the Left Bank with the supposed army splashing out in midstream. Then, congratulating themselves, the Gauls turned over to sleep; and not one Gallic scout reported the march of the main body of Romans from their Montmartre camp downstream to a point about four miles west of the island where the barges put in. So from a spot now called Auteuil by the Bois de Boulogne, where the Empress Eugénie would some day ride with her court under their parasols, the Romans—infantry and horse—were ferried over.

At two in the morning and in a violent storm, the first troops landed. The thunder still covered their advance up the Left Bank and the few Gallic outposts, huddled under the meadow oaks, were looking for lightning—not Roman short swords. They were butchered to a man.

For two hours the barges continued their ferrying. The last trooper was dragging out his swimming mount by the bridle as the rear-guard of the thunder retreated up the Seine; and below the hill to the east, where the Pantheon would be built, and just below the summit of which the Gauls slumbered, the morning star shone in the first green and opal dawn. It went out in the full red just as the one scout who had escaped the massacre rushed into the camp, sending the Gauls flying for their arms. At once there was all too much clamour. Children cried, war dogs yapped. Horses, half-harnessed, kicked off the emblazonry from the war chariots. The confusion was natural. For three ways must the Gauls face. They must look to the east, upstream, for the decoy fleet which might return; over the river and the smoking island to the Montmartre camp, which appeared still full of soldiers (the few left behind kept so many fires burning); and downstream for that just landed army.

Sounds of the gigantic hubbub in the camp of the Gauls came to the Romans who were now but two miles below the island down the river; and there was no longer any need for silence. Like all

of the great Consul's commanders, Labienus could use eloquence
as well as shovels and short swords; and he hurled the militant
bronze of his voice full into the molten brass of the sun, just
coming up over the hill to the east, where the frenzied Gauls were
strapping shields to their arms and throwing their gay cloaks over
their shoulders.

Now that hill would make history over and over. Its brown
fields and green woods would give place to cobbled streets leading
past the Roman baths, exquisite Cluny, the Pantheon—then to grey
alleys threading a maze of convents, hospitals, university schools,
of attics, chimney pots, and famous dormers. On the hill, Clovis,
Villon, Ronsard, Robespierre, Zola, the Curies, a legion of illustrious folk would walk and talk and do much more than walking
and talking. Altogether, it was a dramatic place for a battle. But
Labienus was more concerned just then with the morning's work
than with future history—his commander, Caesar, could write all
of that he wanted to. Now he had determined not to charge up
that hill. He would give the Gauls who were making such a noise
behind it rope enough to hang themselves. They should do the
charging upon his javelins.

At last he halted them. The ground he had picked here, two
miles from that Pantheon site on Sainte Geneviève's hill, was sacred
enough, or would be, though it would have a soldier's rather than
a scholar's glory. A few hundred yards to the east of his legions
lay the Champs de Mars where Charles the Hammer would hold
his spectacular reviews, and, later, Napoleon would harangue his
hussars and plumes and eagles. Here—out of history's mists you
could almost see it taking shape—would rise the great military
school where Cadet Bonaparte would ride at horse rings and Foch
would teach tactics. And just ahead were the meadows where, with
Vauban and Turenne, under a great gilt dome, in a blue-lighted
tomb, Napoleon and Foch would sleep the sleep that knows no
bugle's interruption.

While he waited for the Gauls to come on and entrap themselves,
Labienus addressed his massed legionaries, with their practical helmets, metal-pleated little skirts, and oblong shields, by the river.

"Soldiers of Rome—men of the Seventh and the Twelfth
Legions, Caesar asks that we avenge our defeat at Gergovia. 'Twill
be easy, for these Parisians are vain, boastful, easily pricked. Our
soaring eagles will pick their gay feathers of cloak and headdress.
Their arms are yours and their jewelled bracelets—their youths,
too, for slaves. Their women will prove soft bedfellows! But see,"
he added, "that you take none over forty!"

The rough jest pleased them as much as the speech, and laughter
rang along the ranks. But it was no time for laughter. The Gauls

had left Mont Sainte Geneviève and Montparnasse. Marching west, alongside the river, already they were past the downstream point, the prow of the boat-shaped island. All seemed in great temper over their surprise. The long-trousered foot soldiers were still adjusting their equipment as they came on. The war dogs strained at their leashes. The war chariots bounced over fields littered with stumps. The bards, with their harps, forgot their songs, so busy were they arguing about the way the Romans had gotten into their valley without being seen, and cursing, with Gallic ribaldries, both Caesar and Labienus.

So they came out of the last shore woodlot into the open. The two armies faced one another on the gentle slope that runs from the river, by the Field of Mars, up the little rise now known as Vaugirard. This really is the western extension of the ridge, which to the east is called Montparnasse, and, at its highest point, Mont Sainte Geneviève.

The queerly shaped Roman bugle, which as the trumpeter sounded it looked like a Greek letter written in gold on the sky, called to the charge. Off their shoulders where, when marching, they kept them hanging, came the Roman short swords. On their heads went those visored helmets which looked curiously like jockey caps, not nearly so picturesque as the Gauls' with their fashionable flares.

But magnificently straight was the Roman line of steel—the infantry in cuirasses and skirts reinforced with metal, and bristling with javelins and spears; squadrons with slings and bullets of lead stationed at the company junctures; archers, but not many—since Caesar distrusted the bow—and, at the top of the gentle rise, a troop of horse under a red cavalry banner. Another, without colours, had sifted, for ambuscade, into a little screen of wood on the uphill flank—just before the Gauls had come into sight. All this steel line was pricked out, from the summit to the river, by the cohorts' standards: gold eagles, silver boars, bronze bears.

Even more striking was the Gallic army with its wealth of decorated arms, bright helmets and crests, tartans, baying wolf-mastiffs, and bards with gleaming harps. Though more picturesque, it was also more ragged. Their ranks, this unfortunate morning, seemed not only confused but a little thin, and altogether without the old Gallic confidence. The cavalry in particular had been depleted, not only by detachments sent after the decoy fleet toward Melun, but by the fire stampede of the evening before. Knots of foot soldiers were still trying to straighten themselves out; war chariots were still lumbering into the gaps, of which there were too many in the line. The Gallic right rested where some day would be that Valhalla of the great generals, the Invalides. Their centre and left went some distance up the slope, but not so far as the Roman line opposite them. Indeed it fell quite a little way short of the red cavalry banner on the hill's summit—also the troop masked in the wood.

Now there were more notes from the queerly shaped bugles, waking river and hills. The magnificently straight steel line moved forward, until the metal standards were almost in the Field of Mars. It was scarcely a charge, so deliberate, even measured it was. It really was a bait. Labienus could see that the Gauls were about to take it.

He signalled the trumpeters again. The legions stopped, braced themselves, their bows and spears, slings and javelins ready. The sun, now but a handbreadth above the Gallic ranks, was refracted from those bright helmets straight into the eyes of the Romans.

Then there came an even more dazzling burst of splendour as the Parisii ripped off their gay cloaks, baring their breasts to the foe. A moment these fluttered above the gleaming helmets, like a baptism of blood for this meadow where, down the centuries, soldiers of all the eras would gather. Then the cloaks fell to the ground as the Gauls plunged forward to meet the braced Romans.

The charge was as futile as the traditional gesture had been magnificent. From the Roman ranks, upon the racing waves of fair heads under shining helmets, on careening war chariots, red-throated war dogs, the showers of long arrows fell, then the hail of slingshot, and last the deadly javelins, spears, and swords.

This sequence explains the fatal day's carnage exactly; racing foot soldier, dog, horse, fell, spitted; and chariots cracked up, tumbling the oncoming bright waves behind them. Then the deadly Roman short sword got to work. The Gallic blade could slice, behead, but not thrust well. In the infighting, the Roman short swords, which the Gauls had called "silly," were fatal. The result was that the Army of Paris, both down by the river and in the centre, was shattered into disordered knots. In the cores of these, long Gallic swords could be seen rising, falling, rising again, perhaps, but then falling forever, the bright helmets with them, that of white-haired old Camulogenus in his last battle among them.

Finally, before the sun had reached its meridian, only Roman helmets could be discerned—that is, erect. And the last wolf-mastiff, as he leaped for a hated throat, was stopped midway in his spring. But perhaps the outcome of the day is more clearly explained by the manoeuvre which took place on the top of Vaugirard hill. Swiftly the horsemen under the first red cavalry banner swung down from the summit on the rear of the Gallic centre's disordered knots. The Roman left swung too, uphill from the Seine, as a second nutcracker jaw. Now the Gallic detachments sent toward Melun, having discovered that they had been tricked, returned on the run, but too late. On these the troop under the second red cavalry banner swung down hill from its wood ambuscade.

The shouts still kept up as the sun grew hotter and the Romans pursued, as hunters woodcock, the few fugitives left, far from the site of the great warriors' tomb, over in the woods and fields of Mont Sainte Geneviève and Montparnasse. Where students would throng the Sorbonne lecture halls and the Café d'Harcourt and dance with the *midinettes* at the Bal Bullier, the silver-grey beech trunks were crimson spattered. Springs bubbled red; fern dripped it. And the River Bièvre, which now flows under city streets, was as deep-hued as ever it would be by the Gobelin dyes.

In the afternoon there was singing on the river. The barges floated below their usual water-lines, for there were great cargoes of gold and coral shields and enamelled bracelets, also of women who, as Labienus had ordered, were under forty! Past the island, the city of Paris, a blackened ruin now, with wisps of smoke ascending like sighs of sorrow, and by the old dolmen stones, embryo of Our Lady's cathedral, shouting, laughing, hoarsely singing, rowed the Roman victors for the East.

Bloodily thorough as the victory seemed, it was not complete. Another battle to decide whether, for the next four hundred years, Rome or Gaul would rule, must be fought that fall at Alesia in the east. Something more was at stake, though this was not known to either of the armies. The Gauls, for all their faults of pride, independence, variableness, *naïveté*, and quick temper, had faith in a bright Heaven and in death for an idea much nearer her Son's way of thinking than Rome's gross materialism; yet a Gallic victory would actually delay Our Lady's entry into Paris. Rome would hate her Son and hang Him to a tree, but while far from intending it, would build roads for His couriers to carry His banners and His philosophy. So Rome would prepare a welcome for Him and hasten Our Lady's coming to Paris.

Furthermore, the Gauls, for all their inventiveness and valour, would never be organizers until their blood was mingled with the Roman, also with the Teutonic enemy through the Franks. But this was not yet; and if Rome could win the coming battle, she could handle the nomad barbarians, keep them occupied, at work, fooled with badges. Thus she would bring about a long and productive, if enforced, peace, in which the faith of the Cross might grow. In the great economy of the universe, in which nothing is wasted, the haters would serve the Hated. . . .

The amphitheatre in which the battle in the east took place was fit for so crucial a struggle. Actually it was shaped like a stadium, with the west end open. The other three sides were hills covered with Roman camps. Two little strips of green valley, each with a bright river, separated these fortified hills from the higher hill of Alesia in the centre of the valley. Green with trees by the rivers at its base, but sheer rock from halfway up to the citadel on its tableland top, Alesia seemed like some great acropolis rising out of the valley, the giant ark of the covenant of Gaul.

And here, looking out from these aerial walls, stood Vercingetorix, whose name meant literally, "King of Warriors," and who in his young manhood had been chosen by voluntary vote King of all Gaul. If one could have seen him there with his staff, surveying the besieging armies of Caesar all around him and below, and gazing west for the relieving troops, that name and the unanimous vote would have been easily understood. Tall, fair, handsome, he was own brother to Clovis, Charles the Wise, Saint Louis, the Domremy Maid, and Foch—one with Charlemagne.

Now in the plains to the west he saw them, the relieving troops, his fellow Gauls, and the starving citizens shouted. There were only a few Parisii, refugees from the great battle of Paris, in that onmarching throng, but two hundred thousand from other tribes which would give their names to great cities—the Carnutes to Chartres, the Ambiani to Amiens, the Suessones to Soissons, the Senones to Sens, the Remi to Rheims—a gallant throng, although with rather too many chiefs for unity. And for all of them— though they could not know this—there would be a greater advantage in defeat than in victory. For only triumph for Rome that day could, in the end, bring about the arrival of Our Lady. The descendants of all of these tribes would build great houses for her, one in each capital city, and almost as beautiful as her great home in Paris.

At the west or open end of the natural stadium they paused with their horses and dogs, helmets and shields, to look up at the hill city which was so high it gave all in the valley the feeling, even when they were not looking up, of forever craning their necks. Then they gazed at the machines with which Caesar was everywhere covering the valley—gazed and wondered, then swore in disgust. Almost right then and there they turned around and went home. They had expected a grand charge, the gallant shock of battle, not war with machines! Death the arch-enemy into whose eyes they could dauntlessly look they welcomed, not Death invisible.

But there were the machines—machines everywhere. They were seeing something new in the world. It was as revolutionary as the first cannon at the siege of Civitale, the first planes and tanks which centuries later would appear on fields just a little north of this spot.

Great shields of wood and leather, each on three rollers, had been wheeled forward to protect the legionaries and trench-diggers. Supporting these were metal-springed catapults discharging steel arrows, and great springed *ballistae* hurling stones. There were towers several stories high filled with soldiers and equipped not only with wheels but with drawbridges, which could be let down on the city ramparts so that the soldiers could rush onto the city walls. Of course, these mobile towers would not reach up to the aerial citadel of this valley, but Caesar was using them here to guard his slaves digging ditches or cutting down trees for defenses, from arrows raining down or sorties from Alesia. All these engines of war had protections for their men. Even the battering rams and the giant grappling hooks were manipulated by crews from under little shed roofs.

Everything, in fact, seemed to be done by this Caesar under cover. The whole valley was cluttered, not only with machines but with thousands of little sheds, all on rollers. Through long tunnels made of these coupled movable sheds, men were bringing up, in perfect safety, earth, stone, timber, for the walls with which Caesar was ringing Alesia. The advance workers on the earth walls were protected by squadrons of those great shields and mobile towers. And central galleries had been left in these ramparts so that material brought up to them through the shed tunnels could in safety be added to the forward sides of the earth walls.

With these machines Caesar, whose banner bearing his name in great advertising letters floated from the camp on the southeast hill, had locked up Vercingetorix. He and his hill city were locked up and tied in with a great belt, woven of the two rivers and the three surrounding hills of timbers, trenches, and earth walls. Where there was river and hill, there was little work for the slaves. But there were great stretches where river and hill had to be connected, also low-lying slopes over which the belt must be run.

It was made of this texture: first, a great ditch of water; lines then of iron spurs set in planted stakes; a series of fences woven of thorn branches; and finally, pits lined with stakes and covered with boughs. Sets of such fortifications shut in the Gauls on Alesia; others confronted armies coming from the west. At frequent intervals, too, the belt was studded with high stationary towers. The only weak link was by the northwest hill.

In fact, so tightly had Caesar woven the belt that, while he could not get up and in to Vercingetorix, the King of Warriors could not get down to the corn, metals, and wines of the country.

And so badly did he need provisions that two weeks before he had sent his cavalry down through the belt. Thus there would be fewer men and horses to feed; and then a few warriors might get through to carry the word to all Gaul. Only the night before, one of the nobles had suggested the drawing of lots. The long ends would eat the short ones. Vercingetorix, however, had quoted the maxim which summed up the faith of his race: "Honour the gods, do nothing base, and practise manhood." Eating manhood, he said, was not practising it. Should all other ways fail, he would trade his own person for the security of his people.

It was that belt, the machines and the sheds that were to count now, and not the impressive bright helmets, the gold and coral shields, and war-cries, or even the noble character of the King of Warriors, or the Gaul's way of life—death for an idea. That was the tragedy. An older order, an earlier chivalry, was passing. Chivalry was, perhaps, a little to blame. Its chiefs were so seldom of one mind, while there was only one Caesar.

But though the Gauls might quarrel, for three days and a half now they tried, as one man and with incredible valour, to pierce the belt. They even discarded their bright shields and scoured the plains at night for stone, timber, fagots, to fill the ditches and made endless hurdles for leaping them.

In the morning, they would take up their weapons again, until the whole western end of the stadium was full of their glory. Then the war-cries would sound and they would assault the belt, filling the ditches, leaping them on their hurdles, only, as they reached the belt meshes, to become entangled, foot soldier and rider, on the stakes in the bough-covered pits, on the iron spurs which the Romans, appropriately, since death was in them, called "lilies." When they could extricate themselves they fought with stones or bare hands. This was discouraging. And quite as the lowland countries were frightened in the Second World War by the sirens on the diving planes, they were confused now by a new clamour. They were familiar with the groans of the wounded, the bark of military command, the rattle of stones and arrows off shields, the crash of the armour of those pitched off scaling ladders. But they did not like the endless crunch and whine of the rollers of the sheds and walking towers, the clank and recoil of the catapult and *ballista* springs that violated the peace of the far-distant hills. And the green rivers, the muddy ditches, floated black with bodies. The iron "lilies," the woven-thorn fences looked like hedges thick with impaled sparrows.

Through the three days and a half, Vercingetorix and his men looking down from the aerial walls did more than watch those assaults. As often as there were attacks from their allies in the west,

the Alesians in the east matched them. As soon as the wild cries
of the Gauls came up from the valley, open would fly the city
gates high on the hill and down would rush the Alesians with
timbers and bundles of brush, and so precipitately that the watcher
would have thought they would all have tumbled from the sheer
paths leading down from the city into the rivers below.

After each onslaught the belt would tighten. Whenever the
legionaries were being hard pressed, couriers would dart all over
the belt. Or Caesar himself would appear in purple consular toga,
with those strong legs and shoulders which would have served a
gladiator, the whipcord and rock that made up his face, and that
formidable line of mouth. At once, at galvanizing lash of a word
or incisive wave of the hand, groaning towers would move to
threatened bastions, or fresh companies would race to tired battalions. And back would climb the decimated Alesians to the
city gates.

At the end, the battle continued all night. In the light of a
ghostly half-moon, phantom companies advanced toward the
ditches, filled them, and whole platoons this time got over. Their
war-cries, the dogs' baying, went up to the city. In the light
streaming out as the high gates opened above, those in the valley
below could see the black files of men, looking tiny so far up,
starting down once more with their arms, brush, and hurdles.

So all night these bodies of men who appeared like ghosts, but
with cries quite mortal, hurdled trenches or fell into them, scaled
walls or dropped from them. All night, grappling hooks clawed
at towers as the towers themselves moved weirdly across a landscape shadowed by night and now rendered more murky, again
lighted up by brandished torches, burning tents, and showers of
arrows of fire flying across the face of the moon.

With dawn the tumult died down, the skeleton companies were
changed by the upsurging red of day from phantoms into weary
men making their way back to the Gallic camp west or uphill to
Alesia. And Caesar, dripping with perspiration, cursing everyone
that got in his way, went into his tent. Both sides knew that before
another dawn one or the other must give way, that one of two
stars was for a long time setting—that of the Gauls or Celts, which
for centuries had burned so bright, or the red, upswimming planet
of Rome and Mars. If the Gauls unbuckled that belt, Caesar would
never be master of the world.

There was still one point at which they might break the belt—
where it wound, exposed, over the foot of Mount Réa, the hill just
north of the stadium's west, or open, end. It was the one place,
besides the hill city, from which the Gauls might come down on
the belt from the upgrade. And at night half of what were left

of the Gauls marched to the top and rear of this hill. With day-break, they charged the trenches at the foot, and at the same time the citizens of Alesia made one last try at the belt east.

The Roman legions were under Brutus, a man of fine presence and finer intentions. But Caesar had no use for fine intentions that failed. When, under the downhill charge of the Alesians, the legions recoiled, he cursed Brutus, as Washington did handsome Charles Lee at Monmouth—a curse which Brutus would repay in full in the Roman Forum—and himself, as great Caesar, took command and rushed in those ancient foes of the Gauls, the German cavalry from across the Rhine. So for the last time the remnants of the Alesians climbed wearily uphill to the city gates. There was little use in closing them now. Vercingetorix longed to rush, sword-in-hand, into the battle west, to die there. But that fine person of his he must save for the inevitable trade with Caesar.

Still, looking forth from his sky bastions now, he could see a little glimmer of hope. In the northwest, the Gauls, coming down over Mount Réa, had almost broken the belt. They were not now at their occasional worst, a vainglorious mob, but at their noblest, fighting for a forlorn cause. Caesar too had perceived their temporary success and had rushed in his Paris conqueror, Labienus. He himself, having taken off the purple consul's toga, to don the commander's scarlet mantle for a rallying banner, was racing inside the belt, calling on the reserves to follow him.

There was another manoeuvre which the Gauls did not note. Already troops of cavalry from the hills northeast were trotting around to their rear. And there, upon the top of Mount Réa, just as Caesar's scarlet toga flashed into the bloody angle below, appeared the last reserve of the Gauls. They filled the northwest horizon with a glory so great it seemed as though the fire of the sun just before its setting and the afterglow came together. The fire was the light of the sun leaping from crest to crest of their shining helmets, the afterglow the rich dyes of their striped cloaks. Then, at a sign from their commander, came the age-old ceremony, the baring of the breast—for the convenience of materialism and of Caesar, able advance man of the merchants of Rome.

It was the last time the Gauls were to make that historic gesture. As one man they made it; as one the long line of red-striped cloaks came off, fluttered for a second like banners, then were cast to earth, covering hill and horizon with red as at some vast mass blood-christening. For the last time the battle howl of the dogs resounded from cliff to cliff, as the clashing of sword on shield and war-cry rang through the farthest ranges.

Then this most ancient of the old guards of France, like those at Crécy, Pavia, Poitiers, Waterloo, in bright billows plunged downward, horse, man, dog, chariot, shining helmet for a little time erect, then toppling. So, on the bloody angle, the bright billows crashed. And on their rear rode that masked cavalry, shattering the already broken billows into still bloodier spume. It was—as so many times it would be through the ages—French valour falling reckless under Roman spear, English longbow, Prussian machine gun. That valour would be kept alive, for Nature's breeding purposes, only because from time to time a Clovis, a Charlemagne, Charles the Wise, Turenne, Napoleon, Foch, or a simple Domrémy girl would appear to temper that reckless spirit with strategy to outmatch a foe's vaunted efficiency.

So, with the massacre of these valiant and childlike warriors, passed the glory of old Gaul, never to return until the great Clovis should come riding, to give it a new and Frankish setting.

The next morning, Vercingetorix, bidding farewell to his sacred city on the rock, the ark of the covenant of his race, rode down the steep paths to Caesar. The conqueror had again donned the purple consular mantle. Cursing, for he had a crick in his back from the Italian marsh air, he hitched himself up on a big throne, straightened his shoulders, and as he saw the King of Warriors coming, assumed his best rock-and-whipcord expression.

"There," he observed to his sycophants, "rides a strange fellow. He fought, not for money or glory or his own ambitions, but without thought of self, only for love of his people and his own soil."

With his head, being shrewd, Caesar recognized this, not with his heart.

Around in a circle, then, before him rode the King of Warriors, tall, fair, handsome, his cheeks not mustachioed as you see them on old statues, but smooth, as he looks out of old coins. A gold crown was on his head, on his arms two magnificent serpents of gold. His horse, proud of his master and his own royal caparisons, arched his neck, not knowing this was to be his master's last ride. Dismounting, the king took off the saddle, the gorgeous housings, his own jewelled sword and crown, laid them on the ground before the greater, but lesser man, Caesar.

Two promises Caesar made: the first—amnesty for the King's people—Vercingetorix wanted; the second—mercy for himself—he did not care about. The first promise, Caesar kept because it was a good way to consolidate colonies. The second, six years later, he broke, hauling behind his chariot, the King of Warriors in chains, but still own brother to Clovis, one with Charlemagne. The parade over, the conqueror slew him, threw his body on a pile of offal to the dogs. It is just as well that we have those old coins.

The Gauls who died in the great battle were more fortunate. Believing what they had from childhood been taught, they did not lie there to rot on the field of Alesia. No, on the shoulders of their father, the serene, wise, old river, their spirits were borne past Melun and many a hamlet to the old city of Paris. So they floated by the little forests of masts with leather sails, the remudas of horses sentinelled by the silent, cloaked horsemen, the sugar-loaf houses, the great ones with the silver slabs in their walls, the altars they had died for, and to rekindle a fire on which a sweet Lady was on her way, with her Son. And the waves of the old Seine lapped their tired hearts as it bore them to the Gauls' bright Heaven of the West, over the immemorial sea.

II

Rome has conquered Gaul, but Gaul will be the Victor in the End. . . . Rome is the Heavyweight Champion of Builders. . . . The Temple of Jupiter goes up on the Future Site of the Cathedral. . . . Into it go the Druid Altars.

1 B.C.

DECISIVE VICTORIES ARE SO OFTEN INCONCLUSIVE, RAISING at once the question, who is the victor, who the conquered, in the end? Is it the water that takes possession of the sponge, or is the sponge triumphant when it absorbs the water? Who is the master, the masculine strutter, the dominant race, or the one apparently subjugated which, like a woman, allows the strutting yet completely surrounds the strutter, and in all the things she cares about completely moulds him to her will.

The Romans were not, in some ways, as smart or adult as the childlike Gauls. They did not see that this Gallic sponge that would be France was growing stronger in every cell with all the Latin water it was soaking up. And surely it is a proof of the vitality, a sign of the destiny of a people, when they can absorb the mettle of another without forfeiting their own quality or changing essentially from the manner of men they have been.

Many times in three thousand years France thus changed defeat into ultimate triumph. But the triumph was not so apparent in those years just before that simple event of the stable, when all the world was whirling so rapidly out of the Old Dispensation into the New. The Gallo-Roman picture then seemed so much more Roman than Gallic. Over the new wooden trestle bridge that had taken the place of the one so patriotically destroyed by the Parisii (as the second in the long line of bridges that have crossed the Seine from the Left Bank, where the Petit Pont is now), were passing more Roman togas than Gallic breeches. Forever they were coming up from the south—hobnailed Roman legionaries, merchants, lawyers, light-o'-loves, judges, students from the Latin universities at Geneva, Marseilles, Lyon, also artisans and real estate speculators, for a building boom was now on in Paris. One could see this from the changed skyline. In among the Roman public buildings, shops and villas, already completed and the unsurfaced walls under construction, were a few of the old Gallic sugar-loaf thatches. High in the one or two remaining oaks of the Druid grove there still hung, dimmed and rusting, the once bright helmets and gold-and-coral shields the Romans had taken as trophies. But the city silhouette was now almost entirely composed of the hard lines of tiled roofs, brick walls, marble pediments, varied only by the Roman arch's resolute curve, and with, as high point of the island, the new Temple of Jupiter. Three-quarters up, its rising columns and walls, its pediment aburst with haughty gods, were sketched like an architect's unfinished elevations on the beautiful blueprint of the Paris sky.

And for a while it would pay the Gauls to cleave to the hard, straight line of Rome, its directness, the shortcut through the wilderness it made. The marking of that line had really been done by the legions. Now a legion, which had varied in number with the different régimes, ranging from twenty-four hundred to six thousand men, was officered by two co-colonels, called tribunes, who, curiously enough, alternated in command, and ten redoubtable Roman captains, those almost fabulous cocks of the European walk, the centurions. These, though Latin, were not voluble and volatile, as we now conventionally take all Latins to be; they were laconic and trained, through years of hard campaigning, to a high degree of military finish, efficiency and poise. There were not so many of these legions as one, from the firm control they held, might expect—perhaps not more than twenty-five around all Europe. Their work was supplemented by huge navies—how huge may be guessed from the action off Actium between Octavian, Julius Caesar's grand-nephew, and Antony with Cleopatra, when it was said the whole eastern Mediterranean was covered with great splinters and corpses, and Cleopatra escaped to Alexandria with "a pitiful fragment of her mighty fleet." That "pitiful fragment" was sixty ships! Still, the vertebrae of the empire were not those three-tiered *triremes*, but her veteran legions. Forever they were fighting or building forts and roads, protecting trade routes, booting about barbarians who would not "collaborate" with Rome, pinning badges on all who would. It was they who did most to consolidate the colonies and a world which, without them, would have remained in a most violent state of flux and consequent uproar.

Before Actium, the empire had been not three-in-one, but three, split up among Octavian, Lepidus, and brilliant but foolish Antony. Now Octavian, who had become Augustus and in his own conceit God, had conquered, united the dissevered legions, the scattered navies, built up all the cities and intercolonial commerce, stepped up the revenue flow, and made all Europe and much of Africa and Asia one. That "one" still contained within itself the seeds of its own corruption which in the end would split it wide open with a crack whose echo still can be heard around the world. And the principal seed of its decay was the same old master-race idea which never, never can permanently succeed. But for the time Augustus-God had made the empire solid again. Tap it anywhere, from the Ganges to Gaul, and it would give almost a sound ring.

That ring seemed good in Paris now. And although some of the old Gauls spat in the Seine when the new bridge clattered with the legion hobnails overhead, business was good too. They could sell their fish, firewood, onions, soap, pretty pots and dyed textiles to the villas, and also to the governor's palace which, just as the Druid altars would furnish stone for the Cathedral, would supply foundations for the Palais de Justice where Saint Louis was to pray, Villon and Marie Antoinette and de la Motte to plead for their lives.

The Parisians could, if they preferred, mix concrete, carry brick up scaffolds, cart in stone. Any tramp in a faded red-and-white Gallic tartan stained by the years and the wine-shops, with which the Romans were giving Paris a real city look, could get work if he cared to risk a Roman scourge or boot. If he didn't, he might be impressed anyway, and kicked underground into those quarries which we call the Paris Catacombs, and where by the light of little candles in cardboard saucers we gaze today on twenty centuries' dead.

To be sure, these were not our old Gauls. The wars, as they always manage to do, had killed off the best stock. The new babies did not mature like their ancestors into strength and height; and Paris women no longer felled men with their fists. Gaul was embryo France, and it should be noted by all who felt that the debacle of the nineteen forties was something new and the end of France, that such things have happened before. France has not always been at the top through three thousand years. She has been conquered before as she was then conquered by Rome. She has had her debacles before when rulers were weak, generals inefficient, when the whole strength appeared to have gone out of her. She has known troughs of despair between her shining crests of glory. From the sixth and fifth centuries B.C., when she dominated Europe, down to the Second World War, she has been several times on the verge of annihilation, only to recover. This is the difference between France and all other lands. They have known from one to five centuries of glory, then have burned themselves out. Times innumerable France has risen.

But this was no crest. Gaul was playing the patient sponge now.

And the majority of the Parisians who, in spite of their argumentativeness were goodnatured, were taking on the conqueror's ways— the aristocratic youth wearing togas, studying Latin school-books, aping centurions' oaths, the adults adopting the new coinage, weights and measures and trade customs, and some, deplorably, the fashionable vices of the Roman gods. In remote regions, Druid altars were still lighted. But in the cities, like Agendicum or Sens, Noviodunum or Nevers, Genabum or Orleans, belief in the old bright Gallic Heaven of the West was dead, never to be resurrected, although Our Lady and Her Son were coming to replace it with another and still brighter set of mansions.

What dulled embers of the old faith were left glimmered, but as witchfire superstitions. The old rites of the trees, for example, were still kept up, with ceremonies not unlike our Maypole festivities and that fairy ring which fifteen hundred years later the Lorraine children would weave with a girl in her teens whose military skill would match the great captains', her purity and sweetness—almost—Our Lady's.

Like their altar fires, the speech of the Gauls was vanishing, and they would hand on, through the centuries, but a few words. In this they did not make such a bad trade. Latin turned out an even more resonant vehicle for their oratory.

For that matter, the Roman faith too had decayed. If it never had shown anything like the Gallic idealism, at least it had once had a wholesome, rustic simplicity. Vesta, in the good old days, had been the protector of the hearth, the exemplary housewife whose price even Solomon would have declared "above rubies." Jupiter had been a nourishing husbandman, patron of the sky, the warming sun, and the grape. Janus had been the superintendent of the farm, guardian of the foyer, the home; Mars too the farmers' friend, the kindly squire. And the trees, the familiar animals, the boundary stones of their farms held a special sanctity for the old Roman.

But then as more authoritarian grew the state and as Augustus and Nero ranged themselves alongside the gods, those deities took on some of the inhuman traits of human beings, the ambitious Romans climbing up from below. Janus, gentle guardian of the farmer's dooryard, was promoted to the clanging, brassy gates of Rome which shut out all hope. Vesta, shorn of her hearthbroom of twigs, was made grande chatelaine of the Temple; and her attendants, the vestal virgins, with their thumbs down, became the most vicious spinsters ever known. Jupiter himself was transmogrified into a chest-thumping god of victory. Mars was changed from the helpful friend of glebe and acre into a bloody, fee-fi-fo-fum sort of creature that would have delighted the modern dictators. And by a most curious inversion of the Christian ethic, his pruning hook was beaten into a spear, his plowshare into a sword.

Moreover, where before in the earlier and democratic phase, the people, with the help of a few sybils and seers, had run their own religion, the emperor now manipulated a complicate clergy. The church had become as much an instrument of state as the army or navy; the elaborate temple rites had been turned into propaganda and—how the ancient and modern parallels multiply!—the head of the state threw up statues of himself all over the empire, so easy thence would be the step to dictator-worship.

And now when the average Romans, like the Gauls, observed a few ceremonies such as their old rites of tree and pets and boundaries, it was quite as modern folk might celebrate Hallowe'en while ignoring the sacred significance of All Saints Day from which the secular festival sprang. As for the more elaborate temple sacrifices, they welcomed these, because they brought holidays, circuses, an extra supply of idol meat for all; and religious culture meant employment. Gods had to be catered to when such good wages were paid for stuccoing houses for them or, in the stoneyards, for carving them into the simulacra of life. Augustus should have sensed the danger. For when the gods of a race, even when not of the noblest, lose in veneration and popular esteem, though prosperity seems at high tide, the ebb is at hand. But then he had made himself Augustus-God, at the very time when God was coming to earth, and he could not foresee the ebb. One thing is certain: With all the outward order suddenly come, with the Augustan age to the world, and all the inner decay, there could have been no better time for the entry of Our Lady and Her Son.

And now, not her house, but Jupiter's, rashly built on ground which would seem to have been preempted by destiny for her, was nearly complete. It looked impressive by the Seine, but from the first the contractors had grumbled. The trouble was that they were from Rome, and Paris lacked the abundant materials which they had always had at hand. Rome was the heavyweight champion of builders. She dug her foundations very deep, threw her porticos and colonnades high, crowned all with huge domes. Her monolith pillars were gigantic; and behind all her dressed fronts she slewed in tremendous masses of concrete. She could do this where Paris couldn't—then. The time would come when in the Cathedral, Paris would outbuild her.

It was Rome's natural deposits as much as her short swords that had made her great. Other races had won, would win, world power through things taken out of the earth. Not so long before iron had made the Gauls themselves supreme over Europe and Rome. Gold

would give Spain her brief hour of splendour; coal, England her
industrial hightide. Iron, nitre, copper, manganese, bauxite, a host
of minerals would bring to Germany her dazzling but horrible
burst of glory, and to us the snuffing out of it. Her mineral wealth
had given Rome her masonry and much of her mastery of the
world, because of her splendid forts, roads and aqueducts which
consolidated and guarded the empire, and the arenas, palaces, and
temples that added to her prestige and held the colonials in thrall.

Near the Seven Hills or within ferrying or carting distance of
them, were these priceless things: Rich Tiber beds of clay for the
best brick. The finest building sand in the world, not from pits,
but the finer grades from the clear river bottoms. Albano ash, a
chipped stone, ash, and gravel conglomerate, grand for rubble filling and concrete. Silex lava that made those Roman roads which
never seemed to crack. Creamy limestone from Tivoli. *Tufa,* red,
yellow, blue, a building stone excellent with stucco. Fine lime and
all the marble dust and chips they wanted for that stucco. Marbles
of beautiful hues from Tuscany, a mottled variety from north
Africa. Onyx, alabaster, gold, ivory, from other colonies. And,
most important of all, the *pozzolana,* or earth impregnated with
volcanic lava, which when mixed with sand, cement, and water,
made a concrete as hard as God's own rock. Their sand and cement
were superb, but this *pozzolana*—the union by Nature of lava with
Italian soil—was Rome's peculiar treasure. It was the magic ingredient in her concrete, the real secret of her strength. Not so
much the living Caesars as the dead volcanoes made Rome the
"Eternal City." Not so much from the sword as from this humble
deposit of the earth sprang the "grandeur that was Rome."

Paris did not have anything like this abundance of material;
because of this and perhaps also from affectation, the Roman contractors and overseers cursed all the products of the Seine valley
and the Paris hills. It is true they did have those huge dolmen-
roof Druid altar-stones, which went into the Temple; but as a rule
the native stone was light. They could not quarry the many large
building blocks they were used to in Rome, and which they did
not secure with mortar but fitted carefully one upon the other,
fastening them with oak dowels and iron clamps.

Still, they did pretty well with what was at hand: Limestone and
freestone from the quarries on the Rue Saint Jacques, from Montrouge, and from those where the Paris Catacombs stretch now,
also from Pontoise—brought up the Seine by boat. The brick
fired in the kilns in the Bièvre meadows. The Paris concrete that
had no volcanic magic, only Chaumont cement—from the hill
northeast—and the Seine sand and gravel, or *grève,* which gave its

name to the famous Place de Grève, where criminals were executed and public grievance meetings were held—whence the name, *grève,* for strike.

Certainly the road-beds they made then were to last. It would be, for example, nineteen hundred years before they would pry up the old Rue Saint Jacques to repave it. And we know how the Cathedral, made of limestone like that which went into Jupiter's Temple, has lasted for eight centuries and can last for ages more, unless the sons of men destroy it with nitre, iron, manganese, copper, bauxite, and all their chemicals diabolically used. Indeed, the whole Gallo-Roman city, made of these same "too light" Paris materials, might have endured down to today had it not been for progress and the Gothic and if many builders had not put on, in place of tiles and stone, too many wooden roofs for fiery Norman arrows to light on. As for Jupiter's Temple, which only stayed up about three hundred years, it could not have endured forever if Our Lady's house was to go up by the Seine.

All these building details are important, if the Cathedral was ever to go up. For the building experiments of that age would start others in endless chain. The Roman style would give birth to the Byzantine and early Basilican, the latter to the Romanesque and that, in turn, to the Gothic, architectural heir of all the ages that had gone before. From out Roman arch and supporting walls would spring the half-barrel vault and ogive, then the pointed arch and the high delicate Gothic walls of the Cathedral that were no longer mere supports but Heaven-high framing for gorgeous windows. So a thousand years of trial and error all over the world would solve the construction problem of the ages—of weight and thrust, roofing and lighting—and solve them so beautifully that the Gothic would seem not the work of mortals with metal and stone, but of angels with leaf and branch, petal and sunset hue.

If the Romans were masters, the Gauls served their apprenticeship very creditably. This was well, since that apprenticeship not to Rome, but to a great building tradition that began with Man's first temple, would take a long time, in fact until the greatest of architectural eras would find its birthplace in the Ile de France, with Paris as its core. The apprentices would be masters then, their genius flowering here where dolmen grave roof, Druid altar, Jupiter temple, and early Christian church had been, in the ranged arches and flying buttresses, the panes and towers of Notre Dame.

The same craftsmanship these embryo Frenchmen had displayed in their graceful pitchers, their helmets with the fashionable flares, the very headstalls on their horses and the emblazoning of their chariots, they now turned to Italian tiles and oriental mosaics. With almost the old impetuosity they had shown with their chariots in the charge—for they were a naive if smart race—they now ran up the ladders to the scaffolding stages. This scaffolding, incidentally, was like that of mediaeval days. It did not cover the whole building at once, just a few sections at a time; like snails dragging their houses after them, the workers pulled out the timbers or "putlogs" from the putlog holes in the façade, and placed them and their platforms higher as the walls mounted.

Eagerly they tended the fires in the Left Bank kilns, those in the tile works, where the Tuileries Gardens are now, and which gave the Tuileries their name, and chiseled straight noses for Apollo, round bosoms for Venus, where purer saints and Our Lady would be carved later, and strained at pulleys and chains hoisting Jupiter into place, and stole rides aloft on the Roman gods' shoulders.

If the offender were scourged to death or fell and had a leg jammed in some windlass, that did not matter—that is unless the foreman were short on labour. Then though it was more for governors than for slaves—there was some surgery to help. Here where a long line of famous scientists and physicians—from Saint Landry through Paré and Pasteur—would work in the Hôtel Dieu, country doctors had already set up their signs.

Though these physicians were not as adept as those in Rome, they had acquired some little skill from the surgeons in the capital who had learned much from the Hindus, more from the Greeks—from whom they had taken most of the things worthwhile in Rome outside of their legions and their concrete. Indeed, the very instruments the governor's physician used now—the forceps, saws, probes, syringes, the rectal spatula and catheters—had been modelled on the set the Greek doctor Hippocrates had used almost five hundred years before Christ, when he tried to start doctors out honest with an oath and a code.

In those days the best of the practitioners in the great cities could do a surprising number of things. They could amputate in the method of the Roman Doctor Celsus—published in several papyrus rolls on the Seven Hills—do jobs of plastic surgery on wounded legionaries, open up skulls, help hernia, take out tumours, treat for cataract, operate on liver and spleen, remove pus in cases of empyema, clear up sinuses and reduce piles, and even cut up stone in the bladder. This operation was as fashionable in Rome as appendectomies would be later; and very good fees were paid by jealous emperors to doctors who would prescribe it for over ambitious citizens, especially if the surgeon in removing the stone from the bladder would remove from the world the troublesome patient. One such doctor, favoured of the court, had even had to flee Rome because his toll of both stones and patients became alarmingly high.

Yet not all of the physician's skill could save many of the Gauls who fell under the scourge or were crushed by swinging crane or under falling stone. The dolmen grave roofs that had later served as Druid altar stones, were at last swung into place. Symbols of faiths that had vanished, they went now into the temple of a faith that would vanish too, to be replaced by another even now coming into light in the East. These stones were covered, not only with the blood of innumerable animal and human sacrifices, but with the sweat and blood of the humble workmen. What Jupiter cared about that no one knows. But Our Lady and Her Son, who were coming, would always be just a little partial to slaves and outcasts.

III

The Zero Hour

JUPITER'S TEMPLE BY THE SEINE WAS ANOTHER STEP ON THE long road that led out of the mists of the past to the cathedral. But there was a more important event that happened about this time in the East. And if we are to understand, not only the cathedral, but the pageant of history, the march of men that led to it, we must, for a little while, go back toward the rising sun. The body of the cathedral was of the West, the pattern of it—the cross—was of the East. What went on inside its magnificent body revolved around a life once lived in the East. Cross body, altar, chapel, niche, pane, eloquently proclaim His story. The very structural parts, placed for engineering reasons in the cathedral's beautiful frame, align themselves not only in building harmony but as though by a miracle, in the harmony of the symbolism that points up that life and its objectives.

And many devices that make vivid the story—the chants, responses, music modes, credo, costumes, dialogue—had their origins in the East. Men from the Orient first recorded the story, shaped the scenario, and died to show it was infinitely worth the playing. From the Orient started the progression of playhouses that evolved into the gorgeous one called the cathedral. From the Orient, too, later on, crusaders came back with warm and colourful ideas for its building.

The cathedral, then, lovely blossoming of the cross, and what goes on within its beautiful body, the reliving of a hero's story, stemmed from the East. And there now we must go, to a valley where she lived who was mother of the Hero, and in whose name our cathedral of Paris and so many others around the world went up.

This famous valley of Our Lady extends three hundred miles from where it is watered by the Orontes River, north in the Antioch country, to where in the south the Jordan loses itself in the Dead Sea. And it is so carefully guarded by mountain ranges, one east facing the desert, the other west facing the sea, that it seems as though the Lord who singled her out had set the valley apart. Indeed, some said the choice had been made ages before. Otherwise why should the shepherd king Abraham and his father have driven their flocks from Mesopotamia with its rich cities, fine markets, its lands made fertile by two of the Garden of Eden's own rivers and the best irrigation system in the world? They settled first by the desert's edge, near Damascus; then Abraham crossed over into the southern part of the valley to found Hebron, very near Bethlehem and Jerusalem, in what was to be called Judah, a pocket handkerchief kingdom which a man could cross in two days' walk, and yet to become the most important kingdom in the world. This homeland of Our Lady, which was to be known as the Holy Land, is a harsh if ever picturesque, and, because of its rock hues, a high-coloured country. True, in spring, almond, apricot, plum blooms around old village walls; green fringes the great central river in the valley. But summer brings a violent change to the Palestine landscape. For many months there is little good grass in the highlands, even around blue Galilee. Except in the few brief deliriously lovely weeks around their Pasch, our Easter, festival season, the Brook Kedron in which Our Lord waded as a boy, yawns tawnily empty; Jerusalem lies like a scarred old lion on its sun-baked rock; the Jordan slinks south through fiery furnace gorges.

It is no wonder, then, that a race that could not only survive but flourish there, should prove as tenacious as the twisted, thousand-year-old olives, as passionate as the fiery breath that came over the mountains from the desert, as violent in its judgments as the hard oriental light, so that they were misled when the Prince of Peace of whom they had sung came with such humility into the tiny kingdom.

There were shepherds among them, and fishers and carpenters, as we have good reason to know, but they were inclined to be traders—never natural farmers like the Gauls—loving their cities, bazaars, and markets more than the soil. For this trading, for security too, they very early built strong walled cities on the hard heights, so that warders might see the foe while still far off. Not alone in the spring, when the anemones were red under His feet, would her Son live out His immortal story, but on the stony roads that led to the fortress cities in the hills.

Our Lady, one afternoon, two thousand years after Abraham, two thousand years before us, was on one of these hard roads leading out of Nazareth. That hard Palestine light, so almost violently brilliant on the powdered limestone, the yellow and rose-red rocks, the golden green lizards, the little black skipping goats, showed her figure, as she rode, a little heavier. Her companion, on another ass, was a little solicitous. Exercise just then might be good; but one had to be careful about stumbling.

Looking back from a high turn over Nazareth, where the carpenter Joseph had set up his little shop, she could see through a vista of white domes, old walls, and cypress cones, the home he had established for her. At a certain angle she knew she might catch a sight of his sinewy back as he bent over some new plane he had bought up in Jerusalem. The pile of shavings that fell from it came from cedars cut in the green belt in the Lebanon mountains north of her. It was expensive wood now. Joseph's royal ancestors had been wasteful, sending sometimes as many as thirty thousand men to cut down the green giants for their palaces and navies, and never doing any replanting. Joseph must ask higher prices for his beds, chairs, chests, these days. The odd thing about it was that a man who came from a long line of kings should have to bend over a work table.

But other cares were on her mind and in her heart—had been there frighteningly, exultingly, ever since the great news had come. When her companion, in calling attention to some familiar well or sheepfold or a camel cavalcade in the valley below, spoke her name, it did not sound precisely like Mary. Nearer Miriam it might have been—the name of the sister of their great leader Moses. Wise men were to argue many years about it, whether it was Miriam, which meant "bitter sea," or came from the Egyptian Mery, "the cherished one," or the Hebrew Mara, "the perfect one."

There were other vital statistics which she would not have thought at all important, but over which scholars would conduct long range duels—for example over her father's exact name—Joachim or Heli—and her birthplace. Sephoris, some said this was—a tiny suburb of a small enough Bethlehem. Others insisted she had been born in Jerusalem, just a city square's distance from her Son's own miraculous pool of healing, Bethesda. Churches, which the rival schools thought would be final exhibits, conclusive arguments in stone proving the truth of their claims, were built both in the little Bethlehem suburb and over the Jerusalem pool. Her parents had lived in Jerusalem for a time and had often walked by Bethesda Pool. Later they had lived in Bethlehem; and it is nice to know that Our Lord's mother was born, either in the hamlet that saw His coming or the capital that knew His passing.

There never was any doubt about the name of Our Lady's mother. As Saint Anne, she has a beautiful door—the south one in the façade of Our Lady's cathedral. But there was dispute about the site of the house to which Our Lady was riding now. Some would claim that her kinswoman, Saint Elisabeth—how the two women, in their humility, would have been horrified by that "saint"—lived at Saint-John-in-the-Wood, others at a point north, and churches would go up on both these sites.

The great news she was bearing to her cousin had frightened her at first. Her woman's hour would be like no other woman's in the world. The miracle that came to countless other women would be divine Miracle in her. Memories of the way the news had come still quickened her whole being. Now she thought of it as the accosting by a bright being who seemed to be of very high rank in another world. Again she had the vividly burning recollection of a sudden great light that filled the room and her head and heart, with voices coming out of the light. And despite the wonder of it, there had never been, even for the moment, any gainsaying of its truth, so that the Word that had mystically come to her did not need to be confirmed, as it was a little later, in the old, old way of nature.

Indeed, this great destiny seemed to her now as much of a fact as Joseph's shop or the village well. She did not lose humility in the consciousness of the great part she was to play, sweetly and humanly assured by the movements of the first born, so awing in the first motherhood. Still she went about the common tasks, as she always would even when the Child she carried was launched on His ministry, ever effacing herself, so that the masculine recorders of the gospels gave her but little mention after the birth. She was the perfect mother the world loved, the perfect Mother who had herself borne the Divine yet would never presume or obtrude upon it.

So, little of herself she thought. In this she was even purer than most saints who never see their own halos nor smell the perfume of their own holy deeds. For the heroic deed, the high duty, is performed by the great of soul, as is the little act—with a little more prayer perhaps, but with no pose, no histrionics, above all no standing outside oneself and approvingly looking on, just simply, directly, by one who is but naturally functioning, who while making history, is as quietly as inevitably expressing his or her own nature.

Some centuries later, Saint Athanasius would say, referring to her, "God has created a new thing in woman." This was no ignoble playing with words. This greatest of births was for the early Christians the central, the core fact of the universe. They saw no difficulty in accepting it. Every day they saw all around them two miracles. A millimeter of seed in the earth sprang forth into the giant tree. The microscopic seed in the womb became the prophet with his visions. If two beings who lived on some remote star where the first two miracles did not take place, were transplanted to Earth where these marvels were daily occurrences, would not their wonder over them have been as great as ours over the divine one? It was for them, then, no far-reaching jump from the two daily events to the other. In fact, it was only logical that the Maker of the ever-fresh, ever-startling miracles which all accepted, would choose to join up this life he was every second creating with the source life that was greater. To have failed to do so would have been anticlimactic in the great drama he was creating. So for them, as for many billions since in all generations, this young woman named Miriam, or our Mary, now travelling the stony roads of the Judean hills, occupied a special place. She was the very coupling forged for the linking of the Divine with the Human, toward which the whole universe was moving.

Yet there were the troubling human sides to this immortal drama. There was the putative father, for instance—Joseph, a kindly and Godfearing man who tried to give good wood and honest workmanship to his neighbours in Nazareth. In his consciousness, though more inarticulately, was the same acceptance of the divine miracle. But that it should come so near his humble carpenter shop, so near home, was astounding, baffling. And he was really the only one in Nazareth, in all Judah, who could be fairly certain of the fact, that great core fact of the universe, now to be made manifest.

However, it is to his great credit that he did not voice any suspicions or troubling questions that would have disturbed a sensitive soul like Mary, and at a bad time. She still walked the common ways, dusted and baked, but no more did she go to draw water.

He had made no objection at all when she expressed a wish to visit her cousin who had had news so strikingly like hers. Elisabeth was beyond the age of expectancy, yet she too had been told of a child, one that would prepare the way for the Other. It was quite natural that Our Lady should wish to ride over the hills so that the two women could confide in each other.

When she crossed the threshold, there was no need for any further angelic heraldry. For the babe in Elisabeth's womb stirred, then leaped up to hail the Babe in Mary's. So Elisabeth saluted her in the beautiful speech, "Blessed art thou among women." And Mary broke into that joyous, exalted speech—"My soul doth magnify the Lord . . . for He hath regarded the lowly estate of His handmaiden, and henceforth all generations shall call me blessed . . . He hath put down the mighty from their seats and exalted them of low degree," and all the other lovely words Luke has handed down to us and which, set to glorious music, would ring out in the churches, the cathedrals named for her, and all the cathedrals through the ages.

The nine months had passed when, back in Rome, Augustus the

Golden ordered a census. It was not his invention. Rome's first had been taken in 550 B.C.; and there had been a military one by Judah way back in Exodus times. Rome now counted her populations every five years. Her chief censors were powers in the state, regulating public morals too—no easy task when as fast as the imperial fortunes advanced public morals declined.

Couriers riding through the valley ordered every family to report at the birthplace of its chief. Ordinarily Mary would have welcomed a visit to Bethlehem. Even if she had not been born near there, as many have claimed, she had lived in the neighbourhood as a child. She knew the hills on which her father had pastured his flocks, the houses of the town, the inn, and the stable in the cave. But the hill roads were hard, the hoofs of the ass none too springy upon them, and her time was near. However, the journey had to be taken. In Bethlehem were to register all of David's royal line.

Over this line there would be trouble, for there was dispute about the grandfather of the Child she was carrying over the rough way. That royal lineage we can see in Luke. It is richly emblazoned too in the Tree of Jesse windows in many a cathedral. The name of that grandfather, Heli, is on the white gospel page. It is represented by a branch of the cathedral's bright glass genealogical tree. And Heli, say some, is the name of Mary's father, not Joseph's; and she, not he, was David's descendant. Also they point to one of those commas which have changed so many fortunes, this one in a line of Luke's, "To a virgin espoused to a man named Joseph, of the House of David." That comma, they say, throws that qualifying "House of David" back to Mary, and she it was, not Joseph, who was of royalty.

Most do not believe this. But it cannot matter. If it was Joseph that was of David's line, and Christ not being Joseph's son, was not by blood, only by adoption, of that line, that would still have sufficiently fulfilled the old prophecies. And if the comma, like a little sickle, attacks that great genealogical tree imprisoned in the bright Tree of Jesse windows, that cannot matter either. Already, in proclaiming the strain to be Joseph's, and denying the royal blood to her, who was Christ's one blood parent, the beautiful tree has given itself the lie. If so, it is only an earthy dynasty that has been shattered. He who loves beauty with truth, need not throw out that lovely window. For the Heavenly pedigree remains. He is alway's Mary's Child, and the Son of the Father. He is the great friend of Man who came to rescue him at the cost of His own life. The cathedral still stands. For the sons of men the heart of the immortal story still throbs, beats on forever. . . .

And so Mary and Joseph rode through the Bethlehem fields where a many times great-grandmother named Ruth had gleaned;

by the barn where she had laid her young head against a pile of corn; through the Bethlehem hills where a many times great-grand-father, David, had tended his sheep and practised on his harp; over the brook where he had picked his slingshot stones; by the village well where the great Judge Samuel had waited for him to crown him king—toward the inn.

In the few houses they knew already twinkled the little lamps of the householders going to bed. They knocked at the door of the inn. In the torchlight the landlord's face was churlish as he looked out. His beds and pallets were full, and a king not coming often to a village inn and the landlord not being one to recognize a royal mother without robe or crown, he slammed the door. Others pass-ing by with their wine, seeing Joseph's worried face, laughed rudely. There was so little compassion then in the world—there couldn't have been much, for the Seed in her was to be root of all such things.

Some say a stableboy was wiser than the rest, and slapped the cattle on the flanks, made them move over, cleaned out the foul straw, though he was tired, and shook down fresh bedding, making their resting place a little warmer, for the wind blew through the cave. Others are sure it was Joseph who, after the long ride, did all these things. At any rate, the humble ostler left behind an ancient lantern to light the Prince on His way.

But no one had to show them the well. Mary, knowing every landmark in the town, could tell Joseph where it was. And water would be needed. Since the hour was so late, no women were about to help him, only Mary, with her directions. But the well was a reassuring omen. It was the one used by the many times great grandfather, the king who loved to sing, named David. From it, soldiers who loved him had brought water to him hiding in a cave, at great risk to their lives; and learning this, he had poured out the water on the ground. As she lay there, Mary could see at first, through the opening, the usual stars. But now Joseph, going with his pitcher over the threshold, saw in the east a great star that looked like many stars swollen into one. Then its light came into the stable, and the wind that had whistled through the cave died down, as though to listen and watch with the rest of the universe. Gazing higher, at the hills, he could see in the bright illumination, the shepherds too looking upward, and in the skies around the great star, the shining focus, was a broader zone of light, which suddenly seemed peopled with shining spirits. They all seemed happy and sang melodiously—the same song the morning stars must have chanted in Creation's dawn when they all sang together. Perhaps they thought the Child might remember it.

But Joseph hurried in with his pitcher. Then, in that cold stable, with only the ancient lantern and the breath of the cattle to warm it, and the one little thorn-fagot fire, she went down into the Valley of Death which, even though she bore the King of Kings, with all women she must enter. Then, suddenly, with the highest, the farthest-reaching note, of that multitudinous song, out of the Valley of Death, came Life at its highest.

So there was heard in the stable the voice of a Child which, though tiny, should have been heard around the world.

In later times, some of the skeptical ones would call attention to the fact that none had calculated the exact date of that birth. Instead of being the Zero Hour, they would declare it was B.C., or before Himself. Dionysius the Little, a sixth-century monk, set the Christmas date we recognize, reckoning it by unverified dates of Herod's death and the massacre of the Innocents. But seven years wrongly calculated or not, it *was* the Zero Hour that split Time into two, divided the Old Dispensation, the old way of life, from the New.

Others would point to a bright conjunction of Jupiter and Saturn about 4 B.C., or argue that *nova* stars burn with a startling incandescence, then vanish forever, being chemical seven-day wonders and no miracles at all. But certainly the appearance of that star had a splendid timing for so great an event as the birth of the Child. Most of the skeptics have spent so much time searching for the link between the animal and the human that they should be the first to admit the like logic of a link between the Human and the Divine effected that night in a poor stable. . . .

Our Lady knew well the logic, as the little fist pressed the breast in, the little lips tugged at the fountain within her. There was Divinity reduced to the span of a woman's arms. The human circle now lapped the Divine centre, for the time an atom of flesh. The Divine drew life from the Human to which it had given life. Mortal arms upheld the Immortal that would one day uphold all the mortal that called to them. The round was complete. . . .

That same day, to some of the humble folk by the Seine were born children, ancestors of those who would build on the spot where Jupiter's Temple then stood, a greater house for Our Lady and her Son. Simultaneously they came into the world—babes of no account and the Babe of all account. And all drank in their mother's milk, learned to walk and talk, and dabbled their feet, they in the Seine, He in the Brook of David.

IV

The Cross in whose Form the Cathedral will be built is raised on a Hill.

33 A.D.

THE PEOPLE OF JERUSALEM, THIS HISTORIC NIGHT, SLEPT poorly. It was the springtime, but the atmosphere seemed as hectic as in midsummer. Nerves were taut, aroused by passion to a greater heat than that which burned the desert beyond the dread heights of Moab and Petra whose red rocks showed like dark crimson blots and the weird shimmer that proclaimed the Dead Sea.

Through every watch the Roman sentinels patrolled the streets. They had closed the wineshops early. This did not prevent disputes from arising late at night, behind closed doors, as to the exact spot of the arrest and the price paid to the Dark One who had led His capturers there. Above the roofs were thick with sleepers who turned restlessly at the clash of arms suddenly grounded in the palace guard-room or the bark of a shepherd dog in the hills where even the flocks, this night, did not lie quietly.

In an upper room Our Lady sat, surrounded by friends— friends who could do nothing, say nothing to ease her. Her Son, after supper in another upper room—the last He would take with His friends, had gone to the Mount of Olives, to a garden. She would have liked to have gone with Him. Later the news had been brought by one who loved her Son and who came running, that men with torches and swords had arrested him in the garden.

A little later, she heard that He had been brought to the high priest who, at the lying testimony of suborned witnesses, had rent his clothes, and all the elders had shouted terribly. Then they had stood Him in the high priest's hall and had struck Him and had spat in His face, as though they hated and would have put out the light of the world it held. They would turn Him over to Pilate in the morning. So sure was the condemnation into which they were harrying a not badly-intentioned governor, that, in another house, not far from Mary's, certain kindly ladies of Jerusalem rose before dawn to stir the cup of the doomed. Brewed of frankincense, vinegar, and myrrh, it sometimes brought a little surcease to criminals at executions. It would be presented to Him in the morning at a corner of the Via Dolorosa.

In a nearby palace, Pilate, who would try three times to save Him, paced nervously. He heard the uproar, knew what it boded politically. He did not like it and longed for some way out. When he tried to slumber, he tossed through the long hours, unrefreshed by the plashing of his fountains.

At a fire in the high priest's mansion, Peter had been warming hands which he thought were, but should not have been, cold. Then—so witnesses told Mary—something strange happened. Peter had not been his usual sure self, and he looked frightened. At the jeers of all by the fire, he swore he did not know his great friend and leader. Then He, bound and bruised, passed by the pillars on the way from the hearing, and He looked at Peter. A cock crew and Peter, breaking into bitter tears, rushed out into the night. No one had seen him since. This did not reassure the group waiting with her.

It was in the middle of the night that the cock had crowed, and now it was dawn. The sun came up and shone on the black marble, the gold corners of Herod's Temple. The Levites who watched the five outer gates and those by the inner portals rose. One rekindled the fire under the dome of the hall called Hel, where the priests warmed their bare feet. If the old ones sleeping on divans, with robes rolled up for pillows, were not, like Pilate's wife, startled out of their dreams by fearsome premonitions, they had not slept easily. This Passover week, so soon to flower into our Easter, and which should have known serenity and peace, had been almost riotous and disgracefully political; and they had not been happy. Perhaps Truth, which men lock in the hidden dungeons deep in their subconscious, and which has a way of rising and stalking them in their dreams, had whispered that they had missed their chance.

They were generals of an old army who should really have enlisted in the new that was being recruited out of the old. They were stout veterans; religion was breath to their nostrils; and there was a hard fight ahead for the new army which their vigourous souls would have loved. They might have been commanders in this new army which was to sweep the world. Instead, they would leave the leadership to a band of unknown fishermen and labourers whose names would ring round the world, through the far-off ages. These generals of the old army would have been so much better off if they had enlisted, for their stronghold, the Temple, was soon to be destroyed, and they would lose their posts. The trouble was that the ways of the new candidate for kingship were not royal. He appeared bent on receiving blows, not on dealing them out. And, so spies had reported, He did things as unregal as washing fishermen's feet at a farewell supper.

This reactionary spirit should not be too harshly compared, in the light we have now, with the faith of the unlettered fishermen. The eye sees only that for which it has been trained to look. The eyes of the men of Galilee had been sharpened for currents, winds, the signs of storm, leaping fish, and holes in nets, things as simple and direct as His own parables. The scribes had been taught to seek holes in arguments, hairs to split.

Furthermore, this candidate, this young man of thirty-three, whose back they had striped in the night with scourges, whose fine brow they would bloody with thorns in the morning, and whose body, straight and muscular from carpenter's bench and steersman's seat and pure living, they would nail up by high noon, had set Himself up, not only for king, but architect-builder—of a new temple, a new state, a new scheme of "many mansions." In their eyes He was a novice, and they had for generations been working on sound old school Sinai lines. New designs were hard to grasp, especially those for temples "not made with hands." And what proportion of the old leaders of any land would rush to accept a scheme that would call for the wrecking of their Temple, the institution that had been their chief glory? Any larger percentage, say, than the five thousand Jews who listened to Him by Galilee, the faithful seventy that gathered to see Him go, or any more effective group than the eleven who carried His message to the world?

Already Israel's temple had been wrecked three times. Aaron's staff, the pot of original manna, the reparations jewels, the ark with its gold overlay and the golden winged cherubim of the mercy seat, had vanished. The loss was as great as would be ours were Paris looted of the Winged Victory, Dagobert's throne, the Arc de Triomphe's Eternal Flame, and the Cathedral's north rose window and piece of the True Cross. And now He prophesied the Temple's razing for the fourth time.

But even more than this threat to their Temple, the issue of His kinghood disturbed them. The greatness of the Jews did not spring so much from their conception of a Messiah as from their One-God idea, and their warm personalizing of Him. Their Jehovah might be harsh at times and—to Israel—highly partial. In their magnificent literature He was also the pitying Father. All the race, from beggar to king, hugged to their hearts some thought of His paternal interest, even through all their extraordinary backslidings. This warm One-God idea was the priceless legacy of the Jews to Man.

But, despite a current belief, the Messiah was never quite so present in their consciousness. In their hard struggle for survival, they developed a super-patriotism, a fierce race consciousness. They came to believe that if Man were to be redeemed, as Genesis promised, it would be the best representation of Man, Israel, that would be chosen. Of course, Israel would not go scot free. She had a great awareness of her sins—it was one of the noble qualities of the race, and she would have to go through fire, she knew. Then, purged, she would have hegemony over the rest of the world.

Other races might be redeemed too, but they would come along at a remote distance; and some would go into outer darkness— there would have to be this sombre background for Israel's high light. In their tableaux of the Last Day, from which the Messiah was often left out, the Judgment Seat was not far from Sion's Rock. No New Jerusalem of jasper, but their yellowing old lion of a capital, restored, would be the heavenly capital.

Their immortality was more often than not, especially in later years, a mass immortality. The emphasis was on a golden age for the race rather than on the leader who would usher it in. The average conception was of a military leader who would assure dominion for Israel, and peace, flocks, acres for all. For those of wider horizons he would be the ideal king who would restore both their temporal and moral glory. But few sensed the unique quality of the King who would actually come, as did the great four of the eighth century—Isaiah, the great court prophet; Micah, the farmer-poet; Amos, the Bethlehem shepherd; and Hosea, whose lovely lament for his erring wife was transformed into an elegy for all Israel. And the man in the Jerusalem street could not see the picture so familiar to us now, of star and wise men, manger and angel song. Few could connect, as we can today, those lines, "He was a man of sorrows, acquainted with grief"; "He bore the sins of many"; "He was wounded for our transgressions, and bruised for our iniquities"; "He was numbered with the transgressors, yet made intercession for the transgressors"; with the tragic events of that morning as they were scourging Him and setting up the cross post for Him, on a hill.

So much of the conception of the history and the literature of their race, aside from such foreshadowings, had led to their mis-conception of a Messiah as a returned David. Perhaps this is what He meant by that "They know not what they do."

When He had come, many had rushed to pay Him homage. When they heard no trumpet's defiance, only His immortal para-doxes about those of high degree going down low, and saving one's life by losing it, they were stunned. There was not enough altruism-mindedness in the ancient world for a leap into such high humility, into the realm of such selflessness. And only a few took it.

When the bewilderment of the majority soured into anger and fear, the reactionaries found fault, as people will do when they dread a great catastrophe, with trifles that had nothing to do with the main issue. They toothcombed His least statement in the Temple or their parish churches, the synagogues. At first they were carping. Then, their malice increasing with their concern for their order, they tried verbal traps and read dangerous double meanings into His simplest spiritual pronouncements. They called Him slanderous when He assailed certain rich men for their hypocrisy. When He said to the provincial woman, "What have I to do with thee?," they approved—for one moment thinking He was upholding their snobbishness. At His forgiving conclusions they were aghast; and it never occurred to them that in asking the question He might have meant that He had everything to do with her and with all the wandering and lost.

So, tragically, they misunderstood His noblest irony. This very morning, they would declare Him a barbarian for refusing the Cup of the Doomed, prepared by the band of kindly Jewish ladies. They did not know that He had made a bargain with His own soul—to drain another cup—and so could not dull even the least drop of its agony with any opiate for the Human in Him.

But it would not only be the Old Order, the reactionaries of that day that would misread Him. It is so hard for them anywhere to see something shining and new. The crucifixion was no matter of race. He was to be rejected sooner or later by Man, in his every race, with that blind stupidity which, a few hours later, His gentle heart would insist was ignorance when, dying from their wounds, He called down forgiveness for them from the cross. . . .

In the morning, watchers on the walls saw a squad of soldiers on an eminence which was then without but is now within the city walls. They were preparing for a crucifixion, the cruel punishment the cultured Greeks hated, the hard Romans loved. Others of their comrades were unwittingly building roads that would carry His sublimely subversive message to the world. These legionaries on Calvary were quite as unaware of what they were really doing. By high noon they would raise the cross, the then despised frame for the felon, which he would transform into Man's most honoured symbol. In the end it was to conquer Rome, and would be placed over innumerable towers and altars, and be signed on forehead and breast by countless millions down the ages. From it too would blossom the Cathedral.

So, unconsciously, these rough soldiers on a hill made ready the setting for the last scene of history's greatest drama. These soldiers—it would have stupefied them too, had they been told this—

in performing their simple tasks were but finishing a chain started ages before, in the dawn of Time. And now as with awe we come into the heart of this great climactic scene, it is best for a moment to consider, while Christ waits in the Judgment Hall and Pilate casts about for some way of escape, just what was this universal drama. This is especially necessary since scenes from that age-old drama were to be retold from lectern and pulpit in the Cathedral, sung by choirs and pictured in mosaic, and stone, and bright glass; and one high scene from this very last act would be transformed into the most sacred of mysteries to be performed in the sanctuary. Around it there would be reverently built during the next few centuries a sacred continuity made up of His words and deeds of the night before, and some of those of His companions and the prophets, with the little acts necessary for its celebration, and chants, petitions, responses, and hymns of the morning and evening from the old Hebrew Temple, and later little additions which would be found to add emphasis to His message or beauty to its telling. But never, no matter with what loveliness the Cathedral might clothe this scene, this mystery relived in the sanctuary, was it to be considered as a spectacle, something merely to be looked at, but, rather—since it is real and sanctified by love, the most heroic of deaths, and God's intent—as something to be entered into, partaken of, with every fibre of the surrendered being, not only as one kneels at the rail for the wafer, but every moment as one watches from nave or aisles.

Let us see what they of the Temple—which was truly, if not technically, the cathedral of the East—had so far made of this story, this universal drama of God and Man and Man's relation to his God. For as it was unrolled with vivid metaphor and exalted language in the Old Testament, it was not only the grandest of epics, wherefore dramatic, but it was at heart, in very essence, the most sublime of dramas.

They had a majestic Prologue of the Creation and the First Act, the long pilgrimage of Man. They might not be aware, as they should have been when their usually thronged Temple courts were deserted for Pilate's Judgment Hall, that the Last Act was then being played—they were awaiting one more imperial and militant. But they did have an idea for an Epilogue that would be a grand denouement—the Last Day.

In that Creation Prologue, God had created Light, and with the bright angel squadrons, the morning stars had sung as they wheeled into their appointed orbits. Thus beautifully did the Pentateuch scholar-poets portray the geologic ages of later scholars who would study very near the Cathedral. And very early they established the drama's conflict. The legions of the Dark under Prince Satan engaged the legions of the Light, on the plains of Heaven, were defeated and tossed down to our earth, there, insidiously, to carry on their rebellion. But every allegory, each cloud-capping fantasy was lined with a moral. Here, in the very beginning they were showing, through that sublime battle among the stars, how inevitable and fierce and ceaseless is the struggle between the forces of the Light and of the Dark, Good and Evil, God and the Devil.

Then poetically, with bright parable, they continued to picture the later scholars' Evolution. God made Man out of a breath upon our earth dust. With his fair garden, his goodly heritage, blind, childish Man was not content. Through the re-entrance, with all his wiles, of the leader of the forces of the Dark, and his own pernicious curiosity about the Dark, Man fell. He lost his lovely estate, from it was barred by an angel with shining sword. In this exile too there was logic, for had not Man traded the high for the low, sold his birthright? Thenceforth he must toil in sorrow and pain. With his fall, sin had entered, and, hard on sin's heels, Man's archfoe Death. He would dog toiling Man's footsteps all the long way.

So, as the Old Testament chroniclers and poets unfolded the story of Man's pilgrimage, every scene, whether historic incident or colourful moral tale, under its bright oriental imagery, was cored with truth. But how was Man to be rescued from this fate which he had, by his deliberate choice, brought on himself? This was the solution toward which the whole of this universal drama, the whole march of the race, moved.

Oh! there were, with all his sufferings, some compensating, some very grand adventures. Seas opened up for Man. For him sun and moon stood still. Before his trumpets cities fell. And with all his defeats, lusts, and golden calves, there were his glittering triumphs, idyllic love stories and immortal songs, of which all in the Temple were properly proud. Yet Man's hardships were great. Who would save him from his misery and toil? This, during the First Act, was all that concerned most. But the nobler brooded over the penalty of Sin and Death which—the drama held irrefutable logic here, for Man by his desertion of the Light had earned it—must be paid. It was not mortal death which Man had earned; that was to be blotted out, but, though few guessed this before the Last Act's tragedy made it clear; it was that moral death which meant condemnation into the Dark which Man had chosen. Who would be willing to take on Himself this penalty, and the weight of guilt that went with it and so rescue His great friend Man, and round out the age-old drama?

It was He who was now over in the Judgment Hall where so many of the Temple, though not all, were clamouring to kill Him, not knowing that this was the way the drama would be rounded out. Twice that morning, once before their star chamber assembly, again before Pilate, He had given them the answers they had longed for, which they were sure would seal His doom: "Art thou the Son of Man?" "Ye say that I am." "Art thou the King?" "Thou sayest it." They had shouted in unholy glee. At last, they thought, there had fallen into their verbal traps He who had hitherto so mysteriously eluded them.

Pilate, torn several ways by his sworn duty to quell disturbances, to mollify a subject people as far as was reasonable, by his wife's beseeching him to have "nothing to do with this just man," and by the strange power he himself felt in the divine prisoner, sought a way out through change of venue. He was from Galilee. Herod who had come to Jerusalem should do the condemning which he, Pilate, hated, but which would please the mob.

When the debased, curious Herod asked to see a miracle, which he thought would be an entertaining bit of wizardry, and Christ refused, he turned Him over to his own guard and the palace hangers-on. On the body, bruised and buffeted the night before, they put a gorgeous robe and, mocking Him, led Him through the streets, back to Pilate. The perplexed governor confronting the howling mob and the determined leading citizens of the city, attempted once more to reason with them. "I, having examined Him before you, find no fault in this man." In grim earnest he spoke; the silence answering him was ominous. Then they broke into a sullen roar. He tried his last resource. It was the Passover, and people had come in from the hills and all over the long valley to their sacred capital. It was as crowded everywhere as our metropolitan cities are with the throngs that come up to them in the same season, which we call Easter. It was a Passover custom for the governor to release a prisoner. There was Barabbas, brutish of look, shameless, murderous, of the city's scum. He would give them their choice. Surely they would not, they could not, make the wrong one.

"Whom will ye that I release unto you, Christ or Barabbas?"

Then came the saddest mass cry at which men ever shuddered. "Barabbas! Barabbas! Barabbas!"

Barabbas for Christ! The low for the Most High!

So, while some of their compatriots wept, the Old Order chose. A wearied and saddened Pilate, who had missed the larger chance in taking the lesser, washed his hands and turned Him over for the scourging.

Sometimes callous Rome tied the condemned one to the upright of an already planted cross, and scourged him until, through the gashes, even the bowels were exposed. Christ was to carry His own cross, and they scourged Him in the hall of the praetorium. They stripped Him. The beautiful body, so straight before, was bowed under the storm of the leather and lead. Over Him then they put a robe which some say was purple, others scarlet. It was dyed deeper from the crown of thorns above when they pressed it in. Then alternately they placed a reed, for mock sceptre, in His hand and took it away from Him to beat Him on the head and drive in deeper the thorns. Alternately they knelt before Him, roaring with laughter, and rose to spit at or strike Him. It was as good sport, this striking the helpless, for Antichrist, as it would be for the crooked cross Antichrist in the twentieth century. But the helpless one here was really the all-powerful, though He would not use that power, knowing that temporal displays of it were vain. That temptation had been fought down, long before, in the desert days. And He who, because of indignities, wounds and the cruel death awaiting, should have been the pitied, was the Pitying One. They could dimly sense that, even in the midst of their obscenities, cruelties and rage, and it but made them the more savage.

At last they took off the royal robe and put on His torn, spattered white tunic, and gave Him the cross. The top of the upright above the transverse extended beyond His thorn-bloodied head. The main weight of it rested on the bowed, bloodied shoulders. The low part of the massive post dragged heavily.

From beneath His burden He spoke to the great crowd who sorrowfully followed Him, bidding them not to weep. For there were many tears in the crowd, that day, though none from the Old Order. Those tears did much to purge Israel.

So He passed down the street afterwards called the Via Dolorosa, still littered with bits of palm fronds from His one triumphal parade, mixed with slaughtered lambs' blood and soured goats' milk in the gutters. Several times—sacred tradition says three— He stumbled and fell, for—though He had an unspoiled, glorious physique—scourge, thorns, sweated blood, and betrayals had taken toll of it. Even these stumblings and falls would be a part of the Cathedral, like the crown of thorns which is the chevet, the wound in His side which is the Red Door on the north side of the choir. Enter the Cathedral any hour, and you will find some one making the round of the Stations of the Cross, the little sculptured scenes of this day, that stand out in beautiful, if tragic, relief on the walls. Three of these depict Christ falling under His burden on the Sorrowful Way.

When it was seen that the weight of the cross was too great, a bystander, who perhaps was never conscious of the supreme honour, was impressed into carrying it for Him. Then they came out through the city gate to the Knoll of the Skull where dice rattled, nails clinked in the soldiers' hands. Naked, save for loin-cloth, they bound Him with cords on the prone cross, which was of the *imminsa* form, with the vertical piece rising above the transverse, not a T as so many artists have pictured it. Nor did it have the support for the feet that other artists—in sympathy and after the event—have painted in. The dragging of the body at the pierced hands was part of the ordeal. Sharpened nails quickly went through the hands and feet which millions afterwards would have given their all, not to pierce but to kiss. Up then against the sky, as had been foretold centuries before, as the old nomad tribes had raised the serpent in the wilderness for healing, the cross was raised, with its precious burden and the mocking title above. So, before the world, they raised the holy sign which never afterwards would disappear from Man's consciousness, whether he accepted it or not, from out of which more than the Cathedral would flower, for it would become an attitude, a background itself, and a standard, a code by which all men would be consciously or unconsciously judged, whether they honoured it in the observance or in the breach.

The earth was spaded in around the upright, the iron clinking against the gravel with that sharpness which, at scenes of death, pierces the survivors' hearts. So it went through Our Lady's. The soldiers threw dice now for His poor clothes.

They had raised Him between two thieves, one jeering, one adoring. The latter, Ditmas, had with his passing, an experience like no other's in this world. If ever there was an eleventh hour conversion, it was his. For his salvation came as he hung dying between Heaven and earth, between two worlds. And he hung there with the Saviour of Men, Who forgetful of His multiple agony borne for all, poured out His love to this thief.

At noon—they had chosen this hour for its pitiless publicity—the three figures stood out against a sky all too bright. Behind them lay Jerusalem like a tawny aging lion which had had all its teeth drawn by Rome, and forty years after this day was to have every bone in its carcass picked by the great emperor, Titus, then beginning to work his way up through the Roman legions. On the hills grazed the sheep, whose ways He knew so well, their black and tan muzzles all turned in the same direction. About the Brook Kedron was the green fringe of spring. The anemones, those "lilies" whose red petals He had compared with Solomon's robes, were brightly in bud. And over the hills to the East bent the red-yellow road to Bethany where, when He needed rest, He had so often gone to talk with His friends. An earthly playwright might have given a dying hero a melancholy consciousness of such familiar scenes. But this was a Hero of both human and divine reactions. One cannot attribute to Him any sadness of farewell, especially since He had ages before been co-scene-painter of all the scenes in the world. The human eyes were fast dimming now, as the weight of all mortal sorrows bearing on the Divine was fast crushing out the human life.

Not far from the cross, the women with John, His comrade, had gathered. The other friends, those disciples who would become one day as lions, were not strong enough yet to stand by in His agony. The eyes of this intimate group were transfixed on the loved figure hanging there, which they thought—the bright Easter not yet having dawned—was leaving them forever. So on the Place of the Skull they huddled, their clothes and heads and shoulders all in the unconscious and immemorial curves of sorrow, whose beauty generation after generation of cathedral sculptors would strive to catch.

So they lingered on with Him through the Three Hours, whose dreadfulness and sublimity the cathedral would show every year on Good Friday by swathing its loveliness in black and stripping its altar as bare as the Place of the Skull where He hung. In it would be repeated the little sentences He spoke and which are called the Seven Words: the human "I thirst"; the loving "Woman, behold thy son," to Mary; the "Behold thy mother," to the disciple John; the divine "Today shalt thou be with me in Paradise," to the poor thief; the anguished "My God, my God, why hast thou forsaken me?" torn out of a despair that was not His despair but that of the sons of men, and which they could not bear and which He was bearing for them; the immortal "Lord, forgive them, for they know not what they do," the prayer for His murderers; and the utter finality of the "It is finished," with the ultimate peace of the "Lord, into thy hands I commit my spirit."

The women—they are ever in the majority at scenes of suffering —heard these words as they came from the lips of the pierced body, now moving painfully and wearily, now sagging lower on the cross as Death approached. They broke on the still air of that bare hill of the ancient city, and on all the world. Even the calloused centurion heard, and pagan though he was, horrified at what they had done, cried, "Truly this was the Son of God."

For three hours the sun which at noon had been pitilessly bright had hidden its face. Now the earth shook. And the sacred veil of the old cathedral of the East, over the gorges facing the Mount of Olives, was torn in the convulsion, as though in evidence that the Old Dispensation was passing, and that in His dying, His fulfilment of His mission, He had destroyed it forever.

Trembling, the soldiers who had forgotten their loot, oaths and dicing, went about the last things they had to do. Often in crucifixions they had to break the legs. It was the one merciful act in the bloody Roman calendar, for otherwise a victim might linger on, hanging there in sun and rain for days.

When they had sufficiently recovered from the shock caused by the protest of Nature to look up at Him, they found it was not necessary for them to break His legs. . . .

It was hard at the tomb for a mother to wash the bloodstains from feet she had taught to walk and had kissed and followed. . . .

So the last act was over. The Hero had given His life for His friends. We await the Epilogue when He shall come again. His life, without which there would have been neither so profound a drama nor any Cathedral, was the most dramatic of all lives ever lived. His death was the most decisive event in history. If His coming in the zero hour had split Time in two, His departure had divided a world philosophy. Never would the mind of Man shrink quite back into its old dimensions.

That act had begun with an idyll of angels and stars and stable birth. It ended with death and a broken heart—literally, as surgeons know from the water mixed with blood which followed the spear thrust. Without sense of this one cannot enter into the heart of the Cathedral; otherwise it becomes a gorgeous frame without a picture, a lofty torch without a light. The architects, priests, stonecutters, masons, who built the Cathedral knew this. Scenes from the tragedy they carved all over it.

He had, the night before, made the grimmest decision in history —not to let the cup pass. This was not only to have his body broken, literally, for others, but to assume for others that overwhelming sense of desertion by God, which is the realization that one by his own choice has forever shut himself out from the Light. Others might have stood with fortitude the bodily pain, even the betrayal, the desertion by friends. For Him there was added the crushing sense of the guilt of all men, its piled-up terror. This was the last depth of Hell, the feeling of being forsaken, of utter loneliness, of desolation raised to its ultimate power, which He had not earned by His own pure life but had taken on Himself for others.

There was for Him another heart wound. He was not only purity and selflessness, but wisdom incarnate. Together with love they sacrificed knowledge on that cross. When He told them His simple parables, He also—had they been ready for it—could have unlocked the secrets of the universe, long before the Newtons and Pasteurs. He could have told them of things that would have helped them—of barometers for their fishing weather, the compass, the gyroscope. He could have explained the stars He watched them steer by, the glands, secretions, cells, that made Peter so impetuous, Thomas so suspicious, though never would He have accepted biochemistry as the final answer. That was to be found in the Cross.

But it was going to be, as He foresaw, so hard for the world to take knowledge, to accept the Light. Seldom would His cause be backed by majorities—had He not often said, "Many are called, but few are chosen." Worse, even His minorities would often desert Him, as had His eleven, the night before, in the Judgment Hall and the high priest's kitchens. Sometimes, of course, in crises, the minorities would sway the majorities. And Peter, like many a saint after him, would, after the moment's recantation, turn out nobly true.

So the last scene overshadows all the rest, magnificent Prologue and First Act, and the first lovely scenes of this Last Act when He stilled the waters, sat with the rowers or pulled an oar Himself, raised the dead, took little children on His knee, or talked with lost women by village wells as they never had been talked with before. Never has there been traitor episode like that in which He is betrayed by a friend for thirty pieces of silver and by a kiss, never a trial in which the judge as he condemns the victim, acquits him, washing his hands. Never has there been farewell scene like that in which He washes the feet of His friends, breaks the bread, and fills the cup, or deathbed message more touching than His when He commits His mother, Our Lady, to the arms of His friend, or last words like the Seven. No final curtain ever equalled the going out of the sun and the shaking of temple and city and earth as though nature herself had been violated by what had been done. Above all, no Hero ever made rescue like this, by the sacrifice, direct of the body, vicarious of the soul. No earthly playwright could think up such things, no mortal imagination conceive them. The test of true poetry is its inevitableness, the conviction it leaves with the reader that the lines could have fallen in no other way, that there could have been no other words.

Thus, in three short, crowded years, was made, through life itself, the imperishable drama for the Cathedral—for the stage that is the heart of everyone that looks to the Light.

Then, when the morning dew was distilled in quivering beads upon each tiny green blade, and the East was all palpitant with Eden hues and dawn of the world tints—opal, serpentine, salamander, salmon, rose—a woman came into a garden outside the city walls. This woman, the citizens of the city would have said, should never have set foot on holy ground, but she had a right there, since she had washed and wiped His feet with her luxuriant hair, and washed away her sins with her own tears.

The stone had been lifted, rolled away. The seal of death was broken on the tomb. She stooped, bent in a curve the back that

men had called lovely, looked within. The linen with which she and
the other two women who bore the same name as hers, had swathed
the once perfect but then battered and broken body, was there
neatly folded, the headcloth by itself, but He had gone. She saw,
or thought she saw—which does not matter?—two young men who
were fairer than all the comely men that had ever come to her,
and she had had her share.

And when, feeling an utter desolation, she began to weep as
only one can weep who has utterly loved and adored, they asked
her why she was weeping.

"Because they have taken away my lord!" she said, and never
was possessive pronoun fraught with so many connotations.

There was also a third who stood near, though in the bright
light of the upsurging dawn he was without shadow. He too asked
her gently why she cried. Supposing him to be the gardener or care-
taker of the place, she asked him, pleading with all her heart, to tell
her where they had laid Him.

And suddenly wave after wave of sweetness swept the garden
and valley, not the fragrance of massed spring flowers most of
which were still in bud, but the wholesome sweetness of life in
growing things. And the massed Jerusalem roofs were glorified,
each hovel turned to a palace as, high over Olivet opposite, out of
the desert, which was no withering furnace now, but a reservoir of
healing life, the sun came up as no other sun comes up save that
of Easter. It was not a red disk or gold ball or great yellow coin
set on desert edge or blue mountain cone, but something leaping,
circumambient, all-enveloping, and not so much a thing of fire as
of that light which is life itself. Life for the grass which quivered
in the breeze like wires silvered with dew. Life for the little
skipping black goats that He had laughed at and run after as a
boy in Nazareth. Life for the little lambs and sheep, which He had
heard so often called by the upland shepherds that He knew them
by name. Life for the swallows who hurried to the sun, with swift
successions of dark blue wing-curves imprinted on a pale blue sky.
For the nightingales too, which He, lover of the Nature which He
had helped create, had listened to in delight, and which had filled
the night with vocal silver that had just died down with dawn. For
the red anemone lilies of a greater than Solomon gorgeousness, with
black centres in crimson corollas, like black nail heads in the round
blood stains on his hands reproduced and scattered a million fold
on these fields He walked. Life even for the tomb that no longer
held the still majesty of death and was not shadowed with the
darkness of defeat but invaded now with the bright light of the
triumph of life. And finally life for the woman who had sinned,
who, with her humility and flowing hair and tears had atoned.

Then she heard her name called—"Mary," by Him whom she, not looking up, had supposed to be the gardener, but who, in the sunshine, was without shadow, and not so much a figure as a presence —an all-pervading, life-giving presence like the sun.

"Mary!" It was all of a piece with the rest of the play. No other would have dared to place such a one, the Magdalen, in such a role.

It was a great glory that He had come back in triumph over death, as they sing in Saint Peter's, Notre Dame, in all the cathedrals and little chapels at Eastertide. "The strife is o'er, the victory won!" It is a greater glory that the one to whom He first appeared after He came back out of the black mystery of the tomb, with the secret at last of Life, was one so very human she had greatly sinned and "because she had loved much," had been forgiven by the Divine.

And now, for the play, First Act and Last, the Divine and Human, the round was complete, in the Easter sun.

V

*The Altar of the Paris Boatmen. . . . The Gauls intertwine their
Gods with the Gods of Rome. . . . Rome builds Roads which
speed the News from Galilee to Gaul.*

33=37 A.D.

THE PARISIANS WERE PUTTING UP AN ALTAR BY THE SEINE,
not really to a god, or even a quarter god, but to a man,
Tiberius Caesar. It seems strange that a group of people
could make a gesture so futile, particularly in the days when Christ
could make a gesture so splendid it was no gesture at all, but the
highest expression of life blooming in the dark flower of death.

But this was one of those low watermark periods that come to
France, regularly as ebb heartbeats of time, in between her eras of
splendour. Still it seems almost inconceivable that ninety-two years
of occupation, even a Roman occupation, could make a people so
silly, especially those once alert enough to conquer the world as
far off as their name city in Asia, Galata, to which Paul very soon
would write his flaming epistle.

During the great Roman Peace, which had provided them with
a strong unyielding frontier against the barbarians, the Gauls had
advanced in their businesses, trades, and farms. Unexampled was
the good order of their cities. Indeed, they were forming a bour-
geoisie long before the Middle Ages, which was long before they
had a right to, according to history. But all that was merely a
matter of bread and butter. On another plane they had traded
their birthright of bright imaginative gods and a belief in bright
heavens and immortality, for a deistic mess of pottage. For that
was what this sleek crew of Roman gods really was now.

Here these Parisians were, making their golden calf not of gold,
but of a huge block of limestone. On it the sculptors were chipping away down by the Seine, in the shadow of the city and temple
wall. Their prize achievement was a great animal which the sculptors' chisels had too exaggeratedly pointed out was a bull, for such
ribald details will creep into temples, even into Christian churches.
If one goes across the river from Notre Dame and looks under the
canons' seats in the choir of Saint Gervais, he can see examples.

On the other side of this huge cube, or die of the gods, were a
few deities—Jupiter, horned Keraunos, Esus with sickle—Gallic

68

and Roman gods all mixed up in the interbreeding of the occupation. On another cube of the same light-hued limestone, designed for the top of this monumental altar, the sculptors, or stone cutters rather, had depicted Tiberius. The likeness here was rather flattering, for they had softened his sullen, stubborn, slow-thinking bullet head, as much as a tool could, sweetened him up too, with sprigs of laurel. Below, they were just chipping out letters in Latin. The altar had started out as Jove's, but there was a large gesture and wave in the direction of Tiberius in this dedication. It can and should be seen by every pilgrim to Paris, for it is the very oldest of the Notre Dame relics:

"To the great and good Jove we, the Watermen of Paris, built this when Tiberius was Caesar."

That past tense, put in currently, was their own, that is, the stone cutters'. For the wording had been left to the stone cutters' taste by the Watermen's Guild—of bargemen, longshoremen, chandlers, sailmakers, sailors of Seine, Sea, and Channel, all who made their living from the water, when they ordered the altar.

Some months before, the great cubes had been brought over the south bridge in huge carts drawn by oxen, from the Left Bank hill, later known as Saint Genevieve's. The quarry was opposite the island and halfway up the hill, on the east side of the highway then and still known as Saint Jacques. The Roman baths, whose ruins are now a part of beautiful Cluny Museum, would be built on the other side. One of the first two aqueducts of Paris—from this hill you could see the other over on the Right Bank—ran parallel with Saint Jacques' road. Its high arches were up. A playhouse was going up near it.

So much limestone had been taken out of this quarry for the rapid shrine and villa building of the Romans that great holes appeared in it and tunnels extended in different directions around the slope. These underground galleries would later be called the Paris Catacombs, and there, in the sixteenth century, all the disinterred dead from the Paris churches, in the greatest mass burial of the ages, would be laid—you still can see them, with candles— on little shelves in the dark.

This chart of the famous Left Bank and Saint Genevieve's hill in the Roman era should be kept in mind by those who love old Paris: first, the two arteries, the elevated arched viaduct, and the road of Saint Jacques parallel with it, going from the river up over the hill where the road continued to Orleans southwest. To the east of road and aqueduct, in the meadows, were brick and lime kilns, and the round tiered Roman arena. Halfway up and east of the road and viaduct was the quarry with a theatre nearby; and on the west side of the road the great baths and palace would go up under Emperor Constantius Chlorus. On the summit (in the modern Pantheon and Luxembourg Gardens area) was a great horse market, a second theatre, and also a companion barracks to the one on the island. From this hilltop post the bugles blew telling the stone cutters by the river altar when it was time to drop their chisels, to munch bread made from wheat grown in the great Issy plains west, and to drink the wine pressed out in the Montmartre vineyards.

The limestone from this quarry was light, like real cream in hue with just a hint of sand-colour in it. Though it furnished a fair freestone that could be worked with some ease by the sculptors and stone cutters, it was not so soft or easily fissured as the limestone south by the Loire, an example of which you can see in the beautiful, time-etched towers of the cathedral of Tours. The product of the Paris hills, which hardens with exposure, gave longer life to her temples and cathedrals. There would be a long line of these shrines. That quarry really was the cradle of the gods, and it should have been blessed by the angels too. Except for some wood, lead and glass, and in the foundations rubble, concrete and granite, Our Lady's great house would be entirely made of that stone, though, looking up now at the great façade, the stranger would never guess its original colour. For over the light creamy hue has been laid, by dust and fog and rain drippings, the dark patina of the centuries. You can see samples of it, light as when the cathedral went up by the Seine, creamy as when the stone-cutters outlined on it that bullet skull of Tiberius and made that bull, in the chantiers or repair stone yards, now northeast of the apse, and just back of the ambulatory chapels. The great majority of the cathedral's blocks are the original ones hoisted into place by the mediaeval workers, though vastly darker. But occasionally now the saws must cut out a new arch or pinnacle part for one dismantled by the ages. Or a sculptor must curl a stone cabbage leaf for a weather-beaten balustrade or imitate, on a new gargoyle, the battered grin of an old gutter monster.

But this bright morning of that decade of Christ's crucifixion, the stone cutters' chisels were clinking away around on the riverside, that is, the south side of the temple wall, and in the shadow of the wall of the city. They were working exactly on the spot where the church of Saint Etienne would rise three hundred years later—a few yards west of where you now see Viollet-le-Duc's and Lassus' handsome cathedral sacristy and treasury which house the sacred chalices, Napoleon's coronation robe, Mary Queen of Scots' wedding vestments, and the Crown of Thorns. It is perhaps best to note now that the cathedral of Notre Dame would be begotten directly of two earlier churches, the church of Saint

Etienne or Saint Stephen of the fourth century, and a smaller Notre Dame of the sixth. Saint Etienne would rise on that south transept side; the first Romanesque Notre Dame beyond, and just west of, the great front doors of the present cathedral, its apse extending into the space now occupied by the nave, as far as the first mighty piers. Some would reverse their dates, placing the first Notre Dame in the fourth century, Saint Etienne in the sixth. That is improbable. For this very altar of the boatmen of Paris was found under the Notre Dame pavements in 1711, among the old débris of demolished Saint Etienne. And church builders, if only to demonstrate the triumph of their new faith, like to build the new shrine on the old site. But one church was fourth century, one was sixth—so much is sure, though it does not matter. Authentic too, is that joint parentage of Our Lady's Cathedral.

They were getting ready blocks, tackle, wedges, rollers, to place the watermen's altar where Stephen's statue now stands, under the carved story of his martyrdom and the great southern rose. Here, not far from the temple, ran the island's south wall, for the Romans had belted the island around with new ramparts. Indeed, they had given the boat-shaped city a modern battleship's appearance. There were slitted towers—one a giant prison on the north shore, like gun turrets rising above that belt. The Roman governor's palace, whose stones have gone into the Palais de Justice now there, loomed up amidships, like bridge and superstructure. The square of the Forum, just east of the palace, was like the open waist. And forward was the great palace garden patch, like the low-lying prow over which the waves wash.

Two bridges, one north, one south, heightened the resemblance, seeming nothing more than companionways from boat-shaped city to the shore. The usually efficient Romans had carelessly made these trestle bridges of wood, threatening fire. That threat was often fulfilled during the following centuries when superstitious souls sent little votive candles to the saints in wooden saucers to float downstream against the piles.

But that was later. There were no saints now in Paris. There were gods, as we have seen, and shrines to them all over the landscape. Already there were several deities on pillars and altars lording it over the island, including the very important Jupiter in the Temple and a Mercury near where is now Sainte Chapelle. And over these bridges, the people were flocking to put up still another altar. From the top of the city walls you could see the workmen everywhere—by the new suburban development, where now is the Hall of Wines; laying down their hammers and their hods by the new Roman baths; their shovels in the graveyards, to hurry in to see the boatmen's parade. By the Temple of Isus on Vaugirard slope, all over the Issy plain, the new granary of Paris where daily they were turning up the once bright helmets of the great battle of Paris, they were leaving ploughs in the furrows as the Roman pipes and bugles sounded the march down the hill from the barracks. They were hanging up their pruning hooks in the vineyards on the hill north where Mercury had still another temple.

From walls, scaffolds, ditches, quarries, hucksters' gardens, wheat-fields, vineyards and fishing boats, men hurried in, to fall in behind the watermen and their instruments or to get good places for the rites by the old island wall, near the new altar. Maidens with flowers were in the procession, also a garlanded white bull purchased from the Issy farmers. And four boatmen bore, on silver staves, a miniature ship. This was the device that their descendants would place on the coat of arms of a greater Paris.

These ceremonies were really not so pious as commercial. The Latinized Parisians, so many of whom had lost the faith of their more gallant fathers and had not yet received the new faith of Galilee, were trying to trade their songs, incense, strewn flowers and bulls to the interracial gods for favouring winds, hospitable ports, and exorcised sharks, whales, octopi, and sirens. A little catering to these mixed deities, they hoped, would secure for them better prices for their beer, coaches, draft and cavalry horses, which they sold to imperial Rome. A little prayer or two might bring better bargains in their barter of their crimson cloth and dyestuffs, wine casks, and decorated cutlery and weapons, for Touraine pastel, imported amber, Cornish lead and tin and British wool.

In the celebration over the altars, the Paris workmen made one mistake. The members of the Watermen's Guild had picked the wrong gods, the wrong empire to honour. Tiberius Caesar had started out well, but was winding up badly. Though so methodical as to seem slow-witted, he had shown real ability, had consolidated the empire left him, and all would have gone well had he not tried to get into his bullet head some philosophy. In it the philosophy apparently turned sour, for it brought him to the most dangerous conclusions—first, that he was superman, then a god. And suddenly he succumbed—as have many tyrants from King Saul to Bismarck—to the tyrant's neurosis and turned psychopathic. The cries of his politically-slain now beat against his ear-drums. The stench of mingled sacrifice suet, dried gladiator blood and burning Christian flesh at last went against him. He fled Rome for Pompeii and the Blue Grotto near it, which he thought might cool him while the white Capri maidens warmed him against the approaching chill of death.

They were unsuccessful. Neither Rome nor its gods could sustain him when Death, accompanied by an assassin, came to stifle him in a mattress. For neither Rome nor its theatrical revue of gods was made for the final mystery or any mystery at all—only things like drachmas that could be weighed in scales, or concrete and marble that could be computed in cubits, and slaves and soldiers that could be numbered by the tens of thousands, and maidens whose charms could be gauged by the eye. The Roman could not, like the great Greek poets, see past that Olympian show, and sense a First Cause, so travel at least a part of the way on the road toward Bethlehem. The Roman system might produce a "noblest Roman" and his avenging dagger, but not a Socrates and his dreams. Carry those dreams of his on into the realm of an infinite logic and you have the visions of the King which produced that empire which was unseen yet alone would endure. In a year or so now, the Roman empire would begin its western descent, start its long three-hundred-year decline.

Not that the bargemen, longshoremen, sailmakers, chandlers, sailors of Seine, sea and Channel, Tacitus or any contemporary historian, for that matter, could see signs of it then. The Roman sun, under Augustus, had reached the zenith. It still rode high. Never before had taxes flowed from all the corners of the earth in such floods, like golden lava, upon Rome. Never before had so many coins been stamped with Caesar's superscription—which that other King did not question, in its place. Never before had so many slaves been chained to *trireme* seats, so many chariots yoked, lead pipes soldered, or pickaxes, hobnails, shields, rouge pots, manacles, toothpicks been manufactured. Never before had so much concrete been mixed, Carrara marble quarried, gold leaf beaten out, more hexameters metred, brothels frescoed, abortions attempted, farces written, sewers laid. And never had so much stone been chiselled into gods, snow been brought down from Soracte to chill wines, Tyrrhenian purple extracted from the little swimming creatures of the sea for Caesar's mantles, or clowns, acrobats, apes, peacocks, laurel and maidenheads in such batches been gathered for imperial banquets.

Still, if it was not the above inventory but the advance guard of that invisible empire which was sapping this very visible one of Rome to its fall, none could yet see any of these pioneer scouts of the faith riding over the hills or rowing up the Seine. It was said that the three Marys, with Lazarus, had already set sail from Jaffa for Provence. But that may merely have been rumour, although you are shown the relic of some of them in the fortified church of the Three Marys, by the Sea, in the Camargue. In Jewish cities and along the Gentile Aegean and Nile, the Twelve and the disciples were having trouble enough. They had not yet even properly organized their little army of missioners, deacons, and those presbyters who, by an understandable etymology, would become priests. It would be two hundred years before Saint Denis would sail from Rome and come down the Seine to proselytize Paris.

Still, those Gauls, being by nature nearer the Greeks than to Rome, therefore nearer that Bethlehem road, should have seen the doom of those gods, have sensed the farce they themselves were now playing. The intellectuals regarded their gods chiefly as curse words, devices to hold the mob, at the best as symbols of the Unknown or a very material Chance. Neither in victory and prosperity nor in decline and defeat was there any real faith in them. And it is better in battle to have a strong wrong-headed belief than none at all. A nation's commerce may be its alimentary system, with fleets and caravans carrying its replenishment up its blood vessels of river and road. An army may be its defense mechanism and signal system against the invasion of obvious disease. But religion, of this creed or that, is its indispensable system of glands, with faith the secretion keeping the corporate body whole and strong, moving and alive. When the secretion slackens or grows weak, empire, republic, or commune, the nation dies.

Oblivious of all these truths, the boatmen, or watermen, of Paris had their parade, sent up their sacrificial smoke, poured out their libations of wine, sang their songs and altogether might have been a people not at home in their Paris, but in some Babylonian captivity.

So they dedicated their altar, which you can see today in the hall of the Roman baths they were bricking in the morning of the deification, and which now are incorporated in the west end of lovely Cluny Palace and Museum halfway up the Left Bank Hill. Louis the Thirteenth, on his mincing high heels, Richelieu, with red cap and goatee, came, one afternoon of 1638, to Notre Dame. They looked it over and up and down and decided to bring the cathedral up to date, give it *chic* in short, to change by a little that Gothic which their baroque taste never did understand. Fortunately they did not do much besides ruining some lovely glass, some giant statues, a rood screen, and the high altar. In 1711, however, Louis the Fourteenth began to dig deep, and the workmen disturbed some famous old fellows asleep. For when they tore the paving up they found underneath, a strange potpourri. It was composed—so mixed and sequential of the relics of the ages is the history of Paris—of powdering archbishops' crooks, chariot wheels, fascist sticks, dulled signet rings, and mouldered Druid bards, Gallic chiefs, Roman proconsuls, bishops, kings' sons, and once lovely queens. Soon they were digging even deeper down, where the Notre Dame foundations were mixed up with the stone and the rubble, the earth with the débris of old Saint Etienne, demolished long before. And from this historic compost they pried up the altar stones of the Paris boatmen, dedicated seventeen centuries before and still with that legend that had been chipped out in flattery of Tiberius.

To Cluny they were later transferred. And as the Cathedral of Notre Dame is, after the Seine, the loveliest thing in Paris, those altar stones are the most authentic links that bind Notre Dame and Paris to the past: the Seine boatmen—empurpled Tiberius—Jove—Stephen and his magnificent gesture—the sculptors chipping out the false gods—Bishop de Sulli's workmen tearing down old Saint Etienne as the cathedral towers go up.

But, as that altar of the Paris boatmen was being dedicated—or a year or so later—when the dead Saul had become the live Paul, he, Paul, to make those altar gods even more obsolete, was, with his desert caravans, riding on his way.

VI

*Two Famous Young Men: Stephen, who will have a Great Door
in the Cathedral, points the Way; Paul becomes the Great
Trumpet Voice of the Cross. . . . Shipwreck, Jail, and Immortal
Letters. . . . Paul and Peter show Coward Nero how True-hearted
Gentlemen die. . . . The News is carried to the Gallic "Legion of
the Lark."*

35-66 A.D.

UP THE WHITE ROAD, OVER THE PLAIN FROM THE PORT OF
Ostia to the Roman gates, in a band of pilgrims and
soldiers, all with a shipwrecked look, he loosely guarded,
walked the surest man in the world. He might have been too, had
he cared about it, the world's most persuasive lawyer, was its most
effective orator, a collaborator on what would be its best-selling
book, and the most influential traveller in the empire.

Physically, he did not suggest any such preeminence. Only five
feet six, he was bald and crooked legged. But his nose was eagle-
like and handsome. The eyes, which looked out from under heavy
brows, had been blue, arresting, argumentative, intellectually imperious. Now, just as the whole face had an appearance weather-
beaten almost to the point of being battered from his hardships, the
eyes showed age, but often as he argued or looked toward Rome
they assumed the old strikingly keen, challenging and commanding look.

Even now, after the protracted journey, this veteran approaching sixty hurried on with a slight forward inclination of his body.
This was not as though he were looking for a chance to escape.
Through the long voyage and the shipwreck, in which he had
distinguished himself, the guards had gained a confidence in him.
That little bend forward was that of one who was always a little
ahead of himself, eager to be in the thick of things, in at the death
—his own if need be. His name was Paul, and he was carrying,
eleven hundred years ahead, a message to the Cathedral. For he was
bearing to the non-Jewish, the Gentile world the story, the drama,
that had been lived in the long valley. It was to make Rome a
sacred, instead of a profane capital and would start around the
Mediterranean the chain of churches that would lead up the rivers

of France to the most glorious of them all. More immediately, he was riding eagerly to that death which, he was pretty sure, awaited him within those city gates.

To these he had come a long way from the Judean prison, on an ill-judged appeal to Caesar. He had come a longer way from the Saul he had been—riding through the Jerusalem gates, breathing fire and slaughter, and hunting down all the comrades of Christ— to the Paul he now was. From Saul to Paul there had been a greater change than from one letter to another. The chasm between the two spirits was as great as that; in fact, was precisely that between the Old Dispensation and the New, which the birth of a babe had forever separated. Paul was the very symbol of that division.

His imminent danger did not prevent him, once within the gates, from surveying the capital with curiosity. He knew desert heat and mountain snows. He had pitched his tent by the Red Sea; for a living he had made tents by the Nile delta and up and down the Aegean. He had tried every kind of pulpit, Babylonian temple, that of Herod, shrines of Diana and Egyptian sun-god, underground quarry and upper chamber chapels, though the message in each was the same. And with the ways of Athens student, Hittite beggar, Arab chief, Roman middleman, Sumerian potter—with all sorts and conditions of his fellows, he was acquainted. But he had never seen the aqueducts and villas, the majestic palaces and arches of Rome.

The natural man in him was pleased now by all the detail of the street scene—centurions, melon-sellers, donkeys, bake-ovens, Vestal Virgins withdrawing white skirts from the manholes down which labourers were fixing sewers, striding black Nubian slaves suddenly eclipsing glowing copper cauldrons or bolts of red and blue and gold in the booths, dwarfs collecting coins for acrobats, tinkers soldering pots, flower girls, gladiators with *cestus* or trident and net, solemn immobile faces and hearts wildly thirsting for one more sight, before death, of their native mountain snows. Even in the precociously foul-mouthed gutter-snipes, the beggars in whose skin his experienced eye saw the oncoming leprosy spots, the courtesans laughing down at him from the roofs, he saw potential citizens—citizens of a new empire. That empire might seem to be Caesar's but was another's, just as the body he had come to render was Caesar's, but its soul another's.

Caesar now happened to be L. Domitius Ahenobarbus, but he was called Nero. He was dining often these days around a pool in a palace on a hill above, with girls from all the street and forest corners of the empire, from Circassia to Cornwall, Paris included.

But during the following months L. Domitius Ahenobarbus did not do the expected with Paul. Tyrants of these and later days could be as hysterical and variable as women are said to be and as frequently are not. This one was especially underglanded and over-sexed. Now he could be ruthless, roaring, snarling and sadistic, and pick like a very bad amateur on strings while gentle Nazarenes, some half daft, others magnificently sane, cast flickering red lights as they burned, through his marble windows on his black and white tessellated floors. Again he was lazy, timid, trepidant, or perhaps just plain played-out.

Furthermore, the Roman system itself bred a sort of tolerance, not the tolerance of liberty but of race pride. A man could make any kind of religious ass of himself he chose, so long as he did not disturb the peace—peace which Rome did not love for its own sake, but for its profitableness. But the minute a zealot caused any disturbance, he played his small part in the great Roman economy as lion meat or tallow for Nero's torches.

Reports from proconsuls were accurate in details if not in readings of such things as Paul preached concerning the new Invisible Empire; and they had decided in the capital that if Paul had not started the riots, as charged, he was a bone of contention. Apparently he was very clever at legal manoeuvering, at anything that had to do with words, oral or written; and in the hall of the Sanhedrin he had outwitted his opponents, the Sadducees and Pharisees, tied them up in verbal traps, and set them fighting among themselves. Thwarted, they had arranged an ambush and persuaded the chief priest and elders to ask the chief captain to send Paul to them for examination. But a bright nephew of Paul's had told Paul of the plot and he had sent him to the captain. Later—it was a great relief to Felix, who had been embarrassed by Paul's vigorous attempts to convert him in open court—Paul was rushed under horse guard to Caesarea Philippi in Galilee.

The proconsul Felix now saw a chance for a bribe. The upper chamber chapels had been increasing throughout the valley; their collections were growing heavier. Surely, Felix suggested to Peter, a part might be spared for so valued a leader as Paul. This Peter reported to Paul in prison where the windows looked out on blue Galilee where the Founder had walked and sailed, and talked, too, about ransom. But that of which He had spoken had to do with love and sacrifice, not with Caesar's coin. So Peter brought back an angry "No."

Then Festus replaced Felix. King Agrippa and Queen Berenice attended the hearings and were much impressed by Paul. He might have been released. But suddenly he appealed to Caesar and, turning to the king and queen, just as he had tried to convert Felix in open court, attempted to enlist the royal pair in his new Empire. It was an adroit, forceful, magnificent appeal. It should have been heard by all who have not learned how far from negative, how exciting and fascinating a truly good man may be. Felix had uneasily pleaded his celebrated "more convenient season." Agrippa now cried, "Almost thou persuadest me to be a Christian." Then, aside, he had said, as Pilate had of Christ, "He has done nothing worthy of death or chains. If he had not appealed to Caesar, he might have gone free." He shook his head.

So to Jaffa Paul walked under guard, sailed for Rome and underwent his third shipwreck, during which, from experience, he gave some excellent advice to the captain of the ship. He was marooned on Malta for six months, then landed at Rome in the spring. There they did not know what to do with him. They were not, after all, throwing people to the lions every day; and Paul though a Jew was too by inheritance a Roman citizen. They did not want to ignore the Jewish factions which, disgruntled by any acquittal of Paul, might start more riots, then ask for more legionaries to quell them; that was always a drain on the empire. On the other hand, sales of citizenship were a not inconsiderable item in the budget, and they did not want to lower the value of that citizenship by putting one against whom no serious offense had really been proved into the arena to fight with the gladiators. So they compromised by shutting him up in a comfortable place that was more pension than prison.

They might not have been so liberal had they been far-sighted enough to see that Paul would immediately start in to confirm some of the rabbis' charges. One after the other, he now sent out more of those letters he was forever writing to little congregations like those in Corinth, Galata of the Gauls, or Ephesus, or others dear to his heart. Those letters of his would start a bigger fire than any conflagration of Nero's.

The floors of his cell were covered with stylus and reed shavings. The most welcome presents friends could bring him were papyrus rolls or waxed tablets. And while many who called on him were the persecuted fugitives creeping up from the catacombs, there were prosperous visitors too, half-converted tribunes, fully-converted centurions, and curious lawyers. These last Paul particularly fascinated, as he did so many people of all types everywhere. Perhaps that is why he had so far escaped the more painful misadventures of the martyr, having only been shipwrecked three times, five times scourged, stoned once. However, ahead was Nero. The famous advocates could not understand why with all his gifts Paul had not gone into the law, instead of off the deep end with his transcendentalism started by an obscure Jewish criminal whose very name would have been forgotten by all were it not for those who chose to style themselves by it.

Paul welcomed them for two reasons besides his eternal recruiting: first, because he was a natural gentleman. Of course in his youth bigotry had killed those instincts in him for a while as he had ridden up and down the country on his devastating way. Then when he enlisted under the Founder, Himself the world's first Gentleman, Paul became one again, a truer one this time. Also he welcomed the Roman lawyers because he loved a good argument. An arguer he had always been almost from birth, never irrelevant, but trenchant and incisive, and—when these were needed—the coiner of eloquent phrases which long after him would echo around the world. Had he lived in their respective eras, he would have argued with Abelard over the Trinity, with Pascal over Jansenism, Jonathan Edwards and Calvin over Predestination, Luther on divorce, Pankhurst on woman's suffrage—in which field only he would have been a trifle unfair—on capitalism with Karl Marx.

But arguments and endless epistles and heartening his fellow Christians who came up from the underworld, did not take all his time. Frequently his only companion was the jailer. So the busiest man in the world for the first time in his life had time on his hands. By day he could hear, through the bars, hoof-beats, harness clank, market cries, trumpets ringing from the forts, watermen's hails from mid-Tiber, the tramp of marching legions, the lions roaring in the arena. At night he might fall asleep or he might not. Even if he did, he was apt to wake before dawn and see the lupina lights or Nero's torches burning. Even in those zero hours, when the spirits are apt to be low, though he knew what inevitably awaited him, there was no fear for the body. There would have been none before the great change, for he was by nature the most valiant of men. And now there was no fear for the soul. Had he not written, in his brightest hour, the world's most exalted cry of triumph over Man's archfoe: "O death, where is thy sting? O grave, where is thy victory?"

Such flaming convictions as this had made him the surest man in history, even as he was the most modest of men, thinking himself the most unworthy. It was only of his faith that he was so sure. His words, both the soaring and the humble, were as sincere words as ever were written; their sureness and sincerity would carry them ringing down the centuries. No powers of darkness could dim their light, no mocking cynic make them sound hollow. Perhaps it is as well for inspired writer not to know, as he puts down his words, that they will be immortal. Certainly if, as he scratched it on waxed tablet or set it down on papyrus roll, Paul could have heard the glorious sentence above being read down the centuries, in cathedrals and chapels all over the world, and by countless gravesides, illustrious and lowly, he would have been overpowered.

This greatest of optimists in history had his dark moods, not of fear but—even after his magnificent record—of remorse. At such times the face of Stephen often came to him. This was not strange, for though Paul had hated him, there had once been the strongest of ties between the two young men. Paul would be troubled about that face, for it would appear to him with the illuminating smile gone, bruised, bloody, broken. Always, in these dark hours, he could feel—in spite of the assurance of forgiveness he had had—his guilt in that death.

For he had helped to kill this Stephen who was his spiritual father, who, more even than the womb of Paul's own mother was responsible for Paul, had given him life. It was as Saul that Paul had done this, before the change in his name and soul.

Stephen was perhaps the most gifted, certainly the most influential of the very young men history has known. When the Twelve were busily engaged with their marvellous healings, in organizing the new state, and teaching its constitution's preamble, it fell to Stephen to stress its inmost meaning, its "invisibility," and to stress it to his body's disaster and his soul's eternal glory. Most of the great empires, on the passing of their founders, or very soon after, have returned to the earth's dust from which they rose. This invisible Empire was not as the rest. For where the others experienced dissolution under degenerate heirs, this state, founded not on world-proclaimed victory but on what at the time looked very like defeat, had four powerful heirs. These men not only kept the domain intact, but spread its boundaries, though by the most unorthodox methods: they travelled on foot, in the dust; and being spat upon, scourged, and stoned was the only acclaim they knew. They had no armour or swords, no banners streaming in the wind, only meekness and lowly services and phrases that have rung down the years.

The four were: Peter, Rock of the Church; John, its beloved Mystic and Poet; Paul, its great trumpet voice; and Stephen, the youngest, who died first. While still a provincial youth, just come up to the University of Jerusalem, he was the first to give an absolutely liberal interpretation to the charter Christ had given for the greatest of all revolutions—a charter, made up of His remembered conversations not yet written down. Seeing, with an insight beyond his years, the need of this charter, he desperately strove to save the breath of life their Founder had breathed into it. He was the first of mortals to show that one could die for the Cause like the King, with forgiveness for his very murderers. So Stephen was the first to catch the torch from Christ's hands to carry it on to his own death. At the end, in passing, he handed it on to a dead Saul, who not only through the light on the Damascus Road, but that on the dying Stephen's face, became the real Paul.

In his prison, looking back, Paul still could see the young Stephen of 35 A.D.—thirty-one years before—standing out from all the rest of the provincials who with the Northern accent thick on their tongues, had come from various schools in Asia Minor to this university whose campus was the Temple court, its halls the Temple steps or the shadows around its pillars. Half-Jews—they were patronizingly called by the native students proud of having been born in the capital. But Stephen, undisturbed by this snobbery, excelled in the Law and was highly proficient in the scholarly Hebrew as well as in Aramaic, the language of his own Syria North, in which Abraham had spoken to his shepherds, and the medium that Christ had chosen for His beautiful parables, the Beatitudes and the Our Father which would ring out in the Cathedral.

Gamaliel occupied a position in this university not unlike that held by the rector of the mediaeval university which, without a physical plant, would grow up around the Cathedral. But Stephen got beyond this famous doctor much sooner than Paul, who was a reactionary, though much more gifted and fiery than reactionaries usually are. To the disgust of the doctor and Paul—Saul then—Stephen left the celebrated halls to take up an intensive course in another school, a radical affair run by some social outcasts on lines laid down by a rejected teacher who a few months before had been crucified between two thieves. Only two of the faculty ever had any standing whatsoever—James and John, who came of the rich Zebedee family which, on occasion, had financed the rest. Even they had been ostracized, and the others were fishermen, did work with their hands, and had little education. Gamaliel and Paul could not understand it.

But the boy Stephen drank in with delight all that his new friends, whose healings were as effective as their teachings, had to tell him of the things the Founder had taught them, in cornfields, on the rocky mount, from the sterns of scale-strewn Galilee fishing boats. More deeply than the words of his beloved Greeks were these engraved on his heart. He felt that Plato and Aristotle with the great philosophers of all lands, would have paid homage to this new philosopher who carried on the teachings of all the good and the great to a perfectly logical but higher summation. Young as he was, he determined that this new charter of men's rights should be given no material twist, that His immortal words while they still were remembered, should be proclaimed with all their authentic ring, so that their echo should not die out of the world.

So the then bitter young Saul watched his former schoolmate receive from this sect Saul hated, honours for which he would have been envied by older men had not his loveableness matched his genius. They sent him on every kind of mission, gave him every kind of trust, until he was almost on a level with the famous Eleven who, now that Matthias had been elected to fill dark Judas' chair, were Twelve once more.

And desperately Stephen strove—perhaps because he felt his time to be short—in every synagogue, at every corner, to tell his countrymen that the Old Dispensation was over, that nothing material, no big flocks or big families or even the cold integrity of the "upright man" of itself, could support one in the final hour; that greater barns, even greater temples, could not bring security. This was to be gained not through anything that could be erected, but through something that descended on the soul, something that was not static but dynamic and flaming, and yet was part of an utter peace that calmed and at the same time fortified the soul. And when he found his friends and even some of the older followers of Christ walking, in spite of the new light, with one foot in the Old Dispensation, one in the New, and looking out of the very upper chamber chapel windows on the beloved Temple of their youth and finding its golden corners and porch, its shining ornaments, exceeding fair, he saw as no man yet the danger that lurks in the very beauty of the Visible. With the gravest earnestness he tried to show them of what immaterial material the "many mansions" of which the Founder had told them, and which He "had gone to prepare for them," were really framed. And not only did Stephen, as architect of the Invisible, erect before the eyes of the willing but slower members of the congregations, a new structure, with the arch of spiritual logic, pillars of phrases imperishable. He went out, to the astonishment and anger of Paul—still Saul—into the lion city crouching in wait for him, and flung a challenge to all the old Tories. First on the steps of Antonia Fort, then on those of the Temple itself, he proclaimed a "temple not made with hands."

Fearlessly he beckoned to Death. His murderers were all about. The Founder had prayed for His murderers, and someone had to be not only the first to die for Him, but the first to show that His matchless magnanimity could be matched through Him by mortals, that this noble idealism was an attainable, a practical, thing. So Stephen drove this principle of the Invisible in, nailed it, in effect, high on the very visible Temple steps, above the Kedron's clefts, on the other side of which, grey, gnarled, and twisted, grew the olive trees where Christ had prayed with bloody sweat, the red dew of death which, before the sun set, was to fall on Stephen.

All these scenes came vividly back to Paul in his prison cell. He could see Stephen as we can see him still above the south transept portal—called Saint Etienne's, in the French, after him—of the

Cathedral of Notre Dame, as he stands up to the conspirators' knot, with their turbans, curled beards, powerful noses, and hands in wide sleeves itching to be at him. The handsome dark smouldering eyes of his baiters and the implacable ones of Saul are, of course, missing from that sculptured story. And the sculptor could not completely express in stone the eagerness, the litheness and youth of Stephen, as he preaches to the crowd, that is, as much of a crowd as the chisel could get into the panel. A dozen angry doctors are there, representing the university, and a little group of those that believed in Stephen, including—one of the loveliest touches in any cathedral—a young mother nursing her babe as she listens to him.

In speaking to the Tories, he had added, for good measure, that cubits, cedar of Lebanon, and guarding cherubin did not matter at all. The only temple that would endure was one, forsooth, "not built with hands." It was then that they tore at their curled beards, as you see them in the stone tableau of the cathedral. And this vividly recalled to them another who had said that their Temple would be destroyed in three days. He had been killed on a hill. Well, there were hills all around. So they haled Stephen into court. But first they had to beat him up. In the East as well as in the West, the Old Order must have its thugs to beat up anyone that brings news that is good but which they do not understand, therefore fear.

They led him into the pillared hall. The confusion was great. A striking, cursing, spitting convoy, a mob of many swirling colours, rushed in with him. In the best places were the curious who are always on hand whenever a social rebel who has something enlightened to say which he must pay for with his life, is on trial. Properly planted was a tough-looking crew, ready at the cue for uproar to impress the council, or a rush for the victim. Heads together, within whispering distance of the leaders of the council, stood the distinguished scholar witnesses and other diehards in fine linen. Among them was Saul, blue-eyed, short, restless, but with an air of command. Sometimes, even as Saul, his face could be winning. It wasn't that day. A conscientious, but perfectly hateful zeal consumed it.

The middle-of-the-road people too, as always, were there. One of them, Stephen's old, Saul's present teacher, made a speech urging moderation. It was polished, highly civilized, urbane. It did nothing for his one-time star pupil.

Some of Stephen's friends who had come up with him to the capital were plucking at his sleeves, begging him to be careful. Already, they said, they had been snubbed enough by the university snobs. Stephen by his defiance would only shove them farther down the social ladder. So, standing by his bloodied shoulders, though behind these they should have known stood the Angel of Death, they pleaded selfishly with him.

It came very swiftly then. There was a half hour of eloquent defense by Stephen—not of himself but of the New Code, the new philosophy. He spoke first of the past glories of their race. The antagonistic clamour of the court died down. Some almost cheered. They were stopped by the leaders. Then, while reciting their grand deeds, he began to allude to their desertions of the Invisible for the visible golden calves. Doctor Gamaliel shook his head. It was a pity, he thought, that so masterly a summing-up should be wasted. There was the sheer courage of it, the splendour of phrase, the startling change of pace and attack, and now the sudden shift from the things of the Old Dispensation. The light of the New, Paul then saw breaking over Stephen's face. When they had hailed him into court, Stephen had stood up before them, Death at his elbow, but he young, eager, and lithe. He was just as eager now, as he neared the end of his defense—like a youth running the more strongly and swiftly as he sees just ahead the shining goal. Perhaps it was the light from it that shone in his face.

So, adroitly, he came to the great Golden Age of their race, which had meant as much to them as the Renaissance to Italy, the Gothic Age to France:

"And Solomon built him a house."

It was there that for his body's sake he should have stopped. But immediately he rang, for the third time that day, a change in his challenge to them—to the Visible. From the solid platform of that statement about this house Solomon had built, he soared to a pinnacle of truth that none committed to the Visible can ever scale:

"However, the Most High dwelleth not in temples made with hands. For 'what house will you build me?' saith the Lord. 'And what is the place of my rest?'"

Now he who had been beaten and hailed into court was no longer the prisoner but the blazing prosecutor.

"Like your fathers you are! They persecuted the prophets. Now you are the betrayers and murderers of the Just One!"

Then in a quiet charged with death he spoke more gently, like one who knew "his course was run," as Paul's would be one day, and as though his heart held only infinite sorrow for them:

"The Law"—that Law they were forever throwing up at him as they had at Christ—"you received it from the hands of the prophets and have not kept it."

Then, knowing his doom was on him, he had just time before they sprang, to say, his bright face looking upward, "I see the Heavens open and the Son of Man."

The mob with a snarl that was not more characteristically Jewish than Gentile—all have their murders of those bringing light—were at him. Saul, still the hound of Heaven, not yet Paul the courier of Heaven, ran with the pack that rushed Stephen out of an east gate —the one Saul afterwards passed through on his hurried journey to Damascus—to a hill. Both trial and hill were technically correct; the Old Order is always so impeccably legalistic. And the Law had prescribed a "high place" for "blasphemy," and Stephen had undeniably committed blasphemy—against the Old Law. Besides, "a high place" was such a good one for throwing down stones and gloating over something fallen and broken, though it had brought them good news and had been eager and lithe and young and bright and beautiful.

In miniature you still can see the stones upheld in the murderers' hands on the Saint Etienne portal of Notre Dame. So that they might more easily hurl these stones and their fine linen would not be soiled, Saul offered to watch over these. Later he thanked God that his services that day went no further. As it was, the contribution was heavy. Yet the young man of genius and love tried to lighten the debt for the young man of genius and hate who would live to turn that hate into love.

For as Saul watched the clothes and the stones rained down an extraordinary thing happened. Only once before had there been anything like it in this world. Crushed, blinded with blood, Stephen called out his last message. It was not the usual kind, of love for one's loved ones, but of love for those who hate. For their pitilessness he gave back pity. And here is the answer complete to those who claim that even the apparently noble deed is motivated by thoughts of self: he did not think of his own agony, of his own soul, of the Heaven which he might be approaching. His heart went out to them even as they crushed out his life. His lips, the only part of him that still could move, cried out just before they quivered into their final peace, "Lord, lay not this sin to their charge." It was a noble paraphrase of Christ's own words, "Lord, forgive them, for they know not what they do." They were winged seeds that dropped into the only fissure then open in the rock of Paul's soul. Unperceived they were to root there and blossom until they split that rock open for the light.

In these noble last lines of Christ and Stephen, so alike, is implicit the whole core of His philosophy, the whole burden of the universal drama whose message would be reverently sent over the footlights, the innumerable candles of the Cathedral, through the ages. This completely altruistic beat of the last act Stephen was the first of mortals to grasp. He was the first to show the world that it was possible for the human to follow the Divine.

If Christ was the linking between the human and the Divine, Stephen was the linking between Christ and the rest of men. Where others might have faltered, thinking the great rôle beyond them, Stephen the young Second Actor rushed on the scene and played it to the majestic last line and his death. So he gave mortal plausibility to the immortal drama.

He is known as the "protomartyr," that is, the first, the arch, martyr; and not inappropriate is the great carved portal with the beautiful statue of him and those scenes from his life under the south rose of Notre Dame. It is too bad that in recent years they have kept it closed, so that many have missed seeing its full beauty from the closed garden. And too few realize the full significance of Stephen who by historic right should lead all the sainted citizenry that so thickly populate niche and shrine, the façade and very roof of the Cathedral. Even for those who never enter the Cathedral or any of the little chapels of brick or stone, cottonwood, pine, or palm, of all creeds around the globe, and who express their social service outside the framework of the Church, Stephen should mean much. The kingdom of the Founder was a highly socialized state, His revolution the source revolution of all revolutions worthwhile. Out of its charter, out of its root symbol, the Cross, have blossomed all the things men of good will hold dear, from chivalry, sportsmanship, the Red Cross, the Christmas spirit, to child labour laws and every social enactment. Stephen showed that its superb idealism was not unattainable. Its charter Christ had sealed with the red seal of His death. With his own death Stephen added the human impress.

If Paul awaiting death in his prison cell in 66 A.D. could have foreseen that he would not have nearly so grand a place on the Cathedral, just a niche by Sainte Anne's door and a place first to the left of Christ in the parade of disciples whose band is split in two by the great Last Judgment door, he would not have cared. Could he have been there eleven centuries after, he would have pointed out to the builder-bishop that the sculptor who worked on that particular group could not have known his subject very well. He, Paul, was no member of the Twelve; and should not have been in at all. It was Matthias' rightful place since he had been elected to fill Judas' empty chair. Then he would have gone around to admire Stephen's door and would have been unhappy over certain scenes in it. But never would he have begrudged Stephen his prominent place in the Cathedral or that which he must take in any true story of Paul.

In prison now, Paul saw it all as he could not see it at the time. That illumination in the dying Stephen's face had been, before the light in the Damascus Road, a torch that had been deliberately handed up to him. He had been too angry, too confused, too ashamed to take it. As though it had scorched him, he had cast it aside.

The face of Paul—still Saul—was hateful looking as he rode out of the gate and took the road to Damascus. His heart was full of the Law, self-righteousness, fanaticism and murder. His saddle-bags were stuffed with credentials to the Damascus authorities and lists of Christian suspects he might arrest there, though already he had filled the Jerusalem jails full. That look was the look of Cain. He had just helped to kill his spirit blood brother.

To understand how that look could have come into his face we must know that this Saul on whom Paul in his great humility was so hard, was not mere bigot or wantonly cruel. He was not without conscience. In fact, he had too much of that and zeal. It took a great martyr's tragedy and the most startling rendezvous with destiny man ever had to do it, but conscience and zeal were to be redirected—that was all. A studious, moral young man, he had worshipped the Law. And he had excelled in its three branches—the written Torah, the Pentateuch, the even greater body of laws developed from the Torah, in his time usually orally transmitted and requiring a prodigious memory; and the fitting of all this great mountain of laws to the little moments of every day—the "Halekhah," "The Rule of the Daily Walk" this was poetically called. But there was much more than this. We could only grasp it and Paul's first love and later struggle, had our own Constitution been wedded to some generally accepted articles of religious belief, and from these had sprung our customs, rules of life, our epics and songs, if all our history had been interwoven with it, and it had been fought and bled for through fifteen centuries. The powerful spell it exercised is understandable. Still, the rule loomed large in it. Now Saul, like a young man, admired all the heroes of his people. Their august rectitude he considered sure proof that his Law was the final and only answer to life and to death. The uprightness of these very great men he attributed to their obedience to the rules of the Law which, to be sure, they obeyed; and he overlooked their larger and forward vision. Faithful adherence to an objective code sometimes moulds character; but Paul, as Saul, was convinced that simply by following ordinances one could wholly transform an inner state.

But even before Stephen's tragedy, as Paul heard Gamaliel brilliantly expound the Old Law in the open-air university, he also watched Peter, James, John, Philip, Andrew, Nathaniel, all the pioneers, both teaching and living the New. And he began to have doubts. Could it be that after all he had been putting second things first? That outward rules could not work in, but regeneration must come first? That life must work from within into the outer act? The Old fought back, with all its true grandeur, all its stubbornness and perversities. It was, in a way, the very excess of his conscientiousness that drove him, for a while, to persecution. It was those aroused doubts about the validity of the Law, his dawning disillusion about something he had cherished all his life, that led him even into watching murderers' clothes. These were the pricks the Voice meant when it cried out of that great Light: "Saul, Saul, why kickest thou against the goads?"

Now, in his prison cell—the roar of the arena lions, the creak of turning chariot wheels, the tramp of marching legionary feet, coming to him through the high barred window—he could see it all vividly, feel it all burningly still: There was that desert city just ahead, with its white domes and plum trees, heavy-fruited, against the walls, and the great light and his horse shying. The torch Paul had rejected was in the Damascus Road picked up and handed back to him. A Voice had come out of that Light. It was the voice he might have heard if he had come up but a few months earlier to Jerusalem. Never after could he be shaken from the conviction that it was the voice of their King, the Founder. In vain his foes charged him with epilepsy. An occasional disability he may have had, or a nervous intensity, in common with Darwin, Pasteur, Lincoln, so many of the great. But hysterical visions do not send a man around the world for thirty years, establishing hundreds of churches in savagely antagonistic communities, settling myriads of little local feuds and great council disputes, and training missioners, ambassadors, and generals for a great new state. Out of no brain seizure springs the kind of light he saw or the power and luminousness of a thousand immortal sentences all sweeping with beautiful sureness into the arrow points of the truths he longed to drive in.

They led him into Damascus, blind. But as suddenly as it had come, the darkness left him. With the same intense energy with which he had dealt out blows for the Old Order, he struck out feverishly for the New. He began to trumpet his conversion all over the caravan city. Illy prepared, he succeeded only in making a nuisance of himself, though some saw in him the great leader to be. They had to get him out of the city at night, letting him down in a basket over the city wall. Nearby a camel was waiting. Over the desert he had come, a tormenting guerrilla commander in the armies of the Dark. He rode back, a raw recruit, but now on the side of the angels.

In Jerusalem under Peter and John he started a course to unlearn all he had learned at the feet of Gamaliel. The New Dispensation was being explained, openly or secretly, in the strongholds of the Old. Champions of the Old hated to see such a sharp instrument as Saul, that once had been theirs, now in Nazarene hands. After his record of persecution, too, he would be a most effective argument for the New. Some of the followers of the New, however, did not welcome him. "What trick is this?" they asked. "He threw us into prison. Our backs are still sore from the scourge. And now he rides back and tells us what to do to be saved. Is he not very like the wolf in sheep's clothing of which the Lord spoke?" It took more than a change of name, to convince the more cautious of the sufferers in the upper chamber chapels.

Later Peter and Paul, both fighters for principle, would clash on occasion. But at that time Peter, rock that he was, nobly played elder brother to Paul. He spent much time in explaining why this spiritual leopard named Paul had so suddenly changed his spots. But they had not completely changed yet. The conversion was not over and done with on the Damascus Road, though it had had a grand start. It was for some time, during this formative period, to be a continuing process. Often this is so. The whole world was to be Pauline-minded; but as yet Paul did not know that mind. In the storms that assailed him he had often watched and envied his new friends. Where it had been so easy for them, it had been so hard for one of his passionate and logical nature. They had but one picture. As Saul, he had dimly glimpsed that true life must come from within, not work its way in from without. He had received flaming evidence of that on the hill, on the road. The light had struck within, it had almost purged him, but not quite. The Old Law was not so easy to down. In the reactions such as come to all men, from Bruce in his cave, Jeanne on the stand, to Lincoln in his study at midnight, and usually just before they rise to their greatest achievements, the Old Law would rise up and strike back again. Once more the two faiths would be locked in struggle within him. Even as he went blazing the story of his conversion through the valley where Jacob had wrestled with the angel, the Old and the New wrestled for him. Then suddenly his friends could not find him. Reports would come in that he had been seen near Tarsus where he had learned tent-making and Greek, or by the wave-slapped quais of Jaffa, or where Our Lord too had fought the powers of the Dark, beyond the Jordan in the sandy wastes, or by the red rocks of Moab.

It is awful to have a great tide—and that is what he had felt at Damascus—turn to the ebb and leave the soul bare and sucked at by the last dragging currents of doubt. But this had to be before he could become the surest man in the world. He was fighting not only for himself and the Church on which he was to have an immeasurable influence, but for all honest men, who being honest must at some time doubt. In his own soul he was waging the war for all, of the New against the Old, the spirit against the letter, of liberalism against literalism and fundamentalism.

That is very often an internecine war; it was with Paul. And in the midst of it he would try for the fatal compromise, wondering if there were not some way to harmonize the New with the Old, which he did not want to give up entirely. Wherever he went on these distracted wanderings, from the Lebanon, Syrian, or Desert heights he could see the long valley and its guarding mountains set aside by God as the stage where the First Act had been grandly played, the Last tragically but beautifully lived. And there were crucial hours when it was the First Act that most powerfully called out to him. This was not strange. On hills across a valley, Abraham had grazed his flocks. On Sinai's snowy summit, the two tables of stone had been delivered. From nearby Nebo, Moses had gazed into this Promised Land. In that village Isaac had courted Rebecca. On that farm Ruth had gleaned. That city had fallen before Joshua's triumphant trumpets. On those uplands Enoch had walked with God. Here Gideon with his chosen band had uncovered the little lights from the pitchers. From this brook David had gathered his pebbles. Under those trees were the still waters of which he had sung. Before those walls the Assyrians had lain in their dewy mail, slain by the passing Angel of Death. All up and down that valley Philistines and Hittites and Jews had struggled in battle, and captains had become great. In the yellowing old capital, the lion city, kings like wise Solomon and Hezekiah and Joash had been crowned and temples had gone up, and all but the last had vanished. And everywhere prophets had testified and young men, like himself, had studied the Law which, with its high morality and one Jehovah, had been such a bright light in its day in the surrounding pagan darkness. Other very wonderful and lovely things had happened down in that valley during a short three years, but he had lost sight of these for the time. For it was as though a mighty last chorus of all those old heroes he had admired, of the scenes he had loved, went up from that valley and its hill to him.

Then, there on the heights, perhaps on those very ones from which Our Lord had been shown the glittering cities on the horizon and had refused them, knowing the temporal choice would mean the spirit's abdication, a visitor came. Perhaps it was the old villain of the drama who had been thrown from the plains of Heaven ages before. If we take this for allegory, very sound and true, it was certainly an envoy from the forces of the Dark who, sooner or later, find lodgment within the stoutest walls. This last temptation —we find echoes of all these hours in his later burning epistles— was, singularly enough, barbed with logic, aimed at a weak spot in a man who if he won would become the greatest logician of the metaphysical the world has ever known.

Often, on these unhappy wanderings, Paul must have been famished like his Lord of the Forty Days, so that he fain would have eaten of the shoots of the locust boughs the desert men cut for their herds, or have milked some camel stray, two of whose dugs would be left free for the calf, two tied for man. The whispers then from the visitor would, in Paul's faintness, have been very compelling.

"Majestic," they said, "is that chorus of voices of the past which you hear. And they are true. Never were there sweeter songs or more sublime scenes and exalted passages than in your literature which was written in that valley. Never was there law more powerful and august than that which your literature records and with which it is interwoven. For ages it has endured. Through all the long pilgrimage it has sustained your race. Could it then be so wrong? And is it something to be lightly tossed away?"

And then the visitor from without or from within Paul's own soul, resorted to the scholar's argument, a technicality, but, for Paul, one on which hung the whole issue, the whole battle, life and death.

"Cursed is he that is hanged to a tree." So had said the Law. And if these all now seem shadowy things, we must remember that each pronouncement of the Law was accepted by every soul in that valley, good and bad, as we accept such axioms of the West as, "No man must be condemned without a trial," "Everyone must be allowed to worship as he chooses," or anything in the Bill of Rights. Besides that same Law had an uncanny way of reaching out over fifteen centuries and picking out a coming event. Paul knew, too, that Christ had said that the Law, in its every prophecy and promise, would be fulfilled. If that were so, then was Christ Himself, who had "been hanged to a tree," cursed? Cursed because He was not true! The Last Act was a vain, an empty tale. This King who had turned him aside from his old allegiance, from a solid thing like the Law, and who had been loved for His beautiful life and what he had taken for His regenerative power, was false! Or else the Law was false. Then somewhere, by the Jordan, in the marts of men, on Christ's heights above the gorges, there came this clarifying:

To Abraham on the hills across the valley had been given this promise: "In your seed is Christ." It was a solemn guaranty to the race. Then to Moses, on that summit south, the two tables of stone, germ of their Law, had been delivered. The Law had *not* come first. That promise of Christ had been given ages before the tables of stone. The Law could not have that priority over Christ which the

Temple scholars had boasted. Christ had priority over the Law. Not only the prophets, but the Law itself, had been but the prelude to Christ.

Of what use then had been the Law? It was a check on Man's wayward conduct, and the only one until Christ came. For—there were more than technicalities to be cleared up, more in him than logician and scholar to be satisfied—if the Law had been eternal, it would have been more than a code ruling by punishments and rewards, or at best leading to virtue. It would have been a thing of fire and life, that sort of quickening that had been given to Stephen. Even before Christ the prophets must have known this. It was not the Law, the Letter, that had brought them their grandeur of lives. Implicit in their very songs was the foreknowledge of what was to come, what he himself had known at Damascus, a mighty impulsion such as he had never dreamt could come to a man and which never had been given by the Law. He had seen it carry Stephen on to a noble death, had watched the tremendous results in Peter, James, John, a thousand others. If the Law had possessed any such life secret, there would have been need neither for the promise of Christ nor His coming. The Law would have been enough. But the Law had been designed as a rule. You could obey a rule. You did not obey fire and life and Christ. You either ran away from them or took them in—took Christ in as you would fire, life, light, so that flame and vessel are one.

Still the Law which had done so much for the world, had not been humiliated. Christ had taken its curse on Himself for others, had been its rich fruit. So triumphantly Paul could cry—and later write it down for us to read—"I have died in the Law; I live in Christ."

And as he looked down into the valley now, the chorus of the voices of the past, of the First Act died away, and that of the Second came up rejoicing and strong. He could see now all those scenes to which those in the First Act had, for that unhappy time, made him blind—all the places where He had been, the cornfields through which He had walked and broken the letter of the Law; the cities by whose pools He had healed the sick, made the blind see; villages where He had raised the dead and, in a world that put little children to the sword, had taken them on His knee; the mountains and sea where He had walked and by lovely word and example taught the ways of mercy and gentleness and love; the streets down which He had ridden on His one day of earthly acclaim, the bare hill on which the beautiful life seemed to have been snuffed out, the garden where in glory and the spring it had been reborn, bright with promise for all the world.

So again he cried, "I live by the faith of the Son of God who loved me and gave Himself for me!"

He had found his answer once and for all. This Christ was a living principle, an all-pervading personality, a regeneration, a fundamental activity that wholly possessed one, at once a rest and a peace, a fire and a tide.

The Temple down there, the valley itself with its guarding mountains, the beautiful Cathedral-to-be in its time, the sea beyond, the stars above, might all vanish. It would not matter. There would still remain that fire and that tide.

Paul has been called the Second Founder of the Church. Even those historians who cannot themselves get the lift that came with that affirmation above to Paul, must admit the very real history he made, recognize that sentence as the premise for the world's most influential philosophic system, basic rule for the most powerful humanistic organization on earth. By it Paul and those fighting pioneers, Church and Cathedral, must stand or fall. Without it, the great Cathedral would be bereft of light. That truth alone can start the current.

Very young Paul had been in those days. His joints had been supple, his hair rich and thick. Now he was bald, and his fingers were swollen from much tent-making and exposure in sea water. From long rides on camel back and in the saddle, his back was beginning to bend. His legs had hardened into that crooked bow. But although he had lost a little of his five-feet-six, no one after the first minute ever thought of him as small. There was still about him as he aged an air of dignity, and, with all their friendliness, of command and sharp challenge in the eyes which had been blue in the desert days, but were fast dimming now.

His course was almost run. Looking back, as he relaxed in the little parallelogram of sunshine from the barred window, he could recapture his feeling of exaltation of soul when, after the victory, he had ridden back to the capital of his fathers. There rode through the city gates no split personality then. Henceforth, through that tide within him, he had been a veritable tide himself, going up and down the world sweeping men off their feet and mostly in the right direction.

Swiftly the panorama of those rich, crowded flying years unfolded itself before him as in prison he awaited Nero's summons and Death's. . . . Smoking lamps in upper chambers. . . . Damp walls of crypts and deserted theatres, where worshipped the persecuted faithful. . . . Little silver Dianas, pretty things too, curses of silversmiths, and stones flying on the Ephesus Temple porch. . . . Camel's lope and sweat and oasis camp fire, the waxed tablet slanted in the dark to catch the light of the fire, and another immortal epistle. . . . Waves' slap and crash of mast, with hamper and tackle overboard, and a whole life in swift review, in the down-sucking vortex of the water. All these came back to him, with the smiles too of those to whom he had brought the good news of the kingdom. And stretching over the coastline and mountains and desert, like the ranged pillars he had ridden by at Nineveh and Palmyra, were the endless tents he had made. He could feel the cloth even in his dreams, rough warp and woof, the selvage, eyelet holes, and the big needle flying. Not for him any preacher's soft perquisites. He preferred to make his living with his own hands, even as he preached. Perhaps this rugged independence added force to his sermons. And above all there were the churches he had established and which were proving such outposts for the new Kingdom.

With all these deep and honest satisfactions there had been mixed the disquieting, the disillusioning things, ranging all the way from gossip and snobbishness to sodomy and incest, even in some of the little churches he loved. He was not mealy-mouthed. He was far removed from that puritanism which avoids even the mention of unseemly things, betraying itself as but an inverted prurience. He not only mentioned, he operated on the evil, for the blackest sin to him was but a cancer of the soul; then, in all affection, for in spite of his vehemence Paul was the sweetest-natured of men, he took the sinner to his arms.

But more even than the crimes, it was the sniping selfishnesses that tormented him. There had been, for example, even in the great democracy of the Church, the drawing of a sort of race colour line. If some members had had their way, entry into it would only have been possible through that old Hebrew gate—circumcision. It was truly amazing. Franchise in the invisible empire was to depend on a very visible foreskin.

Again—how like some of these congregations were to certain narrow provincial ones of today!—many of the Jewish converts wanted the Gentiles to be restricted to the outer rooms and to lower tables at the church suppers while they, the orthodox "circumcised," sat with the salt. Even the pure and gentle James, who proved his nobility under Herod's sword, yielded to this rule to save a schism. The new free Church, in some of its branches, seemed alive with formalists and academicians, as the most liberal democracy is with fascists today. And he had thought he had left them on the Temple steps.

So again and again Paul had to write to the Mother Church in Jerusalem and the little affiliate churches of Greece and Asia, that circumcision was nothing "except that made without hands" in the soul. Over and over he had to repeat in a hundred different ways, the Founder's and Stephen's theme of the Invisible Kingdom, which had cost Stephen his life. And for a while Peter, in all innocence and through his very friendliness, almost caused a split. He would sit down one day at meat with the Gentile novices; the next would go to another table to eat with the Jewish members. Again, at the inns he would eat meats that had been offered to idols. To robust Peter it was unimportant. "What difference does it make?" he would ask, "when by that idol meat bait, I can catch another fish for His net?" But sensibilities would have been hurt. The one chief advantage of these feuds was the adroitness Paul gained in exposition, through his endless epistolary correspondence, in trying to straighten things out with all the congregations. Gifted at the start, soon he had at his command battalions of invincible adjectives, whole legions of shining and apposite metaphors. He became past master at coupling arguments in unbreakable chains and building philosophical structures from the ground up, with flawless cement of reason and never a shaky, impermanent logic timber. But never did he reason in a cold emotionless vacuum. He put poetry and passion even into his theology.

Again traitors and saboteurs would try, in the absence of one or the other, to libel Peter to Paul, Paul to Peter, Andrew to James, James to Andrew, and so on. And Paul had to wear out not only many gross of reeds and styli on papyrus and waxed tablet, but much sandal and saddle leather. Many times he had to hurry back from Jaffa, Crete, Corinth, the Orontes country, or somewhere along the Aegean, to the Mother Church councils in Jerusalem, to smother a new fire breaking out. Sometimes the trouble was as serious as that which threatened the Church in the time of Athanasius, or when two vicars of Christ, one reigning at Rome, the other in Avignon, both claimed to be pope. Within thirty years of its founding, the new empire almost cracked wide open.

In the thick of the race feuds, Peter and Paul came as near quarrelling as two forceful and strong-minded, if unselfish, men can come and yet not part. In the end Peter nobly came again to Paul's rescue, confessed his own lack of tact, gave up idol meat and other ways that wounded sensibilities. The troubled waters he so far settled as to persuade the key congregations that Paul was right when he declared that a Gentile's conduct, and not his foreskin, was the proper certificate of naturalization in an invisible empire. And Paul himself was growing. He had at first thought chiefly of enlisting only those of his own race in this army. Shocked by all these unhappy and unworthy bickerings, he emerged as the most glorious of the ambassadors to the Gentiles.

Looking back now he could see that there were many things he had had to cast out after terrific struggling. For one thing, it might have helped to come home, after caravan trek or shipwreck, to the warmth of a woman's welcome. Gentle hands might sooner have healed up the bruises of the stonings, the red trenches left in his back by the leaded scourges. There was no weak ice water in his veins, only a strong man's fire. And a strong man wants sons. But he had put his hand to the plough. A man of great culture and keen observation, he knew the worlds of art and the arena. He had seen that artists, in carving a great statue, runners, before a race, could divert the creative tides from love into other channels, if prize and goal were enough. He saw ahead the most shining of goals. And as any general would, when his army is small, the opposition great, he welcomed recruits who, for the cause, turned their backs on the warmth of the hearth and a woman's arms. He travels farthest who travels light, unimpeded by domestic ties and concerns. But he would not impose this patriotic asceticism and sacrifice of himself, the advance scout and explorer, on others. "It is better to marry than to burn," he, as all the world knows, counselled a puzzled friend, with vast common sense and some humour. It is doubtful if either he or the Commander he followed expected men to quite live up to their own lofty standards. It was only of themselves that they exacted rigid compliance.

"I keep under my body," he wrote again so memorably to another friend, "and bring it into subjection, lest by any means, when I have preached to others, I myself should be a castaway." Here again was no hypocrite, but the same honest man who by his trade would pay his own way, and made no sin, no matter how low, a bar to his affection and esteem once a man had turned, and who, at the heighth of his own fame, wrote himself down as the most undeserving.

Through all these stirring, crowded years, Paul though he was not aware of it, was moulding the thought of the Church, the drama for the cathedral. He was influencing too, for centuries to come, the thought-attitudes of the civilized world. From his "If meat make my brother to offend," which was used by the prohibitionists, the "little wine for the stomach's sake," which was seized upon by their adversaries, "Let every man have his own wife," "The wife hath not power of her body" nor "the husband of his," Paul's proclamations range all the way up the scale of human interests to his ringing challenges of the ancient foe of all—Death—and his assurances of immortality. At all points of the mind's compass —charity, chastity, celibacy, theocracy, psychology, excepting perhaps woman's status, in which he was a little and quaintly unfair— he expanded the horizons of mankind.

It is amazing too, to find how many lines of his, written at white heat and for some immediate purpose, still are read in the pulpits or used as actual dialogue in the cathedral and in the little churches of all creeds: "At the name of Jesus every knee shall bow" . . . "Put on the whole armour of God" . . . "The first Adam was made a living soul, the last Adam (Christ) a quickening spirit" . . . "It is sown in corruption, it is raised in incorruption" . . . "He that soweth to the spirit shall reap life everlasting" . . . "Though I give my body to be burned and have not charity, it profiteth me nothing" . . . "For the things which are seen are temporal, but the things which are not seen are eternal" . . . "Whatsoever things are true . . . honest . . . pure . . . lovely . . . of good report . . . think on these things" . . . "I therefore run . . . not uncertainly . . . fight not as one that beateth the air" . . . "The last enemy that shall be destroyed is Death" . . . "I have fought the good fight, I have finished my course, I have kept the faith" . . . "For I am persuaded that neither death nor life, nor angels nor principalities nor powers, nor things present nor things to come, nor heighth nor depth, nor any other creature, shall be able to separate us from the love of God which is in Christ Jesus, Our Lord." . . . "The peace of God which passeth understanding."

In the ears of uncounted hosts these and a thousand other phrases have resounded, to their hearts have brought exaltation or peace. The ranged bent heads of those who have bowed under "The grace of Our Lord, Jesus Christ, the love of God, and the communion of the Holy Ghost be with you all," would, if gathered together, make an endless chain that would reach to brighter worlds than ours.

Paul preached to the Church, to all the sons of men, more burningly and continuously than any other, the complete integration of this power that was Christ within oneself. Wherever he went— and he travelled far—and in his immortal letters, he strove to change religion from an upward-gazing, objective attitude into an intensely subjective, a kinetic inner life. So he warmly personalized religion and the Christ he had found and the mystery that was to be relived in the sanctuary of the Cathedral.

But that course of which he had written was almost finished. True, rather accurate historians like Theodoret, John Chrysostom, and Bishop Cyril say that for a while they let Paul out of his prison to fulfill a lifelong ambition, to get to Spain. Anyway, it seems pretty sure that he did get back to some of his dear little churches by the Aegean. There stones flew thicker, bribes to gangsters increased, and the riots grew worse. He was arrested again and thrown, this time, into a real dungeon.

And soon, with torches and swords as they had come for Christ, they came for Paul. They rode from the tower, through the city gates, to a grove on the Ostian Way, and about two miles from the place where Saint-Paul-beyond-the-Walls would rise over his dust.

A sword suddenly raised, more swiftly falling, can flash like that light in the Damascus Road or that on a young man's face, a young man named Stephen. One more thing Paul owed Stephen. He had taught him how to die. And no bugle was needed to speed Paul's valiant soul on this last of his many journeys.

"O death, where is thy sting? O grave, where is thy victory?"

If ever literature was related to life, Paul's letters were; and that is why they are supremely great.

News of his death and Peter's—for the two brothers-in-arms, who sometimes disagreed but always fought nobly together, died together, not so far apart and in the same city—was borne up the Rhone and the Saône and the Seine, to Paris. Thence it was relayed to the men of Paris fighting in the legions, among them the famous Gallic Legion of the Lark. The symbol of Rome had been the wolf. Despite their power, the Romans never forgot the wild wolf dugs at which they had tugged. Even their order, if not that of the wolf, was that of the police dog crossed with the wolf. But the *allouette*, or lark, was the symbol of Gaul. From her fair fields it springs to the sky in such swift flight it seems, like a tiny prism, to gather up wheat's gold, poppies' crimson, blue of the sky, the true riches of France.

That Legion of the Lark which had been fighting for Rome suddenly fought, with other legions against her, in the revolution, the last that broke out against Rome before she fell of her own weight. In Besançon, the great battle was fought and the vine-yarded Burgundian hills and valleys were piled, the old chroniclers say, with the victims, and the little sparkling rivers ran red as though with a vast crushing of her grapes. For a little while yet Rome would continue to win. But not only the barbarians, but the armies of the Invisible Empire from the east, were advancing.

Meantime, as the revolt spread, L. Domitius Ahenobarbus, other-wise known as Nero, took fright, and fled one night from his palace to a house on the outskirts of Rome. Then, as pursuers pounded on the doors, Nero took his own life, not knowing as did Peter and Stephen and Paul, how greathearted gentlemen die.

VII

The Merchants of Paris talk with Bishop Irenaeus of Lyons who has studied with Saint Polycarp who has talked with John, the Beloved Apostle who walked with Christ. . . . Men worship Underground, but at last they build their first Fat Little Churches up in the Sun. . . . The Form of these Little Churches, Heralds of the Cathedral. . . . Early Necessary Properties which will be transformed into the Glittering Ones of the Cathedral Sacristy, and the first Pure Robes which will become the Cathedral's Gorgeous Vestments.

120=240 A.D

THOUGH WORD OF THE DEATHS OF PETER AND PAUL CAME up the Seine as an item of gossip, the first bishop-captain would not come riding over Sainte Geneviève's Hill for one hundred and eighty-four years after the tragedies in Rome. But from time to time bulletins came of the progress of the new and paradoxical, the militantly pacifist armies of a kingdom which was itself framed of paradoxes—"He that would save his life must lose it," and the like—which out of the tangle of men's rites and creeds flash like quicksilver with the quintessence of life.

Such reports were brought into the valley by merchants of Paris. Shrewd Gallo-Romans these were, beating out trade routes that would be famous for ages, to and from glamourous cities as far east as the green Ganges, and south past the river horses, the great stone faces and the rose flamingoes of the Nile.

Everywhere, as these men of the North came into the belt around the sea which the Romans called "Ours," they found believers, when lulls in the persecutions would permit, building their fat little churches; then, when the storm broke again, meeting like ghosts in temple ruins, deserted theatres, down old mining shafts, and in mouldering cemeteries. Everywhere, too, they saw humble men and great dignitaries going down into rivers as a sign of their being washed by "a river of blood," which, uncouth but eloquent preachers thundered, would bring them not only life here but immortality.

Now these Gallo-Roman merchants were more intellectual than

men in trade in other countries usually are; certainly far more so
than the big businessmen of Rome. Had not their people produced
the most cunningly-contrived weapons and utensils in the West,
ever since they had wrought those gold and coral and enamelled
shields and their bright helmets with the fashionable flares? Was
not Ausonius of their race in the 300's to prove the noblest poet
of the last centuries of the empire?

For years as they travelled they had watched history being made
in the great Mediterranean belt, and made, not so much by mailed
generals as by unarmed presbyters and deacons and hermits. Near
strange desert evangels they would pitch their tents, under waving
palm fronds listen to vivid narratives of royalty—of a "King" of
a new and most unorthodox kind. With mountain anchorites, they
would eat roast goat's flesh and wild honey, watch Joppa fisherman or Balkan shepherd, at a roofless service, break a loaf upon
an earthen plate and fill a rude cup as though these elements and
vessels were the most precious things in all the world. Now in
craggy cells they would hear wild words of Sin and Hell, again
comforting ones of "many mansions" prepared by Him whom
they called "King," and bright as the stars on which they gazed
from their camp fires, and which stirred inherited memories of
the old brave Gallic Heaven of the West. But those shining halls
had been for chiefs and conquerors. This new Valhalla was for the
lowly as well. Those at the foot were to go to the top of the
banquet board. And—an even more striking and picturesque reversal of the usual order—not the fighters, but the meek, were to
be honoured. Now their old Gallic faith had had its noble standards, the requirement, for example, of its sons never to desert a
burning house or a sinking ship while there remained alive a
comrade who might be saved. There was some common ground
between this new faith and the almost-forgotten one of Gaul. But
never before had moral courage been so held up for the world to
admire as in the new. And it set these men of Paris to wondering.

Sometimes these inquisitive but courteous travellers from France
would be invited to dine on melons and figs at Smyrna, by the
great Bishop Polycarp. Again the Gallic saint, Bishop Irenaeus,
would play host in his cool refectory over the rushing Rhone.
Already—in 170 A.D.—while the Parisians were still paying a
half-hearted lip-service to Jupiter in his temple at the old Druid
end of Paris Isle, the martyr Pothinus had established a diocese
at Lyons, with a fair-sized church, and another, a little sister
church, at Vienne.

Bishop Irenaeus had once studied under Bishop Polycarp who
had intimately known the Apostle John, just about the time he
was sitting down to write his Revelations. And Irenaeus would

tell them—if Polycarp had already told them himself, it would
all bear repeating—things John had told Polycarp: what, in those
Galilee fishing boats, were the King's actual words; what He wore,
how He looked at the Transfiguration, when walking the waves, or
writing those cryptic words in the sand when they brought the
town woman—just such as one would find in Rome or Paris—to
Him for stoning. These Paris merchants listening to Irenaeus, who
had heard these things from Polycarp, who had been told them by
John, as they had actually happened when John had walked with
Him—it was a great chain! Almost as good as firsthand!

Over the lentils and beets, which grew well in this region, and
a little of its wine, Irenaeus would tell them of the way the wind
was blowing—in Rome. Whether it was thumbs up or down. Now
Rome would devour the Christians; again, sated, would lick her
bloody chops and blink at them. And it did not always matter
whether an empurpled brute, like Nero, or a man of culture was
on the throne. This new fellow they called Marcus Aurelius was
a bookworm. Yet, humanist as he was, foreseeing the ultimate
tragedy of Rome, and growing fearful therefore sadistic, he would
send out spies wholesale, light avenues of pyres, and drench the
arena sands. No, the Church was better off when a man of less
culture but of hard-headed practical sense, aware that what was
left of the pristine vigour that had been Rome's was slowly oozing
out of the sprawling limbs of the empire into the mystic corporate
body of the Church, would try to make allies of the bishops. So
the two faiths would exist, side by side, in Lyons, in Rome, and
even up in Paris, where later on the more receptive of the travellers
found themselves starting secret congregations by the Seine. So
they would exist, that is until, paradoxically enough, the fiercer one
was swallowed by the gentler.

There would come, then, these peaceful interludes. But like as
not when the travellers stopped on the way down again, to see
Irenaeus, they would find the good man grieving because the best
men in his congregation, fine citizens too, like his own dear friend
Pothinus, who had founded the first church in that region, were
being marched out to the circus of death at the word of that cultivated soul, Marcus Aurelius. They would all die like men. But
what Bishop Irenaeus could not forgive was that always there
would walk out on the sands with them little children from his
own catechism classes. Sometimes they were even tied in nets and
thrown down to be gored by mad bulls. Great praise, said Irenaeus,
had been bestowed on the manager who thought up that feature.
And one would have thought that the whimpering of these little
ones as they clung to their mothers' skirts when the lions bore
down would have disturbed the soul of the Emperor Marcus. He

could not have lacked imagination. Yet he found their torments boring—where a later fellow-writer, Shaw, found them objects for his wit.

But that "fanaticism" which served as springboard for his humour, was not the secret of their steadfastness, unto death. It may sometimes serve as counter-irritant against pain, but never for so many against such fiendish agonies. Besides, fanaticism does not go with sanity. And a grand common sense, a superb logic, distinguished the books and sayings of many of these heroes. There was more to all these citizens of the new state than the majesty of meekness; there was magnificent courage as well. Men had to die to prove that, like the Founder, Man could conquer fear and death. There are secure ages when men do not have to give their lives so that the light may not go out. But every once in a while there comes the psychological moment when they do. Those early centuries were one long psychological moment. These martyrs were pillars, buttresses of the Church, whose foundation was their Chief. As they fell, the churches rose, rich fruit of their bodies.

So many a martyr went singing to his death. Not all who are called saints, of course. Some worked away at translations, hymns, sermons, furnishing cornerstones of truth, thought timbers, reason cement. The famous scholar-saints fought not only with abstractions, but with obvious sins as well. Jerome assaulted snobbery and the tyrannical rich. Ambrose, the great hymn-maker, relieved poverty and gave his own large fortune to the poor. Augustine waged a struggle with profane love that is as famous as his books. And some of them were persecuted by the pious as well as the pagans. Bishop Cyril, who wrote of the finding of the Cross, was thrown out of his basilica on the trumped-up charge of having sold the church furniture. John Chrysostom, whose beautiful prayer closes the Church of England service, suggested from his pulpit that it might be better if the clergy had no female servants. His church was burned down over his head. Extraordinary moral and physical courage, with their mystical pioneering, made this fellowship historically more important than the thinkers of Greece, the Paris philosophers of the glorious thirteenth century. Their priceless legacy is their continuous joy in the trinity of work, life, and death. You catch this signalling to us, over the ages, out of their books, big and little, their sermons, long or short, and their intimate, sometimes almost folksy, everyday letters.

Justin Martyr, who with Pope Clement left us that first century scenario, was forever travelling up and down the world in his famous philosopher's cloak. He had loved Plato but had found in Christ's words a higher development of the philosophy of the great Greek. "Before, when I was a disciple of Plato, I heard the accusations made against all Christians. But as I watched them standing intrepid in the face of death, I thought that it was impossible that such men could be living, as people said, in evil and love of pleasure."

When Justin arrived at middle age, Death, which had been tugging at his philosopher's cloak halfway around the world, caught up with him. When he was brought into the arena, they gave him one more chance.

"Come here," the asiarch roared down from his pavilioned throne, "and sacrifice to the gods of Rome. They are the only ones who can help you now."

Justin gazed up at the asiarch unfalteringly. "No one," he said, with valour and some dryness, "would trade piety for impiety, a true religion for one false."

The asiarch shrugged a shoulder. "If you don't, you will be tortured without mercy. Come, don't be a fool."

"Why should we shrink," Justin flung back, with the pride of the warrior of Christ, "when to be tortured is what we desire. For that will surely give us courage to undergo a more terrible ordeal, the last tribunal, at which neither you nor Caesar, only the King of Kings will sit."

So Justin Martyr gave himself up to death.

And there was Saint Ignatius, Bishop of Antioch, who eternally preached the reality of the human and divine natures of Christ. "Christ was truly born, truly ate, truly drank, was as truly persecuted by Pilate, truly died on the cross, and was as truly released from the dead." He also fought like a mediaeval champion for the honour of Our Lady, challenged anyone who threw doubt on her virginity. "My true archives," he declared, "my inviolable archives are Jesus Christ, His death, and my faith through Him."

In 107 A.D., the Emperor had him arrested and ordered him to fight with the gladiators in the arena. "The eucharist is the great medicine of immortality, the antidote against death," he wrote, when condemned, to Polycarp, Irenaeus' friend. And then, forgetful of self even in the shadow of death, Ignatius asked him to watch over a little weak church, which because of that very weakness he had especially loved. Then when, after his refusal to draw the sword in the arena, they ordered him thrown to the lions, he wrote this farewell word: "I am the wheat of Christ. Let me be ground in the teeth of the wild beasts that I may become pure bread."

It is hard to match the letters of these old-time warriors for sheer poetry—a poetry made of the very stuff of life, dyed with death.

Irenaeus could tell too, of the death of his great friend, the famous Polycarp of Smyrna. One day in 155, there were twelve acts of death on the circus bill. But having been warned, Polycarp fled. The blood and agonies of the first eleven did not satisfy the crowd. They called for the star. On a friend's farm, the soldiers found him. From his throne this asiarch called down this curiously perverse reversal of the slogan of the martyrs, "Revile that Christ of yours, and you shall be saved."

Very small and old Polycarp seemed, down there on the sands, looking up at the roaring tiers. But as he threw back his white head and answered, his voice did not quaver: "Eighty years I have worked and battled for my King. He has never once gone back on me. He has never done me wrong. How can I, then, speak evil of Him when He has loved me and served me?"

Still the crowd howled; and he died.

History not fable, all this is. The martyr's necrology, from Stephen and James, of Christ's own family, who was thrown from the Temple, down through Peter and Paul, Andrew, who died on the X cross, to the others who died in the later centuries, like those rosters of modern wars that hallow our village churches and squares is, in its listings, if not always in the encrusting legends, authentic. What makes it the more strange is that the satirists cite the small percentage of bigots and recanters as proof of the spuriousness of a cause for which such a host died so nobly.

Often Irenaeus would speak of these things when the men from Paris visited him by the Rhone. Lord knows, he would say, when some called his followers insane, there were fanatics in the crowds facing the wild beasts, but there were hosts more with a sane and sincere selflessness. And would those satirists from the Seven Hills, he would ask, or even this gifted emperor, Marcus Aurelius, die so uncomplainingly for his empire as Christians did every day for theirs?

As they continued on their journeys, the Paris travellers began to wonder with Bishop Irenaeus. That priest of Hellenic culture, Marcus Aurelius, might die with some stoicism in battle. But would he die for his philosophy as these Christians died for theirs? The Founder of this faith, it appeared, had furnished an example in perishing for an idea. True, others, like Socrates, had done the same. But would the disciples of Socrates die for the memory of Socrates? None that they had ever heard of. Yet every day, followers of an unknown carpenter-felon-thorn-crowned king were dying for Him. There was the difference—and all the difference in the world.

And as they died, more churches everywhere went up. It was almost as though these martyrs were like coral polyps and in perishing added to the sum total of their faith, the island of refuge that was fast rising out of the seas of paganism and unbelief in the world. True, a Caracalla or a calloused, but brainy, Aurelian would ascend the throne and down would go the church-building fever. In the renewal of the persecutions, basilicas could be seen lying all about the trade routes, roofless and half-walled. But soon under a tolerant ruler like Septimus Severus or Constantius Chlorus new churches would begin to shoulder the pagan temples in many a city's skyline.

Although many churches have been called cathedrals because of their cities or their size, technically, a cathedral is a bishop's church, the one from which he exercises his episcopal authority, and near which he resides. The name comes from *cathedra,* the bishop's throne it contains. That which might be considered if not technically at least because of its grand history the cathedral of the East, the Hebrew Temple of Jerusalem, had gone down the century before in 70 A.D. The Paris travellers found the Jews all up and down the Mediterranean stunned by its fall. General Titus, with his legions and five hundred and fifty missile-hurling and battering and mobile engines of war, had crashed in the towers of David, hacked half the populace to death, tossed them over the walls among the ever-smouldering carcasses of the butchered animals in the Valley of Hinnom, sometimes significantly called Hel. The last storming was of the Temple itself. Into the Holy of Holies they threw a torch. Then, crowning humiliation, after breaching in much of the Temple, he had yoked the remaining citizens in great gangs and forced them under the scourge to tug at ropes that pulled down the already half-ruined sections. Thus, unwitting Rome forced unhappy Jerusalem to fulfill the prophecy of the King who had wept over her. Not one stone had been left on another. None of the race they talked to could understand it. Titus, too, had burned the sacred Temple veil, and carried off the seven-branched candlestick. The wailing citizens that had been left saw it glinting in the sun as it passed over the Judean hills to the seven of Rome. With its last gleam had passed too, the ancient glory of Israel. To return again? Had He not too said something about that?

The cathedral of the East which He had respected even as He planned the New Order, and which was mother in tradition to the cathedral of the West, had vanished. The bishopric seats of the new Church which the merchants from the Seine saw in the middle of the second century all around the Mediterranean were not the great soaring cathedrals, but steps in a long chain leading to them —halfway houses, really, on the road to the Romanesque, of the period from the fifth to the eleventh centuries, as the Romanesque itself was halfway house on the road to the full glory of the Gothic. And most of these churches were Roman. They did not derive from the synagogue, the parish church of Israel, or from the old Temple. When, after generations of church homelessness and cold worshipping in caves, catacombs, ruins, and hired halls, the congregations longed for meeting-places of their own, erected by masons, carpenters, metal-workers of the fold, and dedicated and blessed by their own bishops, they did not turn for design and plan to Jerusalem or to Athens and its white Parthenon, but to Rome, and not to its domed temples and Pantheon, but to its civic auditorium and townhall, known before its name was applied to these churches that copied it, as the *basilica*.

In the beginning the Romans had preferred to trade and transact all their public affairs out of doors. As Rome grew great they continued to meet in the open forum, but soon they began to roof and wall it in against inclement weather. This new building, re-christened "basilica," from the Greeks, who furnished Rome with half its ideas, they used for markets, councils, political meetings, horse fairs, auctions. Every Roman town of any size had at least one. There were variants of course, but there was a most often used, a standard, basilica plan; and when the building guilds—of artisans and contractors and all who had anything to do with the industry—wanted halls of their own, they followed this standard basilica design. These strong guilds adhered to strict codes and standards and observed rites not unlike those of some modern fraternal orders. They set up busts of their honoured leaders and strewed rose-leaves on these, quite as lodge members of today place violets on a departed brother's breast. And since the guild-hall had a platform in the rear for their officials and an altar in front of this, and often too had side galleries, it resembled the Wesleyan chapel and galleried meeting-house of the West.

The first stout little churches did not follow in the line of Hebrew tradition. There was little about the form even of the larger ones to recall Solomon's cedar-roofed, ivory-appointed shrine or Herod's black marble, gold-cornered temple, both of which were really huge Parthenons enfolded in many courts. When the bishops had collected sufficient funds or had large enough bequests from grateful converts to build, and lulls in the persecutions permitted it, they adopted the civic basilica design. It is true that the very first churches—of the third century, or as some believe, of the second—those that were not buildings donated, hired, or taken over, but built anew by the Christians, were mere crude masonry boxes without pillars or divisions into aisles. But they did have the standard rectangular shape, the low wide gables, and the official section at the rear, sometimes rounded out into a little apse. The tribunes or stone benches which in the civic and fraternal basilicas had been occupied by town or guild officers and judges, were now used by the clergy, the largest one being reserved for the presiding or visiting bishop. The basilica's old altar devoted to the honouring of pagan gods or leaders and placed in front of the official section which was now the embryo sanctuary, was left in its old position but consecrated to the One God.

But in the early part of the fourth century, other features were adopted in the larger basilica churches which the Paris merchants saw all around the Mediterranean belt. Builders were beginning, in Roman townhall fashion, to divide with rows of pillars the ground floor into a large central nave and two side aisles. This became the general arrangement, although fourth century Saint Peter's had five aisles. The side aisles were sometimes roofed over with galleries as in civic basilicas; and these galleries were the forerunners of the great galleries, the *triforia,* of the cathedral.

An open space extended above the nave and beyond the second storey formed by these galleries, toward the exposed wooden rafters of the nave roof. This walled-in space aloft, rising above the galleried second storey made really a third storey. This feature, rising into the clear, became known as the clear, or clerestorey and was like the loftier one of the cathedral. High up in these clerestorey walls were cut apertures to let light in and down on the nave and auditorium below. These apertures, glassless at first, mere embryo windows, would with time be multiplied and furnished with beautiful panes.

This, then, was what the Paris travellers saw, vertically, in the basilica churches: pillar-divided nave and aisles, sometimes with galleries above, clerestorey rising aloft, high openings for light, and heavy roof timbers.

The apse in the earliest churches was built in the west end, so that the priest, who then faced the congregation as he celebrated the *missa,* might also face the East where Our Lord was born and died and where He rose from the dead. When, later on, the priest often stood at the altar with his back to the congregation, the sanctuary and its enfolding apse were transferred to the eastern end, so that he might still in these sacred moments face the home of Our Lord. This eastern end of the church and cathedral was ever afterwards the conventional, the approved place, for the sanctuary. Looking horizontally from the entrance portals past the pillar rows to the apse, the travellers saw this sequence:

A low screened platform for the choir at the head of the nave . . . The beginning of the apse housing the sanctuary . . . An arch of triumph above it . . . A marble wall a few feet high (the *cancellus,* whence chancel) separating the sanctuary from choir and congregation . . . In the sanctuary foreground the altar with a little flight of steps leading to it . . . Over the altar a pillared roof (first called a *ciborium*, later a *baldachino*) . . . Two lecterns at the sides . . . Behind the altar, centred, the bishop's throne, or *cathedra*. . . . Around the throne a curved marble bench or tier of benches lining the carved semicircular apse wall, all reserved for presbyters and deacons. A stairway, unseen by the congregation, led from the altar to the crypt, its relics, and the remains of some saint.

Though some churches, like great Saint Peter's of today, would still retain something of this sanctuary plan, with bishop's throne centred and the same sort of altar, most would later shift the properties. The altar would be placed farther back, the bishop's throne would go to the side. The choir platform and marble benches would disappear, and canons and choristers would be installed in seats at the sanctuary sides. But the apse remained, the official, the sacred, section.

Serving as entrance to this main building was a pilgrims' and catechumens' porch, or narthex, with vestibule. The façade always showed a low, wide gable; and it was often mellowly stuccoed or pointed up with agreeably arranged brick courses or marble and mosaic insets.

This completed the church proper, but a large one usually also had, in front, an open court with cloistered sides and a well, cistern, or bubbling fountain for the ablutions of dusty travellers and for baptisms. Sometimes a building bishop erected alongside the church or in the court a circular baptismal tower. But before many centuries had passed, the font was transferred into the church interior, and baptismal tower and fountained court disappeared, leaving only the rectangular body and round apse. While Byzantine builders followed not the townhall basilica but the Roman temple, becoming involved with monoliths, domes, arcades, the early Christian basilica continued to be the basis for the great Romanesque and Gothic styles prevailing in the West and North. The features of the great architectural grandmother, the Christian basilica, survived in its more stoutly built and more richly decorated child, the Romanesque church, and the even more beautiful and brilliant grandchild, the Gothic cathedral—for that matter in many a church of our own time.

Our Romanesque church would have transept arms, a bell-tower voice, would hide its rafters under great vaulted spaces and would add thicker walls and buttresses, deeper portals, chapel ring, armies of statues, and colourful glass. Not only would the Gothic cathedral take over these features, magically transforming them, and adding new ones all its own, but it would also be marked always by basilica characteristics which the Paris merchants saw in pioneer churches all around the Mediterranean belt. These were: the rectangular shape of the church proper, the three portals, the clere-storey rising up out of the nave into the clear, the rounded apse, and the devotion of that apse to sanctuary purposes. These the Gothic cathedral was to retain even when the Roman arch, trade-mark of the Romanesque, was changed to the new pointed Gothic arch, and was lifted up and multiplied into a new soaring, rain-bowed world of height and light and glory.

In the first churches and even in the somewhat later ones until the Byzantine extended its ornate influence into Italy and south France, there was not much decoration, only the façade treatment, mosaics in paving and on the apse walls, a little carving on altar and bishop's throne and screen, and simple chasing of the sacred vessels.

The altar itself was no copy of the conventional Roman one supported by a pedestal of kneeling figures, or the ancient Jewish copper-covered sacrificial stand, with four horns at the corners, and subterranean sluices to carry the blood out over the cliffs into the Brook Kedron. As a matter of fact, the altar had been either Cain's or Abel's invention or that of a composite Cain-and-Abel. On it had been placed the first fruits with Creation's bloom upon them. In the Christian church it was a simple table in memory of, to perpetuate the sacrifice of Christ. It was not until 250 A.D. that the first congregation ventured to change the wood table altar into one of boxlike shape made of marble or stone, with figures in re-lief, and gemmed vessels on the altar. In the earliest days, the wine had been brought in a simple chalice, the bread as loaves. Later, the wafer, or consecrated bread, the Host, was kept in a receptacle behind the altar. And it would be some time before they would make this receptacle beautiful, shaping it in the form of a dove, then a little pillared house shrine and suspending it over the altar. In the Near East, the chancel had been called "the theatre of the pious." But the first reverent reliving in it of the divine drama had been, like the set, simple as a beatitude. Through the third and first part of the fourth century it continued to be austerely plain but profoundly impressive. The set had been profane; it had been made sacred. The officials', the judges' tribunes, were now the seats of ordained priests of God. That altar of the gods that had failed had been left there but had been transformed into the table which, with the cross, was the heart of the drama, the heart of the whole world now; and the cross had been placed above. Not much change and yet all the difference in the world.

If the first church of the third century was severely plain, the bishops had been too busy with constitution-drafting, epistle-writing, preaching, alms-collecting, consolidating, training a new army, and being martyred to bother overmuch about pigment

fretwork or robe fold. Indeed, nothing could have been more graceful or truly beautiful than their own robes so spotlessly white. No
cave could have been bare for the first pioneers when the earth was
still warm with His presence, when they heard sermons from apostles who had walked with Him, leaned on His breast. No church
was bare for their successors when holy scholars who had sat at the
feet of the apostles or their understudies sat on those semicircular
stone benches, and at the altar parted the bread through which they
could bring back into their circle His mystical presence. In the
afterglow of His life there was no need of putting in bright glass
or of painting even the coldest of stone walls.

There had been scattered instances of artistic attempts, chiefly of
symbols, earlier, but it was in the fourth century that builders
began to look around in earnest to see what they could do to
beautify His house and so to honour Him. Little holy pictures in
both paint and mosaics multiplied; they set great ones of the
Father on the half-dome of the apse; and they started piously to
paint, gild ceilings and inset rectangles of semi-precious stones and
coloured glass, like embryo stained-glass windows, that sparkled
in the candlelight and refracted living little gleams into the dark
church recesses.

The merchants of Paris in the third century rarely, if ever, saw
any holy statues, except perhaps a silver Christ in the Near East.
The pioneer fathers had given too blanketing an interpretation of
the Mosiac interdiction of "graven images." And always there
would be feuds, even civil wars, even among conscientious men,
over beauty. One school—the literalists, the stern, the dour—
looked on the first simple Peters and Pauls as they would have regarded the later gentle brown Francises, the lovely Teresas, the
exquisite blue-and-gold Madonna with the lilies in Notre Dame,
as unholy idols. The others—the imaginative, the religious roman-
tics—even in the most superstitious times, saw these semblances as
representatives on earth of the departed great who delighted in
acting as guardians and counsellors for harassed men. Even those
high in the intellectual scale, men like the great Saint Basil, regarded these holy statues as symbols of beneficent goodness, companionship, help—and these and the paintings all, as story illustra-
tions for men who could not read, as giving vividness, body, life,
to the true tales of the Bible and heroic lives.

The literalists, the all too dour if conscientious, demanded Truth
naked and unadorned. The others, the warmhearted religious ro-
mantics, somewhat submerged those first few centuries by the
austere, thought it no harm to clothe this same Truth in a little
beauty. The gold leaf, murals, mosaics, embroidered robes, images,
and the glory of the later glass, they regarded as tributes, like

Abel's rosy first fruits from the primaeval orchards, presented not only to the God of whom the worshippers in the early dawn were aware, but now to the Son.

But—so it would always be—neither school would ever understand the other. That was the tragedy of it. The second might at times, in all conscientiousness and love, overencrust the divine drama a little under lace and embroidery, violet and crimson lights, sceptres and rings, organ tone and candle flame. The stern, in all good conscience too, but misunderstanding the love, and fearful lest the Truth be buried too deep under form, would think to serve the God of Creation with destruction. As iconoclasts, the image-smashers of the eighth and ninth centuries, as upright but not understanding Huguenots and Puritans later, in mad pursuit of Truth, they would take up hammer and axe. Almost it would seem that they were in bloody pursuit of Him whom Francis Thompson called the Hound of Heaven, down through the stone forest aisles of the cathedral, where they would wreck chapel covert, preciously carved stone foliage, the tombs of great men and saints, and even the final refuge, the altar itself.

But these sorry times had not yet arrived. In the third and fourth centuries, most of these properties, gold cross, couronne, rich chasuble, all the bright things of glittering processional and feast day were still locked up in the sacristy of the future. And the later painters who put mitres on Denis, Marcel, and Peter in the cathedral were guilty of gross, if picturesque, anachronism. Saint Peter never even saw a mitre. The first headdress, the helmet-like *camelaucun*, appeared in 750, the true mitre in 950. And for a long time no cross was used, though as early as 200 men were signing the cross on forehead and breast and great thinkers like Saint Augustine followed this practise. The early fathers were as chary of overdecorating their ritual with phrase or gesture as of putting embroidery on their vestments. It was a long time before they got beyond the plate, cruets, basin, the pure white towel and napkin, the wooden table, and the little side table for the lamps of the first sanctuary. They thought of their church as a ship, and it had almost the same neatness and freedom from clutter. "The house of worship," says the Apostolic Constitutions, "should be long and lie toward the east, with its vestries on each side of the eastern portal, in the manner of a ship. The throne of the bishop must be placed in the centre, with the presbyters seated on each side of him, and the deacons standing by with closely-girt garments, like the sailors and navigators of the ship."

And as on a ship nothing was allowed except things necessary the use of lights and many other aids to the service sprang from necessity rather than from any desire for adornment. In times of persecution torches were used to illuminate, with their flickering pennons, the ruins where Christians assembled, and the long underground galleries where the faithful from the arena were laid to rest and the eucharist, or communion, was celebrated each Sunday. Later, in such improvised places of worship and in more formal basilicas, candles and lamps with wicks floating in bowls of oil were introduced because they did not make so much smoke as the resinous pine torches. In the above-ground halls too, illumination was needed because all the first church services were held at night. When some of these were transferred to the daylight hours, worshippers had grown so accustomed to the cheerful little lights that they were unwilling to give them up.

So the use of lights in liturgy came in a functional and natural way and not even their later more extensive ceremonial use can be traced, as some satirists claim, to purely non-Christian or even pagan sources. It is true that Israel reverently kept glowing that "cloud of light," representing Jehovah's presence, and that Athens kept a perpetual light before her Athena, while Romans placed lights before the statues of their gods and leaders. But these lights of the pagans were considered as votive or propitiatory offerings. They were not used, in the Christian or the old Temple way, as symbols. Some satirists in attempting to throw suspicion on the purity of the faith, go very far afield, declaring, for a ludicrous example, that the church spire, or flèche of the cathedral, is nothing but the old phallic symbol as though it were not natural for men to raise towers to overlook the surrounding country, to be seen from afar, for lanterns that might light the region roundabout, or even to point up to a future country and a higher life. Spires, lights, flowers are common material for all the sons of men for any celebration; and they are not copying any outworn faith when they use them for a new.

In the first century A.D., Paul tells us of an upper chamber being very bright with lights, although it is likely that this illumination was necessary because of the great number who crowded in to meet him. But in that late first century and in the early second, the illumination was not only prolonged into the daylight hours, but the congregation carried little lamps on entering the churches in a solemn line that later became the processional. There were no lights on the altar itself; but the lamps were set around or near it, on a little side table or on the steps leading to the altar. It was in the third century that illumination became important ceremonially. It was then required that lights should be displayed when the gospels were read. This was to indicate the joy they brought by the ever-thrilling, the perennially-fresh "good news." This intent to nurture a living symbolism should ever be kept in mind when studying the history of the Church.

In the third century, history says, a great golden candelabrum was set up in a church in Rome; and burning lights before the arena martyrs' tombs down in the Catacombs were the forerunners of the custom of burning candles before the statues and shrines of the saints in the cathedral. By the fifth, many churches had kindled perpetual lights; an old bishop of the time writes happily of his altar being "crowded" or "crowned" with lamps. But by this he must have meant that there were many lights around, or suspended in front of and above the altar; for in spite of the growing ceremonial use of candles (which were always made of the purest beeswax) and of lamps (which were always filled with the purest olive oil) no lights went up on the altar itself until well on toward cathedral times. Indeed, in the Church of the East split off from the Church of the West and known as the "Greek Catholic" or "Orthodox Church," the old custom of placing the lights on side tables is still followed. In the Church of the West as early as the ten hundreds in some places, and everywhere by the eleven hundreds, they went permanently up on the altar itself.

Since that time it has been obligatory in the cathedral and the sister churches of its rite to have lights on the altar at every liturgical service, and six for a high mass, seven for a pontifical mass which a bishop celebrates. During mass, lights should also be burning on the altars of the side and apse chapels. But always, even when after mass the candles are extinguished on the high altar, the light that never goes out is kept burning before the high altar and before all places where reposes the Blessed Sacrament, to indicate the Eternal Presence.

On Easter eve a new light, source-fire of the perpetual flame, is kindled as a symbol of the Resurrected Christ. These perpetual lights then burn through the year until the following Holy Week, when in churches and cathedrals everywhere they are extinguished to be replaced by the new light of the Risen Lord. By cathedral times lights played a lovely part in the liturgy. Three beautiful purposes they serve. The multitudinous flames of the cathedral reflect the myriad gleams by which the old heroes at the peril of their bodies worshipped, thus forming another link in the unbroken chain that binds us to the past. They dispel the actual physical gloom of the church building. They symbolize the flame that banishes the soul's darkness. Always it was in the minds of the good and the great who have gone before that those multiplied lights represented the light, the fire, that was Christ, His power, and love.

Incense, though never so important or inspiring a factor as the

lights, had also a functional beginning. The censer was not then
the swinging perforated sphere we know now, but was stationary
and set on the side stand or chancel steps with the lamps. Its aromatic substances on burning coals were needed in crowded oriental
meeting places and in the catacomb cells which were near, or were
themselves charnel houses, often containing assemblages of both
the quick and the dead, the live brethren using the tops of martyrs'
tombs for altars and sacrament tables. In 250, incense was used at
a Christian burial in Rome. This, too, was for sanitation as well as
sanctification, for when the bodies were brought down from the
red arena sands above, corruption set in very early.

When, in 326, Constantine's mother, Saint Helena, went down
with her excavators into Calvary and found the crosses, censers
sweetened the air of the Holy Sepulchre at the celebration Vespers.
In some churches, this service is now combined with Complines or
one of the later night offices; and some put it forward as early as
two in the afternoon. But most still start at the orthodox time, set
by Saint Benedict in the sixth century, confirming the early custom—four in winter, six in summer. The lovely service is still
much like the one Saint Helena saw in Jerusalem and which the
early fathers called "Vespers" because it came at the hour when
Hesperus, the evening star, begins to glow in the sky.

As for symbolism, it was a later clergy who had time and peace
enough to write hymns, paint little books, and to develop an imaginative church lore that explained the censer as "a sign of the
graces the sacrament bestows," "the sweetness of sanctity," just as
the mediaeval fancy explained the apse-chevet of the cathedral—a
beautiful architectural formation rounding out the ambulatory
into rayed chapels—as the crown of thorns. And if a little sentiment was mixed in with the early rites, the leaders felt it could
do no harm. Had not Christ as a boy watched the incense ascend
from the inner, cedar altar of the Temple, the candles twinkle in
the seven-branched candlestick? Being realists as well as dreamers
of visions, they would have allowed in the service nothing that
would obscure the salience of the truths they were presenting to
the sons of men. If they had considered dangerous such links with
the old chrysalis faith from which the new had so beautifully
emerged, they would have broken them off.

Quite as simple as the properties were the vestments. Not from
the Temple dressing-rooms, but from the everyday wardrobe of
the man in the street, these costumes were taken. Though there
are parallel beliefs in the old faith and the new and rites common
to both the Hebrew and the Christian services, the premises and
denouements differ radically, and the new dramatists did not slav-
ishly copy the Temple routine. The old tradition had been violently

broken. A new tradition had been started and it would be maintained. The form of the simple garments worn by the first presbyters, or priests, has remained in fashion for almost two thousand years. Their basic design is followed today by the ecclesiastical outfitters of the Paris Saint Sulpice quarter and of New York's Barclay Street.

The original sacred costumes, then, followed the pattern of the secular, the one distinction of the first being that they were scrupulously white.

"We should not," wrote Saint Jerome, about the year 390, "enter the sacred place in everyday clothes soiled with work, but rather in raiment, like our consciences, clean."

And the first Book of Canons declares:

"As often as the bishop participates in the mysteries, the presbyters and deacons shall gather round him, clothed in white, in *quite particularly clean clothes*—more beautiful than those of the rest of the people."

The "more beautiful" did not mean more ornament, only that the clothes should be "quite particularly clean." And the holy women of old saw to it that they were kept so. It is quite likely that Our Lady herself, who was so constantly with the Apostles, attended to or superintended their careful laundering, an exquisite "fullering"; and the holy women along the African and Spanish coasts laid the garments of the Bishops of Hippo and Seville in lavender.

But although they were "quite particularly clean," the priestly vestments were "everyday." The Roman and Graeco-Roman wore a long under tunic, an over tunic, and a cloak. This undergarment, the *tunica alba* or white coat, the presbyters wore and kept it long, after the tailors shortened it for the layman. Of wool at first, then of linen, its name was popularized from *alba*, or white, to the *alb* we know. Later it acquired the familiar deep lace border, which is now unpopular with the strict liturgists who prefer the simpler, earlier ways.

One form of the over tunic, designed in Dalmatia, therefore called the *dalmatic*—a name still in use—was also long and had the edges sewn together in front, leaving a hole for the head so that it was put on, like a shirt, over the head. This *dalmatic* was once worn by bishops and priests. Later, while often worn by the bishops, it was taken away from the priests and allotted, as a distinguishing garment, to the deacons, who still wear it when they assist the bishop or the priest celebrating mass in the Notre Dame choir. It was distinguishing because of two pillars with a H crossbar embroidered on the back. This ornamentation and marking, of course, came later, along about the ninth or tenth century. In the sixth they had begun to vary the pure white with red borders.

When the *dalmatic* was allotted to the deacons, the priests retained another form of the outer tunic similar to the dalmatic. Because of the opening at the top, through which came the priest's head as though sticking up, people said, out of the chimney hole of a little house, it was called, from the Latin *casa,* or little house, the casuble, then the *chasuble.* In the sixth century this also was given a red border.

Gradually the wearing of the *chasuble* became restricted to the celebration of the mass; and it, with the *alb* underneath, was recognized as the uniform of the priest during his highest function. About the tenth century, the *chasuble* was given a sign it still bears to distinguish it for the audience in aisles and nave from the *dalmatic* now worn principally by the deacons. The latter has sometimes on the front, always on the back, the two orphreys, that is, two decorated pillars, with the H cross-bar two-thirds of the way up. The *chasuble* had, as it still has, a broad orphrey or strip, or pillar, with a horizontal or a forked cross-arm, like a chevron. A little later they began to embroider these insignia very heavily with coloured threads and gold, and parts of the vestments and accessories were dyed rich hues to match the colours which, because they were considered appropriate, the Church had officially set to mark Whitsuntide, Easter, Advent, and the changing liturgical seasons throughout the year.

There is a third important garment in the priest's wardrobe, the one he usually wears in the processional and which he doffs in the sanctuary to put on *chasuble* and *alb* and the accessories for the celebration of the mass proper. Its design, derived from the old Roman mantle, cape, or raincloak, you still see in varying forms— as a poncho, on the lay Camargue cowboy of Provence and the *agent de police* who guides the traffic outside Notre Dame on feast days, and also on the priest inside the cathedral, as a *cope* (from *capa*). The edges of the original Roman mantles were secured at the breast with a clasp, and it had, like the poncho, a very practical hood. Decrease the original hood a little to a stiffish, gold-shotted, collar-like shield standing up in back, and you have the *cope* of the processional to the Notre Dame choir.

The clergy kept the ensemble long, with *cope* and *chasuble* three-quarters length, and the *alb* reaching the ground even when, in the fifth and sixth centuries, the civil tunics and togas became abbreviated. This conservatism was, aesthetically, fortunate. When travellers from Paris watched Bishop Polycarp at Smyrna or Irenaeus at Lyons, over the rushing Rhone, or any of the old valiant heroes consecrate the bread and wine, or raise their hands in benediction, the long white robes fell in nobly sculpturesque folds.

In addition to these main garments there were, of course, the accessories, the very necessary things which from the very first were used in the upper chamber chapels and still continue in the clerical wardrobe. This, then, was the ensemble that Polycarp, Ignatius, building Pope Alexander, and—except for the stole—that Peter and John, all the Twelve wore, at each celebration of the sacred mysteries:

1) The *cope*, the hooded cloak in which they came, in which they departed; 2) the *alb*, the long full-sleeved tunic reaching to the ground, like those with which painters usually clothe their angels; 3) the *amice*, or neckcloth, to prevent perspiration from streaming down on clean garments and sacred vessels; 4) the *cincture* or *girdle*; 5) the *maniple*, the long handkerchief for brow and hands; 6) the *chasuble* or *dalmatic*, the long sleeveless, head-out, little-house-like main garment; 7) the *stole*, a long streamer added late in the first or early in the second century.

In the sixth century, under Gregory the Great, they similarly arrayed themselves, but added those blood or cherry-red borders to the chasuble and dalmatic. In the eleventh, when Notre Dame was abuilding, in the thirteenth, when Saint Louis brought into the cathedral pieces of "the True Cross" and the Crown of Thorns, the only changes had been not in lines but in allotting to the priests the chasuble, to the deacons the dalmatic; in placing on the chasuble back that upright pillar crossed by the V, on the dalmatic back the H, and in adding gold leaf and embroidery.

Today, at high mass on Sunday morning, or at any feastday mass in the cathedral, and in many a smaller church about the world, we will see the deacon who, in the processional, has entered the sanctuary, in the *dalmatic*. The priest himself enters, in the all-enveloping cope, with the original hood reduced now to a little bib-shaped remnant extending down the back, also up around the neck in a little stiffish collar, and the main body of the mantle made of the most richly dyed material and blossoming all over with beautiful figures worked in applique, in gold and coloured thread, and clasped in front with a great glittering brooch.

After the priest has washed his hands for purification, the cope is removed, for the celebration, with the deacon's help, leaving him in the more modern black cassock. The *amice*, the old perspiration neckcloth, now of embroidered silk, is draped over the priest's shoulders. Next, the *alb*, the long white basic garment, sometimes with a deep lace border, is donned. Around it is placed the *girdle*; over the forearm, the *maniple*; the long handkerchief, now of decorated silk, and around the neck, the *stole*, a long silken streamer decorated with three gold crosses at each end, or with other designs in gold thread and pearls. Completing the costume for the immortal drama, comes the old high sacrificial garment, the sleeveless, over-the-head tunic, the *chasuble*, today a gorgeous gold or silver brocaded, many-figured over garment, in which the seasonal colour predominates:

White: Trinity Sunday, feasts of Our Lord (except those of His Passion), of Blessed Virgin, All Saints, nuptial masses, children's burials.

Red: Feasts of Christ's Passion, His Precious Blood, Finding and Elevation of Cross, Apostles and Martyrs, Pentecost octave.

Green: Between Epiphany and Septuagesima Sunday and between Trinity and Advent, always excepting festivals, their octaves and ember days.

Violet: Advent; from Septuagesima to Good Friday; rogation (intercession) days, fast day vigils and ember days except those of the Whitsun Season.

Rose: Laetare and Gaudete Sundays.

Black: Good Friday and offices for the dead.

There are, of course, in the wardrobe of the cathedral, the sacristy, other things that help make the choir blossom like a garden in colour—embroidered dais, processional canopies, gold shrines for relics, sacred vessels presented by kings and queens. Also there are many additional costume features—the *pallia,* bands with lappets and six purple crosses on white silk; the *mitre,* with its broad bird-bill shape and fine material—white silk, or damask, or red velvet, and gold plate and pearls; *rings,* with fine chasing and precious stones; and *croziers,* the apostles' staves with which, and their scrips, they set out on their missionary journeys, now transferred into gorgeously gemmed ecclesiastical sceptres.

But all these last appointments are for abbot, bishop, cardinal, or pope. And what one needs to remember are the seven features of the costume we saw in the order of the robing of the priest in the choir. These, by one of the beloved traditions with which the Church links the present with the past, are but the same old articles of everyday clothing worn by the apostles, the pioneers of the Church, with the pure white enriched and given a few distinguishing marks.

So, basically, the old, old costume which the priests must wear has not changed, as in churches all around the world and in the sanctuary of the cathedral is relived the mystery which is its heart, and into the development of which we must now look.

VIII

The Form of the Divine Drama that will be relived in the Cathedral.

The Early Centuries

THE PARIS MERCHANTS AND ALL THE BUSY TRADERS FROM the Levant, as they travelled around the shores of the Great Inland Sea, saw something being developed besides the basilica, its properties and costumes; it was the presentation of the central mystery, what was to be celebrated in this new and ever-expanding church building.

As the outer, the physical, setting derived from Rome, the services of varying forms that were to be given in churches often borrowed from Israel—its chants, the old race responses, King David's songs, the ancient chronicles, the doctors' and scribes' habit of expounding. These, together with Christ's conversations and His life story, the apostles' letters, His cross, a chalice, a loaf of bread, and a table, made up what may with reverence be called the most beautiful scene in the universal drama. And two things, the cross and a table, made up the simple but majestic framework of the whole. The first services served as common storehouse for many churches. But we are following the path from the open cave stable door to the majestic portals of the cathedral, and very easily traced is the evolution of those early services into what was to be relived in the most beautiful, the most passionately built of all Man's sanctuaries, of all his buildings whatsoever—the high and moving sacrifice called the mass.

Its early form was very elastic, with the original Twelve and the presbyters and deacons doing much improvising. It was not at once called the mass, but the eucharist, Greek for "thanksgiving." When, in the third century, its name changed from the Greek to the less flexible but more resonant Latin, it was known as the *sacrificuum,* again as the *passio,* because of the tragedy of the King. The term mass came from the *missa* in the dismissal phrase, "*Ite missa est.*" The first record we have of its use is in a letter from Saint Ambrose, in 397:

"Soldiers were sent yesterday to disperse a meeting near us. The next day, after the lesson and tract had been read, I dismissed the catechumens (candidates for baptism) and explained the creed to the competents (those who had qualified in the baptism course) in the baptistery of the basilica. Then I heard that soldiers were being sent, this time to us, but I stayed and went on with the *missa*."

From the first the service was divided, as the mass would be later, into two parts. That for the catechumens, the beginners, borrowed most from the Old Testament. As the impressive march of the Old Testament led into the Promised Land of the New, the mass of the catechumens led into the fuller drama, the reliving of the last act's high scene, which at first only full members could witness, though very soon it became the custom to admit the catechumens. For several generations a little love feast, or *agape*, with open public confession, was included; but later fear of exhibitionism banished this. Through references in his letters to the practises of the time—such as the breaking of bread, the great prayer of Christ, the kiss of peace—Paul laid down the elements which later scholars crystallized into a set continuity. And Paul and the great missioners left many a phrase like his of the major and the minor benedictions, and the triumphant one for the dead, that were later set down in the dialogue. But the first fairly complete idea of the order is given by Justin Martyr, who was born in the round year of 100:

"We always lead the new believer who is about to join our company after his baptism to the group of brethren where they are gathered together to pray not alone for themselves and the one who has just received the light but for all men. . . . When this prayer is over, we greet each other with a kiss.

"Then a cup of water, the wine, and bread are brought to the president of the council and when he has received them, he sends up praise and glory to the Father of all. . . . After that he offers thanks that He has made us worthy of all these benefits. . . . And all the people cry 'Amen.'

"Then those who are called deacons give the bread and the water and wine, for which thanksgiving has been made, to be tasted by all; and they bear some to those not able to be present. This food is called the eucharist."

And later Justin says, "On the day of the sun, a reunion is held by all the faithful in the cities and on the farms, and the writings of the prophets and 'The Commentaries of the Apostles' . . . are read as long as time permits.

"Then when the president of the council has aroused our desires to emulate all these glorious deeds, we all arise and repeat our prayers. These finished, the president again sends up prayers for all men, and the people cry 'Amen!' And a share of the eucharist is given by the deacon to all."

Pope Clement the First too wrote much about the order of the *eucharist-passio-missa*, which in the first three centuries was this:

1) Reading of the Lessons (four, sometimes five);
2) The sermon;
3) Prayers for the people. One was called "For All Kinds of People," matching the later "All Sorts and Conditions of Men";
4) The kiss of peace, passed on by all;
5) Offertory of Bread;
6) Thanksgiving prayer by presbyter or bishop (president of council);
7) Consecration of Bread and Wine;
8) Intercession for peoples;
9) Ending of prayers with "Amen";
10) The climax, the Eucharist.

Justin and Clement ignore the music, but they did sing hymns —the songs of David and ancient canticles. Christ with His disciples sang a hymn in the supper scene of which we have made a climax for the great mystery and drama. Paul and Silas sang in prison. Tertullian tells of members advancing to the altar, between the placing of the lights on the altar steps and the washing of the hands, to sing, now this one, now that, solos of praise.

Very early, then, they had something like a generally accepted order. And when, in the 200's, the Paris travellers toured the Mare Nostrum belt, they saw, in metropolitan basilicas, cave chapels and mountain monasteries, practically the same affecting drama. Either one of two versions might be given: that set by the church of Jerusalem, or that ordered by the church of Antioch, the two most powerful sees of the day. But only in details did the two differ. No presbyter of either school ever strayed far from the ten-point programme.

For some time the technical directions were handed down orally, or through such letters as those of Paul. But gradually prompt-books were compiled to guide the presbyter. The first, the far-off father of the missal we buy today in the streets near the old Saint Sulpice Seminary, was issued just after the second century began. It was a collection of gospels, epistles, true and apocryphal, doctrinal beliefs, ordinances, and eucharistic directions—a missal-theology compendium, all in one, called "The Teachings of the Twelve Apostles."

Its order of service accords with that of Justin Martyr and Clement, which is authentic enough, for Clement the First was the third in the long line of Bishops of Rome and of Popes after founding Peter.

This first promptbook, "The Teachings of the Apostles," was

expanded into "The Apostolic Constitutions," which Damasus in the fourth century, Gelasius in 482, revised adding later changes to the mass. Finally, for the fourth edition, Gregory the Great per-fected the promptbook, reduced the overburdening four, some-times five lessons to a practical two, shortened it overall, then with resonant phrase and ennobling music, rounded the *missa* out into the mass that is celebrated in the cathedral today.

What had really happened, then, after Christ's death, was this: His friends met in their rooms to talk about Him, the wonderful things He had done in life and those that had taken place in the ten weeks after His crucifixion. They repeated the prayer He had taught them, sang the hymn He had sung with them on His last night in the flesh on earth, and gave little talks, simple fore-runners of our sermons, pointing out the application of His say-ings, so full of beauty, wisdom, and common sense, and His exquisite parables, and repeated His messages of healing and com-fort and forgiveness. It was the loveliest sort of Lycidas composed by a composite poet band of fishermen, artisans, tax-gatherers, wholly unconscious of the high place they would occupy in history, and almost wholly unaware of the tremendous impact their meet-ings would have on posterity. But it was more, for then they com-memorated, as He had asked, His farewell supper. They closed with His benediction, whose peace lingered with them still.

But men being of differing temperaments, their reactions and motives varied. Some even came to the upper chambers in Jeru salem out of curiosity or for purely social reasons. With these the disciples had much trouble. Others looked on these meetings in the early days purely as memorials and feasts of thanksgiving. The more spiritual saw their simple ceremony not only as a memorial and thanksgiving for what God had done for them, and a re-energizer through the uplift of pious fellowship, but as a profound regenera-tion as well. With the supper, the Risen Christ was imparting to them new life. Then still others under the leadership of our Irenaeus and Saint Cyprian, about 250—and it was in the tradi-tion of these that the mass would be celebrated in the sanctuary of the cathedral—saw the eucharist as the three—memorial, thanks-giving, regeneration—and also as the veritable and true repetition of the divine sacrifice on the altar. This is the inner meaning of the mass. When in the fully developed mass of our time, the priest, after a devout and humble preparing of himself for his great and sacred function through the many little impressive acts which have been incorporated in the ritual, stands before the altar and elevates the elements of the body of Christ, the consecrated bread and wine, he is offering up the divine Victim as he was offered up on Calvary. But more—he is at the same time offering up himself with Him, and all the believing in the congregation. So the transmission of the divine life is twofold. It flows in to the communicant as he partakes of the sacred wafer at the rail, and into the celebrating priest as he partakes of the consecrated wine and bread at the altar. But also it is given to all watching and worshipping with opened hearts.

This was a lofty conception and one not to be all at once brought down to earth in the words and directions of script or missal. For a sincere, impressive, and properly beautiful presentation, there had to be a slow maturing, a deliberate technical and liturgical development. At first every step rose out of necessity and was only formalized after continued use. As candles were employed to lighten the physical gloom before they were set up on the altar, as the proper robes were put on in the crypt or a room off the basilica chancel before the robing in the choir was made a significant part of the ritual, so almost every phrase and movement of the liturgy was a functional factor before it was transformed—as it usually was—into a beautifully aesthetic feature. As for the symbolism, this supreme act of devotion by Man was so rounded, so complete, that it seemed that the symbolism was implicit, inherent in it, and naturally flowered out of it, so never needed to be superimposed or artificially injected. It was only the natural acts of the apostles as they went about their simple ceremonies that were later standardized and set down as prescribed in the promptbook, or missal.

In the Jerusalem upper chamber so long ago, hands had been washed because it was unthinkable that soiled ones should touch the bread that was pure life. The washing, years afterwards, was turned into the ablution rite, attached to a psalm, and placed at a fixed point in the procedure. The bread, chalice, or cruets, had to be brought to the altar, held up to be blessed; and the sacred vessels were cleansed and put away. All such simple duties of presbyter or priest, and deacon, were woven into the beautifully rhythmic formalities we know today. It is true, of course, that such ornamental features as stationing one choir to sing antiphonally to another choir, were instituted, but that added great impressiveness to the music. The priest does kiss the gospel, but that indicates reverence. Also the clergy in the chancel bow to each other and to the congregation at certain times. And that but shows the truly fine and beautiful courtesy which the mass and the whole faith breathe.

Never, purely for its own sake, out of pure externalism, without meaning, was adornment applied to the ritual, no more, indeed, to the divine drama than to the gorgeous theatre, the Cathedral, which houses it. And once more it should be noted that although never is

that which goes on in that lovely theatre of God to be regarded
as spectacle, or anything but divine mystery relived, we can in all
reverence call it drama. For that universal overall play of God and
Man, which began with the stars of the morning, continued with
Man's fall, through his long pilgrimage and all his defeats, found
its climax and solution in that high scene which is imperishably
preserved in the mass. The Hero Christ partook of the farewell
supper, then gave Himself to death to save His friend Man from
his own betrayal of the Light. And this, in its very nature, is the
very purest and most exalted drama, as the greatest, the most
heroic, and the most beautiful of actual lives is drama.

And in Man's most glorious theatre, built in the name of God,
for this drama, and in the living play itself, everything has its
appointed part to play. One might except, perhaps, some stone lily
petal, but he would probably find, on investigation, that it is true
even of that. In the Cathedral every horrendous, inimitable gargoyle is in place to carry off rainwater, so that it will not corrode
the walls. The very pinnacles are there not for decoration, though
they add that, but because of the scientific fact that a little weight
added to the top of a buttress just doubles its strength. And even
the carven angels and saints have been installed, for vivid illustration, to give life to some parable and tale.

As the great cross form of the Cathedral was not chosen for its
significance, but grew, as we shall see, out of a beautiful structural
functionalism, almost every step in the relived drama celebrated
within it, was born through a functionalism of word and movement. Out of naturalness, out of little human ways and deeds, the
magnificent drama was wrought. As every arch and buttress assumed a greater beauty through its union with the whole, its
partnership in the plan, so each word and gesture, however simple,
took on impressiveness and grandeur as it was woven into the rich
visual and aural tapestry of the mass. This was because each word,
each movement was needed to carry forward the divine drama's
march, to make more vivid the life of its Hero, to deepen the
instructive symbolism, to strengthen the ties with the original followers of Christ who first celebrated it, and the linking with
ancient origins and the Source itself.

Once all the congregation members brought wine and loaves of
bread to the altar, at the offertory, as their offering, like Abel's.
But those soon mounted up so high that the president of the
council (the leading presbyter) allotted the greater part to the
clergy for home use, and set aside a few loaves and a little wine
for the eucharist. Over these the celebrating priest still reads a
silent, or "secret" prayer "for those (loaves) set apart." The custom of the donations has long since been discontinued, but the

little oldtime prayer remains in the liturgy as "the secret." The kiss was prominent in eastern ceremonial. So still we have in our churches, the "kiss of peace," which in Paul's day was given by all the people, but now is restricted to the priests, deacons, and canons in the choir stalls, and also the kissing of the altar when the priest bends low over it, after the "Brothers' Prayer."

In the Christian basilica the lectern, or reading desk (the *ambo*), was the first pulpit. Its position varied, but in large basilicas there were often two, placed at the chancel sides. Deacons used these for reading the Bible and announcements, the priests for delivering their sermons—the Bishop usually preached from his own throne. Gradually from this lectern, or *ambo,* the large, carved pulpit was developed, and the lecterns were left, the one in the front of the sanctuary and on its north side, for reading the epistle, the one on the south side for the gospel. This was so that everyone, even those in the transept corners, might hear at least part of the "lessons." And still we have in the cathedral the "epistle," or north, side of the sanctuary, the "gospel," or south, side. But though some churches still kept the pulpit too in a corner of the sanctuary of the choir just within the dividing marble screen (as it is, for example, in New York City's mid-nineteenth century Cathedral of Saint Patrick's), in Notre Dame and the large churches of Paris and France and of England too, the pulpit was stationed outside the choir so that the sermon could be heard in every aisle; the usual position being at the side of the nave near the second or third nave pillar.

For petitions they had, first of all, the Lord's own prayer. Later they drew on others like the psalms *Judica me, Asperges me,* and *De Profundis,* and the eloquent one of the thanksgiving after mass, of the Children in the Fiery Furnace, in which they called on heaven and angels, fire, light, frost, dew, heat, fowls, cattle, sons of Israel, and sons of men, and all creatures of the universe, to "praise God and exalt Him above all forever." And there was the unforgettable one of the Bethlehem angels, the *Gloria in excelsis.* Other petitions were improvised to fill a soul need or inserted to accompany some necessary act in a service. Some of these fitted so logically in the sequence that, even before there was any central authority to approve, they crept into the ritual of all sees and cities everywhere and there remained.

Nothing could have been more practical than the insertion of that confession of general principles, the *Credo.* In a faith for which the professor might have to die any hour, it was appropriate for him to stand up and state the articles of his faith for which he was willing to give his life. When the first saints arose in congregation, the first martyrs before the lions, they simply gave a little statement like that which Paul suggested to the Romans: "If you confess, with your mouth, the Lord Jesus Christ, and believe in your heart that God has raised Him from the dead, you shall have life."

Such was the first of all credos. About fifteen years after Paul's death, Ignatius summed up with more detail the beliefs at which they had arrived. From his outline and the writings of his contemporaries, we have assembled the Apostles' Creed. Finally, in 325, the great Nicene *Credo* came in.

There was another, a very human source of much of the dialogue. The leading bishops selected spots where whole psalms and scripture chapters might be read complete and also places where separate sentences might be effective in spoken, intoned, or chanted response. Often the members of the congregation went them one better. Some one, overcome with joy at his enlistment in the new army, a far-off prospect of the invisible empire, would shout out his happiness in an exclamation arising out of his heart or, by way of the subconscious, from far back in Abraham's or Solomon's time. The spontaneous expression would appear to all gathered there as so fitting that it would be taken up by all, later to go down in the missals, ultimately to be sung to the thundering organs of Notre Dame.

So Pope Clement, about the year 100, with great glee, reports: "We, assembled, in unity cried out aloud: 'Holy holy, holy!' " Thus spontaneously was resurrected from the Old Temple service the famous *Sanctus*. In the year 390, the great hymnmaker and organizing bishop Saint Ambrose, suddenly inspired, cried out an "Alleluia," the full musical possibilities of which Gregory the Great developed two hundred years later. Ambrose also started the antiphon, the chanted or sung response from one choir to another, from the clergy to the choir, or from one portion of the choir to the remainder. In 425 Pope Celestine approved this innovation.

As the fourth century ended, the old varying gospel versions, the Old Testament, the promptbooks, "The Apostolic Constitutions," and "The Teachings of the Apostles," were grandly climaxed by the first standard Bible. It was a great event when Saint Jerome made a careful translation of the Old Testament from the Hebrew and took the Latin and Greek and Egyptian and Syriac editions of the gospels and epistles, compared them and issued a new Latin text, which, united with his fresh Old Testament translation, was called the Vulgate. This, with a few nineteenth century changes is the text of the Catholic Bible today, and the one we hear being read from the "gospel" and "epistle" sides of the cathedral choir.

Somewhere along the line, too, a bishop, fearful lest the borrowings from the Hebrew Temple seem too wholesale, and to make sure that the metamorphosis from the Old Dispensation to the New was complete, began to trail off the old Hebrew monotheistic chants with the thoroughly Trinitarian *Gloria Patri*. Another inserted the "It is truly meet"; and, about 600, Pope Gregory interpolated the beautiful salutation of Christ, *Pax vobiscum*, "Peace be with you." And he transferred Christ's prayer to its proper place, at the critical moment of His life, just before the breaking of His body.

The clergy at Constantinople, in the fourth century, added the cry of the sick who at the pools awaited His healing—"Lord, have mercy, Christ, have mercy!" As *Kyrie eleison, Christe eleison*, it rings grandly through the cathedral aisles today. And sometime after Gregory came in the *Agnus Dei*, whose poignant loveliness of phrase, musicians from Palestrina to César Franck have tried to match with their notes.

There is another thing besides those which have already been stressed that one must keep in mind in studying the development of the drama: So many of the early fathers were steeped in the often eloquent, but sometimes lush imagery of the Orient. Others came from near Rome, where signs and portents were all important. In the Middle Ages when so many legends and customs crystallized around the lives of the saints, everyone set great store by miracles and symbols. Even the mediaeval scholars who lived in the shadow of the cathedral seemed to possess that combination of keen intelligence and wonder and of delight in the world which the Greeks had and passed on, over the heads of the Romans, to the French. With people then and for many succeeding centuries so eager for symbols and signs, their very preoccupation with those of the Church, their hunger for tales of legends and miracles of the saints, some believable, others apocryphal, but dutifully pointing a moral, is proof of the tremendous part religion then played in their lives. And there were symbolic rites which, however externalistic they might seem to those not understanding their origins and significance, were very far from being mere incantation. There were those, for example, which had to do with water. In the sacred mystery of the mass, water is mixed with wine, to signify that without which there would have been no Christianity or Christ—the union in Him of the human with the divine.

And there was the baptismal sacrament. In apostolic times, whenever a river was at hand that was used, as the Jordan had been at the first baptism. Not that the apostles were literalists insisting on a river. For Tertullian explains, "It really makes no difference whether one is washed" (of sins by baptism) "in the sea or in a pool, in a river or in a spring, in a lake or in a ditch."

It is the heart that counts. But it was considered a happy circumstance when a river was near, for its water was not dead like that of cistern or pool, but "living," that is, running water.

Gradually they transferred from open air to interior baptism. At first the fonts were housed in those Pisa Tower-like structures which the Paris merchants watched going up alongside the basilicas. But in 311 a new building custom was started, when they sank a pool near the altar in a church at Tyre. You can still see (if man does not destroy it) a built-in pool at Saint Jean's in Poitiers, the oldest church in France. Sometimes the rims of these pools were on a level with the floor; sometimes they rose above it, with steps ascending to the rim, another flight descending into the water. In rich churches like those of Sancta Sophia in Constantinople and Saint John Lateran, the baptismal pools were gorgeous with sculptured marble, silver-lined bottoms and golden lamps on bridges overhead.

For the ceremony there was a long preparation course, resembling that in a modern catechism class but made arduous by fasting. The converts always stood—in those pioneer days, naked—above the pool and recited the Apostles' Creed. They were not always completely immersed. Sometimes they stood only partially covered by water, and were sprinkled on the head three times, that being the number of days Christ lay with the dead. Afterwards they were anointed with sweet-scented oil, clothed in white, garlanded with flowers, in symbolic foretaste of the joys of Heaven, and given a milk and honey drink.

But it should not be thought that any one of these details was a *sine qua non* of salvation. Not only do we have that just quoted word of Tertullian reassuring us, but also a passage from a current ordinance stating that in case of illness a font was not necessary. "For," it states, "the Holy Spirit cannot be hindered for want of a vessel."

Polyeuctes, a heroic martyr of 260, who was about to die for the faith, called down to his bishop standing by to ask if the fact that he had not been baptized would invalidate his martyrdom. And the bishop called back, "When they brought the blind to the Son of God, He never asked if they had been baptized, only if they believed." Ever in the minds of the early fathers there was this sacred baptism "by blood," the veritable stream the brave martyr shed, or when there was no means of baptism at hand, the earnest desire of the heart.

And "holy water" came from no pagan belief but rather from a profound poetic conception. All the ancients venerated fire and water—water as the element of purification and the giver of life. And the idea went even deeper. A prayer of 200 A.D. blessing the waters, gives a clue: "Fountain from the realm of rest, power of Salvation . . . descend into these waters, so that the grace of the Holy Spirit may be perfected through them." They felt that God sent His messengers to charge spiritually the waters, "to medicate them," Tertullian says, as the angels did the Pool of Siloam when they came down, with healing, into its waters. The full beauty of the conception comes to us if we walk a little farther with Tertullian who, born about 155, was the greatest of Christian writers between Paul and Augustine. "Any waters on earth are susceptible of sanctification because all waters generally were hallowed by the spirit of God brooding over them at Creation."

These beautiful connotations then accompanied the idea of "holy water": The spirit of God descending upon Jesus in the Jordan, the angels coming down into the healing pools, and that awesome scene of the Prologue of the universal drama, when the spirit of God brooded over the primaeval waters. No incrustation of legend or superstition should blind us to the majesty of the conception itself. This is true of other rites that are often misunderstood. Their interweaving in the high scene of the drama is justified by a sublime trinity of ageless tradition, mystical logic and profound poetry.

Later the mass was called "high" when there was much singing. The plainer service was termed "low" because the tones in it were low. There was no need for this distinction, however, in persecution times. With spies all about, chants had to be muted. Very early plain song (the *plein chant* of the cathedral) was used. All the voices, high and low, sang the air, without accompanying chords or counterpoint. In the Notre Dame plain chant, which is there interspersed with later music, one hears echoes, not only of early Christian times, but of the Hebrew Temple from which it was undeniably derived. Some trace it back to the Greek. And the plain song scales (in which the piano student would find a dearth of black keys) were called by the names of the Greek modes. The form is particularly adapted to recitative wherever, in singing, words are stressed. Like Temple chant and Greek chorus both, it is slow in tempo, plaintive, affecting, and was ideal, the old bishops felt, for the incidental music of psalm recital, a most fitting way of approach to the far-off majesty of Godhead.

After Constantine's recognition of the Church, Sylvester, the great building pope, started the first canonical singing schools. In the same century Bishop Hilary of Poitiers wrote the first hymn that was not a chanted psalm or canticle, but composed in the measured metrical form with which we are familiar. Saint Ambrose (born in 300; died in 397) wrote a great number. And in 590 they set up in Rome the great Schola Cantorum, where Gregory's musicians added new modes to the old plain chant and created the Gregorian chants. Charlemagne's great singing schools of around 800, at Toul, Soissons, Cambrai, Lyons, Dijon, Orleans, established this music of Gregory the Great throughout the empire. A century farther on, a Dark Ages choirmaster stumbled on the idea of harmonizing parts to accompany the melody. And just a thousand years after the great Gregorian chants were composed, Palestrina developed his rich polyphony. Such were the four great steps in liturgical music.

But when the Paris merchants visited them in the 250's, the pioneers of crypt and catacomb and basilica were still shouting the old Sion hymns or compositions of their own in the same style with no part harmony, all to the same air, as they ringed the altar in their immaculate white. But, remembering the perfunctory rites of the Temple of Jupiter by the Seine, the artificial ceremonies of the guildhall altars, the travellers were struck by the freshness and vitality of the services in these new little churches, so bare and clean. They were impressed, too, by an air of sincerity about all of the pioneers, whose natural dignity was enhanced by the sculpturesque folds of their long robes as they gathered in their austere sanctuaries.

There was one ceremony that the men from the Seine thought particularly moving. Through this the officers of the Church received at their ordination a sort of accolade for all entering into the full service of Christ—into holy orders. When the deacon was made a presbyter, or priest, the squire made a knight of Christ, he received this accolade from the hands of the bishop which were laid on his head. The bishop so officiating had long before been ennobled in the same way by an earlier bishop. That father of the Church had himself received the accolade from some still earlier saint; he, in turn, from some elder of Jerusalem upon whose head had been placed the hands of one of the original Twelve. The tradition had been handed down through many generations. Authenticity, validity, sacredness were thus to be transmitted through the ages. The apostle, the first of the chain, had sat on the rower's seat when the King had walked on Galilee, had gone up with Him on the mount, had looked up at the crossarms whereon were stretched His all-embracing ones. Nay more, the first-link apostle had touched His garments, and some of them even the Source Itself, the nail-prints in the palms of the King.

For nineteen centuries this continuity has not been dissolved. And there are other links in the great chain made by the laying-on of hands. For the ceremony is observed when the children are confirmed. Each year myriads of such new links are forged when the little ones from the Rue des Chantres, the Rue Chanoinesse, all the old Cloister district around Notre Dame—and in all the cities of the world—flock to the altar in their confirmation white, in the months of May and of June. On the cheek of each child at the confirming the bishop gives a gentle tap in the token of the buffets we must endure in life for the love of the King. On each head the bishop places his hands admitting each to the age-old communion coming down from Christ. Uncounted hands of God's priests, uncounted heads of His priests and His little ones, they reach back, a vast pyramid, through the ages, to the Twelve, to the One.

When the priests march in the cathedral today in the processional as did the cloistered mediaeval monks, in imitation of the safari of the Wise Men to the Manger and of the holy women hurrying with spices on Easter Morn to the Tomb, they go to the altar, as the choir sings one of the old songs of David. Their robes fall in the folds of the old Graeco-Roman tunics the Twelve wore at communion, though these have flowered out into their mediaeval gemmed and brocaded splendour. Tenth-century mitres shine above the parade, and rings and golden crooks, symbols of the Shepherd Kings, sign too that the Church is pastoral as well as militant. In the sixth century Gregory's white hands beat time to that chant which ascends in silver purity to the high arches. It was in the second that men began to make on forehead and breast the sign they make now, and that they began to go north to read the epistle, south to read the gospel. In 325 today's resonant *Credo* first rang out. In Christ's own time the sick of Siloam saluted Him with that *Kyrie*. Candles like those which guide them lighted the first evening star service of Vespers over His tomb. Clouds of incense there went up to symbolize her joy as Helena embraced the cross she had found. And that altar in all its glory but stands for the table over which He broke a home-baked loaf of bread, poured out a pitcher of home-made wine and words that are for all time and for all the world beyond any forgetting.

So scores of simple, homely things, sublimated and made immemorial, are done as they go down the aisles and kneel by the altar of the great playhouse built in the form of His cross, for the ancient ceremony of the laying-on of hands. It is the final, all-enveloping linking which, by transmitting touch, takes them all back to the Cross itself, the hands that were nailed there, the gentle yet mighty soul that there suffered, the body that died there, so that they and we might live.

IX

*Flat Figures of the Cathedral Glass that were Three-Dimensional
Fighters. . . . One challenges Jupiter's Temple in Paris and loses
his Head on Montmartre. . . . He is buried by the Roman Crossroads where the great Abbey of Saint Denis will rise and the
Gothic will be born and a Long Line of Kings will lie down
with him.*

250 𝔄.𝔇.

𝕺VER SAINT GENEVIEVE'S HILL, BY THE ROMAN HIGHWAY
that led up from Orleans and the south, strode three figures
in long coarse-textured, dust-covered mantles, with sandal
straps white with limestone, and haversacks, called "scrips," hanging from their shoulders and filled with meagre earthly possessions.
As they came up over the summit and paused there a moment
looking down over the Roman villas spreading out fast now in the
Left Bank suburban development, the gabled brick Roman theatre
on the top of the hill near where Saint Genevieve's shrine would
stand, another playhouse by Cluny Palace, the aqueduct east, the
brick kilns near the river, and the arena with lions roaring and
athletes practising in the sand, the travellers looked very weary.
But when they saw over the river, on the isle, the wall-and-tower-
belted city of Paris, they girded up their loins afresh like warriors
who recognized neither weariness nor wounds, whose course knew
neither truce nor cessation, and hurried down as though they
would by soul assault take that city and its towers, particularly
its citadel dedicated to their arch-foe, known by many names but
here called Jupiter.

Rusticus, Eleutherius, Dionysius later called Denis, were the
names of the three. The first two were deacons, the last an ordained
presbyter. They were saints too. So truly indeed that one of them
would go up many times, with his stone head in his hands, on a
great stone house for a lady built right where then stood by the
Seine that citadel of Jupiter. And all three would go up in bright
glass in a church that would have the first truly great glass in the
world and which would be reared four miles over the Paris plain,
in a town to be called after the leader of the three, Saint Denis.

It is important for us, for a moment, to consider of what a hard

133

schooling this Denis came, and of what fabric and fibre were his fellows, not only the two swinging with him down the old Saint Jacques highway that morning to take the city, but all the great band of devoted local and minor saints, whose lives were not drawn for us with such completeness and clarity as were the deeds and deaths of the major martyrs. Sometimes their careers have been misted up with legend; and this is true even of Denis, though he was to become the first national saint of France. For frequently an author, himself a saint, writing of a Saint Felix or Martin or this beloved Denis of France, would do what Adamnan did so profusely for the great Irish saint Columban, or for that matter what Parson Weems a millennium and more later did for Washington. He would throw in, with a respectable array of facts, a story or so, invented with no deceitful, only a pious, intent, for instruction purposes.

But, as we have noted, legends are not altogether to be despised. They are often truly poetic and inspiring. And, in studying the workings of the baffling, inconsistent, delightful, and often powerfully moving minds of the folk of the Dark and Middle Ages when this lore was built up, we must again and again remind ourselves of these things: first, that there is a difference between the legend which can obscure truth, and the actual miracle and true symbol which illuminate it. In times when people were avidly hungry for signs and legends as well as symbols and miracles, it was fortunate that they were fed by the often very beautiful tales of the Church. The joy they took in the lives of the old Church heroes is proof of the all-absorbing interest, the actual fascination that the great drama had for them. So profoundly were they stirred by its message and its lovely central story that they eagerly drank in all the secondary stories that flowered out of it. And the general and genuine delight in both the piously invented and the verified miracles performed by the ministering angels of another world, at which sophisticates scoff, is bright evidence that they were not, as the scoffers are, wholly engrossed in the world below.

The names of these major and minor saints are legion. As in ancient, crowded cemeteries, the dead are placed in layers, the latest comer above his predecessors, the names of these canonized workers choke the encyclopedias, the missal calendars, or the local histories. And all of them are pictured somewhere, in stone or picture or window, but none more often than this very Denis, who, if all the effigies of him all over France could come alive would, all by himself, make up a populous city.

We have seen the bright and happily the most often evident side of the legend question. But there is the dark, the morbid aspect. Often the legend-makers were mischief-makers who did as much harm to men like Denis as did the more bigoted of the biographers who were obsessed with asceticism or martyrdom for its own sake. But though we see them now impressed and imprisoned in the rich glass, these doughty warriors like Denis and his two companions were no flat figures. Most of that great school could walk from dawn to sunset, swim deep rivers, sole sandals, cure hides, make and set up tents, lay a net on the most favourable side, work a capstan, knock the shores properly from under a ship at the launching, reef a sail, lay a foundation, place a perfect brick course, fell huge trees, lift great weights, shear sheep, barber, knead bread, staunch blood, handle stubborn asses and camels and human beings, wrestle mightily, sweat profusely, love intensely, preach magnificently, pray incessantly, and write movingly in from two to six languages. That is, each of the saints we revere could do quite a combination of, if not all of, these things as well as gaze unmoved at prefects, asiarchs, Caesars, Delilahs, arena lions, the torturing gridiron or the mounting flames. If ever there were three-dimensional fellows here they were. They had to be in a day when if a man had an enemy, it was as much as his life was worth to set foot in a church since he would be reported in Rome. Yet here they were, night and day straining mightily to build more churches. And if ever there were happy warriors, here they were exulting actually, in either living or dying for the cause and sometimes preferring the latter since, in that critical era, that was the greater service. And almost all abode, to the death, by the greatest law their Leader had laid down—the cryptic paradox that he who would save his life must lose it; centripetal self-interest meaning death, centrifugal giving of self alone bringing life.

Altogether the popular conception of the great throng of stout-muscled, stouter hearted warrior-saints, like the three coming over Saint Genevieve's Hill, is surprising. All too often they have been taken for crabbed, intransigent, fanatical, troublesome fellows—which only occasionally they were—or else as austere, emaciated, neurotic figures, even as something very like ecclesiastical valentines dressed up in the lace and gilt of fancy, with the arrow-pierced hearts of a maudlin sentimentality. It was there where the bigoted biographers left off that the legend-makers—who gave us so much that was simple and beautiful—were inept. And the artists helped on the messy illusions. Saint Simeon as a pole-sitter is no good advertisement for an enterprise as vital as the new highly socialized state of the Founder. And Sebastian must always come out of their pot-metal crucibles or from under their brushes like an overstuffed pincushion stuck all over with arrows. Lawrence was always on a griddle. Scalding water refuses to burn Margaret and Lucy when they refuse the lustful prefect's advances.

And by a crazy kind of play on words, the mediaeval *tanners'* guild selected for its patron Saint Bartholomew, because he had been *flayed* alive; the woolcombers Saint Blaise because he had been tortured by an iron comb. And on Saint Anne's two red, iron-embroidered doors to the left in the façade of Notre Dame in Paris, some guild placed a stone Saint Marcel. Now he was the ninth bishop of Paris who, in the third century, had to work hard to keep up his diocese in the intermittent fever of the Roman governors' persecutions. But the sculptors did not think such a sound contribution dramatic. So on the post between Saint Anne's two doors, they pictured Bishop Marcel with a lady in a coffin and the dragon from which he, Marcel, had rescued her.

And there is Saint Theophilus above the north transept door. He was notable for good works and, through modesty, had refused a bishopric. Yet instead of picturing Theophilus as the devoted worker for the King, Architect de Chelles posed him up there as one of the original Fausts, selling his soul to the devil, while a very sweet Our Lady comes to the rescue. You can still see Theophilus above the Rue du Cloître, signing the devil's contract with his own (stone) blood. Our Lady has been coming along for seven hundred years in the nick of time to save him and tear the contract right out of Satan's hands.

This naïveté is fascinating for the tourist. But the artists were shelving for such inventions better stories that were true about real people, that would have left them real and still have held the mediaeval beholders. There was material enough in red fact for all the crimsons of their panes. But they entirely missed the point, which never was the dragon, the woman's corpse, the bloody contract, Our Lady's eleventh-hour rescue, the boiling water that would not scald, or Lawrence's griddle, Sebastian's arrows, or even Denis' head, which he was said to have carried in his hands four miles over the Paris plain to the Roman crossroads.

Chisel off Satan, corpse, dragon, from Saint Anne's portal of Notre Dame. There remains for the record the devoted, hard-working Bishop of Paris in stern times. Throw away Lawrence's griddle. There is still left the courageous man dying, whether by griddle or not, for what he believed, in the persecutions of 258, when the Romans killed the majority of the presbyter priests, and struck down Pope Sixtus in the catacombs. Empty Margaret's and Lucy's cauldrons of boiling water that refused to work. You have the flesh and blood girls who preferred death and a heavenly love to life and a Roman legionary's lust, and so were beheaded. Strip the Valentine legend of its frills down to the truth. There were two Valentines, both buried in the Flaminia Way; they died, not for love of woman but for the love of God.

So one can take baskets and, Salome fashion, gathering up the heads which Denis holds in his hands all over France, toss them in the river, and France would still have the true and undying memory of the valiant martyr Saint Denis, whose banner was borne into battle by her kings, and whose dusty, travel-worn, corded, sinewy figure was, this afternoon in 250 A.D., hurrying into Paris to his almost certain death, as he well knew. He and the long line of martyr saints were no mere stone effigies and dim profiles in rich glass, but foursquare, three-dimensional figures. Always there was about them a vivid reality.

For a moment as they came up over the brow of Saint Gene-vieve's Hill, this presbyter Dionysius, or Denis—as all France was soon affectionately to know him—and his friends, Deacons Eleu-therius and Rusticus, paused by the Roman barracks on the summit, the horse market, and the now filled cemetery. From there they looked down on the city which men through the ages and all their changes have found so fair. Then they passed down the Saint Jacques highway and over the bridge, which should have echoed to the thunder of their coming, for Denis was the first great warrior of Christ to come to the pagan Paris that was to be the Paris of a thousand churches.

Once over on the island, he came to the Roman Forum, a little east of the island's centre, and stood there in the flow of the Gallo-Roman capital's midday life, looking up at the Temple of Jupiter, which he was about to assault. He would go up, too, one day, not on that Jupiter's house, whose marble then was pretty well stained, its cement cracking, after three centuries of wear—but on Our Lady's house, on the same site. In many places—over its portals, in niches close by the doors, on a great pedestal just around the corner from Saint Anne's red doors looking out over the Seine—he would stand, with his head in his hands, also in great stained-glass windows in a royal abbey named after him, four miles over the Paris plain, and in many other bright panes and niches all over France of which he would be the patron saint.

But he and his two dusty companions could not foresee that. They did not stand long surveying the Temple priests, the sacri-ficial bullocks being led in, the housewives with urns, palace chambermaids, fish pedlars or the clerks, centurions, chirurgeons, courtesans, charioteers, who gathered round to stare curiously, then to snicker and jeer and roar with laughter when they started to preach, as the warped of mind always do, at men of heroic mould who somehow seem to the mob ridiculous. Nor did the three listen to that other roar, lazy at first, then gathering power, from the arena across the river and the lions who had not been fed any too well lately, but who were likely to fare better with the new persecution order.

At once Denis began to tell the crowd a true tale from history, not about the Emperor, but the King. So full of it he was that he would not wait even to hunt for lodgings or a meal or to wash off the journey's dust. But the Gauls, long interbred with the Romans, although they were building fine cities and outdoing the Romans in culture, had not yet recovered what they had lost, with their independence, at Alesia—their sense of the old bright Gallic Heaven of the West. They would recapture it again and so kinetically that they would put up magnificent shrines of stone and glass such as the world had never seen, and would start panoramic pageant migrations to the East, called Crusades, just to win a hill and a tomb.

But just now they were busy with things that could be apprehended by the eye and the fingers, rather than the unsubstantial but everlasting creations of dreams. With fish and bread, they now were concerned, properly fired brick-kilns, agreeably tempered hot baths, well nurtured and carefully pruned vines on the hills, rich compost for the vegetable gardens, cunningly wrought keys, locks, bracelets, safety-pins, taxes, tunics of the right length, wineshops, and circuses in the arena (the remains of which are still on the Left Bank's Rue Monge) and plays in the theatre on Saint Genevieve's Hill (near the corner where now stands the Collège de France). Besides, did not a famous Emperor say, furnishing a precedent for modern dictators, that no state could possibly be secure so long as men of the King continued to preach and practise gentleness and unselfishness and to uphold the seditious principle that Right, and *not* Might, *was* Right?

Wherefore, ordered the imperial edict, all the King's Men— which, of course, took in Rusticus and Eleutherius and Denis now in Forum Square—should be apprehended and ground out by sword, cross, bow, spear, exposure, starvation, griddle, fagot-pile, gladiatorial melee, fishnet, bull's horn, lion's molars, tiger's or panther's fangs, asp bite, rhinoceros or elephant charge, or whatever Death's fashion was favoured in the particular community. So more raucous now grew the hoots and jeers, thicker the humiliating spittle, and louder the roars coming across the river from the little barred cages of the arena as even the beasts seemed to sense that three great champions of the interdicted faith were there as prey in their midst.

Lazily the whips of the charioteers flicked this way and that, cutting the cheeks which Denis had just figuratively said should be turned, all too literally. Fast the blood was running down, mixed with the hateful spittle, but Denis kept on with the lovely idyllic

story of the birth and the walks in green fields, the talks on blue
waters, and the great peace and forgiveness and the many mansions
of the King, so in contrast with the outcries and blows of the
sadistic crowd milling around in the Forum. Then from the
Glaucinus tower, guarding the island wall (by the north line of
the present Flower Market) a centurion came with a maniple of
soldiers, on the run, slapped Denis and the two deacons on the
shoulders, and clapped them in manacles.

They took them to the governor's palace. Its successor is still
there—as the Palais de Justice. In the ancient city the palace was
west of the Forum and began where now is the Pont au Change,
or Money Changers' Bridge. The downstream point of the island
was then where the Pont Neuf is now. The land beyond that, now
included within the island and making up its downstream end, was
then separate from the main island of Paris as though it were a
chip of it. At the prow end of the island in the old days, behind
guarding walls, was the governor's garden, and out of the green
of its fruit trees and vegetable beds the palace rose.

The trial was short. The new persecution decree was explicit,
a generous blanket covering a multitude of sins against the state.
There were witnesses enough to portray the innocent victims as
wicked aggressors.

Historians are uncertain about the exact year of Denis' execution. Since we know it was in the middle of the third century, that
cannot matter. Some claim that Denis and his two friends fled to
the Right Bank marshes, a section known after the Bastille and
the Temple had gone up there as the "Marais." On dry islands in
these reedy, miry coverts, he preached, they say, for almost eight
years to the Parisians who found their way to him secretly through
the morasses. Finally the Roman bloodhounds holed him out and
brought him to the island Palais for a star-chamber trial.

But whatever the year of the third century, they rushed him,
the centre of a reviling, striking crowd, bleeding from increasing
showers of stones and hissing charioteers' whips, out of court, over
the north bridge, through the little stretch of plain, to the hill.
Some insist that because of the tragic events of that morning it
was called Montmartre, which means Mount of the Martyr. Others
insist that the hill was already called Mount of Mercury; they trace
it this way:—Mons Mercure—Monsmercre—Monsmarcre—Mont-
marcre—Montmartre. And a little temple to Mercury did stand
on the top. If today you go back of Sacré Coeur, the white pearl
of a church on the south end of the summit, you will come on grey
old Saint Pierre, in whose crypt Ignatius Loyola founded the Jesuit
Society to reform the Church. And in its aisles you will see some

of the old pillars of that little Temple of Mercury which, in the twelfth century, were appropriated by Saint Pierre.

Quite a chain it all is. And up there, on the hilltop, they made Denis kneel. A great fellow took out his sword, ran his thumb over the edge. From the Left Bank arena, far below and across the river, the roar of the lions came up, full-throated, to match the mob cry on the hill.

Oddly the head—some, asserting that the two deacons, his friends, were not executed later but in that same hour, say the three heads—of Denis, Rusticus, Eleutherius, their lips grotesquely twitching, rolled in the gravel. Denis' at least was subject to indignities. Wild women, courtesans who for convenience dwelt near the Roman barracks, dipped their hands in the blood. Boys who had watched the legionaries, dividing into two companies, run with and kick the football, "association" fashion, kicked the head about. It was later that the famous story sprang up that, to save his head, Denis picked it up and carried it across four miles of Paris plain to where in the Middle Ages, at the great Lendit Fair, the rector and faculty of the University of Paris, the students, with such wild heads as François Villon's among them, would come in a singing parade to buy parchment and pick cherries. There, by the Roman crossroads where now is a smoking, industrial town, Denis laid his head down, his body beside it. And there he has rested these seventeen hundred years. And thus it was that his head, he carrying it, went up in all those niches and gay windows all over France.

What remains when the head—and with it the story—is tossed out of those windows is what counts. And it is something very real. The blood this simple, valiant presbyter shed up there on Montmartre was no quaint pretty crimson like that congealed in the bright but cold glass. It was agonized blood, full and red-corpuscled. His burial too was actual. Moreover what happened there afterwards in Denis' name was more miraculous really than the miracle of the legend. In the four hundreds by that Roman crossroad, Saint Genevieve would erect a little oratory, a memorial to Denis. King Dagobert would come there two centuries later to go down into the tomb and sleep with Denis and to erect a bigger church over him. And Suger, great minister of state, in the twelfth century would put up the pioneer Gothic church, the famous Abbey of Saint Denis, one of whose towers we can see over the plain from Paris, the other tower having been, like Denis' head decapitated by time and chance. There, too, Jeanne d'Arc, defender of France, wearied by wounds and battles, would hang up for a little while her armour. And all around would rise the massing factories to build engines and wings for a later France.

With Our Lady's Cathedral Denis would have a very close connection. Three places he would have there: one at the side of the
Virgin's door; a second just around the southwest corner; a third
over the Treasury. This is fitting for one who came to the Seine at
a time when Jupiter reigned supreme over the island as the very
first missionary to Paris, and who in the historic square that has
seen dolmen, Druid altar, Roman Temple, Christian basilica and
cathedral, risked his life in the very telling about Her Son. And
out of that abbey, almost out of Denis' dust, as Woman out of the
rib of Man, would spring the first Gothic arch that was more than
experiment. Germ this was of the Gothic, core of its design, and
seed of the Cathedral.

From Notre Dame kings would carry the banners of Saint Denis
when they went forth to war. To its portals, when they could no
longer uphold those banners, they would return to be intoned over,
then to be borne up the Street of Saint Denis, through the high
Saint Denis gate of Paris, over Saint Denis plain, to the smoking
city and royal abbey named for him too. There with the humble
Denis they would mingle, the long line of them, their royal dust.

X

*Constantine sees a Cross in the Sky. . . . Seven Bishops conquer
All Gaul but the Germans refuse to be Christians. . . . The Romans, who have been trying to save their Empire, now are Christianized. . . . The First Great Church Council meets at Nicaea.
. . . Delegates from Britain to Persia, Gothland to Ethiopia,
attend. . . . They draw up the Magna Carta that will be proclaimed
through the Ages in the Cathedral.*

325 Ã.Đ.

SO GREAT NOW HAD GROWN THIS EMPIRE WE CALL THE
"Invisible," that an invitation had gone out from Constantine, the head of the empire, whose walls one could see
and touch, to fifteen hundred princes, the bishops and council
presidents, of the other. And, in the spring of 324, when the lilies
stood up in little white sheafs between the moss-green boles of the
forests of Versailles and Saint Cloud, the presbyters and deacons of
the Seine Valley gathered—as they were gathering all around the
world—by the south Paris bridge, above the barges discharging
their British wool and Cornish tin, to bid farewell to their bishop
who would join Bishop Nicasius and his delegation to set out on
the many months' long and perilous journey to the city of Nicaea
in Syria.

He was an extraordinary man, this Emperor Constantine. He
had seen a cross of flame in the sky and although he would not
be baptized under it until he lay at death's door, he had raised the
cross, had its symbols painted on his legionaries' shields, and swore
that by that holy sign alone he had won his great battles. And he
now had the idea—arrived at in conjunction with the great bishops
of Rome, Jerusalem, Antioch, Cordova, Constantinople, and Alexandria—of holding this, the very first of all ecumenical councils.
At it, he had said to the bishops, would be settled the "things of
God"—theirs; also, he fondly hoped, needing an ally, the "thing
of Caesar"—his.

An astounding transformation had taken place. Emperors, instead of persecuting or ignoring, were consorting with Christians.
Bishops with great trains were travelling unmolested to a far and

widely advertised council. The tables had been curiously turned. Officials now were not pondering whether to torture or placate the Christians, but whether to allow pagans to slay, as they had for ages, their sacrificial bulls and to kneel to Mars. Something had happened in the seventy-five years since Denis had come hurrying over the hill to defy Jupiter, to die for Christ, and so to take Paris: that cross had been set in the sky. Seven bishops had set out to win Gaul. Decay had set in in Rome, and this council to which they were hastening from all over the known world would finish the matter. Into the causes of the changed conditions, we must quickly look.

They are worth noting. Striking enough was that cross of flame, striking and heroic the seven bishops of Gaul in their sandals and with their staves and scrips, casting lots by the shore. This convention was to be a motley, a picturesque, a very human and yet a profoundly moving thing. And the decay of Rome was, strangely enough, almost as striking as her ascent to her glory. Gaul, as France, might stay in the front rank of nations for an infinitely longer period, but Rome's sway, while it lasted, was complete, unshakable, iron bound. And she is the great and dramatic exemplar of the imperial pride that goes before the fall.

Though it could not be understood in the early centuries of the Christian era, the Church and Rome seeming so antipodal, their fortunes were as inextricably interwoven as are sometimes those of two brothers—the one brutal, self-indulgent, self-willed, dominating, gifted, destructive, the other lovable, selfless, constructive and only seemingly weaker. After her fall, for which she was then heading, Rome would pass on her extraordinary gift for organization not to succeeding earthly empires, but to the Church. And before her fall (in 474) in the third and fourth centuries there was a curious characteristic in their close relationship—as Rome's fortunes fell, the Church's rose.

Rome, of course, had only herself to thank for it. By her system, capital had been bled white, colonies drained to support Augusti and Caesars, tremendous armies, an aristocracy of power and wealth, a too sumptuous imperial pomp, and gargantuan circuses as sops for the masses. Tax-gatherers hung like clouds of locusts over cities and farms. Two classes—rich landowners and serfs—made the state top and bottom heavy. As always, the stratum between—the middle class—was squeezed out, to the empire's mortal hurt. Meanwhile, barbarians were nibbling away at the corners of the too far-flung empire. As the Emperor Constantine studied reports, at first in Rome, then in his new dream city of Constantinople, he could, with no distorted fancy, see their watch-fires gleaming on the horizon, hear the wild thunder of their cavalry. No longer was Rome the unattainable queen. She was the worried matron, fearful of her own slaves. They were getting out of hand. At the same time the barbarians were showing that restlessness which was but the prelude to the violent assault when a wild stream of savage semen would flood the imperial womb.

So even before Constantine, who was the greatest of the Caesars since the founding ones, all had cast about for something to save their empire. Caracalla, at the third century's beginning, made all who were free citizens of the provinces free citizens of the empire. He advised wealthy masters to liberate worthy slaves, slaves to save up and buy their freedom; the latter policy working two ways, cementing aliens to Rome and enriching her treasury. Other emperors opened up the schools and academies of Rome to promising colonial youths, the Senate to gifted provincial orators. Armies accepted commanders from trans-Alpine cities. And for a time an excellent new temper had been substituted for the old vanished mettle of Rome. But too often the colonials became like the Roman cosmopolitans—urban, polished, soft. In 286, Diocletian tried a partnership plan to manage the unwieldy enterprise which the empire had become. He promoted two generals to be Caesars, just a little below him, and another to be co-Augustus, almost on a level with him. Thus there were two imperial general managers and two branch ones. The ship of state had become a catamaran. It was easy to cut the catamaran links and for the two sections to drift apart. So, in the whole empire there was but one source of vigour as yet untapped. The breast of this nourishing mother, the Church flowed with the pristine strength the dugs of the Roman wolf had held before they were drained dry. And many of her sons on whom the emperors cast covetous eyes were potential leaders of integrity, heroism, vision and great capacity for statesmanship.

Six of these leaders had come in 250 from Rome to Marseilles with a seventh, Denis. There, by the Mediterranean shore, these seven bishops of Gaul cast lots for the seven cities: Narbonne, Toulouse, Arles, Clermont-Ferrand, Limoges, Tours and Paris, possession of which meant the unlocking for Christ of all Gaul. It was from this lottery by the sea that Denis came hurrying over the hill to take his Paris. Never since the Apostles went forth at the command of Our Lord, had there been a grander or more striking mission. Bidding each other farewell in God's name, they fared up the bright rivers of France, and by the river roads, for the seven cities which was theirs by lot. Still in those cities you will find, on street or square or borne by church or cathedral, the names of the seven bishops of Gaul. When you come on the lovely Romanesque doorway of Saint Trophime in Arles, the royal abbey of Saint Denis, Saint Sernin's near the old University of Toulouse, or the beautiful example of lace-work in stone, Saint Gatien in Tours, it is hard to connect the soaring beauty you see with some worn saint with scrip and staff, coming into the then little towns of seventeen hundred years ago. But such humble workers for the faith were the sources of the lordly cathedrals.

The seven bishops of Gaul had chosen well. This land they were peacefully invading was fertile ground. As usual, Rome with roads, communications, education, common language, and state of peace had unwittingly paved the way for Christ. Their seven cities and others like that earlier bishopric seat—Lyons—were of fair size in the dimensions of the time, and now getting to be truly metropolitan cities, with forges, potteries, waterworks, townhalls, arsenals. Each had a strong burgher caste which, like the middle class of France today, was united in its fear of two foes—the Germans and the communists, then called *begaudae*. The most alert and gifted of all the provinces, Gaul was beginning in some ways to outshine Rome herself. Her sons furnished more wit and eloquence to the Roman Senate, greater military skill to the general staff, and the best talent to Roman literature. Their poet, Ausonius of Bordeaux, would in the fourth century shine as the brightest star in the imperial firmament.

But Gaul had emulated Rome almost too well. Ever since the sad day in 52 B.C. when the King of Warriors, Vercingetorix, had ridden down the steep Alesia path to unsaddle his horse before Caesar, she had been loyal to her new mistress or rather her new mistress-ally. Soon Gaul became the smartest colony, a sort of junior member in the imperial partnership. She was faithful not only in legal, trade and military matters, and all sorts of fashions and customs, but also in her religious ways. That altar of the Paris Boatmen—which we saw being erected—with its interweaving of both Roman and Gallic gods, is an excellent symbol of the racial ways and rites. But to the seven bishops this mongrel interbreeding was a horrible thing and they wanted to end it forever. It was not always the rustic people who gave the bishops the greatest trouble but often the most travelled. The aristocratic Gallo-Roman young bloods, sometimes even the scholars, more Latin than the Latins, preferred Horace's Falernian wines and golden girls to any mountain sermon or the cross whose ways were hard. As for the farmers, they were very fond of their tree dryads, their Roman and Celtic divinities of hearth and boundary. It was hard to wean them from their pagan feasts and half-magic ceremonies like those of the fairy ring which came down to the time of Jeanne d'Arc. In Touraine they almost lynched Saint Martin because in a great forest he had cut down one tree. In it, the farmers said, dwelt a girl.

But the seven bishops of Gaul and the fervent, hard-fighting warriors who came after them had advanced so far in their conquest of Gaul by the time of the Council of Nicaea, that there were already powerful sees with fair-sized episcopal palaces—in the seven cities they had won by lot, the two that had been Christianized first, Lyons and Vienne, and also in Trier and Cologne on the Rhine, which most historians have believed was designed by Nature as the east boundary of France.

But over the Rhine they could not get. The leaders of the German tribes said that Christianity was not for Germans. They repeated this as late as 754—emphasizing it with an axe which they buried deep in the skull of the grand old saint, Boniface. Long after the rest of Europe was going to church, on down to modern times, their military men forgetting their own sacred bishops and their own immortal *"Stille nacht, heilige nacht,"* would insist that Christ was too gentle for Germans.

It was different over the Channel. Under the white cliffs of Dover, the advance scouts of the seven bishops—Christianized Breton sailors—stood up in the prows of their snub-nosed, leather-sailed craft and shouted over the waters to the British fishermen and sailors the three-hundred-year-old news of an angel chorus on snow-clad hills, and of a King born in a stable who had told other fishermen where to let down their nets. So when Augustine, the second saint of the name, reached Canterbury in 597, he found the way prepared for him by the converts of the seven bishops of Gaul and their successors, the Breton fishermen.

By the end, then, of the 200's, the faithful had come up out of the cave and quarry, deserted theatre and catacomb meeting-places. No longer were churches to be found as the merchants of Paris saw them, lying all around the Mediterranean, roofless and half-walled. No longer did the hired guildhalls, the finished basilicas of the faith, go alternately light and dark, with the ascension of pacific or persecuting emperors. No longer in Paris and other cities did they have to adopt the ruse of banding themselves into "burial societies," disguising themselves in weeds and shrouds so that they might meet and hold their ceremonies in the cemeteries.

Strangely enough, it was a very practical man and politician who consolidated the work of the Founder, His apostles, the early fathers and heroic martyrs and the seven bishops of Gaul. He, Constantine, had seen a cross in the sky near a Tiber bridge, and had imperially sanctioned Christ's Revolution, which had challenged the empire, by issuing in 313 the Edict of Milan, which like that of Nantes by Louis the Fourteenth, provided for toleration. A few years later he made Christianity the official state religion.

There was both method and sincerity in this. Other emperors—
his own father, Constantius Chlorus among them—had tried to
tap the new fountain of vigour and life, the Church. It was the
only source from which, they felt, could be drawn leaders who
might save the empire. This theory was sound even though after
Rome had been brought into alignment if not into actual alliance
with the Church, her leaders did not avert Rome's fall. Perhaps
this was because the strategy of an "Invisible" Empire does not
work so well with one so very visible as Rome. However, the
Church would do something better still and Constantine was even
wiser than he knew. Instead of patching up an old oversuper-
structured and leaky ship of state, when the final floods came in
474 the Church could offer itself as a mighty vessel with all sails
set on which shipwrecked Man could climb.

Constantine had succeeded where all before him had failed. He
was an extraordinary man, a great general, an able politician who
fortunately often rose to the stature of a very great statesman. He
was born about 288, of an emperor and a woman who, Saint
Jerome tells us, kept a tavern. And he owed much to his parents.
His father, Constantius Chlorus, who built Cluny Palace on Saint
Genevieve's Hill, and set out so many vineyards on the hills of
Paris, had been very liberal with the Christians. His mother,
Flavia Helena, for all her early start, was a truly great lady, and
became a saint—Helena. It was she who discovered the True Cross
under Calvary. Her son was half-prince, half-plebeian. That ple-
beian part helped. His mother passed on to him her personality and
her peasant wisdom which was transformed in him into a statesmanship so far-sighted that he transferred the seat of empire from
the Seven Hills to the Golden Gate, where he built the marvellous
city named for him. Though many intellectual leaders were now
taking serious notice of Christianity, the hard businessmen of
Rome, he was sure, would not accept the new faith, which first for
state reasons, then because of a supernatural sign, he was determined to champion. Its mysticism, he felt, would have a greater
appeal for the imaginative folk of the Near East out of which
that faith had originally come.

That supernatural sign had been a cross. One chronicler says it
appeared in a dream. His biographer, who so often talked with
him, says that it appeared in the sky over his armies and also in a
dream. It was in Italy that he saw it. He was there with his legions
because of Diocletian's partnership scheme, which did not succeed.
Always the co-Augusti were falling out or some ambitious imperial branch manager, one of the new Caesars, was starting a civil
war.

It is easier to understand the visions of consecrated spiritual souls than those seen by such practical if sincere men as Constantine. Even although when he saw that fiery cross in a dream or in the sky above his armies at high noon, he was not experiencing such close and beautiful visitations from on high as were granted to Paul, Francis, Teresa and Jeanne d'Arc, the vision was very real to pragmatic, non-mystical Constantine. If it was a dream, it was the most fruitful one in history. If it was an objective cross of fire set in the sky, it flashed on something already working subjectively and powerfully within him. If it were but an atmospheric effect of cloud and light, God could use an effect of His own Nature to set a cross in the sky. In one of the two greatest moments of history the star had appeared over Bethlehem. He might, too, use even an instrument seemingly so unpromising as hard-headed Constantine.

Certainly no greater events ever followed a dream or portent, except those that attended that star. Constantine had always been deliberate. That cross of fire touched even his caution into flame. Immediately he swore an oath of allegiance to it before his generals and armies and took its sign for his device; it was painted on their shields by those most unlikely-looking, fourth-century crusaders, his pagan legionaries. Then he struck decisively and hard. He conquered all his foes. He brought together—for the time—the catamaran sections of the empire that had been drifting apart, and became the last emperor but one (Theodosius) to rule, before its final fall over a united Rome. And religious history he changed equally with the secular. If he had not taken the faith of the cross into his heart at the time of his mission, for he was not baptized until just before his death, he believed in that cross, supernaturally, as an infallible sign. It had helped him to win; and he swore he would repay the debt. The toleration edict of Milan, his establishment of Christianity as the state religion were the first two big payments. This council at Nicaea was to be a third. Powerful as the Church had become, it was threatened by a schism west, a schism east. This was one of the two reasons why Constantine, the one reason why the bishops, had called the council.

Fifteen hundred had been invited; three hundred and eighteen, with many deacon clerks and translators—four-fifths of that body from the East—arrived at the Syrian city of Nicaea with its four famous high carved gates, and its central monument towering over the blue lake and the plain roundabout. They came in varied attire, mantles, togas, cassocks, drawers, trousers; and in various ways, on asses, little donkeys, camels, in chariots, and the torture-twisted in litters. There were bishops from Britain, Dijon, Carthage, the Black Sea country, from everywhere, one from Gothland in the north in a high furred cap, and one in a turban from Persia. Many celebrities rode in: the two bishops from the birthplace and deathplace of the King, Bethlehem and Jerusalem; Sylvester of Rome, later in the line of popes, very happy over just having built Saint John Lateran; Hosius of Cordova; Alexander of Alexandria, the great right-wing bishop; his archdeacon Athanasius, later the arch-champion of orthodoxy; Eusebius of Caesarea Proper, who knew more words than any man there. There were many more, including one of the living causes of the council—the arch-rebel Arius, handsome, ready of word and argument, the idol of over-eager young men and many women.

Constantine himself came in, a little later, from his summer capital near by, Nicomedia, with a great convoy in glittering mail and rich caparisons, the horses' iron hoofs crushing the flowers strewn by the inhabitants and sending up so great a fragrance it seemed as though all spring must have there been wrung out for its perfume.

It was a sacred and yet a very human convention. Politics did sometimes intrude. There were many committee and subcommittee meetings. Delegates would buttonhole other delegates by the pillars, on the rooftops, in the bazaars. In private and open meetings cities would be arrayed in argument against one another. And Constantine added too much pomp. He even tried banquets to please the clergy. He might have been better advised, for most of the bishops were not feast-fat, but fast-thin. The bodies of all but the tortured were hard and fit, from saddle, shipwreck, and cliff ropes. They preferred cress, spring water, goat's milk—at the most luxurious, a little roasted goat's flesh and green vegetables—to the sherbets, melons, and perfumes Constantine ordered. And there was a great deal of peaceful benediction, prayerful thought and consultation, agonized petition, and wrestling with words and phrases to find the inspired ones. For they felt their responsibility to all Christendom then and thereafter. If Constantine was there because of his belief in the efficacy of the cross as a supernatural sign and to ally the Church with the Empire if he could, the bishops were there to unite the Church so that it would not fall like Rome; and it did not.

There were, of course, lesser matters. Some over-literal souls, who wanted nothing of the Old Dispensation, suggested that the Easter date be changed because it coincided with the Passover's. It was not changed. Then there was a dispute over martyrdom. This was not surprising for martyrdom had been a big, a moving, and picturesque thing in their lives. But now Lycopolis, in open assembly, advocated self-immolation wholesale. Alexandria demurred: Death, when one was very surely summoned to it by Christ was glorious. But a deliberate wooing of stake and hunting out of lions was a vanity of the spirit as grievous as that of the flesh. Then celibacy was brought up. It had been practised by many of the noblest since the Church's beginning; and many advocated it for all workers for the faith. They believed with Paul that he who was without family ties and property cares would travel light, therefore farthest, for Christ. They held up the example of the Apostles who had cast aside their domestic ties. But application to all was left for later councils.

So they came to the burning issue for which they had travelled over desert sands, through icy mountain passes, and perilous seas. This issue was ostensibly the disruption threatened by the introduction of alien philosophies into the Church. But it went, as we shall see, far deeper than that.

There had always been orators to trick the credulous Christians. The Apostles had to unsnarl Christian from pagan practises. Irenaeus made long tours to root out astrological rites from the eucharist itself. A bizarre teacher, Marcellus, mixed geometry with theology. At the top of his triangle was God, at one lower angle, Christ, and at the other, none other than he who must have taught Marcellus all this—the devil himself. The Manichees had a theory which held an uncanny fascination for the childlike: two spirits, Darkness, Light, contended in a man's soul-skin for him. All things of joy, even marriage, were of the Dark. Their inferior members might mate, not their choice ones. There was even Darkness and Light in Jesus. It was strange that any who had seen the pure drama of the King should have been drawn by their mixture of merit and morbidity.

A worthier philosophy swept the legions for a time—Mithraism. It extolled the manlier virtues, not the selflessness of Christ. And there were the western Donatists and many others, above all, Arius, the first great Unitarian, and a very able opponent in debate. Indeed, it had been the fond and mistaken hope of Constantine, who though he followed the cross to war had not yet followed Him who had died on it, to find the least common denominator of Christianity, Arianism, Mithraism and the other better religions, and to find unity again for his empire by imposing this composite religion upon all. At the council he found he had been wrong to think that this could be done; and thenceforth he championed Christianity exclusively, first as a state policy, toward the end in his heart.

Arius, the ablest and most intelligent of the rebels, denied the divinity of Christ. And at this point the whole issue of the Council cut deeper than any question of unity. The bishops had come to this council to rout their foes, unite the factions, and more: to settle that awesome question of the substance of Godhead. The majority of them were lovable, searching souls, with an immense capacity for both faith and analysis, and an intense yearning to understand the quality of the light which after so many centuries of darkness, had come to them, and the nature of Him who by His words and bread had so transformed them. They longed to define Godhead so clearly and compellingly that all forever after might have a platform of faith that would not give way. Polycarp, until his heroic death, had spent his life fighting all challengers of the divinity of Christ. Ignatius, before he went down into the arena, had written ten thousand sermons proclaiming the reality of His two natures. Most of them there would gladly have followed these and countless other illustrious examples. They were not at this council ever being merely theological. It was a matter of life and death—of the soul—for them. Arius, who with his attractive ways, gifts, and large following, was dangerous, had introduced a credo which, if adopted, would kill that life.

They prepared their counter credo while the debate was on. It was prolonged. So was the intense heat that summer. Often Constantine would look in, worried at the slowness with which the convention was progressing. Frequently his firm-set, close-cropped head could be seen beyond the windows against a background of trees outlined in oriental silhouettes, and tawny mountain ranges with friezes of swaying camel queues on their high trails, as he sat on one of the Roman X chairs and discussed policies with Alexander, who was so impressive of mien and handled that convention with remarkable poise and skill. Again the diplomatic ruler would be observed by the pillars talking with ascetic hermits, the tortured with their drawn faces and maimed bodies, who would look on this practical man of affairs with a mixture of alarm and yet of faith, for since the vision of the cross he had shown himself just and liberal and merciful to the oppressed. Sometimes tempers became so taut through delays and heat and the near acrimony of debate, that saints whose names were afterwards in the calendar would order their horses or camels to be saddled at dawn only, on the advice of Constantine or the older bishops, to countermand the order in the morning.

When Arius formally presented his credo, the storm broke. It omitted the Third Person, whose great mystery was not understood, many seeing in it a comforting rather than a Comforter. And it demoted Christ whom most there felt they did understand, if not completely, at least enough to pour their hearts' blood out for Him.

To calm the council, Alexander, the patriarchal bishops of Antioch, Bethlehem, and Jerusalem, and Alexander's floor leader, the inflexible, but resourceful Athanasius, needed all their skill.

They were not being over-parliamentary or petty when in debate they let Arius have enough rope to hang himself, and meanwhile buttonholed delegates in the halls, on the stairs, on the rooftops, and tried to win their support. For what? For the Right Wing, yes, and at the same time, for the greatest Left Wing, the greatest Revolutionary that ever came to this earth. They were fighting for a magna carta for themselves, for us, for the cathedral and so many churches, above all fighting for that charter's centre and core and more earnestly than ever Runnymede barons or Independence Hall patriots fought for theirs.

All this time, Eusebius, the world's best educated man, with his constitution committee, was burning the olive oil lamps very late. They had six early credos to draw on, one Eusebius' own. And there were the most popular, the Roman and the Apostles, whose text we have put together from what Tertullian and Jerome have told us. There were no very serious variations among them. The Apostles put in, the Roman omitted, the "Christ suffered." Another credo used the words "He came down" (to earth) for "incarnate." The one of Antioch phrased it, Christ was the "first born of all creation, begotten of Him before all the ages." And another quaintly and beautifully put it—the poetry of many of the old sentences is very moving—He, "for our salvation . . . lived as a citizen among men." The main ones related the twelve central facts of Christ's life and Man's existence; they covered the events that mean more to us than any others in history. Indeed, two of these early credos might have served as synopses of the great drama, reaching from the Creation Prologue to the Epilogue of the Last Judgment. Their fault lay in their mentioning only in passing the Third Person, and covering the marvel of the birth at Bethlehem in five words. And that was the beginning of the life that now quickened them. The framers wanted a more inclusive, a more magnificent and magnetic definition. They were not being over-parliamentary when they fought for their beliefs with all the floor strategy at their command, nor were they being merely theological when they searched long and late and to the point of the utmost fatigue for precise phraseology. The right word, the illuminating sentence was worth many legions, nay more, innumerable armies to the Church. And neither were they being over-technical when they worried nights over one little letter.

It was an "i"—even the layman can understand this—and tiny as it was, it was one day to pit princes and kingdoms against each other. It came in the mooted Greek word, *homoi-ousios*. A like word, *homo-ousios* left the "i" out. But the first, with the "i" in, meant that their King was *like, but not of the same substance as the Father*. The second word meant that He was "*of the same sub-*

stance, of the same being, as the Father." Here was the difference between comparative and superlative, talent and genius, a fair earth and a celestial heaven, the afterglow and the sun at noon. The first, declaring that He was only like God would not do for souls surcharged with faith in and love for their King. And, gloriously for the welfare of Man, the convention was made up chiefly of these. From the first they had accepted the fact that Christ was the link between the Human and the Divine, and therefore could not be merely like the Divine, but of it. An angel might be like the Divine. A saint should reflect it. If they accepted that for their credo, it would make Christ not much more than any angel, a mid-being. But that He was of the same essence, of the same life, as the Father, the Apostles had taught. And one with the Father, Christ had declared Himself to be. Existence without Him for them would have been unbearable. It was also incomprehensible.

Not in the committee rooms but in open assembly Arius, half-wilted by the prolonged heat and fatigued by so many of the redoubtable leaders of the Church—and that then meant of the world—bearing down on him, yet maintaining his peculiar persuasiveness and charm, which was to survive even after his death, and convert vast hordes of barbarians to his unitarian idea, was still insisting:

"Christ Himself did not create, in company with, at the same time as, the Father. He was—and perhaps this is what you are looking for—the highest of all created creatures." Then, at the protest of a score of bishops, "He may even have existed before what we might call time's ages. And if He did not create the universe, He may have created Heaven and the earth."

It is, perhaps, not profitable for the layman after all the centuries' changes in attitudes and thought, to follow through all these subtleties he urged then or those of the venerable fathers in rebuttal. It is only important for us not to lose sight of the bright thread that traversed clearly all that web of debate, and which they were trying with all their souls, to have woven into their credo—the reality of Christ and of the life that had come to them.

Arius soon was through. The great majority of the bishops from Britain west to Persia east, from Gothland north to Ethiopia south, would, after they had given him that rope, have none of him or his voluble supporters. In stormy but very human scenes they argued, then shouted him down. That is, his career then was ended. The emperor exiled him. There was no malice in this on Constantine's part or on that of the bishops. If to have let him and his satellites out to preach in all the pulpits was not like sending out so many Samsons to pull their pillars down, the Church being mighty enough to withstand all kinds of assaults, it would have caused endless trouble. Always the most liberal have to ask themselves: can the champion of a truth, trusting that Truth must prevail, but knowing how gullible with most men are his parishioners, open up his pulpit to the subversive, or should he keep his sanctuary inviolate for that particular truth which he is sure is of the Truth?

Arius was not a bad man. He was virtuous. But he would have turned the Church into an ethical society instead of the living organism it, with all its branches, is. What he tried to do was to take from their unique religion that which made it unique and powerful—the Human and the Divine Christ and His dynamic, woven of strength and gentleness and love. There was worth in some of his teachings, but he would have left a King without legitimacy, an incomplete Christ. He took the leap out of the fire, the wonder out of the Birth, the angel song away from Bethlehem. Christ a good man? Even a superlatively good one? And that only? They might as well have burned the New Testament, closed the convention doors and our Cathedral might as well not have been built.

Years later Arius, weary and no longer handsome, wanted a little rectory where he could lay his head, a simple chapel where he could preach what the majority voted now. He asked for it; it might have been given to him; but it was too late for he was nearing the brink. And all he desired then was that communion bread whose validity he would seem to have challenged at Nicaea when he had questioned the divinity of Christ. Alexander set the date for his re-entrance into the Church and his partaking of the sacrament, for the following Sunday. But poor Arius! Trying so hard to be regular, he was defeated once more. On the Saturday preceding the appointed Sunday, he fell dead of a bowel hemorrhage in the street; and went where all questions of essence and substance are answered, where they should be—at their very Source.

It took a little while at the convention, after he had been so vehemently voted down, for them to finish the drafting of the credo. In framing it, they felt that they were but channels through which God and His truth would speak, so that out of themselves would come the reaffirmation they longed for, of what they had believed.

That reaffirmation came in the halls of Nicaea by the blue lake, with a tremendous majority. This Credo they had arrived at started with the magnificent bugle call: "We believe in one God the Father Almighty, the maker of all things visible and invisible. And in one Lord Jesus Christ, the Son of God, begotten of the Father, only begotten, that is of the substance of the Father."—There was no doubt of it now; then as though that were not enough—"of one substance with the Father, by whom all things were made, both those in Heaven and those on earth. Who for us men and for our salvation came down . . . and was made man . . ."

If it ended with three curt statements about suffering resurrection, ascension, a council in 381 added the familiar phrases about "glory," "Light of Light," "The Holy Ghost the Giver of Life." And the great broad basis was there. And all in that hall had the conviction after they themselves had voted for this relationship of Christ with God, that God's own voice had thundered through their balloting, as it had on Transfiguration Mount when he proclaimed His son the true Heir, and that the Human and Divine linking which meant so much to them was valid and the fire they had received from Him was indeed Heaven-sent. They experienced an elated emotion of vast relief that went far beyond any joy aroused by triumph over their foes.

The triumph, men being what they are, would not remain complete. There would be differences again. But they had saved for the Cathedral and all the men of good will who enter its portals the heart of the drama, the genuineness of its Hero and His sacrifice for His friend—erring, wandering Man.

The convention had also accomplished some other important things. Just before he died Constantine called for his bishop, put off his robe of imperial purple, and donned the white of the catechumen, the candidate for baptism, and became a full member of the faith of the cross which he had followed, a little far off.

The convention had also established the ecumenical council as a supreme court for the settlement of theological disputes. And now that the boundaries of the two empires, the visible and the invisible, or rather the earthly counterpart and framework of the latter, showed some signs of coinciding for the time, there was started the tradition of a strong right arm for the Church. Constantine was the first of a long line of vital and picturesque personalities that upheld the Church—Clovis, Childebert, Charles Martel, Charlemagne, Louis the Seventh, Maximilian, Philippe Auguste, Saint Louis—oddly enough, most of them sons of Gaul.

The fall of Rome had been postponed. And this, in the study of the great drama, general and Church history, and, indeed, the whole pageant and forward march of Man, must ever be kept in mind: before her fall Rome was to split into two, the Empires of the East and West. This division came in 364, the final fall in 474; and from that fall, Rome was never to come back, for all the misfit and miscalled "Holy Roman Empire" of the Middle Ages. The Church also was soon to split into the churches of East and West, the Greek and the Roman. Given the oriental and occidental temperaments, perhaps, both divisions were inevitable. But the Church would not, like the Empire, fall. The Church of the West would take over the old political capital on the Seven Hills and turn it into one sacred. It was indestructible. And the bishops who from all over the known world had attended this council had, in a critical time, helped to save it.

They had had the wisdom that approached the sublime to proclaim in their charter that light that is the source of all other lights, to hold up to the world the Torch personality that is kinetic enough to light, if they will only let it, all the little shards of personality in this world. That light shone in the Nicaean hall, transfiguring their faces, the harsh, the sane, the fanatic, the torture-scarred, the loving, the gentle, as in triumph that their King was of the true line, they repeated the words which ring out in unnumbered churches and our Cathedral today.

XI

Paris now has Twenty-eight Thousand Souls. . . . The Temple of Jupiter goes down by the Seine. . . . Saint Etienne (Stephen), Ancestor of Notre Dame, goes up. . . . Julian, Emperor-to-Be and Gentleman of Culture, tries to replace the Cross with the Agate Lamp. . . . He dies, crying Quarter of "The Pale Galilean."

357=363 A.D.

THE EMPEROR JULIAN WAS A PAGAN AND A VERY CHARMING man. Centuries before the word was invented, he was a great advertiser for Paris. Many letters and verses he wrote about her, with fine adjectives, the most oft-recurring of which was, oddly enough for a military man, "darling." "His darling little Paris," he called her, using of course, the then current name "Lutetia," which meant "the white city." White, some say, because of her Roman marble; others, for the light limestones of her city quarries that went into most of her buildings; still others, for the linen displayed, through the centuries, by the laundresses dipping and beating clothes by the Seine. Julian was also her first distinguished expatriate, starting that long line through Aquinas, Dante, Heine and Karl Marx, who have sought art, liberty or asylum in Paris, to find there a second home which often they turn into a permanent residence. Other emperors before him had favoured Gaul, making Trêves, Arles, Rheims, as Constantine had Nicomedia in the East, their summer capitals. But Julian, while he was still procurator, or governor, had already planned, if he ever became emperor—and there was a chance, his cousin Constantius being an unworthy heir of Constantine—to transfer the seat of government from Rome to Saint Genevieve's Hill, not only for summer when it seldom grew hotter than seventy degrees, but for the winter which rarely fell below forty, in our fahrenheit.

There were other excellent reasons for the choice besides this equable climate and the lovely view. And these were evident to Julian, when refreshed by a plunge in one of the deep pools under the high arches of the Roman baths and by a massaging on a marble slab with the best Provence oil, he came up with the sunset one afternoon of 357, into the palace gardens. The Roman elms and magnolias and the cypress shading the grottos had been set out by the Emperor Chlorus when he had built the palace here, halfway up the hill. Over the river on the north hill called Montmartre, where Denis had died, Chlorus had also done some planting. The vine-shoots he had set out there had already matured into the vineyards which would delight Henry of Navarre when, twelve centuries on, he would come over the hill to take a greater Paris.

For imperial residence only, Julian had reserved this new Left Bank palace, whose ruins can still be seen in what we call the Cluny Gardens now. The law and the courts he still housed in the old structure standing where today rises its much-altered modern version, the Palais de Justice. This faces a wide boulevard now, but then it was within the island wall-belt, between the gardens of legumes up in the island prow and the lofty Glaucinus prison tower which was near where the Flower Market is now.

The island was crowded with fortresses and turrets and public buildings. Because of the marshes, there had not yet been much construction on the Right Bank. But the Left Bank, all around the arena, the Saint Clement-Saint Marcel church, and the Saint Germain meadows, was full of suburban developments. Julian could see arches, gables, foundations, brick course, peristyles, in all stages of construction. And as the shadows lengthened, watchmen with dogs were coming in and labourers laying down their tools, in the quarries. There were three great ones now—the old one on Saint Jacques Road, not yet exhausted, in spite of all the buildings it had supplied for centuries; the one, south, at Montrouge; and a big one on Chaumont Hill, northwest. Each week all three were turning out, in this boom, vast quantities of stone.

This was really remarkable when reports were coming in every day from the rural regions of that depression which was but a prelude to the fall of Rome. The farmers of Brittany, Touraine the Beauce country, because of taxes amounting to expropriation were turning their acres over to the weeds and wolves and, because of the high cost of living, practising infanticide, and on no small scale. Yet in Paris business, both wholesale and retail, was good.

With the sunset, the workmen from the quarries, others from the limekilns and brickyards in the river meadows below the palace, repairing crews from the high-arched viaduct, were crowding across the south bridge to join the fishermen in the island wine shops. Lawyers, clerks, armourers, soldiers off-duty, were climbing uphill to the theatres, one on the summit by the barracks, the other left of the Governor's gardens, on the present Collège de France site. All seemed to have money to spend. And these building speculators from Rome and the home town were making a handsome profit, in which he, Julian, had his share. Yet the boom did not seem inflationary. The old city could take good care of its citizens—by the last census, twenty-eight thousand—though wealth in the provinces dried up and populations shrivelled.

Besides, the empire's fall did not seem so imminent here in Paris. The frowning city wall and its turrets looked impregnable enough. Below him, the Seine navy lay darkly moored in the river glow. From barracks on the top of the hill sloping up behind him, came sharply barked military commands. And into the island barracks marched other legionaries with their metal standards gleaming. Above all these imperial symbols the sky flamed with the last splendours of the dying sunset, which might have been taken for the symbol of the majesty of empire that was fast dying too. But Julian refused to face this fact. With those legionaries above and below, he had just thrown the Germans, out on one of their ever-lasting invasions, back over their silver fence called the Rhine. The Roman wolf had not lost quite all his teeth.

So, looking down on his "darling little Paris," Julian, half-nephew of Constantine, half-cousin, son-in-law, and full brother of others emperors, and to be emperor himself before that night was over, found navy, fortresses, arena, aqueduct, forges, villas, vineyards, everything good. Everything, that is, but one—the cross on a large church which, almost finished now, was appearing above the island's battlemented wall, near the site of the old Druid altar, on that of the Temple of Jupiter and the altar of the Paris Boat-men, and just where the sacristy and treasury of the Cathedral of Notre Dame would rise. That cross spoiled the city skyline for Julian.

Yet the cross had loomed large in his family's history. His half-uncle Constantine had seen a cross of flame in the sky. He had helped to set up the one confronting Julian now and many others in the imperial skies everywhere. And there was a very beautiful and interesting story connected with the memory of his half-great-aunt, Saint Helena. In 326 A.D., one year after the Nicaean Council, when her own son had come to be the greatest man in the world, she had come to the Holy City and had been distressed to see the challenging and mocking pagan temple the Romans had so defiantly and futilely set on the holy hill of the crucifixion, to drown out all memory of it. She wanted to clear it away and all the debris and accumulated dirt of the long Jerusalem sieges, and to build a commemorative church on Calvary. This—and it was one of Saint Helena's many good works—she accomplished. In the course of it she went down with her diggers, led by a friendly Jew, on the first great archeological expedition in history, very deep—the report says—into the earth, and there found three crosses lying in the different positions in which they had been carelessly tossed after the crucifixion. The one of the three that was the cross of the King was first miracle-tested, the account tells us, by the healing of a sick woman who, in tears and to her ecstatic joy at the unheard-of honour, was laid upon it. Then it was cut into pieces by her all-powerful son and sent to chosen churches, one of them Santa Croce in Rome, where it is still cherished. Another lies in our own cathedral.

One account has it that the "True Cross" was discovered by an earlier Roman lady, but it has few supporters. Helena's are many and famous. In 347 or 348 Bishop Cyril wrote a letter to Constantine mentioning his mother's discovery. The famous scholars, Ambrose, Rufinus, Sulicius, Sozomen, also confirmed it. There is also an historical record of the Persians carrying away the Constantinople piece in 614 and of Heraclius returning it in 629. Bishop Theodoret and Pope Clement VIII, with all the historical evidence at their command, were sure of the genuineness of the three crosses Helena found, and of some of the relics claimed to be pieces from it, although not of all later displayed. It is fine to think that this woman who, though humbly born and an inn-keeper, had the personality to attract an emperor, who bore a great son, who did all she could to honour the King, and who tore down the pagan church on Calvary and raised one to Him, was the one who found the Cross. The scholars of Saint Louis in the thirteenth century went very deeply into the matter, examining all the documents; they pronounced genuine the piece of the cross which the Sultan had obtained from Constantinople. Saint Louis then gave a king's ransom for it and a piece of the Crown of Thorns. In 1248, he brought these relics to Notre Dame in a glittering procession, in which he humbly walked barefoot. To house them, he soon built the jewel-like Sainte Chapelle, but later they came back to the treasury of our cathedral, where they repose today. Not that the fathers of the Church ever wanted worship of even such holy relics. Indeed, the Council of Trent and the second one of Nicaea, in 787, expressly warned against it. "Relics," read one injunction, "should not be worshipped because of something we hope to get from them, or because of any divinity that is in them, or because we put our trust in them, but for the honour that is directly related and referred to what the relics represent."

Even if, as very practical people point out, the story is shrouded in the mists of antiquity, there were contemporaries of Helena to relate it to Bishop Cyril. It would be strange, too, if the tradition of so sacred a place had not been kept sufficiently alive for the native son of Jerusalem who led her to it, to guide her accurately. And it would have needed someone official and wealthy and powerful, in a day when Christianity was but recently recognized, to make the extensive excavations. Besides, no one need worry. Even if the relic, as so many and such famous people have believed, were not of the true upright or crosspiece, it would now be priceless and would have a genuineness all its own. In the eyes of all to whom continuity and history and their fellow human beings and the King mean much, it would now, after seven hundred years at Notre Dame, have acquired an authenticity through the uncounted millions who have knelt before it, believing it the true Cross of their King. And, after all, it is not so much the relic that matters as that which houses it, the cathedral that blossomed out of the cross. And finally neither relic nor cathedral matter so much as the Cross itself.

Yet this great-nephew of the lady to whom it had meant so much, this Greek-loving Julian, wanted no more of it than did the Germans he had just conquered. He had even then in mind the idea of tearing that church down or transferring it to the old worship, not through tyranny but by subtler methods, by matching his loved Greek philosophy against the "Galilean's." He was the first great lover of Paris, though his father had been fond of the place, and all the admirers of that incomparable city are grateful to Julian for his tributes to her climate, her sweet air and wines, and even the blocks of ice flowing past in the Seine—pictures which come down to us perennially fresh through the ages. If he was an apostate to the Church, in whose sign he had been brought up, he never was to Paris. He, the gifted imperial adolescent, victim of the stormy, pagan-to-Christian transition period, did not love that cross nor admit that it had come to stay. It did not yet monopolize the sky. There were pagan domes and gables still in Roman cities. Constantine had made Christianity the state religion but he had not ruled others out. In a few years, Theodosius the Great, who ascended the throne in 379, would do that. It would be the final victory of Christ over Rome. And then the cross would dominate the skies all over the empire. But the middle two quarters of this fourth century which saw Julian born and die, still a young man, were very tolerant ones. Rome had co-emperors; she also had co-religions, the two main ones, the old one of the gods and that of the cross. On Sundays Julian could see his Parisians, whom he ruled pretty well, go as they chose, in full liberty of conscience, to the arena, the Roman temples, or the churches. There were at least three temples now that Jupiter's had given way,—one to Mars and one to Mercury on Montmartre, another to Mercury in the island's centre, a stone's throw from the new church. There were two churches—that new one and the little meadow one of Saint Clement, later Saint Marcel.

This large island church Julian watched going up with jealousy was the first one on the island, the second in Paris. He could see the first one, Saint Clement's then, with its Roman arched portal, few round-head windows and spireless ridgepole, standing up bravely in the fields of the Left Bank, about two-thirds of a mile upstream from the island church. This little one was to grow very old and historic. It was built as a shrine to Saint Clement in the late 200's, not long after Saint Denis died on Montmartre. In the late 300's, Bishop Marcellus, one of the earliest bishops of Paris who was alive in Julian's time, was buried there. Soon it took his name, becoming Saint Marcel, and was enlarged in the 500's. So it stood in the Left Bank meadows until 1873 when it was torn down—a gross error of the city and nation when this, the first church of all Paris, had stood there as little shrine or parish church for sixteen centuries! The Bièvre, as small a river as Saint Clement's was a church ran by it in Julian's time, clear and pure as the "still waters" of the chanted psalm which he, quite disgruntled, heard in his Cluny gardens on Sunday mornings. Now the Bièvre flows hidden by buildings and polluted by dyes. And there is nothing left of Saint Marcel now but the name given to the quarter, Saint Marceau, and to the Boulevard, Saint Marcel, which cuts through the site of the old churchyard. There was also at one time a graveyard attached to the church. Occasionally in our days, when a new building goes up in this neighbourhood—around the old royal Gobelins tapestry works—a steam shovel will scoop up with the earth the bones of one of the old Saint Clement worshippers, the first openly organized Christians of Paris.

The church Julian saw going up behind the island's city wall would last (in renovated form) but nine centuries—not as long as the little one in the meadow. But it was to be far more important as the first sizable church in Paris, and one of the parents of the Cathedral of Notre Dame.

This first church on the island, on the site of the old altars and that of Notre Dame to be, was not named for Our Lady, but for some other saint. In Julian's time few of the western cities would have named a church for her. It was still a very masculine world. Men ran it and the Church. Even the great saints and scholars felt that this was very proper. Indeed, although she is recorded as having been with the Apostles, there is in the New Testament very little mention of her after Our Lord had so tenderly committed His Mother to the care of His friend. She was alluded to in early apocryphal writings; she is to be found depicted in bas-relief; and there was one small sect, scarcely orthodox, who lovingly offered little cakes to the Blessed Virgin. But very early in Syria and in other regions the common folk began to tell stories of her. Perhaps, as often electorates have a common instinct

about what is to come to pass before their parliaments are aware
of it, these humble parishioners were a little in advance of their
scholars. If so, the scholars soon caught up, and with their greater
insight analyzed, purified, and gave form to what had been an untutored mass feeling.

In that fourth century Athanasius had written of her, "God had
created a new thing in women." And the greater of the two famous
Cyrils, he of Alexandria, wrote, "Hail to thee, Mary, Mother of
God, to whom, in towns and villages and islands, were founded
churches of believers." Toward the fourth century's end, Saints
Ambrose and Jerome preached about her, proclaiming her as the
ideal of sinlessness. In 431 the great Ephesus Council was opened
in her name. In that fifth century there were built in her name
a church in Ephesus and two in Rome. In the sixth, artists represented her seated on a throne; and emperors carried her picture on
their standards. From that time, too, we have a little sailors' prayer,
"Oh, Lady Mary, Mother of God, have mercy on us."

So the devotion to her would increase until—as was natural, she
being the Mother of God—she became the very first in the "Communion of Saints," which is proclaimed in so many creeds. Her
high place was the logical development of that "Communion." In
the seventh century came from the East the Assumption ceremonies giving reverent festal form to that touching story of
Christ's coming down among His apostles as they gathered around
Mary when she lay dying, and taking her, His own Mother, home
to Himself. And here all who love accuracy with their history
should note that just as the Church did not sanction worship of
her like that given to God, only that adoration which is the highest
and most loving honour, so even in times when such stories and
signs and miracles meant so much, belief in this Assumption story
was not required, only a respect for a conception borne out of
piety and love, and one which so characteristically expressed His
nature. That Assumption story has been engraved deeply in the
walls of the cathedral which was to go up on the island Julian so
anxiously watched that day. You will find it, marking Notre
Dame, branding her twice, as was proper in something that is Our
Lady's—once in the tympanum, high over the magnificent Virgin's Door of the façade, again over the little portal that leads into
the choir—that little "Red Door" which represents the wound in
Christ's side. There in stone, Saint Louis and Queen Margaret watch
an angel crowning His Mother while Christ fondly approves,
seated by her.

Just before and during the building of that cathedral, the feeling
for, this paying of honour to her, became something intensely
personal, a deeply moving emotion. People had grown weary of

the widespread misery of the Dark Ages. Depressions preceded the Crusades, bloodshed went with them. They cried out for some all-healing compassion. But many were very humble, awed by the absolute goodness of God and His justice which in their abasement they felt to be too remote, too far off for them to approach. For a time even the purity of Christ's life, His shining whiteness, blinded them to the tenderness that was His very essence. They had a longing for someone not quite so high that would intercede for them, a pathetic thirst for all those lovely qualities that go with the maternal. The very personification of these was at hand—their Blessed Virgin, Holy Mary, Mother of God. It was she, they were sure, who would plead for them in the mother's, the universal mother's, way. Through her they might reach to that forgiveness, that tenderness, which was God's and His Son's, of which they felt themselves so unworthy. This is affectingly true of the great majority, no matter how many examples of the hypocritical or the merely superstitious one comes across in the chronicles. The clergy and scholars believed that as Christ could not be—as some including the Arians taught—merely a superlatively good man, she who had borne Him could not be just an exceptionally good and pure woman. She who had fulfilled the greatest of human destinies, must be magnificently unique among women. So through the centuries, they gradually recognized as hers a place higher than any held by even the most sainted of women and men. The inarticulate of low degree out of emotion alone, the wise and articulate out of both reason and emotion, all with a feeling of great exaltation and joy, elevated her, the Mother, to the place where a mother is usually found—near her Son. Nor is this at all beside the point, while Julian watches that church go up. It was to be the first ancestor of Notre Dame. All this emotion expressed for her, with the love of her Son, their longing for Heaven, and the amazing vitality of the Gothic Age was the source of the life of the cathedral. Without a feeling of this, no matter how much esthetically you may admire the lofty pile, you can never feel or kindle to its lovely warmth.

In the fourth century, in spite of those foreshadowings and mentionings of her, Paris was not ready to dedicate a home to her. This very first church on the isle, one of the two parent churches of the cathedral, was first called by the name of another saint. No one knows who this was. But we shall at once call it Saint Etienne, or Stephen, for what most who love Notre Dame would call a sound reason: for six hundred years two churches—an early, wood-roofed Notre Dame and a Saint Etienne—stood side by side in the upper part of the island until, in the twelfth century, they made way for the cathedral. Everyone agrees the two were there for that long period. And the majority of archeologists and ecclesiastical authorities believe that Saint Etienne, the one nearer the river, was there before the other. In fact, it would seem that this Saint Etienne began with the unknown saint's church which Julian saw and which soon took Saint Etienne's name. With some additions and enlargements it stayed up for eight hundred years, until its stones went with those of the early Notre Dame as well into the cathedral, quite as the stones of the Temple of Jupiter had just gone into the new church. Julian had seen them.

Before he became emperor and open apostate, Governor Julian had to preside, much to his distaste, as imperial representative at meetings with bishops. When he had looked in the new church he had found nothing like the laurel, the flower festoons and pageantry of his bull sacrifices. A plain auditorium, like those we saw in the Mediterranean basilicas, was divided into nave and aisles by pillars that also upheld the narrow second—or clear—storey, which let in a little light through its arched apertures, down on the nave. Within one saw, in sequence, the choir platform, the marble screen between sanctuary and the rest of the church, the altar in the full front, with its shrinelike superstructure, the bishop's throne directly behind it, and around the throne the carved and curved benches for presbyters and deacons lining the apse wall. But there were some sacred vessels of very fine carved ivory and chased gold. Gleams from these and lamps suspended by chains from the oak rafters of the wooden ceiling and the sparkle of mosaic holy pictures lightened the gloom.

Even when, a little after Julian's death, Saint Etienne was lengthened to a little over a hundred and forty feet, and had much of its timber work changed to stone, it kept its barnlike basilica form. The round apse would be expanded, and what had been mere apertures on both sides of the clerestorey and those on the first storey's north side would become real windows. In Charlemagne's time they were to know the luxury of the first stained glass. The three Roman portals Julian saw would then be more deeply recessed and filled with a great company of saints. But what the cathedral builders tore down after nine centuries was but a longer, thicker-walled, richer version of this same low-gabled, belfried Roman barn that so annoyed Julian.

Always through those centuries this first island church of the unknown saint, afterwards Saint Etienne, would be enfolded and guarded in a peculiar way by the island city wall. It had, in fact, but three walls of its own. Not that Saint Etienne's fourth wall had to be imagined as in a theatre. To save money a section of the city wall had been used for that fourth, or south wall. Furthermore, the round tower apse containing the sanctuary also served as a bastion or angle fort in the city wall. So the City had been incorporated in the Church. So on the City the Church had been grafted. So City and Church, in those ages, served each other.

There was another symbol besides the cross that irked Julian, Governor of Gaul and emperor-to-be before nightfall. On the church, rising above the island wall, was a belfry. No longer was this considered a perch for Apollyon. Its bells were no longer devils' tongues, but angels'. With the sunset, they rang an angelus across the river and up to Julian under his Roman elms. It was like a ringing answer to a challenge he had written. Out of his hate he had made a poem. The envoy of its hexameters he repeated as he looked down on the cross and heard the bells:

"Oh, pale Galilean!"

This grudge the young Julian nursed against the cross was not entirely his fault. He was gifted and had rebuilt some of the ravaged cities of Gaul, reformed her tax system, and had helped her for a little while out of that vast depression that would become deeper when the barbarians came on. But he had had an unfortunate childhood and youth. In the first place he had had too many tutors. Some had been staunch Christians, others neo-Hellenists with a burning zeal for everything that stemmed from Greece. First Mark and Paul, then Homer and Hesiod, had occupied his hours. Education was all a confusion.

Then there had been a massacre in his family. The path of the Church is not always strewn with triumphs, sometimes only with wrecks. There is not always light upon it, often only encircling gloom. And the murderers had been Christian princes, his own cousins, and their allies. They had wanted to get out of the way all of his kin who because of their relationship with Constantine might sometimes appear as heirs to the throne. He did not stop, intellectual though he was, to inquire if these bloody prince cousins were worthy exponents of the faith; he promptly disowned it. He took on himself a strange duel against none other than the Galilean. Not that there was exactly a cruel intent in the challenge he had just repeated. Julian was given to moods, but if he showed temper at all it was in a nervous excited torrent of speech, his only weakness. He would not like his forbears have nailed that Galilean up on a hill. He wanted to beat Him, that was all, by matching a philosophy he preferred against His. Later he would even try in revenge to rebuild the Jerusalem Temple and would be foiled by a miraculous fire. But though a fine strategist and a seasoned soldier, he preferred the humanistic Hellenist's role. He took it as a personal affront that more than half of Paris had gone over to the Galilean's side, that "the glory that was Greece" had paled in a new splendour, that the classic Golden Age had been dwarfed by three intense years of a crucified felon's life. Passionately he longed to take down the cross, to replace it with the agate lamp, symbol of culture, not by blood but by a peaceful counter-revolution.

Thus, unwittingly, he attacked his best ally. For not only would the scholar army of the Church become chief makers of the books he loved, and so through the Dark Ages keep the torch of learning burning and bright, but already it had done much to revolutionize the book. In the library lounge of the Roman baths he had just left, on benches under the magnolias and elms where he loved to read in the sun, there was always some new multiple-paged *codex*, forerunner of the quarto and twelvemo of today.

For the book had come a long way. Thousands of years before Homer it had been but a jar of clay tablets. Wedge-shaped characters were cut in these moist clay pages. These were then baked and put in jars. Later bark and wood pages were substituted for those of clay; bamboo pens being used in the writing. Then boards were glazed with wax and inscribed with a metal, bone or ivory stylus. The waxed tablet soon acquired a hinged cover, was supplied with extra wood, and sometimes parchment pages, roughly laced at the back, and the *codex*, the forerunner of the modern book, was at hand. But though hitherto a bookstore had had to be large, with all the jars and cylinders and boxes that contained the clay and wood pages of the books—and the book itself was a mighty thing—it never contained many words until the coming in of papyrus which grew extensively in Nile waters and the Garden of Eden rivers.

A great gift, like iron and wheat, papyrus had been to man. It not only made books but history. Of it were woven Moses' little floating cradle, Pharaoh's shroud, Cleopatra's mats, Esther's sandals, the bonds with which Joseph was tied when his brethren sold him down the river Nile, sails for the ships which brought the first Phocan settlers to Marseilles and the bark which brought Paul to the judgment of Rome. Papyrus even saved the human race by caulking the seams of Noah's Ark. And cut into strips, its pith mixed with water, hammered, dried in the sun, and smoothed with ivory, it preserved for the ages the thoughts of Socrates and of Christ Himself.

The long papyrus roll could accommodate many more words than could the old tablets. Sometimes the text ran with the width, sometimes with the length, tremendously long parades of words marching unbrokenly over the full extent of the roll. Again the sentences would be broken up, massed into columns, embryo pages, with white margins between. Occasionally writers would make creases in these margins and fold the roll into uncut pages, accordion fashion, compressing them between board sides.

Usually, however, the book in papyrus style was left as a roll, coiled, when not being read, around two knobbed sticks. Labelled with title or serial number, it was kept encased in a cylindrical can. Since it allowed so many more words than the old tablets, it was an advance of course; but the book was still a cumbersome thing, a matter not of inches as now, but of yards. Reading in classic times was a physical as well as a mental occupation and none for the lazy man. When one took out a complete book like the Bible from an ancient library, with all its jars, cylinders, and containers, it was something like going to market in a milk cart; and in the actual reading one had to use both hands all the time, one unrolling, the other winding up. Should the reader become engrossed and wind the roll absentmindedly, he had to reroll it, using not only both hands but his chin and chest as a shuttle for the papyrus.

If this bothered Julian, it was even more awkward for the bishops and presbyters to handle in the pulpit all the rolls and containers of the many books that made up the great one to which papyrus gave its name. Accordingly the churchmen began to experiment with pages made from animal skins, those of sheep and goat called parchment, those of fine calf called vellum which had appeared, though not extensively, before Christ.

All through the early Christian centuries there continued this duel between the book in roll-and-container form and the book in codex form, which was more nearly like that of today. There were then, to sum up, these main styles of the latter class: that papyrus roll when the words were ranged in columns with white margins between and the roll was creased in the margins and the whole compressed, accordion-fashion, and placed between board covers; and the infinitely more popular style, consisting at first of painted wood leaves or those made of linen on wood, but more often of the old waxed tablets, just slates with wood margins and depressions filled with wax for the stylus inscribing, and all hinged together or crudely laced at the back. The wide use by the Church scholars of the new style leaves really brought an end to the duel, for these parchment and vellum sheets were infinitely more flexible than the old wood or waxed wood pages and a far greater number could be inserted between the board covers. They were, also, more easily punched with holes, and gathered together with cords running through these holes. With this mechanical process the modern book was in sight. And Julian was as much pleased with this victory of the book—the triumph of the leaves—as with any of his own sword.

A little later, just after Julian's death and about the time when
that church on Paris Isle would be rechristened in Saint Etienne's
name, the victory would be consolidated, as bookmakers began to
gather up these parchment leaves into regular quires, to sew them
firmly and attach them to a leather strip at the back.

Now even though the soldier who so loved letters, watching in
the sunset in the gardens of Cluny Palace, could not foresee the
desperate fight the army of the Church was to make through
the dark centuries ahead to keep the life of the book, with the
life of the Church, from being crushed out, already he knew that
the Church scholars had made the best books in the world and
that the development of the book was in a great measure due to
their ingenuity and tireless labour. Therefore it is strange, in spite
of his experiences as a youth, that this Julian the Apostate, born
in Christianity, forswearer of it later, did not have more respect
for the church below him on the Seine. In spite of their vows to
the cross he should have had at least a fellow feeling for these
chasubled soldiers, instead of a cold, cultured young cynic's an-
tipathy expressed, so far only in words and hexameters, but later
in expropriations and some unfair edicts against them.

But there he was cursing out, as they rang up the hill, the bells
of Saint Etienne. It was all, of course, very foolish, for those
oaths of Mars and Jupiter and Hades were futile. Already that
church rising above the island ramparts which were now its own,
had been indissolubly linked with Paris. It had used the very wall
of the city for wall of its own, and had swallowed the walls, from
foundation to cornice, of the supposedly eternal Temple of Jupiter.
That structure had now completely vanished from the Paris skyline. Every last stone of it had disappeared, gone into the making
of that church of the cross, ancestor of Notre Dame. So had Saint
Etienne appropriated, been buttressed by, the materials, the very
symbols, of all the ages. The dolmen stones, roofs of the houses of
the prehistoric dead, had gone into the church's foundations. The
Druid altar, chiselled out for the sacrificial blood, strengthened
its piers. Jupiter's pillars upheld its roof. In its crypt were buried
the altar of the Paris Boatmen and its intertwined gods. So strangely
had old faiths been incorporated in, and sublimated by, the new.
So myriad heathen hands had in spite of themselves helped to rear
the house for the King who had slain their gods. All of which
should have been proof enough for Julian, looking down from
his magnolias and elms on the cross, that the Roman dispensation
was about to pass as had the Hebrew.

But Julian's ears were ringing with hexameters and bugle calls,
drowning out golden rules and sermons on the mount. And the
bugle sounding from the island barracks and the hilltop camp, in

challenge to the tongues of those bells, gave him a little heart. Rome might still help him in the strange conquest of toppling that cross, not so much to restore Rome as to bring back Greece. And a voice—perhaps from the tribune of the Rhenish Legion, a favourite of the governor's, or out of his own mind—declared:

"Those bugles sing a prettier tune than the bells."

And Julian, feigning a lack of interest in his own question, to the tribune now at his side:

"You read the order to them?"

"To the maniples below and those on the hill."

A still uncertain Julian must show a little tactful displeasure. "I made no suggestion that the emperor's order should be disregarded."

"Of course not. But they roared at once that they would not go to Persia to fight for the weak son of a great father. It seems impossible, doesn't it, that so mighty a wolf as Constantine could give so unworthy a whelp to Rome as Constantius."

Still Julian hesitated. Below him lay the Seine. It might have been the Rubicon. "Would they fight in Persia for anyone else?"

"Hark!" Shouts were coming up from soldiers pouring out from the island barracks below, answering hails coming down from the hill camp above. "There, governor, is your answer!"

"But Constantius is the lawfully-chosen emperor."

"And you"—tribune or Ambition now—"are his cousin, therefore of the blood. And you win battles for Rome. He loses them!"

"Besides"—from himself or someone who, hearing the tumult, had hurried to the group in the garden—"those Persian armies must be defeated."

"Exactly." And as the sunset blazed in the west: "There in the skies the gods have raised your triumphal standards." Then as those heavenly banners shone on shields and helmets massing below on the old south wood bridge, "If I'm not mistaken, you'll soon have callers . . . Why, here"—at a terrific banging made on the gates by the weapons of the hill soldiers coming down as the island soldiers raced up—"they are now. And," seeing the emperor so soon to be pause, as Napoleon would at Brumaire when his brother Lucien saved him in one of the few hesitant moments of his life, "since it has all worked out so well, we would humbly suggest that you admit them."

Still Julian must demur. "No one shall say I admitted them, inciting them to a revolt I have had no hand in."

There were, however, other and willing hands to unbar the gates for him. So quite as other legionaries had come with swords and torches into another, the Gethsemane, garden, they came to Cluny Palace now for Julian, not to raise him, under a mocking acknowl-

edgment of his majesty, high on a cross, but with a mighty clanging of javelins and swords, and a full-throated cry—"Down with
Constantius, and up with Julian!" high on a centurion's shield.

When he heard about it, Cousin Constantius, being an unworthy
son, made no trouble at all, but after an inconsequential skirmish
or two, faded completely out of the picture.

So the new parchment books were collected in a camp library
for this most cultivated new emperor and put on a pack-animal's
back for the Persian wars, quite as Ossian and Plutarch and Euclid
would be packed in the ship's hold for Napoleon's expedition to
Egypt. Down on the Provence coast they embarked as did the other
Little Emperor. But Julian went farther. Napoleon would stop by
the Red Sea but Julian's army passed through Arabia to the
Persian Gulf, landed and marched inland against the wild tribes
flushed with their recent thrashing of Constantius. And for a
moment Julian brought back the old grandeur to Rome.

But very soon he lay in his tent, far from the vines and the
villas, the Roman elms and magnolias of his "darling little Paris,"
which he had sworn to make his capital. He never fulfilled that
vow. Some say his mortal wound was inflicted by himself and that
as he made it he looked upward, crying, "Thou hast conquered,
oh, pale Galilean!" We like to believe that; and many have. It was
in a fine poem. Military men, however, say, that the wounds came
from others, up in the front line. Yet in a way the poem was true,
for He whom in his hexameters Julian had challenged had conquered Julian, the gentleman, the cultivated, the apostate, the great
lover of Paris, and hater of Christ, and was overcoming his
empire too.

Later the word came to Paris, the palace, and Saint Etienne
church. And now, just as had Jupiter's Temple years before, the
Empire itself was beginning to crack. All over Gaul and the world
you could hear it. All over Gaul, too, the wolves were out—not
the great Roman wolf; her teeth were gone, her dugs spent; but
the native grey wolves, trotting, tongues hanging out, fangs gleaming, in packs. By the Danube, Vistula, Elbe, Dnieper, Ganges, the
tribes like the wolves were on the move.

XII

Of the Four Great Doctors of the Church. . . . Jerome produces the First Standard Bible that will be read from the Cathedral Lecterns. . . . Ambrose gives his All to the Poor, champions the Oppressed and writes the First Great Hymns of the Church. . . . A Mother worries over her Son and an Unknown Girl. . . . He becomes a Saint, changes World Thought and affects the Sermons and Sculpture of the Cathedral.

The Fourth Century

THERE WAS AT THIS TIME A HARD-DRIVEN MAN, WITH A powerful pen, who changed the entire thought of the world for ages to come. He was driven by his restless passions, a clamourous conscience, and what must often have been the Voice of God. He was born in Africa, had a pagan for a father, a saint for a mother, who was eternally worrying about him, also a girl he had to give up to see the bright visions of the City of God. His name was Augustine. And it was he who, in the last analysis, with all his essential sweetness, put up that stern Last Judgment above the cathedral portals, incarnadined more deeply her panes, and added to the tragedy of the cathedral. In addition he poured into the mould of the Church a magnificent strength.

He was not solitary in his genius. It was an illustrious age. The years were filled with great men who walked and talked with Augustine or by whose writings he was strongly influenced. This fourth century was one of those which rise above their fellows, like mountainous waves out of the sea of Time. As the first century was made glorious, not only by the secular Augustus, Trajan, the Plinys and Epictetus, but by the Twelve, Stephen, Paul, and the King Himself; and the second had Justin, Tertullian, Polycarp, Irenaeus, Ignatius; the golden thirteenth, Louis the Ninth, Aquinas, Giotto, Roger Bacon, so this fourth was resplendent with great names. There flourished then two truly great emperors, Constantine and Theodosius; the celebrities of Nicaea, Alexander, Athanasius, Pope Sylvester, and Arius; and a grand galaxy besides. In Gaul alone had been born three outstanding men—Ambrose, later Bishop of Milan; and two hearty outdoor saints, Hilary of

172

Poitiers who ushered in the century, having been born, so many records say, in 300; and Saint Martin of the cloak who, many declare, went out with his century, dying in exactly 400 A.D. Both baptized amazing numbers of converts. You still can see the place where Hilary brought many into the fold—the sunken pool of Saint Jean, the oldest church survival in France, on the hill of Poitiers. Saint Martin, who began as an exorcist—a sort of theological apprentice—under Hilary, Bishop of Poitiers, himself became the famous Bishop of Tours. It is pleasant to think of him as the young soldier, before he became priest, cutting his cloak in two with his sword to give one-half to a shivering beggar at the city gate, and also as the patron of Saint Martin's Summer, swallows, and drunkards. It is perhaps even better to remember him, after his ordination, looking proudly at his new chasuble and writing to his mother begging her to be his very first convert, at the top of his baptism list. No wonder she consented.

Saint Ambrose, Bishop of Milan, who, in addition to his other famous deeds, wrote many beautiful hymns and who was born in Gaul, his father being prefect of Narbonne, was more of a cloister scholar than either Hilary or Martin. They were sturdy, all-sorts-of-weather fellows, able to pace a horse, plough a straight furrow, and fell a tree on the line. They were often in the saddle too, riding up and down the country, preaching, immersing folks in the bright rivers of France, and watching new churches going up—Hilary himself attended the cornerstone laying of big new Saint Etienne, up in Paris. And both were great fighters. They battled ceaselessly against all sorts of wizardry and particularly against the posthumous influence of the amazing Arius, whose ghost was forever popping up in the most unexpected places. Saint Martin performed a much finer deed than most they have since commemorated in the crimsons and azures and violets of the Tours Cathedral panes. The unorthodox prelate of Avila, Spain, where Teresa, centuries later was born, had grafted on the faith the Manichee tenet that righteousness meant celibacy, for priests, the Catharist "perfect souls," everybody. Since celibacy precluded posterity and any recruits, the puzzle was, what use was salvation anyway when soon there would be none to save? One would have thought that such a doctrine would have held little appeal for warm-blooded Iberians and Provençals. But soon Priscillian of Avila had half the peasants leaving their marital beds to sleep out in the barns. Since, should this belief have been generally espoused, both the Church and the Empire would have gone down—much sooner than the Empire actually did—the Emperor Maximus had him condemned to the stake. This cruel verdict was given by the state but certain bishops, overconcerned for a Church that was indestructible, had given testimony against Priscillian. He was, of course, no Stephen, but, like Saul at Stephen's martyrdom, they had "consented to his death." Many other bishops of the time, aghast at the extremity of the penalty, fought for Priscillian's release from this fate, though they had no use for his philosophy. Leading this group were the great Saint Ambrose and Saint Martin. They did not succeed in saving his life, only in saving him from death by fire for the swifter one by the sword. Still, quite as Martin had thrown around the beggar, on the winter night, his soldier's mantle, so now he tried to throw around the poor misguided fanatic his cloak of pity and love.

It was no wonder that Saint Martin's tomb in Tours has been for sixteen hundred years a popular place of pious pilgrimage. A century and a half after Martin's death, Bishop Gregory of Tours used to go mornings to his tomb to collect from the pilgrims who came from all the provinces of France, bits of news, informal recitals, little oral biographies which he used as material for the great source book, his famous History of the Franks.

You would also have found working away many other saints of the first magnitude between these fourth century markers: Cyril (315-386), bishop of Jerusalem; the gifted but truculent Cyril of Alexandria (376-444); Saint John Chrysostom (about 347-407), archbishop of Constantinople, called the "Golden-Mouthed," a gifted and tremendously sincere spirit who had spent ten years in meditation in the desert, who valiantly fought corruption in the imperial courts, and was sent back to the desert time after time for his daring, who preached sermons so magnetic that whole towns turned out to hear him instead of attending the circuses, who widely distributed charities, and who composed the beautiful closing morning prayer of the Church of England; Basil of Caesarea (330-379), the fourth century's Thomas à Kempis; and Theodore of Mopsuestia (350-428), the first higher critic, who was not so critical in his love for a pagan girl who, before his repentance, almost wrecked his career, as another almost did Augustine's.

So we come to the illustrious quartette, the four great scholar-doctors of the Church who moulded and gave direction to many of the beliefs of man: Ambrose (340-397), the able administrator and maker of music for the Church; Jerome (about 340-420), the great scholar and teacher and editor and translator of the first standard Bible; Augustine (354-430), the mighty theologian and elevated author; and one who came after the three yet is linked with them, Gregory the Great (about 540-604), the gifted organizer and statesman of the Church, and father of the beautiful and familiar plain song chants.

The four had nearly been five. There was another to whom the great four owed much. He had died before them all, in the third century. Origen was his name. This should have been spelled with a final "i" instead of the "e," Origen was source of so much. Because he was that, and so much in our modern spirit, sixteen hundred years ago, he deserves at least a passing glance.

An odd figure he was—Alexandrian aristocrat, great scholar, eunuch and martyr's son. He was also a very effective mixture of plain living and high thinking. His fare was as simple as Gandhi's now, his outlay the equivalent of a few cents a day. He had one code he faithfully followed—the Sermon on the Mount, reinforced with a few sterner Stoic clauses. Partly to reserve himself for higher things, partly to fit himself to teach the great numbers of women who came to him for instruction, he, with his own hand, made himself what the Greek courts called a eunuch, the Latin a *castratus*. Later he denounced the step as impulsive and misguided.

But let no one think such a whittling down of the flesh impaired his physical and mental vigour. Often eunuchs made the wisest chiefs in council, the bravest generals at the front. And Origen was both chief and general in the Church and one of her true pioneers. Still, self-mutilation, being a grave canonical sin, cost him his cassock or the white toga that then stood for one. Also it robbed him of a place in the saints' calendar alongside these four great scholar-doctors and the famous Aquinas. It prevented a full fruition of his career as a similar misfortune somewhat handicapped Peter Abelard. Had his place in the Church itself been secure and official, his teachings might have found wider acceptance. As it was they threatened for a long time to outlast those of the illustrious four. But of one thing he cannot be deprived—a very high place in all scientists' eyes. For Origen was a true scientific pioneer. He was the first to point out that science was not *per se* the foe of religion. By his unremitting and parallel studies of all contemporary branches of science and religion, he proved their potential harmony, and with that, the not too distant kinship of the wise men and holy men of the ages, with the greatest of them all, He who summed up the best of their philosophies and added His sublimating touch, the Founder and King. Origen was the great pioneer of the scientific attitude, the reasoning approach, in the cloister. He was spiritual ancestor of the famous mediaeval scholar Thomas Aquinas, in the Dominican convent on Saint Genevieve's Hill and of his fellow-eunuch Abelard and his debating peers up there and down on the Notre Dame porch. Almost this Origen with the significant name made that great quartette a quintette. He deserves a place with them.

Jerome, the first of the big four, came into the world about 340, in Dalmatia. He left it, in 420, from his last home, in Bethlehem, a most appropriate place for a saint. He was one of the band of celebrated figures—Paul, Constantine, Augustine, Jeanne d'Arc, Teresa, Bernadette, are others—who started on their greatest missions because of vision or dream. For many years he lived in Rome where he made a great name, also much trouble for himself. The trouble resulted from his quick pen and quicker tongue. For this admirable but often rough old saint could be cuttingly satiric at times. Usually—and this is just one more proof of how far from anaemic or sanctimonious and how grandly rugged and sympathetic were the vast majority of those old saints—it was his feeling for the underdog, the vigour with which he championed the poor against the tyrannical rich, that brought down anathemas on Jerome's venerable head.

His fame came through his biography of Saint Paul the Hermit and innumerable other writings, and the greatest piece of translating and editing ever done in this world, when he brought together the first standard, adequate, and official Bible, which was later dubbed the Vulgate. With years of patient labour, he translated the New Testament from the Greek, referring constantly to the old Latin, the Origen, the Syrian, Egyptian, Coptic, and other versions, then the Old Testament from the ancient Hebrew, constantly comparing the current old Latin and other versions, both into Latin. Since that was then a much more universal tongue than any we have now, it was a very great gift to the sons of men. For ages it would be read from all pulpits, over the known world. Later, revised a little by that gifted man Alcuin whom Charlemagne chose as tutor for his weak boys and strong tomboy girls, also a little later still, by the abbey-builder Lanfranc, who was called over from Rouen to put some beauty and French ideas into Canterbury Cathedral, this Vulgate continued as the official Bible through the early Middle Ages. It furnished a complete base for the French, Italian, Spanish, German, Dutch versions of the later Middle Ages, and a partial base for the Wycliffe, King James Douay and other English versions. Then, by the reverse process the official Bible was revised in the nineteenth century back again into something very like the original Jerome Vulgate for our own times, and is still being read in this text in countless thousands of churches of the most numerous of all existing sects—and in the cathedral.

So Catholics, Protestants, Jews, men of all faiths, men of none for that matter, are indebted to Saint Jerome for what is, as you wish, a great composite epic and collection of the world's loveliest songs and stories, or a trumpet of faith—for some fortunate souls both. Jerome was one of those who were canonized for their grea services and scholarly achievements rather than for sanctity of life, although his showed that in beautiful measure. And it is highly fitting that this indefatigable translator, editor and teacher, incessant traveller, and doughty champion of the oppressed should before the end find a little peace in the most idyllic of the settings in the great Book he put together. In Bethlehem he passed his last days; and near the cave-stable, the birthplace of the King, he died.

The second of the big four—Ambrose—who as we have seen was born in France, as near as can be determined, in the same year as Jerome, was a man of singularly beautiful character. His influential family brought him a prefecture, wealth, social prominence. But it almost seems as though he were the reincarnation of the young man in the Bible on whom the King had looked, "sorrowing," come back to correct the oft-quoted error. For not only did Ambrose give up that political sinecure and his palatial home to study theology under a humble parish priest, but he donated his entire wealth to the poor. The King would have found many such young men those days to gladden His heart. The very Gregory, who was fourth of the four, for example, was another.

As one of the great heads of the Church, Ambrose had a double fight on his hands, against pagans and Arians both. The ghosts of Arius and Jupiter were abroad again. In one of the temporary pendulum swings away from the new faith, reactionaries stormed his churches and the senate, crying for the restoration of the pagan altar of Victory and the vestal virgins. In another, an apostate emperor and empress and their court stormed the bishop, demanding that he turn over to them two of the churches of Christ for the Arian faith that denied His legitimacy. Facing the ranked power of the temporal world, Ambrose cried, "If you demand my person, I am ready to submit. Carry me to prison or to death, I will not resist; but I will never prove traitor to the Church of Christ. I will not call on my people to defend me. I will die at the foot of the altar rather than desert it. The angry tumult of the people I will not encourage; but, in the end, God alone will be able to appease the wrath you have aroused."

So reactionary Rome and the throne got neither Victory altar, vestal virgins, nor churches for the attacking of the Divinity of Christ. Perhaps it was the great peace that came to one who had given up all to follow his Lord, who had always lovingly looked after His poor, and had now fought for His kingdom against overwhelming odds, a peace now singing in his soul, that found expression in Ambrose's hymns. These, with Hilary's, were the first great ones of the Church. Hymns, that is, as we know them now, with words in stanzas and poetic metres. Also he added to the *missa* lovely adornments—the now familiar antiphons, responses, alleluias, with other liturgical details very effective musically. Though he wrote in the old musical notation, he laid the groundwork for the later beautiful music which, under Gregory's inspiration, would echo out from Notre Dame. To Ambrose, this father of the Church, who was such a musician as well as warrior, benefactor, and administrator, all organists, choir-masters, canons, choristers, and the unnumbered worshippers streaming to the cathedral where the immortal drama is so beautifully relived, should be forever grateful.

From this quartette Gregory, the great organizer, must—since we will meet him in the sixth century—for the time be omitted. Which leaves us but Augustine, the wrestling Jacob and mighty theologian of the early Church, and one who exemplifies even better than the Christian of Pilgrim's Progress, the wandering, buffeted soldier of Christ. To the vast yearning and emotion of the earnest, but untutored, Bunyan's hero, Augustine added the struggles of a mind which, although its workings were of the fourth century, was daring, far-exploring and nothing less than magnificent.

His father was a sort of alderman in a Numidian outpost. His mother, for her tenderness and piety, was later calendared a saint. To offset his father's worldly influence, which she mistrusted, and to ward off evil for the rest of this infant's life—she could not guess how stormy if effective it would be—Monica at his birth and almost before he had been washed and olive-oiled, made the sign of the cross over his brown-tufted head. This holy sign, which had been so laughed at and mimicked by the Romans, had by the second century become so much a symbol among the faithful, that Tertullian swore that half the Christians he knew had almost dented their foreheads in from making it. However, this exorcising did not work with Augustine, for a long time. And he worried the life out of his devoted mother by entering at seventeen into a union by presbyter unblessed, with a Tagaste town girl. He could not give her up.

The youthful Augustine fell under another spell which, in the 'teens, is as powerful as that of adolescent love. For idol he took the eloquent, but unsound, Faustus. He was a leader among the Manichees whom the Nicaea delegates thought they had forever choked out, but who, like wild carrots or poppies, were forever springing up in the orthodox wheat. There were other such sects. For life then was not a duel between the Christian warrior and the sable-armed pagan. It was a five-way fight. Into five main divisions the religious thought of the time had been split.

At last Christianity had become the strongest. But Arianism had a great appeal for young emperors, as we have just seen, and for Vandals, Visigoths, Ostrogoths, all the barbarian tribes who were heading from the east for the setting sun. The old Roman cult was popular with gladiators, circus performers, prostitutes, sailors, and bohemian folk. Mithraism, which unworthily mixed free-masonry, Christianity and mythology, but worthily stressed self-control and courage, had been accepted by many legionaries who had been inclined to Christianity, but who could not be admitted to the sacraments as long as they continued in their profession of arms and blood. The fifth was this erratic faith of the Persian Mani and his Manichees. Under the old arches ranging like the arguments the mighty theologian Augustine later would build, Faustus taught the young Augustine, all afire with the flesh and athirst for the truth, these perplexing things: Two gods struggled for him, Augustine. One was not only symbolized by physical light; physical light was more than mantle of him; it was his very body. It was so with the other duelling deity and darkness. The idea of the contest pleased the potential fighter in Augustine. His new teacher was right! Utterly futile was all this procreation—which had gotten him his little illegitimate son. Yes, yes, would conclude his artful master, Faustus, celibacy was the only scheme for a man of intelligence. And Augustine, all a confusion of mind and senses, would assent, and—a little later—go off to town. So for several semesters Augustine seesawed between resolutions of celibacy and sessions with the Tagaste town girl.

Yet through all this *sturm und drang*, his mind kept clear and he won most of the prizes in school, excelling particularly in poetry, in preparation perhaps for the grand flights of his immortal book, "The City of God." For a time scholastic success went to his head. He began to *tell* his parents and teachers. He was the most typical sophomore in all Africa. To complicate matters he had, by the girl of Tagaste, an illegitimate son. At the christening—not at a Manichaean ceremony, but, to please his mother, at a Christian font—in a sudden access of piety, astonishing everybody there, he had called out to the surprised bishop, "Christen him 'Gift-of-God.'"

The informal arrival of this infant did not trouble Monica so much as her son's heresy, for he had not entirely given up the Manichees. She consulted the bishop, who gave her this assurance, which has since become classic, "The son of so many tears cannot be lost."

It was then that Monica had that dream. In his inimitable "Confessions," in which never does he whitewash himself, never even tries to put his best foot forward, Augustine tells of the vision:

"She saw herself standing on a rule, a little one made of wood. A youth, with face and garments shining, was coming towards her. He asked the reason for her tears. She told him it was I, Augustine; that she wept for my dissipations, my danger. Immediately the shining youth told her to look around. And there was I standing by her side on the rule."

He supported himself now by teaching grammar, first in Tagaste, then in Carthage. There were no wilder students anywhere than those in this town, and in spite of Monica's vision, Augustine again sowed a luxuriant crop of wild oats. But at last disgusted with himself, he left the girl, also the boy in Monica's care, and went to Rome. Still he continued under Manichaean sway. Monica could not understand it. But it was not Faustus that held him then. It was his boyish hope that the Manichaean asceticism might lead him to victory over the flesh.

But soon he deserted Persian Mani for Plato. He could find instead of two battling gods the implication of one in Plato's abstract source—Goodness. Like Stephen and Paul, he had loved the old Greeks; and he sympathized with Plotinus and the contemporary philosophers. Quite as the mediaeval schoolmen would try to link Christ and Aristotle, they were trying to bridge Plato and Christ. Debates were forever going on as to whether there was one universal diffusion through all humanity of a great Oversoul, like Plato's goodness, or if the soul in each of us was individual and identifiable. But also like Stephen and Paul, Augustine decided that magnificent Plato gave ideas that were lofty, but not life. No matter how plain might be the link between Plato and the King, a very human and tempestuous soul had best turn to the source, the One who summed up all the great philosophers, and added His own vivification to them. His mother—he saw it all now—had been right. There was but one place to find light and strength and life.

It was fortunate that at this critical juncture he came under the influence of that great scholar-doctor-saint, Ambrose, at Milan. The older man's nobility and serenity of soul steadied the younger. Though he could not always be with his students, Ambrose, whose labours went on far into the night, let them wander in and out of his study at will to ask questions. He was always ready to look up from his writing of hymn or sermon to help Augustine. In the interim he let him have enough spiritual rope, so that he could work out his own destiny, or salvation could work out its way in him. But those struggles with the flesh increased in intensity. His African sweetheart sailed from Carthage and came to Milan to see him and their son, little "Gift-of-God," who was now with him. But meantime, Augustine, at thirty-two, had become regularly betrothed to a young lady and had also formed a liaison with a Lombardy girl. Never did his sense of guilt let him rest. Con-

currently went on his hearkenings to the voice of Venus and the
barkings of the watchdog conscience, also the inevitable depressing
remorse.

Altogether he was on the verge of a dangerous nervous breakdown when, like Paul and many others, he had a vision. It was
under a fig tree, in the quiet of a garden. He had come to that
distressful state when he could not nap on his pallet for fear of
some sort of Venusberg dream; and that morning had run from
his room, with the sweat pouring down, in a violent trepidation
and passion of weeping, as he tells us in his sometimes naïve, often
lofty, and always virile "Confessions," and under the fig tree
flung himself down.

"Read!" said the voice that went with the vision. He turned to
see a book a friend had left on a bench. It was open at a passage
embarrassing for Augustine: "Not in drunkenness . . . chamber-
ing . . . the flesh and the lusts thereof."

He took this sign literally—even to the renunciation of wife,
fiancée, mistress, all at once. The vision too cured him of lesser
vices, such as his way of swearing, for he had a robust temper.
As they had when Paul went blind on the Damascus Road, folks
now, when the fig tree vision was mentioned, suggested "seizures"
—as though a neurosis could propel one on such an intellectual
forward march as he now started, or a lesion produce such a legion
of works as he now performed.

He set out for Africa, his mother with him. She was overjoyed
at this living answer to a lifetime's prayers. Already she had con-
verted her office-holding husband in Numidia, and now when she
felt death to be near, her son was added to her harvest. Her pride
in him was great—perhaps, with the joy, too great for an overfull
heart. As they were embarking from Ostia, port of Rome, Monica
died in the arms of her son for whom she had prayed and wept
so long.

In Africa then, near his boyhood home, he formed a retreat
which later was to become a model for monastic communities. It
was all very simple. His friends, with Augustine himself and young
Gift-of-God—now fast shooting up and ever near his father to
remind him, when pride came, of early irregularities—would gather
under the lemon and olive trees for discussion, much as had Virgil,
Horace, Catullus, with their idolizers. But the subjects were quite
different. Augustine's favourite was an abstraction which to him
was very real, the powerful mystery and factor of life he called
naturally, then theologically, "Divine Grace," which had transformed him. It was there, in the circle on the stone benches, in the
grass, that he formulated his simple suggestions for the ideal monastic life. Though he was no formal conventual head, he had, after

Benedict, the greatest influence on that tremendous activity of the Church. His ideas were adopted later by the Trinitarians and many other orders. And on the Left Bank of the Seine, just opposite the prow of the Isle of Paris, there would rise in the Middle Ages the famous Grands Augustins Convent, on the quay named after them, devoted to his rule. It was its chapel which Villon immortalized in his lovely prayer-poem written for his mother, who knelt on the Grands Augustins church stones, both terror-stricken and enraptured by the scenes of the hereafter in the bright glass.

For a time after his great change Augustine did not become a priest. He felt strongly that the sins of youth, carried on into early middle age, had left him unworthy. But his fame as a great lay preacher and philosopher increased so that whole parishes clamoured for his ordination. And the shout that went up one morning from the whole congregation gathered in a church porch to greet him was so insistent that the bishop ordained him soon. But he did not remain a priest, or presbyter, as it was then called, very long. Because of his great gifts, he was elected Bishop of Hippo in his native North Africa.

Then, in the prime of his life, he became the stoutest debating champion of the Church. It was a great age for debaters and sermons. Thousands of these Augustine wrote in that ideal convent of his, on Mediterranean galley decks, in Rome, and in Milan, where great throngs turned out to hear him, and in his upper chambers in the city of Hippo when the vandal invaders were filling all the plains with their war cries, the besieged city with the racket of their missiles. Thousands, too, of complicated tracts he put out, many expositions of doctrines, fifteen books on the Trinity alone, whole libraries of pastoral letters, and three great books. The first was the inimitable "Confessions," the winningly frank story of his own wild oats. The second was the "Retractations" of his maturity, in which he humbly calls attention to his early teaching mistakes. The third was the "City of God," in which he frames, out of lofty thoughts and soaring phrases, the ideal Church, rising in splendour out of the Roman wreck to come.

And there were his duels with words, which ranged all around the Mediterranean. The great champion of the Church, he routed the omnipresent ghost of Arius, the Donatists, his old associates the Manichees. But his principal opponent was the Gael Pelagius, big of body, deliberate of thought, and very good-natured. Augustine courteously alluded to him as "a very saintly man."

Now Augustine was to affect the doctrine of the Church, of the several branches that later split off from it, and the thought of the Western World at many points—at most of them constructively even magnificently, at one unfortunately. Here, too, it was in a large way; there was always, in writing, debating, preaching, even in sinning and repenting, something spacious about Augustine. The critical, the unfortunate point he reached now in his debates with Pelagius. The issue was not one of the old ones, the celibacy, twin god ideas of his former foes, or the Arian denial of divinity in Christ. It was Man's most troubling tendency. In the great drama he, Man, through his failure to live up to his first natural and pure estate, to the Light, had passed on to his heirs the inclination to explore, and usually to yield to, the forces of the Dark. Over this perversity as evidenced in others, more especially in himself, Augustine had deeply brooded and now debated. It was, obviously, not original with him, but since it was in his time that a new and more depressing term for it came into use—"Original Sin"—and he was such a doughty wrestler over it, people down the ages believed the theory was his or at least in his especial province. And as he wrestled with, wrote about, or spoke of it, men did not like it at all. It did not flatter them or the Augustine he himself sincerely presented as exhibit A. It made men out as decidedly frail when not actually base, incapable of rising out of their lusts unaided. Pelagius' view pleased them more. He pictured men as inherently noble, Adam's fall hadn't hurt them. They could rise to any heights of themselves. There was small place now for the rescue by the Hero. The debate over it would go on through the ages. Great men—Thomas Aquinas, Duns Scotus, Calvin, Luther, Arminius, Wesley, Whitfield, Puritan and Victorian leaders down the centuries—would take sides.

The religion of all men is coloured by personal experience and this sense of the natural depravity of man implied in Original Sin was intensified in Augustine by his prolonged struggles with the flesh. But there were other theories that further complicated these long duels. First was the Fall, not through serpent or apple, but through Man's turning his back on the Light. He lost both earthly and moral estate, sank deeper and deeper into the pit and could not climb out. So came Divine Grace to help him. This was a heartening idea, but there was then introduced a factor which would darken the atmosphere not only for a millennium and a half of theologians but for our very childhood, tingeing, up until almost yesterday, not only our sermons and revival meetings, but most of our secular, even our juvenile books, and moulding half the codes and attitudes of the West. Known first as Election, it was soon given the fearsome term of Predestination. God had chosen beforehand those who would choose good. He had predestined those who could and those who could not listen to Divine Grace. To make the matter more insoluble still, Free Will, it was said, still existed. God had chosen those who could choose, yet men still could choose.

So into the centuries-long duel over the natural depravity or nobility of man was injected this question of the amount of control God kept over Man's will.

It should not be hard for moderns, who are so inconsistent themselves, to understand the ancient mindedness out of which this paradox was hatched. Man has always been intrigued by conceptions of Fate; and this awesome one of God sorting out destinies for men, before they were men, seemed to many sublime. The Church, while accepting the bulk of Augustine's doctrines, did not like his extremes; and he himself modified this one, even as he softened his harsh baptism theories, when he grew older. But many went all the way with him then, the sixteenth-century and nineteenth-century men even farther.

There were explanations for the paradox. In God's creative conception which became the great fact, the universe and our world, there were all sorts of lives to make the complete picture. Many were inclined to be good, therefore were subject to good influences, others were subject to the bad. Others laid emphasis on God's foreknowledge. God did not forewill, He but *foresaw*, evil. He was aware of the basic nature of each. Some had potentialities for good; others did not. So much of Fate, they said, one had to accept; you could not get further behind the curtain. Knowing all, God "allowed" the set of motives in each case that would let the individual develop into what he intrinsically was.

Augustine recognized, with gratitude, a fourth factor, but rapt in his contemplation of God, he had somewhat subordinated it to his early more fateful theories. This was the Atonement, which is the coldly theological technical term for something not dark but very beautiful, the sacrifice of the Hero. Those later sometimes lost sight of it entirely, while paying lip service to it. They had taken his milder though troubling form of fate and exaggerated it into a more extreme predestination. God, in Augustine's first scheme, through what might be called some mysterious inevitability, had chosen some for salvation, overlooking others. But now the Luthers and Calvins—upright men, too—had God actually and deliberately damning people. They were not being wantonly cruel. So profoundly were they convinced of the truth of their findings that they were willing to abide by that fate even though it hit themselves. They were magnificent in their consistency. They hoped that somewhere all the apparent unfairness would be proved to be fair. But—and this is one of the most extraordinary things in history—men were willing, if so chosen by the workings of this scheme they proclaimed, to perish for it, not by a mortal death, but by one eternal.

There were strange concomitants of these beliefs. Ideas of dam-

nation and Hell, although for ages in the air, were intensified.
Augustine was ever courteous, chivalrous to his foes, the most
tender-hearted of men. Yet when he injected into the pure drama
the Fate motif, he burned these images deeper into the minds of
men. Gleams of splendour often shone forth from his life and his
books, but from this theory a little of futility and darkness seeped
into the Christian consciousness everywhere. It even crept into our
cathedral, the sermons, the counsels given there, and through the
thought patterns and moulds he hardened in men's minds, up into
the awesome scenes of the Last Judgment portal. Because of this, details there were more vivid and fearsome. In the red panes the flames
of Hell leaped a little higher. Later he wanted to let these flames
die down. But the men who came later whipped them up. Though
never did he go to their extremes, they were his children; and
Augustine reaches down over the bridge of these other minds into
our own time. The town girl of Tagaste touches hands over the
years with Hester Prynne of *The Scarlet Letter,* even as Augustine
with Hawthorne, Wesley, Moody, little Victoria, and some unhappy yet singing souls like Pascal, Bunyan, Cowper, and Francis
Thompson. Those who love to reflect on what history might have
been had that mooted inch been added to Cleopatra's nose, might
ponder on what would have happened had that Tagaste town girl
not looked up from among her lemons and olives and donkeys and
smells of a North African market to smile at a harassed young man.

The strangest thing about it all is their misreading of the drama.
Augustine sent a little shadow over it. The others—in all conscience too; that is the tragic part of it—tried to bring the curse
back. The First Act's curse of Sin and Death had been laid in the
Second Act by the life so beautifully lived in the valley and the
heroic rescuing death. Why must they try to bring back again that
curse of Sin and Death?

But lest this be considered too final we should remember that
though the Church accepted the major part of Augustine's doctrine, they did not go with him all the way even in his milder
Predestination. Over and over the Church leaders stressed Free
Will, that Man had full liberty of choice, God a burning desire
to save him. The greatest scholar of the Middle Ages summed it up
when he wrote as he looked down from Saint Genevieve's Hill,
while they were putting the finishing touches on the Cathedral
towers:

"If an infidel or barbarian really does what is in his power, God
will reveal to him what is necessary for his salvation, either by
inspiration from within, or by sending a missionary. God does not
refuse grace to anyone who does what he can."

The great thirteenth century master of theology knew that

not believe this. Two famous poets, however, did. One, Longfellow, in New England, wrote:

> "Saint Augustine, well hast thou said
> That of our vices we can frame
> A ladder, if we will but tread
> Beneath our feet each deed of shame."

The other, Tennyson, in Old England, linked the two—the Saint and Longfellow:

> "I hold it truth with one who sings
> To one clear harp in divers tones,
> That we can each make stepping stones
> Of our dead selves to higher things."

Augustine was a saint, but he was also a grand salty old man, admirable for his prodigious activity, essential gentleness and a humility refreshing in one so mighty and renowned. And more often than most saints he preached and proved to the world this possibility: that the lower nature of a man can be conquered by the higher, aided by a still Higher.

He fought on to the end when he fell sick of a fever, just as the Vandals filled the air with their missiles and shouts and ringed the city round. As their catapult stones and arrows of flame rattled on the Hippo roofs, he turned his face to the wall and died, having leased a lodging in another city, the shining one of which he wrote.

XIII

*Attila and his Huns come up from Hungary. . . . Great Race
Rivers and Immigration Tides. . . . A Woman now protects Paris
and the Ancestor of Notre Dame. . . . She enlarges the Hôtel
Dieu, the Hospital that will stand in the Cathedral's Shadow
through the Ages.*

451=495 A.D.

SEVERAL HUNDRED THOUSAND MEN WERE TROTTING TOWARD
Paris. They had high cheekbones, deep torsos, and shortish
legs swung over small horses. Once they had lived in Asia,
but impelled by one of those unaccountable tribal urges when the
earth seemed to melt into rivers of men, they had come to the
Danube. They had rather liked it there. But fighting and roving
with hunting and fishing, were their chief occupations, and soon
they grew restless again. They had heard that the rivers of France
were many and full, her acres fertile, her cities fair. So here they
were trotting by Châlons, on the Plain of Langres, where Vercingetorix had fought his last battle, to possess them.

It was the fifth of these main fifth-century rivers that flowed
out of the East or North or vague far-off primaeval sources,
Visigoths, Vandals, Ostrogoths having preceded them, with Burgundians still to come. They did wild and picturesque things, like
sacking cities, decking out their women with plundered jewellery
and high-coloured mantles until they and their high wagons looked
like a travelling circus, and turning aside rivers to bury their kings,
then re-turning the rivers again. But, though they were called
"barbarians," they—and particularly the various Goths—performed some deeds that were quite civilized. They built great
fleets to chase the Mediterranean pirates, for they had their own
"enemies of God." Though heathen or Arians themselves—for the
ghost of Arius still stalked Europe—they listened to prayers and
saved orthodox churches; Alaric, the Visigoth King, galloping
around Rome, and ordering the fires his celebrating soldiers had
started put out. And their kings even heeded the requests of
noble Roman ladies not to be raped and sent them presents
instead. And finally they settled in the cities and often whole
countries they took and ruled them well. Theodoric the Ostro-

189

goth, for example, proved, in spite of some examples of cruelty, an exceedingly able king of the Italy he conquered.

Attila, though his Huns were never so cruel as the German armies to which their name would be applied, was a byword in France. Paris hearing of his coming, with his half million, and with her tiny army, was afraid. Through the three thousand years of Gallic history her citizens have been spectacularly courageous many times, as in the first Crusades which the French dominated, and under Philippe Auguste, Charles the Wise, Turenne, or at Marengo and Austerlitz. They have been steadfastly heroic in such sieges as those of Calais, in 1347, Paris in 1870, Verdun but yesterday. But there have been ebb eras when her morale was low. Luckily such occasions have been rare in the long colourful history of France. And now when the couriers galloped on foam-flecked horses over the north bridge, crying, "The Scourge of God is at hand!" it was only for an hour that they were afraid. For they had a real leader. A woman! Who had tended sheep! It was perhaps a fortunate training, for dwellers in cities too often are like sheep. It may have been more than chance that three of the great saint leaders of France—Jeanne d'Arc, Vincent de Paul, and Genevieve —were shepherds, and followed the calling beloved of the King and so often drawn on by Him, in His tenderest moods, for His figures of speech.

In the shadow of the southwest hill of Paris, Valerien, in the little suburb of Nanterre, Genevieve tended her sheep until, at the age of seven or eight, she took the vow of virginity. Even then she knew what she wanted—in fact, it was one of the great things about her, and a grand thing for France when she faced enemy kings, that though a woman of sweetness, she always seemed to know what she wanted and pretty much got it until, at eighty, she was laid to rest on the hill named for her, which was what she wanted too. And already, at so early an age, she had seemed to sense her vocation—to bind up the wounds and to lead her people of Paris.

A famous bishop passed through little Nanterre on his way from Paris to preach to peasants in Brittany. Bishops in those days had become very powerful. Just as in feudal times the downtrodden would look to court or duke for protection, the underdog then turned to these princes of the Church. Often kings as well would turn to them for counsel in matters of state. They had come a long way. It was two hundred years almost to the exact year since the populace had jeered and spat upon and the State had beheaded him who was now known as the first bishop of Paris—Saint Denis. Sometimes the bishops were self-made men, risen from the ranks. Often they came from families of education and wealth and had chosen their vocation because of what, in that age at least, was a clear "call." It must have pleased Him exceedingly, who had looked around Jerusalem and observed that it was easier for camel to enter the dwarf gate, the "needle's eye," than for a rich man to enter the kingdom, to see in the early Church, so many men of riches giving them up, taking up His cross and following Him. It was not so much from any personal ambition as from a genuine longing to protect the weak in troubled times and to advance the Kingdom's cause, that these powerful bishops turned their once so very democratic sees into powerful principalities and soon began to fortify their abbey walls.

When this bishop of Paris passed through Nanterre, Genevieve's mother had just died, and somebody spoke to him about the girl. He talked with her and saw in her an unusual quality. It was something like that which illuminated Bernadette of recent memory. Already there was the suggestion that there might be united with this spirituality in Genevieve a dynamic energy as a leader. As the bishop talked with little Genevieve, he must have felt as the elders of Israel felt when they conversed with that brilliant boy Samuel who became the great prophet, writer and judge. He gave her an invitation to visit Paris on his return. It wasn't much of a journey, only five miles to the city gate, and when both her parents were dead, she left her sheep and came to Paris to start her unique career.

Since this bishop showed such discernment in recognizing the potential greatness in one so young, his name should be recorded. It was Germain. There were two Bishops Germain of Paris, both able men. They lived about a century apart and both had very famous landmark churches named for them. They were built about the same time in the next, the sixth, century. This friend of Genevieve who discovered her in Nanterre, and who lived in the middle of the fifth century, was known as Saint Germain l'Auxerrois, because he had been born in Auxerre. His church, on the Right Bank, was known as Saint Germain l'Auxerrois too, and that should strike a chord in almost everyone's memory. For its successor church, known by the same name, still stands on the old site which is now opposite the east end of the Louvre. This mediaeval survival has an ancient porch in whose ceiling an old blue heaven and dimmed gold stars still show; from its belfry rang the tocsin for the Saint Bartholomew massacre, as Catherine de' Medici watched from behind the draperies of the tall Louvre windows across the way.

The other, known as Saint Germain of Paris, though both were bishops of that city, lived in the middle of the sixth century and was a counsellor of kings, particularly Childebert. He was really the Cardinal Wolsey, though a better and more sanctified one, of his age. His church, Saint-Germain-des-Près, that is, Saint Germain in the Fields, because it was for centuries outside the city wall, is on the Left Bank; and below its rebuilt and sole surviving spire, in the twelfth-century masonry, one can still find sixth-century sections. For these if for no other historic reason one can always remember the two famous Bishops Saint Germain of Paris by these immortal Paris landmark churches.

So into the city of which she was to become patron saint and saviour, and which she was not to leave for seventy-two years, and which was never through the centuries to lose memory and sense of her, this child of eight came. Bishop Germain of Auxerre and Paris welcomed her. From that time their interests never clashed. He was content, even proud, that she become a greater personage and saint than he, true saints never worrying about their own sainthood or honours.

At once he told the clergy of the high hopes he held for her. Report of this travelled through the Seine valley. From the beginning she became a legend. She made the legend real by giving it the flesh and blood of good and great deeds. Long after Germain had died, people would recall his prophecies made at the time of her entry with delight that they had come true.

As she matured she could have had much attention had she wished it—from very great men when she became celebrated for her sweetness and charm and charities, the Lady Bountiful of Paris, a great figure and the confidante of kings. But she never married. She preferred to walk the common way rather than live ever near thrones. It was social distinction enough for her to be, as they reverently put it, "the bride" of the greatest of Kings. She was as completely as any who ever entered convent. She had taken the vow of virginity, and she devoted every waking hour, even her dreams, to His service and prayers for and care of His unfortunates. If ever there was a devoted, completely consecrated life, it was hers.

From her entry, then, at the age of eight, she spent all the time she could take from her studies and prayers in tending the sick, the crippled, the poor. She was twenty-five when the invading Hun came, and already she had turned into a fine hospital—they called it "Hôtel Dieu"—the little hospice she found running on the island right near the long church, Saint Etienne, which Julian had watched going up. It was in an appropriate place for a hospital. If the island was the heart of the city, this, the upstream end on the south fork of the Seine, was its upper right ventricle which for centuries had throbbed with religious life in various forms and would rise to a feverish but dynamic beat when the Gothic arrived. In this sacred part of the island, a hundred feet of the island's southside city wall served as south wall for Saint Etienne, Saint Etienne lending its apse tower for a turret to the wall. As the inclusion of the old grave roof dolmen stones in the Druid altar, then the Temple of Jupiter, and in Saint Etienne, finally in the Cathedral itself, was mute evidence of the unbroken continuity of religion and life, this buttressing of Saint Etienne by the city ramparts, the very identicalness of church and city walls, was no empty symbol of the incorporation of the Church with the heart, the very life of Paris.

By Saint Etienne, in the lee of this south island wall, was the little poorly kept hospice which Genevieve had found and turned into a strong vital institution. Some two centuries after her Saint Landry would build, on a spot about ninety feet west of Saint Etienne's front doors, a larger successor to this hospital of Genevieve. And this Hôtel Dieu would grow with annexes and alterations until, in the Middle Ages, its half timbered gables stretched for quite a distance along the river, and its annexes even crowded over onto the bridges. Today, of course, the square in front of the cathedral has been somewhat changed and enlarged. On the old Hôtel Dieu site, on the south side, there is now a long strip of green lawn on which a mounted Charlemagne rides high. Fronting the square to the west, rise the grey police barracks. Opposite this, across the square on the east, loom the cathedral towers. And just across the square from the old hospital site, on the north now are the acres of palatial buildings to which Napoleon the Third transferred the Hôtel Dieu. So that too has had a continuity like the cathedral's. Since there was also in Roman times an infirmary for the island barracks nearby, there has always been a hospital in the shadow of the church—of the old gods or the true One. Then, early in the Christian era, Saint Julien le Pauvre (whose grey barrel-vaulted church still lies across the river from the cathedral) had a little oratory by the river, a tiny house with a few pallets for storm-tossed travellers and invalids. He did more than care for the sick. Julien the Poor was an enthusiastic ferryman. His stand was there by the Seine, on the island; and his greatest delight was in rowing pilgrims over the river in the worst sort of weather. Those who love Paris can see an illustration in a stone lintel on an old house on the Rue Donat showing him at work, rowing a tubby little boat with oddly foreshortened oars. A fare—or guest—for he never charged sesterce or sou, got him out of bed, they say, on so stormy a night that his lantern blew out. But he found he needed none. Never had he known passenger so poorly-clad or unlikely-looking before. But suddenly there glowed on that passenger's face in the stern a light brighter than had ever been seen on sea or land or river. When they reached the other bank, Julien could see that the poor garments had vanished, that the passenger now wore those of a shining splendour. Then, with a blessing for Saint Julien the Poor, the stranger suddenly departed. So, long before there was a house there for Our Lady, the dwellers by the river declare, Her Son came to Paris and was ferried over the Seine.

No wonder that Julien the Poor, believing that he had truly seen this blessed vision, founded a little hospice with a bed or two. And whatever the age of the name "Hôtel Dieu," whether seventeen hundred years from Julien's vision, fifteen hundred from Saint Genevieve's foundation, or thirteen hundred from Saint Landry's larger hospital, the tradition of continuous hospital service there is long and sacred and unique. The lame, the halt, the blind, have been coming for cure for more than two thousand years, into the square of the Cathedral.

None of these founders, Julien the Poor, Genevieve or Landry, had fine equipment, only much love and great diligence. Indeed, it is a question whether medicine at that time had not retrogressed. Even Rome knew few instruments besides the probes, knives, lancets, saws and catheters that had served for centuries. In the Mediterranean capitals they were trepanning, cutting out tumours, performing rectal operations in the age-old ways; only in facial surgery and in kidney operations had they invented anything new. They still believed in the four elements of Hippocrates—blood, phlegm, yellow bile and black—in which modern doctors see some point. But they had lost sight of—as men would continue to lose sight of, for twelve hundred years more—Hippocrates' teaching that disease did not come from unseen or supernatural powers but from the breaking of natural laws.

But Hippocrates himself could have found no doctor that kept his beautiful oath better than the head of this hospital of Paris, Genevieve. She and her nurses and all her assistants did not, like many modern doctors, insist on regular hours; they answered all calls of distress at any hour of the day or night. And if they lacked blood-count gauges and hypodermic needles, she had a great store of soothing cordials and balms, of mandrake concoctions for the easing of pain, and of clothes fresh-laundered in, and beaten snow white alongside, the Seine. And her way of smoothing pillows and caressing fevered brows, with her prayers, cured more than did the doctors or at least helped the patients more peacefully, when the hour came, over a river much deeper and darker than the Seine.

So Genevieve of little Nanterre Village, under Mont Valerien on the southwest outskirts of Paris, became the most helpful saint and benefactor that ever came up to the city, the greatest woman too, in that land of remarkable women until the coming of Jeanne

d'Arc. For seventy years in life, for centuries in death, she continued as the patron saint of Paris.

Altogether, it was natural that the oncoming couriers, clattering
over the bridge with their news of the oncoming half million
horsemen, should ride, once they had passed the bridge gate,
through the open space of the old Roman Forum toward Saint
Etienne and the hospital in the shadow of the wall. By this time
half the population of Paris was calling for Genevieve to come out
and pray for them.

The litany in the old church over, she led them through the city
which most picture as grey and very old looking. But Puvis de
Chavannes, the nineteenth-century painter, was not so far wrong
in the soft tones, the pastel shades he gave Genevieve's Paris when,
in his murals in the Pantheon on her hill, he pictured her guarding
it. The tenth and eleventh centuries would find the city grey, low,
hulking, Romanesque. Mediaeval times would see her greyer and
browner, but gilded and painted up a bit, a mysterious, narrow-
streeted city, lofty, pinnacled, and aspiring. But Genevieve's town
was low, with many pillars and round arches, open squares, and
something of the Roman spaciousness left. And while the Palace
and Glaucinus Prison near it might show a little of the hue of
age, Saint Etienne's foundations and the city wall, the green stain
of Seine damp, the marble and Saint Jacques quarry stone of the
dwellings had not been smutted in her time by any mediaeval mire
or modern fumes. The gardens, too, at the end of the island's prow
and the vineyards and farms on the farther shore were still un-
walled and fair, and the Seine flowed by, an uncorrupted green,
so that the ensemble of Gallo-Roman Paris showed the charming
light tones the mural painter put on the Pantheon walls.

Genevieve now led the citizens to the north bridge. Below her
they massed, some already armed, others in everyday togas, smocks,
and smutted aprons. She climbed the narrow stone treads and came
out on the parapet on a level with the palace windows. As Jerusalem's holy men gazed up at their tawny hills, she gazed at the
four that looked down on the island city. Directly ahead of her,
when she turned to look to the east whence the invaders would
come if they were not driven back, lay Chaumont or the Butte.
On the north rose Montmartre, where in 460 she would build over
the tomb of Saint Denis a chapel, the start of the royal abbey
where the Gothic would be born. Over her shoulder loomed
Valerien under whose shadow she had played as a child and, as a
child, tended her flocks. South, across the river, was the hill that
would be named for her and on which, in a great abbey, then in a
Renaissance church, she would lie through the years.

"I will lift mine eyes to the hills whence cometh my help."

Not only mystically but literally those hills were bulwarks. For fifteen hundred years after her, foes of France would set foot on those hills but five times, and for brief periods at that—the Norsemen in the Dark Ages, the English in the Hundred Years' War, the Germans and their allies at Napoleon's fall, all by themselves in 1870 and 1940, although they had tried to get there eighty or more times. Whenever, after Genevieve's death, they came down on Paris, the Parisians would call on her spirit to rise from her hill again.

In addition to this mystical help from the hills, there were two other sources of strength on which Genevieve relied. The first, Aetius, was that moment riding at the head of veteran legions that were but ghosts of their former selves, towards Châlons to meet Attila's hordes. But if his command did not have its old morale, Aetius was very far from being a shadow himself. If the last Roman, he was one of the noblest of them all. To what was turning out a pretty dingy sunset for a passing great empire, he would add a little flare-up of glory.

Although hopeful, Genevieve could not be sure of the second source of help, also marching for Châlons. For Merovée—his name had other forms, Merovic, Merowech; but in France the French one should do—was a relative, a cousin-germain of the Germans. They did not have so much in common. Existence for Merovée's merry men was not so much a mere matter of wassail bowls, begettings and blood as it was for the out-and-out Teutons. The Franks could do a little slaughtering on their own, but they were not so consistent and methodical about it. And they had something approaching a sense of humour, the lack of which and of the sense of proportion implicit in it, has caused the Germans much of their trouble in this world.

Furthermore, these Franks though durable enough, could be fused. And they had come just in time not only to stop Attila's hordes and to save Gaul when Rome was spent, but to add a new race ingredient in the fusion which was fast becoming that something we call French. Already evolution had tossed in Ligurians, Iberians, Basques, Phoenicians, Phocan Greeks, Gauls, Middle Europe Celts, Latins. The Franks were at hand. And last, four centuries on, would come the Normans. Then complete, this new strain would be added to the English—after Hastings—for did not William the Conqueror fill up his army with Ile de France knight and say "We French have conquered"? It was a cousinship which the English might with profit have honoured, rather than eternally dwelling on the Anglo-Saxon tie.

That spring of 451, in Genevieve's young womanhood, there
were four of these race rivers circling in and around France. First
was this one of the Huns, with Attila as its wild and picturesque
crest, which had flooded over into France and had overwhelmed
Bourges, Troyes and the Orleans country. To meet it, a new generation of the Visigoths of Alaric had rushed up from Toulouse
and had forced the Hun stream to veer toward Châlons. South,
coming on was a third stream—of Romans under Aetius. Once
this last would have been a current that bowled everything over;
it was a rapidly diminishing one now. And it was really the
fourth, the strong Frank current, to which the statesman this
gentle woman Genevieve had turned out to be, looked on as potential ally and source of strength. A doubtful friend for a time
it had seemed, for it had sucked up half of the cities of Belgium
and north Gaul. Then suddenly this great river, with Merovée
as top wave, turned and went swirling toward the east. Indeed,
all three—Franks, Romans, Visigoths—rushed precipitately for
Châlons and a confluence there against this raging flood of Huns.
Into this maelstrom Genevieve proudly plunged her brave rivulet
of Parisians.

When past Châlons town, by Mauriac village, the mad Hun
flood stopped, to settle all over the plain in great pools of men.
With skill too they had deployed. For Attila was more than mad
dog, more than the hissing "Scourge of God" they made him out
to be. He could do his share of wrecking, but on a scale no more
wholesale than the so-called civilized, the history-acclaimed conquerors. And libel it is to link his Huns with modern German
armies—a libel, not of the German armies, but the Huns. Not
half the anathemas heaped on his singular, but striking-looking
head, did he really earn. Chroniclers too often being mere special
pleaders, so much depends on historian's birthplace and biographer's blood. And when Attila returned to his Danube home from
his last foray he would leave behind (with a little later Magyar
addition) quite a legacy for civilization, in a race named Hungarian for him, which would prove a stout bulwark against the
Turks and other wild riders from the Balkans and Levant when
it was their hour to run amok.

For an ancestor, he was far from impossible. If looking down
from a gilt frame, he would have appeared striking, he was even
more picturesque on an iron throne or gazing from a saddle out
over a battlefield. Never, of course, without being laughed at
could he have disowned all his little horsemen, with their eyes
so near the slant, their red or swart-yellow complexions and little
legs curved around the bellies of their nine-hundred or thousand
pound ponies. Bull-torsoed, short of stature—at that dispropor-

tionately short of leg—he looked as if he had sprung as their archetype up out of the ranks. But his stride was swift and regally imperious; and his eyes, though they were set on the sides of a very squat nose, could blaze forth in a magnificently royal anger. He could also display a chivalry quite as eccentric and spectacular as any of our fancier Christian majesties. One wild ride Attila made down through the Brenner Pass, and pounced on Italy and shook her until all her towers chattered and a fortune dropped out of her rich pocket cities—all for a lady with whom he had just fallen in love.

When the little Paris contingent arrived at Châlons, they saw Attila's men spread thickly over the fields to the east as far as the eye could reach from the north to the south horizon. They looked like the "vast cloud of locusts," they had been called, all alighted and since their swords, spears, and javelins now hung straight down from saddlebow or shoulder, like locusts with wings closed, but ready at a word from their king to fly, swoop down, and devour. Or—since the confusion of names they fastened on Attila breeds a mixture of figures—they waited there, tense, a half-million lashes, ready to be swung by him, the "Terrible Scourge of God."

With all those lashes, his half-million swart-yellow horsemen, then, he struck at dawn. All over the plain, far and near, they fell on Visigoths south, on the skeletons of the old Roman legions under Aetius; and also on the Parisians and the soldiers from the Seine Valley in the centre; and on the gusty, heroic-looking army of the Franks under Merovée, north. Again and again the dread "Scourge of God" swung back, let go. The little horsemen charged all over the plain. The lashes sank, cut in deep. And if they left many behind after each withdrawal, they had cut great gashes out of the defense.

So time after time, as one possessed and actually swinging a scourge around his head, Attila, the flat-nosed, deep-chested king with the blazing eyes, reached way out over the plain and whirled and flailed away with his army. And in the evening, this barrel-torsoed, little-legged, half-Oriental figure, Hun, scourge, lover, cavalier, crazy man, fox, paced in royal anger up and down under the stars, by the eastern campfires. As deeply as had his lashes, his tongue and his imperious glance cut in, as he upbraided officers who with the dawn must mount, charge, close in their ranks, retreat, only to charge all over again.

Three hundred thousand slain, the old chroniclers computed. It will do. At least the "Scourge of God" thought so after the last countercharge when the allies—Franks, Visigoths, Romans, Paris and Seine men—still more terribly reduced his numbers. The Huns had come out of Asia driving ahead of them other barbarian tribes, like lesser game before the more royal beasts of plain and jungle. Now it was their turn to flee. It was a new, bitter, and perhaps wholesome experience for Attila. With half of his lashes extracted, he gave the command. It ran angrily, shriekingly, along the ranks to the clang and clash of arms. Then suddenly, leaving half of their supplies behind, all the little swart-yellow horsemen wheeled and, digging three hundred thousand (now) pairs of heels into the flanks of their wearied ponies, vanished like locusts over the eastern horizon. So, in Pannonia by the Danube, they settled down, to found that highly musical and civilized race of namesakes.

Merovée's stout Franks rode away toward the Soissons country to suck up more of the Roman-Gallic cities. Aetius, last of the noble Romans, disappeared in the south, having given the imperial sunset its last flare-up of glory. And soon at home, on the isle in old Saint Etienne, Genevieve and all Paris with their returning brave men, celebrated with a grand *Te Deum* which rang musically out over the Seine. But, to tell the truth, the old river, being so much more ancient than Man's city which it embraced, and all his churches and altars and wars, was beginning to grow weary of all these victories and rivers of blood.

But there was more trouble ahead. For first, victorious King Merovée, the founder of the Merovingian line, then his son Childeric I, then his grandson Clovis, who established it right royally, paid attention to Genevieve in a way she did not like.

XIV

Rome has fallen and the Whole World still echoes with the Crash of it. . . . But Franks and Gallo-Romans build up a real France. . . . Clovis conquers Many Peoples, but Genevieve locks him out of Paris until he becomes Baptized. . . . Genevieve is buried on her Hill in a great new Abbey, but they will bring her Ashes out, to encircle the City with them, whenever Paris and the Cathedral are in Danger.

495=512 A.D.

ITH PEACE SETTLED DOWN FOR A WHILE ON PARIS, Genevieve kept up her walking of mean streets, which she preferred to sitting in palaces; and of these she could have had a fine assortment. On the sick and the poor she continued to wait, and let the kings wait—on her.

The first monarch she snubbed was victorious Merovée. Courier after courier whom he sent down from North Gaul she left to cool horse and heels on the north bridge outside the Paris walls. But he continued to send them, so bent was he on winning his game. Not the game of love, but the other, equally old, of sponge-and-water, whose object is to see which—invading water or conquered sponge —will absorb the other and so eventually become the victor. It is a waiting game and very wholesome sport, making as it does for an eternal political balance, as timid liberals who fear modern dictators so much should remember. After five hundred years the Roman Empire had just lost the last round to Gaul.

Already in preliminary moves King Merovée had consolidated much of the west Rhineland, Belgium, Picardy, the Meuse country, or else they had, sponge-and-water fashion, consolidated him and his ebullient Franks, all unconscious of the true process. And he wanted the sponge-core, Genevieve's Paris, very badly. But in spite of his great victory over the Huns, in which her Parisians had fought, Genevieve would not open the city gates. She stood up on the parapets and to the waiting heralds signalled a most vigorous "No!" For King Merovée had not been baptized.

Faithfully all Paris followed her cue. For a quarter of a century even when in 476, twenty-five years after the great Châlons battle, Rome fell and Paris had lost her great protector and needed a new one, she still kept the kings waiting, the gates closed, her city locked up. It was not Merovée now. With his sword and bracelet and pottery, he lay in his tomb. His son, the first Childeric, capable ruler too, reigned in his stead. But the same sort of official love he made to her, as patron, therefore proxy for Paris. It was no use. Still she persisted, shook her head. By now, she called down over the Seine, their royal master should have known the conditions. Had she not twenty-five years ago laid them down to his father? In church, in Seine, Marne, Loire, or Bièvre water—it did not matter which—he must be baptized. Angered, Childeric threatened to besiege Paris, cut off her food supply. "To the font!" he cried.

And because of the courage of this indomitable woman, the spell which even after her death she cast on the sons of men, or for very shame, Childeric did not carry out his threat. He beat the Visigoths south of Paris, on an island in the Loire just opposite the first chateau of Amboise where later Catherine de' Medici hung rebel Protestants from her balcony like so many blackbirds on a rail. He stopped the Germans once more in the northeast; saved Angers city from the Saxons, in the west; and, south, barred some more German cousins, the Alemanni, from crossing the Alps. In fact, he built up his territory all around Paris but left it an untouched sanctuary city, a real island in the heart of a great surrounding France. All the time he kept up his overtures, sent forth his couriers to Genevieve. Paris has often been wooed but never with such ardour. This suit of the Merovingians is the longest in any record, whether of artists, poets, burghers, merchants, conquerors or kings.

In the end, he won and lost. Kept his point and lost the city. Not even when Childeric was near death up in Tournai, where later one of the fiercest battles of the great World War would be fought, would he send for the priest. Henry of Navarre thought Paris worth a mass. Childeric coveted her yet would not pay the price of a few drops of water. They found him, twelve hundred years afterwards in 1653, in his tomb, with arms, precious stones, his signet ring, even a royal tooth that would bite no more. All these you can see in Charles the Fifth's library (in Mazarin's palace, now the vast Bibliothèque Nationale, on the rue Richelieu). You can see also the sword with which Childeric conquered Goth, Alemann and German (but did not draw on Genevieve) with its bright colour-scheme of maroon and gold. And still on the scabbard, which he did sometimes rattle in her face, there swarm, uncrushed by the weight of the years, the exquisite raised gold bees, which must have given an idea for a device to Napoleon.

After his imposing funeral, in 481, there came a greater than Childeric, the ablest of all the kings of that age, and one worthy to rank with Charlemagne. His name was Clovis; and, for his role of first ruler of an emerging France, Nature had well equipped him. He had a powerful sword-arm, considerable military and organizing skill, great hardihood, and some good humour. He was, of course, an autocrat like the rest of his family, and kept an order of serfs in his kingdom. But they were not as numerous as under Rome; and even before the dramatic conversion of Clovis, the Church had eased their condition. Constantly, sincerely, and without political design, the bishops had preached neither emancipation nor revolution, but loyalty on the part of the serfs, consideration on the part of the masters, so that all might live as one big family in the eyes of God. There was too, about his lordly Merovingian manner a royal, even large-hearted effect. This the crowds both of freedmen and slaves found far more agreeable than the ways of most autocrats, and actually at times as contagious as his bursts of good humour, the whole ebullient drive of him. If citizens must have tyrants, it is perhaps better to have them like that.

Needing Paris to round out his grandfather's, father's, and his own territorial acquisitions into a complete France, Clovis continued this extraordinary courtship of saint and city. By now Genevieve was known, far and wide, for a prize, a woman of holy deeds and earthly charm and of a decisive habit of mind that was to say the least, unusual. Never in this world did a woman take so long to say "Yes." This courtship of three kings, and her everlasting "No," had become more than an intriguing fireside tale. It was a legend, a great tradition. And to both tale and tradition Genevieve stuck, sending out curt messengers from the gates or signalling that "No" with a shake of the head, when she walked with her women and the warders on the walls and a new string of ambassadors, proxies for Clovis as she was for Paris, shouted or trumpeted up to her from the other shore. Always some seemed to be on hand, like the Greeks, with pack animals loaded with gifts and now lounging, with the spring, among the Seine lilies again making fagot fires as the leaves yellowed to their fall or, in the winter snows, waving arms to keep warm and stamping spurred heels. So much like suitors trying to sit each other out they were that even the old river seemed to chuckle in his ripples as he flowed by them under the bridge and past the prow of this island city he knew so well, on his way to the sea.

"Like grandfather, like father, like son,"—so, in effect Genevieve, from her walls, told these ambassadors in mail. "Surely by now, the Merovingian family should have known the conc

:ion"—which was to say, the great tradition—"no baptism, no
:ity! If, for a few drops of water, your proud Clovis will but bend
his head, unlocking his heart, I will unbolt Paris—but not before!"

So time after time the ambassadors rode back, with the gifts un-
distributed. And at first Clovis simply threw back his great head
and laughed.

"The game," he would observe, "begins to grow interesting."
Most people thought it had long before. "Grandfather, father," he
would ruminate, often aloud, in his battlefield tent or the corridors
of Tournai Palace, "have played it, lost, and, losing, died." But *he*
would win, he swore.

There came a time, however, when that laugh did not ring out
so infectiously among the walls of Tournai Palace. A string of
sound Frankish oaths rebounded back instead. Suddenly that royal
cursing made an ally for Genevieve. Not among men, but her own
sex. For Clovis' wife, Queen Clotilde (who is eternally memorialized on Genevieve's own hill, by a street called Clotilde, right near
the Rue Clovis) did not like this bombastic blasphemy at all. Not
because she had been born a Christian. This lady—another striking personality of the age—though a woman of culture, had been
born a barbarian, a princess in the palace of the Burgundians who
had but recently taken over the rich lands southeast whose wines
would give their name so pleasant an immortality.

Not long before she had become affianced to the great King
Clovis she had, through a good bishop's introduction, taken a
greater King to her heart. And now she resented this cursing that
woke the palace. Of its futility too she was sure, knowing better
than he her sex and the staying powers of this representative of it
whom he cursed and who so resolutely kept the gates barred in the
city by the Seine. And when the oaths had died, their ribald echo
tailed away, she suggested to her decidedly masculine husband,
in her gentle woman's way, that, after all, it might be a good way.
"Which way?" he roared. "To have Genevieve dragged by her hair?
Or damned by that new god they all—Genevieve, Clotilde, and
Germain—who was nothing but an old woman—seemed so taken
with, and burned in this bright new, rather interesting Hell?
Cheerfully, with a right willing heart; he would watch that fire,
even toss a fagot, or better, some charcoal on it, so that it might be
slow. Not that? What then? *Be baptized?*" Less mirth there was
now, and more reverberating profanity in Tournai. "Well, anyway, they had given him an idea—a good one—that damnation.
Damned she, Genevieve, should be! Damned all three!"

So turning on heel, he mounted and rode south, by more conquering to show them—show all these weak, variable, unpredicta-

ble women, who fell for religions, cults, fads, gentle gods!
Especially one woman, who was so weak that she held out for a
principle for so many years, when all the kings roundabout were
hopping on his wagon train!

Of course, there was more to those expeditions now than pique.
There were statesman's objectives. And there was something more
basic even than these. From the start, Nature seemed to instill in
French sovereigns a deep and abiding sense of the design she had
drawn when she had made the earth rock, folded up these hills
creased in the valleys and the riverbeds for this same France
Fenced in by two main mountain lines, Pyrenees and Alps, by
two great seas, and one river—the Rhine—France should be. Such
was the age-old plan and when conquerors like the wise Charles
Philippe Auguste, Louis, and Foch, accepted the pattern, clove to
the design, they usually met with success. When, like Charlemagne
Francis, Napoleon, they overlapped it, tried to stretch it out, they
met with disaster, at least with no success that could be called
enduring.

Clovis was now trying to stretch his lands, not beyond but up
to, these natural limits. He was far from them yet. But in a way
he *was* showing his women; and Genevieve should have been just
a little afraid. For first, in 486, at Soissons, he overthrew con
siderable of a guerrilla revolt under Syagrius, a general of the ol
Roman legions, one of the last of them too, but not nearly s
noble as Aetius. A little while then, Clovis spent in an extensiv
déménagement, a grand moving-day, urging on, from the ol
palace in Tournai to a new one in captured Soissons, a great parad
of wagons piled with benches, spears, high beds, arras, shield
drinking horns, furs, skins, silver pitchers, bronze plates, blac
cooking pots, gold chamber ones, Clotilde's coverlets and robe
and his own throne of good iron. There were many peoples he ha
to defeat to get near those boundaries, even his own wife's famil
At Avignon, over whose bridge the whole world would one da
dance, he defeated her uncle Gundebald, the Burgundian king
who had come over the borders of his beautiful wine country int
Lyonnaise lands and Provence. Hating his wife's family, all h
in-laws, never did Clovis better relish a victory. Near Poitiers,
507 he felled with his sword Alaric (the Second). Not conter
with that he cut off with his own hands the leather-dark head an
held it up so that all his enemies might observe the defeat which, th
silly frozen smile of death seemed to say, was so utter and fina

Meantime, through all these years he had been conducting h
suit of Genevieve and Paris. Some ten years before these oth
battles he had turned his suit into a siege there by the Seine. H
father's, Childeric's, sabre-rattling apparently had had no effe

on Genevieve. He would give her a taste of the real thing—a fillip of war. So up he marched his soldiers by Rhone, Saône and Seine, took the bridgeheads north and south on the river, encamped there and stole all the pork, flour and wine going toward Paris in the valley tumbrils. But the spell still held. He could not keep up the siege. Something about the indomitable old white-haired woman made him—as it had his father when her hair had been iron-grey, his grandfather when it had been bright—just a little ashamed. As a mere matter of form, he sent his heralds in with new proposals, knowing they would be refused. Then he marched his troops away to the Rhine, for like pigs in clover, the Germans were in again.

Now, as do all masterful men sooner or later, great Clovis got into trouble. For unlike the Burgundians, Visigoths and Romans, his time at Tolbiac field the Germans refused to run for him. In fact, they showed signs of winning here and then taking Paris. If they had, it would have gone badly with Genevieve. The Merovingians might be, on occasion, just a little ashamed, the Germans never. For them a woman, even one so courageous, would have held no spell. The place of their big blond helpmeets was by the hut hearth, drawing water from the river, roasting haunches, in bouncing begettings, not on the city walls nor in the seats of the mighty. Clovis might curse Genevieve, but he did not want these big cousins of his Franks to have her or, more particularly, her city. But now his great fists, his mighty sword arm, did not seem to work. And since Kings, like all men, when things go well will laugh at their wives for their suggestions, but when things go wrong will listen to them (and forever afterwards claim the credit) he suddenly decided to try Clotilde's idea and Genevieve's. Up to high Heaven went his once-powerful hands in helpless appeal. If this new fad of his wife's was more than a fad, if it worked, if this new gentle god she and Genevieve fancied would turn the scale, send those hard-pressing Germans racing for the horizon and the Rhine, he would—he would, indeed—give in to Genevieve and, what was harder for a masterful man, give in to Clotilde, his own wife, and be baptized!

Of course, the hairy-armed, boyish Clovis laboured under a misapprehension. It was with the God of the Old Dispensation that men made bargains. The King of the New rejected all earthly triumphs and trades. But Clovis' gesture, like Constantine's exclaiming over his heaps of slain that he saw a cross in the sky, may have been inspired by a little unconscious or—and more probably—conscious showmanship, for, as we noted when we traveled to Nicaea, both were so well-timed. The first came when the empire needed the Church's upsurging strength, the second when the membership of the Church was so rapidly increasing that if it did not already compose a political majority in France it would with the addition of the Frankish army, soon reach it. And certainly there is no law against a king, any more than any other mortal, mounting a bandwagon.

There is also the chance that Clovis was more deeply touched than he liked to show by Clotilde's telling him about that King whose birth in a stable so sharply divided that Old Dispensation from the New. Her simple recital of the old, old play had come years before, in Tournai Palace. And this Frankish king, on he concluding the story with the moving and tragic death on the hill outside Jerusalem, had cried,—"*By God, had I but been there with my Franks!*" Oath or no oath, his boyish heart spoke out on this naïve and forgiveable boast.

There occurred then on Tolbiac Field, as soon as Clovis had lifted on high his hands and made a vow to be baptized, one of those seemingly significant coincidences of history that may have meant everything, again nothing more than that some of Clovis reserves had just come up or the Franks had just gotten their second wind. Anyhow, quite as the blaring notes of Joshua trumpets seemed to acquire a new and mystical power to blow down Jericho's solid walls or as the prophet's arms, held up until the setting of the sun, brought another triumph to Israel, Clovis bargain prayer brought an almost magical might to his sword. As quickly as the ebb of the tide can turn to the full, those German (for the fiftieth time) were racing for the horizon and the Rhine. And whether or not France had ever done anything to deserve this apparent intervention, or the Church had earned it, victory came at the psychological moment for the consolidation of France and the Church by her most picturesque convert, Clovis. As for the event itself, it was so dramatic it did not need the wholecloth story, made up in the ninth century by Hincmar, of a phial of sacred oil sent by Heaven in the beak of a dove for Clovis' iron crowned, sweat-ringed head.

Drops of this mystic ointment are still preserved, they swear in the cathedral of Rheims which the Germans tried to shatter all the more viciously because it and the site had so much to do with their cousins, the Frankish kings. In Rheims there was joy and a great paean of bells (now considered not devils' but angel voices) and of shouts and *Te Deums* in Paris. For in 497 Genevieve threw open the gates. There was in Clovis' heart a great exultation which even his steed must have felt, so blithely did it prick its way over the north bridge, by the Palace and Glaucinus Tower, and under the old Maximus Arch in the Roman Forum by the Seine

And gaily it caracolled under its heavily crowned, maced, and cuirassed king, as he started to dismount to take Genevieve's hand, before the portal of Saint Etienne.

Fourteen years Jacob had worked for his bride. Forty-six, the Merovingian line had waited for their Rachel, Paris. Heartfelt were his thanks as he knelt on the mosaic pavements before the gold-chased altar. And if he and his newly-christened Franks did not know the words of the *Te Deum*, they watched and copied Bishop Remi (good Germain had died) and Genevieve, and to her soprano added a great roar which rang out over the river to the four hills. By rights those hills should have skipped like the Old Dispensation lambs, for the first French or Frankish, King had come to Paris to stay, to make her the capital. At last a recognizable France was on its way.

Once again the King's heavy wains rolled south, this time from Soissons Palace to the Seine. Then, except for expeditions of war and occasional chateau visits in season which do not count, there would be no more voluntary royal moving days for thirteen hundred and ninety-nine years, that is until Louis the Sixteenth and Marie Antoinette should slip out of the Louvre's Saint Honoré gate, headed for the Rhine and a sanctuary among the ancient enemies of France—that foolish, ineptly ordered journey which ended so ingloriously in a village grocery at Varennes.

But there still goes on a slight dispute about Clovis' actual residences. It is known that he set up bed and board, also his throne, on the island shore by the north bridge—known later as the Moneychangers' Bridge—in the old gubernatorial mansion, the Palais de Justice we know today, then in its Gallo-Roman, the fifth century edition. No one, however, is sure about his tenure of Julian's old home, the palace at Cluny across the Seine which, some insist, was not a palace at all. Rather extensive remains there are, it is true, of brick-and-tile course walls with wide gables over deep concrete hollows that once were pools, all picturesquely attached to, and incorporated with, the west wall of the beautiful mediaeval palace that now stands in Cluny Gardens. But some archeologists declare these ruins are not those of any royal residence proper, although Julian was often there, but of a very elaborate set of Roman *thermae* or baths with an intricate system of water pipes, cellar furnaces, hot and cold rooms, reading and writing rooms, bedchambers, and gymnasia.

But it is a question whether Clovis and his warriors would have done any lounging or bathing there at all; they were so busy, so used to fording and swimming rivers surfaced with winter's bright isinglass, and must have been astonished by this sybaritic warmth loved by the over-urbanized Romans.

A little beyond Cluny and higher up (near today's Luxembourg Gardens), Clovis put up a great church with a roof of beautiful tiles, three high doors, stout rubble and surfaced walls in the grand Roman style, and within, high floral-capped pillars mosaics, and bright swinging chain lamps in the Byzantine fashion. Larger than Saint Etienne below, this church of Saints Peter and Paul, or "of the Apostles," as it later was called, stood up against the sky on the city's south hill as Sacré Coeur now does on the north. It was the city's great landmark.

The Franks soon were won to the new church. Their dark northland deities stood up no better now than had the old Olympian gods. It was so with all the gods of these invaders. "In the glance of the Lord," like Sennacherib's hosts and the snow, they melted. Almost at once these fourth and fifth century rovers of all strains became nominally at least orthodox Christians, Arians and so on, according to the custom of the country they conquered. Clovis did not content himself with merely adding to the Church these new external walls. As though it were all a fascinating new game, he delighted as much in presiding at ecclesiastical meetings in appointing priests, as he had before in cracking Visigoth skulls. The Nicaean bishops had agreed that kings might be the strong right arms of the Church, but Clovis entered with such savage earnestness into the rôle that it was well that some of the Church veterans retained their sturdy independence.

The fusion of Frank and Gallo-Roman changed the ritual little. By their retelling of Rhineland myths and Baltic legend the Franks gave new vigour to Celtic imaginativeness; and gradually a little more colour and adorning details were added in the Church of Gaul. The "rite of Rome," which in these centuries was not followed in England or France, was majestic, sonorous austere. As Gaul and Frank met under the mantle of the Church the "French rite" acquired a little more aural and visual richness than the other.

The homage that had been paid to Rhine Lorelei, Celtic tree maiden, Roman wine god, and the heroes of the old bright Gallic Heaven of the West soon was transformed into reverence for the saints and Bible heroes. The peasant who had been robbed not only of Roman bread and security but of its circuses and folklore found a substitute in the appealing new legends and tales of brave and helpful saints, though they had not yet been placed before him in the cathedral panes, only in rude stone and mosaics. But when depicted in the words of the priest, they came alive in the peasant's heart, furnishing a never-ending escape. In the Dark Ages it was to mean more than that. Then all that would make life endurable was the sense of protection and beauty the Church gave. And most folk being but children, it was reassuring for them to have in addition to the great central story of the Hero and King these little side stories of those picturesque and valiant personages, the saints. As the poor knelt in icy forest, draughty hut, cold church, there was warmth in the thought of the shining company ever hovering near who might aid them.

As a rule, whenever migrating invaders settled down, they settled down, too, to the old Roman ways of conducting legal, business, and social life. The Franks, like the rest, preferred to take over and adapt rather than to remould. Their contribution was a fresh vigour rather than any genius for ideas. Even the language, both the pure official Latin of forum and court and the corrupted patois of the street, absorbed Frankish words so slowly that they were very smoothly modified, with the Latin, into the crystallizing mediaeval French. So even in defeat Rome prevailed over the migrating tribes that had conquered her. And above both contestants the Church rose as the ultimate victor. Yet Church and Empire continued, even after the fall, to react on one another. In rite, music, above all, in that organization which was the great legacy of the Empire, the Church showed the imperial influence and thus made dead Rome immortal. Dead architects of Rome still seemed to be designing all the churches that were being built. Latin rang out in all the chants. Roman discipline strengthened the clergy for the struggle of the Dark Ages just ahead.

In spite of the ready acceptance by the Franks of established forms, Clovis unknowingly laid the seed of new orders to come when he arrived with his warriors. In part for political reasons, in part through an easy good nature, he had handed out to bishops he liked large benefices and thus increased the strength of these already powerful princes against the time when they would form the second of the great mediaeval estates and help to keep the balance between nobility and king. He bestowed land grants, with duties, on favorite generals who distributed these to their favorites in turn, and thus made the pattern for the feudal system which Charles Martel would intensively get under way.

And yet, unwittingly again, Clovis planted the seed of another system that would destroy feudalism. High-handed and rough as the Frankish chiefs often were, they had been chosen by oral suffrage. Clovis had but ten thousand men for his infiltration of Gaul, but swiftly they took the lead. Whenever disgruntled burghers or farmers grumbled against the tyranny of the rich, the Franks would get them into open assembly where they aired their grievances in the Frankish way. The oral suffrage was the foreshadowing of universal franchise. The open assembly or town meeting was the forerunner of the Estates General in 1302 when, under Philip the Fair, the people would crowd into the Cathedral to pour their souls out, not in litanies, but in *viva voce* votes on political affairs. These assemblies were first models, too, for the rump convention that, with solemn oath, met on the Versailles tennis court to confirm the most earth-shaking, and consequential of revolutions—after that of Galilee.

As she walked in her hospice ward in the shadow of Saint Etienne or, from the hill to be called for her, looked down on the island city Genevieve was aware of all these political currents, although she could not discern their ultimate goals. A very old lady now, her work almost done, she found the altered physical aspect of the city's life even more disconcerting. Since its peaceful conquest when she had opened the gates to Clovis, Paris had not been the same city to which and to Bishop Germain's welcoming arms she had come when a child. It had not been completely transformed like towns in a boom or gold rush, but changed as all cities are when a different order peacefully and gradually takes over.

There were so many strange faces, costumes, furs, in the streets, a wealth of beards and mustachios. The famous gold hair of the oldtime Gaul and Parisian had long been toned down, his height discounted. But once more tall, blonde women tested wool, examined the dyes of fabrics in the booths, held up looking glasses, tried combs in their long hair. Large-limbed, big-buttocked children struck at and assumed leadership over the native gamins. All around, from marching squads, the markets, the wineshops, palace, the sterns of Seine fishing craft, came phrases which at first seemed uncouth but which before long would become deep imbedded in the softer Latin-Celt patois. And there were gusty meetings at street corners, such as once would have been immediately broken up by centurions, more naïve, guttural answers from rough witnesses to the sleek Latin lawyers of the court, deeper bass and mezzo notes in the chants in Saint Etienne's where restless warriors and the blonde women craned their necks to gaze at the great chain swinging lamps, the huge bronze coronas of candles, the gold-work on the altar or stared covetously at the bishop's chasuble, which had a border so gorgeous it would never, in the old austere days, have been allowed. What worried Genevieve most, however, was that while there still remained a devout and independent clergy making their merciful rounds of cloister, island and suburbs, many of Clovis' too-hastily chosen candidates for clerical orders and the actual holders of benefices he had given out, mingled long after midnight sprawling, drinking, and singing, in the old Roman wineshops below and the Cluny "Baths" on the hill.

These superficial aspects of the new Parisian life did not greatly impress the workmen and serfs when they drove over the bridge and into the gates with their tumbrils filled with grapes, flour, legumes, wine, and building stone. Through the still unglazed windows of farmers' and charcoal-burners' huts, the keen wind howled. The same wolves or their progeny, in famine seasons, nosed at the rattling doors. There was no decrease in taxes that anyone could notice; in fact, they tended to increase with Clovis' largesse of benefices and titles. As had the Italians, when Theodoric's Ostrogoths came in to drive out Odoacer's Pannonians, they had but exchanged one profit-loving set of landlords for another. Those games too, in the amphitheatre down by the river (now on the Rue Navarre) had been run pretty well. They liked them better than all this rowdy horseplay of the Franks.

But for all that, the Franks had come to stay. The old orderly way of life, the official control of all phases of it, had vanished, the pattern of existence was disturbed. The great Roman Peace which had so long kept back the barbarians while the Church grew strong, had flown. New invaders kept coming in. Forever on the warpath were Clovis and his sons, Theuderic (or Thierry), Childebert, Chlodomer, Clotaire. King Clovis was busy every minute not alone in protecting French borders, the churches and abbeys of which he was now guardian, and with all his enemy beheadings, but with private murders on the side, of Salian princelings and Frankish kinglets, his own kith and kin. Still, if he worried the gentle Genevieve, who preferred binding up wounds to inflicting them, she could reflect with a sigh, as she looked down on the city, that his murdered victims would have done no good to France. To be sure, Clovis was a strange, a bloody sort of Christian. That anointing oil, brought in the beak of a dove, may have been sacred, but it and the baptismal water seemed to have run off his great head like water off a duck's back, carrying its virtue with it. The mystic yeast of the Kingdom Invisible had not worked very deep. But since men *would* make wars, it was preferable that strong, hairy "right arms of the Church" should win them.

When Genevieve at last approached the portals of death and lay almost expiring on her pallet, all the people of Paris, it seemed, came to uphold, in a last prayer, those hands which had done so many capable, beneficent, lovely things for them and for all who waited outside her chamber, before her hospital and in the cloisters. At her bedside you can see them still—and it should not be without emotion—in those great mural panels on the walls of the Parisian's Hall of Fame, the Pantheon, built by the spot where she was laid. It was not for herself but for them that those last petitions went up in a broken whisper. And when her lips trembled in the last of the so-often repeated Latin phrases, then were still, all the population of Paris and the Seine Valley, by the Loire, in the south country too, mourned her with sincerity and many tears. Daughter of Heaven, mother of France, as well as patron of Paris, they had lost. And on the third day, all the Parisians except those in her hospital who were unable to be moved, climbed or were carried up the hill which would henceforth be known as hers—La Montagne Sainte-Geneviève. When the bishop covered the aged features, so pure and lovely and young again in death, made the commitment and sifted the symbolic dust, there were few that watched who had not either felt the actual touch of her healing fingers or whose families had not been so blessed. And many had gone forth, with her benediction, to save Paris—forever, as they thought—not knowing that, like liberty and all things worthwhile, over and over it must be saved, so frequently repurchased with blood.

She was buried in Clovis' great Church of Saint Peter and Saint Paul, or "Of the Apostles," which, like the hill on which it was built, was rechristened in her name. There too, the great king was laid—some say, a year before her; others, so great is the confusion in the records, a year afterwards—both to be followed by Genevieve's good ally, his own good wife, Queen Clotilde. Mighty had been his achievements in consolidating and protecting the Church and in stretching France almost up to her natural limits of Rhine, Alps, Pyrenees, and the two seas, which his fighting sons would soon reach. But great as was his work, it was so much the fruit of theirs, that it was fitting that these two women should in death be close together and also near him. An abbey-annex, added to the old Apostles', now Sainte Genevieve's, church, carried her name, with her dust, on through the middle ages into modern times. In the eighteenth century the noble Pantheon, also at first christened for her, joined the cluster of buildings on the hilltop that bore her name or guarded her remains. The last was Francis the First's Saint Etienne du Mont, or Saint Stephen's on the Hill, behind the Pantheon and across the street from the old abbey. Of that abbey where so long she was housed, one old tower, rebuilt in Gothic style after a Norman raid, remains to look down on Saint Stephen's from the Rue Clovis; and the refectory still stands on the Rue Clotilde.

When the French Revolution broke out, the mobs forced their way into the venerable pile, pried up her bones from under her rock tomb and carried them across the river to the criminals' place of execution by the old Hôtel de Ville, on the Place de Grève, and started to burn them. A pious soul, however, had followed the mad cortège and, when it danced on to some other desecration, put the fire out, scooped up some handfuls of dust, and hid them. When the Reign of Terror was over, he took these poor remains to Saint Etienne's where once more back on her hill she was again laid to rest in a new gold shrine set on a piece of rock taken from her old abbey tomb. Not an hour, not a minute of any day of the year passes without some child of Paris, old or young, kneeling there. And each year, on the night of the third of January, they take her out from the chapel by the side of the exquisitely-carved rood screen of Saint Etienne's, to circle aisles and nave on the shoulders of Sixth Arrondissement mechanics, postmen, nobles and Sorbonne professors, while fine ladies of wealth, concierges, midinettes, and poor *femmes de chambres* and charwomen chant out their humble homage.

So too, whenever danger comes for the hundred and first time down on Paris from the Rhineland, or from any other quarter, in her gold shrine on the shoulders of some of the sons of Paris she circles the streets of the city she loved and which she still seems to guard with a spirit that springs alive out of the motionless dust. They did not, for some reason, take her out in 1940. Perhaps that was the trouble—or the failure to do so was symbolic of the trouble. But there will be other years!

XV

Benedict recruits the Earth's Greatest Army for the Church. . . .
The Contemplative Life and Active Service in the Religious
Orders. . . . A Grand Review of them; Hermits, Cenobites, Men-
dicants, Militants, and Missioners. . . . This Great Leader teaches
the Dignity of Labour and shows how Abbeys may become Self-
Sustaining Cities. . . . He lights the Candles for the Dark Ages
on Mount Cassino.

544 A.D.

AN OLD, OLD MAN WAS DEAD. THE MOONLIGHT COMING
through the slitted windows of the fortlike abbey on the
mountain-top gave a cameo clarity to face and hands.
Sharply-cut were the features, both by the moon and one who,
if the Creator is a potter, is a sculptor—Death. The finishing touch
he gives is very evident to the eye in twenty-four hours. The
hands were folded in a quiet that is much more than the cessation
of activity that comes in life. It was the cessation of life itself. If
absolute black is the complete absence of all light, so this utter
quiet was the final vanishing, from hands that had been so very
active, of all activity, even of the potentiality of it.

On the breast was a crucifix. Sometimes it gleamed a stationary
cold silver. Then it was in accord with the stillness of the cell.
Sometimes the moon refracted light-splinters of its silver into the
eyes of monks, four praying in the corners of the room, four at
the corners of the pall marked by the four tall candles. Then it
was the only discordant thing in the austerity of a cell whose white
walls the moonlight rendered even more sepulchral. That restless,
roving gleam of the crucifix seemed to symbolize the activity
there had been in the form that now was the very negation of
activity. Picked out by the moonlight on its silver, that unquiet
cross, in the centre of the breast, in the centre of the room, seemed
by its very form to outline the central plan, the self-sacrificing
design of the life that had been. Over and over its sparkle tele-
graphed, reiterated the motif and theme of that life that had been
so super-humanly active and now was so supernaturally still.

The candles were not of the tallow variety used since early

214

Roman days for household tasks. For the melancholy, distinguished purpose of this night they had set up tapers of the costlier
wax taken from the abbey hives. Their flames were much more
golden than the moon; and they added a little warmth to the
room, a little naturalness perhaps, to what was so unnaturally
lying there. Almost companionable they seemed, with their arrowheads of light pointing ever up to where, in the conviction of the
praying monks, in the soul geography of the times, was their
leader's new home, the capital of the invisible empire, Augustine's shining City of God. They could not conceive of it, nor
could anybody then conceive of it, as being anywhere but "up,"
located as ceiling is over apse, bells over roof, spire over bells, sky
over spire, directly over and above their tonsured heads. It was
impossible to think of chalcedon towers, jasper ramparts, the great
throne itself, inverted, or robed angels floating upside down. Such
was the almost universal orientation to the Unknown.

Sometimes those little arrowheads of flame trembled as though
the soul they lighted on its final journey might have found trouble somewhere along the dark way, an obscure valley perhaps, or a
deep, tempestuous river, or experienced the old mortal trepidation
of even the doughtiest souls during the great transfer. But the
wind was coming now through cell-windows narrowly slitted as
though for arrows the flames resembled. And it blew the more
because the fortress-like abbey had been set, to be safe, on the top
of a hill. It was quite a rocky hill in places, rising above green
plains and with aged olives near its base, twisted as though they
had once been engaged in struggle with the devils with which the
still form on the bier had wrestled, and had been stopped short
and forever in their agonized wrestlers' pose. Near the cell-windows outside were cedars, pointed as the candle flames, but very
dark—like sentinels too, or watchers for the dead, with pointed
cowls.

The mountain was in Italy. Mount Cassino it was called; and its
name, because of the dead man, was to become famous throughout
the world, though the last thing the still form between the tall
tapers and the corded figures uttering *misereres*, had ever thought
of was fame.

Benedict, from the Latin *benedictus*, or "blessed"—very properly for once—had been his name in life; Saint Benedict it would
immortally be in death. In France, though, with that lazy French
habit of slurring which later Academy grammarians would make
formal and elegant for all the world to study—they would turn it
to Benoît—Saint Benoît for many a church like his last resting-
place, the great abbey named for him on the Loire and the one on
Sainte Geneviève's Hill where Francois Villon got his man. These

namesake churches were legion, and no wonder. For Benoît, or Benedict, was more than scholar and man of holy deeds. He was a great organizing genius, recruiter of the greatest army ever gathered together, commander-in-chief emeritus of all the monks ever tonsured, corded, burned or beatified in this world.

It was not that the monastic idea had been actually born but that it had most strongly taken root under that fine dome of a head lying so emaciated there, covered, it seemed, only with the thinnest-shaved parchment for skin. Nor were the Greeks—whose word *monos*, for "alone," had given the name to the religious fortress in which he lay—the inventors. It had been an age-old notion of man motivating men of all times and races, that he could free himself from the toils of the flesh, sometimes considered as Sin, again merely as hobbles of the intellect or spirit, by giving up wine for water, a couch for a stone, a kiss for the scourge, or at least the friendly company of men for walled-in solitude. In short, not just to take the thorns of life with its roses, but to toss away the roses and embrace the thorns. Through the vision that had been the dead man's, that age-old root of an idea would blossom one day into abbeys, vineyards, refectories, hospitals, illuminated manuscripts, melodious chants, Cluniac spires, and love and care for little lost children, and lost souls.

But before that final harvest it would bear, as it had borne, some pretty sterile and wizened fruit. In the name of asceticism, men of both the Old and the New Dispensations had done some unaccountable things. The Manichee self-disciplined himself out of meat because he thought a human soul lodged in the slain animal's hide. Other cults substituted fish since the procreation of fish was such a detached and platonic process, while meat, sprung from a mating as carnal as that of mammals, might prove too powerful an aphrodisiac for the eater. Egyptian kings turned down the glass when informed by their priests that grapes grew out of the rotting corpses of Lucifers of the Nile who had rebelled against the Sun-god and had been tossed down out of the sky. To quaff of wine was therefore to drink inciting and insurrectionary blood. Emigré Jews of certain sects abjured it in their belief that its crimson bubbles were caused by the breathing of devils mixed up in it. And even the ancestors of the civilized Greeks, followers of Pythagoras, too, banned risen bread because of the devilish things they, with their own eyes, saw yeast work in it.

Very early the sons of men had found that new heights were to be gained by fasting. That was why they required of their prophets abstinence in some form, and often took mere emaciation for a truly holy look. By this denial of the body, dominion over it was won by the soul or will. To cast that body down was very often to soar with the spirit, at least to feel a body-free, mental exhilaration and sense of adventure. Through senses subdued or sublimated? No one ever quite knew. But thus the Buddhist acquired his sought-after "merit," arrived in a great calm. So Zoroaster, Confucius, Israelite prophet, many a seer, caught hitherto unheard music, discerned the faint far coastline of continents undreamed of before.

When the sons of men found themselves over in a new era, that of the New Dispensation, they did not all at once slough off all the old habits of mind. Some of them continued to withdraw from life for the same old reasons. But there was now a new and powerful and, for many, an irresistible motivation. The pagans would honour their own philosophers, but would not leave the Christian alone to his thoughts and that new dynamic form of thought, the Christian prayer. Great persecutions, like the one of Decius, forced many a contemplative Christian, trying to follow his reading of Christ's command to desert all and follow Him, to flee to the desert, the lonely places where he thought He might be found. And there the far-seeing eyes of Rome would not seek him out or her long arm bother to drag him back to lions or stake.

But it was not fear alone that drove these early solitaries away from the haunts of men. Many were utterly courageous. Even when Rome grew careless of the new philosophy of gentleness and love that was to prove so devastating to her, men were impelled to seek the Perfect Life which Christ had preached and which, they feared, could be attained only in solitude. They not only had an all-absorbing desire to come nearer to God, but they distrusted their ability to come to that nearness in the midst of the great Vanity Fair that is this world whose glittering enticements proved too strong when united with the snares within their own bodies.

It is true that Christ, except for the Forty Days of His own spirit's battle and conquest and for occasional hours on the heights for refreshment of body and soul, had not sought this Perfect Life in solitude. He had not only attained it in the haunts of men: He was the Perfect Life. And He did not counsel His Twelve to any continuous withdrawal from life. Being fishers of men they had to be where men were. But He realized, as did Paul and the Church later, that only the few have the genius for the lofty leadership which involves complete self-surrender to God and service for others. Some of the early solitaries used solitude, as certain of the religious orders did so widely later, as a preparation for that service to others. And from the very first there were the supremely great who attained the great calm, that perfect peace that passes understanding, in the tumult of men to whom they were bearing Christ's message.

But there were sincere and helpful souls who did not have this destiny. All they felt they could do in an age when men were beset, as never before or since, with infinite perils to both body and soul, and when this beautiful philosophy was such a new thing, was to extricate themselves. Christ had pointed out so often that man must give up the things of this earth for those of Heaven. And how could imperfect man keep his mind on those things when those of Caesar, his chariots, arenas, circuses, banquets, brothels, the cries, too, of his tortured brothers, kept ringing in his ears. All he saw ahead was to escape, not for his body's but his soul's sake, which in those days was considerable of a task.

Christ had often remarked too, how difficult it is for a rich man to enter His kingdom. And many of these solitaries were men of privilege and wealth who followed what they considered was His intent. They sought the perfect life, but first they sold all they had for the poor and gave up the world except such shards of it as are to be found in the desert or a bare foot or two of it in a mountain cell. And there, as they advanced from out of their more selfish estate, men were to pray for more than their own souls. They would find that prayer has a power to reach out very far, that men can use their prayers even for those who do not know how to pray. And all the socially-minded who mistrust this withdrawal from life for any purpose, and consider the work of the contemplative orders as inferior to their own civic programmes might reflect on these things: Self-castigation, which may be sterile, is but a small part of the monastic story. The asceticism which they also deplore goes far beyond any asceticism. There is a miraculous dynamism in mysticism, a definite power in prayer, as true to higher laws as radioactivity is to those of physics. As Christ saw, the worthy Marthas do not complete the round of life. There is room for the Marys and their quiet, their inner illumination.

Saint Anthony, the idol of Benedict's youth, was the great monastic founder. Born in Coma, Egypt, in 251, about the time Saint Denis was martyred up on Montmartre, he lived until—no, it is not a typographical error—356! He was not, as the satirists would have it, merely an oversexed and overconscienced man, afraid of the world, the Devil, the flesh, and particularly the feminine phase of it. Indeed, a fact about him more astonishing than that age of a hundred and five years which speaks so well for the austere life, is his continuing, though he lived apart from men for twenty years, not only pure, but the bravest and most cheerful of men. He was a greater optimist, with his bamboo shoots and spring water, than the citizens of the imperial cities with their circuses and banquets and brothels.

His first retreat was in a deserted fortress by the Nile. When too many came out to see him at his devotions, he sought the sandy hummocks by the Red Sea. Always he kept away from the main caravan routes and the strait and ancient canal which, linked, made a short cut to the Orient ages before de Lesseps. So strong was his desire for seclusion that he hated to see even the man-made masts of the ships being oared through the first Suez Canal.

Still, like Paul, he felt the goads. And people would not let him alone. Once more they came out to the desert to see, not a reed, but a holy man. He was distressed. Then it occurred to him that the lone hermit root might bear rich fruit. He took the sincere among the visitors to a mountain by the Nile where they built huts to pursue the perfect life together. Here, high up, at Pispir, was the first Christian monastery. It was primitive and self-sustaining in the meagerest way. They performed a few domestic tasks and did a little tilling to keep diminishing body and ever-expanding soul together. They formed a loose band of what were semi-eremitical monks—it is no misnomer, for though they met sometimes at wells, at a planting, or for a psalm on Sundays, they lived out of earshot of one another. Though other chapters were formed with Anthony as patron, no solid ties bound them to the mother house.

Now there would always be two main classes of monks. The first was the eremitical or the solitary. There were not, after the first centuries, many simon-pure hermits, and since they have vanished altogether. So the first group really comprises the semi-eremitical, like Anthony's men, who most of the time did their little work and extensive praying alone. The second division was made up of the cenobites or communal monks who lived in family-like settlements, eating together, often sleeping under a common dormitory roof, going to mass together and holding chapter meetings, though they spent many hours in prayer and study and work apart. Two corollary, though not official distinctions might also be made. One would be based on asceticism, in some orders severe, in others moderate. One would be based on activities. For some orders incline almost wholly to the contemplative life with a minimum of work, while others pursue a variety of interests that not only help their abbeys but the outside world. But through the centuries the two—the eremitical, or solitary, and the cenobite, or communal, monks—were the main divisions.

Even before the great centenarian pioneer died, two very clear-headed saints tried to give body to the purely contemplative life by mingling with it more work than the few tasks absolutely essential to life which Anthony had required of his monks, also more organization. Pachomius, by the upper reaches of the Nile, established a slightly more formal chapter of his own, then eight more stretching as far south as Abyssinia. Now not only did the knee bend in prayer for long hours in the cell, but the back too for long sessions over plough, hoe, kitchen pot. Pachomius called yearly conclaves, appointed a superior-general, and made of his men not only devoted and sincere praying and studying monks but excellent farmers.

Saint Basil (329-379), in his convents by the Black Sea and in the Balkans, further and very efficiently developed monastic labour. He came from as religious a family as ever was in this world, almost all of his near-kinsmen serving in some ecclesiastical capacity, and one brother, Gregory, and a sister, Macrina, becoming famous saints. One would have thought Basil would have increased the emphasis on the contemplative side. He did carefully nurture this. But he was a man in whom the ideal and the practical were beautifully combined. His conversations were stimulating, his sermons full of fire, his companionship warm and sweet. And he had a head for budgets and system. Though Pachomius had increased the percentage of work that was so slight in the Antonian huts, the monks of Pachomius, as long as they filled their spiritual and industrial quotas, could pray and dig, eat and sleep, almost when they pleased. Basil introduced a fixed, though not too severe, schedule. There were abbots and ranked officials, with clearly-defined duties. Constantly he preached that both prayer and work were indispensable in the monastic round. Physical labour, he pointed out, was not only productive of the necessities, but it was a fine balance against too long contemplation, a guard against hallucinations to which the fasting recluse was prone, and an absorber of those energies which in too static a life might expend themselves sterilely in lustful thoughts and dreams.

And Basil the Great tried to take the religious life further out of the morbid, not only for his monks but all churchgoers, by exhorting the artists of every parish to illustrate the churches with their plastic parables made with pigment, gold leaf and mosaic. He was the pioneer of this policy. By it, he not only brought more beauty into the world and added colour and holy romance to the churches, the only retreats the poor knew, but he enabled those who could not read, to read vivid little biographies of their King and His Apostles and moving incidents from their lives, on the walls. Saint Augustine, too, had written a book about labour for monks; and his simple rule, followed in his convent at Hippo, was to be adopted by a tremendous number of chapters of religious orders, but not so much by monks as by friars, canons and clerks and not until on in the middle ages. It was Anthony, Pachomius Basil the Great, whose kind smile and keen brain did so much to

bring wholesomeness and sweetness into the monastic life, that
paved the way for the great leader of the monks, Benedict, who
lay, this night of 544, in the cell where the chant went up in the
moonlight:

"Kyrie, eleison,	"Lord, have mercy,
Christe, eleison,	Christ, have mercy,
Miserere nobis!"	Have pity on us."

It was a great and picturesque parade of religious orders of all
sorts which the four founders and Augustine started down the
ages—all the Benedictines, black Dominicans, Bernadines, Augus-
tinians, White Carmelites, Cluniacs, Cistercians, Jacobins, Jesuits,
Capuchins with pointed hoods, brown Franciscans, Carthusians,
Celestins, Grey Friars Minor of Saint Francis, Passionists, Brothers
of the Trinity, Brothers of the Common Life, Barefoot Friars,
Saint Gilbertians, Camaldolese, red cross Templars, Knights Hospitallers, Saint Charles Oblates, Knights of Saint John, Olivetans,
Silvestrins, Regular Canons, English Clerks Regular, corded Cor-
deliers, Barnabites, red Austin Friars, Irish Columbites, Men of
Fontrevault, Grandmontines, silent Trappists, Friars Crutched and
Crossed, Little Leaves, and whole regiments of others, to say nothing of the sister orders of nuns. Not all in that long procession
were monks. Many were friars, clerks, canons, who came on in the
Middle Ages. Canons and clerks were usually cenobites, dwelling
communally. In more modern times friars did too, but for centuries the friar was a solitary—not knowing a home, not even a
cell, and working alone though hardly eremitical he was so much
out in the world. But the main distinction between monks and
the friars, canons, clerks, was in aim. Friars, canons and clerks
devoted time to contemplation and prayer, but the prayer was
only a support for their main objective. This was always some
external practical service in the world—ministering to the poor,
for the friars, in general; preaching for the black Dominican
friars; clerical tasks in the parish churches for the clerks; music
for the canons. And these things must be kept clearly in mind
before we follow the path that led to the moonlit cell of the
requiem on the historic heights of Mount Cassino where the dead
leader lay: Rules, habits, secondary, though important activities
might vary, but the monk's chief purpose was always the same.
It was never asceticism or chastity. These were but helps. And that
purpose had sprung out of a striking and beautiful statement of
the King: "Greater love hath no man than this, that he lay down
his life for his friend." Their greatest friend was their King, who
had laid down His life for them. They believed that in forsaking
the world they were, in turn, giving up their lives for Him.

And their contemplative life meant more than any idle dreaming of higher things. It was communication, growing ever more frequent and clear, with the Divine, through the channels of prayer and intense study of His words and those of the great saints and scholars—an existence rapt, all absorbed, and self-surrendered. How completely may be realized from the quaint words of the old monk who sold his Bible: "I have sold the very book that bade me sell all." And what sainthood any of these strivers attained added merit to and enriched the Church, the whole body of believers in the world, through the Heavenly fellowship called "the Communion of Saints," whose mystic power is recognized in so many creeds.

And yet, for all their withdrawal from the world, the monks did great things out in it. Some were elected to the papacy because of their qualities of leadership. Many were celebrated for achievements along intellectual and artistic lines, and even in statesmanship—the Jesuits, for example, as scholars, Cluniacs as splendid architects, a Cistercian as the trumpet of a great crusade. There was not a monastery whose monks did not entertain strangers at their gates, visit the sick, bury the dead, clothe the naked, relieve the poor and afflicted; but the larger external services were byproducts. Although an order might become noted for extensive missionary work, theology, authorship, building, horticulture, medicine, teaching, illumination, all the monks within its walls or away from them on errands spent long hours too on that inner plane, supposedly inactive, but whose activities are so powerful and intense.

None brought greater honour and truer riches and health to the system than Benedict, born in Nursia about 480. Until the night before his death he had been at the very height of the cloistered world here in the monastic capital on Mount Cassino. But the ladder the monk, every religious, must climb has many rungs. And it would have surprised the younger monks praying in the chapel for the repose of his soul had they been told that Benedict had said it was at a very low rung that he had started. The older monks intoning alongside their dead leader who looked, in the mingled moon and candle light, the picture of white holiness, knew what that rung had been, also that it had not been as low as Benedict had pictured it. He was given in his humility to abasing himself, he of the highest degree in the only world that counted with them, bringing himself down, as the Scripture says, to be with the lowest.

Still, it had been a rung of fear if not of devils at least for his own soul; and that is way below the rung of perfect love which, James the Greater tells us, surmounts all fear. He had in his youth been afraid of both his body's death and his soul's. For years now he had prayed more for others than for himself. But then, back by Nero's old deserted palace, he had trembled, even after he had tried Christ's own solution. Like the gifted Ambrose who wrote the great hymns, Anthony whom Benedict idolized, Gregory the Great who would idolize Benedict, in turn, Saint Francis who would come to study in Benedict's first convent hundreds of years later, he had given all he had to the poor.

In addition to the sense of unworth every religious man must feel profoundly at times, he had other despairs. He loved a girl whose name has been lost to us, though that of his sister, Scholastica, whom he loved too, has been preserved. Her refusal wounded him deeply but saved a very great saint for the Church and the world. Like Augustine he was troubled by the dissipations of his fellow students in the private school and college he attended. But where Augustine had been attracted and had to wrestle hard against the flesh for many years before he became a saint, Benedict's sensitive, almost virginal soul had been repelled. After giving away his wealth, he, through the old way of withdrawal from life, tried to find the door to that perfect life. In his first retreat at Abruzzi he was left quite alone to his devotions and studies. His second choice, though the place later became famous because of his connection with it, was at first unfortunate. At Subiaco, a little way out from Rome, was an artificial lake with man-made waterfalls around Nero's old palace that had once been the voluptuous epitome of every thing a hermitage is supposed not to be. Since it was deserted, he took for his first hut or cell this many-chambered ruin. Here at Subiaco, as anchorite, he took the first step, scaled the first rung on the ladder and began to work his way up through all ranks, up all rungs, until he stood at the very top of both monastic officialdom and that ladder, and had stayed thereon until—as the veterans in the funeral cell explained to the awed acolytes—Death, the night before, had lifted him from that ladder over the Heavenly ramparts.

The danger at Subiaco came just as he felt he was making some progress in the holy way, and from another convent. It had been started some two hundred years before by a very great man, Athanasius, the floor leader at Nicaea, and the framer of a great credo, after the Nicaean, and a noted debater on the theory of the Atonement. He was a very stern but upright man; but the monks here, two hundred years after him, did him no credit; in fact, they were almost renegades.

Benedict was not for a time aware that these unhealthy neighbours were so near. The only one he saw regularly was a friend, Romanus, who like the modern camp attendants who bring supplies to the lonely sheep-herders on the Mexican and American ranges, visited Benedict at intervals with food and writing materials he longed for quite as much. Except for Romanus, the cultivated youthful recluse, a penitent who had far less to repent of than the average man, dwelt far apart from all mortal sinners, feverishly seeking the way. Too feverishly, perhaps. The old Antonian recipe of time, prayer, solitude, did not work. There were none of the liberal convents of Basil or Pachomius at hand where a highly-strung young man might find necessary relief from too long contemplation in varied outdoor work, the library or the arts. The ruins of the old pagan palace, which once had resounded to banquet mirth and scream of terror, now echoed with a troubled young man's despairing petitions.

This particular period, however, was soon over. Men had gone out to hear John the Baptist by the Jordan, to watch Anthony at his Red Sea devotions. To this day they delight in looking curiously at people wrestling with the Invisible. And now they came out to Nero's lake to admire young Benedict. But Anthony's audience had been submissive. Benedict's now was suspicious and boded no good. It was the neighbouring monks who, from the reeds and lilies at the lake-edge, watched him at his prayers or studies in the ruins, among the myrtle blooms clambering blue over the stones and the little lizards all green and gold that sometimes crept near his worn sandal soles, so still he was at certain hours when sunk in his reflections, again scurried in all directions into the palace crannies when he grew anguished or vehement.

The monks liked this display of penitence. The appeal for them did not lie in its genuineness and unself-consciousness. Not being sanctified themselves, they coveted for their own convent this young man whom they took for a talented performer. They held a council among the reeds and the lilies and then approached him and asked him to come to their convent, not as guest, but its abbot.

Their hasty step—as the older Benedictines reported to the younger at Mount Cassino this night of death—was soon repented by the unworthy monks. They were a savage and bigoted lot. They did not like Benedict's firm but sympathetic rule, nor he their hypocrisy. They tried to poison him.

Sick at heart, Benedict returned to Subiaco and Nero's Lake. But so great already had grown his renown for gifts and piety that he was tormented as Anthony had been by an almost daily lay gallery. And like his idol of the Nile, he selected the most promising, established a chapter on Subiaco, and engaged the help of all who admired him in building his first monastery.

He had very early matured and gained an unusual poise and

balance; he had surveyed the field and did not repeat the mistakes
of the great Anthony or any of his predecessors. Though he had
idolized Anthony, Benedict inclined to the communal ways of
Pachomius and even more to the enlightened and liberal system of
the great Basil. But on this too he made a great advance.

Experience had taught him also that the life of the actual hermit
could only be for the very few. And those few must be seasoned
veterans in the hard way before they attempted it. For the majority, the communal life was best. He was certain that idleness
was ruin even for most of the very spiritual, even if their intense
devotions kept them busy enough. His was not the old proverb
that cleanliness is next to godliness. He would have substituted
work. *Ecca labora!* "Go and work!" over and over the brethren
heard him say. And prodigious labour they gave to their leader and
the Lord when they built on Subiaco a holy house where had
once been the infamous one of Nero. It was one of the services
which are sometimes overlooked in enumerating those the monks
have rendered civilization. Here was a ruined and deserted place,
and elsewhere they have chosen sites far worse, which other men
would not have looked at twice, often seemingly uninhabitable,
and where only so intrepid and farsighted an institution would
have dared to locate its headquarters. In such unpromising places,
these cowled and gowned soldiers of Christ and civilization have
often worked through years, draining swamps, felling trees, pulling stumps, filling in rutted roads, quarrying, cutting out ladders
in the cliff, and often have made the wilderness around to blossom
like the rose. They made for the sons of men more strongholds,
refuges, centres of culture, places of beauty in their times, considering the populations of their day and the means at their disposal, than ever did the dukes and sun-kings and the financial
barons of later ages. Not one of their lofty skyscrapers begins
to rival the wonder the monks put up on Mont Saint Michel, with
the sky-gardens on plots above the sea cut out of the lofty rock.

During his life Benedict built fourteen houses, including the
Subiaco mother house and his monastic capitol on historic Mount
Cassino, by the celebrated highway that connected with all parts
of the peninsula and with Rome. None of these were primarily
intended as training schools for religious leaders although, as has
been noted, by accident or as by-products they bred some of the
very greatest. Benedict had longed to help men, laymen, as he
himself had been, troubled as he had been, "to put off the old man
and put on the new." His idea was to build retreats where average
men of sincere desire for better things could have the chance,
away from the world's turmoil, to study and apply the injunctions of the Gospels and of the Christian Fathers, and to attain

more nearly to the perfect life. His first broadcast invitation breathes the warmth of his intention:

"My words are addressed to all those, wherever they are, who renouncing their own wills, put on the shining armour of obedience to fight for Our Lord Jesus Christ."

Bossuet, the eloquent preacher, who like the old prophet Nathan thundering at King David, was bold in denouncing the sins of the Sun King, and whom you will find beautifully memorialized in the Fountain of the Four Bishops in front of Saint Sulpice, Paris, emphasized this objective of Saint Benedict, eleven hundred years later, when he wrote of his inspired programme:

"Benedict's Rule" (his schedule of regulations) "is in itself a digest of the Gospels and the teachings of the Fathers." Certainly no book of ordinances compiled on this earth ever won so high a tribute.

Moderation, proportion, balance, characterized it and indeed everything Benedict did. And these qualities are not always found in the religious life or even in all its celebrated followers. As the monks on the wind and moonlight-swept heights of Mount Cassino—talking affectionately in intervals between the offices for the dead of things they remembered about their leader—sadly observed, he had made that Rule with such consideration for them. To begin with, though the older ones said it was not the most important thing, he had made only one interdict in their diet, that against the eating of flesh meat. This was to be reserved for the sick, to replenish their strength. But they always had all the fruit, vegetables, fish, eggs, game, with which the improved and well-managed lands of all their abbeys rewarded their scheduled labour. And if he had asked that they do not eat until early afternoon, why, that but made them the more clear-headed. And each had one pound of bread daily, a good portion, and two cooked dishes at each meal. They could have, too, for the stomach's sake, as Saint Paul had said, a little wine; but he hadn't particularly encouraged it.

Sleeping on the bare cell flooring, with a stone for a pillow, might be a reasonable practise for some, he said, but he wanted the bodies of his men healthy for continued service. He issued to each a mattress, coverlec and blanket. They were not to possess anything beyond the essential, but holiness was not to be attained by looking unkempt and bedraggled. Their garments must be warm, clean, and whole. And he did not see the point of having them up for prolonged hours after midnight through the winter, reading and kneeling on the rheumatism-radiating stones. They were to be faithful in religious observance and discipline, but the more severe tasks and hard hours were allotted to them by turns.

So each brother averaged eight and a half to nine hours sleep. He was insistent on that.

On weekdays his religious duties took up only four hours, on Sunday, the important professional day, but seven. The secular activities of farming, housekeeping, industry, teaching and the care of the sick occupied another six. Four were devoted to study and reading—of such books as Jerome's translation of the Bible (The Vulgate); Tertullian's and Justin Martyr's accounts of the eucharist and the martyr heroes; Cyril's letters describing the finding of the Cross; Saint Ignatius and all the early fathers; and, by the better educated, Boethius' *Consolations of Philosophy*; Theodoret's inquiries into the substance of Christ; the object lessons in the ascent of the ladder of self-discipline by that magnificent climber, Augustine; and the organ prose of his *City of God*—and to all the phases of the contemplative life for which the monastery was primarily created.

Altogether it was a happy, wholesome round of toil and interesting craftsmanship, much of it in the open air, of companionship with their brethren, and through the inscribed word, with the great fathers of the past, of care for the unfortunate and devotion in choir, confessional, stalls and at the altar, and refreshing sleep to knit up the not unduly "raveled sleeve of care."

That is, at first. Later they would undertake their hazardous missionary journeys and other ventures in the outside world.

If he prescribed rules for the monks, there were some for the abbots:

"Never must those of superior position drive too hard their brethren or keep them so continuously at work that they sink into melancholy or abuse them so that they have cause for murmuring, sullenness or any dissatisfaction whatsoever."

"Let him who leads study to be loved rather than to be feared."

"Let him hate the sin, but love the erring brother."

"He should temper all things so that the strong have something to strive after, the weak nothing to fear."

Some of these injunctions were aimed at himself:

"If I cause my flock, through over zeal, to be over driven, they will all perish in a season."

And it was his constant prayer to "serve my flock in the spirit of Christ rather than to rule over them."

There was one of his admonitions to his abbots that the older monks loved to dwell on, so clearly it showed his nobility of spirit. And as one quoted it in the quiet of the night which was so still now that the arrow shafts of the candle flames stood up straight as though pointing the direction in which the true Benedict had gone, it seemed as though it might be a rule that would serve well not only the innumerable Benedictine houses, but all houses and institutions and organizations of any sort in the world:

"Let none that has authority be violent or anxious or too exacting or obstinate or prone to suspicion or else he never will be at rest."

This Benedict had unremittingly followed. He should have rested well, all his nights with them, on earth, the oldest one said.

He and all there crossed themselves, murmuring with soft voices:

"May his soul and the souls of all the faithful departed rest in peace."

There was not a single soul in the cell, in the dormitory, at watch in the chapel, who was not grateful for this considerate treatment. If Benedict had ever been missing, all had known where to find him—in the cell of some brother weaker in spirit or slower in mind than the rest. For long periods he would abandon his important work as leader to help another grope through the mental or spiritual fog to the light. He was always ready to get up at any hour of the night to hold the lantern for the wanderer in the dark.

And, the wiser there remarked, this noble spirit was the reason why so many statesmen, patricians, generals, had sent their sons to Benedict, not often perhaps to prepare them for the perfect life, but for the broadest, the most liberal and humane education then obtainable on earth.

About austerities he was particularly cautious. Within bounds, he told his monks, they might be salutary. They could free the soul for contemplation. Perhaps through striking self-denial, early Christians had turned the dimmed eyes of others Heavenward. But he mistrusted the extremes of the East. There, striving to outdo each other, they had made of piety a game, of holiness a Roman tug-of-war. They even spilled their own blood on the sands. He had already saved the system in the West when wild dreamers and fanatics might have wrecked it. He did not know it, but his convents far and wide were to save the West again in the early Middle Ages when, in a pendulum swing, not only would many orders return to Antonian recluse ideas but many others would introduce into the West the cruel and bloody excesses in self-mortification. It would be the beautiful Benedictine balance of the three activities, the three planes or chambers for the conventual life—the outer one of the hands, the middle one of the mentality, the inner, of the spirit—that would right the whole system.

Christ, he told them, had exemplified the justification for withdrawal and fasting. It was freeing the soul or preparation. He prepared Himself for His later great trials, by the shore, on the mountain tops, in the desert, through the forty days, for his first temptation. It was impossible with His purity, of course, but if one could imagine such a catastrophe and He had reached out to take the glittering cities on the horizon, not for themselves but for the earthly power they represented, so that He might sooner free the oppressed for whom His tender heart ever bled, instead of waiting for the truer and longer way, that would have been to beg the whole question which He had come to answer. And there would have been no Cross, no Resurrection, no coming to Him for the salvation, the rest He, in one of His most beautiful phrases, had promised the heavy-laden. It was for such high purposes that He went apart from men.

Another distinction between Benedict and other contemporary and many later religious leaders was his insistence on sanity even in selflessness. He had given all he had to the poor, but he doubted if it were a good practise, lovely as it might seem, for his Benedictines to go around every day giving away their mantles. He wanted independence in all his houses, so he did not want his monks to become beggars for alms even to give away, like the later friars of Francis. His houses, he said, should be in a position not of begging alms even to give to others, but of having alms on hand to dispense to all who came. Francis and Benedict both were great spirits; they worked in different ways, that was all. The world would have been poorer without the blithe wanderers of Francis with poverty-stricken bodies and their singing souls, who preferred sleeping in a hedgerow to rest in a cloister, who owned no allegiance to chapter or mother house, as did the Benedictines, only to a word and an ideal and God. And the world would have been poorer without the balanced, calmly reflective life of the Benedictines, their great deeds and books that were born of that deep reflection.

Benedict, had he been alive to know Francis for what he was, would have embraced him as his dearly beloved brother, as he would have embraced too, Teresa of Avila, who climbed so high and so often on her mystic ladder that her whole being was flooded and leaping with Heavenly light, the very fire of God. And he would have told his monks, who would have multiplied so amazingly by then, that there is a great variety of flowers in God's garden. His own monks would plant and tend certain kinds. The Carmelites of that great genius among women, Teresa, would plant her flame-like blooms; and the friars of Saint Francis would cultivate theirs which would shed a very sweet fragrance on the air. There was a place for sublime mystics and inspired beggars. They had invaluable lessons to teach the world. But all could not be sublime mystics or inspired beggars. His own Benedictines had their own important, constructive and very wholesome principle to instil. There was one kind of glory to God and another and another kind of glory. All were acceptable to Him.

And Benedict was perhaps the first in this world to apply vocational and aptitude principles to working groups. After their first tremendous labour in rearing their strong monasteries, he allowed each monk to do the work for which he was best fitted. He did not want to see round monk pegs in square monastery holes. This policy, always followed by the Benedictines, gave interest and variety to the activities of their ever-expanding convents and to the host of houses of other orders which were established with Benedict's broad and liberal rule as base. Anthony had started the first communal or cenobite monastery, though he left it rather solitary, with his monks not seeing much of each other, and having only a minimum of work and a maximum of reflection and devotions. Pachomius, as we have seen, added the work in an increasing quantity making his houses self-sustaining agricultural as well as religious communities. Basil added organization and variety to the work. Benedict rounded out the whole with his liberalism and balance. Many borrowed from him and even the footloose friars in the later Middle Ages grew so numerous that they had to draw on Benedict and ally themselves with mother houses too.

This opening up by Benedict of so many channels to the monk in his own great family house, by the time of the first Crusades had turned the abbeys into great hives of industry, model farms that would teach both by precept and practical example scientific tilling to the peasants, thus raising their standard of living, and refuges for oppressed bodies as well as distressed souls. It was not only his houses, forming the greatest abbey chain, with their innumerable chapters by cathedral times, that contributed in such ways to civilization, but all the innumerable orders patterned largely on or at least in some measure on his rule; and there was scarcely a communal cloister in Europe that did not owe something to him. It was he too who, carrying on much farther Basil's ideas for the completer monastic life, by his insistence on intensive study, built up the great corps of scholars who, working in the monasteries through the Dark Ages, preserved learning and art for all, including many millions who never think of this far-reaching service of the monks at all. And it was some of his houses, like the great one at Cluny, with its church with the famous five spires, the largest until the cathedrals came in Europe, that would foster building and develop the Romanesque whose glory was second only to that of the Gothic, and out of which the Gothic would be born, many of its features going intact into our Cathedral.

Gradually, too, the Benedictine houses would, if only in that accidental and indirect way, extend their activities out into the world. Their contemplation, prayers, and study, had always been for the world. Later their teaching, preaching, nursing, medicine, science, and art, which at first had served only those, including the strangers, within their gates, came to embrace a very wide circle. And an illustrious succession of men went out from the Benedictine houses: Gregory the Great who, choosing Benedict himself for model, made his palace a chapter house; Augustine, the second saint of the name, whom Gregory sent as missionary to England; Boniface, whom Charles Martel sent as a light to those gentiles called Germans, who dashed both his torch and brains out; Saint Dunstan, the famous English saint; the Venerable Bede, first great scholar of Britain; Hildebrand, the pope who first proved to mediaeval emperors that the Church had a suzerainty beyond that of any earthly empire; Lanfranc, the greatest of the Norman builders; Bernard, mighty theologian and reformer; and Suger, the abbot and prime minister of kings, at whose abbey of Saint Denis the Gothic would first really see the light. And there were hosts of others very famous, to say nothing of those who, though they later joined other orders, were Benedictine alumni, having studied at his houses—Thomas Aquinas, for example, the foremost of mediaeval religious thinkers and scholars, who spent a long time at this very Mount Cassino Abbey where the Founder this night lay, and the incomparable Saint Francis who matriculated at Benedict's first pioneer convent, Subiaco.

Nor does this even suggest the great sisterhood of Benedictine nuns, who have done a great service for the world. Wherever there is work to be done, the women will gather, to follow, sometimes to lead, always to inspire the men. Often, too, you will find them following the great leaders, not only in the general and anonymous way, but in one more intimate and personal. There were the Four Marys of Christ. Basil the Great had his devoted sister, a saint too, Macrina. "Poor Clare," herself a great founder, purely loved Francis, and in death she lay near him. The sister of Pius the Tenth gave him something of the family affection that even men in exalted positions need. And Benedict had a sister too, named Scholastica. Often she journeyed to see him, and since women could not be lodged in the monastery, he would leave Mount Cassino for a little house in the village where he had dinner with her. Then they would talk lovingly of the past and even more of the future in the heavenly kingdom for which, they prayed at grace, not only they two but an ever-increasing number of men with whom he came into contact might be headed. Benedict dined with her in this way at the little house three days before she died. Knowing that her time was short, she had come to him and there they had said farewell. But though she could not lodge in the abbey in life, she did in death. They buried her on Mount Cassino.

"*Kyrie, eleison; Christe, eleison; miserere nobis!*" so on the chants sounded through the night. In the morning they buried him beside her. "May their souls and the souls of all the faithful departed rest in peace!"

But he was not always to lie there at rest. It was a stormy place. Even before he had built his capital monastery there, the Goths had laid waste the town at the foot of the mountain. Then, as it commanded the high road, the Langobards, later Lombards, scouring the country between Rome and Naples, came across it in 660 and gutted the pile with fire. In the ninth century the Normans did it all over. So it went through the centuries, until the last barbarians, those Germans who hated the cross—fortunately not all of them do—came and took possession of his mediaevally rebuilt abbey, installed there their engines of war and so brought it down in ruins again.

Not long after that Lombard invasion, a far-off abbot, Aigulfe by name, having read Gregory's loving life of Saint Benedict, and also having learned of the destruction of the abbey, made a vow in his cell up on the Loire, rode down the Rhône, over the Alps and hunted among the Mount Cassino ruins, until he came on the tomb. Then he took the remains of the great saint back over the mountain passes, up the rivers of France to the Loire and his little Merovingian church, which he renamed after the saint, giving it the French form, Saint-Benoît-sur Loire. It was not the las resting place but the first that the Germans in the Second Worl War violated on Mount Cassino.

So did his work flourish even in death that the abbey grew unti about Charlemagne's time, it housed five thousand monks, teacher and students. Even when the Normans came up the Loire, as the did too at Mount Cassino, though they fired it, somehow the overlooked his tomb. To replace the old Merovingian Abbey, larger and truly noble Romanesque pile was built. This still hous the remains of the great commander-in-chief of the monks.

The little candles that shone that night of 544 on the sign an seal of the King, the silver cross that lay on the dead saint's breas did not go out. They would flame through the Dark Ages ar others which are quite as dark, though they are not always call so, upon myriads of his followers, working with missal and cro and crucifix, stave and chord and organ key, hammer, and chis and anvil, balm and phial and retort, parchment and inkpot ar brush, chisel and pigment and gold leaf, chemicals and micr phone and printing press, a thousand other of God's instrumen for Him and His children.

XVI

Our Lady at last comes to Paris. . . . Hosts of Mosaic Workers,
Goldsmiths, Glassblowers and Artisans arrive from Venice and
the Golden Horn to work on the First Notre Dame and to make
for the Unlettered Great Picturebooks in Paint and Stone and
Glass and Marble.

550=558 A.D.

WHILE GENEVIEVE, CLOVIS, AND CLOTILDE SLEPT THEIR LAST
sleep in the new tombs in the great abbey on the hill, and
Childebert—when he was not away at his wars—reigned
in the island palace, there could sometimes be seen, coming down
the river road from the east, bands of southern pilgrims distinguishable from others that came that way by kits of tools on
pack animals or slung over their shoulders. They were not as great
in numbers as the itinerant artists and artisans would be in the
seventh and eighth centuries when the Lombard guilds moulded
the architecture of western Europe, or in the twelfth when representatives of the building trades and crafts flocked to the Seine
from all over the world; but already the tide had started.

Other workers came over the hill every day, either from the
southern suburb quarries, or from down Orleans way, looking for
jobs. And they would have, from up above, a better view of the
city than the travellers by the river road, whose first glimpse of
Paris was blocked by the turreted island wall, with only the palace,
Glaucinus Prison, and Saint Etienne visible over it. For Notre
Dame was not yet; at least it was only a hole. The men above,
carters or pilgrims, would always pause a moment on the hilltop,
by the ever-expanding abbey of the Saint, and the old Roman
horse market and barracks, now resounding to Frankish, not
Roman, commands. Looking to their right, they could see in the
river meadows, the little parish belfry of Saint-Clement-Marcel;
the round Roman amphitheatre, from which the lions had long
ago vanished; and thence a succession of low houses, and brick and
lime kilns, of wheelwrights' shops, smithies, and armourers' forges,
running from the east to the bridgehead of the Petit Pont. Running north from the hilltop, down past the old Roman Left Bank
palace and baths to the same bridge, were the high arched aqueduct

and the Paris ending of the Saint Jacques Road over which the Orleans workmen came.

From the two hundred and fifty foot elevation of Saint Genevieve's Hill, they could look over the island wall to a space back of the old Roman Forum, and a little northeast of Saint Etienne's, where there now gaped a great hole. Heavy carts were constantly rumbling over the bridge with loads of timber, stone, lime, which they dumped by this great hole; and boats were ferrying more material from downstream for it. From that height too the travellers could make out two figures who seemed to be constantly urging the men to swifter work with pick and shovel, trowel, cart, and crane, and otherwise seemed to be very much in evidence. But at that distance the newcomers could not guess that the two were neither contractors nor superintendents, but the bishop-premier and the King of France. The one in his cassock who bent over once in a while, to etch out a detail or outline a design in the loosened earth was the famous Saint Germain. The one who gestured impatiently or, with buskined foot, autocratically and most unarchitecturally amended the impromptu design, was the conquering Childebert. They were bent on making a fine house for Our Lady.

Once this would have been incomprehensible. Now no longer at church councils did they table motions to honour her. In 431 at the Council of Ephesus had occurred something that seemed startling and yet was a touching indication of how the sons of men longed for some supreme representation of the maternal. At the first direct and official recognition of her, sober and consecrated deacons and presbyters had actually danced in the streets, no irreverently but with holy joy, as David once had danced before the Ark of the Covenant. The sons of men, after their long neglect had recognized that her function as fleshly forge for the beautiful link between the human and the Divine, as chalice for the wine of the spirit that had come to refresh the hearts of men, had a importance, after all, in the universal scheme which they of the Church were trying so hard to reduce to simple terms for Man understanding.

The workers that came from over the hill and those who came by the river road were delighted with the operations, all the bustle about the great hole. Those who came over the hill were the unskilled workers, but those who travelled by the river road, who had come from Milan, Venice, Byzantium, had tools and bright colours on their backs, and grand designs for tower, capital, mosaic pattern, and gold altar in their heads. Some not only had the shoulder kits and implements and sacks on pack animals, but huge wheeled, high stake-sided tumbrils, rumbling and rattling and bumping along in their wake. The others were much interested when the foreigners came into the open space east of the old forum about the great hole, and exhibited, even before they found lodging places, their cargoes—the forges and crucibles, the instruments for glass-making, the chests of pigments, gold-leaf, cloissons, the thin partitions set between rows of mosaics, sample small marble cubes, or *tessarae,* also larger marble slabs. With the antique yellows, Tuscan reds, and African onyx shades of these, they hoped to tone up their designs if the native French marbles turned out as bad as they expected.

They received a warm welcome. Bishop Germain, the Suger of his day, head of the diocese, assistant head of the state and King Childebert saw that huge loaves of bread, sheep and beef quarters were supplied by the palace seneschal to the new workers, and great beakers of wine, both the red made from Theodorus' grapes, blooming on Montmartre, and brown Gallic "wine of hops." There was earnest, too, of good wages to come in the coins handed out.

For Childebert, son of Clovis, had recently turned from the destruction of war to the construction of churches. For a while he had the time. The Merovingian kings, like all the Franks, had the fault of splitting up their domains among their sons, so starting endless family quarrels. But the four brothers—Childebert, Chlodomer, Clotaire, Theuderic, or Thierry, builder of the chateau of American memories—who took over the divisions of the kingdom, fought more with outsiders than themselves. Somehow they had hewn to Clovis' line, finished his great unfinished work, kept the core of France intact, and added to this heart great limbs and a mighty body. Together they had bested the Bavarians and Thuringians, two more German variants, to the east, the Burgundians and Visigoths in the south. In doing so these four sons of Clovis had stretched their land up to the Rhine, Alps, Pyrenees, and the two seas, matched their France with the blueprint long ago furnished by Nature in her configuration of the country, brought their boundaries up to what were considered, not only by autocrats like Louis the Fourteenth, but by some very reasonable kings, the true fortifications built, not by Caesar, Napoleon, Vauban, or any man's hands, but by Time and the ages, for France.

Of course in this consolidation all of the imperfect but rather capable Childebert's deeds were not so laudable. Like his extraordinary father, Clovis, he had had his private murders on the side. Among them was one thoroughly deplorable, executed in a model Richard the Third style on three princeling nephews in—of all places—the Palais de Justice. Under hired daggers two of the little fellows went down. The third, Clodoald, escaped. In the dead of night he was ferried downstream to a wider part of the Seine, on the hill above which he built a monastery when he grew up. This and the town which expanded around it, and also the Renaissance palace there which saw Napoleon's first *coup d'état* and was burned by the Germans in 1870, was called for the fugitive prince who escaped Childebert's dagger Clodoald—Saint Clodoald; the French *patois* characteristically whittling it down to Saint Cloud. But all these measures were rather hard on Germain and the other bishops who needed strong right arms of the Church but wanted them to be consistent and good examples. Though in the end such murders proved disastrous, through the very precedents they set for rule by assassination, at first it appeared to the bishops as though, in some ghastly illogical way, all the bloodletting actually helped the State. It was not at all to their liking. Already they had been forced to forget so many things. These strong right arms, even Childebert and the otherwise admirable Clovis, to say nothing of that batch of inept heirs ahead, were such strange and bloody Christians. Too often their conduct seemed to be scarcely adult.

However, Childebert was capable enough. Having now through deeds, some deplorable, others quite worthy, turned out for the monastery map-makers a pretty complete France, he thought it high time to climb on the day's bandwagon, or chariot. This strangely enough, happened to be Our Lady's. Now that her spell was at work, her star in the ascendant, he planned to welcome her heartily into the Isle, to build, for her residence there, a truly fine house.

It was not his first ambitious church-building attempt. Already he had thrown up by the two down-river gates, on each side of the Seine, the two great Saint Germain abbeys which the pilgrim coming over the hill always noted when they looked west. The one on the north side, built where the first Saint Germain met Genevieve, near the Louvre side, Saint Germain l'Auxerrois, was round and of moderate size. Saint Germain des Prés on the south or Left, Bank, was truly great. For it had been built to house the liturgical cloak or dalmatic of Saint Vincent of Saragossa, a martyr under Diocletian. On one of his wars, King Childebert had seen it carried by the starving, but singing population of Saragossa around the walls of their city which for months he had besieged. Rubbing his eyes at the daring and faith of it, he had let them—armed defenders, priests, the tottering and aged—come out of the gates, make the complete circuit of the enceinte and reenter the gates without challenge, without charging on them at all. So impressed had he been by the miraculous powers of the tattered cloak that he himself proved these by raising the siege, so saving the city—in trade for the cloak! With this sacred relic, or its double, for Saragossa sacristans continued to show a duplicate which the

said was authentic—he marched north and raised a shrine to house
it. A beautiful shrine for a rag of a cloak this Saint Germain was,
with that great Toledo cross of gold by the pulpit, and Saint Eloi's
most marvelous gold tomb for Germain (a few years later). A
mighty house it was, for so small a thing, with the three high
spires (one of which is still up) the wide-circling, deep moat and
the far-flung fortified walls, and all the ever-increasing abbey dependencies within, that made it a great factor in the history of
Paris as well as a landmark on the horizon.

Altogether, there were native crews sufficiently large and eager
and experienced enough from their work on these two great abbeys,
to put up Notre Dame without any imported labour, particularly
if all the veterans who had helped build Clovis' great church on
the top of Saint Genevieve's Hill, were included. And they were
deep in those island excavations now, or engaged throughout all
the plain, or up and down the river, bringing the material in.
Still, Paris had not yet developed anything like the great school of
bishop-designers and monk and lay foremen or the craft skill of
the artisans who, in the twelfth, thirteenth, and fourteenth centuries, would cause the Ile de France and, by example, all of
western Europe, to blossom out in stone. To the south and east now
was the talent. Dead Rome was still a very live source of construction ideas, Byzantium a golden fountain of artistic inspiration.
There might be no emperor now on the throne of the West, but,
there in the east, was a very great one, Justinian, a mighty builder.
And just eighteen years before, this Justinian with his dazzling
retinue had entered a new church, the very greatest in all the
world, built on the old Roman principles, or rather, adaptations
of these by Constantine's and this last emperor's designers. And
when he had surveyed the high marble portico of Sancta Sophia,
gazed up at all its multiplied domes and semi-domes; then, in the
interior, observed their great bell-shaped mouths, the main apse
recesses, all the niches, the towering walls, and galleries aloft, the
inverted carpet of gold painted on the ceilings, the flowering pillars
with the new dosseret tops, the precious metal fretwork of the
altars, the great Last Judgment pictures, those of the Christ shepherds and Apostle sheep in glass, enamel, and marble fragments
on the walls, if he did not quite fancy himself Deity, gazing on
His Creation and finding it good, at least he was beside himself
enough to shout down the corridors:

"Great God in Heaven, I have beaten Solomon!"

Some of the traveling merchants and clerics hailing from Paris
may have heard the emperor. At any rate they were vastly impressed with his, or rather his artists' handiwork, and longed, if not
to imitate Sancta Sophia, at least to tap this new source of inspira-

tion. And here by the Golden Horn and in the Italian cities, which were clearing houses for Byzantine ideas and labour, they dropped hints that very soon there would would be lots of work up in Paris. The exodus did not immediately start. It would not, in full force as we have seen until the next century when the last wild nomads to come over the Alps to North Italy, the Langobards, should become orderly Lombards and grand builders themselves. Thus the Roman architectural influence, before transferred to the East, would be returned to Italy and the Adriatic cities, to be passed by them, to the Lombards; finally, with many of its Roman, some of its Oriental, features and fresh vigour, to extend up into the Rhineland and France.

Already an advance trickle of this great cultural stream had begun and the Paris authorities were glad of this infiltration of the immigrants who were trained in the latest screen and altar and painted ceiling fashions. With their tools and intelligence these artisans brought along a fine tradition. When civilization outside of the Church seemed to be going back, many of these building men were faithful to the ideals of the old Roman guilds. When one speaks of these the hearer usually thinks of the powerful bodies which in mediaeval times brought beauty and strength to the Cathedral, and prosperity and charters to the cities. But ages before that, these building guilds of the old empire had reached a high state of development.

Their rules were sound, providing penalties for disloyalty and inferior work. They had dues, ceremonies, fees for initiation (about a dollar and a half, a considerable sum those days), and compulsory holidays and sick benefits, also well-run schools supported by their treasuries for apprentices, and postgraduate course for the journeymen. They never knew deficits. And very often wealthy contractor would donate ground and money for construction of a basilica guildhall, his only stipulation being that he should receive after death the annual tribute of rose leaves strewed on his bust.

A majority, from the man with the hod on the ladder up to the master of works, contributed an invaluable professional pride. Even the less conscientious were forced into a creditable output. For the guild members were very jealous of their honesty and craft integrity. The interests of both the employee and employer were safeguarded. Only by furnishing the best material and work could a member remain in good standing. The giving of sincere service to the employer was considered as important as the securing by the employee of just returns. This grand tradition of Roman building was transmitted to many of the workmen by the Seine and made have had more to do with the triumph of the Cathedral than most have realized.

From the minute these itinerant workmen crossed the Petit Pont and looked into the excavations, they knew what the completed church would be like. They needed no drawn plans. If they wanted a model, all they had to do was to look up from their excavating (in the ground covered now by the front quarter of the Cathedral and some rods of the paving in front) and study the old grey and damp-green church of Saint Etienne. It was still in its old and unique position, its southern wall being identical with a section of the city's; and its apse serving as an angle fort. Thus embraced by Paris, Saint Etienne ran alongside the Seine for a hundred and thirty-six feet, on the site of the cathedral presbytery and the south transept portal. The old church and the new (this first Notre Dame) were near neighbours, Saint Etienne's three front portals coming abreast of the ditch they were digging for the other's apse. This was appropriate, for the two were to be parents of a greater Notre Dame, their stones and their ancestors' going, bone of their bone, into the Cathedral.

The travelling workers knew Saint Etienne's type well—a descendant of their own basilica-townhall-guildhall. Now Romanesque is the name given to buildings stemming from Rome but coming after Rome ceased politically to count. It began in Christian basilica times and much of it was, as we have seen, born of the basilica. There were regional variants—Lombard, Sicilian, and so on. The French Romanesque, common in northern France, was now very recognizable, though it would only completely mature in Charlemagne's reign. As time went on, it would grow more stoutly buttressed, would more boldly vault over great ceiling spaces and more competently treat half barrel vaults, while its glass would grow brighter, its portals recede more deeply and become alive with statues.

Some would soon begin to add transepts, the first of which came in the third century with two churches built by Saint Ambrose and Rome's Saint Peter's, and were designed to give more audience space and to support central belfries. Saint Etienne, which had begun as pure basilica, would in periods of alteration add many of these features. It had no transept yet, but with its strong bell tower, impressive portals, narrow high clerestorey, fortress-like apse, and the long line of Roman-arched glazed windows down its landward side, it already had the grey, wise, immemorial, northern Romanesque look.

Now, names of architectural schools did not worry builders men; in fact, the names were added by later scholars. These builders did not think of themselves as belonging to this or that school. And the great mediaeval cathedral men were content to do the building and—had they heard of such activities—would have gladly left to drabber souls the shoving of their mighty works into little phrase pigeonholes.

But they did complain about materials. Quite as had the builders of the Temple of Jupiter once there by the Seine, they longed for their clear river sand, and that volcanic soil, the *pozzolana,* for their concrete, all the abundant materials of their homeland about Rome which we noted in the first century. As soon as they had tossed away the last bone of the sheep the royal cooks had roasted for them, and drunk the last drop of Germain's welcoming "wine of hops," these southern men began to examine the cut building-stone, the surfacing, rubble, climbed to the quarries, tested the freestone there; and they laughed at the chancel carvings and the faded gilt in Saint Etienne's. Also they looked very glum when told there would be little copper, Saint Germain and the King had used so much on the great gilt-copper roof of Saint Germain des Près, for copper was needed for their gold leaf base, since it flaked off less easily from this chemically treated metal than from stone. And they grumbled about the qualities and colour of the marble the boats brought up the Seine when they compared it with their many-hued Lombard and colonial varieties of which they had brought but a few samples.

For days they experimented with the native cements, trying to find a composition that could be smoothly worked into the interstices between the tiny marble and glass mosaic cubes. They were anxious to make this new church an illustrious example, to anchor their saints forever to the Notre Dame walls. And they were discouraged when they agreed that this first Notre Dame would not reflect much of the glory of Sancta Sophia. For though most of the north and west France builders did not copy structurally the Byzantine which elaborated the Roman ornate temple style, while the Romanesque adapted the Roman basilica, nevertheless the Byzantine school influenced all builders in interior decoration. In that Sancta Sophia had been magnificent, as some of the artisans there had seen when they had visited the Golden Horn and of it an old bishop of the day has written almost in ecstasy

"Its very walls seemed bathed in light. Its ceiling, like the New Jerusalem, is paved deep in gold. Bright are the walls with marble fresh green as the sea, blue like cornflowers in the spring grass.

The one encouraging thing they would admit they found was the replacement of the old-fashioned skin "blowbag" by the new rope-and-treadle worked "bellies," as the first bellows was called This was a great help in the forges of the Left Bank and in the in the palace courtyard where, incidentally, though men had been shoeing horses in Asia for seven hundred years, they were for the first time outfitting the king's horses. It was of great assistance too, to all making tools to work on Our Lady's house, and glass and all forged and fired things that would beautify it.

As for that material, they need not have worried so much. If it was not as heavy as Rome's, it was quite like that of Lombardy. And it had this advantage over the old imperial material: slighter tackle and smaller cranes could be used to swing the larger building blocks up to the hoisting stages; and the rubble and *voussoirs,* or arch stones, could be carried in baskets up the rope-tied ladders. When finished, the first Notre Dame would last until the ninth century when a fire gutted it. Saint Etienne would have a life of more than eight hundred, coming down but to make way for the cathedral. And the cathedral, though built of the same light material, has been up now for over seven hundred years, and can last forever unless man, with his viciousness and chemicals, attempts to destroy it.

These workmen did not have the lifetime's employment they would have had if they had been born in the age of the cathedral. This first Notre Dame was completed within a few years after their coming, the last stone being laid in 558, the year before King Childebert died. With the two island churches, the first one in Paris, little Saint Clement's, rebuilt as Saint Marcel, great Saint Genevieve on the hill top, and the two Saint Germains west, one north, one south of the river, six churches had edged their way up into the Paris skyline. With the old Temple down, the pagan statues destroyed, once-heathen Paris began to have a Christian look.

In the interior the builders departed little from early design. Pillars divided side aisles from nave and upheld the clerestorey whose windows lighted the nave. Looking toward the apse with its domed ceiling and half arch in front one saw, in order: the space for the choir, barred by a three-foot stone screen and two lecterns near the sides; the altar, with three steps leading up, a pillared stone canopy overhead; the bishop's throne behind; the clergy bench circling it and lining the apse wall.

One could pass in the rain from Saint Stephen's front porch to the Notre Dame portal, of which it was abreast, without getting cope or chasuble wet. Yet though the furnishings in each were almost identical it was like going from one world into another, the new Notre Dame shone so in glory. There was little work on statues. Recently there had been one of those iconoclastic spasms which come every century or so, and well-meaning, but utterly warped, people had swept through Paris with hammer and axe, thinking, like Puritans and Huguenots later, that it was a service

to the God of beauty to destroy it. They had wrecked the sculpture
in Cluny Palace, every statue on the Isle, thus robbing the Louvre
in advance. Bishop Germain had tried to stop them, but could not.
He did not think it wise to risk mob violence again by setting up
many more statues, but he was firm about painting and had
preached sermons in all the six churches, saying what Gregory
the Great put officially in words a few years later, "Painting i
proper in churches so that the unlettered may read, so that they
may get from the walls all around them what they never could
get from books."

Also he quoted Basil's eloquent exhortation to the artists: "Arise
ye illustrious painters of the good deeds of the King's Army. Make
beautiful by your art the body of Our Lord. And by your craft
render immortal the martyrs who have died and who by our word
are far too feebly painted."

Perhaps the men with axes did not think two-dimensional saints
offended the old Mosaic injunction. The statues were to come late
in the Romanesque age and very thickly to the doors and niches of
Notre Dame. But the artists did their best work with brush and
mosaic. The furnishings of the sanctuary were in themselves, of
course, very beautiful. The chancel screens, the altar, the great
bishop's throne (the *cathedra*), were handsome with carving and
fine bas-relief. The altar cloth was a lovingly-spun, exquisitely
threaded piece of fine linen. The vessels were of ivory, gold-edged
or of gold, bead rimmed, chased, and gemmed. The pillared canopy
over the altar, was of the most richly-toned marble. Under it the
pyx, containing the Host, blazing with gold, pearls, and emerald,
crimson, azure, and topaz-hued precious stones, made a special
little high spot of glory even in the night.

But it was the makers of pictures with mosaics that outmatched
anything yet in northern France. Their masters had seen Sancta
Sophia and were on their mettle. If they could not here, as in
Constantinople, fling gold leaf about regardless, carve endless flocks
of the eternal little lambs, squander bushels of sapphires, and lay
literally acres of mosaics, they made all Paris gape. For three years
they were busy with pliers, chisels, pots and frames. Every day
Bishop Germain would stop in, he found so fascinating all the
processes: The tinting with oxides of the glass sections, later to be
broken in pieces. Painting these with gold leaf. Pouring over these
a thin transparent film of liquid glass. Laying rubble and stone
shard beds for the mosaic pictures. Getting marble dust or brick
dust matrixes in which the glass and enamel and mosaic pattern
were laid. Mixing the lime, crushed marble, and water cement
be poured into the interstices of the patterned rows. "Fixing" the
bright blue and gold backgrounds. Polishing everything smooth

down. And always they strove to reach the standards set by the bishops who drew up the art formulae as carefully as they would any church canons. This was one direction:

"Of wheat colour the complexion should be, with eyes and hair of brown. Grand-looking the eyebrows should always be made, with beautiful eyes. In beautiful clothing too all should be arrayed, with mien humble, impeccable and beautiful." In his earnestness, at a loss for words, the old bishop art teacher had used three times, in that short space, the "beautiful."

The stained glass sunsets had not yet settled around Our Lady's head. They would not come until her head was much higher. But in promise of the full glory to come, on the walls around the sanctuary were pictures, some in pigment, the majority in solid marble and glass cubes and shards, which gleamed with a surprising number of tints and were sparklingly offset by minute glass insets. The subjects were like those which later would appear in the great Gothic windows, but were more naïvely depicted in mosaic—a large Christ shepherd with Apostle sheep, the popular "Doom," as it was called, or Last Day tableau, with fires, harps, trumpets, chains, and lost and saved souls, a "Pentecost," with far-ranged heads and tongues of flame, and endomed on high, a "Majesty," from which looked down a cloud-riding "Our Father."

All these figures were two-dimensional. Most faced front no matter what the pose of their bodies; therefore sometimes defied anatomy. And the layman, looking at the mosaic bits before they were assembled, wouldn't have expected much of a picture. But so skillful had been the artists in arrangement of blues, greens, browns, and the Tuscan reds, Lombard "antique yellows," the African onyx shades, that they had surrounded the sanctuary with an impressive and colourful company of saints, all on a background of fresh blue and gold that was actually breath-taking to the Paris parishioners.

And all this splendour was capped by the apse ceiling of copper chemically treated so that it would hold the gold leaf. And when at the dedication, the burnished lamps hanging by bright chains from the glittering ceiling, lit up the gilded vault overhead and shone on all the tinted and jewelled magnificence of the chancel below, and on Bishop Germain in his new red-bordered chasuble, the people of Paris, exulting, forgot the solemnity of the moment and almost shouted in their joy. If they had, Our Lady, the great Mother, would have understood; and so would her Son who had brought wine—and laughter—to Cana.

If the artists had not matched Sancta Sophia's superlative splendour, they had at least let some of the Golden Horn glory sift through on Notre Dame. A Saint Etienne mass, even on a bright day, seemed as though celebrated in twilight, while a Notre Dame matins, just after midnight, in all this fresh glory might have been a nones chanted out in the meadows under the sun. There was no need now for bishop and priest to exhort to church attendance. All the Seine Valley, from nobles to serfs, flocked to see in the first Notre Dame's sanctuary the great mystery, the high scene from the universal, the most moving of dramas, woven of a stable-birth, a few walks and talks, and cures, a loaf of bread, a chalice of wine, a death on a hill and an immortal spring.

XVII

A Horseman rides forth from Rome on his way to preach to the English. . . . The Principal Parish Priests of Rome, Forerunners of the College of Cardinals, send after him and elect him Pope. . . . As Gregory the Great, he makes Two Churches to grow where One grew before and consolidates the Papacy. . . . Also he distributes Bread and Gold, makes the Most Famous Pun in History, sends out many Missionaries, among them Augustine (the Second) to Canterbury, and creates some effective new Chants for the Cathedral.

590 A.D.

𝕿OWARDS THE END OF THE SIXTH CENTURY, A HORSEMAN could be seen riding up an Umbrian highway at the leisurely pace a long journey demanded, with another rider not far behind, in a cloud of dust made by his break-neck gallop. In a short time the first horseman turned as though he heard shouts from the other, let the other come abreast. For a moment the second horse, excited, caracolled restively about the first. The two riders conferred, the first glancing toward the north now and then as though eager to be on his way. It was evident to one watching from the hill that the second, at this, expostulated with the other, for his hands went out in wide explanatory gestures. At last the horseman who had been stopped in his journey looked steadily toward the north, almost as though he were, like Moses, looking at, and bidding farewell to, a promised land. Then he turned his horse's head and rode back, unwillingly it seemed he rode so slowly, toward that Rome from which he had come.

Thus was a great natural missionary made pope, one who wanted to be an advance scout for the kingdom made commander-in-chief of the whole army. Indeed it is conceivable, that if he had started on that ride but two days sooner, if his horse had gotten a pebble in the frog and gone lame and he had gone aside from the high-way, the soldiers of that army, the six churches of Paris, the twenty-eight of Rome then, might not for some time have had a commander-in-chief who would with such signal ability have led them and the whole Church into an impregnable position.

When the hard-riding courier came abreast, he shouted:

"Turn back, turn back! Pope Pelagius has sent for you."

So vanished the rider's, Gregory's, dream of his holy adventure. He rode back to become secretary to the Pope.

But Destiny had overtaken him and summoned him back for something more than a secretaryship. Gregory served so well that when the Pope died, his own name was mentioned everywhere as the successor. Hearing this, through modesty, a longing still for that holy adventure, or because of what he took for a hatred of the administrative work for which he was so eminently qualified, he rode away once more. Again he was overtaken, brought back to the Roman gates. Destiny or a Higher Power knew that his hand, whose strength was in inverse ratio to his reluctance, was the hand indispensable.

In the ranks of the Church there was uneasiness. Gaul, Spain, so many lands were ever loyal to the Holy City. The Christian emperors, the strong right arms of the Church, recognized the authority of Rome, constantly referring to it all ecclesiastical disputes brought to their attention. Some of the Eastern patriarchs, however, now Antioch or Jerusalem, again Alexandria or Constantinople, in which city would come the final split between East and West, wanted an oligarchy of their quartette and a fifth, Rome. They acknowledged the prestige of the see of Rome, whose throne was in the old imperial capital, which had been Peter's first bishopric and death-place, Paul's too, and which had further been sanctified by the martyrdoms of so many in the arena, their burial in the catacombs. But they did not like its power of veto, of official direction, and asked for more local autonomy. What the Papacy needed now was a wise head which could assert its power in major matters, resign it in minor.

Since early times so many of the greatest saints and thinkers like Ignatius, Jerome, Clement, Polycarp, John Chrysostom, Tertullian, had joyfully recognized Rome's preeminence. They could give no other reading to Christ's commission to Peter, as the first of the Apostles to recognize the Kingship of the King. "Who say ye that I am?" "Thou art the Christ, the Son of the living God." That was an awesome, a sublime moment in human history. So had come the command: "And I say unto thee that thou art Peter and upon this rock I will build my church . . . And I will give unto thee the keys of the kingdom of Heaven, And whatsoever thou shalt bind on earth shall be bound in Heaven, And whatsoever thou shalt loose on earth shall be loosed in Heaven."

There is an old law beloved and often quoted by historian

called "the Law of the West." And for some centuries now, religion as well as politics seemed to have obeyed its decree—that victory must travel from east to west, that dominion and power must, with every new epoch, be given to some land nearer the setting sun than the one which in the preceding age had prevailed. The first leaders of the Invisible Empire founded in the east, in the valley where the King had been born, had chosen for their capital their fathers' city, outside whose walls He had died. But when the Gentile recruits began to outnumber the volunteers from the King's valley, the tides of Empire Invisible followed those of visible empire, which long before had turned toward the west. With the coming to Rome of the first great missioner to the Gentile world, Saint Paul, and the arrival there of Peter, he who held Christ's high commission, a strange thing happened: the same city, Rome, became the capital of two empires, both the visible and the Invisible. Then when under Constantine, secular authority, by way of exception, reversed that "law of the West" and began the return drift to the east, and the barbarians put out what temporal glory had been left Rome, nonetheless it was still considered by the majority as the fortress city of the faith. The eastern and African dissident bishops were but fighting Destiny. That mystic authority represented by the joint terms "Bishop of Rome" and "Pope" which most of the world accepted would, when the rider twice brought back by Destiny to the gates, had had it thrust upon him, be accepted by the whole world of the West. He would make it a very real high command. This rider who incidentally, whether on a throne or on horseback, looked the great part he was to play, would, before he left the city for the last time, return to a desolated Rome her lost preeminence and set up a throne on her Seven Hills more widely recognized than that of the vanished Caesars.

Yet the horseman, Gregory the Great, as he was to be called, had not wanted anything like this power at all. He would have much preferred to look into the bright face of danger up in the front line, in England, for which he had been happily headed in that first flight. He saw now ahead of him in this elevated post an endless round of executive duties, with infinite detail and vexatious diplomacies the chaotic times demanded. But if, as he passed on the return journey under the Trajan Arch, his head was lowered, it was not from lack of courage or vision. In these no contemporary matched him, except one, perhaps, whose star now arose in the East.

Missioners occasionally brought word of the flaming battles, the equally fiery sermons of this new celebrity—Mamoud, Mahmet, Mohamet, Mahound, Mahommad—something like that was his name—in Saint John Lateran they never could be sure of the spelling. But his philosophy was distorted, not magnificently altruistic like that of the King or of His generals who, like Gregory, manfully fought for His least word.

If Gregory when recalled again was grave, it was because he was renouncing a life-long dream—of far seas, white English cliffs and adventure of body, above all of the soul. His dreams, his self-will, his youth, he was leaving forever outside the city gates. Perhaps that is why his pace was so slow, and his whole distinguished person appeared so reluctant.

The Rome through which he rode, with the twenty-eight churches, had an even more Christian look than Paris with its half dozen. The soldiers of the peaceful army of Christ were always fond of military terms. The names of the hours when the Roman garrison changed guard were applied to services held at those hours, and you still find *terce, sext, none,* in the missal. They gave to the twenty-eight churches the group name by which they are still known, "sentry churches," because, during Lent, the Pope stood guard or station in all when he preached sermons in them in rotation.

The priests serving these were called *incardinati,* from *cardo,* or hinge. They were attached permanently like hinged doors, as the head priests, to these historic churches. Besides their parochial duties they assisted in certain papal ones, and, above all, cast ballots for the pope, forming with the seven Cardinal Bishops and seven Cardinal Deacons the famous College of Cardinals. Through the centuries the number fluctuated, in our modern times about seventy. There is an interesting link with the past in the titles still borne by many of the Cardinals. The names of these pioneers, the ancient sentry, or "Station Churches," still appear in the title of some of these powerful princes of the Church.

Some of these old churches, like Saint Mary Major, Saint-Paul-without-the-Walls, are still represented by impressive mediaeval reconstructions. Many, like Saint Clement, Saint Lawrence, Saint Agnes and Saint Sabina, still retain within their rebuilt bodies bones of their old selves, arches, buttresses or crypts of the very buildings by which Gregory rode.

No rival bishopric seat could show such an array of shrines. If other reasons were needed for the location of the holy capital on the Seven Hills, there were two of the largest churches in the world—Saint John Lateran, much of which is still as it was then, and the first Saint Peter's. He rode by innumerable holy spots where the saints had met their deaths, among them Saint Peter. Not far from his saddle opened up the catacombs. This vast netherworld was honeycombed with rock crypts, chapels, sacristies. In the tragic age that was past, no gorgeous robes or decorated vessels had been kept there, only snow-white everyday clothes and altar cloths and simple pitchers and plates. Tomb tops had served for altars; and there had been congregations of both the quick and the dead, the martyrs lying on burial shelves all around. The pillars of these persecution chapels were the pillars of the Seven Hills. To Gregory it seemed a sign of the destiny of the Eternal City.

Often when he saw people staring at the holy places he felt like tapping them on the shoulders and reminding them that once they would have been arrested for doing just that or even looking in a church door. To bend the knee now was not to bend the neck for the sword. To make the sign of the cross was no longer to sign one's death warrant. All on these hallowed spots should fall on their knees in gratitude. But children's children never value enough the liberty their fathers or their fathers' fathers have, by their deaths, won for them. At least they take their freedom for granted until, because of their carelessness, it has to be won all over again.

If, as he rode into the square before Saint Peter's, Gregory resented the fate that had prevented him from continuing on his journey to battlefields in foreign lands, and had assigned him to the home office, he did not underestimate the importance of this post to which he had just been summoned back. Though he would willingly have transferred the honour to someone else, he was convinced that the overlordship of this diocese extended beyond the environs of the Eternal City to the whole Christian world. In churches, tombs, bloody arenas, holy spots, he had just ridden by overpowering proof. And it was overwhelming for him. None had lived who would not have been awed by the thought that a conclave awaited, insisting on investing him with such mighty authority. He could hear voices everywhere echoing back from the walls of places where Paul had written his immortal letters, where heroes had died, where the first bishop, Saint Peter, had chosen his own college, twenty-four priests and deacons.

The church named for the first Bishop was his goal. And now Saint Peter's loomed over his head. Not with a dome; there would be none for a thousand years. In 1590 the great Michelangelo and Bramante dome, one hundred and forty feet across, would be completed on a magnificent Saint Peter's replacing this fourth-century church which the troubled Gregory was now approaching. But it was a great church, two hundred and seventy feet long, the same dimension in width, and covered two acres. It had a great porch, with three high portals, a long high clerestorey with long rows of

Roman arched windows down the sides, and the first transepts in Christendom, dating from the fourth century. It was a worthy seat for a bishop, also for that higher authority which the horseman named Gregory had just ridden in, against his will, to have offered him.

A crowd had gathered in the square to see him arrive, for watchers on the city walls had given word of his approach while he was way out on the Campagna. An appreciative murmur ran through their ranks, but they did not cheer. They were waiting to give that when the cardinal electors, now in the chapter room, would bring him out for their acclamation. At one time the shout of the crowd in front of the church had been all that was necessary for the election of a bishop—even of the bishop of Rome. The clergy would show a candidate they thought likely to the crowd and they would shout him into the throne or how him down. In some sees, as the Fathers had sorrowfully noted often the choice had been decided by lungs rather than by the Holy Spirit. It was to guard against the perils of a *viva voce* vote by an emotional crowd that the election had been turned over to a council of priests. But while the balloting was theirs, the confirmation still had to come from an acclaiming crowd.

The forty-two of the cardinal clergy, predecessors of the illustrious College of Cardinals, had arrived from the "station churches" and suburban sees, at Saint Peter's, and were inside the chapter room. They wore none of the familiar red velvet cassocks and red skull caps. These the thirteenth century would bring. And there was no voting urn and no fire sending up columns of white and black smoke to announce to the throngs on the hill and roofs the result of the balloting. They wore their simple robes of red-bordered white with a fine and solemn dignity that made up very well for the lack of the later pomp. And so wise and mature and, most felt, Heaven-guided had been the voting of this body that never had there been any dissent by the crowd.

If ever they feared such dissent, it was not at this election. One and all sat in their Roman X chairs with serenity on their venerable and spiritually seasoned faces. None in all Rome doubted the fitness of the man of the hour except this horseman, the man himself. Both patricians and populace were pleased. Of his record there was no question. An aristocrat and ex-prefect of Rome, he had risen through many ranks of the Church—priest, deacon, archdeacon, "seventh deacon." And very recently he had been sent by Pope Pelagius as nuncio to the Golden Horn where he met the dissident bishops who strove to have transferred some of the authority vested in the office he was now going into to chapter room to refuse if he could. But this very experience of his counted with the statesmen among them who realized that the era had come for the consolidating of the forces which had made for the establishment of that office beyond all rival claims.

What delighted the crowd most was that, though Gregory was one of breeding and wealth and decidedly not one of the crowd, his heart ever beat for them. Already his benefactions, foretastes of those for which he would become famous as Pope, had been princely. One more and very great figure he added to the line of aristocrats from John through Ambrose, Augustine, and that idol of Augustine's youth, Saint Benedict, who when they started their magnificent service to the Church, had not simply put on the cross, but at a cost earned their right to the wearing or bearing of it, and had shown the world that "rich young men" *could* follow His royal advice and literally give up their all before taking places in His train. Visible proof of his observance of this beautiful and immortal rule was in sight of that crowd, up on the Coelian Hill, in a palace on the skyline. It had belonged to his father, the old senator who on his death had bequeathed it to Gregory. And at once Gregory, in honour of his adored Benedict, had turned over to the Benedictines the whole of the splendid pile, except for one little room which he reserved as a cell for himself.

But there was one thing he could not slough off with all the trappings of rank. This was his look of the right to rank, the true mien of the prince, of either Church or State, his manner both of charm and authority. There was no ruler of either empire who more truly looked the ruler's part. His beard, scarcely hiding the lips whose fullness at once betrayed his generosity, had been yellow in youth, but now was tawnily grizzled. The aristocratic nose was not sharply hawklike but had a noble and smoothly-curved aquilinity. The splendidly-domed head went very well with the great arches of his own Saint Peter's. It was lighted by a pair of very lively and curious brown eyes which took in everything—so many things for his white, shapely, beautiful and extremely capable hands to do.

These were now handing the reins to an attendant at the transept door as he dismounted to go through to the chapter room. Once inside, he did not do the expected at all. His greeting of the conclave of cardinal electors seated there was courteous and gracious, but not grateful. Immediately, those shapely white hands went out in a plea to rescind their action, take back their votes.

They glanced at one another in amazement. Never had anyone they had known, so summarily thrust aside proffered power. Those fine brown eyes were not so lively and curious now as burningly

faded backgrounds given new gold coats. No monk or priest went with undarned cassock or sandals needing resoling. And not a cracked bell jangled in any parish.

Because of his faithful stewardship, revenues flowed in ever-increasing streams. He was the mightiest and best landlord on earth. Because of the great respect he won for his régime, more and more of the hold-out bishops came to be convinced of the validity of the age-old claim. Ever he pressed this, but with infinite wisdom and tact; never once overurging it in any way. A legitimate favour he would do for Carthage here, accept a grudging half-inch there from jealous Milan or Smyrna, and turn both into diplomatic ells. When he outmanoeuvred Visigoth Toledo or venerable Antioch, it was with the greatest graciousness and good humour.

And half of the generals of the temporal empire and the governors of the Italian cities, owed their appointments, in whole or part, to him. Always like, but with better conscience than our modern statesmen, he kept his political fences mended. He had to, if he would match wits with kings and keep them from burning down all his churches, with his congregations inside.

As he so sagely saw it, this Church-State, for all its mystical foundation, was a very visible expression on earth of an invisible empire. Though a divinely-motivated affair it was also humanly-wrought-and-run and designed to carry on Heavenly-ordained functions in a decently earthly way. After all, even a religion founded on so supernatural a faith inspired conduct which had to be related to a social framework. Gregory, and in a disordered, chaotic time, did a magnificent job of coordinating a heavenly scheme with one temporal.

He began, on his assumption of office in that chapter room, with that sizeable kingdom within the great empire—his bishopric of Rome. And so powerful did he make this, that the secular kings looked on him with awe. Visigoth, Ostrogoth, Lombard, whatnot —all of these Arian or pagan barbarian kings, were still too abashed by the spell of a vanished Rome which Gregory reinvoked to seize the power that should have been theirs when they came over the Alps to conquer the peninsula. He had not been long in office—the episcopal one and that mystical and still occasionally challenged higher office too—before he began to be regarded, not only as a lieutenant of the King but the true heir of the Caesars.

On the holdout factions this had a strong effect; and it could be seen now by all the adroit, that golden Constantinople, ancient Antioch, legendary Alexandria, and holy Jerusalem had forever lost. Through the efforts of Gregory more than those of any other —at least, through that culmination his work proved to be of all that had gone before, what had been accepted as an ancient tradition, strongly based on sentiment and history both, was suddenly crystallized into a permanent status.

There was nothing for the rival bishops to do now but admit it or else split off from the main body. It had been a remarkable exhibit of statesmanship, without cynical and stultifying diplomacy too, this taking by Gregory of what had been a moral influence, the prestige of the bishopric of Rome, and developing it into a real centralization of the power of all sees in one head, on one throne, in one capital. So the high command was made official in the eyes of the West. Many eastern prelates acknowledged it too, but others, while accepting its moral prestige, still tried to curb its authority.

There arose a credal difference too. The East stuck to the reading, "The Holy Ghost who proceedeth from the Father"—"and the Son," the West added. Many in the Levant too resented the conscientious efforts of Gregory and popes before and after to extend celibacy among the clergy. And they did not like their limiting the right of confirmation to the bishops. Though the complete and final dissevering of the Church of the West from the Church of the East, later called the "Greek Catholic" or "Orthodox Eastern Church," did not come until 1054, they had not been homogeneous for centuries.

With the consolidation, in the time of Gregory, of the temporal power and spiritual hegemony of the Papacy, political evolution had, of course, something to do, and also an overwhelming legacy of rich memories of early altars and sermons and epistles and martyrdoms—of an infinite number of examples of sweetness of spirit with unflinching valour combined, that had hallowed this same Rome. But the elevation and expansion of the bishopric of a once-pagan city into the Christian capital and perpetual seat of the high command was, above all, due to the logical and practical concluding of a very beautiful premise. This was that a humble fisherman, a traitor turned indomitably loyal, a craven transformed into immortal hero, had once been touched on the shoulder by his King and made His earthly regent. A lovely, a touching, delicately-told story was respun into a world-wide social fabric. On its base the world's mightiest institution was reared.

Gregory had long been a monk, but even after his installation he was forever going out into the world. He was a great monarch but he did not sit much on his throne. Almost every day the Paris choir-boys who came over the sea in the boats with the wine-coloured sails to enlist in that nine-year course in the Schola Canorum came across him in the streets. Very kindly would be his greeting, but his lively brown eyes seemed to be taking in everything, that noble dome of a head, which went so well with the grand arches of Lateran and Saint Peter's, to be thinking up something new for his staff, and, particularly, for himself to do.

They were forever doing things, those hands. With dawn, they would be waving up, like magic out of the air, great arches for some one of his legion churches; the next hour, within some one of them, elevating the Host. Still, without breakfast, in Benedict's way, when it was almost noon, he would rein his horses around a city wall or up a hill road to a lonely and needy parish. With his first meal he would listen perhaps to a steward's report, checking it carefully as he pared a plum or seeded grapes, then confirm a new roof outlay or phrase, with fine indignation, an order forbidding the persecution of the Jews and the expropriation of their property, though it was an infinite sorrow for him that they still refused to acknowledge his King. But that, over and over he would say, was no reason why we should not show them the King's mercy.

If he grew tired then, from industry and rising at dawn, he would, for rest, inscribe thick choir parchment with the old musical notation *neumes*, humming, as he worked, in one of his four newly-discovered keys, some sonorous new chant. At midnight some departing courier would receive his last instructions or some blundering, inept envoy feel the force of a righteous wrath. Then, the candles guttering down, but his energy seemingly unspent, he would write away at his "Life of Benedict," a saint most fortunate when so few great men have Boswells equal in ability to themselves and so rarely do Plutarchs rise to the level of their own "Lives." And every hour in between these diverse and multiplied tasks, those beautiful hands would pause to open the papal purse, dig down into his own, or to unlock the doors of one of his innumerable almonries. Whatever the day's cares, at the end of it, with the setting of the sun, they would weave a benediction with those beautiful motions of theirs which of themselves brought grace and peace to troubled souls.

In so many places besides Saint Peter's and the "Station" churches which lay strung like a rosary on the Seven Hills, the Paris choir-boys saw him. When curiosity took them to one of the smaller *fora* where slaves were sold and there were men of all climes, colours, coiffures, and characteristics at whom to stare, they were likely to find him there, patting some slave-boy's head as he shook his distinguished own over this slavery problem he longed to, but could not, solve. On occasion, he urged slaves to be diligent and honest with their masters, and far more often, their masters to be considerate of their slaves. It seemed as though this were all he could do, and it was such a half loaf. The King could never have envisioned these conditions for the kingdom He planned to come in His name on this earth. For men free of body and soul, His charter had called. As Lieutenant of the King, Gregory sometimes felt he had very truly made His kingdom, that Invisible Empire, expand, had set its frontiers far forward. But question this advance he always did when he came into the slave markets. Yet he could not hasten by one hour the coming of the psychological moment for the abolition of the practise he hated. Only Evolution, which they then knew as "God's good time," could do that. And in "God's good time," a thousand years are as a day. Just one day, then, of "God's time," and an hour or so over it, or more than twelve centuries, it would take before Europe would effectually abolish the slave trade. There would be steps before that. Louis the Tenth, from the shadow of the cathedral, would issue an edict in 1315 for the abolishment of slavery in his own imperial domain. And in 1788 Condorcet, Mirabeau, Lafayette and some of the fine spirits active in the French Revolution formed a society for the freeing of all blacks, but it was not until the next century that the shackles really fell. Even if he could have foreseen the event, twelve centuries would have been a tragically long time for an anxious, greathearted man like Gregory.

Perhaps it was not only the pity of which his heart was full that turned his steps so often to the slave forum. The objective may have been the English slaves with whom he talked most often. They always aroused in him a nostalgia for a land he had never seen and from a journey to which Destiny had called him back.

He had, one day on a trip to the slave market, come upon a group, ranged on the pavement for purchase, with particularly blonde hair; and he paused to run his long tapering fingers through the light curls of a tall captive standing by a pillar. Curious, hopeful too, that this kindly, distinguished-looking man might purchase him, the youth did not stir. Curling the strands like golden floss over his fingers, with a reflective light in his eyes as though he were recalling his own vanished youth, the days when his beard, now tawny and grizzled, was as yellow as the boy's hair, he asked the foreman:

"And from where do these fine-looking fellows come?"

"From Britain," the market man said. "They are Angli."

The Pope smiled. " 'Angli!' Why, *angeli,* then! Angels—not from God but from overseas!"

And the old face lighted up with visions of the chalk cliffs he had never reached.

"From what kingdom in Britain?" then he asked.

The interpreter questioned a tall bright-haired youth.

"From Deira, your Holiness," he reported.

" 'Deira'!—*De ira!*" In the Latin he played on the British name. "*De ira*—from the wrath"—so he translated. "The wrath of God! And from the wrath of God shall they be saved!"

Once more he turned to the market man. "Ask them who is their king."

"Aella—he who took Wessex."

Almost uncontained now was the old man's delight. " 'Aella'! Alleluia! In Aella's land shall alleluias be sung!"

So he finished the triplicate pun, the most famous witticism in history, and went back to Saint Peter's and sent out Augustine— the second saint of the name—as his own proxy to save that England of which he had dreamed in his youth. Augustine's mission was to convert the tens of thousands of the British unbaptized and to consolidate the faith of the little Christian congregations. The religious tie between Britain and Gaul was ever very close. These little congregations were descended from those who had long before heard the good news from Breton fishermen and advance scouts who had carried it down the Seine. The English clergy when oppressed sought refuge in Little Britain, our Brittany or Armorica, as it was then called. The Bishop of Troyes, France, in 429, with Bishop Saint Germain of Auxerre, the friend of Genevieve and the one for whom the Paris Church of Saint-Germain-l'Auxerrois was named, had come over to England to help the leaders reform the English churches which had been sadly depleted by the perverse Pelagian theories. And now this Saint Augustine the Second who with the great Pope Gregory did so much to foster the infant English church, when he was made the first Archbishop of Canterbury, was consecrated by the French archbishop of Arles.

As Gregory the Great had strengthened the army of the monks, then that of the secular clergy, so now he gave new life to this other branch of the service, the missionary. The little candles lighted by the first twinkled in abbey windows everywhere as the monks toiled and the tall tapers gleamed up and down Europe by thousands of altars where priests celebrated the divine mystery. And he was the great missionary father. In every land on Gregory's great map, in many whose outlines had not yet been charted, the torches of his heralds, the missioners, shone. This was not for the glory of great Gregory—he was under no egoistic illusion about that—but to proclaim One before Whom he acknowledged even his princely self to be as dust.

The lights those years burned late too in the John Lateran library. Gregory was a notable scholar himself, he with Ambrose,

Jerome, Augustine, making up the quartette, "The four Great Doctors of the Church." He had constantly on hand a great corps of learned men in the John Lateran library, editing the works of the early Fathers: and he had made an intensive study of Augustine. His greatest gifts, perhaps, lay along the lines of administration and the conducting of energy into the channels of the Church through his own powerful personality. But he and his scholars simplified, summarized the expositions of the great thinkers. They codified what had gone before and laid the groundwork for the theological textbooks of the Middle Ages.

And he explained clearly the eucharistic beliefs of the Church and its stand in such matters as those of angels, demons, and Purgatory. The mighty intellect of Paul had recognized the existence of the bright ministering mid-beings. As for Purgatory, most of the early fathers had considered only logical that some souls should undergo a probation period after death. The scientifically inquiring Origen, Gregory of Nyassa, had written of "purifying fires." Cyril said, "We believe that the departed souls for whom we pray receive very great relief." Augustine wrote: "There are some who have departed . . . not so bad as to be deemed unworthy of mercy, others not so good as to be entitled to immediate happiness." All such matters Gregory made clear.

He did not change the sequence of the *missa* from that followed in the fourth and fifth centuries which we have already noted, except to add an alleluia or two, a few words to the *Hanc Igitur* prayer and to transfer that of Our Lord to its more proper place just before the breaking of bread. As he had consolidated the work of his predecessors in shaping the organization of the Church, he crystallized and gave the Church sanction to the continuity to be observed throughout the centuries, in the cathedral. Changes thereafter would be local and inconsequential.

Nor did he change the vestments we saw in the basilicas, except to add one little accessory to the bishop's, the pallium or Y-shaped lappet, also a border of red to the usual white vestments. These, however, were to be beautified in time, especially up by the Seine, though the design would remain the same.

Another grand service he performed by adding to the *missa* a beauty for the ear. It was to learn about the new music which was as revolutionary in its day as the polyphonic discoveries of Palestrina and the new harmonies of Debussy were in theirs, that the choir-boys had come down from Paris. This new music, like all so far heard in the churches, was entirely vocal. Instruments, because of their pagan associations, were still considered, as bells once had been, tongues of the Devil. The strains of pipe and lyre reminded the congregations too strongly of the lascivious festivals of

Dionysius and Nero's playing as Rome and the Christians burned. So not even the portable organ, which had long been used in the east, was then allowed within church walls. And no organ would be allowed there for another hundred and fifty years, when Charlemagne's grandfather would install one up in the city where Jeanne d'Arc would be captured one day—Compiègne.

The choristers of Gregory's Schola Cantorum, the first of all the great singing schools, the clear trebles, the incipient tenors, and those in the later teens whose voices had definitely gone down, were not divided as now into groups of sopranos, altos, tenors, baritones, and basses, singing different parts. All sang the same tune. With all of Gregory's improvements, music remained a thing of two dimensions—melodic line and pitch, and without the rich depths of polyphony. Harmony and counterpoint would not be dreamt of until in the Dark Ages just ahead, some obscure choirmaster would one day grow impatient with boys who finding themselves, per- haps because of changing voices, incapable of reaching the higher notes, would improvise, and very badly; and he in despair would himself compose separate melodic lines for them that would har- monize with the air instead of forcing them to sing an octave below it.

So, like the iron weapons of the once masters of all Europe, the Celts and the Gauls, the glass of the Phoenicians, and other things that would go into the cathedral, the polyphony that would enrich its service was discovered quite by accident; and in the most backward of eras, out of sheer darkness, the great light of music was born. Unsung, his very name unrecorded, that Dark Age choirmaster was spirit father of that long line from Des Près of the mediaeval motets, Palestrina, bringing his melodious thun- ders to the Seven Hills, through Mozart and Beethoven composing requiem and mass, to Saint Saëns, César Franck, and Pierné work- ing out their harmonies on the Saint Severin, Sainte Clotilde and Saint Sulpice organs by the Seine. A greater benefactor of man- kind was he than the greatest of the Caesars.

But that golden time was still two or three centuries off. And from the one choir sheet of thick parchment held up for all to see, the entire choir sang, reading the odd musical signs called the *neumes* that indicated time and pitch, but only approximately! From them the singers could tell when the voice should go up, when down, but not how far up or down or for how long. Arrival at unison came only from memory and heart-breaking practise, so that it took many rehearsals for a group to learn one tune. Often Gregory would drop into Saint Peter's, Saint John Lateran, or his palace which he had turned into the convent of Saint Andrew, to watch with delight the mouths of his choristers opening in arches as round as those over his venerable head. The ensemble, however, was not always as perfect as the arches. Often his eyes would go up towards the high vaults and oak rafters in horror. One can readily understand why he decreed that the course of the Schola Cantorum, started by a predecessor but enlarged by him, should be extended to nine years.

Though they had banished all strings and reed and brass, the vocal music was quite as pagan in origin. Those very intervals and modes on which it was based had been arrived at, ages before, in Greece, and had formed the structure of the old battle songs and dirges, the hymns and invocations to the Olympian gods whose followers had sought so to discredit the King when He came. But this had been forgiven long ago by that great authority of song, the gentle soul, Saint Ambrose. For there was an atmosphere which the old intervals aroused, through the ear, in the soul, that was appropriately ecclesiastical and majestically solemn. Those far-off echoes of the Attic stage added a richly theatrical effect to the songs of a drama, still new, ever fresh, and the most dramatic ever conceived. The Greeks had bequeathed to the Church something besides its capitals and the arguments Plato and Aristotle unconsciously served up for Abelard in his bouts with the scholastics in the Notre Dame cloisters. One more race had made its contribution to the cathedral.

From these intervals, the old Greek modes, Ambrose, in the fourth century, had worked out four fine tonalities for his resounding Latin hymns. And someone in the group—perhaps Gregory, probably his musicians, discovered four new modes as effective as those used by Ambrose. And now chants keyed on the eight scales, as impressive as the songs of the old warriors of Troy and prophetesses of Homer added new glory to twenty-eight simultaneous celebrations of Vespers at sunset on the Seven Hills. Those chants to which had been given Gregory's name are still sung, each Sunday, in a more majestic choir by the Seine.

Gregory himself liked nothing better than to listen to them. Often, he was sure, as the beautiful notes went up to the high oak rafters, that the angels came to the clerestory windows to listen, even as he listened each day of his years, until the distinguished old head, with the aristocratic nose, sank, the lively brown eyes which took in everything took in nothing at all, and the beautiful white hands ceased their beating time—since time no longer existed for him—and he fell asleep.

XVIII

*The Churchbells ring out in Paris as Charles Martel gathers his
Soldiers on the Field of Mars. . . . There the Feudal System gets
a Fresh Start. . . . Swift Horsemen led by the Ghost of a famous
Armourbearer - Caravanguide - Wholesalegrocer - Bandit - General -
Genius named Mahomet, ride toward Paris to replace the Cross
with the Crescent. . . . The Armourers by the Seine make a
Great Hammer for Charles Martel. . . . With it he stops the
Invaders by the Loire, saves Europe, and sets up a Throne for his
Grandson Charlemagne.*

732 A.D.

ONE MORNING IN THE YEAR 732, THE PARIS CHURCH BELLS
rang out in continuous clanging acclaim over the Seine.
They were summoning, not the populace, but the nobles
and leaders to an assembly on the Field of Mars in the river's bend.
A throne had been erected here, not for Charles Martel, the mayor
of the Palace and truly the first man in Europe, but for the king.
Other thrones would be set up there later, among them one for
Napoleon, with red velvet and gold Bonaparte bees. Charles Martel,
not the king, was starting, that morning, not only a system that
for ages would prevail, and an assembly that would turn into
something very like a parliament—and the first—but the grand
tradition of fêtes which, through the centuries, would be held on
this very Champs de Mars, where now stands the Ecole Militaire
in which Cadet Bonaparte rode at rings and Strategist Foch prepared the soldier manhood of France for victory in the First
World War, and near which the Eiffel Tower rises up against
the sky.

The Gallo-Roman-Frankish warriors were ranked before Charles
—mighty men, too, with acorn-shaped helmets, two-handed
swords, and leather shirts covered with protecting chain links. The
king was not exactly led to the throne but there was that suggestion in his manner, though Charles the Hammer kept a pace behind. The name of the puppet cannot matter—Charles set up three
himself, and a cipher, even a royal one, should be left in its

round anonymity. The Merovingian dynasty was following the old shirtsleeve law—only three or four generations between shirtsleeves for gentlemen and kings: first a tough young Frankish battleaxe, rising from the ranks; Merovée next of the Attila victory; the peak of glory with Clovis; a capable Childebert; then, with inept heirs, the swift tobogganing down. This had been stayed, but only temporarily, by good King Dagobert. After him the dynasty had gone to seed, petering out in this dried-up pod on the river throne. The Merovingians were as definitely on their way out as the Carolingians under Charles the Hammer were on their way in.

But they would follow the same road. Charles had had a stout Pippin for grandfather, would have a well-glanded Pippin for son. Then, like Clovis, Charlemagne would come in glory; only to be followed by foolish heirs, and the shirtsleeve sequence would begin all over again. In the ninth century a butcher's son, Robert the Strong, would pave the way for the usually mediocre, only occasionally brilliant, Capets who would break the rule, hanging on the throne until they came to the shirtsleeves again and with a sad literalness—for the guillotine.

Charles the Hammer had more than courage and a strong arm. He had a head. He never tried sitting on thrones himself. He was content with placing his puppets in them and with being an ancestor himself. An ancestor like the Hammer may be as fit to sit on thrones as his descendant, like Charlemagne, who finally perches there; but Charles was wise, reserving that honour for his seed. If he had not been patient, his seed would never have gotten there or he himself permanently. If that morning he had seized the sceptre he deserved from the shadow king, the nobles would have cried "Usurper!" and there would have been blood on the Champs de Mars. But Charles knew they would stand for a more gradual usurpation. So he continued in his father's old post of mayor of the palace, enfolding in this portfolio those of prime minister, chancellor of the exchequer, secretary of foreign affairs, commander-in-chief, quartermaster general, and national hero. His puppet held the sceptre; Charles held his battle axe. It was the stronger. With it, and his brain, he had made France supreme in Europe and had added many realms to her, among them Germany. He ruled this Germany in the puppet's name in all departments but one—religion. All the rest of Europe might go to Church, but for liberty of conscience the Rhinemen stood firm, calling out to the great emissary Charles sent to them, the eloquent Boniface, "Christianity is not for true Germans!" They were to say this at other times too, but this was the occasion before referred to, when they accented it with an axe, deep in the old saint's skull.

In such proselytizing efforts Charles Martel was, considering the elementary character of the times, remarkably sincere. Former strong right arms of the Church, Clovis and Constantine for examples, had recognized the moral power of the Church as the asset that made her their strongest ally. Charles Martel was the first of the great temporal leaders to see that the State itself could not only rely, but itself draw on, that moral power, from it derive the only true authenticity. Greater he was in vision even than his grandson Charlemagne.

And Charles was starting on the Field of Mars something more than a series of fêtes and a parliamentary habit. The feudal system —which for five centuries would prove such a blessing, insuring something of order and protection for the weak, and for five centuries after that such a curse, breeding the worst extremes of caste and privilege which only a great Revolution would destroy —there, that morning, got under way. It was but the farther carrying out of the old Frankish custom of dividing the king's own realm among all the princes instead of leaving it whole in the hands of one. Feudalism, after one or two tentative starts under such kings as Clovis, began in real earnest with the handing out of pieces of parchment for which the boisterous battle-axed audience had assembled. A long line of beneficiaries in chain links was now called to the throne by the river to receive the deeds to the new fiefs. Carved out of conquered lands, from the royal domains, sometimes even from church territory, these were farmed out in a sort of perpetual lease. Loyalty, concretely expressed in gold, steel, manpower, was quit-rental. These deeds were to remain a long time with the families of some of the lucky link-sewn, leather-shirted soldiers, many of whom were turned into nobles by these ivory-hued sheets with the royal seal. When these were presented, all bowed in the general direction of the throne, but their eyes smiled gratitude at the tall figure at the throne's right. The king's hand might be passing out the patents, but it was that of Charles which had made up the list. It took that mighty integer of a Charles Martel to turn the royal cipher into Authority.

If the bells of pioneer Saint Etienne, the first Notre Dame, little patriarch Saint Marcel in the Bièvre meadows, the new Saint Paul on the Right Bank, Saint Genevieve's spreading abbey on the top of her hill, the two picturesque Saint Germains, one north, one south of the river, rang out in these festivals of parliament, above all, of Property, they were to ring out more wildly and in general alarum very soon. As all the inverted bowls swung, clamouring, in and out of all the belfry louvres up and down the river, the warriors came, with spurs, swords and accoutrements ringing into the square, strode clanging into the Notre Dame nave, where mass was celebrated, then kneeling and elevating their swords, swore on the uplifted hilts that the design of those hilts, of the giant crucifix in the nave, of the emblem up on the very rooftree, should never come down. There was reason for this mailed mass oath. For other men, by the hundred thousand, had sworn the opposite. Warriors too, slighter and darker with more mobile lips, they had taken an oath that that cross should be supplanted by another symbol—the design of their swords, the swift scimitars —the crescent! It was for this that the horsemen had swarmed in clouds over the Pyrenees. And couriers on froth-white steeds had clattered over the Petit Pont as riders so often had before Genevieve and after, with news of oncoming foemen. They reported now that these latest invaders had filled all the southland with the muffled thunder of daintily-fetlocked horses and the multitudinous jingling of bridle, bangle, accoutrement, also myriad little bells on the ankles and wrists of dancing girls cavorting in the van. Gaily those tiny laughing notes seemed to mock the grave deep tones of the Paris bells.

Who was it that rode at their head? Why, a spirit. Of one dead a hundred years. And to the very year. It was in 732 that these brazen tongues were clangouring out their alarum by the Seine. In 632 that leader had died, and yet his phantom still led onward these graceful, adroit and picturesque horsemen. Since his ghost, then, had brought the East way from the East to clash head-on with the West, it is best while the armourers of Charles are firing and cooling and beating a mettle into his last battle-axe, to flashback for a moment to see what this Mahomet in real life had been.

As a boy he had a dreamer's brown eyes, an over-thin body, an overlarge head. As a prophet he had an El Greco-like length and emaciation, over-large hands that swept the heavens as though they would pocket the stars, and the head was spaciously domed with its vaulting visions. It had been crammed—in between boy and man—with the religious and historical lore of the sacred beige-walled city of Mecca, with its huge cubical black memorial rock, a host of bazaars and thread-thin, balconied alleys set in harsh, violently-coloured hills. It was devoted to revenge, piety, and profit. This affected the boy. And the four-months-long fair, in which all the desert came in and, forgetting their feuds in the traditional truce, traded and feasted, further drenched his mind with tales of other tribes and bright Arabian Night scenes of his city so gay by day with striped pavilions, ruddy wineshops, the stacked arms and gleaming copper utensils, of nights magical with torchlight, dance and lute and lovesong that made all the hills murmurous in the moon.

For apprenticeship in battle, Napoleon had his Toulon. Mahomet, great conqueror-to-be, became an armour-bearer for his uncle, and was dishonourably discharged. At the first sight of blood he had become sick at his stomach. He tried caravan conducting then, going as far south as Abyssinia. Sometimes there was a little banditry or what moderns know as "highjacking," on the side. But more scenes, casts, codes, tales, dialogue, went into that amazing catchall that was his memory. Tours as a wholesale grocer and jobber of supplies added more. The cash for this was furnished by a widow of twice his years, fifty times his fortune. She also gave him an oversupply of children, among them one Fatima, whom he truly loved.

But domesticity could not hold him. He had been as a youth a Samuel in Islam. Visions, theology, genuine zeal for reform, ambitions made a ferment in that overlarge head. He had decided on one God, so he first tried alliance with the two major monotheistic faiths, going to study at Jerusalem. Though he excelled at oratory, he was so poor at the Torah and the Talmud that the rabbis expelled him. This was unfortunate for Israel and Islam both. Yoked, they might have overcome Charles and his Hammer and possessed a good slice of west Europe as they had of the east, and of Asia and north Africa. Some overtures he also made to the Christian bishops. But his puzzling admixture of sensuality with religion, they thought, had little in common with the pure philosophy of the Cross. He had his own morals, some better than those of the West, but revenge was a weak point. He swore to have it on both rabbis and bishops.

Rebuffed, and striving then for a faith all his own, he went up into the mountains, wrapped himself in his mantle and lay down to his dreams. Very far off sometimes are the shores which a ripple started by a pebble incident tossed into the ocean of evolution, will finally reach. Mahomet's ascent of more than a century before started the ripple that grew into the enormous wave of horsemen now at the Loire.

Other leaders had gone up into mountains. Moses had come down with his face shining and his Law. On one Christ had given the greatest and shortest of sermons, the highest of philosophies complete in a few phrases. Mahomet came down with a new faith which, he reported, he had found on the summit with Gabriel's help. To his father-in-law and other secretaries he poured this out. They took it down, all the flaming poetic passages and the sluggish ones of directions, and through twenty years edited it and boiled it down, giving it the continuity, syntax, and the grammar it had sadly lacked. It was a glittering conglomerate, an astonishing joblot, a brazen and golden treasury of many things: Old Mesopotamian myths popular in his holy-wicked Mecca. Tales from other faiths. Rococo sets for grandiose heavens. Characters from other celestial casts. Arrant ramblings and sound moral sense. Jingles and impassioned dithyrambs. Sheer poetry in majestic flights and sheerest nonsense. His chance utterances, his sex instructions, even his grudges. In short, his balanced contemplations and all the frothings-up out of that amazing subconscious of his, all the things past and things remembered from a life that had been one-third crusading, one-third ascetic, and one-third vagabond.

Each race should have, he said, its special prophet. He did not reject Christ. He put him with Moses alongside himself. He kept too one the three faiths had in common, Abraham—he called him Ibraham. An imposing hierarchy of supernatural beings he placed around his Allah: secretary angels who helped him; scout angels who reported on our conduct below; traveler angels who surveyed the universe; battalions of seraphim who spent the ages in carolling around his throne; and two very appealing ones, Azrael, the dignified and noble Angel of Death, and Israfel whose heart strings were a lute, the angel of the Resurrection. Core of his universe was a new Trinity, One Person, Two Things: Allah, the great floating Throne, and the Book of Truth, his Koran. And Heaven had three planes, one each for Jews and Christians, and the highest for his followers. Rivers of milk and honey, silk carpets, springs with diamonds for pebbles, and seventy-two wives would reward each saved Moslem. For recompense each wife had thousands of servants. But if his heaven was rococo and to it had been transferred these delights which had always been thought mundane, there was often an exotic but genuine beauty and poetry playing around the queer jumble of Mahomet's script—in the ninety-nine imaginative names he gave to the Most High, for example. And there was tenderness in the prayer that might be considered the Koran's Pater Noster:

"In the name of God, the Compassionate Compassioner, praise! To Allah, Lord of the Worlds, the Compassionate Compassioner, the Sovereign of the Last Day, praise! Thee do we worship, of Thee beg aid. In the right road guide us, in the way of those to whom Thou hast shown favour, for whom there is no wrath and who go not astray."

Often in his little breviary he counsels "help for the brother in the road"—the beggar; and speaks of "the perfume of good deeds."

And if he allotted in paradise so many wives to each of his warriors, in this sphere below he looked out for the wives. No man, he said, should have more than four. And he provided for their property and other rights. Oddly enough he was one of the very first of woman's champions.

With his creed set, his reforming zeal blazed forth—first at the unlucky Meccans. They gambled too much and furthermore always cheated at it. Their wives were too numerous, their adulteries prodigious; and their infanticides had become as common as their daily assassinations. His neighbours did not like his prophecies of doom for them. Though they were breaking so many laws there was one they had kept, that against assassination within the city. All murders must take place outside. But now they would have broken even this to get at Mahomet. They stole up his staircase at nightfall but, warned, he had escaped like Paul over the city wall in a basket.

Without honour in his native Mecca, the now established prophet found it in a desert oasis. A wild tribe there nursing its wounds and longing for vengeance over their rivals, regarded this figure with the domed head of the visions, the forensic glance and gesture, the large hands at the end of pipestem arms sweeping the heavens, and thought he might call down a little of victory for them. They got it. And they joined up. Other tribes too. Soon there was a great snowball in the desert, as chief after chief followed the procession of the camel cavalry and stallions, the rude wood and leather artillery bumping and creaking along the desert sands. Where califs demurred, he threatened them, fought or overthrew them by boring within. He knew all the stratagems. One frequently used was becoming betrothed to the daughters of the rulers of the tribes, who thought this a great honour on the part of the prophet. There were scores of such alliances, most of them nominal as may be gathered from the fact that some of his fiancee had not been weaned.

He did not fight in his battles. He left the inciting examples of personal valour to his lieutenants, "Faithful Friend," "The Lion of God," and "The Deliverer." They were very careful of that stomach weakness of their leader. What prisoners they took they executed at a distance where he couldn't hear. Always he laid his plans, disposed his troops, gave his orders, then when the battle was about to be joined, retired to his tent at a safe remove. But he prayed there powerfully. Once—so they repeat at the festival they call "The Day of Deliverance"—when great regiments of evil spirits had joined with the foe and Mahomet's ranks were in grave disorder, he prayed down whole squadrons of angels and won that famous day.

So he fired the Arab pride beyond quenching. From moral crusade to moral crusade, battle to battle, on he rode, a strange half dervish, half-prophet figure, now pointing to his Paradise and its peris, now warning of the perils of Hell. And this armourbearer-bandit-caravanconductor-wholesalegrocer-general-reformer-poet-genius had dominated Arabia and many bordering countries, and was well on his way to laying an actual hand on the garments of his dreams and the conquest of many other lands when, near By-zantium, he was conquered and laid low forever not by the sword, but, as Genseric had been, by a fever. But he had permanently aroused the pride of his people scattered far and wide, and left to them a new religion-and-race consciousness, and a great book. If this was often marred by a hectic quality, chromo pictures, diony-siac flights, and an immature morality, it was at times constructive and beautiful and moving. The whole of his book, of the great politico-religious structure he had reared, and the heavenly ladder he thrust up toward the paradise of his dreams fairly trembled with the vigour of his climbing.

As a spirit more powerful than he had been in the flesh, he had ridden over the continents through the years at the head of his horsemen and had now come over the high Pyrenees passes, had reached the Loire, and was headed for the Seine. His horsemen lived and fought by that book. They travelled fast but at the appointed hours they always dismounted and knelt, facing the once pious-wicked, the now sacred city of Mecca, in memory of him. They were bound to meet some time—this irresistible race-wave of faith of the East and the immovable breakwater of the faith that had been taken over and now seemed to be of the West rather than the East. The at times worthy and moral and improving re-ligion of Mahomet with its revenge and over-physical rewards for good conduct, now collided with the faith of the cross with its purity and its quite different selflessness and inner spiritual re-wards. Mahomet's code, being not so elevated as the other, was perhaps more scrupulously observed. But at least the warriors of Paris observed their faith well enough in letter, particularly when they wanted something or were in danger. And one and all they marched now into the first Notre Dame with a great metallic ac-companiment of chain links and accoutrement to the bronze many-tongued alarum of the bells and the angrier, snarling clan-our of the armourers hammering on their anvils across the river. They were, however, unalarmed. Invasion was nothing new for Paris. A hundred times the hostile hoof-beats had sounded, the dust had arisen on the horizon. More often than not, it had been the Germans that were coming—almost always unsuccessfully. Over the bugles, the oliphants, the churchbells were calling men of France to drive those invaders off. It was a long and picturesque one that had answered and would answer the call to drive off

German, Swabian, Burgundian, Goth, Roman, Moor, or cousin of England: Vercingetorix, Merovée, Aetius, Genevieve, Clovis, Philippe Auguste, Charles the Wise, Jeanne d'Arc, Duguesclin, Bayard, Turenne, Vauban, Dumoriez, Gambetta, Foch, Joffre, de Gaulle. And we have not mentioned the *poilus*, the men in the ranks —all those who through the centuries would throw down hoe, trowel, mould, shears, pastry pan, wrench, crank, riveter, acetylene torch, to take up spear, pike, sword, gun, parachute, wings. To take them up so that between wars they might plant their peas, pollard their plane trees, pleach their pears, plaster their chimneys, shoe their horses, design their engines, fill their retorts, blow their glass, dip their sheep, print their books, distill their perfumes, chisel statues, search Nature for her secrets, trim their inimitable hats, bake their little cakes, throw great bridges over canyons, paint pictures, sing gay and wistful little songs, write organ chorales, build blue ribbon liners, carve umbrella handles, and rear mighty cathedrals in air, all in peace—in peace.

But to be quite fair, if there were beautiful things in Paris then, like the lovely ivory and precious metal vessels of Saint Eloi (the goldsmith of King Dagobert who had gone down into Denis' tomb to spend the night with him) and the exceedingly beautiful tomb of Saint Germain (the Left Bank Saint Germain), the invaders had too made beautiful things—more indeed up to that time than the Gallo-Roman-Franks. Some day the men of France would surpass them, but not yet. They should all have joined forces and made more beautiful and useful things together. The trouble was— as it still is—that the fashion is for one set of men making beautiful and useful things to go out, every once in a while, and destroy or steal the lovely and helpful things made by another set.

It was truly astonishing how much beauty, in a century's short space, these horsemen had created in Spain alone—palaces, fountains, gardens, mulberry and almond groves, damascening shops, bright bazaars, graceful grilles, looms weaving exquisite tapestries, arches lovelier than any of the Romans and Byzantines, also universities in which were taught algebra, medicine, an advanced horticulture, astronomy and astrology, the right-hand and left-hand studies of the stars, and a host of subtle things of which the scholars crowding the Paris hills would one day know so much, but of which those hard-riding, hard-fighting, smashing nobles on the Field of Mars, in the first church of Notre Dame, knew next to nothing.

Now this dark invader could not be strictly called a Moor. He might be known as a composite Moor, perhaps better an Arab-Moor-Berber. In the ranks defiling through the Pyrenees, debouching on the lovely Touraine plains, one might see the lineaments of some old Red Sea vagabond, Damascus pickpocket, Garden of Eden rascal, or a fourth generation descendant of one of Mahomet's desert veterans. Often one might note the noble aquilinity of the pure Arab. There were simon-pure Moors from Mauretania, the old Roman province of which Carthage was the capital, the nomad Berbers of the Sahara wastes, the Atlas foothills, all as great horsemen as the original Moslem adventurers who had absorbed them into their ranks and cause and faith. The Arab, and at his best, this composite "Moor" was the most perfectly coordinating specimen Allah or the universal God had ever made. He had an alertness and an elasticity with strength that went well with his keen and perfectly tempered scimitar. A grace, too, like that of his personal ornaments and the headstalls of his stallions, the rich grille work and arabesque in his Spanish cities which he had found so heavily Roman and left so bright and light and gracefully oriental. And there was a subtlety not only in his poetry and thought but in his very hospitality and his revenge. For he was a paradox. He liked his horses slender as gazelles, his women plump as quails. He could stab a foe adroitly in the back, in the same hour defend with his life the stranger within his gates. For the beggar by the wayside, "the brother in the road," all in that army would show consideration even as they planned as on they rode the lewdest and most unchivalrous things for Our Lady. Indeed, what had been true of the Gauls in the millennium before Christ, was true of these "Moors" and Arabs then—could they have added to their other talents one for organization they might have controlled all the contemporary kingdoms. As it was, they came near doing it. All in all, Ferdinand and Isabella did not do so bright a thing as they thought when, in 1493, they drove the descendants of these horsemen from Granada and lost their knowledge and craftsmanship forever.

If people later made a mistake about this Arab-Berber-Moor-mongrel army travelling north to dispossess Our Lady, the armourers of Paris made another when, as they plunged hissing steel and spat into the great cooling casks, they cursed these invaders for "blackamoors," "black Mahounds," and "black monkeys trying to climb our towers to tear the cross down." They were no more black than—modern producers to the contrary—the Othello of Shakespeare's conception was really. Not negroid, never black, they were—when not pure Caucasian, as was often the case—of a leathern, walnut, or café-au-lait complexion or of some fine tint dyed by centuries of sun, sand and simoon into the flesh as colour is wrought into the very texture of the porcelain.

In the Paris forges the armourers worked in an atmosphere of flame-lit murk, their straining bodies casting giant interlocked shadows on the walls, to a terrific banging of iron hammers on resounding steel. All who looked into the doors knew that the sharp-edged, heavy-hafted bludgeon of a mace was for the mayor of the palace, Charles. No royal cipher could wield such a weapon, let alone swing it in great circles around his head. It was fit only for the great shoulder muscles, all that magnificent leverage system of tendons that rippled smoothly under the chain-link sheath whenever Charles rode, strode, lifted high his axe or brought his fist crashing down on a council table.

The armourers were also making swords almost as mighty. They were very sure of the merits of these compared with the daintily made weapons of the Moors. The Frankish two-handed scramasax, tall, broad, strong, like its wielders, and with hilt in the design of their symbol—the cross—they swore would beat down the scimitar, so like the supple dark horsemen, slender, elastic, and in the curve of the crescent.

So scimitar against scramasax it was for them, a dead Mahomet against a live Martel, the sensuous crescent against the austere cross. One should not add what would also seem obvious—revenge against love, for most of these armourers and the men for whom they made the swords were not always keenly aware of the difference in essence between the two versions of the great drama of Man's relations to his God, the one worthy at times but adulterated, the other simple and lofty and shiningly pure.

There were now ten churches to ring over the Seine: on the Left Bank, south, an enlarged third-century Saint Marcel; Saint Genevieve's great abbey on the hilltop; Saint Germain-des-Près to the west; in the centre on the island, ancient Saint Etienne, Childebert's Notre Dame, and a new tiny Saint Martial; on the Right Bank, north, Saint Germain l'Auxerrois, two tiny new ones, a Saint Merri and Saint Paul, and a rebuilt Saint Denis across the Paris plain. It was pleasant going to church now. One could feast his eyes on soft-toned mosaic pictures, great gold and blue, cloud and wing spreading murals, silver lamps suspended by gold chains from Our Lady's gilded ceiling, and altar ivories and altars, crosses pyxes, chalices worked in precious metals and gems, with two splendid gold tombs made by Saint Eloi. And further to confirm them in the good habit of churchgoing, the bells of the ten churches through the day sounded the hours for matins, angelus, complines, vespers, salut, all the offices, and the masses. So perhaps they forged swords and fought with them for the cross because they were so used to the cross and it was their own. Sometimes it would seem so, so quick were they to resort to the sword, forgetting the message of the Cross. And yet something of that message and its beauty must have pierced through the heart's darkness, or those ten sanctuaries never would have remained there and the cross would have come down.

Whatever the cause of the fidelity of the workers and warriors of Paris—habit or sheer faith—on one thing they were resolved as they knelt on the cold stones or beat steel out on their anvils—that design of their sword hilts, of the cross, the symbol of their faith, should not be changed into anything else. But they had to hurry if they were to prevent it. Already the dark horsemen had reached Poitiers. On third-century Saint Jean, much of which you can still see, the crescent was in place, and the Moslems were bathing in the baptismal pool. At the rate they travelled they would soon be at the very doors of Our Lady. And at last, the great hammer finished, half of Paris and much of North Gaul followed it with a vast arsenal on their backs and in high-wheeled wagons, a sun-glinted army, down the Orleans highway for the Loire.

So they came to "Caesar's City," which we know as Tours. There Charles stayed long enough to be blessed by the bishop who was the seventh or eighth in line from the famous Gregory of Tours who wrote the great history of the Franks. The old walls between which the Hammer rode are still there, running from the square of the mediaeval bishop's palace and the cathedral of Tours which, night or day, seems wrought of cream lace.

Charles did not linger long in the old capital but marched to a hamlet of a half-dozen stone cottages, a forge, and oratory called Sainte-Catherine-de-Fierbois. Another conqueror would pass that way one day—a girl in mail. Later she would send messengers from royal Chinon to the mediaeval church of Sainte-Catherine-de-Fierbois that succeeded the oratory, for a sword which she had been told by her Voices was buried there. You can still see the cleft in the stone through which it was disinterred from the original altar. This history confirms, and there is good reason to believe that the sword of Jeanne's was one left there in gratitude by Charles Martel on his way back from the battle to which he was now riding.

Sometimes it is called the Battle of Tours, again of Poitiers. It is hard to set the exact spot, for the foe fanned out all over this country. It is all fertile ground for those who love to relive history. The hill city of Poitiers is thronged with old monuments and with ancient churches where *Te Deums* were sung for victories. And one can visit three famous battle sites in the suburbs: by Vouille, in 507, the Unitarian Alaric the Second was defeated by the newly-baptized Trinitarian Clovis; at Maupertuis, in 1356, the English beat the French in the Hundred Years War battle of Poitiers; the third neighbouring little hamlet, Moussais-la-Bataille, is pointed out as the site of Charles' great battle. Though some high point or critical charge took place there, one cannot chart out the exact progress of the battle. The violent action took place between the two famous cities, by one of the full-bodied rivers which keep France so fair and so envied, and which ran so green at the beginning, so red before the struggle ended. Those dark horsemen came on their magnificent mounts, not in battle waves but in clouds. Clouds of flowing white garments ballooning out over saddles and streaming manes and tails. Clouds with myriad dark eyes meshed in them and shot through with lightning flashes as the sun caught headdress, headstall and raised scimitar. Clouds as musical as Alpine heights with goatbells, from the far-flung tintinnabulation of the belled dancing girls who, until the actual moment of contact, raced on singing in the van. It was the oddest battle divertissement ever seen by the soldiers of the West.

So like cumulus clouds billowing up from the southern horizon, with lightning playing in and out and driven as though by the winds of a Great Idea—and the Prophet's breath—up to that destined meeting, they, buoyant and singing, rode, only to break in fragments, like clouds torn on low mountain tops or sea cliffs. Clouds of white garments on cliffs of iron-ringed, leather-jerkined Franks. The delicate curved scimitar bending on the two-handed scramasax. Above all, breaking on the Hammer of him called "The Hammer," rising and falling everywhere as he towered over the battlefield. And if it did not in one day crack the ten thousand Moslem skulls accredited it by later minstrels, at least it cracked the composite Arab-Berber-Moor-Mongrel-Mahound skull—broke the back of Islam just as it was riding on, singing, to world dominion.

The chief pity of it all—besides that implicit in the silent wind rows of the slain, man and horse, dark warrior and blonde, in the long Loire and Vienne and Clain grasses indiscriminately and bloodily mingled—was this: could they only have gotten on together, the oncoming Dark Ages might not have been so dark and the Renaissance might sooner have come to Europe. For the Phocan-Punic-Liguric-Iberian-Basque-Romano-Franco-Gallo-Celt (so soon, too, to add the Normans) whom we know as French could, despite that Gallic and Phoenician artistry and imaginativeness, have done with a little of the knowledge and skill of these polite and highly-civilized "infidel dogs," "black monkeys," and "blackamoors," these same Semite Arab-Berber-Moor mongrel. But they waited until the Crusades before profiting by the contact. Perhaps, too, had they not waited, the Gothic might have been born sooner. For certainly those Arab arches were much easier on the eye than those in Rome and Childebert's Notre Dame.

However, in its destructiveness, the Hammer of Charles did do something constructive. That high colour and nervous sensuosity of the Orient would never have done for the hardier West. And the cross stayed up. And Notre Dame had no domes. The play did not close.

XIX

*Charlemagne founds a School and Choir at the First Notre Dame.
. . . He buttresses the Church, mourns Roland, conquers most
of the Kings, has Trouble with his Wild Daughters, distributes
Education, tries to sing, to write himself, makes a New Empire,
a New Europe which unfortunately will not last, receives Gifts
from the Land of the Arabian Nights, Keys to Many Cities and
the Tomb of Christ, takes a Swim, gets Pleurisy, and after a busy
Life, which he has tremendously enjoyed, is buried sitting up with
a Bible on his Knees and a Gold Crown on his Head.*

813-814 A.D.

IN THE RAMBLING CLOISTERS AROUND KING CHILDEBERT'S
Notre Dame, already almost three hundred years old, and
Saint Etienne, almost five hundred, the *ecolatre*, or chancellor
of the Cathedral—the first one—signalled to the boys. They were
scattered under the round arches and by the great pillars in groups
and without regard to race—Frankish boys, Belgians, youngsters
with a Latin look, and many rather purely descended from youths
who had once put bright helmets on bright hair by ancient altars
here. Some squatted on their haunches, in a little straw against the
pavement's cold, giving the Latin phrases a chattering, sing-song
accidence. Others stood at sloping desks, clicking their quills in
inkpots and, with heads cocked at all angles, made cross and down
strokes for letters, that already had a Gothic appearance, resembling the choir carvings that would come there some day. A long-
gowned group stuttered in their spelling of psalter words and
between whiles leaned against the walls, sighing as the creak of
wagon wheels on the old Roman road that led over the island, the
cries of sailors on the quais of the river, gamins' shouts as they
dove into it, all the seductive sounds of the great outdoors came
into the world of shadowed pillars. But there were not many pauses
in which they could listen to these siren calls, for their masters
were ever alert, and there was usually a great clamour, sometimes
very melodious, again off pitch, from a considerable company that
stood up elbow to elbow with mouths as roundly open as young

robins, scanned the choir sheets held up by a deacon, and sent silver flocks of notes through the round-head windows, up to the belfry and out over the Seine.

But all this lively industry suddenly stopped when the chancellor, with a hand as waxen as the parchment on which the musical *neumes* were written, rang his handbell. It was the tenth time that winter that he had exhorted them to do their best. For their patron, the school founder, a very great man, the most glorious indeed in the whole world—called then Charles, but to be known as *the* Charles, Charlemagne—was on his way down from Aix, and would visit them soon. Each week now for ten the chancellor had said the same thing. Sometimes he added that all the boys from the choirs of Paris, Cologne, Trèves, Aix, Toulouse, and the rest of the schools he had started, owed to him lodging and food, shoes and choir sheets, gowns and knowledge, fires and puddings and silver pieces at Christmas.

And then the chancellor, extending his parchment-like hands as though to take in the full round sum of the Emperor's deeds, told the older scholars how his empire had grown from the west to the east. Bretons and Danes had knelt to him. The English had sent gold. The Scotch had begged for treaties. Before his sword the Iberians had surrendered the Spanish Marches and the Balearic Isles of the Inland Sea. The Pannonians of Odoacer's land paid him tribute. Italy opened up to him her fabled cities. He had marched off with the gold of the Huns. All his cousins—Saxons, Frisians, the proud Bavarians, the Alemanni—had gone down before him in battle. The Avars had yielded by the Danube. His sword would not have stopped there had not his prestige now won for him without use of steel. Irene, fascinating Empress of the Empire of the East, had become friendly to him, indeed almost married him. The rulers of the Near East, vastly impressed by his presence when they saw him, by his prestige when they did not, by his organizing skill which they took for military genius—and which in truth brought him more than half his victories—and his onward sweep, sent him keys to their cities. On their rugs awed Persian delegates bowed down to him. Haroun-al-Raschid sent him peacocks, carved chessmen, silks from the Land of the Arabian Nights, and later, through the Patriarch of Jerusalem, made him a present of the Tomb of Christ. So peacefully he won what the Crusaders would win and lose, wading through seas of blood.

Picking his words well for immature minds, the chancellor told them of grave errors the Emperor had corrected, the worship of images, for one thing, which had crept into many parishes, particularly those toward the east, and the sale of Christian slaves.

And he fought the Saxons time and again before they would give up their worship of devils.

Also the great Emperor had, with large heart and hand, distributed charities, regulated coinage and weights and measures, drawn up codes, and added to ancient Roman and Frankish laws new ones embodying Christian principles. And he was constantly asking for reports from distant lands, like Africa, on destitute Christians. Sums of money were always going overseas to help them.

He had even given to the months the very names children learned —all taken by this great outdoor king from the great outdoors, for instance: Shedding Month (February) when the deer shed their horns; Breakground Month (June); Ears of Grain Month (August); Wood Month (September) when they gathered fuel for the winter fires; Vintage Month (October); Holy Night Month (December). And he had his scholars and musicians gather together in a collection that would always delight men's hearts the *catilenas*, as he called them, folk tales and songs of the bards out of which, though they could not know this, would spring the immortal *chansons de geste*—in which he and his paladins would greatly figure.

Of all of these things the chancellor of Notre Dame told them as the sunlight, refracted up from the river waves, wrote the rhythms of the Seine in wavering gold on the old walls. And there was that date so nicely even, and of all dates in history—except those of the King of Kings the easiest for young students to remember—Christmas Day, 800. Then in great Saint Peter's he had been crowned Emperor of the old Empire of the West, and called Augustus by the Pope. So the chancellor, as well as the Pope and Charlemagne himself, was sure that he was bringing back to enduring life the old Empire again, which would have been quite a different thing from that shadowy and troublesome state which later emperors would call and pretend was truly "the Holy Roman Empire." He came near to reviving it; and would have, if his son had been half so wise and capable as he.

The chancellor went on to explain to the older and more knowledgeable ones that Clovis did not equal, Constantine did not out match Charlemagne as the support—what we know as the strong right arm—of the Church; even, he might have added, as Charlemagne himself did not surpass his great and usually underestimated grandfather, Charles Martel. Like the most pious peasant, he was always a consistent church-goer, thus setting a good example for all, for the students and choir-boys there in these old halls assembled. To his home church in his residence capital at Aix-la-Chapelle he donated solid brass rails, ornamented lamps, pillars from

Provence. On Saint Peter's, in another city very dear to his heart, to which he made a pilgrimage every four years to renew his vows, he had spent a fortune to repair, enlarge, and adorn it. He high-handedly had had his clergy add "*Filioque*—to the Son," to the Creed. He could not change the vestments, but he had designed new uniforms for all sacristans, nightwatchmen, and even the door-keepers of all churches. He had increased the holdings of the Pope around Rome and in central Italy so that the capital of the Church might have a domain commensurate with her dignity. And he was ever ready to spring to protect her, as he had the Pope when he was in grave danger. Regard too he had for that learning which was so dear to all of them there. Not only had he founded all these schools but he had imported the most eminent scholars from other lands, not only to teach his family and his most august self, but to reform the system of education and to make for all in the empire a new grammar.

So, resonantly the chancellor of Notre Dame finished his tribute, omitting, however, a few things that might have interested older heads. The great man could at times show a certain highhanded-ness, and did not like to be disagreed with. He had buttressed the Church, but sometimes he overinterfered with its management. At the coronation he had written down for the Pope the divisions of their respective provinces as he saw them, and he had by no means scanted his share. Too often he had his way. At that ceremony, he had paid respect to the Pope, but His Holiness had made obeisance to him. All this, however, was but the virtue's fault. He had for the most part influenced the Church for good. That effi-ciency and system of which he was a master and which more than any flair for strategy made his armies so powerful, strengthened the Church to her farthest barbarian parish. He was a helpful ally at ecumenical councils. His very staging of the coronation in Rome and his receiving the emblems of power from the Pope, started the custom of religious coronations. Before it had been a purely civil matter. Hereafter no monarch was true monarch unless crowned under the aegis of the Church.

Also the *écolatre* might have mentioned, could he have looked forward as well as back, that Charlemagne had made the same mistake his cousins from over the Rhine would make eleven hun-dred years later. He had extended his empire to cover a large part of Europe, and sovereigns beyond it acknowledged his power as unofficial chief potentate of the known world. But he had failed to protect it by water. Once or twice he tried to build, oar and launch a navy, but the result was futile. He had a magnificent land army, a near cipher of a navy. He had neglected sea power; and consequently the Moslems ranged the Mediterranean with their galleys bent on war and piracy. They boasted, almost without exaggeration, that without their permission no one in it could float a plank. Successors of these Notre Dame students might note another historic parallel. King Alfred of England, before the ninth century had gone, would not make the same mistake of the continental conqueror. Across the Channel he would build what was for the time a magnificent navy.

The loss of the sea to the Saracen sailors had greatly inconvenienced the chancellor, all the palace and cloister cooks, and Charlemagne. He loved good eating—it was one of his two weaknesses—and wanted pepper with his roasts. The corsairs had stopped the trade in all such things. The Jewish merchants who had journeyed along the river roads and the trade routes were now not bringing much silk, gold, papyrus for parchment and lantern glazing. Gone were the perfumes called "of Araby" but really only of that peninsula through transit on their way from the Far East and the spices—cloves, cinnamon, cummin, pepper, sweet-smelling nard and hot garum. The caravans of camels which before Charlemagne had gone through Spain, looking with their merchandise sacks as though they had many humps instead of one, were not seen very often. Sometimes the lamps of the eleven Paris churches were dimmer now. Though those of Our Lady were by custom supplied with oil from Provence, much had come from Africa; and seldom could cargo galleys get across.

Incidentally, Charlemagne had to do what kings from ancient to modern times have disliked: go off the gold standard and coin much silver. This did not help his finances, which were in none too good a state. He needed a large income for his armies and generous gifts, and this had come from property sales and taxes and imposts on merchandise, the stream of which was now reduced to a trickle.

However, this control of the sea, the eternal blockade, had one good result. It turned the north and west of Europe further in on itself, and tended to make the nations there self-sustaining. Europe was breaking away from the classic chains which had bound her to Athens and the Levant. Thenceforth she was to nurture a new Western culture of her own, derived in part from the classic, but different, a little rougher at first, more Frankish, but full of life and gusto, with nothing of the effete, the too urban, the over civilized about it. Charlemagne had breezed all over Europe with an invigorating freshness after the decadent Merovingians. And if he had lost trade and pepper and gold, he made up for it by all his schools and songs and grammar and great scholars. He sounded in advance a horn mightier than the famous oliphant in Roncesvalles

It presaged the dawn of the more modern Middle Ages, of the
Gothic and the Cathedral.

The chancellor had not, of course, seen fit to mention the peculiar
and gusty royal ménage at Aix—Charlemagne's wives that succeeded one another, his concubines or his self-indulgent daughters.
They were a wild lot, those girls, but he loved them well. Whenever he could, he would have them at dinner with him. He would
listen as they studied with their celebrated tutors, take them on his
hunts and when he went swimming—his favorite exercise—in icy
rivers. Indeed, so fond was he of them that he did not want them
to get married, and, as a lesser evil, allowed them their lovers in the
royal palace. He would rather have them a little frail and at home
where he could see them often than spotless in their virtue and far
away from him. He was very, very human.

Instead of such details, the chancellor, speaking of the Emperor's
great grief for his friend, the hero Hroudland or Roland, which
time had not dulled, called on one of his scholars to recite the
catilena of the glorious death in the pass of Ronscevalles, in preparation for the Emperor's visit. He never seemed to tire of this tale
of his paladins being caught in the mountain death trap, by the
less heavily weighted and the swift moving Basques and Gascons.
The chances were that in whatever school he visited, the master
would have some prize scholar on his feet reciting this. And
Charlemagne took a great delight in the accomplishments of his
gowned waifs.

The great man had these past few months been staying in Aix,
which is now on German but was then on French soil. Only a few
foundations of his palace remain and these are under the Aix
townhall. But in Saint Mary's Church we get a little closer to
him, for it has been there a thousand years. It was rebuilt one
hundred and seventy years after Charlemagne's death but on the
old lines and in the octagonal shape he had ordered his architects to
borrow for the first church from San Vitale, Italy.

This season when the Notre Dame schoolboys were faithfully
practising their pieces for him, Charlemagne who had been all
his seventy years so exuberantly active, was beginning to feel his
age, and to show it just a little. And he had been so good to look
at, seated on throne or horse, or striding along. Tall, finely-muscled
with a good brow, fine hair, merry and ever alive eyes above a
long nose (which so many great kings of France have had), and
always dignified but carrying his dignity easily and humanly, he
had been as fine a specimen as one would want for man or emperor.

Now that grand figure was beginning to give just a little and
to lose its resilience. Its one defect, a pudding prominence of stom-

ach from his love of good eating, was beginning to round into actual corpulence. And this fall he had suffered a good deal from rheums and fevers. From his continuous hardships, his riding at the head of his armies through arduous campaigns, he had been troubled with them before. But now they threatened to become chronic. And with them went at times a lethargy annoying to one who had been the most active man in Europe.

He fought against it. It had been his custom to take a nap early in the afternoon after a good dinner. Now he was tempted more often to drowse, to nod on the throne or in his great chair by the fire, with his aging hounds at his feet. But still he rose early, put on, without help of wardrobe man or groom, his linen underwear, brought the hose up over his long legs, fastened the leather thongs about his thighs, donned a silk tunic with its silk cord and laced his shoes. This, with his martin or miniver trimmed mantle, was his everyday dress, the national one of the Frank, and no better than that of his poorest noble. On feastdays, of course, he did better, wearing an embroidered tunic and a cloak fastened with a gold buckle, carrying a jewelled sword and wearing a great gold and gemmed crown on his head which, if ever man's did, looked truly majestic. Often while he was putting on his clothes he would dispense justice and settle quarrels for rich and poor who came into the spacious, draughty chamber, sparsely but handsomely furnished with great high carved pieces and voluminous arras. None of the litigants thought their king looked less judicial or majestic in his drawers.

Dressed, these days he would often attend to his studies. He was like many big and able men who have not had too much learning in their youth, very eager for it. Indeed, he was as much in love with learning as he was with swimming or the hunt or the charge. Often his robustious girls or his inferior sons would find him seated in the great chair by the fire, practising at his Gothic pothooks. For though he was a great patron of the arts, he was none too skillful at them. Other rulers have dabbled at these. Richard Cœur de Lion, Marie Antoinette wrote love songs, Frederick the Great composed string quartettes, modern prime ministers and chancellors try painting, all with who knows what help from courtier critics and shadowy ghosts. So they get, perhaps, overmuch praise for their accomplishments. And Charlemagne was rather an entrepreneur of scholars than one himself.

True, he would converse at length with Alcuin, Peter of Pisa, Angilbert, and Lombard Paul. They would speak in a fine Church Latin; but he would lapse too often into the universal Latin vernacular, to receive courteous corrections from his distinguished teachers which he would take with good grace. He would read

Greek to them too and they would nod approval. Also he was very fond of the lofty ideas and lordly language of Augustine's "City of God." At night, he would go up on the crenelled top of his palace with his teachers to talk of the shining constellations—it was from staying up there too long that his rheumatism had increased of late. But he was a little slow at writing. Perhaps his hand was too coarse and thick from handling the great scramasax, the boar spear, the battleaxe, for the little quill and inkpot. He had been an outdoor, a hard-riding, hard-fighting king and he could put together great armies and an empire, but he could not always make those little letters behave. However, he was so eager to learn to write well that he kept little sheafs of parchment under his pillow. Nature got him up four or five times a night and each time he would also try to write a little.

It was often his habit, by day, to go into the huge chamber allotted to the ever-increasing palace library. There at the sloping desks his scholars were always at work, illuminators too, with black, green, indigo, crimson inks and gold leaf. He would look at all this paraphernalia and the manuscripts and chained books admiringly and wistfully because, great as were his triumphs in the fields of war and statecraft, those he won in the scholar's field were chiefly vicarious.

Then, restless again and craving activity but shut up by the blizzards, he would stalk gloomily through the halls to stare down from the windows at his hounds, leaping up at the sound of his voice, or at the armourers welding the chain links for his leather shirt. In his depression he often wondered if the sword of foe, or friend's in practise, would ever ring on his armour again. It was very hard to be shut up in the draughty fortress-palace, full of arrow-slits, and so many of whose windows were unglazed and protected only by arras and hangings against the North Sea winds which swept the Rhenish flatlands.

There were other things besides books and studies on his mind. He was very lonely. Five wives he had had, four officially wed, one informally in the way later called morganatic. The first, Himiltrude of the Franks, had had to go and bear him—Charlemagne of all men—a crippled son. He was an affectionate man not only to his daughters, but to his mother and sister, of whom he was very fond, and to all his friends. He pitied the poor boy; it was not his fault; but a prince could not be a prince with a crooked back.

Besides uncrowned Himiltrude, there had been four crowned helpmeets—Italian Desiderata, repudiated when her father's treaty was broken; Rhenish Hildegarde; the false Fastrada; the Alemann Liutgarde. Very near too he had come—after the last three had died—to wedding the gorgeous Empress Irene of the Golden Horn. His concubines, he was sure, couldn't count, though Alcuin and his confessor had chided him about them—it was the one irregularity in a regular, well-disciplined life. Yet of all his women those concubines had been the most appreciative and cooperative. This he had proclaimed to most of his queens in turn, when they had harassed him about favourites in a palace wing. Very vividly stormy scenes came back to him—the anointed bedfellow bolt upright against the bolster, big braids against it, her nails biting deep into palms, as he protested that he had raised her to a great height, lavished on her great riches, that she was envied of all women, and should be very grateful. To boot, he would protest, he had been a faithful husband—within the limits prescribed by Nature for strong, blood-running monarchs—a Godfearing one too, going to mass every Sunday and feastday and very frequently to confession. He had always started with what he took for sweet reason but had wound up by overriding each queen with his great voice and blazing eyes as he rode down all in the world except his daughters whom he called now his "little fawns," again his "hound-sluts." But that too was his fault, when he had loved them so he had wanted them not properly wed and far away, but near even if erring, so that he might stroke their dear heads.

The worst of it now was that as there came back to him some scornful remark of a queen about how his virility would vanish one day, a rheumatic twinge with its agonizing barb drove that prophecy home. Was the great Charlemagne, King of the East, King of the West, growing old? Was Time sending his messenger ahead? And Death's?

But when the north winds continued to howl across the flat white wastes and beyond the outmost barbican, the wolves seated on their haunches in a ring repeated that howl, and the palace arras flapped in the windows and the log flames now died down, again gushed up the chimneys in geysers of sparks, the great Charlemagne would take up the struggle again, wrestling with his pothooks as his ancestors had with pots. Almost as consistently, before they brought the flagons of mead and the trenchers with great smoking joints upon them for the noon hour, he would bid the illustrious doctors, Einhard and Alcuin, to go, not to God, but to the devil. He would make as short work of his stewards bringing to him accounts of his household, his treasurers bringing the accounts of the kingdom. And not a letter a clerk would write, to be conveyed by couriers to far-off regions, would please him. He could write, he would roundly swear, a better one himself; then as if that touched on a sore point, his one great defeat in the lists of learning, he would stride off to the looms again, to examine the last hour litter in the court, his kitchens, or to the falconer's to look at his "hawks of the lure" and "hawks of the wrist," perched on their blocks, finding fault with the bewits, or bellstraps, the jesses, or leg-strops, and brails, or wing-thongs they had made, to end by throwing a great lot of them on the stones, with a great jangle of bells that showed the distress of his disposition. It was not like him. And all in the palace dependencies said he was a great hawk himself, hooded by Age and belled for Death.

Again he, the great emperor, who, on horse, on wings, had ranged Europe, would confine his moody pacing to the draughty halls. In the tenderer mood of a fatherhood that had been astounded then sorely wounded by the vagaries of his get, he would look in on his boys—at their books and pothooks too, under Father Peter of Pisa. They were a bit more moral, considering their sex, than the girls. But that was small consolation. While they scored over their sisters on the moral side, they lost very heavily to them on the side of ability. Once he had had hopes of his sons learning at least their letters and a little of governorship, if they couldn't absorb hunting, broadsword play, and military tactics. Now he had no hopes, only a vast and brooding despair and foreboding of what might—and did—happen to his great empire under them.

Nature was a jade—and a sorry one. Why couldn't she have made his girls boys? His girls. He loved them. He would smile at the thought of them; and would turn towards their chamber; hoping he would find them at their tapestries. For in the work of the looms of every kind, as in all useful arts and crafts, anything that might help his empire and his people, he was deeply interested; and scores of *missi dominici*, his official inspectors, he had sent, all up and down Europe to nurture the industry.

Or he would go up a stair to break in on them and have one of the old jolly, affectionate tussles when they would rumple his hair, even playfully pull that long nose, which would come back in every king of genius in France and in some that had no talent; and he would take the biggest on his knees by the fire and feel warmed by the leaping flames and their lapping affection.

Again, as he entered the chamber of one of his daughters all too hastily in his affection, he would hear a masculine voice and see some lover sliding behind the bed curtains. And his hand would go for his sword or, needing no weapon, it would clench in his might as though to strike them down or drag them, lovers and all, by their long hair and the scruffs of their necks, to the windows to throw them over the walls. But always he would think better of it. His great fist would drop to his side. He would return to brood by the fire which now too seemed to have no heart, no warmth. Then, inevitably, he would wind up by telling himself that if not good girls they were fine girls. They in turn would feel sorry for him, not so far as to repent and turn to the domestic tasks which, in his heart, he felt proper for girls, even fine strapping capable ones like his, or to things that would have pleased the priests, but to waiting on him when he was tired of cupbearers, tutors, and chancellors, sitting by him when he had the rheum or fever, or playing chess on a board which some chroniclers insist, some deny, was sent him by Irene, the Empress of the East. And they would romp with him, even play leapfrog in the big banqueting hall when no one was there and he was jolly with mead, and sang in big round sopranos and deep altos—the same tune line, of course—around the roaring log fire at Christmas.

But that seasonal gayety and wassail passed. In the depth of winter, locked deep in cold and snow and ice, with the great forest firs on which he looked out, never green, always white, he grew so moody that he forgot even his sprawling attempts at learning, his kingdoms, soldiers, horses, hawks, concubines, and girls. Back and forth he went on his endless journeys; now not to the Pyrenees or the Hellespont, but from barbican to barbican without, wall to wall within. Back and forth went that endless patrol—at night too, down the cold corridors, around draughty angles, past the billowing arras, his aging hounds at heel. In the great, gusty, indefatigable Charlemagne, it was pathetic. It was the twilight of a god, a king, or—better, a very great man.

But there was one last flame in it. For then came the spring—the last spring. With the first zephyrs and the breaking of the apples into white and pink against the grey walls, the fevers went and he burst out of the castle donjon and over the draw, to strip off wool and leather and plunge, a naked and very muscular king into a river just released from the bonds of ice as he had been from those of illness.

And he broke into song, harsh song but lusty and jolly; and coming into the castle then, roared to seneschal, grooms and equerries, to saddle and make ready. For suddenly it had occurred to him in the resurgence of his strength that while great victories of which he had his fill, might be all right, and priceless his possessions—all the crowns, thrones, cities, the royal jewels, the key to Jerusalem, of Saint Peter's and Christ's own sepulchre which Pope and Patriarch had sent him, and the rare singing birds of Haroun-al-Raschid—all, all, taken together, were not worth the simple ability to read and write. If beating would have done any good he would have beaten letters into his own boys' heads. Since his own had failed him, he would ride down to where there were boys who could learn all the beautiful things books could teach—like that memorial song of his old friend, Hroudland, for example

He would visit his schools, and Paris should be first on his list. In fact, with spring, he had an uncontrollable urge to visit Paris— he did not know that it was for the last time. Ever since the Emperor Julian, and long before him, people had been going to Paris for one thing or another, as they would be resorting there down the ages. His paladins might be glad to go because of the girls of Paris. The objectives of Charlemagne were boys and books.

His attendants, seeing that the fever flushes, the rheumatism twinges, the advance scouts of time and old age, had at least for the time been banished and that he was himself once more—which meant just about the gustiest, most vigorous picture of energy in Europe—soon had inner and outer wards of the castle ringing with hammer, horseshoe, chain mail, and bugle. And with a kiss of the lady in the wing, and warm hugs, with playful buffets on the buttocks, of his lively bouncing girls, Charlemagne was over the draw, with a plain steel helm on his great head that needed no gold casque to look royal, and bright blue eyes ablaze, as he cantered past the farthest barbican.

So the cavalcade of paladins and sergeants, bowmen and spear-men to the rear, with bright smitings of the sun upon their mail, rode southwest through great forests and by the river roads, to the high chatter of the trumpets. They went, too, at a pace a little fast for one so recently in thrall to a fever. And to his further jeopardy, he resumed the long swims of his youth in the dawn-cold currents. He was the first of all to plunge in and the last to come out, lecturing his paladins on their over-big breakfasts. His own frame might be large, his torso big, but until this past winter he had not been stout, but deep of chest, rather. And now he would thump it to show them. He and Roland—before Roland fell "at the craven hands of those dog infidels of the Spanish Marches"—had outlifted them, all his paladins, at weights, out-distanced them at throwing the hammer, outwrestled them at "catch-as-catch-can," because the two had always risen from the east before they were full. All his life he had done everything (except being busy) in moderation.

So this great group of hardy outdoor knights in chain mail came to Saint Denis, and their commander strode into the grilled chapel King Dagobert had—after his sepulchral nap with the martyr— raised over his bones. Then almost within the twenty minutes he was at the Seine, over the bridge, whose successor today is called Of Moneychangers," and under the gate-arch, to the roars of all Paris from chimney sweep to count.

Shouting still, they followed him toward Notre Dame. And now for one hour of his recaptured prime he was his old ebullient self, a king to follow; on horseback, with back straight and head a little up; on foot with his swift breezy step, the great beard, eyes curious yet compelling and his whole manner like an effective and powerful wind that blows great ships to prosperous ports, and which seems forever just starting or just completing some grand voyage and high adventure. Through the narrow way that led from the palace to the old Roman Forum and to the little open space beyond, he and the animated crowd at his saddle skirts and all around came to the first house of Our Lady. He dismounted near the spot where now, in a strip of green lawn by the riverside and in front of the last Notre Dame, he never dismounts but ever rides high on his great bronze horse.

Then the gusty cheery figure strode in after the welcoming bishop and the elevated cross, through the central King Childebert portal and the gloom of the nave, towards the little twinkling altar lights and the great one they never put out. And a goodly pageant they made of it, he and his paladins and squires with their standards and his toothed silk oriflamme on a spear, their pointed helms, spurs ringing and chain links clashing through the nave and aisles. But for him it was not as fine a pageant as once it had been. For Roland was not there. And Oliver was not there. Nor, for all this cheery temporary showing, the youth of Charlemagne. And these latest paladins whom war had spared were too heavy in purse and poundage now, too light with true piety. And Charlemagne, despite his women, placed a premium on that. Indeed for these new-fangled paladins he was too much of a churchgoing man. They would have much preferred to stay outside the portals dicing in the shadows or with the Paris girls.

Still, it was a great show, if only the revival of the grandeur that once had been. Then, his homage paid to Our Lady and the King greater than he and Whom he was ever glad to acknowledge, he went out of the side portal into the cloister school. It was characteristic of him that no sooner had he come into the school quarter than his contagious smile had all the students, little ones and big, actually at their ease as before a comrade, a great man with a boy's own heart. With gravity now he listened to some as they read or looked over their shoulders at the books, again commended others for perfect spelling, a correct sum or psalm quotation, a sweeping capital curve or an azure and gold and crimson illumination in a Book of Hours they were making for him. Then he beat time to their chanting of Gregory's lovely phrases with hand so much thicker than Gregory's beautiful long tapering fingers that had thus beat time when they were first sung in Saint Peter's two centuries before. And as their massed treble and the deeper voices rose to the vaulted roof, he tried to join in cautiously, in a voice very subdued for so powerful a man and king. He appeared fearful of singing off pitch, and even envious of the skill of these poor waifs. Quite as when he wrestled unsuccessfully with his Gothic pothooks, the great conqueror of the world seemed pathetically like a wistful little boy. When the singing had ceased he told them that he himself had never had such advantages. And when the prize scholar recited the oft-rehearsed tale of his old comrades-in-arms, the great blue eyes that in the face of the foe held lightnings in their depths shone misted through tears. But his hand soon dashed away this mist and his laugh rang through the halls at the answers some of the boys gave. Almost too many prizes he handed out, not only to the best scholars but to those who had missed, saying he only wished his own boys could do half as well.

They say that if you listen keenly you still can hear that great ringing laughter of his by Notre Dame. Sometimes it seems to come down from the high horse he rides, across the way from the Cathedral's Sainte Anne door, by the riverside. Again it seems to bubble up from below, from the waves of the Seine, which forever carries in its old heart memories of great men and great things past.

Whatever the truth of the legend, the next week, after seeing that things were in order in the school, Notre Dame, the palace, and Paris, he went over the north bridge for the last time and rode by plain, wheatfield and orchard, through the forests and up the river highways back to Aix and home. It was his last journey to Paris. He had had an attack of pleurisy a few years before. In the fall of 813 the fevers due to his over-exertions in a hunting excursion struck him down again almost as soon as he had crossed the threshold of his castle-keep—brought him to another threshold which all mortals, sooner or later, must cross.

He seemed to feel the time was now. With his robust health and common sense, he had despised omens. But his family recalled an abundance of portents that had occurred that year. There had been many earthquakes and eclipses. Black spots had appeared on the sun. Lightning had struck his church in Aix, hit the pinnacle and fallen on the bishop's roof. Bridges Charlemagne had built had burned or had buckled with crowds upon them, killing many people. And a great ball of fire which, they were sure, could only have signified something momentous—and what was of greater importance in the world than his life? —had shot across the sky and past his window with astonishing brilliance. So they were much alarmed when he was brought low.

He rambled a little during the few days before he took that last step over that other threshold, crying impatiently to one of his dead queens that she should not fuss so much about the ladies in the wing. They were not pages out of his life or words like those he found such difficulty in getting down on parchment, but only unimportant little dots in his existence. And once suddenly sitting up, he repeated the words of a decree he had handed down long before when he had established all the schools for the boys of his empire:

"It was his purpose that in these schools they might learn to read, to correct the psalms carefully, to make all the signs of writing, and know the songs, the calendar, and the hard grammar, for all the sons of men desired to pray to God in the proper way but prayed very badly because of the very badly written books."

Often these last days, the old tales tell us, his daughters sat by his side holding his great hand, so wasted, nervously making motions as though writing on the coverlet all the letters at which he was so awkward. Or they would lift the great body once so amazing in its strength, so that he might swallow a few drops of water or wine. And "Good girls!" he would say one time, "Poor girls!" the next—the last as his eyes followed them wistfully about the room, longing for something he might say, perhaps, that would dissuade them from so many lovers and would lead them into the ways the Good Book and the priests always said were the wise ways for a woman.

Then his mind would drift away from visions of candlelit chancel and nave, shot through with petition and chant and churchbell, as his daughters their cheeks against his cheeks would tell him little things of his household: how his pet hound bitch had littered, or the wild gray wolf had been shot by an arrow from the east battlements and of the legions of wild huntsmen riding through the forest, the night, and the wind. And they would sing to him what they said was the song of the wild huntsmen down the wind—sing it first in crooning fashion lulling him to sleep, again in heroic Valkyrie mood, wild-syllabled and high, until his eyes seemed to follow them out of his fever and he lifted his great head from the pillow to follow after them—after his singing girls whom he took now for the wild huntsmen—after the wild huntsmen whom he took for his old armies riding after the Saxons, the Spaniards, all his foes of Europe, to the death, and his own voice joined in with what he must have taken for a great battle cry but which was only a shrill one ending on a death-rattle note in his throat.

So the eyes that had been blue and lustrous became dim—and the light went out. The lines about the curious long lovable nose, that had poked into every corner and kingdom of Europe, deepened. A shadow fell over it, was not lifted. And since the passing of a king is not so different from that of a peasant, the last curtain of the sheet was drawn over the great face that had been Europe's sun for a generation. . . .

For years after his death in 814 all his people, the burghers of his cities and particularly the peasants of the lands he had ruled, dreamed that he, the great Charlemagne, would come again—in the time of France's need. When two hundred years later, they opened his tomb they found, so the chroniclers reported, this most energetic of personages characteristically sitting up. So he was most properly interred—as another most gaucy personage, Clemenceau of the Vendée, would be buried. And the sceptre was in his hand, an opened Bible on his knees, and a crown on his head—a gold one, not the famous iron one of the Lombards. That iron one the god-of-the-machine which is history would keep above ground for Napoleon, whom Charlemagne would have liked and yet disliked.

But that crown, though of iron, could not bind all the kingdoms he had conquered. Only worthy heirs could have done that. And like Napoleon, Charlemagne, though he could breed victories, could not breed capable sons. And his empire was too far-flung. In the end, for all the glory, it might as well have been made of cardboard, that glory only have been gilt. He had dared greatly, but essayed too much. Long before his death, taxes had reached the "groaning" stage. Of people that disagreed with him the prisons were full. His best marshals, like Napoleon's, had been killed. The ablest and mightiest of world superintendents he was, but he could not hand over his organizing and galvanizing gifts, with that iron crown and all the saints' sepulchres and the Holy Sepulchre keys. His empire was not made for the long pull. But it was a grand, glorious, furiously-going enterprise while it lasted.

Like Napoleon, he left a legend to thrill men, which would endure longer than anything recorded on a map. Which is immortality enough unless one goes in for a sort of immortality so quietly exemplified by quite another kind of king—He whose figure stands near the mounted Charlemagne, above the Last Judgment Door of the Cathedral.

XX

In the Dark Ages the Wolves of the Sea and of the Woods lay waste All France. . . . The Abbeys save the Souls, the Bodies too, of the Poor Folk. . . . Alert Farmers build Wood Towers and become Dukes. . . . Lovely Legends are born out of the Dark. . . . Notre Dame burns; Saint Etienne becomes "Notre Dame." . . . The Normans sail up the Seine. . . . Abbo the Abbot writes Verse during the Bloody Battle by Moneychangers' Bridge. . . . Hugh with his Little Round Cape is the First Capet. . . . In the Year 1000 A.D. Men climb the Hills to see the End of the World, but it rolls on and Men are left to build the Cathedral.

885-1000 A.D.

ABBO THE ABBOT, HEAD OF SAINT-GERMAIN-DES-PRÈS, THE historian of Paris, walked the island city wall. Each morning of this year of 885 he could be seen there pacing the ramparts parallel with the palace and ending his beat by the north bridge. When he looked into the window slits of the palace whose foundations were below him, he could see, working with his stewards or generals or scribes, Eudes, Count of Paris, who like Charles Martel was the real power, the uncrowned king, in France. For brains, a backbone too, he had, whereas the last of the Charlemagne whelps, Charles the Simple, Charles the Fat, Louis "Overseas" and Louis the Stammerer, had been prodigious bunglers when not actual cowards.

It was strange how many bunglers, lollers in litters and retreaters in battle so mighty an organizer as Charlemagne could breed. He did not transmit to his heirs a single spark of his great spirit, a single volt of his tremendous energy. On the throne there had been one of the three greatest of Charles ("The Hammer" and "The Wise" being the other two). Now on it was Charles the Fat, one of the three worst in history (Charles the Fourth and Mad Charles of Saint Bartholomew's being the others). The old shirt-sleeve sequence we noted long ago was at work again—down. Merovée, in the 400's, Childeric, Clovis, had mounted Fame's bright ladder. Childeric, in the 500's, had clung there a while, then his successors had tumbled off. In the late seventh and eighth centuries the stout Pippins, then the great "Hammer," and Charlemagne had become kings of the mountain, only to see, from Valhalla, their heirs taking a swift tobogganing down it. Charlemagne's great French empire had been split into three longitudinal strips—one running from Baltic to Danube; a second from Lorraine into Italy; the third from the North Sea through the Low Countries, the Ile de France, down toward the Pyrenees. All three of these strips of old France had been clawed into shreds by the ravening wolves of the woods, the roving Norse raiders of the sea. Under monarchs almost as bad as the "Do-Nothing Kings," the mighty Carolingian structure was collapsing. Its walls might as well have been built of playing cards, its buttresses of jackstraws. Wherefore Count Eudes (whom the Germans called Odo) was forever at work, bolstering up the king, beating off the Normans, mending walls and patching up this third torn strip, the heart of which was Paris and the Ile de France. Also in intervals between his battles, he burned tapers very late in a groined cabinet of the palace, on a level with Abbo pacing the ramparts outside, as he tried to put some order into the palace accounts.

Eudes was at work too, though he could not know this, at becoming an ancestor. For he was a third step in a new shirt-sleeve sequence which would succeed where the Merovingians and Carolingians had failed. A butcher, Eudes' grandfather, had been the first rung. Not an ordinary butcher, but the best butcher in the kingdom he had been. Also the best man. And a far better breeder of sons than Charlemagne. One was a truly great one, Robert the Strong. The butcher's stamina had gone by way of this Robert into Eudes, and in a century would be handed on to the first king among them, Hugh Capet. So would the old shirt-sleeve law be broken. Not three or four, but thirty generations of Capets there would be between the butcher's bloody smock and the return, all too literally, to the shirt sleeves, for the guillotine's convenience, by Louis the Sixteenth.

When Abbo the Abbot, on these mornings in the year 885, reversed his patrol of the wall and walked downstream to the prow-end of the island where in an angle of the wall grew the vegetables for the king, he could see the reasons for his recent retirement from his abbey of Saint-Germain-des-Près to the security of the old island. They were to be seen across the river, in the ruined towers of his church. Two of the loftiest of these had gone up in smoke. Only one of the three tall spires still landmarked the southwest horizon. The others had been burned and pulled down by the Normans on one of those many occasions when they suddenly rowed around the river bend. Vanished with them was the great gold Toledo cross Childebert had brought to the church, and all the precious metal work of Saint Eloi on Saint Germain's high tomb, within. Every gem and cunningly wrought figure had been pried off and pocketed by the vandal Normans. Half of the churches in the Paris belt, half of those on the Loire, half, in fact, of all the shrines in central and south France, had gaping roofs; their naves and altars were open to the weather.

The majority of the nobles' villas in the wooded suburbs of Paris and Chartres and Rouen, of the peasants' farmsteads in Beauce and Grenelle, were black charnel houses. Every last hayrick had been charred down to the meadow's edge. Hundreds of thousands of fair French acres so painfully carved out of the wilderness had returned to the wilderness. If a census of the wolves could have been taken, the number would have exceeded that of the Great Depression of the third century when parents killed their children to save them. By day the tangle of the countryside was red with the curling flames of their tongues. By night it was lighted by the green fire of their eyes—also the smoking torches of the two-footed wolves from the Norseland and the Rhine. And often, as Abbo had scoured the land, he had come upon and startled creatures munching on corpses—not vultures, but human beings feeding on their own kind.

No, the sun these mornings might be very warm and bright on the Seine flowing by, but the age Abbo chronicled was very dark. Still as a leader he must keep up good heart, like his own monks and all from the abbeys roundabout. Some, in spite of the destruction wrought by the fiery Norman arrows, were forever putting out fires with little buckets or putting on new roofs; one could see scaffolding all about. Others in battered cells, sometimes opened to the stars, worked away by tiny candlelight, at grammar, translation, illumination and part song, thus keeping the Torch of Learning from going out quite. And all turned their peaceful abbeys into grim fortresses to keep the race itself from being extinguished. As in pioneer days in the New World, imperilled settlers would flee into blockhouse and stockade, now when the Normans rowed up from the west or the Germans came over the Rhine, the peasants fled into the abbey enclosure. From the very church towers and arches the molten lead of the roofs was often poured down on blonde Teutonic heads and thick, wild, yet very practical Norman ones. The soldiers of the vast corded and cowled and crucified army must not only keep their candles trimmed and burning, their hoes and plowshares filed and sharp, but their skirts tucked up as they worked so that they might swiftly lead their flocks within their gates when the wolf packs, animal or human, appeared.

And if raiders and wolves and king-whelps gnawed away at the heart of France, the cancer of slavery was deep in her vitals. It was not so bad, of course, as it had been in old Rome. Then the great, the cold and calculating Caesar could auction off six thousand three hundred slaves in a batch one pleasant afternoon. And chains and penalties were multiple—even the "trusties," the Roman house porters, wearing shackles as they watched over their masters' homes—so that not only Christian preachers but pagan essayists protested. In fact, the latter were more violent than the clergy themselves. The Christian bishops, deeply impressed with the "No cross, no crown" slogan and the martyr way of life, though they freed every slave who worked about a church, stressed resignation, urging masters to be kinder to slaves, slaves more loyal to their masters. But like the chateau intellectuals of the eighteenth century in France, who supported the cause of the underprivileged and so brought the chateaux down on their heads in the Revolution, these heathen liberals of ancient Rome cried out at the whole system of slavery as inhuman and against all natural law. It is odd. In the *nineteenth* century, Christian sermons in the "sweet land of Liberty" upheld the institution of slavery. In the *third*, these "cruel" pagans attacked it, and the early Christian bishops persuaded emperors, like Theodosius, to present to each slave with his certificate of baptism one of emancipation. In 1863, the forward-looking American Republic issued its Emancipation Proclamation; in 1315 King Louis the Tenth wrote his for the Ile de France. The world does move!

But it was not yet 1315—only 885—when Abbo walked the walls writing his chronicles in rhyme, with an eye cocked downstream for the Norman galleys. And a serfdom, though not as bad as the slavery of Rome in 250, America in 1750, still persisted. Clovis, even Charlemagne, autocrats both though grand ones, thought some form of it necessary to a strong state. So they changed the old institution to one of forced labour. Serfs did not die under the scourge as slaves had once upon the Seven Hills. They did not even faint with pain of it as often they had under Marcus Aurelius or would in America until 1865. In France in the Dark Ages they possessed actual rights under the Law. Their persons were their own and, with a few restrictions, free. That is, they were not subject to the old cruel punishments but they had still to stay on the farm or stick to the trade to which they had been born. It was as harsh a system as sharecropping, yet an advance on the old slavery; and it would be further liberalized in 1106 by the fighting king Louis the Sixth.

There was another institution of the age which Abbo, had he cared for historical causes as much as for the quaint verse and thumbnail battle pictures he left us, might have written up: Feudalism. Later it almost wrecked society, but then and for some centuries it was one of the two buttresses, the other being the Church, that saved what of social framework was left. Foreshadowed by Clovis and his Frankish ways, definitely gotten under way by Charles the Hammer with his fief-giving on the Field of Mars, further confirmed by the grants of Charlemagne, it was more deeply engraved on the body politic by nothing less than those Norman boats with the painted ravens flapping their spread black wings on the sails, which were forever dropping anchor unexpectedly in the Seine and Loire. Feudalism now fastened its hold because there were not enough of those fortified abbeys to hold all the farmers and peasants fleeing from fang and brand and flame; the wolf-packs and galleys had become too numerous.

So embryo dukes who then held no titles, and fancied themselves as nothing more than the best farmers of their regions, who stood out because of sturdiness and common sense, dug ditches deeper, built stone walls stronger, wood towers and palisades higher than their neighbours. These crude strongholds contained inexhaustible wells and storehouses stocked well enough to sustain the less provident and capable folk of the countryside who at the sight of Norman raven or German helm would rush into these rude towers on the hills. In return for such sanctuary, ever open, they would let the owners of the primitive castles put foot symbolically—and often all too literally—on their necks.

The bargain thus sealed—provender and protection in trade for tribute and military service—would in many instances be kept, sometimes with benevolence, sometimes with rigour, for nine hundred years, until the tumbrils rolled with the condemned over the successor to that north bridge at whose head Abbo turned back in his round of pacing. These wooden towers on the hills of France would be expanded into the great Ile de France, Norman, Angevin, Provençal keeps. The simple ditches and palisades would be multiplied into the folds of deep moats, inner and outer wards, barbicans, curtains, crenels, and hoardings of the mighty Coucy, Pierrefonds, Chateau Gaillard, and Carcassonne castles all over the land. From these well-muscled and shrewd farmers who had the foresight in the Dark Ages to supply the first crude refuges would spring the Valois, Condés, Orléans, Montmorencys, and all the great families that would determine the fortunes—now up, now down—of the colourful land we call France.

There was another trend of the age which affected the mentality of the people and which at the same time brought to them release and delight. The old heroic and supernatural tales of the saints of the earlier centuries—the sacred *chansons de geste*, as it were, of the Church—had been handed on. But now there was a fresh flowering of their faith and fancy into an infinite number of new legends and tales about famous and more local saints, all having to do with miracles. This was quite natural in a day when it seemed that new wonders and miracles must be often performed if millions of hunted, harried people were to survive.

If abbots like Abbo not only kept alive the old miracle tales and countless true stories of the old great figures of Christian history, but also welcomed fresh ones conceived in pious dreams, it was for love of their people. If in a dark age their souls as well as bodies were to remain alive, hope had to be kept before them. The story of the great drama of Man and his God from the sublime Creation through the Fall and the long epic pilgrimage to the salvation of Man through the love of God and the selfless sacrifice of His Son, was the greatest story ever set down, and the greater because it had been lived and was the source of all life. That sacrifice was relieved for all at the altar in the sanctuary. And a flash of its light, a fraction of its power, penetrated even the childlike souls of the harassed peasant parishioners, the charcoal-burning communicants of the day. But naïve and elemental as they were, they could not often stay on the highest spiritual plane. It helped them when for long months they were immured in castle or abbey to have in addition a religious folklore, most of it true in fact, more of it in spirit. Quite naturally this had evolved from the continuous recording of the lives and miracles of the great church heroes and the simple annals of the holy experiences of the equally heroic and selfless, but obscure provincial saints. All these corollary little scenes of pious deeds and miracles clustered around the great, the core, mystery in the sanctuary, as the chapels dedicated to illustrious saints circled the sanctuary.

Even these local accounts bubbled up from pure springs in the hearts of consecrated religious or lay people of humble origin but lofty life. The concepts were moving, the morals sound, the imagery exquisite. These chronicles of sight restored, wounds healed from other flowing wounds, of veils, trees, cherries, ferries, flowers, of visitations of Our Lady, of the King Himself in beggar disguise, sometimes seem to the over-practical man of today—who is happy only in that he does not know that he is unhappy—as naïve. But very often they were true recitals, confirmed by exhaustive and critical examinations of the Church, and like the Voices of Jeanne, indisputably proved by magnificent results; and when they were not factually true, they were always wholesome in moral, and in spirit true. Beyond any reckoning they brightened the lives of forlorn Jacques and poor Pierre. And never could they, at their most fanciful—which for some is to say superstitious—take away from the people's engrossment in the central drama, quench the light or the life or the ineffable beauty of the altar's mystery.

And they needed hope in the heart then, both layman and priest. It grieved Abbo, as he paced the battlemented walls along the north fork of the Seine, to see on every hand the evidence of the sorry estate into which the kingdom of France and the Church had fallen. At least half of the property and of the personnel of both had been destroyed. The very appearance of Paris now in its decrepitude suggested the unhappy pass to which all things French had come. Seated in a crenel of the wall and looking toward the city within, Abbo could see his Paris, all bulky, hulking and low and Romanesque. Nowhere in the skyline was there even a hint of the oncoming Gothic, of its inspiration and aspiration that would lend hope and grandeur to the most tortuous-alleyed of the narrow, pinched-up mediaeval cities. The whole capital looked what it was—a peeling, stucco-sloughing, broken-arched ninth-century city, yellow with lichens, blackened with fire, green with Seine damp, built on a boat-shaped island moored in one of the melancholy ebb tides of Time.

The very phrases Abbo heard all about, the corrupted Latin of the curses of the fishermen in the river below, the pure Latin of the palace assizes and of the church chants, sounded like sad echoes of a once masterful tongue, of an old and vanished glory. All Paris and France seemed waiting the day when a new life would revivify a polyglot tongue and all that Iberio-Ligurian-Phoco-Phoenician-Basque-Latin-Franco-Norman mixture of a race into something fresh, vigorous, ebullient, and very French.

As for those chants which Abbo now heard on the island, they came only from tiny Saint Martial and from the older of the two big island churches and parents of the Cathedral to be—Saint Etienne, now five centuries old. Silent were the Notre Dame choir and bells. The flames which in the Paris ninth-century fire had sprung up from the old Roman barracks and old villas by Notre Dame, then from that church itself, somehow had not leaped the little space between the Notre Dame apse and the neighbouring front porch of Saint Etienne. The two churches with their narrow second storeys like ships' superstructures had seemed like two boats racing side by side downstream. The higher and shorter one, Notre Dame, which had always appeared ahead, was now a blackened hulk, while Saint Etienne was untouched save for the new roof tiles which showed where fiery Norman arrows had more recently fallen. The salvaged Notre Dame treasures, a few mosaics and altar appointments had been transferred, after the fire, *with the*

name itself to Saint Etienne. For since there must always be by
the Seine a house for Our Lady, Saint Etienne was now the cathedral. And it was no longer Saint Etienne. It had been rechristened
Notre Dame. Until the next (the tenth) century it would be
Notre Dame.

Forty-two years before this of 885 when Abbo the Abbot
walked the walls, Charlemagne's grandsons, in the famous battle-
city of Verdun, had attended to the shredding of Charlemagne's
empire into three. In 866 Robert the Strong, butcher's son but the
uncrowned king of France and forefather of thirty generations
of Capets, after keeping the third, the true French strip, from
being wholly shredded by these Danish and Norman sea wolves
who had left their clawmarks all over, in roofless abbeys, charred
champaigns, and sacked cities, had valiantly died in the bloody
battle of Brissarthe. And it had fallen to Robert's son, this Eudes
who worked so hard again and again to beat the Norsemen off.
But they were indefatigable; and here was Abbo now watching,
as he paced or between cantos he put down on parchment, for the
raiding galleys to come round the bend.

It was not long before his voluntary patrolling was rewarded.
He saw one morning nosing upstream around the curve below
the city gates, a fleet of the dragon beaks, with shields like rows
of bright buttons down the sides, rows of jackstraw oars shattering
into silver splinters the sun-smitten Seine, and aloft the great
raven-illustrated sails. In a moment they were beached where the
south windows of the Louvre Hall of Apollo are now. Then in
short order they felled the trees skirting the north shore meadows
and set up towers by the north bridge, on the Right Bank, where
today rise the waters of the Place du Chatelet fountains. At sunset
they stood, black against the rose and just out of arrow-shot,
roasting stolen cattle whole, munching sheep's quarters, bathing
naked in the Seine and shouting bawdy jocosities at the inhabitants gathered on the downstream end of the island walls, as the
bells rang out from churches they now desecrated but would
one day reverently imitate in their new kingdom down by Rouen.

In the siege of Paris that followed—the fourth by the Normans,
and the most bitter of all—Abbo the Abbot was to gather abundant material for his battle-written, blood-baptized book that was
half-history, half-epic. From the fragments left us, his verse
seems to glow out of the gloom of that age as Chaucer's later
shone out of the darkness in England just before the Elizabethan
dawn. All the first night and for many nights thereafter, Abbo
writes, "the arrows came in a great whistle over." And showers of
lighted ones, with trailing comet tails, wrote in fire on the sky
as they described their bright arcs over the island walls and down

on the roof of Notre Dame (now the rechristened Saint Etienne). It seemed as though they were celebrating with fireworks some anniversary of the queen, Our Lady, instead of trying to burn her house down for her.

But Abbo not only wrote. As Count Eudes threw down his quill with which he had been checking palace accounts to take up the sword of his father Robert the Strong, Abbo also laid down his pen to help in the battle. Eudes, whom Abbo admired, seemed omnipresent now. One moment he was inspecting his archers, the next his supplies; and the next instructing his engineers how to prepare the loop devices to snare the enemy's siege hooks or the battering ram heads with which the Normans had fitted oak timbers felled in the meadows. Then he would dispose his bucket brigades on the walls, ladders and roofs, to put out the fires started by the arrows and dispatch crews to scour all the island forges for the last ounces of lead. And almost simultaneously Abbo would see him high up somewhere ordering men to pry off the metal overlooked on the roof of the palace or on the churches, for melting down to pour on the Normans, and hurrying off the tumbrils for the blackened building stones from the Notre Dame ruins. These too would be let down on the Normans when they came over in the daily attacks from the wood towers they had built on the Right Bank side of the bridge.

These new strongholds stood just across the river from the corner tower of the palace built in 860 by Charles the Bald. And, though somewhat reconstructed, it is still there, on its face a great red and gold clock, the one that ticked out the seconds for Marie Antoinette when she passed that way on her last ride. It was by that tower (without Marie Antoinette's marigold clock then) that Eudes disposed his veterans to meet the first assault. It was in force; the Normans raced over the bridge under an arrow barrage and partially protected by wood bucklers held overhead, carrying both sharp and blunt battering rams, scaling ladders and siegehooks, while assisting forces in small boats they had knocked together rowed over the river to the attack.

It was a warm greeting they received from Eudes. Upon these racing warriors, many still with the sea-brine in their mustaches, the sea-rust on their chain links—down upon their rounded, crazy, yet practical Norman skulls, fell smoking, scalding, stinking casks full of pitch and the molten lead from the roofs poured out of great cauldrons tilted over on the walls. For further welcome the men on the walls pried over and down on them the building blocks King Childebert's masons had once used for Our Lady's house. Thus, said the Parisians, did Our Lady with her gentle hands, get in some powerful buffets on the foes of France. And flat on the banks, the bridges, in overturned boats, in the river, like so many human nine-pins, under the building blocks, they fell. Our Lady had bowled them over. Then, as the Normans sank in the river, Eudes cried out—so Abbo on parchment reported—in delight at all this cracking of skulls:

"May Father Seine give you fresh and better-combed wigs!"

However the jest may seem to us, it was pat enough to all on the west walls. In joy at it, they slapped each other on the shoulders and sent up a roar of laughter to the hills, a tumult in which all the churches that had not had their brass tongues torn out from their belfry throats by the Normans, joined with a joyous resonance.

But this delight was short-lived. Now the Norman flames ran over farms, ridge-poles, church spires, meadow wheatfields, leaping, licking, devouring. Half the warriors could be seen climbing down from the walls and racing through the streets of the besieged isle to the fresh fires springing up in different quarters, to form chains and hand up ladders buckets of Seine water, to figures ghostly in the swirls of smoke on the roofs. It was almost as though Abbo wrote his famous apostrophe to Paris, in requiem now:

"Our Paris, who calls herself 'The Big City,' which shines like a queen with a diadem above all other cities with all her towers and ramparts looking out over the river and whose praises all the sons of men sing."

As the weeks went on and supplies could not come over the bridges, north or south, and the children of Paris were weary from drawing bowstrings, dropping boulders, plunging swords, climbing ladders, and ladling molten lead; blind from the swirling smoke and showers of arrows; deaf from the ceaseless pound and bite of the rams; faint from starving and the smoke and sweat and scorch stench, Abbo continued (not in the azure, gold, and vermilion letters which came later, but in hurried black downstrokes) his climax chapter, which is the bravest and most picturesque thing in words that has come to us out of the Dark Ages. Just as the food was giving out it was; the battering rams had at last made their breach in the north island wall by the bridge—near that palace corner tower of Charles the Bald.

"And when the wall tumbled and that wide breach was made, our soldiers looking through that great hole, saw all the Danes" —so he called the northmen who had settled down by Caen and Vannes and Rouen—"all mightily helmeted and rushing on.

"But then"—and here came the magnificent curtain—"Seigneur Dieu looked down on His big city of Paris and on all her towers with His children inside. And He listened to the cry Our Lady herself sent up to her Son, pleading with Him to save Paris!"

It was Abbo then who, as he pointed to the sky above the walls, cried out not with pen but with voice, "*Regardez!* See! From the Heavens Saint Germain rides down to aid us! And with him a goodly company of men all in shining armour!"

Perhaps the vision came through faintness from famine and all-night watches. Still, all the soldiers and citizens cried out that they saw these dazzling reinforcements too: all the goodly young men in armour and Germain and Saint Denis, walking back with his head in his hands just as you see him today in his post on the façade of the Cathedral.

"And then," triumphantly records Abbo the Abbot, "those sea wolves, the men of the North, looked in from their side of the great hole in the wall and saw our valiant men and *counted* them and dared not come in."

Accordingly it was Eudes who had to make the first move. He burst through the breach with his men and fell on the staring Normans, cleaving their helms and skulls and piled them up on the bridge and both shores like shoals of dead fish with gleaming chain links for scales. Then those that were left ran out from their wood towers to the Louvre beach, shoved their galleys into the stream and leaped in them so frantically that they shipped too much water. There was little of the old rowing rhythm left as they headed downstream for the sea, only a deal of crabcatching by the oars and a great jamming of block-and-tackle as they tried to hoist the sails with the great black ravens spread on the white.

In the decades following there was much parleying with these foes. Despite this decisive victory, there had to be bargaining, for the Norman group was still a world factor. After Alfred the Great, whose latest Wessex galleys boasted more banks of, and longer, oars—the measure of power then—the Normans still had the best navy afloat. And they had thoroughly established themselves in western France, Italy and Sicily.

In the end, however, they did get together, these Parisians and the Normans, so that the Norman ingredient was added to those already in the Alps-and-Pyrenees-sea-and-Rhine-rimmed melting pot. It was the last step of a long process, the final admixture The forging of the Frenchman lasted for at least a thousand years He was emerging now, not—again it should be pointed out, so persistent is the illusion—as the Latin, but as that lively yet tenacious, industrious yet brilliant amalgam of Gaul-Celt, Ligurian Iberian, Frank, Roman (fifth place), Norman, Asia-Minorian Greek, Phoenician, Basque, and pretty much in that order of preponderance. It would not be long (only 1066) before descend ants of these oarsmen who rowed away so fast, would call them selves "We French," considering themselves blood brothers to th thousand Ile de France knights William the Conqueror would take with him on the invasion of England.

Altogether that charge of Eudes by the north bridge not only made a great chapter for Abbo, but changed the destiny of Europe as much as had the Poitiers battle of Charles Martel. For like the Moors, the Scandinavians had set out to establish their empire over the whole continent. These fiery sailors of the North had come as near doing just that as had the dark horsemen from the South. It was another of history's close shaves.

So this feat of arms which in Abbo's fragmentary epic shines brightly out of the night of that dark age, helped to establish a new dynasty and stability for France. True, it would wobble around for a while, but very soon a great block of peers assembled in Compiègne voted for Eudes as King in 888. This victory on top of the heroic deeds of Eudes' father, Robert the Strong, paved the way for the complete and official recognition of the line to which, in 987, Hugh's little round cape gave the name.

Even then, of course, theirs would be such a little kingdom, a fragment of Charlemagne's far-flung realm—just Paris, the Ile de France and a few cities around it. But this was the throbbing heart of the country. To it the heirs of Eudes, Robert the Strong and his father the butcher, would through the ages add great limbs.

So thanks should go to Eudes in that dark age, as well as to all the little monks. For a long time after Charlemagne, France had been pretty well kicked about. There had been too much of wolves and firebrands, of hunger, retreat, and fleeing into abbeys. A charge was something new. France was on her way out and up.

There was, however, one last dark night, just as the millennium closed, before the gloom of the Dark Ages was dispelled. Because of the roundness of that year, 1000, all the Parisians went up in great groups on New Year's Eve to the four hills that looked down on Paris—most of them on Saint Genevieve—quite as all the other people of Christendom climbed mountains near them to await the end of the world, the Last Judgment—the *Dies Irae*, the Day of Wrath of which the Notre Dame priests sang on the island below.

From the hilltops they craned their necks all night, scanning the skies for flashes of everlasting fire or heavenly glory, waiting for all the scenes they had gazed at in the stained glass to come alive. And when neither Gabriel with trump nor Michael with shining sword appeared, and the abbey tomb did not release Genevieve, a sigh of relief went up that turned into a great shout. It was the greatest shout the world had ever heard that went up that night, from trembling mortals everywhere around the world.

The world was to go on, whether standing flat and upheld by

monsters, as most of them thought, or as scholars knowing old Greek books believed, spinning in a crystal sphere between chanting stars.

So, too, Time was to go on. The ebb tide had turned toward the high—the culture of Cluny and the great abbeys, and the still higher, the flood tide of the Gothic, with all its breadth and sweep and splendour.

Meanwhile, so much had been lost in the darkness—millions of bodies and souls and so much learning and beauty with them. Nothing, indeed, would have been left had it not been for the little monk soldiers equipped not with the sword or battle-axe, but with hoe, quill, brush, paint-pot, music sheet, salvebox and crucifix, working away in choir, garden, at forge, on ramparts, or in their bare and often ruined cells with their candles. The tiny flames of these pinpricked the long European night with hope.

XXI

A King waits in the Snow. . . . A Stammering but very Great Pope disciplines the Royal Penitent and makes an Earthly Empire a Fief of the One Invisible. . . . Also he proves that Effective Reform can come quite as well from within as from without the Ranks of the Church.

1077=1085 A.D.

POPE GREGORY THE SEVENTH LOOKED AT THE HOUR-GLASS. It was a bitter January afternoon in 1077; and he was not in his Lateran palace at Rome but, as a guest, a transient, high in a vaulted chamber of a cold castle in Canossa at which he had arrived a week before as the storm broke, while his arch-foe, Henry of Germany, came hard riding and black wrath in his heart down over the mountains from Bavaria.

The sand, slowly sifting from the upper half to the lower through the fine-blown neck of the hour-glass had almost left the upper cup. He waited for the last grains, nodded with satisfaction, waved toward the window, then turned the timepiece.

"It is almost time," he said to the deacon-amanuensis at his side. There was a hint of a stammer as he spoke. He had never quite conquered the impediment since, like Demosthenes, he had first attempted it not at the great abbey of Cluny in Burgundy—as the story later ran—but in a Cluny branch chapter at Rome where he had been a poor monk of sincere purpose and powerful mind, working indefatigably away without a thought that he would one day be elevated to the throne of Saint Peter.

His taking of the name of Gregory on his election had been appropriate. On the long roll of two hundred and sixty-odd popes there have been some Agathos, Landos, Zozimuses, Hormisdas, Deusdedits, Adeodatuses, and such unfamiliar names. But there are more celebrated ones that had recurred and would recur many times. Eight urbans would appear there and nine Bonifaces, nine Stephens, twelve Piuses, thirteen Innocents, thirteen Leos, four-teen Clements, fifteen Benedicts, twenty-three Johns, and—second in number on the list—*sixteen Gregories*; several of them truly able men too. Furthermore, Gregory (the First) had been the official name taken by the great organizer of the Church, he of the chants, the noble head and beautiful white hands, the grand exemplar of all pontiffs to come. And this once-poor monk with the powerful eyes, deep-lined face, and speech impediment, who though anointed as Gregory the Seventh was always, informally, the Stammering Hildebrand, kept in the line of this great tradition.

As he turned up the hour-glass, with the remark that it was "almost time," the Pope rose, went to the window and looked out and down from behind the arras which their hostess had doubled to guard against the storm sweeping over the North Italian plains, and his waxen features relaxed in a smile. For down in that court was a man standing out in the snow. And that man was a king! A proud king but at present a very damp one—from the flakes sifting down from the grey bowl of the sky as swiftly as the sand from the hour-glass cup, until it seemed as though the Pope had mystically commanded that the royal rebel be buried under both snow and time. Certainly he was keeping him out there long enough. And it was evident that he was very cold as he stood there in the courtyard centre and apart from his retinue who shivered in their cloaks, not understanding this turn of events at all. Once their spirited but arrogant king had baited the old Stammerer up there. And here he was now after his defeats in the north; an unwilling, chafing, smouldering suppliant, come knocking seven times at the castle gate to be admitted at the last, it was true, but not into the Pope's audience chamber, only to the cold stones of the court whence he could enviously watch the flames leaping in the deep-throated fireplaces within. And there was no sign of relenting from the thick arras above when the ruffled king, assuming a placating smile, cocked a cautious eye up at the window. So, his young man's choler overtaking him again, he let out a round curse, quite audible to his retinue though not to the eminent guest above, and turned his royal back on the window to stamp his feet (not bare as in the story, rather booted and spurred, but burning with chilblains) and took off his gauntlet to blow with white-misted breath on his red hands. His train, meanwhile—drenched dukes and generals and princelets and such—dared never a word, let alone a curse.

But though the amanuensis might smile at the sight below, His Holiness, this Hildebrand-Gregory, did not. No humour at all lurked in the deep furrows of his face, only a profound purpose and a wrath for those who had thrown down the gage to him and his Church. No pity, only an implacable rectitude, looked out of his powerful eyes. The belated penitential stand out in the storm of this hotheaded, now thoroughly uncomfortable, Henry the Fourth of Bavaria—chief, too, of Austria, Burgundy, Germany

Italy, that Empire without rhyme or reason called "Holy," also "Roman," in memory of grander days and by a sort of wishful thinking—was a more serious thing for him, the Pope, than for the royal culprit himself. Not that there was for Gregory much of the personal element in the feud. He did not hate this German Henry for himself. He was not without his points. He was stubborn, insolent, rebellious, licentious, had badly treated the wife joined to him by the Church. But he showed at times a catching good humour, was liberal with the poor and had, curiously enough it seemed when one considered his whole life, a rather pronounced fondness for the underdog. Also he was young—only twenty-seven. In spite of the unyielding uprightness and the relentlessness so often expressed in the Pope's face, he might even have liked Henry, would have bidden him in out of the cold to the warmth of the fire, had not so momentous a decision depended on the one who first gave in—the decision whether the Holy Roman Empire in particular, the temporal power in general, or the Church, that is, the Invisible Empire, should be sovereign. And far-sighted Gregory had sensed that the verdict of the campaign, ranging over a number of years and now climaxed in the snowy court, would be final not alone for his own régime here at the eleventh century's end, but for many more centuries to come.

The shivering young king in the whirl of snow down there had been altogether too bold. It was something to challenge the authority of Hildebrand-Gregory himself. It was more to go against that of Constantine, Clovis, Charlemagne combined. And that was what he had done; had ventured to change their policy and that of the emperors of seven hundred years. That immortal trio of kings had been content to be allies of the Church and its strong right arms. But not young Henry. This Bavarian hothead would have had Church and Pope kneel to him. To build up a faction favourable to him in the Church he took advantage of a practise of his day, since called "investiture," which Gregory particularly wanted to root out. For by it through gifts, deeds, grants of land given by monarchs and nobles to abbeys and cathedrals, they and their heirs had been exacting a dangerous *quid pro quo*—nothing less than the right to appoint their own favourites to such abbacies and bishoprics. These were often totally unfit, usually unconfirmed and unendorsed by the Church and always supporters—naturally—of the king's claims against those of the Church authority. And out of this custom had sprung another and worse practise called "simony." Kings not only honoured their friends with clerical appointments for which they were not fitted but sold them. Venal and wholly unsanctified clerics bid for higher preferment, bought their bishoprics, bribed their way to archepiscopal thrones. Like the sloughs of despond which every once in while slow up the course of earthly empire, these depressed time would occur in the history of the Church.

Henry could afford to laugh at Gregory when his armies wer winning in the internecine wars up north, but soon his rebelliou subjects, exasperated by his wild ways and arrogance, arose in great revolt and victory deserted his banners. Then came the mor powerful blow of a weapon wielded by Gregory—excommunica tion. Half of the State and nine-tenths of the Church now arraye against him, Henry sent messengers galloping down to the Pop with a plea for a truce, then galloped after them himself. Thre times he had come knocking at the castle gate. Three times admit tance had been refused. On the third day the draw was lowered an he walked, not rode in. Not for the three days of the legend bu all that day, he had stood in the snow.

A little lesson given to a bad boy of a king! But the quarrel wen far beyond the Teutonic hotspur of a Harry biting his lips in tha court before a dazed and crestfallen retinue parched for warmin wine, and aching for the flames they could see across the snow brightly bellying up the kitchen chimney hoods. Earthly Empir and the Invisible, at least as represented by its vicar on earth, ha come to grips. The shivering Henry represented all earthly kings A pope simply could not truckle to earthly kings and keep hi kingdom pure. Nor could he afford now to relent too soon, no because of any personal spite, not even for the three times whe Henry had declared him, Gregory, the lawfully elected pope, de posed!—but for the Invisible Empire's sake. Though Gregory wa not one to gloat, Henry was paying now for all those things a modern jesters say "through the nose." But Gregory was no minded, just to establish a legend and make a good story, to mak him wait there the whole of the three days certain historians al lege, and so die of what later was called phthisis or pneumonia. S he looked at the hour-glass again. Several times it had been turned It had been enough to keep him on the cold stones all that long grey, white-dotted afternoon. He set down the glass with a thud

"He has had enough," he said. The deacon-secretary pulled th cord. A lackey appeared, received the signal, descended the stairs The great doors opened. The king came in, shook himself like drenched dog, was ushered up. On the threshold he bowed a littl uncertainly; then, as one swallowing a bitter pill, fell to his knees And now on Hildebrand-Gregory's face came the missing smile The spoiled boy who was emperor of the Holy Roman Empir he took in his arms, gave him a forgiving and paternal "My son!" escorted him to the fire, handed him a great goblet to drink an a little later bestowed on him absolution after confession. He wa

a just man and could afford to be generous. There was no doubt
now in the mind of the king who had three times deposed him as
to who was the pope. In that cold castle of Canossa, on the Italian
heights, two thousand feet above the sea, Gregory-Hildebrand had
raised the papal pennon and, more important still, the banners of
the Invisible Empire above the standards of earthly kings. It was a
great precedent that was more often than not lived up to through
the ages. There was another: that reform could very well, and
might better, come from within than from without the ranks of
the Church. Such vigorous souls as Saint Francis of Assisi, Francis
de Sales, Ignatius Loyola, Bossuet of Meaux, and Lacordaire would
be born to prove it over and over.

And veritably Hildebrand the Stammerer who became the great
Gregory the Seventh, had for a long time to come "smashed this
thing"—simony and investiture, the buying of bishoprics, auction-
ing of abbacies, of directorships of the great drama by those who
did not understand it and had not one tithe of its spirit. The king
thereafter, except in rare cases of usurpation or decline, was not
to run our Cathedral. Neither he nor his appointed favourites were
to take part in the greatest of mysteries, except as the humblest
out in front of the sanctuary participate in it. Hildebrand had
crushed these evil practises when a deflated prince, a cooled hothead
named Henry, rode back to Germany. And Gregory's successor,
Urban the Second, would make the ban official and complete when
he preached the fiery sermon for the First Crusade in the cathedral
of Clermont-Ferrand down in the volcanic Auvergne country.
But first, before the high Romanesque vaults echoed the "Deus
vults!" of the mailed warriors and they sewed the red Saviour cross
on their breasts, he stripped the nobles of the last vestige of the
privilege of ecclesiastical appointments so that they might also be
stripped clean for the high adventure to the Holy Land. Like a
great wind he cleaned the profaned holy places. With scourge of
word and sermon and bull and excommunication he finally drove
the titled, ermined moneychangers out of the Temple.

There was another great battle in which this genius of the halting speech and never-halting action won a victory before he died:
the age-old one of celibacy. Though Christ (while giving especial
praise to those who for His Kingdom's sake in the perilous times
of its inception foreswore domestic ties) never enjoined celibacy
on His apostles and Paul did not command only commended it,
and for the chosen leaders, the heads of the Church were more
and more inclining to what was so evidently Paul's feeling: One
could not very well buckle on the "sword of the spirit," with too
many loved ones hanging around his neck. In early times he was
not so apt to risk martyrdom if he knew he also risked leaving a

family without a head. Later one would not be bold on missionary journeys with women and children tagging along. This growing conviction among the bishops was intensified by the hosts who chose the contemplative life and the accompanying celibacy. If it worked so well in the monasteries of Pachomius and the very balanced and useful ones of the great Basil why, many asked, would it not be salutary for the secular clergy?

There were, of course, always the two schools; the one which would put curb bit, to say nothing of blinders, on that dangerous mount, the body; the other which would give it a little rein. Many non-Christian sects from the old Essenes to the Catharists and Manicheans, had been constantly arguing the matter. Dispute over it disturbed the air everywhere; some even in the congregations of the Church had been influenced by the tenet of certain of these sects that the body was a wholly despicable thing. Many among the faithful sincerely believed that the onward march of the Church was stayed as much by domesticity as by wantonness. Others saw no harm in the wearied soldier of cassock and crucifix being warmed by hearth fires all his own.

Realizing the human side of the issue, the early Christian bishops veered between outright bans on marriage and compromises which limited the clergy to one marriage (that to a virgin, never a widow), or permitted him to retain a wife taken before ordination but not to marry after it.

In 305, a Spanish synod tried officially to forbid marriage to bishops, abbots and the higher clergy. At Nicaea in 325, the question was opened, then tabled. In 385 Pope Siricius brought it out of committee and tried to establish celibacy by fiat. He said that if the consecrated men of the religious orders could attain to it profitably, the secular clergy could too; it was only logical. But human nature is very often illogical. Less than fifty percent heeded. For centuries priests with wives and celibate priests dwelt harmoniously in neighbouring parishes. The difference of conviction was accepted.

Pope Gregory, the First and the Great, tried banning marriage in the diocese of Rome and adjacent regions. He succeeded there; elsewhere half of the priests continued to marry. But constantly the leaders preached what Paul had taught and so excellently exemplified in his own person—that the energies of a man can be diverted from lower to higher channels if the cause the higher channels supply is dear enough to his soul. And what cause could be or should be dearer to the men who had entered the Church as vocation than the cause of Christ's kingdom? But, alas, too many of the rank and file were not capable of this lofty and valiant sublimation.

So all through these centuries Church leaders experimented in the great laboratory of the Church with three powerful elements: this clamorous and mercurial body of man, which they devoutly hoped was growing less insistent with the years and their study; his mind; and his ever (so they also hoped) expanding soul. Constantly they strove in their research to land on some proportion of mind, body, soul, that would be a combination that would work in a difficult, explosive world. That is, the wisest of these leaders—magnificent men they were too—did. The less enlightened still treated the body as a poor relation; tried to keep it below the salt, often to shove it completely away from the elect company of mind and soul out in the cold. But it was hard even for the determined to keep tripartite man at two-thirds of himself.

This confused condition was what Hildebrand, seventh Gregory, had on his election in 1073 received as papal legacy; and it both puzzled and pestered him. A thousand years, nay, eleven hundred of them, and still some of the most valiant of the sons of men, sworn officers of the Church who would bleed and suffer and die for their King and His symbol, the Cross, continued to marry and be given in marriage. They simply could not become as the angels.

But now with his powerful mind and relentlessly determined nature, Hildebrand decided that the time for experiment was past. He would harden, congeal the old more or less fluid bans into an edict that could be enforced. And he was confirmed in this purpose by the unalterable conclusion to which he had come—that the whole problem was not one of animal expression merely. Real estate was involved as much as any passion or lust. In marriage, the thirst of the flesh might be slaked; but with it a new thirst—for property—arose. Everywhere he saw otherwise devoted priests growing all too concerned over their acres, the education of their sons, the patrimonies they would hand on to them. Such an interest, Hildebrand admitted, was to be expected. There was in it nothing inherently wrong. It was natural, human, decent. But so many among the married of his great flock had lost all sense of values.

Hildebrand became more worried, with time, over this property-mindedness of his married and perfectly moral priests and deacons than he was over the occasional frailties risked with celibacy as an iron-clad rule among the less controlled, the black sheep that appear in every flock. Though Thomas Aquinas had not yet explained it to the world from his cell high on Mont Sainte Geneviève in Paris, Hildebrand knew full well that as no coward can taint a true cause, so no timeless and immortal sacrament can be invalidated by an errant priest merely because he happens to be the one on whom, at a certain scheduled hour, falls the duty of celebrating it. Any rôle in the great drama is bigger than the mortal actor in it, the drama itself greater than the whole cast.

So now Hildebrand went further than Saint Paul, carried Paul's premises to their ultimate and not so illogical conclusion. The celibacy which Paul commended for shock troops and advance scouts like himself, Hildebrand now commanded for all ranks. The pioneer days of the persecution era might be past. Sword and flame might no longer threaten, but a danger that Hildebrand felt was just as grave lay ahead. If women hanging tearfully around the Christian warrior's neck had kept him in the old days from advancing into the danger zone, the thought of golden harvests on his own acres, or bright hearth fires and goose feather beds, could still keep him from ministrations to the sick, the visit at night in the winter cold to the bed of the dying, from long prayers and litanies on bare sanctuary stones for a sin-ridden world. And it was not as bad for the body to go up in smoke and flame and glory at the stake, or down triumphantly before the lions of the arena, as for the soul to die of covetousness within contaminated church walls, in the betrayed fortress itself.

Now not only did Hildebrand campaign among the clergy for a stricter observance of the celibacy law, with sharper teeth in it —but also among the laity far and wide urging them, with sermon and prayer and threat of the Church's grave displeasure, to avoid all churches in which stubborn married priests still continued to celebrate the mass. A great part of his time toward the end of his life was devoted to the final rooting out of matrimony from the priesthood.

In this great issue he was helped by Evolution. Still, he had won where all his predecessors had failed. And coming in one of those eras when through too great interest in wordly things and alliances with temporal princes, bad practises had become current in many a diocese, he had cleansed the "fabric" of the Church vigorously and effectively. It took unbounded energy and courage to do this, for it meant the loss to the favourites of the princes and to the erring prelates of power or position or both, and very wide circles were affected. Great as was his power, hosts within and without the Church never forgave him for this, quite as hosts sulked because of the change in their family estate. It was not the least valuable lesson this great pope gave the world, when in his smashing of investiture and simony, he showed how the son of the Church, loving dearly and serving his mother all his life, could cure her of grave ills without waiting for outside diagnosis and violent remedies.

And finally he had defeated Caesar. He had not only established beyond rebellion the dominance of the papacy at Rome, but he had carried to a success Augustine had never dreamed of, that saint's idea of the overall power of Christ's Church. He had varied Augustine's ideal of the identity of Church and State (because of God's moving through all the activities of life), to a recognition of the separate individualities of the two and their coexistence side by side. But he proclaimed (and backed up his proclamation by vigorous action) that the Church was superior to the State, or any one and all of the separate kingdoms that might at any time compose it. It could chide and punish the sovereign at will; and chide and excommunicate Hildebrand did. Many of the kings like the tamed Henry became, with princes' favourites and sulky priests, the foes of this indomitable old man. So great became the defections that he died in exile at Salerno.

So many of these Church heroes of all ages deserve the most careful and intimate study. They are worth it. And agree or disagree as they will with Hildebrand's policies, all historians must unite in their admiration for his great courage, his never flagging energy, his marvelous statesmanship and his utter sincerity. The Church of Christ was his great love. He longed to impose and see accepted her beneficent and benevolent rule as the representative on earth of the King of Kings. For this he fought with dogged valour to the end against them all—until one sunset when, as the reflection from the sea rippled on the wall of the lonely house in Salerno, he turned his face to that wall and went to the one Sovereign he acknowledged.

Greatly he had affected the condition of the whole Church and with it our Cathedral and its ministering clergy, and even of the kings who would help in its building. For so helpless and confirmed a stammerer, Hildebrand had been most articulate.

XXII

*The Abbey reaches its High Tide, the Romanesque its Autumn.
. . . Abbey Capitals, that really are Great Self-Sustaining Cities,
save Souls, protect Bodies, spread Culture, teach Everything from
Farming to Pharmacy, and bring Much Beauty into the World.
. . . Cluny raises its Five Towers over the World's Largest Church,
and off Brittany Saint Michel touches Heaven with his Sword.*

The End of the Eleventh Century

IT WAS THE ABBEY BRANCH OF THE CHURCH THAT FLOWERED
out of the dark soil, Time's alluvial deposits, in the Dark
Ages just ended, into the richest culture and architecture,
the most vital intellectual life, and the ablest personnel. Indeed,
if an institution can be the protagonist of a history, no human
being—neither that sturdy stammering Hildebrand, adroit Premier
Suger, stout Bernard nor Stormy Petrel Abelard—but the Abbey
itself was the true hero of the eleventh and of the twelfth century
now dawning.

It had, that eleventh, seen new things enough when one con-
siders the tempo of the era. There had been the first persecution of
the Jews in 1016; the first of heretics in '22 at Orleans; the first
plague in '43; also, about that same year, the first Truce of God,
when men really threw down their arms not only for Advent,
Lent, and the Virgin's, Twelve Apostles' and other sacred days,
but over every single weekend and later from Wednesday night
to Monday morning. Time sometimes does go backward; and it is
doubtful if a custom so advanced could be instituted in these modern times. Otherwise the Big Bertha, in 1918, for example, would
never have killed seventy-five and wounded ninety worshippers
at Saint Gervais across from Notre Dame on Good Friday; and
an Italian dictator would not time his invasions on the same holy
day.

Also the battle against simony and investiture had been won in
these ten hundreds; in 1077, the bridge at Avignon had been
gotten under way; in the 1070's were started the churches of
Canterbury and Winchester (in Romanesque form). About 1077—
glorious news for democracy—several communes were started in

France. And in 1066 William the Conqueror had defeated England, not in the name of Normandy but of France, and very properly for had not Rollo, his ancestor, declared himself vassal to France, the century before, in 911? And as we have observed, William, when he crossed the Channel, brought along with him a great contingent of Ile de France knights and before the conquered English called his whole army "we French."

So already the French sponge had absorbed the invading Norman wave as it had the Latin, the Frank, and all the others. Therefore the French through that conquest transmitted to the English something more than a few proud and resonant names for their county families—much blood and many customs and a certain quality. It might have paid the English better to have remembered this before 1939 so that they might once in a while have thought of the French as cousins instead of so eternally dwelling on their relationship to the Germans which was not, in the end, to bring them too much luck.

Finally in 1095 the First Crusade was preached; in '97, Godfrey of Bouillon arrived in Palestine; and in 1099, as the century was coming to a close, they stormed Jerusalem and bloodily took it. There had also happened in that extraordinary century something that had very much to do with Our Lady and her house by the Seine. In 1095 there met an ecumenical council, much expanded from the old one at Nicaea almost seven hundred years before. It was no loose federation of independent bishops now but a harmoniously functioning officerhood of a splendidly organized army. And it did something for Our Lady. It "recognized," that is, made official the canonical offices which had frequently been observed in her honour. Thenceforth all the lovely phrases so familiar to us in praise of her, in plea to her, and all the beautiful hymns like the famous *Stella Maris*, "Star of the Sea," would float out at evening over the Seine.

The great rôle which the Abbey as an institution, almost a protagonist personified, was to play through these centuries and others to come had been earned with suffering. Long and harsh had been its apprenticeship. Child of Saints Anthony, Basil, Pachomius, in the early days of the Church, ward even more completely of Benedict who slept now by the Loire, the Abbey had been nurtured by him in his twelve mother chapters into maturity, and so for three hundred years had worked away as a brave pioneer. Then, for three centuries more—from Charlemagne's death on—it had had to exert all its strength, to call on every last ounce of vitality and willpower, for mere survival.

But the Abbey was a veteran now, mellow and rich in learning, art, wisdom. Through the long night just ended it had been a community harsh and austere. A place of discipline and devoted labour. A thick-walled, stout-buttressed, fortified sanctuary, for defense and long vigils of prayer, for healing bodies and souls. A refuge from very visible assailants and the invisible foes of the soul.

Now, in its high summer and early, bright-foliaged autumn, its bells sounded less often in alarum than for "offices" and school. It was the centre of culture, crafts, church ceremonial, scholarship, aesthetics, medicine, agriculture; the joint cradle, with Notre Dame's porch, of the university—in the less solitary, the broader orders like Cluny, that is. For ages the monks had spent half their lives on their knees, either in prayer or blowing life into the sparks of learning on man's hearth. Those sparks had now leaped into flame. The little tallow dips of the half-ruined cells had become great coronas of light. Paris' Saint Victor and Saint-Germain-des-Près, England's Fountains and Kirkwall, Frankish Fulda, Benedict's last home, Saint-Benoît-sur-Loire, his first houses at Cassino and Subiaco, Cluny of Burgundy, the great abbey capital, Saint-Michael-of-the-Sea-of-Peril, scores of others ringed and illuminated the world.

What had been simple, sometimes almost cruelly bare, became now more involved when not actually ornate. Theology, grammar, dialectics, mass, chant, altar, choir carving, turned complicate in so many abbeys. And abbey acres were far-flung. Abbey pastures were deep in sweet grass. Orchards were heavy with pears and plums, ewes with lambs, altars with ornaments, libraries with books. Earlier in this eleventh century, the Bishop of Rennes had described the indispensable buildings of an abbey as four:

"One, in which to store God's bread; two, in which to eat God's bread; three, in which the brethren may stretch their limbs, wearied with God's work; four, the holy one in which to sing God's praises."

Later the ideal plant had been expanded to include besides these four (the church, granary, refectory and dormitory), a flue-warmed meeting or chapter-house, a library, almonry, hospital, pharmacy, a storehouse for clothes and bedding, a guesthouse for kings, one for beggars, a brewery, bakery, bathhouse, dairies, sculleries, kitchens, big barns, physic and vegetable gardens, besides all the tilled fields and orchards, wheelwrights', farriers', saddlers' shops, smithies, tanners' vats and a *chantier* or building yard. And it further supplied rows of houses for leadsmiths, trenchmakers, masons, weavers—shelter for everyone who could feed a hopper, weed an onion bed, mix a plant-lice potion, make a halo for a saint, carve a stone acanthus, tint a letter, gild a wood lily, geld a bull, or attend to any of the thousand and one tasks that kept a great abbey going.

Looked down from on high, the famous abbey community resembled the chart of a Roman walled town. It was as populous with buildings as the name-sake university of a modern multimillionaire. It was a practical experimental farm, an ideal institution like the famous Brook Farm, also an instructional one where peasants were taught such things as seasons for planting, cattle midwifery, and the use of insecticides. It served as clinic, well-equipped for the times; as theological seminary and singing school; as college of construction, forestry, the humanities and the liberal arts; as guardian of all crafts until the coming of the mediaeval guilds; and as the cradle, workshop, refuge, Gethsemane, and resting-place of man's soul. It was a great destiny. But magnificently the Abbey filled it—that is, the more liberal orders did.

The capital country of the monks had once been passionate, high-coloured, miracle-loving Provence. Now Burgundy was the centre. The shift was natural. Burgundy is the great gateway of France through which came both travellers of good will and hostile invaders to take her rich treasures. And Burgundy had in France, land of full-bodied rivers, the best river-system. Therefore this province was a very great centre of cities and of trade. Other provinces and kingdoms might hold important fairs. There were Beaucaire and Saint Denis, for two picturesque examples. But Burgundy had a whole flock of them—at Autun, Auxonne, Beaune, Châlons, Chatillon, Dijon and Tonnerre.

Where commerce throve there was gold for rich abbeys; and in the fertile valleys on the wine-clad slopes of Burgundy they rose —Saint Bernard's Clairvaux, Porthières, Saint Pierre de Bèze, Benique de Dijon, Cîteaux, where the famous order of the Cistercians was born, and Vézelay from whose porch the Second Crusade got off to a shouting start.

And here on the Grosne, fourteen miles north of Macon, Burgundy, was the capital of Abbeys—Cluny, one of whose lovely branch city residences we have passed so many times back in Paris on the site of Julian's old Roman palace, on Saint Genevieve's Hill. Almost as many pilgrims came to Cluny after it was finished in 1109, as ever reached Rome. And its church was larger even than old two-acre Saint Peter's—the largest ecclesiastical building, in fact, in all Christendom.

Five towers it showed, rising above the mighty cluster of roofs and chimneys of the conventual buildings and its fields and groves. Not so much in form and design (though those five towers and the five broad aisles were startling innovations then) as in prestige, Cluny Church was the eighth wonder of the world.

The order boasted an abler government than any of the other ecclesiastical groups of the time. Seven truly great abbots, all wise and powerful men—Berno, Odo, Aymard, Mayeul, Odilo, Hugh, and the extraordinary Peter the Venerable, following each other in dazzling succession from the abbey's founding in 910 to 1157—formed what might be considered one continuous régime. And since, unlike the first Benedictines and their very active rivals, the loosely federated Cistercians, their order was strongly centralized, each abbot was as supreme as any generalissimo or the General of the later Jesuits. He ruled not only the great regiment of monks at rich and populous Cluny but all the other abbeys the Cluniacs had erected and also a great number which, like Saint Benedict's own mother chapters at Lake Subiaco and Mount Cassino had followed the changes the Cluniacs had made in the old Benedictine rule. Three hundred and fourteen of these chapters there were in 1150 with over ten thousand monks, besides the less formally vowed but equally faithful lay brethren.

It took a great outlay now to provide entertainmen᷍ for the pilgrims who came in hosts to Cluny. For Cluny was a word to conjure with, not only in Europe but all over the civilized world. And on sandals, dusty, perfervid, and waving branches, they arrived, also velvet-mantled and golden-spurred with famous insignia on their saddleskirts, and with the grave melancholy of sinners of high degree. As it happened, this institution of making pilgrimages, like the Crusades, was an idea of the French. As long ago as 333, the first pilgrim had set out for the Holy Sepulchre from Bordeaux. Only forty-seven years later (380), the famous deaconess Paula, friend of the great Vulgate saint, Jerome, grew as enthusiastic over the numbers that came down her road as over the whole idea of which she wrote to him:

"Surely to add the finishing touch to Virtue is to adore Christ on the spot, to stand where His blessed feet have trod, on the hill where rose the Cross."

Responding to her enthusiasm, Jerome who died in Bethlehem, raised a hospice, the very first for pilgrims, near the Holy City.

Even through the Dark Ages this half-fanatic, half-consecrated parade intermittently kept up, though the way led through hostile countries where they were constantly beset by armed bands. Priests like the famous Bernard of the early, the ninth-century Mont Saint Michel, princes like Willibald of Kent, with many more whose bones were left without any graven Requiescat along the Danube roads, hazarded the perilous journey on foot to Jerusalem, which often took seven years more than that for the nobles who are on record as coming from Iceland.

There were also popular pilgrimages to other shrines—to Saint

Magdalen of Vézelay, the Second Crusade city; Saint Denis, because of the legend of the famous head and the fine mausoleum King Dagobert erected over him; Saint-Germain-des-Prés of Paris —that is, before the Normans destroyed the high golden tomb Eloi made for the saint; and to Chartres, which guarded a large piece of what was believed to be Our Lady's tunic. But the favourite journeys, after the grand tour to Jerusalem, were three: to Rome, to Cluny, and to Saint James Compostella in Spain. The Cluny monks, besides taking care of the pilgrims enrolled in their own order, provided shelter for all others taking the very popular Spanish tour, by opening hostels for them at Vézelay, Tours, Le Puy, Arles, all the larger cities along the route in which they had branch chapters. They even had barbers in waiting to trim the pilgrims' beards, cobblers to repair their worn sandals. And they prepared a handbook entitled "Advice to the Traveler," which gave lists of the churches to visit en route, relics to see, rivers and springs of which it was safe to drink, and an appendix of Basque words and phrases to ease the passage through the Pyrenees. This twelfth-century guide was the world's first Baedeker. Merchants added to this fine service rendered free by the abbeys by providing great stocks of plums, almonds, pomegranates, pastes and other refreshments for sale in gaily-striped booths by all the city gates.

The conversion in the tenth century of the Hungarians, *en bloc*, decreased the perils of the Grand Tour of the Palmers to the Holy Sepulchre; for Attila's descendants and the later settlers by the Danube, the Magyars, thereafter more often played the part of Good Samaritan than that of the Jericho Thieves; at least they offered a more peaceful way through central Europe. But soon, almost at the journey's very end, there was trouble. The Saracens grew tired of the long truce that had been observed by them and the Church of the West ever since the Patriarch of Jerusalem had sent the keys of the Holy City to that strong right arm of the Church, Charlemagne. Caliphs who had been courteous now grew impolite. They fell upon and murdered the peaceful pilgrims almost within the Sepulchre's shadow. The wayfarers who once had come waving palm-branches now had to brandish swords. Violence and treaty-violation increased. And when the gathering murmurs of all the congregations in Christendom swelled into a great angered roar that they would not be denied Christ's Tomb, it was the sermon of a Cluny alumnus, Pope Urban the Second, that climaxed the tumult and indignation, galvanized that into action, and sent them forth on the first of those great mass pilgrimages, the Crusades. The Abbey was not only the alma mater of the scholar of the Dark Ages, but the mother of the crusader of the early Middle Ages, with the archetype abbey, Cluny, his especial cradle. It was a headier wine than any made from the grapes of Burgundy that the abbeys of that fair land distilled when Urban sent all France out shouting for the Holy Sepulchre.

And these monks of Cluny, with their hospices and travel hand-books, nurtured a grand tradition of song. Pilgrims on their way to Spain often heard in the rest houses minstrels chanting the *chansons de geste,* those epic songs of Charlemagne and his hero marshals, his paladins, and other striking figures of the times. They chanted them, too, as Taillefer had rendered them, at Hastings, without the later weakening rhyme and in the original assonant form. It was a wilder version than the rhymed one, but more forceful and picturesque, and it wove a spell on all hearers as the minstrel, ever on fire himself no matter how many times he had recited the songs, made the most of the martial assonance, the colourful figures, and the almost torrential yet measured and ear-catching rhythms of his lines.

As the Roman empire declined it was Ausonius, a poet of Gaul, who wrote the greatest verse of his age. Now France again, with the pulsating Middle Ages ahead, made all Europe articulate with her songs. In them she poured out her heart and that of all the West, so long harassed and shackled but about to break free. In those songs you heard the first introductory notes of a magnificent literature to come which would be a glory to France, a treasury for the world and a stimulus to all civilization. Thus did the Abbeys of France in still another way serve France which itself in a thousand ways—let this be remembered when eclipses come upon her —has served the world. The pilgrims in these Benedictine-Cluniac hospices heard these great songs. Some even ventured to become minstrels. More carried away staves ringing in their heads, in their memories unforgettable pictures of Roland blowing his great horn in the Vale of Roncesvalles where Basque and Gascon came upon him, and "high are the mountains, dark are the valleys, dark grey the rocks, marvellous and intricate the defiles" . . . of Peter the Hermit's followers staggering along toward the Holy Land, "their sides naked, their stomachs a hole, their knees baked black, their shoes all broken" . . . of ancient knight crusaders, "with beards whiter than the flowers of the field, their grey hairs showing under their helmets, old men of valour who had fought well in the Spanish Marches" . . . of ladies in the Crusades, "who, serving the Lord, ran into the houses to seize swords and spears, tied veils over their hair to prevent it from flowing in the wind, and filled their sleeves with stones to throw at the Saracens or brought big ewers of water for their lord husbands to drink."

They hummed and quoted these everywhere and thus added to the great lyric campaign of the ever-increasing strolling jongleurs.

So through France and the West swept this prairie fire of song. And it was from parchment scripts found in some of these old rest houses on the road to Compostella that later scholars transcribed for us some of the finest of the *chansons de geste* which, after nine hundred years, are so vivid and fresh and exciting. Many consider that Song of Roland the greatest single epic; and they would not trade it even for Homer.

If this Cluniac influence extended over the Pyrenees as well as over the rest of Europe, it was culture's bread cast upon Time's waters. Ideas and designs came back over the Pyrenees. There was that Hispano-Morisco arch-frame, for example; also the arcade and the alternate plain and coloured stone pattern which the monks of Cluny adopted for some of their chapter houses in southern and central France. And what the Cluniacs approved became a leading fashion. Cluny dominated architecture as she did learning.

To understand this and the position of the Abbey as the Middle Ages opened, we must for the moment consider the progress the religious orders had made since Benedict. As we noted when we watched with the chanting monks and the moonlit cedars by the candle-ringed body of the great saint that historic night on Mount Cassino, in the beginning the monks withdrew from the world and its lures to attain, through sacrifice, self-discipline and seclusion, a more perfect life. With the eremitical, the "solitaries," the seclusion was absolute. With the cenobite or communal it was partial, for though they spent much time in solitude, they lived in a community. Pachomius, in Egypt, started the first of these communities with a self-sustaining agriculture and considerable efficiency. Basil the Great rounded out the monastic cenobite life with wholesome and varied activities. But since very early the pioneer monk, the eremitical Anthony, had gathered other hermits into a crude settlement where they prayed apart yet frequently met, the proportion of absolute hermits decreased; one could no longer divide the monks into two classes, but rather three—the purely eremitical; the semi-eremitical like Anthony's men; and the communal monks, the cenobites. There were other finer distinctions, based on the degree of discipline and austerity and the amount of time allotted for the manual, artistic, intellectual activities and to the contemplative life. Benedict with his lofty spirit and keen intelligence as we have seen, brought the completely cenobitic life to such a high level that his rule became the pattern of the two leading orders under Hildebrand who added much strength to all the orders, and for many a one that was started in later centuries.

But no matter how rounded and agreeably varied became his regimen the main purpose of the monk continued to be the perfecting of himself for the indwelling of God's spirit. Their charities were many but through all these centuries they had been restricted to those dwelling or visiting within their walls or in the vicinity. Until the century called "the glorious thirteenth" came along and with it Saint Francis, these loving services did not extend beyond the monastery circle. Where a monk was chosen pope or selected for some high outside post it was accidental—this has been observed before, but since the monastic world has so many ramifications, it must for clarification be repeated here. And the men so honoured had not entered the monastery and had not been expressly trained for such careers.

There were, however, two services of inestimable value which the monks had rendered the world in addition to preserving through perilous times, the arts, crafts and sciences and keeping alight the torch altogether. In the fields of radioactivity, thermodynamics, all those of physics, there are infinitely fine instruments for the gauging of energy—Pierre Curie delighted his wife with one, and to great results—not so long ago. But there is no precision instrument for measuring the galvanic power of prayer which despite the wistful scoffing of purblind pragmatic skeptics, has been proven time and time again by lofty and consecrated souls to be limitless and as potent and as positive as only the truly ideal can be. And very early the monks, particularly those of the more purely contemplative orders, projected their prayers, if not their practical service, out from their cells, over their walls, to the remotest corners of the world. They prayed not only for themselves but for all sorts and conditions of men, for their enlightenment and salvation and their acceptance of the love of God. This had always been one of the noblest purposes of the most consecrated orders.

There was that other power too which is as little susceptible of measurement but which myriads down the ages have had proved to the joy and reassurance of their souls. Whenever one through sacrifice and complete surrender to the inflowing currents of God's love, becomes truly a saint, not only do those in Heaven rejoice quite as they do over the finding of the parable's lost sheep, but the whole Church, the whole body of believers everywhere, is given strength, enriched. There is a heartening and beautiful principle of the higher life which every creed accepts that speaks of the Communion of Saints. And all of the higher vision know with that knowledge and certainty that is born of faith and experience that this law, mystical yet in its results so practical, works in this way By every increment of such holy and sweet lives the power of the Church is increased; and there is an enrichment of a vast treasure and reserve of the spirit which helps all believers, even though they are unaware of it, and on which every soul can draw for sustenance and comfort.

When in the thirteenth century, Saint Francis came singing down the highway, there followed a great revolution in the world of the religious order. Great new ones were formed with prayer and devotion still a purpose—for what would external service be without it?—but with some external service, in the name of Christ, for the main objective. Friars sprang up all over the countryside. The first little Friars Minor of the great saint—in grey then, later they donned the familiar brown—took care of the lepers, their first loving charge, then the sick, and finally began to minister to the oppressed of the great cities. Sometimes they went out, like the disciples, two by two, to preach in the city gutters. Their leader preached to the poor, to the birds—the loveliest lyric of a sermon —and later to the sultan on his throne in the Holy Land. This was the greatest sermon men ever heard except those preached on the Mount, by the sea, and in Jerusalem by the One Francis followed. And it had more effect on the Moslems than all the crusaders' swords and battleaxes. Francis formed another, the third Order, a lay army of pious men and women who led a deeply devotional life in their homes and cared for the sick and poor in the Franciscan way.

At Toulouse—it is amazing to see how many orders first saw the light in France—Dominic in 1217 with sixteen other devoted charter members, had formed another order of friars, those great preachers, the black-over-white Dominicans, who preached their sermons very far out in the world not only in the great city pulpits but as devoted missionaries, in savage wilds, where they died heroic deaths.

There was an important post- or neo-Augustinian influence at work too in this revolution. Some on the rebound became hermits, living by the simple semi-cenobite rule Augustine had ages before framed for his convent at Hippo. Others became Augustinian "canons regular"; and there were also orders of regular clerks. The regular clerks served the parish churches in clerical and similar capacities, often in the services as well. The canons regular attended to the music and officiated at many offices in the parish churches and cathedrals. Father Peter, wry-tongued Precentor of Notre Dame, writes in 1190 of the canons of the cathedral being so late sometimes that they picked up their skirts "and ran through the cloister like old women after a greased pig."

One of the very greatest of institutions in history, was to start as an order of clerks—the Society of Jesus. This too was born in France, in 1534 at the instigation of Saint Ignatius Loyola, who attended the famous College of Sainte Barbe on Saint Genevieve's

Hill. Formed for another of those reforms from within such as Hildebrand, Gregory the Seventh, had conducted, its work soon covered many fields.

Now a man may be in an order but not in holy orders. Those monks who have not only taken the monastic vows but have also been ordained, are called "regular priests," in contradistinction to the "secular priests" who serve the parish churches and cathedrals. From the beginning the majority of Jesuits were ordained as "regular priests." They baptized, buried, celebrated mass, and preached—very eloquently. They became famous as scholars and as writers on the Church, sometimes on temporal themes as well. And they were tireless and self-sacrificing missionaries. One of the brightest pages in New World history was written in the life blood of the Jesuit heroes of the Great Lakes and our inland rivers.

There were two great distinctions between the monks and the friars who in the thirteenth century sprang up everywhere in such great numbers. The first was one which has been described before, —but of which one in this maze of the cloistered world must never lose sight—the difference between their primary aims: the monk's prayer for himself and others, the coming closer to God through the whole contemplative life; the friar's (the clerk's and canon's too) of outside service. The second divergence was in loyalties— not, of course, that to Christ in which they were one—but to headquarters. For the monk his monastery was headquarters and home. He dwelt and worked there. Even when later his services sometimes took him into the world, to his monastery he reported while afield and to it returned. Though in later centuries the friars would acquire common property, they started out poor. The little gypsy of the Lord knew no attachment to any particular lodging. His home was where he hung his hood. He often preferred sleeping under a hedge to resting in a chapter dormitory. Here the canons and clerks who resembled the friar in their aim of external service were like the monks, being attached to certain communal halls or cloisters. The friar's allegiance was not to any chapter house or fine abbey but to the whole order itself, to an idea; many to the memory of a man whose singular charm equalled his great love of all waifs, feathered, four-footed, and human. The monk's was not to his order, for he was often rather loosely federated but to his home and alma mater, the monastery or the great and powerful abbey like Cluny.

This revolution had as far-reaching results as the Renaissance or the Gothic Age of which perhaps it was itself a phase. The world was all astir and it seemed bent on getting the monk out of his cell, and very often unfairly. What does old Guy of Provins, expressing the general lay feeling of the time, say?

"No, my brethren; a monk may read a whole lot and chant very long and work very hard and even suffer, but if he has not charity, he means nothing to me. He is no more than one of those spiders which spin their webs in old deserted houses, then destroy every thread. To chant and pray can never save souls, only charity." And charity, he meant, overlooking the monks' great service, out in the world.

But with Saint Francis and Saint Dominic a new spirit did come in, in that thirteenth century. No better evidence has come down to us than the words of one of these more celebrated preaching friars, the black-and-white Dominicans. It was during the Crusade against the Albigenses, a prim and orderly folk who had followed the old Catharist ideas and declared all the Church rites vain, substituting one of their own which they said perfected them beyond the need of any church ministrations. Also they preached the hideous old theory that was forever in some new guise raising its dragon-like head, that the world and all its products and ways were evil, and that even procreation and childbearing was a sin. In short, though so orderly, they were public pests and dangerous doctrinaires, and soon they had all the Provençals by the ears. Which, however, could not excuse the hate against them, the consequent crusade, the massacres and the destruction of so much of the old Provençal civilization that only a fragment of its old glory has been left us. But in all that quagmire of blood and cruelty, in an era when cruelty had been so general, a Dominican made this grand plea which should have pleased that great liberal Voltaire himself:

"When the men of France attack the men of Toulouse, because they consider them heretics, it is not, in my opinion, a good thing. *For there are good and bad men in every country.*"

Under that general urge to more active service some of the monastery men also extended their services farther out into the world; the black Benedictines, for example, later founded a vast number of well-run schools. But the majority of monks and their sister nuns stuck to their spiritual last, clove to their old high devotional standards. For example the Carthusians—another order created in France, at Grenoble in 1084, on Chartreuse mountain, whence the name of their first chapter house, the Grande Chartreuse and the liqueur, and whose homes in England are the famous Charterhouses—continued their austere life almost as "solitaries" through the centuries. They ate one meal a day, wore hair shirts, also their white serge habits until they were threadbare. The money they made from their celebrated liqueur they spent not on themselves but on schools, hospitals and churches. And there were the Carmelites, called "White Friars," because of the white mantle over their brown cassocks, and whose first home was on Mount Carmel on the site of a very ancient Hebrew monastery and by Elisha's cave. The tradition, perhaps apocryphal, was that hearers of Peter's great Pentecostal sermon went out and founded the order on the mount. Certain it is that there was a going chapter on Carmel during the first Crusades.

In the late 1500's, that consecrated and rarely endowed genius Saint Teresa and her able collaborator, that purest of mystics and poets and souls, Saint John of the Cross, persuaded many Carmelite communities both of nuns and friars to return to the original severe rule. Under her powerful spell so many flocked to take their vows as Discalced, or Shoeless, Carmelites—as the reformed branch was called—that several new monasteries and convents had to be opened. But the bare sandalled feet (even in winter time), and the other rigours of their life were only outward signs of a sincere, an utter devotion to the wholly contemplative life which for centuries they followed, though later on some of them went out as missionaries into the most dangerous places. The Trappists would observe their old rigid silence in their semi-eremitical houses even in the Kentucky of the New World. By the Picpus Cemetery in Paris where Lafayette lies, on the rue d'Ulm, near the Curies' old radium shed, the contemplative nuns of the Adoration Perpetuelle still decorate their altar with infinite pains and guard it lovingly, prostrating themselves before it day and night while keeping up their lovely charities. So through the years the followers—there are so many other examples—of the contemplative life have continued to furnish to the world that mystical service which, though many are not of the temperament to understand it, is nonetheless indispensable.

Few orders had come into positions of influence by the end of the twelfth century. Not including the earliest like those of Anthony, Pachomius, Basil, or the first houses of Augustine, the main ones were: the Carmelites, with their white over brown garb; the white serge Carthusians; the black Benedictines; and two great off-shoots from that great Benedictine trunk—the grim grey Cistercians, another French-founded group (Cîteaux, Burgundy, 1098) and the very powerful Cluniac-Benedictine group with their splendid capital at Cluny, also in Burgundy. Cluny was the great Abbey exemplar in what we have called the Abbey's Golden Age; which does not mean that the accumulated deeds of all the later orders would not in total surpass those of even so powerful an abbey chain. But never again would the Abbey be so completely and splendidly a self-sustaining unit, with planted acres, heavily-weighted orchards, smoking forges, shops, libraries, so varied and all-around an equipment. Never again would it be a great college, experimental farm, craft centre, art school, seminary, and the fortress for both body and soul in times when religion and civilization threatened to go entirely and forever out of the world.

The Cluniacs had kept to Benedict's wholesome and moderate rule. They were vegetarians, went without breakfast, but had food from the greatest farms in the world at their other two meals, possessed mattresses, attended to their devotions for five hours on week days, on Sundays eight. They worked six hours daily in the gardens, forges, the barns, dairies, or at carving, gilding, illuminating or other skilled labour, read holy books and reflected on them for another four hours, and slept an average of eight and a half hours, for even the night vigils were handled in relays.

There had had to be some changes in routine in Norman times when monks had to fortify and to fight for their abbeys and half of the countryside milling around within their gates. Then often their hands were engaged with pike rather than with crucifix; and instead of telling the old-fashioned pebble beads, they dropped boulders on enemy heads. Also in the Dark Ages they translated and sang more—the new part music, accidentally discovered when boys with changing voices dropped an octave below or tried some crude harmonizing, since they could not keep the pitch, and choirmasters wrote in parts for them. But when the Dark Ages ended, after so many centuries our composite monk had gotten tired of hoeing. The Cluniacs especially began to soft-pedal the manual part of the rule. They ran more to mental, to desk, or art work—and with some historic results. They added to the world more good books, architecture, students. But they lost contact with the good earth and with it something of balance and vigour. That is why the Cistercians, who stuck to their farms, became the best cattle-breeders in Europe and by 1150 surpassed their rivals in influence and power.

During all this time the Cluniacs, to be sure, kept their goodly farms going, but they left all the haymaking, horseshoeing, and plastering to their lay brethren, and spent their time in expanding their theology and in decorating their litanies and their walls. They were no longer satisfied with the simply beautiful lauds and vespers, but must finish a whole book like Genesis in the services of one week. And each day heard a hundred psalms chanted in each Cluny church until, like coins too often banged on a counter, half their poetry was blunted.

But none of these extravagances affected their architectural taste and skill. Cluny builders were as functional as critics could wish; and yet they refined almost everything they touched. All these experiences at Cluny had much to do with the coming of the

Gothic now just around the corner. It seemed as though the Gothic spirit that would in the mid-twelfth century blossom so exquisitely in stone, was at work impelling these Cluniac monks. They might at times overembroider their masses, but in their building were never guilty of bad taste. And they erected buildings stronger and higher than any others. They incessantly studied all the new structural problems raised, with geometry and drawing and all sciences indispensable to the architect, and taught these too, to their talented lay assistants. They had many students now, for while the bishops' schools of the time took in the sons of the nobles, the abbeys gave special care to the children of the poor.

Not content with making their chief church at Cluny the largest in the world with a tremendous nave, they had five aisles and five towers (then an unheard-of number), and a very long and wide narthex or vestibule for the ablutions and sleeping quarters of the countless pilgrims that came that way, and chapels raying out behind the choir and wide ambulatories so that great companies of pilgrims could circle the sanctuary in singing processions. With such innovations at Cluny, capital of the world of culture, they were getting well on the way to the vast spaces, the great weights and height and nervous strength of the Gothic. It remained but to learn how to handle the pointed arch. Even with this problem builders here and there, in a Cluniac church at Vézelay for example, were experimenting as they had years before in the Near East without, however, realizing its magnificent possibilities.

While the architects of the Cluny school were employed with construction, her plastic artists were busy enough inside. If, exercising more restraint, they did not smite the eye with the old Byzantine's glitter, never had gold and carved capitals been so liberally used in the North. As for glass, though the Romanesque could not match the great style that succeeded it, the panes were now multiplied, the colours higher in key.

"The gloom of the nave," wrote an old monk, "was absolutely irradiated with these pretty windows." It was a great advance toward the splendour of the Gothic rose.

There was another monk working at a sloping desk among the waist-high folios of an abbey *scriptorium* or library, who did more than go into raptures over these new building fashions. Bit by bit he gathered the common knowledge of the artists and architects of his day and wrote it down in his elegant hand whose capitals looked like little galleons, and made of the whole a guide to art. "Theophilus' Guide to Art," it is called, and it is one of the oldest in the world. That Theophilus was consecrated to more than art is revealed by his beautiful charge in it to all workers with paint-pot and chisel:

"Let him who possesses the understanding of technical arts glorify not himself, since his achievement is not any conquest, *just a gift*. Let him therefore be happy in God, without Whom there is no art, not any thing at all."

There were others, however, who looked askance at all this art. This was in part because, as they beautified church and service the abbots, after so many hundreds of years of pure Benedictine routine, had gone back on their earth and relied now for their incomes on mortgage-interest and rents, instead of on leather and wool. Even Abelard, stormy petrel of the Church, who was destined to die in Cluny, became worried:

"We abbots," he said, "who ought to live by the labour of our own hands, as Benedict said, now incline toward ease, that serpent of the soul, and seek our income from the labour of other men whom we but superintend."

In the reaction, the grey-gowned, black-aproned Cistercians returned to the Benedictine rule with a Spartan vengeance. In fact, they went back to the good earth so hard that they added two hours of manual labour to the original six, on top of all the offices, reading and prayers, and got up at two a.m. to work in the morning mists. Not content with this, they reduced the two Benedictine meals a day to a spare one and threw out from their fare, with the forbidden meat, even their own brook fish.

So the old feud was on. Between the ascetic, the dour, and the esthetic and romantic. We watched it in the early Christian days when Saint Basil ordered his chapel walls painted with pictures. We will see it again when Scotch Presbyterians order the organ out as the mouthpiece of Hell and fall back on a pitchpipe, when Huguenots and Puritans stone the bright panes and smash the white tomb angels.

The Cluniacs thought it no harm to make, in all reverence, as beautiful as they could all the sacred ceremonies leading up to and following the celebration of the divine mystery of the tabernacle, and continuously to strive to add loveliness to the sanctuary and the church that housed it. Perhaps in their loving zeal they occasionally overdid it. The Cistercians—they could not help it, either—looked on loveliness almost as a synonym for lust. They thought of adornments if not as actual enticements to sin, as distractions taking the worshipper's thought from the clear line of flight to God. The mighty shepherd of the Cistercians, Saint Bernard, the most intellectual of the Puritans of his day, who preached the Second Crusade and scotched brilliant Abelard, and the intrinsic worth of whose brilliant soul no asperity or bigotry could spoil, wrote and preached often about this. From his house at Clairvaux on the Aube, he shouted this challenge over the vine-clad Burgundian hills to Peter the Venerable, Abbot of Cluny on the Grosne:

"What is the object of all this decoration? Is it to show the repentance of the contrite? I doubt it. For while the walls of the churches are resplendent, the poor are not there [Bernard was a little libellous in this]. When they do go to Cluniac churches the curious may amuse themselves with these decorations, but the miserable find in them little of peace and cure."

What can one do with a good man—a thoroughly good man—like that? He wouldn't even listen when friends quoted great men like Basil and Gregory the Great in defense of ecclesiastical art, but kept grumbling and preaching away:

"And, anyway, what has all this imagery to do with monks? I challenge you to tell me, all you monks and abbots, professors, tutors, wise men, what place has gold in a sanctuary? What is the meaning of those ridiculous monsters you carve?"

Thus Saint Bernard, the indomitable and so very difficult—the magnificent as well. In fact both rivals, Bernard and Cluny's Peter, were magnificent men. Their age resounded more loudly to their disputations than modern eras to the duels of Lincoln and Douglas, Gladstone and Disraeli. Bernard was no respecter of persons. He even stood up to the great Abbot Suger who built the Gothic Saint Denis and who was the powerful confidant and, to all effects, the prime minister of the king.

"True," he said, "Messer Suger renders to Caesar the things that are Caesar's, but God's to God? *Bah!*"

However, this ascetic, non-aesthetic Bernard showed at least enough tolerance of art to allot a place—though such a little place —in the Church, to music. As a strangely poetic justice, it was his bare, cold Clairvaux that gave the setting for that exquisite thirteenth-century tale of a minor artist, who like many a monk worked lovingly and humbly at his art for Our Lady, "*Le Jongleur de Notre Dame.*"

So, in the eleventh and first half of the twelfth centuries, the grey Cistercians could be both noble and narrow within abbey walls, the black Benedictine-Cluniacs liberal not only with alms but in art and education. It was this breadth of spirit that gave Cluny its dominance in art, learning and architecture, from the 900's until 1150. In duels with stone as well as with words they overcame the grey Cistercians until that last year when the grimmer but younger monks outstripped their mellower but older rivals. But these had seen and done much service and had had glory enough.

The great Cluny cluster of buildings and the great five-towered church was one of the wonders of the Middle Ages. It was a pi that Napoleon who often showed consideration for churches, opening hundreds after the Revolution, saw fit for some War Department reason to tear it down, so that only fragments of the church and the abbot's palace remain. But perhaps Cluny was not the greatest visible monument of the Abbey movement. Leaving out of the question all the art and the hosts of books and manuscripts the monks have saved or created for the world, the work of their hands which with the most beauty and majesty still stands up before the world, is far from Burgundy and over by the sea.

It is up on a mount, a tricorne upside down, chiefly of rock but on the north side forested to a deep green-black; and that mount is an island for part of the day when the tide rushes in. Some ninth-century cataclysm of the sea (just about the time Robert the Strong or Eudes beat the Normans and Saxon Alfred the Danes) burst in over the Breton shores, uprooted the magnificent forests there, and forever cut off the island-mount from its motherland Brittany, so that it is only by the umbilical cord of a causeway moored to her at high tide.

It was a faery sort of island then, to which, legend said, the dark ferryman Charon had rowed his dead. In this twelfth century, a company of black Benedictines dwelt on top. On the topmost turret they set a martial but silent Saint Michael to keep guard. He is there still with his star-pointed sword.

This abbey of Mont Saint Michel was not quite finished when Cluny was dedicated in 1109. But it was well on its way. It would take some centuries for the Bretons of the mount and shore and neighbour Normans, under the influence of a great mass faith, to transport all those hundreds of thousands of tons of granite from the mainland quarries. These Benedictines were determined to build their high abbey not of the mountain's rock but of other stones upon it, so that it should rise as far as possible above the sea. So they decapitated the mountain's head for a partial base; dug out, farther down, other recesses as planes for the granite piers and buttresses, the stone for which had to be brought from the mainland—between tides too, and hauled up the one mountain road. Modern builders, with steel girders and beams, locked with rivets, never had a task like that. But then, though they plan and estimate superbly, they cannot dream quite so well as monks. And neither monk nor man unordained ever dreamed better than here at Mont Saint Michel, or put more heroic foundations under his dreams.

So in terms of stone transported with incredible labour, and the rock of the mount, the monks worked out their vision. They laid great foundations on the mountain's decapitated neck; set supporting hundred-and-fifty foot buttresses on excavated stands farther down the slopes; and built upholding as well as useful crypts deep within the mountain's heart. Thus they wove, welded, transported stone and mountain together, and as the centuries went on and the great new style came in, spun out of both a great Gothic jewel set in the noblest Romanesque and held up high over the shining sea for all the world to see.

But it was more than jewel. It was a nobly-made and practically-functioning structure—a sanctuary, architectural masterpiece, little stone city and fortress, all in one. It was girt below with warrior walls—which it was going to need many times; equipped with great crypts for stores, and for water thousand-ton cisterns such as are ordinarily underground and here were under the earth, yet high above it; high-vaulted refectories where monks and visiting kings might dine very near Heaven; aerial cloisters with grass plots green as those of earth; gardens by towers with the common growing things we know below, though here in the company of the clouds; and a whole mountain-side of ranged buttresses which to the far-off mariner looked like gigantic organ pipes adding the church's lovely Gregorian notes to the flood music of the sea. All of these architectural tiers and factors rising around, in, and out of the mountain, and made one with it, were accented by, gathered up in, the top tower and flèche crowned by the most triumphant of all the saints—Saint Michael. On this Gothic-wrought summit like no other summit on earth, he stands, the happy apex of this sanctuary-eyrie, high over the wet satin-smooth shimmer of the surrounding sands, the agitated shimmer of the sea. And there his uplifted sword joyously hails, as no spire can hail it, high Heaven by day, by night seems to rally all its glittering stars.

XXIII

*Peter the Hermit, William the Carpenter, Walter the Penniless
and a Parade that took Four Hundred Years to pass. . . . The
Signal Sermon is preached by the Great Pope Urban, Oaths are
sworn, Shields are painted, and even the Little Children join in.
. . . So the West goes to the East. . . . When it returns, it leaves
behind the Castles it has built on the Palestine Heights, Miles of
its Bones along the Danube, and Seas of its Blood in the Valley
of the King. . . . But it brings back Something of the East, of its
Courtesy and Chivalry, also of its Colour and Culture, which will
enrich the Civilization of the West and also the Cathedral.*

1095=1144 A.D.

FROM AMIENS A RIDER SET OUT IN THE YEAR 1095, ON A
little ass, to change the world. The warders in the gate
towers roared and slapped their leather-jerkined sides in
laughter as the two passed through. They thought the pair comic.
They could not know that the little man with the rude wood cross
in his zeal held high would become the world's greatest circuit-
rider, and that the small grey ass would come to be regarded as
sacred by all the peasants in the land.

The day was auspicious for the start of any enterprise. The sun
was up; the dew had thrown a far-spread shimmering cheesecloth
on the green which was spread with the innumerable gold chalices
of the flower cups. The little monk wore a gown of coarse wool,
with the hood hanging down below his tonsure. His bare sandalled
feet toed in the little animal's hairy sides. He held a little forward,
its tip rising above his head, the three-foot cross of rough unbarked
wood. His face was olive hued, more happy than fanatic. Animated
black eyes sparkled in it, shining with holy zeal in his purpose, and
with an earthly joy in the supreme fairness of the morning.

Though the little ass was to be regarded as sacred, he did not look
the part. He lazily chewed the last wisp of hay from the abbey
stables. His little rump was still caked with straw and dung. His
tail now flicked around it, scattering the flies that had pursued
him from the gutters of the mediaeval city out here into the green

333

open, again hung neutrally downward. His ears, however, were not neutral. By their contortions, the queer angles at which they cocked themselves back at their master, they appeared to be asking questions—of his intent—of the objective of their journey. It was curious, but in all France only two ever posed such questions, this little ass who brayed and pantomimed his unwillingness to proceed at times, and a great saint—Bernard, the grim shepherd of the grey Cistercians. And later Bernard withdrew his objections. It took fifty years, but at last he gave in, grew crusade-conscious, and preached the sermon which got another, the Second, Crusade off to a shouting start.

Now one should not misunderstand the little animal to whom Saint Francis, with his affection for all creatures, dumb and articulate, paid tribute in his lovely canticles in whose very naïveté is the essence of all wisdom. He whom the good saint loved and called Brother Ass had participated in too many historic events to be considered any mere symbol of the ridiculous. He had been present in a celebrated stable, at the birth of the King under a great star. He had carried that King, while still a child cradled in His Mother's arms, to safety in the swift flight by night into Egypt. He it was whom the King had chosen for His mount on His one solitary day of earthly triumph. These holy occasions should take him far beyond the realm of the merely comic. And the ironists are wrong when they say Fate properly placed him as a symbol of the ridiculous in the van of that four-hundred-year series of pageants called the Crusades, to show them up, not as the great epic romantic novelists make them out to be, but as a tragi-comedy. Waste there was—in blood and cities, as the Christ Who wept over Jerusalem knows. Commerce, economic conditions played a part. But there had to be a more kinetic motivation—that spiritual tide of the times which would build the Cathedral and swept all men, the skeptics with the believing, on to this mighty adventure. Hosts there were who believed they were expressing their love for Christ in the salvation of His Tomb. And nothing could be considered tragi-comedy that so intermingled, as we shall later see, ideas of the West, ideas of the East, and imported into the West so much knowledge, art, and culture.

It was Pope Urban the Second who gave the first signal in his great sermon at Clermont-Ferrand in Auvergne. But Peter out-preached him, east, west, south, north, in France and all along the Rhine. He himself led the first French columns and, with his prairie-fire recruiting, mobilized other armies. And it was he and his little grey mount that headed the intermittent, four-hundred years long parade of Crusaders, in mail or rags, of base blood or blue, who sewed red crosses on shirts, painted them on their shields

and painted a very vivid crimson the Holy City of the King. Very
properly we can think of them—the little ass, no symbol of the
ridiculous, but of service, the little monk, of fervour—in the van
of all the great crusades from the first when Pope Urban changed
his text from "The Soul" to "The Tomb Must Be Saved," through
the seventh in which that king and saint and very great man,
Louis the Ninth, died, crying in his delirium, "Jerusalem, Jerusalem!" There were appendix crusades, of course, afterwards. En
train in all were ghouls, grain speculators, peculators, paramours,
knighted murderers thinking to pay their way into Paradise with
decapitated Saracen heads. But there were greater hosts who burned,
like Peter, with sincerest zeal, and longed to show, even unto
death, their love for the Christ Who had died for them.

So great forces which the Amiens warders did not, and no modern ironist could, see were abroad and riding with Peter. The
warders laughed their sides out, the world shouted its lungs out
and followed after this little dark Don Quixote on his hairy Rosi-
nante, with no windmill for goal but Christ's Tomb.

Their success was astonishing. They made a circuit of all the big
towns, hills and valleys in France and on the Rhine. Their schedule
was always the same. They would enter the city gate, the rough
branch cross lowered during the journey once more raised, Peter's
black eyes ablaze and he shouting "Christ's Sepulchre must be
saved!" The gate passed, Peter would sometimes stop at hospice
or private house for crust and cress and spring water, rarely, when
he was greatly fatigued, for a little fish and wine. More often he
would make at once for the church, he tight-packed in the crowd
that had gathered at his cry. Arrived at the portals, he would
tether his ass in the square—before they got through it was tied
in almost every church square in France—and taking a swift
drink at the well and dashing water across his dusty face, he would
go inside into the pulpit. When the gathering was great, from the
porch outside he would leather-lung the square, the milling city,
and the hills. Sometimes it was Pope Urban's own sermon from
which he quoted. Most frequently he preferred, the crowd with
him, his own fiery improvisations. These made up what was then
called a sermon. It would be "propaganda" now. Anyway, it was
great recruiting plea. A modern nation would quickly vote a
million pounds for a Peter who could put today's issues in today's
terms as magnetically as he put into patois, Latin, *langue d'oc*,
langue d'oïl, the then burning issue of Christ's Tomb. If they
were wise they would give at least another hundred thousand for
the little ass.

Peter had figures, too, at his tongue's tip. He spoke of all the
pilgrims with branches murdered by Saracens with scimitars. It

never occurred to them that the Saracens might be paying back
for Charles Martel; and angry murmurs at once swept the ranks
of his listeners. The actual figures were bad enough, and Peter was
not given to understatement.

The citizens thus incited by bloody statistics, he would begin
painting the most vivid rhetorical chromos. It was as though with
weaving hands and tongue he created the most lurid murals—up
on the vaults above the heads of the audience inside, for the overflow without, on the house walls of the square, the hills, the very
clouds. In startling colours they came alive, these verbal tableaux
of the Storming of Jerusalem by the Infidels, and the Defiling
of the Tomb. The mouths of his hearers, though soundless, would
be open with horror. Moans would be heard from the tender-
hearted, the unstrung. The atmosphere became supercharged with
his burning pictorial oratory, crackled as though with fire.

Then all of a sudden he would lower and sepulchrally hoarsen
his voice to tell how the King must feel at this desecration—as
though He were crucified once more. Every phrase and intonation
then would be as dolorous as a wayside calvary. The pity of it,
the utter lugubriousness would set the sensitive to trembling, the
warlike to pitiless murder in their hearts.

And once more Peter would change his tempo and beat up their
blood by denunciations of the defilers that sounded more frightful
than the lay curses outside in the square.

Thus his audiences would be variously worked upon. The neurotic and near-epileptic would be at the point of hysteria now
The soft of heart would swoon with terror and ecstasy. The sadistic
would thirst for blood, speculators for grain-corners, others fo
loot, the silks, gems, harems of the "wicked Moslems"; and the
yelps of "God wills it!" from these were—to egg on the rest—
more savage and piercing than any. As for the normal and robus
now whipped up, they would feel as a father when child of his ha
been violated by a pervert, while even the finest-fibred, those i
spirit most truly following the King, would be glad that a tim
had come when they could die for Him who had died for them

So, on the ending of one or another of Peter the Hermit
galvanic sermons, every Picard, Poitou, Provençal town church
every Somme, Saône and Seine cathedral would ring with thes
responses, these frenzied antiphons—the *"Diex el volts!"*—Go
wills it! God wills it!"

Everywhere scene and set were the same. Just restaged, that
all. Always there were the Jericho entry, the milling parade, wil
sermon, the same old parish crowd, half-wolf, half-sheep, with th
poor ones prone or twitching on the cold church pavements, ar

the wild guttural "God Wills!" Followed then the clanging of great swords on church stones or square-cobbles as the nobles enlisted; the banging of strong boxes; the grind open of their intricate locks; the clink of the gold poured out at the altar. And the shear and rip of cloth, the sewing of red crosses on peasant smock and noble mantle, and ever that daubing of red crosses on shields, with the drip, drip and splash of red everywhere. From brushes then. So soon from swords.

And it was the snowball all over again. The bands following Peter, his rude cross and the little ass grew astonishingly. And his preaching helped in starting other divisions under William the Carpenter and Walter the Penniless in the Rhine country, under other leaders down by the Loire.

The trouble was that the nobles did not get in line as speedily as the poor. The seigneurs had wives—or substitutes—of whom they must take lingering farewell, even if there were no chastity belts to lock, which some museums suggest, unfairly, was the rule and not the exception. But there were certainly suits of armour to be forged, and striped pavilions to be woven, estates to be set in order, ships to be leased, last testaments to be made. Often, too, those strong boxes were very low in gold. Loans must be negotiated from social inferiors, burghers and guilds, who would collect their interest in charters later on, also from those loan sharks who had been so vociferous with their "God Wills," but somehow never got to buckling on the sword. Word had to be passed down the long feudal chain from rank to rank, so that the fealty which had been sworn to long before under Charlemagne or Charles Martel on the Field of Mars, might now be paid in cash, men, and steel.

All this, like the mobilizations of modern democracies, took time. It was more than a year after these sermons of Peter before the nobles got themselves and their horses down to Marseilles and on board. But the poor always travel light—in the case of those who followed Peter, William the Carpenter, and Walter-without-a-Penny, far too light for the brigands along the way, and the jealous Church of the East, and the Saracens when they neared their goal.

In 1096, the warders of the Paris gates saw a pathetic division of the *pauperes*, "the Poor Ones," as the first devoted but indigent crusaders were known, down the Orleans road, limping, shuffling through the dust after the rude, unbarked cross, the small grey ass, and the little olive-faced, black-eyed commander. A cry went up through the city announcing their coming, to be followed soon by Peter's "Sepulchre!" hail, so astonishingly resonant from so small a frame. And all in Paris, except the bedridden of the ancient hospital, the Hôtel Dieu, met at the top of Saint Genevieve's Hill, to escort the patched crusaders down it.

It did not matter that the arsenal they carried was worse than that with which their descendants would assault the Bastille—just a few old pikes and swords and a lot of farm tools, or that the red crosses on their rough tunics were so poorly sewn. Paris had been caught up in the crusading fervour that swept all France. And the Parisians formed a running, ejaculating fringe all around the motley parade, threw their arms over the sweating shoulders of the pilgrims, and handed them loaves of bread, pitchers of wine and pasties, until the wearied army that had limped up the hill took on an excited and almost alert look. The rusted weapons and farm tools were, with the rude cross, now held high. Even the withered branches which they had dragged through the dust were now exalted like hosannah palms, while the rejuvenated chorus of "God wills" from ragged guests and city hosts aroused in the ancient quarries and the hills echoes as resounding as ever answered Genevieve's warriors or the shining-haired, beast-and-bird-helmeted Gauls.

In the jam as many as could touched Peter and his cross or took hold of his stained gown as though virtue might issue through it as it had through the hem of His garment Whose tomb they were on the way to save. But many of the townspeople were more fascinated by the little ass than by Peter's burning, holy look. In greater numbers they crowded in on the beast, patting him, stroking him, some even plucking hairs from his little round rump to save for relics. He had been treated as great enough personage all the way up to Paris. But so much fuss did they make over him here that one would have thought him the very mount which had served Our Lord.

With similar acclaim, the rude cross held high, Peter the Hermit's procession came down the Rue Saint Jacques and crossed the river into the square bordered by the ancient Hôtel Dieu, bulging with cheering invalids, Saint Etienne's now deserted long grey bulk flecked with wallflower gold, and King Childebert's restored Notre Dame, all alive and lighted again.

Above, from the central belfries, the old bells jangled out a welcome. Then suddenly there was an almost magical transformation. When they marched through the three high Roman arched doors of Notre Dame, the altar lights at the far end gilded the old pikes and farm tools with a new blazonry. The long rows of roundheaded windows down the sides which presented to the outside world black cobwebbed faces, within revealed in the lights the old Charlemagne glass, not so glorious as the Gothic rose to come, but still glowing with warm if subdued azures, emeralds and crimsons. And when the sun came through the panes they enriched the faded garments of the little army with lozenges and patches of bright colour, until with the incense burning, the rich chants going, these crusaders almost looked their parts. It was then, not later, that the romantic novelist should have looked in on these *pauperes*, the famous "poor men," who were to march on to their doom. Then he might have gone down to Marseilles to feast his eyes on the shining nobles with their rich trains, boarding their bannered galleys, long after the plain people.

While Peter mounts the pulpit on the south side of old Notre Dame and becomes the little living volcano of zeal, it is best perhaps to linger without—on the wrong, the dark, side of that Charlemagne glass—and consider some of the economic and political causes which while not so important as the religious, still played a part in the Crusades. The historians of those days, engrossed with piety, too often ignored them; the modern analysts, in their turn, dwelling on them too much and ignoring the moral factors.

In part, of course, the Crusades were all a part of a grudge fight. The Moslems had not forgiven Charles Martel or forgotten his hammer. His grandson Charlemagne, three centuries before Peter started out, had smoothed things over. Never did human glands work more perfectly than in Charlemagne's breezy, gaucy person. Like the rest of men the Moslems admired him. He had made them forget their defeat. They turned over to him the keys of the Holy City and the Sepulchre. In the afterglow of his genial presence, for many generations after his death, they kept the roads open for the pilgrims, that is for those hailing from Rome, not for those who owned allegiance to Constantinople and the Church of the East. This vexed that organization very much. It grew jealous of these prerogatives of its ancient rival and its guardianship now of the holy places, and threw all the obstacles it could in the way of the faithful when they came to the Danube's mouth and near the Golden Gate. Indeed, after the Hungarian bandits had been baptized *en masse* by Rome and forebore further belabouring of the pilgrims, the hardest stretch of the long journey to the East had been, not through pagan, but through Christian country.

For two and three quarter centuries, then, Calvary had remained a quiet little Christian oasis in the midst of a tremendous desert of sand-brown Moslems. Then suddenly there came two changes in policy—one just an odd shift, the other a complete and bloody reversal. The festering hate that Caucasian Islam had long before felt for Caucasian Christendom (there was a bitter *vice versa*, of course) came to a head in a wild caliph named Hakim. He saw that the Carolingian strain the Moslems had admired had petered out in inept heirs. The glow from the robustious personality of Charlemagne no longer irradiated them—no more, indeed, than the dark, bleak sides of Charlemagne's glass did the overflow crowd outside Notre Dame by the Seine. And feeling an utter contempt for the West now, in 1071, Hakim destroyed a good deal of Jerusalem and the Church Constantine had built over the Sepulchre, then tossed the suzerainty of the little holy plot to the jealous Church of the East, with its capital in Constantine's old city. For a price and a treaty, he gave them the privilege of rebuilding the ruins he had made. It was now the time for the West to be jealous. And the West had to pay a tremendous sum. Never had the Moslems imposed such tolls and taxes on the wayfaring pilgrims as the Church of the East enforced on them now.

And then—almost as swiftly again—instead of being driven further apart, the two churches were almost thrown into each other's arms. For the Seljuk Turks had been welded with the Arabs who were often too artistic or polite or else easy-going, to work long enough on this revenge on the West. And the newer race had added to the old a new fibre and fierceness. If ever they had a chance, it was now. Soon it would be too late. Martel had driven them out of France, the Iberians out of much of their peninsula, the roving Normans from Sardinia, Sicily, Italy's boot-heel, and northern Africa, the Byzantines from Syria. Like a three-hundred-and-fifty-year tide that would never turn from its ebb, bit by bit their grand empire had receded. And trying to turn it now, they turned on all Christendom, in both its Eastern and Western forms.

The Eastern, the "Orthodox" Church, which had for centuries been aloof from Rome, and in 1054 broke off entirely, was thrown out of Palestine, saw its priests being murdered as fast as the Roman celibate pilgrims. And a cry went up not only from Laodicea but from all the Hellespont, the Byzantine and East Danubian country, to come over and help the East and, incidentally, save the Sepulchre. Never since the empire had split into two, the two churches parted, never again down even to our day, would the great schism, the breach between East and West, come so near to being healed. Unfortunately, Hildebrand and his successor had a great civil war on their hands. They were too busy, putting an end to simony, investiture, establishing celibacy among the clergy and placing the spiritual power above the temporal, to see the opportunity and hear the cry. To the hurt of succeeding generations, domestic affairs submerged the foreign at a critical time.

Meantime the pilgrim casualties grew. It seemed that the more the Paynims, as they were called, set on them, the more the recruits for the Holy Sepulchre processions increased. Peter the Hermit's figures (given out in his sermons) of the pilgrim murders were not by any ridiculous margin too big. The way to the Tomb was indeed blazed now by the bleaching bones of the pilgrims.

There were for this grand parade Peter led, one division of which was now kneeling on Notre Dame stones, seven reasons, which follow, though not necessarily in order:

FAITH (The most callous could not deny the presence of that)

PIETY AND PIETISM (There is a difference)

CREDULITY (which could have something to do with the second)

REVENGE (on the Moslem side, though many of the Crusaders had enough of it in their systems and expressed it before they were through)

GREED (and enough to have wrecked any enterprise)

SOCIAL UNREST (which was not called that then and was left for the social schools and lecturers of the future)

AND THE WEATHER

If one thinks the latter rather sillily tossed in, let him look to the contemporary and wise Guibert de Nogent and his quaint and understanding book:

"The French at the time suffered from famine. There had been so many years of *bad weather*. Poor harvests, year after year, had raised the price of grain to exorbitant figures. Avaricious merchants took advantage of the universal misery. There was little bread. What there was was very dear. The poor had to eke out what little flour they could get with roots and herbs.

"But when the cry of 'Crusade!,' of 'Save the Sepulchre!' echoed through the land, all the bars and bolts that had closed the granaries were like magic, in the spreading piety, suddenly opened. And strangely, provisions that had been too high in price when everybody was at home, sold for little when everybody was packing up to depart.

"Famine had now disappeared, giving way to plenty. As all hurried to take up the road to the Sepulchre and to God, they hurried to change into money everything they owned that was not needed for the expedition. It was a buyer's time, not a seller's. The former fixed the price. And it was a new thing in the land to see everyone selling cheap, then buying dear. For immediately everything they required for the journey had gone up in price. Everything of which the new-fledged crusader wanted to get rid went for next to nothing!"

Peter's columns, however, were chiefly composed of those who literally had nothing to sell. As they were singing behind the Charlemagne glass the beautiful Crusaders' hymn, there were other columns gathering who had just as little in this world, at most the share-cropper's bare necessities for tilling the land. And over these Guibert's heart bled.

"It touched mine," he wrote in the words which still so burningly survive, "to see these poor crusaders shoeing their *oxen* just as though they were horses, then hitching them to their two-wheeled carts in which they had piled not only their clothes and bedding but their children! At each town in France or Burgundy they would stretch out their hands, as they saw its towers and ask, these poor ignorant ones, if this were not the Holy City, the Jerusalem they were seeking! And seaports were flooded with ragged itinerants who spoke in unknown tongues, then, finding they were not understood, held up their fingers in the sign of the cross to show that in the crusade they wanted to be enlisted."

Some, of course, in the old days wove a sprightly romance of it all. But this was later, from the Second Crusade on, when knights in mail and with bright pennons made of crusading both a game and a business. An old monk of Mont Saint Michel tells to what a pretty start—for something that would have so bloody an end— the crusade got off from Brittany:

"Clear was the day and windless. The young men and the maidens all recited verses or sang. Even the old joined in this singing and everyone seemed to have a look of joy. The ones who knew little cried '*Outrer!*' or threw in a 'God help!' And as they started, the musicians struck up the viols. The weather was fine, the happiness great. All the chargers and the palfreys, the hackneys and the laden packhorses too, neighed for very joy. And in the woods the little birds tuned in. And everywhere there were victuallers' tents with all sorts of wines and bread and sweet pasties, fruit too, and venison, fish, birds and cakes, plenty for all that had money to buy."

But then that monk wrote in an abbey near the stars from which everything looked fair. And that was the Second Crusade, a few years farther on and a much better-dressed and more fashionable affair than the first half of the First Crusade which Peter and the little ass led.

In this First Crusade they were at last on their way, crowding out of the three high Roman-arched doors, with candles, rusted swords and pikes, mattocks and axes and billhooks raised and following the rough unbarked cross, in a great gust of *Diex el volts* shouted up to the Paris hills. Many buckets of Seine water the charwomen had to throw over the Notre Dame stones to clean up after them.

They took the old river road by which the Gauls of Paris had gone to help Vercingetorix against Caesar. Their way, after they passed the old battlefield of Alesia, was through the gateway of

France, Burgundy, thence by the Danubian highways toward Constantinople. There they had planned to meet other brave and crosspatch divisions which, partly because of Peter's own eloquence on his Rhineland tours, partly because of the personalities of William the Carpenter and Walter the Penniless, had joined in the "Poor Men's Crusade." Five grand divisions in all there were, counting those led by Fulcher from the Loire which had started out from Orleans.

The Rhineland divisions, however, started out badly. They began for one thing with a mass murder—of Jews! Ten thousand they slaughtered. A considerable number when Europe's population was but a fraction of what it is now. They were going, said some of the fomenters, to save the Tomb; why not kill the descendants of those who had killed the One Who had lain in the Tomb? It all had, they insisted, some connection! So they reasoned in those days too, by the Rhine.

The ten thousand done in, they also got into fights all along the way with Attila's descendants and the Magyar Hungarians. The Hungarians seem to have had the best of it. They had their case. Not the best of motives but the worst apparently inspired quite a section not only of the knights but of the *Pauperes*. "God wills it!" was on the lips of these, murder and pillage in their eyes and hearts. The Balkan wild folk took care, in their own fashion, of the Rhenish fragments the Hungarians had left. Only two thinned-out corps under Walter the Penniless, who truly had thought to do God service, reached Constantinople to fall in behind Peter the Hermit. Then suddenly because of some internecine fights, a neurosis he had or simply because his zeal, endless circuit-riding, and preaching had burned him out, Peter's spirits began to droop, his black eyes lost their sparkle. When they were so near their goal, he let them cross over, some say, and stayed in Constantinople or returned there quickly after his armies began to dissolve. It was almost as though Joshua, throwing down his trumpets, had refused to assault Jericho or Moses had balked at the Red Sea. So he stayed and waited in Constantinople for the first-class fares, the crack part of the parade, the princes and knights in shining mail under Godfrey of Bouillon, his brother Baldwin, and Raimund of Toulouse, who came a year or so late.

There is not in any chronicle the verified record of a single company of these "Poor Ones" who so tumultuously, joyously and naïvely—and at least a half of them so sincerely—enlisted in the People's Crusade, returning to their native land once they crossed over the Bosporus. Many great pyramids their bones would have made had they been piled up together. Still, they had blazed the trail, striped white with skeletons the road to Jerusalem for the knights who had procrastinated but would make a better fight for it. But then their armour was splendidly plated and riveted. And smocks and tunics and farm tools had not seemed to stand up so well against the scimitars.

Peter rode along with the knights and was with them when after massacring their way down through Syria they stormed Jerusalem. The knights did not pay much attention to him. He had been the grandest circuit rider in Christendom. Now he was what was called in the West *Outre Mer,* an "exploded phenomenon," or, as our Guibert de Nogent put it, a "fallen star." On the outside looking in, he watched them constructing rams' heads, gathering boulders for ammunition, stringing the great steel bows, building stationary offensive towers and great high walking towers, tenanted thickly with men-at-arms, that rolled right up to the walls. And then, in 1099, just as the sands of the century were running out, he saw the breaching of the gates; then, high in air, the pouring out of men on the walls from the walking towers; the race down on the ground through the breach, the flowing of streets with crimson instead of the customary white of soured goat's milk, and the spitting everywhere of Moslems, like quails doubled up, on Christian lances and swords. All, all, making, in the name of the King, butchers' carcasses of those He had so plainly indicated were their brothers. They painted red the Holy City, splashed even Calvary red. Happy, happy, insensate warriors!

Peter the Hermit got out of it all somehow and back to France. Somewhere, though, he had waylaid his cross. He died, very peaceably, as the head of a priory. How he managed to do it no one knows. Not that that should be a reflection on him. Some, like Peter the Hermit, are built to hold a short, fierce flame, others, like Saint Bernard, for a long and enduring and hardening fire. What became of the little ass no one knew, though someone certainly should have recorded it.

The fifty years period following was by far the most prosperous cycle during the long series of Crusades. Romantic novelists might really have found something of glamour in this period. The Crusaders scalloped the Syrian sky with crenels, thrust up the squarely doubled fists of donjon keeps all along the Palestine heights so that you might have thought you were in Touraine if the landscape had only been more lush and green instead of so rose-red, fiery and tawny. And Godfrey, once seigneur of Bouillon, now King of Jerusalem, set up there as splendid a court as ever was seen in Arles or Paris. So they made a little France out of the Holy Land. The French tongue was the official one in court and the courts; French laws were observed; and French feudalism was here transported bodily. The French Song of Roland and the *chansons de geste* were recited in halls and glens that had resounded to David's strumming, where Ruth had lain in the great hay barns, where Gideon had broken his lamps at the Hebrew Thermopylae. French songs of love were heard by the well where Isaac had wooed Rebecca, French lullabies on the Bethlehem hills, French rowers' songs on blue Galilee.

It was a most profitable appendix kingdom to France. In spite of battles, bargaining went on. The modern song to the contrary, there the West did meet the East—met to fight, to make up, to trade. This prosperity lasted for fifty years until the Second Crusade after which the whole movement or institution degenerated into a seesaw succession of mass attacks and mass retreats, the alternate losing of Acre, Tripoli, and those splendid strongholds on the heights, and the Holy City, and the storming of them again. And there were queer, compromise phases in between that did the West no credit, when in illy-defined truces the pilgrims were on humiliating sufferance allowed in the holy places.

But by 1144 the Saracens, all the Turks and Arabs, the desert peoples, had become merged together. And there was mighty good material among them. Did not the chronicler of the famous "History of the Holy Wars" almost go into ecstasies over it, for all his patronizing Occidental manner of which he was so unconscious: "Brave and proud and wonderful are the citizens of these cities. *If they were not unbelievers, better men never would have been!*"

The noble Godfrey, his brother Baldwin, and Raimund of Toulouse had been replaced by Norman Franks who had deteriorated two ways. They had gotten soft by sitting on divans and listening to lutes, and greedy from pouncing like robber barons from their lordly castles down on peaceful Saracen travellers.

So when the aroused Saracens struck, the cry for help went back to the cradle of the Crusades, France. In all that land there had been but two that had asked questions, doubted the sense of them —the little ass, and the great Bernard of Clairvaux, shepherd of the grey Cistercians. Somehow now they persuaded even him to a *volte face*. He, the Cistercian leader, in the rival Cluniac church of Vézelay, became the new bugle. In some ways he was more effective than the first one, being resonant where Peter had been shrill, even as he was intellectual where Peter had been but emotional.

"Edessa is taken," he challenged that Vézelay audience. "You know it well! It is news which dismays every Christian! Bare now and desolate are the churches! And God is no longer worshipped therein! You knights, ponder this well! All of you who are famed for your feats of arms, give those arms to Him who on the cross was lifted up for you!"

Then, intellectual though he was, he made the old plea:

"He who will now go forth with Louis need not fear Hell! His soul shall fly to Paradise with the angels of Our Lord!"

More of that red-cross-sewing, shield-splashing, then the thundered "God Wills!," the swearing, borrowing, financing high and low, and the Second Crusade was on. Eight principal ones there were supposed to be through the hundred and seventy-five years. Actually, if you throw in all the post-, or neo-Crusades, there were over twice as many, covering a period of precisely three hundred and forty-nine years. This was the order in which they marched in history's greatest parade:

I. First Section, First Crusade, 1096. "The Poor Man's Crusade." Almost every recruit but Peter the Great Recruiter was lost.

II. Second Section, First Crusade, 1097. Godfrey's, Raimund's, Baldwin's regiments in shining armour. They took more cities, spilled more blood than any and turned Palestine into a Franco-Norman-Arabia for fifty years.

III. Second Crusade, 1147. Saint Bernard's sermon struck the bugle note. Louis the Seventh was chief marshal. In it he lost some prestige and eventually his wife, Eleanor of Aquitaine. She went over to England, soul and body and *dot*—a goodly section of France; which laid some of the seed for the two-hundred-years-off Hundred Years War.

IV. Third Crusade, 1189. "The Poster Crusade." Here the spark was not a sermon but a poster, a great "twenty-four sheet" affair, painted to show the Saracen stallions defiling the sacred spots. Richard the Lion-hearted; the equally brave, but shrewder, Philippe Auguste; and Redbeard Frederick figured in it; brown Saladin too. They kept a few of those lordly castles in the north, lost the others, and Richard failed to interest Saladin in a trade of Richard's sister for Jerusalem. They still talk of his muscles, though, and sing his love song written behind bars.

V. Fourth Crusade, 1202. They now shifted their objective from saving the Sepulchre to beating the Moslems, taking Constantinople instead of Jerusalem, and continued to drain dangerously the West of its best blood.

VI. First Section, Fifth Crusade, 1212. The pitiful "Children's Crusade." Unhappily, a child—two of them—did lead this one, but not the Child. One column a lad named Nicholas led out of Cologne, to leave behind—its only trace—a legend out of which grew "The Pied Piper of Hamelin." Stephen, a shepherd boy of France, led a great army of children, promising them that the waters would let them through dry-shod. But the Mediterranean refused to act like the Red Sea. All that did not perish of the hardships were sold by traders into slavery. The story of this had best be told not in chronicles or any words but in the strains of Gabriel Pierné's music. His chords and dominants may resolve some of its horror into classic tragedy that can be borne after all these years.

VII. Second Section, Fifth Crusade, 1218. Frederick the Second of Germany accepted the leadership but he arrived eleven years late. The command devolved on John of Brienne, who was elected "King of Jerusalem," when they didn't have Jerusalem. He didn't win it back and signed a treaty by which he gave back to the Sultan the Holy Cross. In this Crusade Saint Francis preached one of the greatest sermons ever in this world. It had more effect on the Sultan than the Crusaders' swords.

VIII. Sixth Crusade, 1228. Frederick, who had missed the Fifth, arrived eleven years later, in time for the more successful Sixth. But he was in trouble with the Church. The Church had excommunicated Frederick and an excommunicated Crusader is an anomalous figure. Indeed, the Pope had declared a crusade against him in his own lands even as he was winning back the Tomb, not by fighting, but by bargaining with the Saracens. He got the three most historic towns on earth, Jerusalem, Nazareth and Bethlehem. Sometimes the Moslems had murdered the pilgrims entering the Tomb, sometimes had sold them entrance tickets, very high-priced. Now it was in the hands of Christians, if excommunicated Christians, and for fifteen years.

IX. First Section, Seventh Crusade, 1248. No enterprise of those ages could have had a nobler leader than Saint Louis of France. But he did not have much success in the Crusades. His own court felt that in advance, and he had to wheedle them into the Seventh by a ruse. At Christmas he handed

out to each noble a brand new and beautiful costume,
neatly folded up. When unfolded and held up by the
shoulders, each tunic and mantle showed a nicely-
embroidered red cross. By their acceptance of the
gifts, the nobles were willy-nilly enlisted. There
were some prodigious battles, hammer-and-tongs
sieges but they could not recover Jerusalem which
had been lost all over again.

X. Second Section, Seventh Crusade, 1253. "The Pastoral or
Shepherds' Crusade"—they might as well have been children
and, as had the children before, they vanished like Villon's
snows.

XI. First Section, Eighth Crusade, 1269. James of Aragon mobilized, sailed down the Mediterranean and saw a storm
coming up, so sailed back again.

XII. Second Section, Eighth Crusade, 1270. Saint Louis made one
more attempt before he died. A little nearer home, though.
The objective was now to cripple the Moslems, not by
taking Jerusalem or Constantinople but Tunis. And he had
more trouble in recruiting. The nobles were sick of
crusading. And they were on the lookout for Christmas
suits. But Saint Louis kept seeing the Holy City in
all his dreams. A famous and extraordinarily capable
earthly monarch, he cried out, like his Heavenly
King,—"Oh, Jerusalem, Jerusalem!" These were
his last words as he died. It should have been the
note on which the Crusades ended, for they were
so evidently over. But there was one note more
sour. Louis' brother talked the bey into a great
tribute. And Prince Edward of England, who
was another that was late, arrived as the
tribute was being handed out. He didn't
get a penny and sulked all the way home.

It was clear now that the whole movement had petered out, for
all practical purposes, if the expression can be used of a movement
so wholly impractical.

And yet there were other attempts, inept revivals. Still the Crusaders came on now like phantom columns:

XIII. Ninth Crusade, 1344, of the Knights Hospitaller and the

Venetian Doges from the Bridge of Sighs. All they did was
to take Smyrna and its dates.

XIV. Tenth Crusade, 1353, by the Prince of Vienne, which wound
up simply as a sail over the Mediterranean.

XV. Eleventh Crusade, 1365, in which Peter of Cyprus sacked
Egypt and Syria but never reached the Tomb.

XVI. Twelfth Crusade, 1396, Jean sans Peur of Burgundy was not
fearless enough to get beyond the Balkans.

XVII. The Thirteenth and last of all, even the Ghost, Crusades,
started in 1443 by the Kings of Poland and Transylvania,
aiming at Sancta Sophia, but not getting even that, and
leaving the Tomb where it had been since Mahomet's
death, where it would be until Allenby came in 1917 —
in the hands of Islam, which had no use for it except
as a trade.

But even when the Crusades were ended, their ghost was not
laid. Often the idea would be resurrected into enough life for a
court argument at least or some propaganda campaign. And sometimes it served as a slogan, frequently as a holy cloak for a most
nefarious enterprise. In 1492, however, Columbus used it for one
worth while when he suggested to the pious Isabella that if she
gave him her diamonds and pearls so that he might sail into the
sunset, he might wind up in the sunrise and at Our Lord's
Tomb.

So was America, in a manner of speaking, a by-product of the
Crusades. There were many such by-products:

For the first and most obvious one, there was the centralization
and strengthening of the Kingdom of France. Too highly feudal-
ized it had been, so that the countless counts and dukes and
princelets who were presumably vassals of the King had strained
at the tether of the oath that bound them to him. The only domain
of which he had been sure in the eleventh century was the kingdom's core and heart—the Ile de France. Over the other states
roundabout he might legally and nominally hold suzerainty but
he could not seem to exercise it literally. The Crusades now changed
the empty lip-service of their oaths to a genuine limb-service. With
his great vassals the King of France had ridden and sailed, had
charged, fought and suffered, commanded them too, and not infrequently had shown them impressive examples of personal valour.
Not so often thereafter would they be curt, indifferent to, or

downright rebellious against the King. In real earnest he was their liege lord.

At the same time the deep abyss between noble and peasant or burgher was bridged. Sometimes the link was made of sentiment, for by his prowess at Alexandria or Acre, or—on the few occasions when he did get there—before the Jerusalem walls, the seigneur had been transformed from a rude baron or large-scale farmer into a highly romantic figure in shining armour about whom legends were nightly woven around the hearth-fires and whom the whole countryside admired. But often that bridge over the social gulf was built of gold. Those oriental voyages and sieges, with bannered galleons, new castles and all that went into them, took money. Strong boxes showed bottom too soon. The more prosperous farmers, the burghers, towns, guilds, could lend. After a big loan the most feudal of lords would not be too tyrannical toward a vassal if he were his creditor. A mortgagor in mail would not crack down his gauntleted fist on a mortgagee in wool. And it was simply impossible to ride the high horse in the town hall before a composite creditor like a whole city in ranks assembled. For too ready to play off commune against noble was the king. So the commoner, he at least of the shops, counting desks, merchant ships, the three balls, often he too of the farm granary, began dimly to sense his power. More things than the discovery of America were tied up with the Tomb. When in 1095 the knights of high degree began to borrow from them of low, the day of the mediaeval guilds, the free cities, was just ahead, and—looking back, one can see it now—signs of the Third Estate, the commune, and the labour union were on the horizon.

These unsuccessful wars which did not gain their objectives and swallowed up so much gold and blood and so many reputations, somehow did add to the prestige of France. In the rich eastern court which Godfrey of Bouillon set up, French was used in some measure by everyone from Dauphiné duke to Saracen scullion. Even their most jealous rivals, the English knights, could not object to this; after the Conquest of 1066, half of them were French or Norman-French. Then, too, warriors, ambassadors, traders, travellers of every nation came to this new West-East kingdom and its capital, ancient Jerusalem, during that fifty years' tenure. All up and down the Palestine valley and coast, in a bizarre setting of grey western keeps and oriental fountains, tournament lists, and silken ottomans, falcons and little singing bulbuls, saw-toothed *porculles* and graceful grilles, oxen roasted whole and dainty sherbets, they heard French spoken, learned it, took it back home.

And all the troubadours and minstrels, in all the holy spots and spots unholy, by all the rivers along which they passed on their return and in the home cities, sang to oriental lutes they had imported the French *chansons*. So that soon this liquid old French became the polite language of all the capitals of the known world, also the medium of exchange, the common verbal currency of all peoples who bordered on the Mediterranean or came within sight of its waves.

A French culture had started sixteen hundred years before they took up the cross for conquest. Then the old Gauls made beautiful dyes and tinctures and textiles, exquisite pitchers and pots, and put on these cunning traceries, silver slabs in their walls, enamel on their shields, and designs in the gold helmets on their golden hair. They gave them smartness and style and used trousers before the rest of the world of the West, and mattresses and coaches before other men, and put oil in their shampoos.

This grand tradition had conquered their Roman and their Frankish conquerors in the end. It had been given a new glory by Charlemagne and all his schools and scholars and singers. After the Dark Ages it was revived again by the Crusades to flame up with unmatched splendour in the Gothic; never again to be extinguished in spite of conquerors—of any vintage. At least this is the hope of half the world. And now, quite as the monks, who through the Dark Ages kept learning's torch alight, brought back from their pilgrimages into Spain many good ideas from the Berber-Arab-Moors, the Crusaders borrowed many things from the pure Arabs.

This was always evident as soon as the bronzed warrior crossed the threshold into his own vaulted *foyer*. His mantle and tunic were longer cut now in the oriental fashion. The sword on his hip was exquisitely damascened. After the later Crusades, the toes of his felt shoes were turned up and curled in some Damascus manner. And he did not forget his chatelaine, whether mistress or only wedded wife. Ostrich plumes he stuck in her hair. Sugar, spices, sweets, he held out in his gauntlets under her nose. He displayed furnishings to brighten up her stern castle boudoir—gay rugs, silver ewers, silk hangings, chairs with pearl inlay, oriental crystal and threw down before her silk ottomans and pillows.

To match all this new splendour the Crusaders tried to make themselves brighter all over. They succeeded! A far more picturesque parade they made as they came down the gangplanks of the homefaring ships than they had when they embarked. That is the luckier ones did, not Saint Louis or the Poor Men or the Children or the Shepherds. There was no homefaring for them.

These luckier ones now rode on handsome Arab stallions which they had bought both because their arched necks and caracolling showed the knights off as prettier riders and because they could be bred to the sturdy French mares to improve the stock. Their shields and pennons bore more than red crosses; these were decorated now with a magnificent blazonry. The heraldry of the East they had transported bodily. Soon they turned it into as colourful a code as a modern Lloyd's yachting register with all its gay flags. And they developed it into a complex study and created for it colleges in which grave men made a lifelong study of these bright labels and posters. So they transformed Western chivalry into a whirling world of dazzlingly bedecked mounted sandwich men.

During the Dark Ages, France with the rest of the world had lost some important things—for one striking example, the knowledge the Greeks had handed on to them in their great books written in crystal images and crystal-clear phrases, that the earth was round. Many scholars and monks still cherished this secret. But the man in the mediaeval street thought his world too flat for anyone to go near the edge without danger. With the decline of medicine and surgery, the Hippocratic investigating spirit had vanished, awaiting the days when Doctor Paré of Paris and Harvey of London would recreate it. The Suez Canal and waterway which had been in use for a millennium and a half had filled up or disappeared. Eleven hundred years later the French would have to reconstruct a Suez Canal all over again.

It was the same with libraries. The monasteries had them but not often the State. There was nothing in any capital to match the ranked tomes of ancient Alexandria, which had ages before gone up in fire. Of books not devotional the Paris palace was actually bare. It was during his first trip to the Holy Land that Saint Louis conceived the idea of enriching his kingdom with a royal library. Also the oriental dye-stuffs attracted him. There was nothing in all Paris now to rival the hues of the glorious old tartans and cloaks worn by ancient Gauls who had once fought for this island. And he made this loss good by importing from the East pigments of fresh and delightful hues. *Madder rose—Indigo—Saffron—Ultramarine*, whose very name came from *outre mer*, "over-seas"! Like Columbus, Isabella, the United States, Burke's Peerage, the guilds, communes, Paris fashions, the artist too was in debt to the Crusades.

Furthermore, though they had lost their main objective, they had gained in commerce and foreign exchange, which some mediaeval business men thought even better than taking the Tomb. Saint Louis himself started a sort of international exchange by making merchants' marks which could be used by traders in countries whose language they could not understand. And all large commercial centres established consulates in important foreign cities.

By the year 1250, in Saint Louis' reign, Arles, Montpellier, Narbonne, Marseilles, of France, and Genoa, Pisa and Amalfi of Italy
were represented by consuls in many places of the Levant. When
they did not go 'by land the main crusading bodies, of course,
sailed in ships chartered by powerful nobles or the king. But the
shipowners, to encourage individual travel, offered the following
"special rates" as they called them, to all who would make the
water pilgrimage to Palestine:

Table of Fares for the Pilgrim to the Holy Land

First Class—with privilege of sleeping in fresh air on top deck. .60 sous
Second Class—sleeping between decks........................40 sous
Third Class—on lower deck (near sweating oarsmen)..........30 sous
Fourth Class—in the hold................................20 sous

Now no country has been basically sounder—over long periods,
that is—than France, but its volatile franc (of which a sou is the
twentieth part) has taken terrific punishment since the Middle
Ages. The franc is the descendant of the louis of the late Louis'
time, and of the Carolingian *livre*. The *livre* equalled an English
pound, a sou the shilling. A mediaeval sou was worth, then, twenty
cents, from which height it had tobogganed, in the Second World
War, to an eighth of a cent. But a shilling or twenty cents in
those days, had almost a hundred times its present purchasing
value. Whence can it be easily seen why one of those horses which
the Crusaders took to ride round Jerusalem walls cost but ten sous
then, where now it would cost two hundred thousand sous of
Second World War value—also that the poor pilgrim paid enough
for his cranny in the hold, and those rates were not so very special
after all.

But astonishingly businesslike were the shipowners of the Crusades. They also installed a good deal of almost modern system.
To all the pilgrims and passengers numbered tickets were given;
and duplicates were filed in the guildhall at Marseilles.

Yes, profit and business, as well as lust, attended the Crusades.
But this extended phenomenon, this seemingly endless parade to
the wars, can not be charged to these or social unrest or any single
cause whatsoever as much as to faith, though expressed in a way
that seems naïve, anomalous, impracticable, and often like credulity
to so many now. But the credulity was often very like faith. And
at least the credulous knew that which the too practical never
know at all: what it is for the heart to sing and the soul to soar.
Too often, it is true, those "God wills! God wills!" turned to "Kill,
Kill!" in frenzied throats. And it is hard to drown them out. But
one can if one listens for the Crusaders' Song coming down, all
those years:

"Fairest Lord Jesus,
Ruler of all Nature,
Thou both of God and Man the Son,
Thee will I cherish,
Thee will I honour,
Thou, my soul's glory, joy, and crown.

"Fair are the meadows,
Fairer still the woodlands,
Clad in the lovely robe of spring;
Jesus is fairer,
Jesus is purer,
Who makes the downcast heart to sing.

"Fair is the sunshine,
Fairer still the moonlight,
And great the twinkling starry host;
Jesus shines brighter,
Jesus shines purer,
Than all the angels Heaven can boast."

So it comes down, "Fair are the meadows . . . Fairer still the mountains . . . Fairest Lord Jesus" . . . from the Jerusalem walls in the watches of the night, from the Bethlehem hills where the shepherds saw the Heavenly host, and even from the little children who were lost yet never lost.

There was one art and its masterpiece which, above all others, was influenced by the Crusades—architecture and the Cathedral, now just around the corner of the years. The Holy Land might be arid but for the architect it was a well-spring of ideas. And there the inquiring mind, under cassock or coat of mail, drank deep. This man of the West built his castles strong. Grand and sweeping were their lines on the Palestine as well as the Provençal heights. But in France they did not then have so much in the way of gardens and parks. They did not show such delicacy of arch or lightness of shaft. They were not so familiar with fountains or even with colour. But he who saw palace interiors modelled on Solomon's or had gazed on the Lord's lilies, the red anemones that outmatched Solomon's splendour, could never forget it. Borrowing the Saracen heraldry, he put that colour on his shield, on his back, on his manorial walls. But the poor were not warmed by that. They seldom came beyond the courtyards of the castles, except with tribute. To warm the poor folk, then, to open the channel for refreshment of the soul through the delighted eye, the priests and abbots put the hues of the Lord's own lilies with that of the northern fleur-de-lis—imprisoned them, dyed them deep in glass, up in the church windows. In the great rose. Under the great towers. Over the row of kings.

And there was the arch. It was not with the Arabs, Gothic, but a horseshoe. Still, it was not that old round Roman arch that had held up everything in Paris for more than a thousand years. This Arab arch had a point, though not for bearing much stress like the Gothic. Already the man of the West as artisan, builder and architect, in Normandy, Bourgogne and in the churches on the Oise, had been experimenting with the arch though as yet but tentatively. But nonetheless he had been trying to break it, point it up. And now as he came back from the East, his mind seething with new ideas gave impetus and drive to the long engineering search that had been going on in France for a wedding, or a great harmonious triangle rather, of strength and height and light. For such a union the mighty Roman arch had proved unstable. But very soon now, between the Second Crusade and the Third, that long search would work out in the heart of France high and bright and glorious, its great miracle.

XXIV

The First Notre Dame is the Mother University, the Alma Mater of Alma Maters. . . . The Ancient Cloister of Notre Dame. . . . The Famous Schoolmen wrestle in the Campus of Cathedral Square and in the Church of Old Notre Dame. . . . One of the World's Great Love Stories that was lived in its Shadow, and Three Immortal Letters of a Paris Girl.

1079=1142 A.D.

WHEN THE OLD ORDER WHICH BORE THE STAMP OF ROME was passing and the Gothic dawn was about to break there lived in Paris a man and a woman who are immortally connected with the story of Notre Dame.

It is easier to tell the woman's story, for she revealed with a mental power that almost matched the man's and an equal fortitude, much more forthrightness. His course, though so meteorlike at times, is harder to follow. It was both bright with fame and dark with disaster. No one was ever more popular or had more relentless foes, though he was not king or general or bishop or in any command except over some schools and desolate abbeys and over the hearts of many men and one woman. Part scholar and headmaster he was, part cleric, and wholly the worshipped idol of Paris until, through a scandalous operation, he became half a man; and even so he won back much of his former popularity and an even greater if stormier celebrity.

His manner in early life held an infinite charm, in his older years, a desert harshness. His logic was magnificent, his grudges were irksome, his self-pity often a pathetic thing to see. His pen was now a flame, again a whine. For thirty-eight years his life was a grave open book for all to look at; then for a stormy space, though he tried hard, he could not conceal its shameful pages. His heart was filled with bitterness, so much of it self-brewed; yet he drank one long, heady, wildly sweet draught of love such as few mortals have ever tasted. And his glory still shines down the years, in part because of his gifts and achievements, rather more for his offense and its tragic punishment, but chiefly because of the devotion of a Paris girl.

But while the world has reckoned the high point of the story to be that "affair," which should have very little to do with cathedrals, his story must be relived. For he was the founder or co-founder of the mother of universities, the nourishing father of the alma mater of alma maters, there at Notre Dame and up on Saint Genevieve's Hill. He played a greater part than any of the famous contemporary "schoolmen" in establishing the great philosophical tradition that wedded dialectics and debate to theology, logic to faith. And none exemplified the Gothic spirit better than he in his intellectual explorations, his lofty, soaring climb up after Truth.

The mother university with which Abelard had so much to do did not have its first life in any set of buildings devoted to education. It functioned informally but with glorious vigour in the porches of, and the dependencies around, the two churches, Childebert's Notre Dame and Saint Etienne, then on the site of the later cathedral.

The so-called "Cloister of Notre Dame" was not a cloister as we now picture one. There was a pocket-handkerchief plot or so of grass, but the quarter was too crowded for much of that serenity and greenness one ordinarily associates with the lovely old ambulatories of the monks. Abelard and his gowned rivals did not debate against any background of delicate pillars, moss-green fountains, or velvet lawns. There was a deal of broken paving, cobblestones and mire all about. This Notre Dame cloister, except for that little green breathing space or two, was a great conglomeration of ancient heavily-masonried buildings in which dwelt and worked all who preached, baptized, or buried for Our Lady, wrote *neumes* or sang staves for her, tutored, embroidered chasubles and altarcloths, dusted canons' stalls, mended lace amice borders, inscribed psalms on old vellum in lovely colours, moulded wax candles or fluffed up goosefeather beds for visiting prelates.

For several acres this ecclesiastical warren stretched at the island's end, curving around its upstream rim, pressing out against the island city walls on the north and the south riversides, and crowding in on the cathedral square and the hospital, the Hôtel Dieu, and the two churches that fronted the square.

But the inhabitants of the quarter loved its every scent and sound. For it was most mixedly aromatic with thurible incense, kitchen smell and dungeon river damp. And it was alive with school babble, mothers' scoldings, the clink of stone-cutters' chisels and masons' trowels repairing church walls, the clack, clack of tongues accompanying needles sewing on holy things, the cries of fishermen and gardeners delivering produce at clerical doors, fullblast "alleluias" from deep bass throats, gamins' trebles in the exquisite *Agnus Dei*, wails of infants in the cold *chapelle de bap-*

tême, and the solemn, hauntingly beautiful *"Resquiescant in pace"* for the dead.

To this Cloister of Notre Dame came Peter Abelard, aged nineteen, fresh from his father's farm down near Nantes. He disagreed with his father, for he hated his native place, the plow and hunting-bow and fishing rod, and he fairly itched for the quill and rostrum. Yet despite this difference, father and son were alike in religious temperament, for the latter later went into a monastery. Heloise was not on hand to greet Abelard. In fact, she was not in the Cloister or anywhere on earth. She came into the world three years later, just as this boy wonder of an Abelard was beginning to make a stir in Paris, and as the old century was going out, and the clerks, with jaunty up and down strokes, were expressing the hope that lay in the new magic figures, the 1100's.

High up—that is, as high as those old Roman and Romanesque buildings ever went—he started out in an attic room, bare save for lumpy bed, out-of-kilter armoire, ewer, ink-splotched sloping desk and crucifix. There he would write to the burning out of his candle and the paling of the stars, even in winter, every bone aching with the cold but his soul on fire. Then, the dawn breaking, after a knob of bread, a lump of cheese, a swallow on holidays of wine, he would go out to one of those many halls or chapels.

There he would sit, in the none too clean straw that protected the buttocks from the chill of the stone flooring, and always in a front place where he could take in every word of his new teachers and present his own brilliant, but too often assured, arguments. He was always on time and never missed a class though the hours were long, the lectures in winter often continuing so late that the torches smouldered low before the masters left and the lanes were filled with students flocking to inn or lodging-house. Even more prolonged were the debates in summer when they were held outdoors. Often a half-past nine sunset, burning red down the Seine, would spread its bright banners above the buildings lining the square, before the massed gowns would break up into twos or threes to thread their way through the Cloister.

Always in the warm months young Pierre Abelard would head not long after dawn from his attic for the square, the college campus. It was smaller than the space before the great cathedral today, and irregular because of the way in which there had grown up around it the old Romanesque buildings on the west; the Hôtel Dieu, oldest going hospital in the world, on the south; long Saint Etienne east; and the first Notre Dame on the north.

These two landmark churches had always appeared from the other shore like two boats, with their narrow second storeys for superstructures, belfry towers for bridges, rising above the city wall. Both were headed downstream and were almost parallel, Saint Etienne running due west, Notre Dame having tacked a trifle to the northwest. There was a little strip of cobbling between them, and Saint Etienne had almost caught up with Notre Dame, its porch prow being just ahead of Notre Dame's apse stern. There Saint Etienne seemed to have stopped in the race, to be moored to the city wall. And there for many ages Saint Etienne had been plastered up and into the city wall, its fourth or south wall being part of the city wall and its curved, fortress-strong apse guarding the city wall as well as its own sanctuary. Never had church and city closer link.

To the students on the island pouring each day into the square, the two churches seemed like bulwarks that never would be crushed. Arch expressions of their age they were, typically Romanesque in their low, thick-walled, stout-buttressed strength. The centuries had not changed their features: the low wide gable, the three recessed portals in front, intertwined with saints and devils, the clere (second) storey extending over the nave and letting light in and down on it, the sides stripped with vertical stone buttresses, the chunky round apse behind. Set in the bays between the buttresses on two sides of Notre Dame, one side of Saint Etienne (its riverside wall being blank) were window eyes, looking immemorial and very wise under their Roman arched eyebrows. Those of Notre Dame were often aglow showing when the candles within were lit, the old Charlemagne glass, like bright irises. But old Saint Etienne's eyes were dimmed now. They stared blankly through the smoke, grime and cobweb cataracts of the ages.

A little later Abelard on his expulsion from the Cloister would start a rival college up on Saint Genevieve's Hill, but it was here in this Cathedral centre that the ancient school of Notre Dame, founded by Charlemagne, flowered out into the at first informally organized University of Paris. That open space, if not a quadrangle, nothing in geometry fitting its irregularity, at least served for one. The two churches were its Whig and Clio Halls, for if Saint Etienne no longer heard mass celebrated, it did hear lectures, particularly in its porch. An abundance of chapels and dependencies in the maze of the Cloister served as study and lecture halls. In the Romanesque rookeries were dormitories. And for the very poorest there was shelter under the sanctuary, or in the crypt with the dead.

As for the square, it was more than a mere cobbled campus. It was the celebrated arena whither came gowned contestants from many lands to wrestle in debate over the strangest of issues. And the two church porches were not only the main university amphitheatres where often very important and violent debates were held, but the most famous cockpits in Europe. The decisions handed down there in these unique contests of the mind, were eagerly awaited in other capitals. The cries of triumph in the Notre Dame and Saint Etienne porches echoed around the world.

Now while a little of natural science had been introduced into the best medical schools and the applied science of horticulture and some botany were taught in the abbeys and the fine Arab and Moorish-Spanish schools, the standard university courses were mathematical and academic. The chief subjects down to the time of Francis the First and the Renaissance, were advanced arithmetic, geometry, grammar, rhetoric, the languages, astronomy, music, philosophy, logic, with medicine, civil or canon law for specialties. But the famous lecturers and debaters in Notre Dame and the other universities which followed her lead, covered provinces far beyond these. With them philosophy, theology, logic were closely intertwined; a special facility in a branch of logic called dialectics was required; and they made forays into the field of a not yet scheduled subject, physics. This intellectual game, which could have been played to such crowds and with such enthusiasm in but one other city in history, the elder sister of Paris, the Athens of long ago, was very ambitious. For under cover of their programme, they were trying to pin down what they called "universals" that is, the bedrock things. They strove to get at the back of the universe to know just what was the substance of God and just how much of it went into man.

The whole faculty of Notre Dame and the student body were aligned into teams, based on their respective ideas of these bedrock things. And it was astonishing that these spirited adolescents played this intellectual game as excitedly as though it were one of hard knocks and blood which young men ordinarily like. They pursued these intangible universals as hotly as modern young men chase a football.

The teams had as captains men famous in their day, though some have been forgotten by all but the scholars: Anselm of Laon and William of Champeaux of the Realists, Roscellinus of the Nominalists among them and, as soon as he won his spurs which was very soon indeed, Abelard of the Conceptualists.

Since the Realists were subdivided and leaders often modified their opinions, precise definition of these terms is difficult even for scholars and unnecessary for those who are looking over the students' shoulders for Heloise, or who are interested more in Notre Dame with which the girl and the genius were so intimately connected. It is enough to recognize the general issue on which the masters lectured and over which the students struggled with as much zest.

This issue had sprung out of Aristotle's and Plato's philosophies. Plato, obsessed with the transcendence of the ideal, taught that the only reality lay in pattern ideas, archetypes in the mind of God. Aristotle denied that the true reality lay in these archetypes and magnificently tied it up with the object, be that object tree, river, planet, man, or something supernatural.

Neither would ever win. The issue would never be settled. It had been started on the steps of the white Parthenon over the blue Aegean by these two Greeks who would influence the minds of men for longer periods than any but Christ and Paul. It had been taken up by that last noble Roman philosopher, Boethius, and by Erigena of the Dark Ages; it was being worried now by that young hound after truth, Abelard in the Cloister shadows; would be thrashed out by Victorian thinkers like John Stuart Mill. And an energetic woman of the New World would start a populous sect based on one side of it:

"Is the object or the concept of the object more real?" it was, or, more explicitly, "Does the greater reality lie in the general idea or the particular thing?"

The teams had made slogans out of it: Plato's *ante rem* (concept before object); Aristotle's *in re* (reality is in the object); and the compromise *post rem* (concept comes after the object). As in the twentieth century before the German machine guns silenced them for the time, one could hear on Saint Genevieve's Hill, the cheerful staccato rallying cries of the students of the Sorbonne Law School and the Arts Decoratifs, so, in Abelard's day, anyone walking through the Cloister could hear these old Latin philosophical slogans of the first University of Paris echoing back from the ancient walls that hedged in the irregular cobbled campus and the immemorial halls.

These students, half of them in tonsures and clerical soutanes or mediaeval cassocks, half in secular gowns reaching below the knees, would flock into the square day after day to chatter these old phrases, to argue over them, or absorbed to watch the masters from far and near engage in their duels with rapier words, fights with cudgel phrases, bludgeon arguments over such delicate abstractions. On days when champion lecturers or imported debaters were on the bill, the listeners would be swirling around the two churches, massed up against the grey walls of the dwellings on the west, or against the façade and Roman-arched portals of the Hôtel Dieu from whose windows the crutched and bandaged invalids looked down, wondering how the young folk below could be so full of joy and vigour. One had to arrive before dawn to get on the porches or near the doors of Notre Dame or Saint Etienne, the favorite places for all who held forth.

There was one who during those years of Abelard's study in Paris took particular delight in watching the young prodigy plunge into all these verbal *mêlées*. Not Heloise—yet—but her uncle, Canon Fulbert of Notre Dame.

And Abelard was worth watching. No matter what competition he had—from the city, from Chartres, Rheims, Soissons, Ireland, Trêves, Fulda, Cologne, Bologna—the young man always stood out in boldest relief as though there were a spotlight on him. He had a fine equipment: a winning address (on the tribune, not always off); gestures now graceful again thrusting and incisive but always effective; a sort of harsh handsomeness of feature; eyes which darted this way and that as he took advantage of some weakness in an adversary or pressed some argument home and ever with a burning-coal glow in them; and a vibrant resonance in his voice. Now it issued through the hall, out over the square, in a flowing legato, like that of the father of all Paris scholars, Father Seine. Again it broke into a rapid crescendo like the brilliant course of a flashing Alpine stream.

On fair days, Canon Fulbert, when he was through with his baptizings, reciting the offices, and chanting in the choir stalls, would take his place now on Saint Etienne's porch, more often— some afterwards thought it significant—under the tumultuous carvings of the striving sinners, fiends and saints, on the sides and tympanum of the Last Judgment Door of Notre Dame. As he watched these tremendous scrimmages over the Trinity and the nature of God, the endless object and concept tug-of-war, his heart was filled with delight.

For Canon Fulbert's heart, those days, was warm. Later his eyes might grow furtive, envenomed with hate for the man whom he had adored. In the earlier days he was not like one of the fiends all around him in the portal but one of its more amiable saints. Before the blow fell, he was at peace with his fellows and happy in his deep love for his orphan niece and a growing affection for Abelard.

In the porch he would enthusiastically comment to his brother canons on any keen thrust his young idol made. He would even cry out *"Touché!"* when Abelard stopped in his swift, reflective pacing of the cockpit that was a church porch or in the cobbled arena between the old houses, the hospital, and the two churches and would hurl a most brilliant conclusion at the rows of dazzled young students packed in on the porch steps, or would explode some inflated hypothesis right in the beard of his arch foe and master, the redoubtable but decidedly inelastic William of Champeaux.

Later, Heloise would have ears for few but Abelard. But she di not listen to him then. In the years when Abelard was arriving, rapidly becoming the idol not only of the students but the Paris crowd, she never saw him except perhaps once or twice when she ran away from her nurse in the old stone dwelling where Fulbert lived. A little north of the two churches this stood, backing on the Rue Chanoinesse and fronting on the river and the north island wall—at 9 Quai des Fleurs you will find the site now. And then she saw her lover-to-be through chinks in the student crowd or from a perch on her uncle's shoulder. For when Abelard first—as he with his sometimes amusing, frequently annoying self-confidence puts it—"first mastered my master" (William of Champeaux) Abelard was twenty-two, Heloise only two.

That summer Abelard perhaps overplayed the boy wonder role. "I had become," he afterwards wrote to a friend, "a serious burden to William of Champeaux, because I argued with him and *usually victoriously.*"

Now bright rebel pupil and wise experienced old master often do not get on with each other. But in quarrelling with, then crowing over, William, Abelard had been just a little too smart. This happened in the last of two historic verbal duels he fought. The first of these made him; the second brought him more renown and got him expelled from Notre Dame. But before he packs up in his little attic and leaves Paris and Heloise behind him, she to grow into an extraordinary knowledge of such academic subjects and an astonishing beauty and capacity for love, those duels must be set down briefly.

They were over two new twists of the old concept-or-object controversy. Roscellinus, very strong for the object, the substantial, declared one morning in the Cloister that concepts did not exist in the mind until they were associated with or derived from their objects. Now this was Aristotle's fine reality carried to an extreme. But here was Abelard's chance. The champions of the theories of the two great Greeks—*ante rem* and *in re*—were forever locking horns. He would proclaim a compromise and, by Heaven, form his own team. So looking, then pointing, down the space between the Hôtel Dieu and Saint Etienne walls, to a boat whose red sails could be seen above the city wall passing down the Seine, he cried:

"Behold the boat, messieurs! Roscellinus gives us but half the truth. He declares that 'Boat' does not attain reality until it is tied up with that boat or all the boats in the world. Quite correct. But his opponents are right too. The concept 'Boat' exists in the mind as a 'universal' (one of those bedrock things, he meant, like genus and species, general attribute). It does exist in the mind as an idea, though it does not have reality until associated with what we see sailing by there. Wherefore, both schools of thought being right, I would advocate this acceptance of both points of view, and this union between them."

Now all these debaters are dust. But that "Boat" parable would go down in all histories of the progress of thought since written. On that boat Abelard had built a new school called the Conceptualist—had his own team. He was at so early an age a captain at the University of Paris.

In the other encounter, the stately William of Champeaux had declared that there was no essential difference between individuals, stones, trees, beasts, men, anything. The only difference between Socrates and the bell-ringer above, trying to drown them out, came through superficial characteristics. Socrates was but an "accident," a drop, of the substance called humanity, and only distinguishable from others through slight variations in form. And further—here he sprang his own trap and among the massed gowns Abelard almost chortled—the substance of humanity was present in its entirety in and was wholly absorbed by Socrates.

"You say," shot back Abelard, "that humanity is present in its entirety in Socrates?"

The old master nodded.

"Also that humanity is wholly absorbed by Socrates?"

An irritated, "Of course."

"Is humanity not also present, Messire William, in Plato and say yourself? Yes? Well, then, if humanity is present in its entirety in Socrates, and is wholly absorbed by him, how can it also be present in Plato—or yourself where Socrates is not?"

So he ran William of Champeaux out of the Notre Dame Cloister for the day, himself out of it for seven years! That flash of Abelard's, listed as "the Socratic man argument," was to go down too in all the encyclopedias. But the victory and applause had cost Abelard his job.

But before we go back with him to pack up his few belongings in his little attic, it should be understood that he had not just been subtle. Those great theories of the Greeks about the universe and ourselves have long engaged men. They had engrossed the Church scholars who had forever been trying to find some common ground in them and Christ's teachings. Some felt, for example, that Aristotle's proclaiming of reality in the thing, even if it were supernatural, strengthened their own theory of the sacred reality in the eucharist. And, according to which philosopher you accepted, you believed, with Plato, that there was one great Over Soul distributed through many or, with Aristotle, that there were many individual souls.

Furthermore, what Abelard and his rivals were really doing was establishing a grand philosophical tradition, developing a method of inquiry by reasoning, of fortifying faith by intellectual analysis, which the great thinkers would follow for centuries.

Nor must it be thought that these great men of long ago had closed minds. There was a noble liberality in many an utterance. Augustine had said, "Faith aids Reason; Reason helps Faith." Anselm of Canterbury had declared, "We commit a grave fault if after we have attained faith, we do not strive to understand what we believe." And Abelard, "Honest doubt is the gateway; inquiry the open road to Truth."

But it was all over with Abelard, for the present. And he was passing over the Little Bridge, to travel with his little pack on his back, youth in his face, genius in his mind, dark choler in his heart and a chip on his shoulder, up the river road for Melun.

With a frankness that one often finds in him and which goes far to disarm one, even when he is thinking most of himself, he tells about it:

"Presuming on my talents, which were beyond my years"—he was right about that—"I aspired, boy though I was, to the headship of a school" (not one of thought now, but an organized institution of education) "over which I might preside. I secured one of my own in an old royal palace at Melun."

With his talents and a charm which surpassed that of many women, when he was not angry, and a poise and *savoir-faire* that outmatched the weighty greybeards', he did well at Melun, but tiring of that place soon transferred to Corbeil, a town near Paris. He taught there until he had what we would call a nervous breakdown and he went down the Seine, back to the little hamlet of Le Pallet and the farm which his father, who had by now gone into a monastery, had left to his sister.

There were some who said that Abelard should have sowed his wild oats early, then he would not later have had so great a fall. But he had learned, or instinctively knew, the rule of sublimation which Paul had kept all his life. And great minds can be gripped by an obsession with a worthy cause that is more powerful than the flesh.

Abelard's objective in those years of his life was more self-seeking and worldly, even though it was of the mind, than Paul's. Still it had power enough to keep him for thirty-eight years debating and burning the midnight oil rather than burning himself out in beds of love. Strange the fate that made him virgin for thirty-eight years, voluptuary for a delirious season, then eunuch for the rest of his days.

When he had recovered enough to teach again, he still continued the old warfare with his rivals over the issues which neither the

Cloister nor any man has yet decided. When exiled from Paris at Melun, then at Corbeil, he had kept up a long-range running duel with his old master who remained in possession of the Notre Dame citadel, maintaining his theological barrage about God and essences, accidents and universals, often even when William was very quiet. Wherefore Abelard was not unjustly charged with keeping up the strife, not so much for the sake of truth as for increasing the glitter of his own reputation.

Then, after his exile—seven years now—and after the convalescence, he, edging thirty, came back to Notre Dame. But he did not stay there long enough to get acquainted with, or at least to know well, the girl named Heloise, who already at ten, was showing such promise of beauty and learning, picking up phrases of Latin and Greek from her uncle in a way to amuse him and arouse his pride. For from that sacred citadel of Cathedral and Cloister, William of Champeaux again had him thrown out.

It happened this way: William had secured another post for himself, as Abbot of Saint Victor (in a quarter then outside the city but now within it—near the Halle des Vins) which he thought would prove a splendid retreat for his scholarly old age. In his place as headmaster of the Cloister school (there was a chancellor, too, who didn't count) he had left a one-time pet pupil of his, now in holy orders. But Abelard, who so often complained of the ruses of others directed against himself, now tried one of his own. With angelic, or fiendish, persuasiveness, he got the substitute to turn over the headship of the school to—Abelard! Naturally, as soon as William heard of this, he saw to it that Abelard was once more expelled.

It was a sorry sort of proceeding for Notre Dame. Abelard returned for a while to Melun Palace. But he could not get back to Paris quickly enough. He was as homesick as the Emperor Julian had been, or Villon or Marie Antoinette or Rachel ever would be, for the fair city. And now Abelard began to slash the new appointee with his satire whenever he met him and in circles when that unlucky fellow was not present, making him and his master so lose face that William returned from the Abbey of Saint Victor. At once Abelard started a new school in the precincts of Saint Genevieve's Abbey, whose porches and halls now served Learning as had those of the two churches below for so many years. This loosely organized institution of Abelard's some have mistakenly considered the first university of Paris. It was the first on Saint Genevieve's Hill, and started a grand tradition there which Robert Sorbonne would make permanent when in the thirteenth century he founded there the college named for him, the Sorbonne. This name would be transferred to its successors there down to the latest, which technically is known as the Academy of Paris of the University of France, though everybody knows it as the Sorbonne. This, in spite of its technical name, is the University of Paris now. Its forerunner on the spot, on that hilltop, was this school of Abelard; but the great mother of the University of Paris was the Cloister of Notre Dame. On the island in the porches of the first Notre Dame and its sister church, the still more ancient Saint Etienne, it was conceived and born.

From his seat on the hill Abelard now unloosed his dazzling rhetoric, his oratorical ordnance down on William reinstalled in the Cloister below. He enjoyed the battle; and was not always quite fair to his foe who was a man of parts. To show his delight, he writes again:

"I had returned from Paris, hoping for peace. (!) He had given my post to another. And I wanted to beleaguer him and his puppet. Hearing of my intent, he *shamelessly* (!) returned to his old school with *such pupils as he could* muster, as though to help out his substitute in the siege. But he only injured himself and pigeon both. *He lost the few scholars he had left*, and so entered a monastery . . .

"As to my conduct of this siege, well, I can but quote Virgil, 'Would you know the issue of this fight? I was not conquered by my enemy'." Though past thirty now, he was still the boy wonder, the prodigy, the eternal sophomore, for hear this:

"I now" (while Heloise was learning more philosophy and beginning to look in the mirror) "took up the study of theology at Laon with the master of my one-time master. This was Anselm who once had taught William. *He was dripping with words, but these contained not one whit of wisdom. He tried to kindle a great fire, but all he did was to fill the whole Temple of Thought with smoke.*

"I did not linger long idly in his shadow. *From his lectures I stayed away*." (And Anselm of Laon had some truly great things to tell.) "But soon, after an argument with him, certain of Anselm's favorite scholars got me aside and asked me to go on with my thesis. *They admired my words and argument so much* that they *begged me* to develop them into a complete course.

"So this old man, Anselm, stirred with anger, *persecuted me*. But this *only increased my fame!*"

He was right about the fame if not about the persecution from a rather admirable Anselm. But thus he went on, as he himself puts it later, "presuming," brilliantly, fetchingly, "presuming"— as the born champion "presumes." And in all the cities in which he taught, the students loved him for it.

At last, in the year 1115, and his thirty-seventh, he came back for the third time to Notre Dame; and they took him in as head of the great school from which he had been expelled. He was no longer the prodigy but the established champion, arrived and acclaimed, in the fine full flower of his attractive figure, genius, eloquence; with now, in place of the old "presuming," a compelling, even charming, arrogance.

Thirty-six he was, Heloise sixteen. That might be very young for some, but not for her. She had flowered out into a willowy figure, an elastic mind, a fetching ankle, and an extraordinary capacity for a doglike, yet high-spirited devotion.

Often she came out from the many-locked house that backed on the Rue Chanoinesse and fronted on the island's north wall and the north fork of the river, to mingle with the crowds in the halls, the porch, and the square. Indeed, the relationship of this canon's niece (and, it is said, the daughter of a canon named John) to this mother of universities was similar to the bond between a daughter of a professor and a college of today. Only her loves were not to be found among the students of the campus and the quarter. The heroes of this perfectly lovely girl were jailed—in those half-calf, full-calf, board-backed vellum, gold leaf decorated and precious stone-set books chained in the Cloister *scriptorium*. With them all, from Solon through Origen and Erigena, she had more than a speaking, almost a lover's acquaintance.

But it was not alone the champions of the dim and dusty past that she followed, but every new champion that came to Notre Dame. Their names she could call, their slogans, and could discourse brightly on their every superficial mannerism or profound article of faith. For she was, as folk of the theatre say, a "quicker study" than almost all the male students whom she envied but could not join. Often she was to be found lingering on the edge of the church porches listening to the arguments, or to the lectures when she could slip in the halls.

In the tumultuous mediaeval ranks of black cassocks and tonsures, shoulder-length haircuts and long rusty secular gowns, she struck a new note. Her face was already luminous with both reason and sweetness, her mouth eloquent with both passion and selflessness, her hair full of lights and shadows, her form well-cinctured, her tongue ready and witty, but never hate-provoking. She had also what seemingly was at variance with some of these gifts, yet in her seemed to bind all to each other—an unconquerable longing for learning and, above all, truth.

Altogether she was admirably designed to get the mind of a genius, flaming but so worthily self-disciplined—until she came along—off on a tangent from his work. Never, never should Fate have set her in the fringe of that crowd.

But Fate did. And there, just as the modern professor's daugh-

:er follows every move of the gridiron game, so this canon's niece,
from some discreet position followed every move in the porch, in
:he square, as in these tiny plots they were trying to assay, assess,
and weigh the vast imponderables of the universe, and she, with
her precocious mind, her normal girlish enthusiasm, was all for
:heir trying it.

As for arguments, she had a bag of them herself. She would try
:hese out at night when the crowd had dispersed and she and Fulbert got home; she from her marketing or the visits which she made
as often as she dared to the scenes of the debates, he from the
:quare, the choir stalls, or from burying some Island seamstress,
a Bièvre brickmaker, or some poor soul who cared not a whit for
Aristotle scheme or Platonic substance, only for rest and a little
:orner in Heaven.

Often their talk would go on through the evening as the prim-
·ose and peach and serpentine green of the western sky faded into
blue and the stars came out over Montmartre, which they could
:ee from their high-up windows. And she would listen all the
:ime for special word of someone, a campus hero, when her uncle
·ambled academically on as he twisted a huge knob of bread from
:he long brown loaf or delicately dissevered the backbone fronds
:rom a flat river fish, or shoved his bowl toward her to be filled
as sparingly as befitted his clerical abstemiousness.

Always she attended him half dutifully, half affectionately. She
was fond of one who might then at least—until the blow fell—
have been called a good man. And he was very fond of her—of
Abelard too, whom every day he watched, admiring and smiling,
not yet envenomed, still a man of good will. Fulbert was well aware
of her superiority of mind to him, though he did not openly
admit it. His feeling, therefore, was compounded of pride, of
vanity, and of much pure affection. This was natural. She was
beautiful, magnificently gifted, and she was of his own flesh and
blood.

Sometimes in these talks in the cool of the evening, Heloise would
not argue, but would let the old canon wander on, because there
were weeks when some sudden access of delicacy, a fear in her
who ordinarily showed such a refreshing independence and can-
dour that she might have been too rash mingling so often with
the male students, kept her from Notre Dame. On such dearth
days for her, he could tell her personal things she longed to hear
about their hero. She could thrust in questions too, about how
Abelard looked. Did he seem in good health—well-fed? Did Uncle
think they gave him warm enough covers in that run-down lodgings?

For they knew each other now. In the shadows she had lingered far back in the crowd. Still, over the heads of the crowd, eyes can meet and souls interlock. And that is just what had happened. True when he had first begun to talk to her he had addressed her with the air of some matinée idol speaking to an adoring girl, though she was already so much a woman. But that was to fool the crowd and himself. Any who had noted how, even before he had addressed her in the fringe of the crowd, their eyes had met, then strayed away, only to meet again above the ranged heads, had known that there was something in the air. Had they been especially discerning, they might have seen that Heloise was in for trouble. For, despite all the sheer dazzle of his flights, Abelard was when you came down to it, a very self-centred, sometimes too moody, often too cocky, again an all-too-self-pitying stormy petrel That chip on his shoulder, with which he had started out when he was first expelled from Notre Dame, had been transformed into something very like a persecution complex which showed its head in certain moods between his most brilliant efforts. Though he was back, with the siege lifted, in the citadel of the Cloister, a canon now and the *cher maître,* the bright particular star of his alma mater, he often felt himself misunderstood. For all his deceiving older brother air (he could have been her father) he had first spoken to her because he had seen the clear light of understanding in her eyes. And who is to understand a misunderstood man and genius, unless it is a woman.

Fulbert, still the man of good will smiling his blessing on them did not foresee the trouble ahead. In fact, he was proud of the first apparently casual notice the great man had taken of the girl. Nor did Heloise cherish any presentiment. She was exquisite joy itself when he first talked with her of the great philosophers and of "universals," but never of the universal thing called love. And up into Plato's lofty stratosphere he took her, into that over-realm of abstract ideas where goodness is supreme; then into the world of his, Abelard's, own exploring—though it was not necessary Already, under her own piloting, she had voyaged there. And she would not have been walking on earth anyway with Abelard at her side.

That first walk after the meeting in the crowd fringe, took them up the Rue Chanoinesse, perhaps, and as far as the corner their next, say, around the apple-peeling bend of the street to the door of the many-locked house in the shadow of the island's north wall. But certain it is that Abelard did not go inside yet. The bolts were not yet withdrawn. That would require some intriguing on his part. There were not many of these walks. A man who was a canon and the most distinguished master of Notre Dame and who thought of becoming a bishop some day, since that would add authority to his writings, could not walk out too often through the devious Cloister lanes or by the river with a beautiful young woman. So for the first few months they fell back on letters.

Just as Heloise was a swifter translator than Fulbert, a quicker study than any of the male students of the quarter, she was, though a woman, more direct than Abelard as his intriguing now shows. One hates to come to that. She was beautiful, gifted, and showed an incomparable devotion of soul. He was a very great man, later an extremely brave one. And their love story ranks with the truly great ones of the world. But to its earthiness we must for a moment get down before we can understand the high courage and the deep and pure love that later flowered out of it. It was by a ruse now, by what he later admitted was a low-down trick, that the high-thinking Abelard, virgin for so many years, now got past all those bolts and into her room. He makes this admission in a letter to a friend written long after the event, but which now, after eight hundred years, still crackles with its self-excoriation, burns with its passion's fires.

"There was on this island of Paris a certain woman named Heloise who lived with her uncle. Great was his love for her and equal to his affection was his admiration for her mind. For while in looks she was not behind other women, in learning she was far ahead. And so unusual in this gift for letters was she that she had become renowned throughout the realm."

Never did true love tale have a more idyllic beginning or more tragic consequence in the end.

He had tired of the letters that had passed between them in the Cloister, though never had there been ones sweeter or more eloquent with love. If the bolts of her house were not yet drawn, those in his soul, placed there by years of discipline and sublimation and intellectual ambition, were now suddenly shot back by his long pent-up passions.

"Seeing in her all these attractions of the mind, coupled with the allurements of the flesh, I thought to join myself with her in love. . . . I longed to get to know her better than by mere correspondence."

He was shrewd enough not to make the advances himself. He had a friend drop a hint to the gullible and still good-natured Fulbert, that the progress of Abelard's so great studies was hindered by the management of a *ménage* in that "run-down lodgings" Heloise had been so concerned about; furthermore, that he could not afford the expense of a separate apartment.

Never did unworldly clergyman fall so easily into a snare. He fairly leapt at that hint-bait, at the chance to have so celebrated a man under his rooftree. Fulbert not only admitted him into the house that back on the Rue Chanoinesse, fronted on the river and the island's north wall, but into her room. He saw here a grand opportunity to enrich that girlish mind of which he was so proud, and begged his famous guest to teach his niece, whenever he could, at any hour of the day or night when he came home from his activities.

"I was shocked within myself," said Abelard, "at a man who could entrust *such a lamb to a ravening wolf!*"

So he called himself, not then but later, in that letter whose sackcloth mood and breast-beating phrases, and its sheer honesty, go far to redeem his earlier conduct.

"It was only through his blind love for her and his pride in her and his reliance on my reputation for purity that he could have placed her in such a situation. We were now in the same house, in the same room, of the same mind."

Like Paolo and Francesca now they truly were. "And in that book we read no more that day," wrote Dante of the Italian pair. And now Abelard: "Meantime our books lay idly open before us. More words of love than of literature rose to our lips."

But nightly for a long time before their complete ensnarement put them past all caring, and often during this passionate interlude, this girl of eighteen and this most fascinating lover, old enough to be her father, continued in this most extraordinary set of lovers' dialogues ever, thrashing out between their lovers' phrases and kindling kisses things philosophical, theological, dialectical, recapitulating the day's debates in the Cloister and counting up the arena scores. That they could discuss such subjects at such a pass, be so metaphysical while so physical, is amazing. Great men have loved and philosophized in the same hour, but rarely the man and woman both.

Night after night this went on. The most idolized man, the loveliest girl in Paris, would mount out of a voluptuous valley to the high tableland of some Logic's Olympia. For a while they would sun themselves on these far shores. Then they would descend from these heights of speculation into the depths of love . . . So a sleep and a forgetting . . . And an awakening. A very rude one, one night, which held for all three—the lovers and Fulbert—the elements of tragedy. It was strange, but after the first few lessons, they hadn't taken him into account at all.

It broke Fulbert's heart. This was more the fault of designing thirty-eight than emotional eighteen. Abelard had said that Heloise and he were of the same mind, but she was not quite. Love had come to her with all its brilliance, its honeyed persuasiveness that this thing which, had it been known, would have been condemned by the Cloister and convention, was, because it was so overwhelmingly beautiful, overwhelmingly right. Barring the extremes sometimes of her physical passion and her temporary deception of her uncle, which, tenderness said, was for his own good, her experience was not alone a receiving like Abelard's but an all-out giving of herself, a holding back of nothing, not even of that which it would have been safer to have withheld. Her love had, therefore, a certain integrity; his, those days, only the forceful directness of desire. And hers did not violate so many things within as his did every hour. Because his love did that, it left him for the time, gross. For—hear him out in more of those flagellating phrases whose very honesty of self-humiliation compels admiration:

"I who had considered myself so profound a thinker, so lofty a philosopher, and who, up to this time, had lived in a virginity so immaculate, fell as low as I had risen high. The depths of my infamy now matched the height of the eminence I had gained on the ladder of philosophy.

"And the more I became absorbed in these novel pleasures, the less time I had for my school. I now taught perfunctorily, by rote. I became a mere parrot. When I indulged in poetry, it was not hymns to Learning that I wrote, but odes to Love. And these lyrics of passion are now sung by those to whom only sensual love appeals.

"Profound now was the grief of my students. All knew of the affair except the one whom it most concerned, the uncle of Heloise. Not that he had not been told. But resolutely he refused, because of his deep love for her and his confidence in my reputation for integrity, to take any stock in the tales. As Saint Jerome says, 'We are the last to learn of the evils in our own house.'"

At first the old man angrily waved all the tale-bearers away. And yet gradually there came a new stoop in his shoulders as he walked, so much more slowly than had been his way, to the house by the Seine. And there crept a new quaver in his voice, a narrowing of the eyes, a tenseness of pose in his symbolic stand in the Last Judgment portal, until it seemed as though not only every gossip in the quarter were whispering in his ears, but the fiends all around him.

And soon he became furtive, began to roam the house on tiptoe at midnight. He even took to listening at the door of his, then her room. The tales had worn him down. No wonder when every shufflefoot and hook-nose gossip in the quarter knew it, also those who deplored it, the orderly burghers who folded up their shop-counters into their house walls at night, the chancellor and faculty, the clergy, and all the students who had worshipped Abelard. To make matters worse, Abelard, as men will when they have forsworn a high purpose which for years they have unswervingly followed, degenerated. He thought himself immune from gossip, from all consequences. He even became careless, singing the very passionate love songs he had composed out of his experience, so unsuitable for a canon, right out loud in the Cloister and on the quais. Like Chanticleer he fairly crowed out his love. No one could understand in so famous a man such a fall and lack of discretion.

The shock and grief of his idealistic young students was especially pitiful to see. But very soon their disillusion frothed over into desire for revenge. There were outright threats against what now was regarded as the soiled person of a once loved hero. They swore to soil it further. They planned to egg Fulbert on, then to use him. And it needed only his confirming discovery when he broke in on the lovers, the one night when they had neglected to draw the bolts, to set the Cloister as well as the city beyond the bridges into a chorus of mixed indignation and raucous, ribald, derisive laughter. For on the first morning, after Fulbert's outraged cry at discovering them, his shaking, and passion of tears, he had babbled it to some one.

Then suddenly, he stopped. His mouth became a thin line. His face was as unmoving and set as those of the still folk all around and above him in the Last Judgment Door, from which he still listened—and listened—and watched, unmoving, for Abelard.

Then it must have occurred to him that all was not lost, that something might be saved from the wreck. Abelard might be persuaded to give up his ambitions for high Church preferment which, despite his wide celebrity, he felt was needed to give more authority to all the books he had in mind to write. Then he might marry her. So Fulbert might even save from the ruin, for himself, a little of the girl's love. But first he demanded that they separate. They did. It was a little late. Already she was with child. She wrote of it to Abelard, not with shame but with joy. Her lover came and took her away by night. They rode on horseback down the Seine, taking some weeks now because of her condition, to the farm near Nantes, once his father's, now his sister's, where a child, a boy, was born. They named him Astrolabe. This star-bearing name was apt. He was not to linger long to endure his father's infamy or his later glory. This child born of so vivid and vital a union was the shadow of a ghost.

Abelard was man enough to suggest marriage. Because of her love, which was far from being merely a thing of passion, Heloise spurned the offer. She did not agree with what he said then, but with what he had felt before: that ordination, which he had not yet received—he was only a canon—and a high church office would help his career. To a bishopric, bride and babe were insurmountable barriers.

Meantime, her uncle was almost mad with sorrow and casting about, Abelard says, for some means of revenge, but could conceive of none that would not equally injure his niece. He felt, he writes, "a little sorry for the old man. I went to see him and promised to do what he wished by way of amends.

"I told him, too, that he should not take it so hard or consider ours so extraordinary a case. No one who had ever felt the powerful force of love or seen its effects, or who had considered the ruin to which from the very beginning of time it had brought the greatest of men, should wonder at it."

If the phrasing, under the circumstances, seems a little cavalier, it must be remembered that he is quoting his words of the time of the tragedy. Such was not his attitude when he wrote the confession. The "presuming" of his youth, the charming arrogance of his thirties, had then been changed to a lifelong humility and an iron fidelity to the faith.

He offered then "to marry the girl, provided the union could be kept secret, and my reputation were not endangered." Fulbert assented with a kiss, so that he, once the man of good will, "might the more easily betray me!"

But again, for his sake, she balked. "The world would be justified in punishing us both if I robbed it of so bright a lantern, so glorious a light."

He was man enough to stand up under this, also objective enough to quote the flattery entire, in his letter, with her further clever elaboration:

"It would be a great tragedy if one whom Nature has created for all mankind, should devote himself to one woman! For, as the good saint says, 'What harmony can there possibly be between pupils and serving-maids, desks and cradles, pens and spindles, Latin and infants' squalls, diapers and grammar?'"

Still, Abelard was obdurate, and they repaired one night to a chapel, probably Saint Aignan's, at the corner of the Rues Chanoinesse and de la Colombe (all gone now, but a few posts and lintels) for he says it was "very near her house." If so, it was a good choice. Saint Aignan's, whose Madonna now stands by the Notre Dame chancel, as "Our Lady of Paris," had often to do with secret things, its priests, for example, serving the guillotined by pronouncing absolution in signs from the crowd during the Revolution.

"There we held vigils all night"—because of their sin—"then were privily married, to the witnessing of a small group of friends who were sworn to secrecy.

"Right after the ceremony we began to live apart, stealing to each other in the dark. But her uncle was so pleased and proud that immediately he began to shout the secret from the housetops."

For a girl of nineteen, Heloise was very determined. Never did any woman so flout—unselfishly—the bond which many of her sex make life's main objective. And a curious situation arose. Each time the uncle publicized the news, the more blithely did she, a holy abbess later but then the perfect actress, deny it. The affair at last seems to have made the old man slightly mad. Enraged by his bell-ringing and sandwich-boarding of the marriage through the Rues des Chantres, Chanoinesse, de la Colombe, every lane of the Cloister, over on the Rue Parcheminerie and Saint Jacques and the alleys of the Left Bank and the roads of the Right, Abelard took her on another secret flight by night, to a suburb, Argenteuil, where there was an abbey of nuns. He stood in a peculiar relationship to this foundation, having been its adviser, patron, and mentor. Like the purer-souled Saint Vincent de Paul, who later invented a habit for his Daughters of Charity, Abelard had designed one for this order. This he now, with the hands that had caressed her, put on her, so taking her away forever from those hands. Then he rode home to Paris and went to sleep. He did not sleep long.

For now Fulbert had gone completely off his head. Two great shocks and one intoxicating period of elation in between, had unbalanced him. He had discovered their liaison, then had been raised to the seventh heaven of delight by the marriage and his connection with this famous man, and then was prostrated by Heloise's repeated denials of the marriage. One minute she was a wife, the next was not a wife, and the next a nun. And Fulbert did not think of sparing her now, only of vengeance on the body of the one who had robbed him of her who had been the apple of his dimming old eye, breath of his wheezing old lungs, very beat of his cracked old heart.

He had bribed the concierge of Abelard's lodgings and gathered his band. There were theological students from the quarter. There were roustabouts from the wineshops, the more unsavory places on the outskirts of the Cloister, those on the Left Bank, and the hangers-on of the brothels in the shadow of the bridge, and heartsick young people like those from the Rue Parcheminerie who had delivered parchment to him, who had worshipped and had been badly disillusioned by Abelard. He had lectured and hectored them but they had loved him for it. So, for one reason or another, had most in the band who clung close to the old thick-walled houses as they made their way towards Abelard's lodgings with ropes and a knife in the hand of Fulbert who led the way.

Admitted by the bribed concierge, they ascended the stairs, stole in, found him asleep. In a minute they had flung themselves on him, some fearfully cursing, others like the heartstick parchment boys and students, cursing and crying all at once, which was more fearful still, and had him, the hem of whose garments many once would have kissed, trussed and on the floor.

So they performed on him a hideous rite; and left him with torn flesh on the reddened floor. Left him with more than the torment of a body's wound—with the door of the priesthood, which opens to none with mutilation, forever closed.

But if the manhood of the body, its integrity, had been lost, he was to gain through the years in manhood within, integrity of soul until he could write:

"It was a most equitable judgment, this infliction of the punishment on that corner of the temple of the body where had been committed the fault."

Over and over, in his confession, he drives in the poetic justice of his most unpoetic doom.

But that was later. As for the next morning, "the whole city," he goes on, "thronged around me." By the cathedral door whence he came forth, was the figure, with uplifted forefinger, of One Who had spoken so immortally about casting the first stone. And yet, "I saw I was being pointed out and that everywhere I went and forever more I would be an object of ridicule."

He was overmorbid in this. If his tragedy was one for the books, for the busy crowded city it was not so much more than a seven days' wonder. The notoriety, the ridicule did not last forever. It is true, of course, that just as the hand of Origen, the father of the spirit of scientific inquiry, had ruined his own body for the priesthood, the vengeful Fulbert's hand had barred Abelard from the then most advantageous position for philosophical teachers and writers, in the officer corps of the Church. But all outlets and audiences were not denied him; in fact, he was to have the last in a spectacular way. It almost seemed as though the deprivation, which in his first horror at it appeared ruinous, held a balancing compensation, not for love, but for his work. And he soon recovered to a new and tremendous vigour, indeed, to an activity almost too great, to Laocoön wrestlings in debate, feverish writings at night, and violent daytime disputes, also—until that final humility should come—to a continual, restless and frequently frantic beating of the wings of his stormy petrel of a soul and into a great desert of life and time, without any oases of love.

They both were bitterly lonely. She would later devoutly adjust herself to this new life she had chosen and to that heavenly loyalty of her vows; but at first she could only regard it as a choice made under duress—of Fulbert and Fate.

"So sweet," she says in one of those immortal letters, "were those delights we enjoyed together that the thought of them cannot be banished even here. I cannot blot them out of my memory. The sweet images come to me in my sleep. They visit me even in the solemnity of the mass, so that I dwell on them rather than my prayers."

Abelard was about forty on the night of Fulbert's vengeance. The priesthood closed to him, he took his vows and became a monk, at first joining a brotherhood in the Abbey of Saint Denis. There, too, his efforts on the rebound from his humiliation were very great. For one thing he wrote an important, controversial book. But also, because of the enforced operation, his thwarted ambition and frustrated love, he became very querulous for the time. With the monks there he quarrelled over both big and little things; very technically, for example, over the identity of the revered founder of their Abbey—whether Denis was or was not the same man as Dionysius the early Bishop of Athens—and, for a big one, over the Trinity. The latter feud, after complaints from monks who disliked him there or whom he had injudiciously offended, got him into court before an august tribunal at Soissons. And the only mental picture Heloise could arrive at for some time from the reports, was of him there in the dock, before the ranged gowns and eyes, being subjected to a merciless cross-examination.

It brought up old questions of the Trinity, which had been end-lessly argued from Tertullian through Augustine to Abelard, and even by schoolmen who quoted pre-Christian theories of Plato or Aristotle to support their stands: Does God show Himself in all three manifestations as the same? Was Christ co-existent with the Father at the Creation? Did He, as the Chosen Man, acquire divinity afterwards? There was, in these debates, some theological hair-splitting, of course; in this case at Soissons something of grudge and rivalry, but also much earnest inquiry and sincerity. But since it was such an intricate and awesome subject, and very great men were puzzled by it and disagreed and misunderstood each other, it cannot be simplified.

But practically that debate can be simplified down to this: There, in the Soissons market place, they took him out, before the old house fronts and the church, the sheds and lambs and cabbages and carts, tongues-up, and made him burn his book.

Now passionately had Abelard loved books. Heloise could re-count endless stories showing this. To the parchment boys deliver-ing sheets to him he would deliver impromptu lectures, finding fault with the hairs left in the sheets from the hairy sides of the skin. Or he would go posthaste over to the Rue Parcheminerie and instruct their employers in what he thought was the proper way of dehairing, liming, scraping, chalk-dusting and pumicing the parchment, declaring that their way left too many smudges and hollows for his pen to trip in. Again he would spiritedly conduct, for the clerks in the Cloister *scriptorium,* a tour of the book industry from ancient to his own modern times, describing the first book of wedge letters on clay plates, those next in cylindrical cans, the volumes in sewn quires that made the Emperor Julian so happy, the later ones of parchment sheets attached to boards so that the edges would not curl up and bound at the back in calf, the first "half-leather" books, and then the great chained tomes with gorgeously decorated sides of Charlemagne's day. And often he would expound to the veteran Left Bank bookbinders on the best methods of making dies, of blind-stamping, applying gold-leaf, making ivory covers and of inlaying these with garnets, topazes, and emeralds.

On his own book were no precious stones. But it was dearer to him than anything in the world but Heloise. And now they made him burn it! "Sobbing," he says, "I saw my little book go up in smoke."

So it vanished. There were no duplicate sheets, no galley proofs then, and we have lost that forerunner book forever.

These sobs reached the Abbey at Argenteuil, where in the cold cell, white from frost, blue-white from the sun when it came through, a very white Heloise prayed for him. She had at times loved, at some times mistrusted, that arrogance of his; but she thought it pitiful to see her lover so stripped.

From his noble defense of Reason and Tolerance at his trial, Abelard now descended to more of those carping little quarrels with the monks of Saint Denis. From that time forward he became in very truth the stormy petrel, now on little darting flights after small fish, again on magnificent explorings in the teeth of Adversity's winds. Like that wild sea bird, too, he lived on harsh rocks, on fen and moor and in lonely places.

True his first home after the bonfire, was in a pleasant abbey with gardens, kind brothers and a godly abbot, at Provins. But soon the Saint Denis foes smoked him out, and he went to what he calls "a wilderness place" at Nogent-sur-Seine, near Châlons, where he built with his own hands a little oratory and a hut of stubble, mud and reeds.

It was "a wilderness place," but again, as before in history, men came out to see no "reed in the wind," but a very vivid and alive personality. And scholars flocked there from all parts of the country, seeking knowledge from his lips, inspiration from eyes so like burning coals now. Soon the harsh wastes around hummed with activity. They put up great barracks of huts and tents and rebuilt the oratory with timber and stone. "The Paraclete," (The Comforter) it was called; and it was to be very famous. There the two, Abelard and Heloise, would rest in death, before they were transferred to lie with the hosts of Paris dead, under the loveliest monument of Père la Chaise cemetery. Abelard was very happy for a season. "It was a pleasure to see how," as he puts it, "all these scholars from the city had willingly sacrificed their homes and all the advantages of the city to dwell in little huts of osiers and mud, to sit down to meals on banks of turf instead of at carved tables, to partake of coarse loaves, cold water and herbs in place of their accustomed city delicacies.

"And since I could not dig and to beg was ashamed, my scholars did everything for me. They really took everything in hand, furnished what we needed in the way of clothes and food and attended to the tilling of the fields, the cutting of the wood, and rebuilt the Paraclete and dependent buildings for me, so that I should not be distracted from my reflections and teaching by other duties."

In short, Abelard was himself again—so much himself, indeed, that of that period he could write later, with one little flare-up of the old vainglory between his passages of genuine remorse and devout humility:

"Though my body was confined to the Paraclete wilderness, my fame extended throughout the entire world. Like the poets' fancy, Echo, it resounded everywhere."

But still the persistent persecution of his foes into whose hands he, with the irascibility of high-strung genius, always seemed to play, drove the stormy petrel to another rock, a veritable pile of them, on the shore of his native Brittany at Saint-Gildas-du-Rhys.

His experience here was like that of the sainted Benedict with the outlaw monks at Lake Subiaco. "If I had tried to force them into an orderly life, I would have lost mine."

But now fell one of the worst blows of all. His foes came down on the fold once more, not on his but on Argentueil Abbey, on her whom he had once called his love and his dear wife, but now addressed as his "dear sister in Christ." She and her nuns had been expelled from their abbey; and here was a chance to make amends. Because of ambition he had driven her from his heart, his bed, to a cold cell. Now, in her need, he could give her a home. The very abbey he had left, the Paraclete which his students under his directions had built, he turned over to her and her nuns. And so had the old arrogance been dissolved into something finer that he wrote:

"The bishop loved Heloise as a daughter, the nuns as a sister, the lay folk as a mother. And her flock at the Paraclete increased far more rapidly than any chapter of my own would have done, had I remained there a hundred years."

He stayed himself a little over ten years at Saint-Gildas. Then he fled once more. It seems that the ghosts of his soul and the hounds of conservatism who hated him, must chase from every wilderness hole and seaside rock this hunted fox. Ever the sequence was the same: flight, the gathering together again of the clans— his students; his periods of eloquence and fire and clear creative thinking; then the academic controversies; his foes' pursuit with his own fret and irascibility driving him to despair; then flight again.

In the last five years of his stay at Saint-Gildas, however, there had been added to such heavenly consolations as he could muster in such a savage place, this new relief: he could make several trips, though quite a journey it was, from Brittany to the Paraclete near Châlons, there to converse with the love he had lost. But converse it always was, even at such rare meetings down the years, on questions of faith and abbey housekeeping. Literally. To such subjects he kept their talks confined when all the time her heart cried out for another relationship than that to brother of "dear-sister-in-Christ."

She had fought hard to keep it on that plane. But the old fires, banked for years in the calming abbey round, flared up at the reunion. Not into physical desire—that at least she controlled, but into a desperate longing for words that had nothing to do with abbey management or even faith—that would show more than a "dear-sister-in-Christ" affection.

There he had a great advantage over her. In the first five years of his stay at Saint-Gildas by the grey Breton seas, the seaweed-greened rocks, as he wrote with a pen of wings and flame, swept up his audience of cell or moor or fen into great visions, or like the wild gulls called down a curse on his foes, again, with the wild winds' wailing, cried out a piteous *"Kyrie eleison, Christe eleison!"* he, if he did not fight through to peace, at least wrestled down his earthly passions. But this had been easier for him than for her. Up through most of middle life he had kept that iron control, until the beauty of body and the beauty of mind of Heloise came along to break it. These removed, it was like settling back into an old, old habit.

But she had yielded almost in the first flowering of love. That was all she knew until she came within the abbey. There still were hours when as the storms came up out of the sea and the waves tumbled over the shore, so over the rocks of his vows and pledged faith broke memories of the rosy hours of passion in the warm, many-locked house by the Seine. But with an even greater violence did such memories break over Heloise. It was a long, long pull before she could drag herself a little way up the shore of consciousness, out of the reach of these billows and their power to overwhelm her, into a safer place where the emotions of men could be viewed with resignation's perspective. There were times, those first years after taking the veil, when as in agony she prayed, it seemed as though the whole essence of her, the whole yearning of her, was pressed out in drops of blood such as she saw on the thorned brow above her, on the cross to which alone she should have given heed.

It is not abbey walls, only a sanctuary-fortress one erects within one's soul that can bring perfect peace. Still, if she had not arrived at that, she had at least come into a reasoned calm during her years at Argentueil Abbey. She had gotten past the tortured days when —it is such realities and the fight they made against them that, in the final analysis, make their love story supreme over so many —the recollections of abandoned passion had pursued her even into the chapel.

Even so, when she had pulled herself up on that shore, away from those overwhelming waves of emotion and into a sort of God's calm, still she did not lock her lover out of her heart. She divorced him from the now indicted things of the past, but she kept his image bright in her mind. In fancy she followed him in his every battle, to his every refuge, thrilled with him when in some measure he got back at his foes, suffered with him in the continuous humiliations they heaped upon him and which rumour brought constantly to her. In the Argentueil cell she had sobbed with him when his book was tossed into the flames. In the austere chapter room, in the refectory where she sat at the table's head, presiding over the soberly-clad rows clattering spoons in bowls at their frugal meals, in the kitchens where she had to reprimand little wastes, in the cool and colour of the gardens or the calm order of the linen room, often her spirit was with him in the Saint-Gildas cell, or by the resounding Breton shore. With him she endured all these long lean years as he preached to gaunt cassocked ascetics flocking to him from near and far or brooded upon his thoughts, little ones of complaint and recrimination, truly great ones that would bring light to the sons of men. And she almost shouted out with him, in a wrath inappropriate for one withdrawn from the clamours of this world, when he protested the latest infamous libel the world had concocted:

"Now, God in Heaven! they must have it that I visited the Paraclete of which I am the spiritual head, and where she has been installed with her nuns, only because of my lusts, when I, of that charge, of all men should be acquitted."

Yet even such things she forgot in her joy in these rare visits when after almost ten years of separation she could look on his face, harshly handsome of old, more harsh than handsome now, and hear his voice, with some of the old resonance gone but to her ears like familiar, never-forgotten music played for her once more.

That is, it was like that at first. Then suddenly everything went dead. Her heart which had leaped up into life under that rigid nun's habit turned cold. That he would make no gesture of love, she had known. That he would not speak in the old terms and that the themes now would be rule and rite rather than love, she had expected. But she had hoped that some inclination, some connotation, some warmth, would creep into that voice. But there was no such sign. He had schooled himself. The iron band was on his will again. After thirty-eight years of what he had taken for rectitude, he had erred, had fallen. Now he would make up. Ordinarily it is the woman that is supposed to hold in her hand the issue of all such situations. It was not so then in the Paraclete. He was fighting for both. He could see that under that nun's habit, the uniform of the King's army which she had joined, under its sign, the crucifix, her heart was wildly leaping. That harshness, which it had wrenched him violently to assume, he had assumed to still her heart, to reassert the King's uniform, the cross, to raise her eyes aloft, to rededicate her to the love of the King for which she was supposed to have cast aside the love and all the memories of old; that it was he and not she who in this critical hour had to make the fight. That it was his heart that was under control while hers beat so wildly leads one to think that perhaps, back in the Notre Dame Cloister, emotional if inexperienced eighteen had been as much to blame as thwarted and inexperienced thirty-eight.

And though once she had been the more direct, now she did not see as clearly as he their clearly marked course. It would take a little more time before his will and the King's would wholly prevail in her. She was waging her last fight, not now with the more objective flesh—that at least she held in rein—but with her desire for some token, some protestation from him that she was still first in his heart.

If she did not beg for these reassurances in the chapter room of the Paraclete, in the refectory where, after these journeys so far apart, he meagrely refreshed himself, or in the gardens that had bloomed in the "wilderness" place, she at last began to pour forth her anguished pleas for words—just some little words of tenderness from him, in the three now immortal letters.

These were written in interludes between his rare visits to the Paraclete and just before his return for the last time to Paris for his one little flare-up of glory before his earthly light went out forever. He was fifty-six then, she thirty-six and in a fuller beauty than when she had stood out, the budding girl, so vividly in the fringe of the crowd by the Notre Dame porch, or in the dawn in her chamber window high over the Seine. But that bloom now was sharp-edged by the coif, dimmed by the veil. And yet her loveliness could not be regimented out of her by that austere habit or the rigid abbey rule. It was far more than enough to have tempted them to a last disaster had he not been fighting for them both.

If, while rejecting the sin of the flesh, Heloise in writing those letters pleading for some sign of his continued love, committed an error of the heart, all of the sons and daughters of men should sympathize with and profoundly pity her. The little boy Astrolabe had gone with the vanished summers, and the other children of her womb her heart had hungered for were not and never would be. And now that heart was not nourished by one little bone-word of human affection tossed it by him, her soul was not lighted by one little warm candle-gleam of a loving look. In her loneliness and her nature's denial, she thought him heartless, blind. She could not see that he was not untouched, only desperately fighting her battle as he was his own.

And yet even in this baring of her heart, her very abjection in these written appeals, her forswearing, if not in the body's letter, her vows, which she was to reswear again and to a lifetime fulfilling—in all her attitude—which the most austere might condemn—there was a loveliness, a nobility that cannot die.

The very salutation is affecting: "To her master, husband, nay brother, his handmaid, nay daughter, his spouse, nay sister—to Abelard, Heloise."

So love and duty struggle in her from the very beginning. And then the phrases, of which only a few can be given here, tumble out not so much from that splendidly clear head of hers, though that was working too, as from her agonized heart, each word a throbbing, pulsating beat:

"In His name who still in some measure at least will protect you, I beg you to keep me, as His handmaid, informed of the storms and shipwrecks by which you are tossed, for I at least am left to you to share in your sorrow as once I did in your joy. . . .

"For it is you who alone can make me sad, can comfort me or cause me to rejoice. And it is you alone who owe to me the debt of the little letter I crave, since I, to the last jot, have done all the things you ordered. I, at your command, changed both the habits and the habit of my body and the way of my life and heart, so that by such holy vows I might prove to you, in my obedience, that you were the one and only owner of my heart, body, and mind. And God knows I never wanted anything of you but yourself, desiring you alone, not anything you could give. . . .

"Who among all the philosophers could equal you in glory? What capital would not, with all its citizenry, turn out at your approach? What maiden, what wife in all the cities you visited did not long for you when you had gone? What queen did not envy you my bed? There were two graces you had which I must admit would have captured any woman—that of composing the loveliest songs and singing them to your love. . . . But what woman who once envied me the possession of your love would not now pity me in my desolation? Tell me, tell me, why, after my taking the veil, which you did decree, I am not comforted by a single letter? . . . Let me tell you what I suspect, that desire, not love, led you to me. When I was placed beyond your body's reach, all your demonstrations of love ceased. . . . Give some attention, I beg of you, to what I ask. It will be such a small thing to do. If I am forever robbed of your presence, send me the counterfeit of your sweet image in words, of which you have so many!"

(And later when he, fighting too, though she did not know this, had sent her a letter filled with paragraphs about the saints and prayer, a letter which she took as stone for bread—very cold stone in return for the bread of her love, made of the earth's own wheat, kneaded by adversity and baked in the oven of trial):— "How can I expect you to be liberal in great things if you are so niggardly with words? Until now I had believed I deserved better of you, since for you I had done so much and, while still a girl, was argued into the convent to please you alone. I, God knows, would have followed you into the fires of Hell. . . . My heart did not go into that convent. It remained behind with you. . . . And all I ask now, in place of the great deeds I might have had are little words. . . . When I entered into forbidden pleasures, many were sure it was from desire rather than true love. But this conclusion, in this immurement here, shows the spirit in which I yielded to you. . . . And so, in His name, to Whom you have given yourself, I beg of you to write me some little word of comfort so that I, a little relieved, may devote myself with the greater heart to Him. When, in those dead days, you came to me for earthly pleasures, by your continued songs about me, you placed the name of Heloise in all men's lips. With 'Heloise! Heloise!' every square and house wall resounded. The girl whom you awoke to desire you should, with compensating justice, inspire toward God. . . . Farewell, my all!"

Sometimes he gives her the cold ash of words in directions about abbey management, the duties of infirmarians, chantresses, cellaresses, of herbs, poultry, bees. And sometimes his cry is poignant: "Weep not for me, your seducer but for your Saviour." Again: "No reverence for personal honour, anything sacred, for God Himself, even on Good Friday, the day He died, held me back. You protesting and resisting as much as your weaker woman's body would allow, I forced to consent."

Finally the fire seems to die out of her own words and she sang at last to his own dulled ordered pitch:

"Upon the words of my unbounded grief is set the bridle of your injunction. And I must temper in writing the words which never could be governed in speech. For over nothing do we have less power than the heart. We never command, only obey it. But I will keep from writing that from which I could not restrain my tongue. Would that the heart of the writer were only as amenable as the hand! There is, however, some little salve for my wound which is still in your power to give, though never can you wholly cure the hurt. Still, as one nail may drive out another, so may a new thought from you drive out the old."

She hewed thereafter to the hard line he and her vows had laid down. No term of endearment did she afterwards permit herself with the pen. Only once, in protest against the injunctions he felt he must give and behind which he hid the beatings of his own never quite tamed heart, did she utter reproach:

"Oh, please, please, do not write so much of 'victory after strife!' I long now to avoid all struggle. If God will only preserve me for some little corner in Heaven, it will be enough for me." And when she wrote that she was thirty-seven!

There were two more short passages which she could hug to her heart.

The first was a prayer which he who had filled the arena of Notre Dame Square with his resonant periods now humbly composed for themselves:

"Thou hast joined us together, oh Lord, and Thou hast separated us when it pleased Thee, in the way that pleased Thee best. Now, oh Lord, what Thou hast in Thy mercy begun, as mercifully finish. And those whom Thou hast divided once upon earth join forever to Thyself in Heaven."

No one could ever take that from her. And once he had unloosed his heart sufficiently from the bonds he had imposed upon it to write asking for her prayers, adding this pathetic plea:

"If the Lord should deliver me into the hands of my enemies, so that they should prevail over me and slay me, I beseech you that wherever my body may chance to lie, it may be brought to your country."

She had replied, in her third letter—the last we have:— "You ask, my all, that I shall have your body brought here so that in the abbey you may have a rich harvest of prayers. How could you think that your memory would ever die? The very suggestion of that death is death itself to me."

Still, that was a second treasure none could ever take from her: He had asked to be buried "in her country."

After this correspondence ceased, he was forced by his enemies and his own mistakes to flee once more, this time from Saint-Gildas. A little while and then he came out of his last hole. The gifted prodigal of Paris came back to the capital; the gifted and beautiful daughter of Paris never again in life, only in death, returned to her city and Notre Dame.

There were no brilliant lectures by him in the Cloister now; he taught up on the hill. Fulbert no longer stood watching in the Last Judgment Door. He, poor disappointed man, lay in one of the city churchyards. And no longer did the eyes of Heloise burn out of her hood in the fringe of the crowd or her foot and laughter sound light in the house by the Seine. There were ghosts of many people, many hours, many things haunting him now when he stood by the city wall and looked up at that house or over the river to boats with red sails, one of which had helped bring him to the fame in which she had so rejoiced.

He was soon to be one with those ghosts. The hounds were after him, poor hunted fox, even now as soon almost as he had begun again in Paris, taking up his trail. When the gods arrive, the half-gods go. And all of Abelard's lesser enemies pale now in the fierce flame of the wrath of his new archfoe, Bernard of Clairvaux, the same who so greatly preached the Second Crusade, champion of orthodoxy, apostle of unwavering faith, and sworn crusader against all doubt and exploration and inquiry which Abelard upheld—in short, the Grand Old Conservative. But if rigid Bernard was, he was a magnificent sort of bigot, sincere of heart and loyal to the death to what he believed. It was too bad that they had to be on opposite sides. But they were, and Bernard, from his earliest days in Clairvaux, had watched the genius at Paris, Corbeil, Melun, Maisoncelle, Saint Denis, Provins, "the wilderness place" called the Paraclete, sea-washed Saint-Gildas, and his every refuge, and had gathered en masse evidence of what this great bell-hound of the conservative pack considered heretical beliefs, with the purpose of crushing Abelard forever when the day came.

He had not liked Abelard's Trinitarianism which, certainly not basely, had declared the Trinity to be not three supreme creative persons but rather three qualities or phases of Godhead—Power.

Love, Wisdom. And he had hated Abelard's Cloister pronouncement: "We believe our religion, not merely because it is revealed,
not because God has said it, but because our reason tells us it is
profoundly true."

What more would they have had? And this must be said for
Abelard, now that the day has come and is set down on the calendar at Sens: He had seduced a lovely passionate girl. In the days
of his glory he had been arrogant, charmingly so, still arrogant.
Even during these days of his wanderings, his persecution, and
darkest eclipse, that pride had flared up now and then in a strange
and most inappropriate sort of vaunting, pitiful perhaps when one
sees it as only a whistling in the dark. He had hugged tight a
persecution complex, carried that chip on his shoulder through a
good part of his life. Yet he had been indefatigable in his search
for Truth, and ever with striking courage he had upheld two
standards.

The first was a very personal one, for just the two. He and
Heloise must keep their vows. When she who stood up against
the world with magnificent defiance for the personal man, wavered
in her allegiance to the invisible, he held her to it. The other,
which like a bright banner he held aloft through storms and
disasters, had emblazoned on it his motto that Honest Doubt is
the gateway, Inquiry the open road to Truth. By these two he,
once as the idol of Paris and all the capitals, then as the veteran,
warped and crippled and scarred, had dauntlessly lived.

So in his last stand at Sens, Tory and Liberal, they confronted
each other. Never once in his fighting, obstinate life would Bernard accept any such open road policy. As sedition he regarded
all inquiry. Faith was the only yardstick that he knew. There
should have been great drama in the air. Could Abelard, one of
the most agile minds in Europe, with a dazzling gift for presentation, with his history first a series of triumphs, then of reverses,
and with his once bright fame tarnished by a scandal only half
forgot—could he, the aging champion, now come back? Or would
the indomitable, ruthless, yet sincerely motivated Bernard—the
Wellington, the Gladstone of orthodoxy—demolish him with one
blow?

The setting too was fitting. The trial was staged in the old
Carolingian palace of the bishops when in this year of 1140—
just twenty-three years before the cathedral of Notre Dame would
be started—already the first stones were going into place alongside the palace for the new cathedral of Sens. This cathedral was
the first representative of the transitional style which bridged the
gap between the Romanesque and the Gothic which Abelard's
ranging, aspiring genius was not unlike.

Through the windows of the bishops' palace came the sounds which were trumpeting the new era, the din and clangour of the building yards, of the carters, the hammers, chisels, of the chains and pulleys hoisting the new blocks up aloft. And as though to give the dark-gowned judges and prosecutor signs that the old order was passing—signs they would not heed—the wind blew in the powdered dust of the ages from the demolished limestone of the old church, sifted it on their black shoulders, making arguing Bernard and the old judges seem hoarier than ever. The mitres of the bishops in ecclesiastical council assembled, the canons' caps, seemed like so many snuffers which would be lifted soon to come down and quench forever Abelard's last flickering little light.

Only twenty miles from Sens, in Abelard's abbey—hers now— of the Paraclete, at Nogent-sur-Seine, Heloise waited in fear and trembling, hoping for a great triumph for him at last. But the drama in the trial was a perverse or reverse drama. The old champion did not come back. The flame had gone. He was old, weary, without will to live. Before the charges were half in, without a word of rebuttal, by the windows giving out on the cathedral of the new order going up, even as he, the old champion of Notre Dame, was coming down, he gasped out to the court that he would appeal his case to Rome.

For Rome he started out. As soon as he had mounted, they passed sentence on him. To beat him the indefatigable, resourceful Bernard sent galloping messengers on to Rome to forestall him. Horsemen brought word of this to Abelard while he was still on the road. With his body's strength deserting him, only his mental powers left, and these fast diminishing, he stopped in Burgundy, at Cluny Abbey.

A little while only he listened to the bells of its five high towers. Then, seeing there was so little time left, certain of the brethren taking pity on him and thinking he should be nearer home, secured a litter and bore him, not to the Paraclete—since Heloise and her nuns were there—but to a priory, Saint Marcel, only fifty miles away.

She did not see him at the end. But later, secretly, she bore him to the Paraclete whose first little oratory he had built of osiers and mud with his own hands and to which a great throng had flocked to hear him, one of the world's great teachers, in that "wilderness place," in the chapel of which she laid him now and where for years she said, as he had asked, her prayers for him.

They could not take that from her. He had asked to be buried where she was—"in her country."

Meantime her renown as a holy woman, as before her fame as a lover, had spread throughout the world. Then, in 1164, after eighteen years of her lonely prayers, others said their prayers for both. For now she lay with him.

So their tale was told, this story both of the way of a man with a maid and of a search for truth. His hand was cold and from those fingers had dropped the torch. But others had picked it up. And because he was the seeker and set the way of life and the tradition for centuries of thinkers and was the founder of universities, and loved her well; and she was so gifted, intrepid, lovely and true and, more, because their tale is made up of beauty and error, of weakness and strength, of faintness of heart and extraordinary valour—for all these things, then—theirs is one of the supreme love stories of this world.

It is imperishable and indissolubly connected with Notre Dame. You cannot walk the streets where the Cloister was, by the Seine and the flower market near her old home, or enter the great Last Judgment Door of the last Notre Dame, started as she died, without hearing the sounds of his eloquent orations and his love songs, of the troth they plighted, their lovers' exulting and ensuing despair, and of their prayers in life, hers in death for him—echoing, echoing everywhere.

Happily they rest now within sight of Notre Dame's towers, under the beautifully carved white stone in Père la Chaise. For in 1817 a great crowd that thrilled to their story after seven hundred years took them out from the Paraclete to Paris, which was more particularly "her country."

XXV

*A Fat, Fighting King, an Abbot Prime Minister and a Queen with
a Wandering Eye. . . . A Battle Cry and the "Oriflamme," the
Banner of Saint Denis. . . . Queen Eleanor takes her Dowry away
from France over to England and breeds Many Centuries of Wars.
. . . The Abbot waves a Hand, an Arch is uptilted and out of the
Romanesque the Gothic, so long in Gestation, is born.*

1144 A.D.

ONE MORNING IN 1144, WHILE HELOISE MOURNED HER
lover, another Magdalen—a royal, but not a penitent
Magdalen—knelt over Denis' dust. She had ridden—and
how this beautiful and superby modelled Queen Eleanor could
ride!—out of the city gates, in the June sunshine, over the flower-
carpeted plain of Paris to the saint's city, four miles away. She
thought she was going to the dedication of a great abbey that
would house Denis' tomb. But the occasion had more to do with
life than that. What she had really come to see was a birth most
important for Notre Dame, the world, and history—the birth or
at least in this great abbey's dedication the christening, of the
Gothic whose key and symbol and its Word, the pointed arch, was
first made manifest in the stone flesh of Saint Denis' church.

Before high noon she dismounted in the midst of her glittering
train at the old Roman crossroads where, since the third century,
Saint Denis had lain. At first it had been under a mound of earth,
starred in spring as the whole plain was now, but unmarked for
some time, until a daring Christian, in the night, dared to put up
a wayside cross. At the end of the fifth century Saint Genevieve
erected a little memorial oratory over the martyred remains. At the
beginning of the seventh, King Dagobert, after piously spending
the night sleeping with Denis, his bones and dissevered skull, built
a fair-sized church which in the five centuries following became
the core of a great group of monastic buildings. There Abelard
had brooded after the burning of his book and had quarrelled with
the monks over the identity of Denis who had given his name to
the abbey and the town and who would go up in niches on Notre
Dame and on so many of the super-churches we know as cathe-

drals which through the next five centuries would be springing up all over France.

Now they were disturbing the saint's nine centuries' sleep with a tremendous racket of chain and chisel, hammer and cart, as they built over his bones his new and final resting place. It was half up, with a great promise of glory, when Eleanor, in a scintillation of silk, jewel gleams, and armour flashes, rode to Saint Denis over the daisies and little plain lilies.

The crowd in front of the great façade, three-quarters finished, and in the roofless nave and the already roofed-over apse and sanctuary was great. They had ridden or walked in from all over the Ile de France and from beyond its borders. For not only was this a famous new-style church, rumour of which had been carried everywhere, but Denis was now the patron saint of France as Genevieve was of Paris. The late King, Eleanor's father-in-law, fat, fighting Louis the Sixth, had so declared him. "Montjoie and Saint Denis!" he had cried in a great battle with the Germans, and had thereupon won it. That had been just a little while before this Louis, a great eater and drinker but a most pious and valorous man, had died. Feeling the pains of death upon him, he had ordered ashes to be strewn on his bedchamber floor, in the form of a cross. And there he had stretched himself, dying on that penitential ash cross, and with the name of his Saviour on his lips, had won his last victory, this time over Death.

Eleanor, now that she was queen, did not think so much of the new king, Louis the Seventh, her husband. She liked a man that could fight. And as his record in the Crusade shows, he was not nearly so good at that as had been her father-in-law, the adipose but most courageous Louis the Sixth, who always had to be helped up on his horse but once up there had done the most prodigious deeds in battle. He had held off the invading English Henry the First, and had gained a great victory over the Germans who once more had come over their silver fence, the Rhine, as they would continue to do down the ages, only three times to triumph and scores of times to go down in defeat.

The peasants had helped Louis the Sixth in this important campaign and so had the town communes which he had nurtured and which, in turn, would do much for the cathedrals. But the spirit of Saint Denis had always been there, as everyone knew, and the ghosts of the Gallic legions that had beaten back the Germans so many times before.

There was another factor in that great victory: the banner of Saint Denis. Before that year the cloak of Saint Martin, he who gave cover to the beggar and had compassion on swallows and drunkards, had been the emblem of France. Now, with the coming in of the Gothic, this banner of Saint Denis became the standard. The "oriflamme," Golden Flame it was called, being of a bright vermilion silk, set on a staff of silver and gilt which in the sun seemed alive with fire. For many generations the kings of France would carry into battle this oriflamme of Saint Denis. When through with the battle they would reverently return it to its shrine, just as when, through with their warfare forever, they themselves would be borne to Saint Denis there to lie with the royal dead.

The oriflamme, some say, was utterly destroyed, others, captured, in the battle of Agincourt. After that the kings of France carried banners with the fleurs-de-lis. Jeanne d'Arc had an oriflamme of her own. She had two banners, one with Christ on a gold cross between two haloed figures, one green, one blue. But her favourite was, like this old standard of France, gold fringed, with a cream-hued field, gold fleurs-de-lis on it, and a picture of Jesus in a great gold sun ray and His name in mediaeval lettering. She carried these in her defeats of the English who were forever coming over the Channel west because of that dowry of good French lands which this same Eleanor brought to England when King Louis the Seventh let this first beauty of Europe go. He was an upright man but too strait-laced for the seductively full-blooded Eleanor. Still Louis blundered when against Suger's advice he secured an annulment of his marriage to her because of affairs of hers in Palestine during the Second Crusade, which started in 1146, two years after this dedication of Saint Denis. After this annulment, Eleanor dallied with a few personable nobles, but married a man her junior, Prince Henry, who became Henry the Second of England; and she had five quarrelsome sons, among them the idol Richard Cœur de Lion and the despicable John.

As king, Henry the Second held through his Plantagenet blood, Normandy, also Anjou and Maine. Eleanor took back from her first husband, Louis the Seventh, her dowry, the rich duchy of Aquitaine with Guienne, Poitou, and Gascony, and turned it over to Henry. For three centuries the English fought with the French over that dowry. Sometimes, as in part of the Hundred Years' War, the English were very successful. But the Black Prince did not dominate the age to the extent romancers make it appear. There were very great French kings, Philippe Auguste and Charles the Fifth and Wise, who had their own superb victories, which drove out the English during their reigns. And in 1429, Jeanne started the campaign which eventually won that dowry back to France forever. The peasant girl, through her goodness and genius, retrieved what, through her vanity, the Queen of France had lost.

Some good, it is true, Eleanor was to do through her patronage of painters and poets. She reconciled her husband and hothead son when embroiled in a quarrel that had upset kingdoms. Through the spell of her beauty she frustrated a plot that would have wrecked England. And she married her granddaughter Blanche of Castile (mother of Saint Louis) to Louis the Eighth of France. But that was all the good she ever did for the land of which she had been queen. Though French dukes considered themselves independent then, those rich lands of hers by geography, by very nature, should have been part of France, not of England. She was a dangerous beauty. Because of her, many men died in the long ago. Because of her, many have died in modern times. For the feud, the jealousy between France and England, though perhaps natural to neighbouring countries, was immeasurably strengthened by her divorce and dowry and desertion and the consequent wars through the ages. All this was not the least cause of the misunderstanding that kept England from full support of France until almost the eleventh hour, before the invasion of 1940, which almost ruined both.

To greet the beautiful Eleanor at Saint Denis, that June day in 1144, just eight centuries to the year before the high tide of the Second World War, there were on hand, military, clerical, professional representations; large groups of peasants; a great army of masons, carpenters, lapidaries, sculptors, painters, leadsmiths, goldsmiths, scaffold-makers, wood-carvers, and metal-workers; and a crew for stained glass, all cleansed of building smut and dust and arrayed in their festival best. Suger had been able to gather these artisans in part because of the religious fervor that had been gaining in France ever since 1095 and which, continuing for an incredibly long period, drove men both to the sword and the Crusades, and to inspired work on the cathedrals and churches. His attractive way and compelling personality also helped Suger; and he was wise enough, Ford-like, to offer higher than prevailing wages to tempt workmen from other cities preparing to erect handsome shrines—Laon, Chartres, Noyon among them, and in particular, Sens, which had already started excavating.

In recruiting these men Suger had done something more than pay honour to the great patron saint of France, Denis. He had mobilized and trained a great army of artisans, many of whom had already had a grand beginning under that benevolent branch of the Benedictines who so benefited architecture with all art and learning, the Cluniac monks. And this great industrial army, many of whom were veritable artists, would soon move over the plain to Paris to astonish the world with Notre Dame, then move on to Chartres.

The façade before which Queen Eleanor dismounted, had reached within a few feet of the line where the towers would begin. No glass yet glowed in wheel or rose window. Notre Dame was to be the great transitional cathedral which marked the flowering of the Gothic out of the Romanesque and yet retained features of it. But the Abbey of Saint Denis was the first church to step out of the Romanesque. And yet in this, its first form, its façade did not bear anywhere on its stone face the brand of the Gothic, the pointed arch. Eleanor saw the first of these new and revolutionary pointed arches when she passed through the central portal, which was still Romanesque, and came into the aisles of the choir, now roofed over.

There on a historic morning two or three years before, Suger, after a talk with the master-of-works, had like magic—so it seemed to those later describing it—waved a pointed arch out of the air. His magic, of course, was merely the crystallization of a long process of thought on his part and the end of many years of search by engineers everywhere. He had directed his workmen not to build over a certain aisle the old heavy Roman vaulting, with round half-barrel vault and much weight and masses of heavy concrete slewed in, but to try a new treatment. First, diagonal arches were to cross over the aisle space diagonally from the pillar springers. This would make six arches for each choir vault bay or section (the nave bays later had nine)—two wall arches running with the aisle at the sides, two transverse arches crossing above the aisle at right angles, and the two new ones crossing diagonally. He had seen architects experiment with the diagonal arches in the great Abbaye-aux-Hommes at Caen. There, these diagonal arches, being semicircular and of longer span than the side and wall ribs, met at a point higher than the summits of the others. It was the brilliant, epoch-making idea of Suger, his master-of-works or some anonymous assistant, to leave the diagonal arches as they were, but to make the arches at the sides and those crossing over at right angles, pointed. At Caen they had stilted them a little, but awkwardly. Here, at Saint Denis, on this exciting morning which was as eventful as that on which Watt read meaning into the rise and fall of the steam kettle lid or that on which Clement Ader flew his aeroplane in France years before the Wrights tried out their improved one, they arrived at the glorious solution.

When we get over with the crew to Paris Isle where the spaces are greater, the vaulting loftier, the arches more multiplied, we can see the mechanics a little more in detail. It is perhaps enough now to realize that the new treatment made all the vault bays symmetrical and gave the builder a most practical framework. For the arch bay, he had a skeleton of light but exceedingly strong ribs which, with the help of the comparatively light pillars and buttresses, would carry safely great roof weight at greater heights than could the old heavy Roman walls and pillars, and on this could be woven a fabric much lighter than the old Roman vaulting. They did not need, either, all the old heavy Roman trusses during the course of construction to uphold the vaulting. They could build directly on the rib structures, with sometimes a few light templates or timbers placed across until the courses were laid. And the stones of the arches were wedge-shaped. They fitted into each other. The weight they bore on their backs actually fitted them into each other more snugly and strongly, in fact, interlocked them. All the thrusts out were made to support rather than to burst the whole asunder.

Suger was delighted when he saw that his experiment—which was really but a perfecting of experiments of the Arabs with the horseshoe arch, of the builders at Caen, engineers in little churches in the Oise country nearby and engineers everywhere—really worked. Now he could really thrust his abbey up high, and because the new structure was elastic and strong, he could without danger do what the old Roman men never could do: place much glass all around and up high in his walls. The Romans needed every foot of their heavy walls to keep the roof up. But he now could pierce his walls almost at will. He could pin down to earth those rainbows of which he had dreamed, anchor them in his high walls. It was for this that he had assembled his army of stained glass guildsmen and had kept them at their pots and fires long before there were any windows for the glazing. And the glass of Saint Denis, with its beautifully toned violets, deep blues, and rich crimsons, was among the best in the world.

Suger planned to finish the great nave and the main aisles and transepts in the new way which a little later on would be called the "French style," Raphael not yet being on hand to dub it satirically "Gothic," thereby revealing a very bad blind spot. The famous abbot did not live to see complete fruition of all his plans, but his successors carried them out in his spirit, lifting up the nave and transepts with this new exciting, aspiring feature, the pointed arch, and even substituting it in alterations for the Roman arch in the earlier finished portions.

By June 1144, Suger had completed the sanctuary choir—which, as the heart of the church, is always started first—and the façade. And even then, as Eleanor saw it, without the high towers, the great west front, if not a complete fulfillment of the Gothic still retaining Roman lines, was a magnificent beginning of the Gothic. It was almost wholly so in feeling. Eleanor who, though a siren, was a woman of great taste, could sense the grandeur as her eye travelled across and up the façade, and took in these features: The spirited sculptures the artists were wreathing around the already completed front doorways. The disposition of the round windows in which the roses were yet to bloom. The relationships of horizontal to vertical lines, a more open and gracious arrangement than in older façades, the whole seeming very spacious as one looked across it, yet at the same time, with its four great vertical buttresses, challenging the eye to the skyward climb. More lofty and lovely this church was going to be than the stout-walled, chunky-apsed, lower-lying Romanesque churches that had covered France, though they had had a dignity, serenity and an immemorial quality all their own.

If Eleanor, Duchess of Aquitaine, Queen of France, Queen-of-England-to-be, had been all suppleness as she rode over the plain, she was all feminine grace and graciousness and royal dignity as she walked through the portal and inner porch, with the king—who was not much noticed when she was in his train, and the abbot prime minister, five archbishops, fourteen bishops, the crucifer, and a great company of chanters, censer-swingers, canopy-upholders, and velvet-mantled and jewelled courtiers. To solemn measured music they proceeded through the nave which had no roof; only the lower wall, the high pillars and the great arches just beginning their upward springing curve toward the as yet unhidden blue of the sky. So the marching glory came to the sanctuary-choir, now completely roofed in and vaulted with the new wonder-working arches at which all gazed.

The place was ablaze with countless refractions from myriad candle flames, embroidered vestments, and the gems of sacred vessels, as well as from this shining parade, a river of glory that marched to the crossing and the screen of the choir. As Eleanor came forward, she seemed as much of a flame as the oriflamme that stood by Denis' tomb. Even when, at such ceremonies, she did not wear bright robes but royal hues, purples and harmonizing lake crimsons cinctured with gold, she gave the effect of a flame housed in flesh. Voluptuous and indolent and full of fire, she was all at once. Her very languors were dynamic. Her eyes had invitations, nettles, spurs, promises in them.

Girdle of gold she had, circle of gold too on her amazing hair. Every man there, from noble to artisan, knew that she was there, not as a mere principal, something exquisite to be looked at by all, but very personally present for himself, no matter what his degree. For all her royal dignity, she was the beautiful feminine personified, challenging the possessive male. And every man there longed to stroke that amazing hair, though later he might—like Louis and Henry and Suger, at times—itch to drag her out by it. Still, it was such a lovely head to bend low over a skull—of the head Saint Denis was said to have carried to the Roman crossroads here. But so Eleanor knelt in the perfect curve of prayer. So she prayed and her eyes slanted and she was aware, not of God or Denis, but of man. Because of straying eye, straying thought, she was to leave this too upright king at her side, unnaturally desert this France of which she was anointed queen, dissever it, and start men to killing each other in droves for years uncounted.

Suger, as he stood there above the fair head making the absolution sign, could sense that desertion, even if he could not see its direction over the Channel; and he felt the oncoming tragedy. For he was very wise and far-sighted. From that chancel, twinkling with lights and resonant with rich chanting from many voices, he could look farther than down that unfinished nave with arches just beginning to bend against the sky. He loved all this beauty he was causing to rise around him, for though he had architects he was the driving force, the fountain of inspiration, for this church that would play John the Baptist to Notre Dame.

But he was more than a mere man of culture. He was a great man of affairs, the Wolsey of his time, though not a Wolsey who would go down in disgrace. Eleanor's father-in-law, Louis the Sixth, Louis the Fighter and Fat, of the oversized body and great heart, and her own husband had recognized Suger's genius, though the latter king had not always profited by it and particularly would not when it came to this woman there. She recognized it but spurned it and fought him, knowing he knew her for what she was. Often kings had valued him so much that they had stood before him while Suger sat on a stool dispensing light and wisdom. And Suger looked the great personage even when, without mitre, he appeared so very bald, and when, without his gorgeous cope and chasuble, so small of stature and almost painfully gaunt. He might spread glory all around him in this church and the abbey buildings, but that was for the glory of the Lord and to lead men to Him. He himself fasted regularly, and in the midst of this splendour slept in a bare cell on a pallet of straw.

But if he was thin to the point of emaciation, it was also to the point of extreme efficiency and tremendous activity. There was nothing in his abbey community, in the royal palace in Paris, in that city itself, or in all France, that escaped his penetrating eyes. These were very black and would have been called beady had they not been so animated, shining with an extraordinary liveliness out of a face sharp-cut and hollowed and shadowed by fasts and penitence.

One fine and charming thing about this great man was that he made no display of his austerity. When alone he lived on water and herbs—a little bread and fish rarely—though in the grandeur of the new abbey palace. But when with others at their ceremonies, he would, like the Christ of Cana, sanction their wine, even partaking of a little so as not to dampen their joy. And though he was as filled with noble thoughts as the panes he was putting in were with bright parables, he did not preach any sermons or exhort folks at their festivals, but told them engrossing and witty stories. He was a very great man, though another great man, Saint Bernard, who frowned on so many things, did not understand his essential goodness. Had Eleanor listened to Suger she might have aroused, instead of the empty adulation of suitors, the reverence and love of millions of her countrymen down to today.

When Eleanor, out of her simulated devotions, caught his shrewd glance reading her, her lustrous, all-conquering eyes could not subdue, as she longed to, his penetrating black ones. He read her, all of her, as she knelt above the sacred dust, near the spot where a wounded and very different kind of woman named Jeanne would lay down her armour. And he was almost relieved when the great pulsation of chant and song, which reached Paris over the plain, died away and she, the vivid focus of a splendid train, rode off to her desertions.

When the five archbishops and fourteen bishops rode away from the porch on the asses with the silk housings and little tinkling bells, they talked earnestly and enthusiastically among themselves, not about Eleanor at all, for they realized that something new and very important had come into the world. Their eyes were still full of the height and reaches of that vault, the serenity and spaciousness of that façade, the heavenly blues of Suger's first panes.

Saint Denis is still up, housing the royal tombs put together again from fragments collected after the Revolutionary mobs swept through, and with just a little of the actual dust, though where Saint Denis himself is now only the winds know. The abbey church looks much as it did when Eleanor was there, and even more as it did after Pierre de Montereau altered it in 1251-1281, though the ordnance both of men and the skies have attempted to destroy it. Lightning, in the nineteenth century, struck down the north tower. It has vanished completely from its place as the left crown of that grand façade. For—and this is significant—the modern architects who restored it after the bolt, built so much more poorly than the mediaeval men, that it fell never to go up again.

Now all the prelates riding away over the plains did not understand the full significance of what Suger had started when, after so many experiments by architects through the ages, he woke the arch out of its long sleep in the Romanesque and pointed it up. The trick, of course, was the use of this new arch in the old, the ogive vaulting, as shortly the wise master of works of Notre Dame will illustrate for us. They could not see, either, the larger implications: that this simple arch and device, through its immense possibilities for beautifying the world, for revolutionizing all construction, would give a new impetus to the fresh life already evidenced by the Crusades and by the vigour everywhere running as sap in spring through the veins of man. But many of the bishops were building patrons, some actual builders. And they did know that now they could build larger and lovelier churches and could gather in immense congregations for the glory—of themselves, a few perhaps calculated, but the majority for the glory of the God to whom they had devoted their consecrated lives.

Four leaders among them were particularly stirred. These were the Bishop of Sens whose excavating had already started, but who after what he had seen was hurriedly changing in his head all his building plans; the Bishop of Noyon who had already collected from the guilds and nobles a good-sized building fund; and the ambitious bishops of Senlis and Paris. The last, as he rode toward his ancient city, mulled over a scheme for a greater building which the new style would enable him to build and which could crowd in six thousand communicants at one mass. The archdeacon who rode at his saddle girths had a broader vision. This young cleric who called himself de Sulli, after his native town, had been like Suger a very poor but exceedingly capable boy. His superior then, the Bishop of Paris, might be planning a big church, but it was he, de Sulli, who as Bishop of Paris would, in nineteen years, start it.

Already he envisioned it as seating not six but ten thousand communicants and springing up on the horizon of Paris out of the two parent fortresses of the faith, Saint Etienne and old Notre Dame. He saw a new Notre Dame, of spaciousness, of strength and grace, of far-flung arches and sunset panes and of whose whole lovely and powerful ensemble the new Saint Denis, startling as it was, was but a foretaste.

XXVI

*Workmen from Many Parts of the World now head for the Seine.
. . . A Renaissance that was greater than the Renaissance. . . .
Fifteen Sister Cathedrals of the Ile de France. . . . Who designed
and built these Great Masterpieces? Recorded Architects and Build-
ing Bishops and Anonymous but Immortal Masters-of-Works. . . .
Maurice de Sulli, the Peasant Boy who rose to be Bishop, digs the
First Spadeful for the Cathedral. . . . The Last Days of the Two
Parents of Notre Dame. . . . In a Shining Procession the Pope lays
the Cornerstone of the Cathedral. . . . Holy Ground.*

1161=1186 A.D.

SAINT DENIS WAS HARDLY UP, THE PAINT WAS STILL FRESH ON
all the devils and angels, and the leads that bordered the
heavenly azures, violets and crimsons of the windows had
scarcely congealed, before these crews Suger had mobilized took up
their kits and moved across the plain. So they set up their forges
and portable crucibles, erected tents or hired lodgings in several
cities in turn. All of these were within the perimeter of the heart-
of-the-kingdom region, the Royal Domain, called the Ile-de-
France. This famous dry island, divided from the surrounding
provinces by no sea, only the barriers of feudal ownership, in
Suger's time covered but the territory around Paris watered by
the Oise, the middle Seine, and the Marne. By the 1300's the chart-
makers allowed it a little more elbow room, stretching it to take
in Amiens and up to the Normandy border west, Verdun east, and
south the land to the Loire. The farthest out of these towns in
which the Saint Denis crews erected the most gorgeous of man's
monuments, the cathedrals, were then not more than a week's
travel with heavy equipage, now three hours by rail, from the
capital, Paris.

As once a similar upsurge of artistic, intellectual, and spiritual
life had manifested itself in a little land, Greece, so now the richest
flowering of this rebirth appeared within a tiny space, this heart of
the kingdom, the Ile de France with Paris as its core. No other
realm ever revealed in so short a span, so small a space, a greater
splendour. Here was the lovely garden of the Gothic. All Europe

would borrow seeds and slips from it. The Gothic spirit was expressed in its supreme glory in these cities spread out over that Ile-de-France wheel, at varying distances from the hub, Paris:

AMIENS, 81 miles north. Notre Dame also, with a magnificent library of tales expressed in stone on its high façade. Erected 1220-1288.

BEAUVAIS, 49 miles north. Saint Pierre, with the loftiest vault of all the cathedrals. Under construction from 1247-1548, it was never finished. Though but half a church, it is very beautiful.

BOURGES, 144 miles south. Saint Etienne, of the five great portals and lofty aisles. 1100's-1500's.

CHARTRES, 55 miles southwest. A second Notre Dame, with beautiful flèche and most glorious glass. Started 1194, the greater part ready in 1240.

LAON, 87 miles northeast. A third Notre Dame, with six huge towers. 1163-1225.

LE MANS, 132 miles southwest. Saint Julien, with gorgeous glass. Gothic sections of nave and choir 1100's and 1200's; transepts 1400's.

NOYON, 67 miles northeast. Another Notre Dame. One of the first two Gothic cathedrals—Sens was the other. Started in 1140, its choir was dedicated in 1157. The church was complete in the following century.

ORLEANS, 77 miles southwest. Sainte Croix, with beautiful tiered belfry towers. 1287. Burned by Huguenots, 1567; rebuilt 1601-1829.

PARIS, THE GREATEST NOTRE DAME. The Bishop of Paris outlines it with his crook in 1160; the foundations are laid in 1163; the nave is ready for worship by 1208, and by 1235, except for side porches, chevet chapels, and a few details, the whole pile shows complete against the Paris sky.

RHEIMS, 98 miles northeast. A sixth Notre Dame and the royal coronation cathedral. It contains all that Gothic has to offer in such full measure that had an iota of ornament, a featherweight of stone, been added, its lovely harmony would have vanished. 1212-1300's.

ROUEN, 87 miles northwest. A seventh Notre Dame, crowned with the highest of all cathedral turrets. 1201-1500's.

SAINT DENIS, 5 miles north. An abbey church and not a cathedral, but still the sire of all cathedrals. 1137-1281.

SENLIS, 35 miles northeast. An eighth Notre Dame. 1155-1500's.

SENS, 71 miles south. Saint Etienne, first of the large Gothic cathedrals, was started, as was Noyon, in 1140; it was fairly complete by 1190.

TOURS, 145 miles southwest. Saint Gatien, woven of stone lace. 1170-1547.

This swift survey of that little realm does not take in a host of other noted cathedrals within its confines, like Soissons, Troyes, Meaux, Saint Ouen at Rouen, and all the incomparable, though smaller, gems of the Gothic like Sainte Chapelle. It is notable that of the eleven most famous cathedrals—Amiens, Burgos, Canterbury, Chartres, Cologne, Milan, Paris, Reims, Saint Peter's, Seville, Sancta Sophia—six were inspired by Ile-de-France architects and four went up in that narrow strip scarce two hundred miles wide. Never in any age, in any land, did man acquit himself better. Before these infinitely complicate but harmonious piles the lovely one-storey efforts of the Greeks pale, and our skyscrapers are dwarfed in art and even in engineering.

It should be remembered too, that while they were wrought without our speedier modern processes and machines and our high tension financial drives, and with such exquisite art and infinite care for details, only half of the cathedrals in that Ile-de-France wheel took the alleged three or four centuries to build. The rest, including the big four, took decades only—Amiens 68 years, Laon 62, Noyon 80, Chartres 46, Rheims 95, Sens 50, and our own Notre Dame at Paris 74 though some changes were made in after years. In 1160 Maurice de Sulli, once the poor peasant boy, now Bishop of Paris, stood by the old, already twice-rebuilt Notre Dame and Saint Etienne and indicated with his crook, the space in the two churches and in the square outside, which would be occupied by the beautiful cathedral of his dreams.

We are fortunate in having such vivid impressions of the instigators and patrons of Saint Denis and Notre Dame, for when it comes to architects we know so little, not even the names of most of these "masters-of-works," as they were then called, who spent their days around the piles and piers and on the scaffolds and at night stayed on the job, sleeping in tents that served as offices, ateliers and lodgings, and which were always pitched at the very foot of the rising walls. If you can persuade a Notre Dame guide of these days to show you the seldom-visited south transept porch, you will find the name of de Chelles, who was responsible for this lovely entrance, carved in the stone under the beautiful Saint Etienne. But architects do not often follow the custom of painters, who sign each and every fragment of their work. Very rarely did these great artists sign their cathedrals. An autographed cathedral is hard to find. De Chelles' successor cut his name there.

Only a few drawings have survived. There still exists one of the Cologne west front. Villard de Honnecourt who built a cathedral at Cambrai besides that tremendous Cologne left us a sheaf, really the only other mediaeval sketches besides the Cologne rendering that we have. These are charming. Ideas for capitals. Windows of Rheims. Laon's six huge towers. And drawings of quaint birds and animals and of native plants and flowers which the thirteenth-century builders, throwing off old classic chains, were beginning to copy in stone, in place of the eternal acanthus and laurel, for their gorgeous new churches.

As for records, there is little more. We do know that the name of Robert de Luzarches should go up somewhere on Amiens' high façade, of Jean d'Orbais above Rheims' three magnificent portals, Robert de Coucy on its splendid twin towers. A Jean Langlois designed the beautiful Saint Urbain in Troyes which is lovelier than the Troyes cathedral itself. William of Sens did much work on the famous transitional cathedral for the town that gave him his name; and for this pioneering effort was invited across the Channel where he transformed Canterbury and fertilized all England with French building ideas and taste. Pierre Montereau finished in a few short years that Gothic marvel in miniature, Sainte Chapelle, which looks as though it were made of three parts stained glass to one part stone, and in the sun gives to the beholder the effect of having been spun of violets and rainbows.

A few more and less important names may be gleaned from records, and there is the Notre Dame roster which we come to now. But the rest is pretty much silence as far as the great cathedral creators go. So that one can understand how men have come to believe that not only was every cathedral the result of a gigantic united movement of clergy, nobles, paupers, guilds, giving their all and actually harnessing themselves to carts, but that the plan and design was always the work of a composite architect. This was true, of course, of those cathedrals whose construction covered several centuries. And on every job, conferences about matters of construction, design, employment, were held between the Bishop and his chapter and the practical men who gave beautiful body to the others' dream of a lovely house for the immortal drama.

Usually the bishop of the city was the first dreamer of that dream, the selector of the building corps, the collector of the funds from nobles, burgesses, the commune—and often chiefly—as was the case with the Bishop of Noyon and our de Sulli of Paris, from his own private purse. Sometimes too, the guiding spirit of the bishop revealed itself in the arrangement the mighty project assumed. So that there was much of team work in the designing and directing, joining in with the great mass urge of the communal movement in shouldering those aspiring towers up so high.

Yet often it was one commanding spirit that moulded the cathedral of short span into its final form, again one great designing genius that left his impress more than did any other on a pile that was centuries abuilding, giving pattern and plan for all who worked with or who succeeded him. But the majority of these great artists who bequeathed such incomparable and imperishable beauty to the world, both those who contrived their designs in groups in the chapter rooms and up on the rising walls, and those who thought them out at night, alone in their construction tents at the foot of the towers, are lost in anonymity—it should be added, an immortal anonymity.

Therefore we are fortunate in having from Notre Dame something more than a shadowy payroll of bosses—this Jean de Chelles who chiselled his autograph in the south transept porch and who, in 1257, started work on that entrance; Montrueil, who added finishing touches to the whole pile in the last half of the thirteenth century; another de Chelles, called Pierre; and Jean Ravy who in the 1330's rayed the apse with the beautiful chevet chapels.

Above all, there was the fountain of both inspiration and funds, Maurice de Sulli, who dug so deep in his own purse for the latter, the one-time peasant boy whose rise from the farm would have pleased that arch-chronicler of worthy boys, Alger, and whose good works would have equally delighted Saint Paul.

But once the Gothic Age had begun, the bishops though they attended to the raising of funds did not, as a rule, direct the raising of the arches. Before, in the Romanesque era in France, the clergy had built their own churches. The peasants and city workers were called on for the rough labour, but most of the parish Romanesque churches, as well as those of the abbeys, had been designed by architects in soutanes. Master masons, goldsmiths, painters, carvers, all had worked with cassocks tucked up. All the talent had been frocked. But now few, if any, of the great masters-of-works—the four whose names we have learned from the old Notre Dame rolls, the half-dozen of other cathedrals just listed in that all too short roster, or any of the unknowns who worked on these magnificent piles from the time of William of Sens on—were ordained. They might have been trained in youth by the great clerical builders but they were not, usually, in an order or "in orders" themselves.

Already in this year of 1163, Bishop de Sulli had ordered several old houses torn down and a road constructed through the square in front of the two old churches for the bringing in of the material from the valley. Much would be needed. For he had decided to build this new high house for Our Lady big enough to receive all her children, all his communicants in Paris and the suburbs if not in one body at one service, at least before all the morning services were over. And his foresight and vision went even farther. He extended the dimensions noted on the plans so that when completed the majestic pile would hold all the throngs which in the centuries ahead would come with Philippe Auguste, Saint Louis, Charles the Wise, the Sun King, Napoleon and Foch, to thunder out *Te Deums* for the victories of France. Ten thousand, he swore by the crook with which he had first traced out the extended outlines in the square, he would crowd in at one mass within the glorious new walls. The hour of Our Lady had come at last on Paris Isle. That highly successful yet very good man, Maurice de Sulli, struck the hour with the spade when he tossed up the first earth at the ceremony that began the excavating.

This took place east of the square which, as all of us who have walked there with Heloise and Abelard, Saint Genevieve, Charlemagne and so many of the illustrious now should remember, was smaller and more irregular in shape than the great *place* in front of the cathedral today. It was bounded on the south by the Hôtel Dieu; on the west by old houses; on the north by the side of old Notre Dame; and on the east by the porch of Saint Etienne. The first digging, which was for the choir, was started near the island's upstream end and about a modern city block's distance from these two old landmark churches. We can get an idea of their relationship to each other if we recall what has been noted before: that the old Notre Dame, could we summon it back, would stretch under the cathedral's west organ loft into the nave for a little way beyond the great piers under the cathedral towers. Its front doors would be beyond the cathedral's, over the street, and a little way out in the paving of the square. A resurrected Saint Etienne would cover much of the cathedral's side gardens, stretching from the cathedral's beautiful east transept door to the little isolated building at the cathedral's side called the presbytery.

One of the two ancient churches disappeared very early in the operations. Some say it was Notre Dame that first made way for the cathedral, since the foundations for the nave began soon after those for the choir were finished, and the nave at the west end took over much of old Notre Dame's ground; Saint Etienne, they claim, running alongside the cathedral, did not encroach on the cathedral's ground plan and stayed up to see service while the cathedral walls were rising. Others, however, declare that Saint Etienne, though at the cathedral's side, did encroach on its groundplan and came down first. But it cannot matter too much which of these two aged parents of the great cathedral came down first when we have so accurate a record of the steps in the development of its giant and handsome offspring. And each old church had had a long and full life. Old Notre Dame, finished by Childebert in 557, had now seen six hundred and thirty-seven years. Through all of them except thirty (from its destruction by fire in the 880's until its restoration in the early 900's) it had been alive and alight.

Oddly, this six-hundred-and-thirty-seven-year-old Notre Dame was known as the "New Church," while Saint Etienne always was for the Parisians the "Old Church," though some since have given it a sixth-century birth. But then Saint Etienne had never undergone rebuilding since Notre Dame went up, and Notre Dame had been reconstructed twice. There was also so much evidence, as has already been noted, that Saint Etienne went up in the fourth century in the name of another saint, and then was enlarged and rechristened Saint Etienne, that the majority believed it was then eight hundred years old. And it also had been a cathedral and had even been known as Notre Dame in the years when Notre Dame was dark—which makes the number of Notre Dames three—Childebert's Notre Dame, this Saint Etienne-Notre Dame, and the great cathedral. But Saint Etienne's possession of the name had only been for a short thirty years. For most of its eight hundred years it had been itself, Saint Etienne, and for most of that time, indeed for all of it except for a little space in the beginning of this twelfth century, it had been a going church.

But it is time to take leave of both, regretfully for they played a great part in the history of Paris, the one on the north side, the other on the east side of the square, each with their familiar and common characteristics which we can never forget: The three deeply recessed, sculpture-wreathed portals. The long narrow clerestorey. The belfry midway. The round chunky apse behind. The sides striped with their vertical buttresses. And, set in bays between these, the window eyes under their arch eyebrows, now blank and dark with the cataracts of the grime and cobwebs of the ages, again, when the lights went on within showing gaily their bright emerald, blue, and crimson irises. There had been so little difference between them, only Notre Dame's richer decorations within, the greater length of Saint Etienne, and the curious situation of the older church which used for its south wall a section of the city wall, and its own fortress-like apse for a turret on the city wall, so guarding its own sanctuary and altar and the city ramparts and thus being incorporated in the city as the city was in the Church.

But the bright Charlemagne pupils in the eyes of the one church had been forever dimmed; those of the other soon would be. For Abelard and Heloise who once had walked these ways, to have come into the square would have been like meeting an old friend who had lost half his teeth. There were so many gaps. When at the island's upstream end they began to dig for the choir, the Hôtel Dieu still stood at the south side of the square, streams of the sick ever flowing through its Roman-arched doors. And one church—logic and evidence say Saint Etienne—was still up. There was a gap then where the other church had gone down, one west where old Roman and Dark Age houses had been torn down to let Bishop de Sulli's road through for the carrying of material. And there was an even greater area of demolition stretching from the square toward the island's upstream end, where many cloister dependencies had vanished to make way for the cathedral.

The gowned doctors with their physics, the old porters, crutched hobblers and bandaged invalids of the Hôtel Dieu deeply resented the change, not seeing the glorious rebirth it all portended. Willingly they would have exchanged for the old clamour of the students, all this building tumult and the clutter of ropes, pulleys, hooks, piles of sand and lime, carts, winches and hoisting machines that lined the square and the cleared cloister ground to the east. Even more melancholy for these ancient pensioners were the piles of bones that lay stacked up by the hole where the church had gone down, and all along the cloister clearing. They saw the human bones of Gallic warriors, Roman conquerors and Christian bishops disinterred by the excavating, and also the greater bones of Notre Dame and Saint Etienne—the building blocks, the old dolmen and Druid altar stones, and fragments of the old Roman temple. These had been carefully laid aside to be knit into a giant skeleton on which would come alive, clothed in a gorgeous fabric, the most graceful and enduring, the most vivid and spiritual architectural entity man ever conceived.

The first spadeful had been tossed by Bishop de Sulli in 1161. Already he had gathered a great army of workmen from the Seine Valley. Others were beginning to come over the bridges, men from the original Saint Denis crews, others who had been apprentices on that great abbey, but who had since learned their trades on the first two Gothic cathedrals. Those were gracefully spired Senlis, begun six years before Notre Dame (in 1155), and the larger cathedral started twenty-five years before Notre Dame (in 1140), at Sens and which, if Saint Denis had brought the Gothic dawn, was the true halfway house on the road to the full glory of Notre Dame.

The first to be mobilized were masons, carpenters, excavators, carters, piledrivers, quarrymen, concrete-mixers, scaffold-makers, and hoisters. But the men of the artistic crafts, goldsmiths, sculptors, painters, stained-glass experts, would start to drift in very soon with their wagons of equipment to put up tents and huts in every vantage point of the city.

It was a large crowd that pressed into the old, that remaining church, one day, and watched the Bishop give his blessing to the great hole that stood awaiting the choir foundations. Ghosts that morning haunted the square, not only those of old Gallic warriors with bright helmets on their still brighter hair, Druid priests, Roman centurions, Frankish kings, but more particularly those of all the craftsmen who, like the later cathedral workers, had come up to Paris. In King Childebert's time they had come by the old river road from the south, many of them from Venice and as far off as the Golden Horn, to make the first house for Our Lady which was only a third as grand as this new one was to be, yet a very fine one for its day.

This new crowd was vaster, almost wholly French, and more intelligent. They had thrown off the old yoke of Rome, its famous arch, which had prevailed for seven centuries after all its armies had been routed. That arch was cut, branded deep, in the one church that remained and in the buildings all around. It had marked those which, with the one old church, had gone down to make way for the new and greater church. And that would bear a new brand, which would be the secret of the cathedral's grandeur and aspiring climb—the Heaven-beckoning pointed arch. No wonder that as Bishop de Sulli raised his fingers in the old sign they all stood gazing with awe at a great hole, dark and bare, as though it were a grave out of which they knew would come a miracle, a glorious resurrection.

Two years later, in 1163, through working at great speed, they had widely extended the excavations and had finished the foundations for the choir and part of the nave. They had used some granite—it was much rarer in the Paris region than farther east and at Limoges, for example—and much rough concrete, all of it dressed. But they were good foundations. Now the Greeks, relying on the Nature they loved, always looked for rock support for their temples. Those dynamic builders, the Romans, scorning Nature and relying on themselves, did not bother to look for rock, but built where they chose, driving deep to virgin soil. No matter how far they had to go to reach solid ground for their foundations, they would get there, then on this virgin base throw in their superb concrete. The French, when they encountered shifting or damp soil at great depths, did not continue the excavating, but drove in gigantic piles down to the solid ground. On these they placed great platforms of oak and on the platforms laid foundations. In the cathedral of Paris they used granite as often as they could get it. Fortunately the Notre Dame masters-of-works did not find on the isle, though the Seine flowed by, as much seepage as the builders of the seventeenth-century Marais mansions and Garnier, who built the nineteenth-century opera house, found over on the Right Bank. For the cathedral foundations they did not require so many piles.

And while the Romans always left their foundations, though very strong, quite rough, the mediaeval French in keeping with the character of their race always dressed their concrete foundations, encasing much of this unseen part of their work in carefully surfaced stone. With their masonry above ground the French were even more particular.

It is perhaps significant that Troyes and some of the very handsome but second-flight cathedrals have only fair foundations, while Paris, Amiens, Rheims, three of the big four, not only make a grand aerial showing but are grand underground too. Beauty and superb strength they have in every part. From foundation sole to tower head they are magnificently built.

When the building operations were turning into their third year, 1163, and the rear, the choir section was about ready for the walls and the first shafts—the first stone shoots of this forest-aisled dwelling of Our Lady—were about to show above ground, Bishop de Sulli planned a grand ceremony. By many relays of horsemen he sent a plea south to the Pope, begging him to come to Paris. Fortunately he was not too far away. There was more than one era in the history of the Church when rash temporal princes rushed in where they had no right and had interfered in matters of Church government. As in the time of the famous "Babylonian Captivity" of the fourteenth century when there were two false popes and the true one fled to Avignon, so now the truly anointed Alexander III, forced out by usurpers, had fled to welcoming France, whose hospitality usually so notable would, in the twentieth-century world wars, come near to killing her.

It was not so long a trip from the south of France as it was from Rome up to Paris. Besides, like Bishop de Sulli, this true pope, Alexander III, was a man of vision. He sensed that the letter with the great royal seal of Louis the Seventh of France, whom the bishop had gotten to add his persuasions, was more than an invitation to a mere cornerstone-laying. Something was very generally in the air. That ceremony was likely to be an epochal event.

Alexander could not, of course, know that it would be a "Gothic" cathedral. Classifying and codifying would come with the later scholars. The sturdy, spacious-minded mediaeval men were content with creating the mighty works themselves. It would be the academicians and bookworms who would shove the mighty works into little pigeonholes.

Nor could the Pope tell that Notre Dame would be known as the best "transitional" cathedral, the first truly great representative of the Gothic and, to many minds, still its loveliest representative on earth. But Alexander was keenly aware that it was an innovation in the world, that it was bringing in a new era, that it would be a more glorious summation of what had been started in the dawn at Saint Denis and nobly carried on at Sens, and was farther reaching than any mere innovation in building styles; in short, that the building of this magnificently designed God's theatre was in itself a revolution or else the most strikingly visualized symbol a revolution ever had.

It is to his immense credit, therefore, that he set out on the journey up the Loire and the central river system of France, which, if not so fatiguing as one from Rome would have been, would still require with the return trip many weeks at the pace a pope dispensing alms and blessings through a vast countryside must take. As the last dressed stones were being laid in place on the top tiers of the foundations of the choir, he rode over the Petit Pont into the building tumult of the Isle which almost drowned out the jingle of his lone train of belled jennets, little donkeys and white asses in red velvet caparisons bearing a host of singing canons, cowled and cassocked clergymen of many ranks, and heavily wrapped packs. In these were presents for this Columbus of a building bishop, Maurice de Sulli, the other prominent prelates who would attend the ceremony, and for Louis the Seventh. Also there was a gift *en train,* all of gold, for Our Lady Herself, with much assorted currency for Alexander's innumerable donations and benefactions in Paris.

The next week spades and chisels were laid aside, pulleys and hoisting machines were stilled, and the clouds of masonry dust which for three years had hovered over the Isle had settled when the Pope came out of the bishop's palace to attend mass in the old church.

A procession then moved with pomp through the gaps toward the new foundations. The Pope, crowned with a glittering mitre, walked under a gorgeous canopy. In the sun his gemmed crook and large papal ring sent sparkles like pentecostal flames leaping into the crowd. The elaborately decorated robes of tradition were individualized by Alexander's powerful features above, just as Bishop Maurice de Sulli's alb and billowed-out cope and chasuble were strongly and humanly accented by his practical, intellectual old peasant's face so rich in earth colour and earth wisdom.

There was no sanctuary there yet, only this great rectangle of masonry enclosing a crypt, before which the bright procession came to a halt. And this was the foundation not for the vast audience chamber, the nave and aisles, but for the sanctuary, which, by 1185, would be complete.

A long train of ecclesiastics made a wake of colour reflecting the officiating Pope's own Solomon-like glory. The King and his court, regally arrayed, were in line. An army of citizens in forest green, meadow flower yellow, and mountain blue, waved branches. Chanting sections of priests from the churches of Paris answered each other in song until, in a deep hush, the Pope laid his white hand on the huge block which had been set in place with chains and crowbars.

It rested where had stood the altar stones since incorporated in Saint Etienne's body, that long before had served as roofs and posts of the old dolmen houses of the dead, into which had been thrown the letters to the world of spirits, man's first articulate attempt to reach the Unknown. Here, too, the Druid priests had stood and hither had come their high priest from the Druid capital in the Carnutes' country (where Chartres is now), to cut with the golden knife the mistletoe and the victim's throat.

That mistletoe had grown on oaks that had stood where now would spring the forest of stone. In excavating for the foundations of that miraculous forest, they had dug up the once-bright helmets of the Gauls which the Romans had hung as trophies on the oaks which had long since vanished. Some of these trophies, mouldering links with the past, lay at the Pope's feet. Where he now blessed the great cornerstone the Roman priest had called on his gods which had vanished too. A hundred yards back of him were the bones of the ancient church which had been torn apart. Its aged sister stood, holding the bones of so many altars, so many temples, its ancient bells going lustily, its dimmed old eyes once more alight. Soon these would go out too. But these would be replaced by greater eyes, the great round rose-window eyes of the Cathedral.

Surely this was holy ground, a grand sequential ground of memories and ties and links, on which Pope Alexander called down a blessing from the Unknown on this first stone above ground for the mighty, the exquisitely wrought, last link in the chain.

Yet as the light from the processional candles illuminated the faces of the masons, stonecutters, concretemixers, all the labourers tricked out in their Sunday best, one might have guessed that piety alone could not rear the majestic pile, foreshadowed in the wood model which was shown to the Pope in the architect's tent after the ceremony. Under the inspiration, unaided, of the powerful men of God of that age, those towers would have been thrust up against the sky. But if there had not been added to the piety something which ordinarily would not seem to have much to do with religion—though it may have sprung out of religion—something which we must look at for a moment now, those Notre Dame towers and the new ones all over France might not have risen quite so high.

XXVII

*The Mediaeval Commune does not destroy Churches; it helps
build them. . . . The Unions of the Middle Ages, the Famous
Guilds, their Pride and High Standards. . . . Good and Evil Titled
Employers. . . . Gaudry the Gory of Laon. . . . The First Strike.
. . . The Guilds give their Names to the Old Paris Streets. . . .
"The Men with Blue Nails" help with the Cathedral. . . . Clergy
and Communists unite and work together for the Glory of God.*

1186 A.D.

𝔄 NEW LIFE VERY OBVIOUSLY POSSESSED THESE SHOUTING,
chanting, milling workers at the laying of the cornerstone
of the cathedral. It was evidence of something not born of
religion but working with it that was astir, not only in Paris but
in cities everywhere. All Europe was seething with new ideas,
bursting with a new and constructive revolutionary spirit.

The first concrete form that this newly aroused sense of power
in the people took, the civic commune, had little to do with the
Communism we know now under which the distribution of privilege is not so general as was envisioned in its first pure scheme,
and the power, in practice, still seems to be in the hands of a comparatively few. Nor was it one with the all-out-against-capitalism
Communism of the Karl Marx phase or that which in 1871 burned
Marie Antoinette's Tuileries, the Archbishop's Palace alongside
Notre Dame, and set barrels of oil, tar, pitch, and cotton and
plumber's waste in the very nave of the cathedral. Notre Dame
would have been gutted and ruined for us then had not the doctors, internes, nurses, almost the entire staff of the old Hôtel Dieu
across the square, with some of the aroused invalids, rushed in to
put out the fire. You can still see one trace of the conflagration,
by the cathedral treasury door, in the charred back of a high chair.

The commune of mediaeval days did not burn churches; it
helped build them. Cathedral chapters and merchants' guilds
worked together. A new industrial faith, this new sense of soli-
darity among the workers, assisted an ancient mystic faith in
these giant building operations.

This was not the first time a secular movement had helped ad-

vance the Church. In the first centuries Rome, even while persecuting the Christians, had organized a vast peace in which
Christianity developed, had established a great system of communications and roads that would speed to all the world its beautiful
yet revolutionary message. This new movement which brought into
being the guild, the commune, was not alien to the Church like
the old empire, but sympathetic. Certainly leaders like Bishop
de Sulli, whose powerful peasant face revealed, with all its light
of consecration, a shrewdness and practicality, felt that they could
use it as an earthly instrument for the glory of the Lord. And
surely the cathedral was for His glory.

This was an unparalleled spring that was breaking on the world.
And as many factors—sun, air, rain, dew, soil—unite to make the
vernal miracle, in France now there had auspiciously combined a
general air of trust in the Church and its leadership, the sun of
faith, the dew of constant prayer, and the rains of the continual
presentation of the immortal drama drenching the minds of all
with its message. The communal movement now united with these,
as the chemical in the soil—the people to bring on this extraordinary
spring of the mind and the spirit.

The feudal system had started in 731 on the Champs de Mars,
downstream from Notre Dame around the river bend, when
Charles Martel had given out to his soldier chiefs all the fiefs
which later became the mediaeval baronies and duchies. And it
was feudalism which, without any such intention on the part of
its beneficiaries, had brought into existence the guild and the commune as counter-agents to itself.

The commune at first was nothing more than the city corporation taken over by the guild of the more prosperous city merchants, the patricians, not of "blood," but of wealth. The
artisans' or craft guilds made up of skilled workers, not employers,
followed the merchants' guilds a long way off and did not have
anything like the others' power when the Notre Dame choir was
begun. It was not until the next, the thirteenth, century that the
craft guilds gained the right to elect representatives to the govern-
ing boards of the city corporation or commune. Which is one of
many reasons why that century was called the "glorious thirteenth."

Rome, in a way, left a precedent and something of a pattern
for the mediaeval guild. The membership of the old imperial
sodality may have been a trifle more comprehensive. The building
sodality of any Roman town, for example, took in everybody
connected with building: masons, carpenters, architects, rich contractors. A mediaeval craft guild kept to its craft. It admitted
all the artisans in any way connected with the industry but
the members who had become prosperous employers and investors

graduated into the rich merchants' guilds which controlled the city when the old feudal noble was overthrown. But the old Roman fraternity and the mediaeval guild were not unlike in their charities, standards and protective measures. The members of the builders' sodalities of the empire, whom we watched putting up their basilica lodge-halls which the building bishops would copy for their first churches, had rules for sick benefits, holidays, insurance and the maintenance of standards. And the last worked both ways. A high living and wage scale had to be maintained for the employee. For the sake of the employer the quality of the work and the material furnished had to be high.

In much the same way the guilds of mediaeval France protected not only themselves but the public by their self-drawn ordinances. Butchers could not expose unsalted beef or venison for more than three days. Blood-puddings were prohibited. Venders of spoiled food, bakers who sold two days' old bread for fresh were fined. So was every tailor who spoiled a bolt of cloth or cobbler who botched a boot—and by their own guilds!

And when, in the thirteenth century, the people of France, still filled with all the atmosphere they had brought back from the Crusades, tried to brighten up their old grey cities by lavishly colouring their house façades, no housebuilder could apply his paint to a single half-timber until the owner had tested it. No saddler could decorate and befringe a saddle until the customer had seen the bare leather and wood. And the statue of a saint for the Notre Dame porch could not receive its Joseph's-coat of many colours before the master-of-works had examined the body from its haloed head to its chiselled toe.

Meanwhile, so far did some of the cities go with their provisions —most of them initiated by the guilds themselves—that the shops had to be open to the passerby so that every part of the process of making glove, shoe, hauberk, whatnot, could be observed.

Some of the guild rules cut even deeper across the social fabric, reweaving it in fact. A man, for example, could not be wholesaler, jobber, retailer, all three in one, or serve in any two of these capacities jointly. Restraint of trade, conspiracy and the fixing of prices, too, were forbidden. And they guarded against speculation by banning all purchases for future delivery.

Meantime, the craft guild mantle was thrown around the little people. The number of places that might furnish them with dubious entertainment was cut down by statutes of the vintners' and brewers' guilds, forbidding their members to sell to low dives. Night hours and Sunday work were prohibited. One shop only in each trade could remain open on the seventh day and on holy days. The owners of the rest had to see that their counters were folded up into the housewalls. And the number of apprentices was limited, in some cities, to one to a shop, so that the bound youth who served from four to eight years might have the very best bodily care and special instruction. The woman worker was also provided for. No employer could assign her to the rougher labour. No male fellow-worker could with impunity insult her.

But most of these social reforms were arrived at only when, several decades on, Notre Dame began to show itself as a real body as far up as the tower line. The trade association idea brought up to Paris by the Venetian, Lombard, and Levantine artisans who came to work on King Childebert's Notre Dame, had been lost in the welter and chaos of the Dark Ages when the only thought was not for social betterment but for soul salvation and bodily survival. Then the only sanctuaries for the torn little people, the only nuclei around which such human hopes as still remained could coalesce, were not guildhalls but the fortified abbeys. During Charlemagne's time a few guilds, survivors of the old powerful Roman bands, existed in France but only as shadows, for though they are mentioned in the old Carolingian Capitularies (779-789), they are alluded to with disdain, as though they were outlaws. It was only in the first half of the eleventh century that the artisans began to group themselves into unions again. At first they banded together merely as the workers of the large castle households of the lords to whom they owned allegiance and sustenance. No distinction as to kind of work was made. All who worked with their hands within the castle walls, from pickler to armourer, could join. As the village, which with its clustering houses nestled around the stronghold like a brood of chickens around a mother hen, began to expand, the harness-maker and tailor and tinsmith who lived within the castle wards had clients beyond them out in the growing town. Finally their trade would so increase that the tradesmen would hang their coloured signs on the town streets. They would still work for milord, part-time, but they plied their trade in shops set up in the town. And gradually their numbers and incomes grew until the old all-trades union was dissolved into separate craft units.

There was that other type of trade association limited to the industrial upper class, really a super- or over-guild, in which all industries were represented, this body taking in the most successful in the crafts, those who had risen to be employers and, by the same token, investors and capitalists. It was the members of this over-guild, the merchants' guild, that first began to arm themselves for protection, then to raise their heads and banners proudly, to really assert themselves in the city. They wound up by taking over as a body the whole city corporation or commune, and winning the control of the town away from the old liege lord of the castle to whom the town had been a composite vassal or an aggregation of vassals.

The commune did not win control of the city wholly away from the liege lord in this era. There were still revenues to turn in to him, services to perform for him. But these now were always reduced, very greatly, sometimes, by the winning of franchises or charters which were granted to the commune by the King or were purchased by the payment of huge sums to some noble impoverished by his own dissipations or a jaunt off on some Crusade. The commune then attended to the policing of the city and often it took over the general administration and a share in the judicial authority. As the city corporation, it had its seal and coat-of-arms, its banners and banquets, its troops and a garrisoned keep to which the officials and citizens could flee when the hand of the duke-landlord became too heavy or a baron turned berserk and, on blood bent, rode with his jack-riders into town. And frequently the commune was, as they would say these days, "sitting very pretty" with a debtor suzerain lord and the king himself, who always tried to expand his power at the expense of the consolidated nobility, each bidding for the favour of the populace.

But it is wrong to make out the feudal noble as always a cruel usurer and a fearsome landlord bogey. The greater proportion of the tithes and fees the citizens paid and the services they rendered had for centuries been justified. It is true that here and there some baron or count would run riot over the countryside. While the poor starved, his granaries would be bursting with grain, his vats with wine, his sacks with wool, which he had exacted in overwhelming quantities from his vassals. Sometimes a "verray, parfit gentil Knyght," in a moment of whimsy, would hang a miser merchant or a sullen peasant by his thumbs and would add to the natural weight so precariously suspended by placing boulders on the shoulders. Or in a playful moment, he might leap at the strung-up victim and seize his genitals, tearing these off, causing the entrails to run bloodily out. But by no means did all liege lords act that way; it was a startling exception.

Through the centuries there had been many who in troubled times had served their country and their people well. In the Dark Ages at first, as we have seen, the abbey had been the only refuge for the little people. But monks and priests though they fought valiantly had not been equipped for natural soldiers. So the strong man of the region, the leading farmer, the embryo lord in homespun, took over when the abbeys had been burned by the marauders. He built wood towers, dug deep ditches, reared stockades, and when the foe came down, brought the weaker folk under cover.

With the years, these stout squires became counts and dukes and instead of timber stockades, now offered strong castles, moats and keeps. There were abundant wells, food, fodder within the castle wards in time of siege for the whole countryside. Bandits, too, the lord had driven off, he had policed the highways. He had built bridges, forest roads, established hospitals, infirmaries, set up mills and looms. In a majority of cases, therefore, the feudal noble- man had earned his power, his tithes and tolls. He had been bul- wark and buttress of the land, patron and protector and great meal-ticket for all those former tailors and cobblers and smiths who had once made shoes and uniforms and swords for him and his garrison and then, when the hamlet he had nursed had grown up into an adult town, had struck out for themselves sometimes to defy him and flaunt their signs and their banners in his face.

But you could not have stopped the workers from striking out for themselves any more than you could have prevented the Ameri- can colonists from severing, when the destined moment came, the ties that bound them to a once-nurturing, but later dominating mother. It was evolution. Feudalism had been a faulty but a most necessary system. Now it had served its time, yet was living beyond it; and against its one-time virtues now turned to vices, the com- mune with its virtues and vices too, fought. It was an advance in or toward Democracy, wresting many privileges from the great upper class and transferring them to one cross-section of the people, those in trade but the wealthier of those in trade.

And these in turn took on the complexion of another feudal caste, slightly lower than the nobles. The controlling merchants' guild, these ex-workers risen from the ranks, these new employers and budding capitalists who ran the city corporation as the com- mune, had their ethics and standards. No one could be admitted who was in debt or diseased. They could be charitable at times. Never did they finish one of their grand banquets without dis- pensing to the poor a gallon of Beaune or Moselle for every gallon they drank.

Still these nobles of factory and market, lords of ledger and loom and peers of the pound, could be very snobbish at times. They formed an industrial Four Hundred and dressed the part, wearing cloaks of velvet, chains of gold, mantles of miniver, and put a like fortune in textiles and gems on their wives' ample backs. From their gilded and bannered height they looked down on all but the bishop and some of the lesser knights inside the town, with whom they allied themselves against the great duke or count without.

In the 1070's the first commune had been formed at Cambrai— the town for which de Honnecourt, who left us the few mediaeval architectural sketches we have, built the cathedral. And from then

on until well after the Notre Dame towers were up, no merchants'
guild would take in any one who worked with his hands, no matter
how great was his skill. Their rules explicitly barred all whom they
describe as "Men with Blue Nails"—that is, those whose nails were
the worse for wear and toil. These splendid-appearing, but newly
arrived aldermen, councillors, magistrates and sheriffs were like the
Unjust Steward of the Bible. Having climbed up themselves, they
would lock the "Blue Nails" out.

And yet in bettering their own estate they improved the lot of
the artisans. They brought power and privilege to themselves and
a peace and hitherto-unknown prosperity to all the rest, including
the serfs, the lowest feudal order, who were not slaves (Louis the
Sixth having abolished the remnant of slavery in France, ages
before our own Emancipation Proclamation) and, though they
paid a forced rent and could not own land, often made a profitable living and sometimes fortunes.

Though the degree of liberty, of course, varied in the different
cities, in all the towns that gained their charters, these new leaders
through their shrewdness, money, and sometimes their blood, had
secured for all a considerable easement of taxes and of the burdens
of excessive marching and fighting for milord, and the eternal
baking in his ovens and grinding in his mills. And they had with
their civic guards checked the tyrannical and lawless peers.

Not that any millennium of peace had immediately come. Drums
had sometimes to beat, alarums to sound, civic guards to come
tumbling out, and the brave new aldermen and magistrates to flee
into their keep.

There was, for example, Laon whose cathedral-to-be would turn
out a twin of Notre Dame of Paris, for it would be started in the
same year that the Pope laid the Paris cornerstone (1163). The
commune of Laon got under way the century before, in the
1170's, with shocking violence and with high-lighted scenes which
the wildest of imagined melodramas could not match.

Now if other nobles had evil hearts, that of the liege lord of
Laon was like midnight, total and unrelieved. He was one of those
ignoble nobly-born whose degenerate conduct tended to condemn
all his peers, even the gentle ones, in the eyes of the contemporary
world and to smear his caste in history for all posterity.

His name was Gaudry. It should be known.

He was never seen, except by some ravished maid, without his
armour. Like Louis the Eleventh, he loved to surround himself with
villains. His private executioner, a huge, grinning black, always
rode with uplifted axe alongside. But unlike that superstitious
monarch Louis, who prayed to the saints each hour, Gaudry loved
to rob churches, to chase his foes into them and there to kill them.

Yet, despite his ferocity, the commune had managed to wrest something very like a charter from him. It did not hold long. Almost the first week after signing it he violated it. So came the first notable strike in the Middle Ages. Butchers, greengrocers, saddlers, bakers, tradesmen all, closed their shops. The name of Commune became a battlecry. "Commune! Commune!" it rang through the Laon streets. Armed with everything from the formal weapons of the garrison to the informal ones picked up in the stable-yards, the torrent of the enraged citizenry broke into Gaudry's palace. He fled to the cellar. But from a wine vat they yanked him out and stripped him of his armour. They did not behead him as men of the later communes would have done. They simply split his skull open. Since it was so thick a one, this was a hard job. Then they heaped, as persecuted folk turning human worms will, many obscene indignities upon him. This savouring of blood having incited them, they swept on to the massacre of all peers they could find, the gentle with the cruel, the bad with the good. But it was not entirely an ill wind, since the mob took it into its muddled composite head to burn down the old Romanesque cathedral and they shortly afterwards replaced it with something new and big and fine with six towers—and Gothic. It was a long time, however, before all the violence that had so worried de Sulli died down and Laon became a settled city with an established commune.

But in the main the merchants' guilds which absorbed, embodied, and interpreted the civic corporations, these communes, made for peace. They did arm themselves, but it was for defense not for raids. They drew sword, but it was to guard their shops, their purses, the city walls and their daughters, not to despoil. More interested were they in the honest web of the loom than in the tortuous one of diplomacy, in butchers' rather than battle-field carcasses. The old seigneur of the sword spent three-quarters of his time in mail, in going to the wars, in tournaments or in feuds and but one-quarter in useful pursuits. These new patricians of the yardstick and scales spent one-quarter of their time in rounding up brigands and dropping stones and cauldrons of pitch from their walls on their assailants, and three-quarters in turning out goods. They brought to the cities a measure of peace in which the artisans might thrive. So though these non-noble men in trade and furs continued to look down on the non-noble men in trade and jerkins, they had helped the manual workers on toward the day when the unions, the guilds of the skilled crafts, would have their place in the sun and their treasures would be full and they would take their watch on the city walls under their own officers, their seats in its councils. And they would acquire whole sections of the city where they would live and work, and these quarters were restricted to the different crafts whose names still survive on ancient streets.

One comes upon these everywhere in old Paris now—Parchment-making Street (de la Parcheminerie) which had been devoted to the trade before Abelard came to town; Glasswares Street (de la Verrerie), Ironmongers Street (de la Ferronnerie), where Henry of Navarre was killed, near Lingerie Street, and many another high-way and alley, to say nothing of the quays—for example, Gold-workers' Quay (Quai des Orfèvres) south of the Palais, and across from the Palais and Marie Antoinette's last prison Leatherworkers Quay (de la Megisserie) where today tiny gold birds, and red and blue, imprisoned too, sing out their little throats by the Seine.

This union heyday, this crafts high tide would not come until Pierre de Chelles had finished his south transept porch of Notre Dame and written his name in it. But the craftsman was now on his way up—with the cathedral. And, after all, if the affluent aldermen in miniver and the snobbish sheriffs with new coats of arms did look down on the "Men with Blue Nails," it was the "Blue Nails" who put the cathedral up. They gave the exciting and aspiring point to arch and *flèche,* the heaven-high curve to its vault, grace and beautiful raiment to its great population of saints, humour and *diablerie* to its monsters, those sunset crimsons, unforgettable violets and blues to its panes. The merchants gave speeches and gold.

Still, the services of all were needed. It was a powerful trinity—merchants' gold, artisans' skill, the clergy's eloquence and inspiration—all united by a professional and civic pride and a mystic faith, and extraordinarily stimulated by memories of delicate, colourful and exciting things which men had seen when they marched off to the Crusades. A great burst of light, too, which dawned as the Dark Ages went out, and the rush of a life sap in the veins of the race in this miraculous spring that reared Notre Dame and its sister cathedrals all over France.

XXVIII

Philippe Auguste, a Very Great King, adds Towers to his Capital,
drives out the Plantagenets and all the English from France, de-
feats the Germans and makes a Strong France. . . . A City Wall,
the first completely to circle Paris, goes up with the Cathedral. . . .
Notre Dame starts Romanesque and winds up Gothic. . . . The
Choir rises, the High Altar is consecrated, a Stranger Prince buried
in a Roofless Cathedral. . . . The Crusades cripple the Building
Fund. . . . Rich and Poor, High and Low, harness themselves to
Carts to hurry in the Stone for Notre Dame and pour out Gold and
Treasure into Our Lady's Lap.

1186-1191 A.D.

THE KING WAS GETTING UP VERY EARLY. IT WAS TO BE A GREAT day. He was a great king and he looked it. Tall, with great broad shoulders, he would have been called strapping had not his figure been so trim, ready and fit. He was bald—no fault of his in the eyes of Paris—for it was wearing his helmet at wars for France or a sickness incurred in them that had made him so. He had the grand royal nose of so many of the wise and capable monarchs of France, an agreeable and cheering high colour, also a cheerful smile for his subjects, particularly the workers, though he could be cold towards his foes and his wives with whom he had no end of trouble.

Impatient of the attentions of courtiers with fine linen towels, ewers, basins of rosewater and clothes, statesmen itching for a word in his ear, he stepped out of the crowded chamber onto a little walk circling the corner tower of the palace. He wanted to greet the morning, the sun, to look on the Seine and this city he loved as much as any in her long line of admirers who paid her tributes in song. But being no poet, he helped her not with words but with deeds and towers.

He had, for example, just made over the old hunting lodge called the Louvre into a great fortress castle with four corner cone-cap towers and strong central keep. But he did not sleep there. He still kept when in Paris pretty much to this old island palace which he had also reconstructed. And he had made over the clock on the face of the tower—still called the Tour d'Horloge, or Clock Tower —on which he stood. Charles the Bald had built that tower there by the river and the head of Moneychangers Bridge and had put there some sort of clock. Philippe Auguste had just painted it a grand red and gold quite as you see it, refurbished of course, today. He was always doing that, this Philippe the Second called Auguste, making things over, little and big, or building anew. There were other strong towers he had put up besides the Louvre at critical points in Paris: the Tour de Nesle, by the Left Bank shore on the west, and the Grand Châtelet, which was to be so famous in Paris history, on the Right Bank just across from the royal palace. He had given Paris its first paving since the Romans had laid down the old cobbles ages before. The sound of the many shoes clattering on it as they came out with the morning was music to the king's ears. In 1190 he started a city wall looping around the hills. And there was at the upper end of the island a new great high building, or rather the portion of one, that loomed up above the empty space torn out of the cloister. In almost a generation it was the only portion of the cathedral that had been built, but it was a pretty impressive fragment, though without a roof, and was already higher than the four dozen other churches in the town except Saint Genevieve on her hill and Saint Pierre on Montmartre, and possibly the tips of Saint Germain-des-Près' spires which the cathedral towers and main roof would of course far overtop.

If this great enterprise was conducted by citizens and clergy, the king had ever to be in the van with appeal and subscription. There was another interesting building which he could see by the Grand Châtelet tower and just across the stream from his clock tower. This was the new brightly painted and highly carved guildhall. The merchants' guild of Paris which met there, indeed all the communes of France, were very grateful to Philippe Auguste for his help. In turn, they had turned out well with both men and cash for him and France in all his wars.

Incidentally, he was one of the few kings that had done fairly well at a crusade—the Third—in which he equalled Richard Lionheart in all sound, not the foolhardy, demonstrations of valour and brawn, and outmatched him in all things that were done with the head.

And being so great and wise a ruler, he had made over the budget too, and had appointed just and capable officers who restored the royal revenues throughout the domain, administrative provosts who looked after his interests, and yet treated the citizens with consideration and a set of circuit judges, called bailiffs, who impartially administered justice. It would have been incomprehensible that the great tide which urged men on to new and resplendent building and to the Holy Land should not have swept France on to a new and more powerful estate. Philippe Auguste had guided her to this. He had made her strong, Paris too, which was fitting, for she should be worthy of and able to guard and protect this new marvel, the cathedral.

Persistently he pursued his perpetual purpose of propelling the Plantagenets from the purloined provinces. The bells had rung for Philippe Auguste when he had been born in Paris, and very properly. For he was to make up for his father's fault in letting Eleanor and her great dowry go from the land of which it was a natural part. This Philippe Auguste, the son of Louis the Seventh's second wife, Adela, beat roundly his marriage connections, the sons of Eleanor by the English Henry. And though it would all have to be fought over again in later centuries, Philippe got back for a consolidated France Eleanor's dowry, rich Aquitaine with Guienne, Gascony, Poitou and the lost part of Touraine. He even won with all this Normandy and Anjou and Maine.

More, he enriched France with another dowry, that of his own wife. She, Isabella of Hainault, brought him Artois and the Arras region. Her father with the Count of Flanders had been making war on Senlis and Champagne and north France towns. He asked her to win her father to his side. Though the queen of France, she would not at first go against her father. Philippe at last threatened her with repudiation. Isabella then, a slight, sensitive but determined slip of a girl, took a leaf out of Lady Godiva's book, though not the whole volume. Stripping herself, she donned only a smock and walked barefoot through the town in protest against the king's decision. The townspeople had hated her as their descendants would hate the foreign Marie Antoinette as an alien favouring the foes of France. But won by this Cinderella demonstration, which appealed to their sense of the dramatic, they cheered and marched along with her to the palace, where they shouted to the king, begging him to reinstate her in his favour. Both reconciled, she won over her father, detached him from the coalition against France; and Philippe freed another large region for a greater France. This tall broad-shouldered king, with the sanguine complexion and disposition, was one of the truly big men in French history.

Meantime, he had been belting in Paris. It was curious, but of all the European capitals only Paris had gone through the ages unfortified. She had had her island wall to defend her heart; but her ever-expanding districts on Right Bank and Left had gone unprotected. Philippe's grandfather, Louis the Sixth, had started

to erect a section of wall in one suburb, but until Auguste no
monarch had undertaken to wall in completely this fair city. It
seemed almost as though they had relied on her "sweet air," of
which the Emperor Julian had sung, and her famous charm to
save her. But though robust charms may soften conquerors, subtle
charm does not seem to. It had no more effect on Germans then
than it has had on their even more ferocious counterparts in modern world wars. And Philippe, in addition to beating the English
roundly, had soundly to thrash the Germans. He did this at
Bouvines Battle in 1214. This was a little later, when the cathedral
was farther along, far enough, in fact, for him to march grand
companies of his bloody but victorious army with their banners
down through an almost completed nave to the high altar.

Besides those strongholds just noted, placed at critical points,
Philippe had built many more of those towers which he gave to the
Paris he loved instead of the poems her admirers usually laid at
her feet. There were scores of them, eighty yards apart, at junctures in the new wall wherever it had been finished. High double
ones with drawbridges guarded the great city gates. The wall would
not be finished until 1211, twenty-one years after its start, but it
was well under way. From the tower he could see it curving like
some prehistoric monster python which had been petrified as it
coiled around his royal city, part of its long carcass whole and
spiked by towers; part of it where the courses were only half up,
the rubble visible, seeming to have been gashed and despoiled.
Being of fresh stone, it was white with a moat running alongside
in the low places, filled by green water from the Seine. The gaps
in the wall caused by the river were guarded at night by huge-
linked chains.

On the west, running between the Louvre and the old Saint Ger-
main-l'Auxerrois church, it curved about Les Halles, the city markets, which are still there, and which the king had just renovated,
fish, cabbages and pears being as necessary to his Paris as castles
and gold. Extending east, it hit the river opposite the middle of the
Ile Saint Louis, the island back of the cathedral choir. A huge chain
standing for barrier there, it crossed the middle of that island,
gave way to another chain over the south fork of the Seine, and
began again at a point on the Left Bank about a hundred yards
southeast of the choir. Running up the hill it looped around Saint
Genevieve's high abbey, then ran down, leaving outside Saint Germain-des-Près, to the river where then stood the Tour de Nesle and
now stands the Institut de France. There are portions of this wall
of Philippe Auguste, whose building was a great event in the history of Paris and the cathedral, still to be seen: in Charlemagne's
ancient "Little School" on the street named for him; in Saint

Julian's tiny park across from the cathedral; in the Cour de Rohan; and behind the Panthéon on the Rue Clovis—a high section of it there.

The city was all astir now with the clatter on the king's new pavement of folk coming out of their houses as the sun came up over the Seine. Ordinarily they would all have been at work. Every morning the industry of their tools woke the king in his palace, the bishop at the other end of the island in the cloister. From sunrise to sunset, except for the noon hour, there was a continuous tumult of hoisting machines, pulleys in blocks, the dumping of carts, unloading of stone on the quais, of boatmen yelling the ancient watermen's calls that came down from Roman days, the cries of warning when huge stone blocks in chains swung too near a workman on the scaffolds of the cathedral, and the multitudinous clink, clink of tools, sounding at a distance like the melodious ring of musical glasses, from cathedral *chantier*, the distant walls and the quarries in the hills. For seventy years that assault on the ears of all Paris kept up. All over France in all the great cities there was a din like this, but in Paris it was triple, coming from cathedral and towers and wall. Still, it was music to the cathedral chapter, the bishop, the king, to every Parisian worth his salt. Any one on the island wall could see rubble being poured into the shell of the cathedral, dressed stone being put in place, blocks being lifted in chains, and similar processes on the city wall in the valley or on the hills. Always they went on together, the industrial chorus of the tools on the cathedral in the half-demolished cloister, the antiphon of the machines and tools working on the wall. And the pious men of the chapter and even the king saw the walls of the invisible kingdom, represented by this beautiful cathedral, and the temporal walls of the city going up side by side in harmony, the things of Caesar not being separate from the things of God but the first guarding the others; and it was true for at least a blessed little space in this world.

The voracious demands of the Crusades for men and money might dim that seventy-year chorus a little at times, but could never stop it. Indeed, the Crusades seemed a parallel activity, a fitting accompaniment to all this building. The passing pageantry of the Crusades was reflected forever in the enduring pageantry of the glass.

Perhaps not even the king nor the bishop, certainly not the plain folk (who were getting ready for their great holiday, such a festival of giving and of work as never had been seen before), were aware of just what, historically, they were doing. But they felt it was something big in this world. And they were sure that they were building for Our Lady a house that was properly beautiful for her. Woven in with all the chivalry there was with them a tender chivalry for her.

It was at the behest of the bishop that the king himself had set aside a season for contribution and mass work on the cathedral. He had a fondness for the old man. In fact, this wise ruler particularly liked men of ability who had risen from the ranks, from the soil. And Bishop de Sulli for all his look of dignity and force had an especial tenderness for the poor. He had never forgotten what it was to plough for fourteen hours a day as a boy, and in winter to tend cattle and sheep and clean barns. One would have some idea of the man who was Bishop of Paris when the cathedral was abuilding if he had known a great recent Archbishop of Paris —the rank has been raised. Cardinal Verdier—he was made Cardinal too—who came from the crusading town of Clermont-Ferrand built in his time over two hundred churches in his Paris archdiocese and died in 1940, just two months before the Germans broke into Paris. Those who loved him were glad that he was not there when they sang the bloody Horst Wessel song under the north rose window of Notre Dame each day and also shot so many of his unarmed parishioners. Paris will not forget that strong church warrior, his sturdy walk, the broad peasant face like a rich brown farmland with wisdom and sunshine lying deep in its furrows. The eyes which saw everything burned with an inexhaustible energy and fire out of that powerful face, but they could grow very soft when the little white-robed communicants came to the altar rail in the month of Mary which we call May. The two bishops, the one of the twelfth the other of the twentieth century, were much alike in spirit and mould. The present Parisian, who has felt in his heart the warm afterglow of the presence of the one, knows what those old Parisian parishioners felt when Maurice de Sulli died.

King Philippe Auguste did not like to see the old Bishop worried. He had gone over to the building site in the half-torn down cloister a few days before. The choir, though roofless still, looked impressive enough standing at the end of the long trench excavated from the ground where the first Notre Dame and adjacent buildings had stood. Like the high stern and poop of some great beached galleon the choir seemed, the stained glass giving the bright look of old painted vessels, the first flying buttresses resembling the shores that hold up a ship.

In the interior, the arches waited for the roof. There were three tiers of colourful windows, all round-head, thoroughly Roman. For Notre Dame began Romanesque and wound up Gothic. Some of the first features would be transformed before the operation was over, but some details never. You can still see at the ambulatory turns the original Romanesque pillars. But the Gothic feeling was evident in the increase in colour, the whole spaciousness and the audacity of height attained, not yet through Gothic arches which would soon appear in the nave, but by the first flying buttresses which were as Gothic as could be.

When Philippe Auguste that day, not long after his return from the Crusade, called out the people to help on the cathedral, the choir had been well furnished with fine screen, carved canons' stalls, a high throne and many beautiful vessels. And Maurice de Sulli's friend, the Bishop of Rheims, had sent ten handsome lamps, "so that," the letter said, "the altar might be eternally lighted for the glory of God." And under the roof, first of canvas then of temporary wood, there had been some stately ceremonies in this first fragment of the cathedral. The high altar had been consecrated by the legate of Rome in 1182. In 1185 Bishop Macarius of the Holy City had preached a great crusade sermon. In 1186 a requiem mass had been celebrated for one who for centuries would lie under the high altar and who though called English was still kin of France. This was Geoffrey Plantagenet, a son of the Queen of France who had taken away from it her dowry, and on whose brothers Philippe Auguste had well revenged France. So not exactly a stranger prince nor yet a native son, this son of the wandering Eleanor was the first to be buried under the high altar of Notre Dame. That very year of this visit Philippe was making to the choir his queen Isabella, the slip of a thing who had marched barefoot through the city streets, would be buried here. You can read her name now in the quaint lettering of the dead inscribed among the carvings in the wall surrounding the choir. Strangely enough, though the choir had been consecrated, there was no ceremony for the finished pile until 1864. Kings would be crowned, queens married, princes baptized, but they overlooked the little matter of the consecration of Notre Dame for seven hundred years.

All these events had taken place under the storm-stained canvas or the unpainted wood. Surely, the Bishop had said in his sermons, it was time that this blemish over the glory of the high altar should be removed. And that day with the king he had pointed up at the place where the roof should be, then down at the great trench stretching in front of the choir awaiting the nave. So far it was filled with the great piles driven in deep, oak platforms on these and tremendous granite pier foundations. A few piers for the nave were also beginning to show above ground near the choir and down the sides. That was all they had done, he said sorrowfully to the king, in nearly thirty years. The guilds, he admitted, had been lavish, the nobles—some of them—generous. His Notre Dame chapter had poured in half of its tithes. The *écolatre* that very morning had complained that it seemed as though they were pouring all the church revenues into that great hole of a trench. Oh yes, he knew; the cost of building cathedrals and city walls at home and running crusades abroad concurrently was staggering. But none should neglect the works of God.

So the king had proclaimed a season of universal giving and work. As he stood on his tower he heard the ever-increasing clatter of the people turning out and music which was not the usual morning tattoo of the tools but of drums. Like so many brass Chanticleers trumpets greeted the dawn from the towers of the city wall. And the sun arrows struck the bright jewelled bulls'-eyes in the panes until the whole choir stood out, all a glory now, not a fragment, but itself a mighty tower in Sion.

So the king joined his queen and his train and they rode to the square to greet the people gathering in as impressive and practical a pageant as the world would ever see until the one very like it down at Chartres. From all over the plain they came, the armies of the rich, the medium-pursed and the poor, all the columns from the outlying districts to join those of city and Isle. The banners waved and the trumpets continued to play and mighty hymns in sonorous Latin went rolling up to the hills. And it was not all pageant. Every man brought what he could. The poorest came with a bottle of homemade wine, a hamper of corn at least, or carried a little kid or a ewe lamb, all for Our Lady. Here marching were not three but myriad magi, twenty thousand Gaspars, Melchiors and Balthazars—in velvets, shining mail, smocks, motley, rags— yet all magi! It was one of the most wonderful things that ever happened in this world. And it would be repeated in other cathedral cities. At its height this cathedral movement was not a fever; it was an ecstasy.

In the processions converging on the city were countless solid-wheeled, high-sided tumbrils or carts. These had been donated by the farmers and a labourers' union, the Guild of the Paris Waggoners, whose members were sworn each day to serve Our Lady and Her Son with all their might. "The Fairest Lord Jesus," they called Him as they called her "Rose and Tower of Ivory and Star of the Sea," in the hymns that swelled up to the hills. The wagons conveyed an almost incalculable weight in building stone, iron, timber and lime, with stores of lambs' quarters, slabs of beef, hams, sometimes whole steers, and corn and wine for "the labourers in the vineyard," which was now Paris Isle.

Sometimes it took as many as nine yoke of oxen to draw a single one of the carts heavily-laden with building stone. Other carts were drawn by knights and nobles who had thrown their mantles on the carts and harnessed themselves to them. The peasants and beggars did not have any fine clothes to discard, but one and all rushed into line and pulled on tongue or chain to hurry on the slower wagons. Often the rich were yoked with the very poor, sometimes even with the ragged and the thieves. Among those that first reached the bridge, Bishop de Sulli saw many he knew: a count of the realm, perhaps, whose confession of murder he had heard; some brick-kiln worker whose child he had buried; a prostitute from the darker ways. None did he upbraid. All were made pure by this service of love.

So the ragged and the rich, the virtuous and the stained, marched shoulder to shoulder or yoked to one another in the bannered, trumpeting processions that moved over the plains upon Paris. Even the little children, laughing with the joy of it, drew alongside the huge lumbering wagons, their tiny toy carts filled with pebbles in imitation of the others' building stone. And their tiny trebles joined the deep voices in the hymns that went up over the river and the hills.

Never had there been such generosity *en masse,* so much fervour, chivalry and true gentleness. Next to the Crusades, this was the greatest pageant the Middle Ages presented; and all without a trace of bloodshed. So in this hour of what might be called high but holy hilarity, Christianity seemed for once to have come to this earth, the spirit of the King to have been exemplified in that parade when for a common purpose people of high and low degree went, hand-in-hand or yoked, singing together.

Before high noon the processions had all rolled over the bridges north and south on to the island. All the people that could get into the square or the cleared spaces of the island knelt for the great outdoor mass. There had to be many priests assisting at the celebration of the mass, the bishop officiating at the high altar before the king and as many as could crowd into the choir. When he came out he passed down the line of those who had been prevented from drawing closer and who now knelt in the choked streets and even on the bridges to receive his blessing. Then one by one the carts rolled through the road the bishop had made and the waggoners, the knights and the peasants unloaded their offerings of material all around the excavations in a great line.

As the crews finished their unloading, many went into the choir and poured into the cathedral basins great amounts of gold and silver. The wealthy stripped from their persons bracelets, armlets, signet rings, and laid them on the altar. Others took their costly, elaborately-decorated mantles and cast these down around the altar so that the whole place was radiant with rainbows like those the sun intensified in the new glass just put in the windows above.

And some were just as generous, only more practical, laying on the altar deeds to quarries and privileges engraved on parchment to cut down forests for timber for the Cathedral. Even after the chants and bells had ceased, this voluntary tribute of work for God and Our Lady continued for some time.

XXIX

1196 A.D.

THOUGH A GREAT GAP HAD BEEN TORN IN THE CLOISTER, THE field of operations seemed very crowded when each morning after *Lauds* was over the clergy of the chapter of Notre Dame hurried over to see how the work was progressing. Eagerly they flocked about the bishop and the chancellor, who had been so alarmed to see the way in which their funds poured into a great hole. He was not so worried now. For in the years immediately following the great tag day, the nave walls had risen reassuringly high.

It was hard for them sometimes to get through. For the ground all around the nave and scaffolding and the finished choir was like a battlefield covered with an army of men and a Caesarian collection of engines of war engaged in a long siege. The supply system had kept up pretty well and trains of carts loaded with sand, rubble, stone, timber, continued to roll through the street cut through the houses west of the square. Flotillas of slow, snub-nosed, leather-sailed boats unloaded their limestone on the docks and quais below the wall. Like Caesar's springed catapults, winches and pulleys creaked and clanked away. Like his *ballistae* and stone-throwers, the hoisting machines groaned and shrieked and clattered as they worked with their stones, though these were not hurled to destroy but elevated to raise on high the greatest and most beautiful house of God.

Everywhere the chapter went, often with distinguished guests, archbishops, lean, brown, whipcord-faced returned Crusaders, builders from Caen, heavy-skirted and furred men from Nizhnii Novgorod or Muscovy, architects from Canterbury or Winchester, dukes, sometimes the queen, their mantles were splashed with the débris of battle. They were brown with sand, grey with concrete globules from the nave walls. And shards of rock, grains of powder from the scaffolding, chalk dust from the stained glass workers' designing tables lay on the queen's miniver-trimmed velvet mantle and the bishop's familiar old black hat.

But the men of the chapter loved every fragment of it as they loved every phase of the activity from the poorest worker's mixing of the drab concrete, to the cutting of the individual stones, the *voussoirs* they were preparing in the *chantier* back of the choir, where they still cut and dress stone today. But now they shape the great blocks that are so creamy at the start, so grey with storm and drippings after a few years, only for replacement, there being in the cathedral's as well as in the human body a constant replenishing of cells. And for every two stonecutters today there were fifty then keeping up that incessant choral of the chisels.

When with their guests, the clergy were dignified. When alone, these fine upstanding and consecrated men were actually vivacious, so happy were they over the unfolding of their beautiful cathedral dream. They often chattered as happily as do a flock of the holiest nuns when in their hour of exercise they read to each other and even play ball on the lawns of their nunneries.

The scaffolding around or under which they passed on their daily tours did not cover the whole building all at once. The Parisians were economical even then. They had to be. When they had finished a section to shoulder height, they would pull out some of the timbers called putlogs that supported the scaffold planks, from the holes in the wall section immediately below, thrust these putlog timbers in the holes cut in the section just finished and on these place the plank platforms. So they drew their supports up after them as the building rose higher, leaving below just enough scaffolding for ladder and hoisting stages. All over the cathedral, even on the west front, you can see these putlog holes cut so long ago.

All around the choir and rising nave walls were tents and huts. In some of these the master-of-works and his assistant architects worked on the plans and models. In others stained glass men bent over tables on which they outlined their designs. Others of the guild copper-wired bright panels around the iron armatures in the first windows in the choir; and everywhere their portable furnaces glowed like the watchfires of an army set to guard the cathedral.

The bishop came to know almost every worker from the mighty

men who drove the giant piles deep in the moist soil to the lead-smiths who, in the last years of his life, helped on the roof. It was the stained glass workers putting up the first glass who could never seem to leave their canvas workshops and sheds and their fires, except on holidays when the Montmartre wine, made from grapes a Roman emperor had planted, flowed too free. During part of the period of the Notre Dame operations the Chartres ateliers had the ascendancy in this field and other cathedrals ordered their glass from there, but gradually Bishop de Sulli built up a force of his own. His work would show in the following century when Paris took over the leadership in the artcraft and by 1240 furnished all the incomparable glass for the Notre Dame roses and for that lovely little shrine, Sainte Chapelle.

Never had there come to the island a gustier crew than these itinerant artists who rolled into town from time to time with their wagons piled high with household goods, portable crucibles and children and who, in spite of their devotion to their work, had given the chapter much trouble with their feuds, artistic rivalries, knifings, a drowning or two in the Seine, and babies born without banns.

The gypsy look of this crew was fitting, for it was Egypt, motherland of the gypsies, that long before Christ excelled in the making of glass, though it was the Phoenicians who discovered it. A group of shipwrecked Phoenicians found when they looked under the nitre blocks which they had rescued from their ship and on which they had set their pots, that the nitre had combined with the sand under their fires in a translucent silicate, a crude glass. This incident or accident—many inventions are little more—took place at the foot of the "Holy Headland," Mount Carmel, Elijah's retreat and the site of the ancient chapter of Hebrew monks that was the ancient forerunner of the Christian Carmelites. Very soon the Egyptians were making glass pastes, and simultaneously—for just as many inventions are accidents so they often have more than one source country—the Gauls were inlaying their weapons not only with silver, enamel and coral, but with bright glass. About the time of Christ, the Alexandrians conceived the pretty device of imbedding sheets of silver and gold leaf between plates of glass.

As eagerly as Germans now seize on basic French inventions and efficiently apply them—often to the inventors' undoing—the Romans took the craft they found flourishing in their colonies and used glass, plain and coloured, in body ornaments, villa appointments, mosaics, goblets and toilet articles. The old classic temples, as a rule, had no windows, only metal or marble skylights which gave good ventilation. The Romans had tried gypsum, mica and alabaster in windows, but in imperial times they replaced these with glass.

The Byzantines too had a rough glazing of alabaster and translucent stones, but in the early Christian era they substituted glass in their palaces and churches, with particular splendour in Sancta Sophia. The first stained glass windows really went up in the early Golden Horn churches. They were made of bright, variegated bits of glass coloured in the crucible, with framings of plaster and stone and looked like gay jewellers' trays set up on end in the walls.

The stained glass workers' guilds of Constantinople and Venice proudly carried decanters and scent bottles of exquisite workmanship in festival parades. By the fifth century they were working also in southern France, for we have a little poem written in the fourth century telling of the installation in a Lyons church of one of these Byzantine windows that looked like little treasure chests of haphazardly arranged emeralds, rubies, sapphires and topazes.

But very soon they were placing the pieces of bright glass in well-thought-out designs. There was no reason why, the bishops thought, they could not arrange these pieces to make up the figures of their heroes and place ever before the eyes of their parishioners the saints whose example they urged them to follow. They had but to call in the painter to give outline to this big red piece of glass to turn it into a robe, to that flesh-coloured piece to make it a face. Other lines could be added to indicate hair, features and, of course, the halo.

All Christendom was overjoyed when its heroes thus came alive. In 550 we watched members of the Venetian and Near Eastern guilds flocking over Saint Genevieve's Hill to put some of them up in the windows of King Childebert's, the first Notre Dame. The Parisians whose ancestors had inlaid their mansion walls with silver, decorated so exquisitely their weapons and shields, designed the helmets with the fashionable flares and made the graceful pitchers with the little horse-wreathed handles, naturally became adept pupils. France soon became so famous for its own stained glass workers that Saint Benedict—not the father of the monks but an abbot of Britain—sent over to Paris in the 670's for artisans to glaze his great new abbey.

In the Dark Ages, which after all could not have been so dark as they were painted, having their own periods of illumination, the workers began to bind the fragments of glass solidly together with lead tapings or ribbons which enabled them to make larger windows. The Pope had one or two of these windows, so leaded, set up in the first Saint Peter's for Charlemagne's coronation on that date even dull pupils remember—Christmas Day, 800. And when Charlemagne came up to Paris, flushed with his crowning and all his victories, he enriched Notre Dame with these new glowing windows, down both her sides. Also he put in on the north or landward side of Saint Etienne a long row of bright-pupiled window eyes.

Made of irregular pieces of glass these were, all deeply coloured and held together by the new lead ribbons. Naïve in composition, they still did not tell a complete story, though often they implied one in depicting the saints with significant symbols and appointments. But it was a great gallery of crude but heroic figures with all their bright-coloured parts, that hung for ages over the Seine. And there were hosts of these holy halls of fame burning themselves into the consciousnesses of the sons of men all over Europe.

Then, having their heroes on the scene, they wanted them doing things, and in the tenth century they began the bright window tales. The Church fathers had never been content with mere ornamentation. They insisted on a purpose even in their decoration. And they longed now to make their stones, their glass, into sermons, to have these windows illustrate their preachings, to emblazon the truths they were telling on the walls above the heads of the congregations for the eyes of all. It was about 988 A.D. that the first of what might be called the "illustration windows" went up in a church—Saint Remi at Rheims so unfortunately mutilated by the Germans in the First World War.

With their recent invention, the window armature which is as typical of the Gothic as the pointed arch, the flying buttress and weighted pinnacle, the stained glass workers were coming into their own. The armature of iron was set in the window opening. To its arms stretching across the window space glass panels were attached by copper wires. The new device enabled them to have larger expanses of glass than ever before.

Before the thirteenth century dawned the choir window framing was round-head and Roman as we have noted. With the century's turn, when the builders had gotten thoroughly into the feeling of the Gothic, all the windows that were going in, all the arches over the nave were made pointed. A fire, which in 1218 destroyed a portion of the cathedral as the nave was nearing completion, proved a blessing, for in the necessary reconstruction the builders decided to change the first round-head windows in the choir, made before Bishop de Sulli died, to Gothic so that they would conform to the rest of the church.

This pointed arch construction, as we shall see more exactly when we get away from these fascinating stained glass men and over on the scaffolds with the master-of-works to watch the major construction, not only resulted in higher but in much thinner walls. And this revolutionary treatment helped no one more than the man working in glass. Much of what before had been wall now would be glazed and the work of the windowmakers became almost as important as that of the masons on the piers and walls. It was this Gothic construction with the invention of the invaluable armature that enabled them to make those lofty and extensive windows and to set up high toward Heaven the splendour of the great Gothic rose.

The members of the chapter, the guests, the townspeople, even the gamins of Paris, were forever looking into the sheds at the foot of the walls where the forgemen, blowers, and designers worked in places that were oppressive in summer but comfortable in winter and always acrid with the smoke and smell of molten glass thrust into ashes and the sweat of many men working in close quarters. There was such a fascinating clutter of furnaces, smoking ashpits, designers' chalked tables, long blowpipes, crucibles with white-hot glass mush and sacks open to show river sand, metal filings, manganese, red ochre and a blue glass called "sapphire." Figures in the fire-glow, throwing distorted doubles on the wall, mixed sand and beech fern ash in the monkey pots. Others stirred in metallic oxides, manganese, thin Greek copper shavings, red ochre, Spanish iron "sparks," or blue Bohemian cobalt to give the rich blues. Newcomers were always astonished by the obedience of the molten substance. It formed a sea glowing like sun fire, but of such consistency it could be stirred, ladled or poured out. And it could be snapped from the blowers' pipe like fiery ingots.

To make the sheets, the blower picked up from the crucible an ingot, a mass of incandescent glass, and blew it into a gourdlike shape. When the bishop saw it magically transformed by the blower's lips, sometimes into flowerlike forms, he often expressed the wish that God might so breathe on some souls he knew and change them into lovelier forms for His glory.

This glowing flower or gourd the blower held near the flame until one end was melted. There appeared then in the glass an opening which was prodded by a piece of wood until it equalled the size of the blob at its widest point. The mass then at the pipe's end turned to a figure 8 and was broken off the pipe. The pipe was reheated with bits of burning glass still on it and was attached to the middle of the glass figure 8. The upper end was placed in the flame and enlarged as had been the other end. The whole was then separated from the pipe and carried to the annealing furnace. When removed from there the glass mass was flattened out.

The designer worked at a large table, one-half of which was reserved for the "cartoon" or sketch of the window under way. On the other half the pieces of coloured glass were cut with lines, arranged to match the "cartoon" alongside, then soldered and bound with lead. The designer's half of the table was covered with a cloth and sprinkled with moistened pulverized chalk. With a stylus of lead or tin he traced on this prepared surface the design for the great outer border, then the lines for the compositions in the various panels, the figures, lineaments, gowns, appointments for the little scenes making up the window. These were as simple as Elizabethan stage sets. A tree indicated a forest, a gable a house, a brace of towers a city. In the outlined segment of the cartoon, that is the sketch traced on the prepared top of the table, were inscribed numbers corresponding with a colour key and indicating the designer's chosen hues. Usually it was red for the saint's robes, yellow for his halo, carnation for his complexion, green for the earth on which he stood, blue for the sky above.

Then he added to the cartoon additional lines to indicate drapery folds, hair, beard, other details and shading, which later would be painted in enamel on the stained glass. These lines were made heavier on the cartoon with red and black.

The cartoon completed to his satisfaction, he turned to trays nearby, filled with pieces of glass of all shapes and colours. From these he selected and placed over each section of the design pieces he thought could be shaped to follow the pattern and of the colour indicated by the colour key number written on the section of the cartoon. With lead or tin he then traced on the chosen piece of glass the cartoon stylus lines below it and showing through the glass because of their red and black markings. If the piece turned out particularly dense in colour he chose another, unless he happened to admire the intensity of colour resulting from the density. He would then have to follow the minute directions in Monk Theophilus' invaluable handbook on art, and trace the cartoon lines of that section on a piece of plain glass. Then he would hold both fragments, the plain and the densely coloured one, up to the light and copy on the coloured glass the lines showing through the plain piece.

Next, the glazier would take not a diamond (a seventeenth-century device) but a red-hot iron, and cut each piece to the dimensions and shape of the corresponding pattern segment on the cartoon or to the shape necessary for its fitting in with other pieces that made up that segment. With another hot iron he would notch each piece to make the soldering easier.

Now, the pieces having been prepared and arranged like bits of a picture puzzle in their panel groups as indicated by the cartoon, the painter appeared. He first made his pigment in a little pot by mixing one-third metal filings, one-third of the blue-glass "sapphire," and one-third green glass which had been powdered on a marble slab. When the queen was a visitor, he would be polite and use for a solvent some of his noonday wine. But usually he would be economical, spare his wine and call on his urine for the mixture—so sometimes are holy things compounded of the earthy. The result was the brownish-black pigment which you see depicting detail in tens of thousands of windows all over France. And with this, using a brush of fine ass, miniver or squirrel hairs, he painted on the coloured glass fragments the lines already cut by the tin or lead stylus on them, to represent gown hems, beards, curls, eyes and shadings. If he wanted more high light he might scrape down the brown-black enamel a little to let more light through the panes.

But this painting was a supplementary and not a major operation. The rich colour of the glass came at the source, in the melting pot, the crucible. It was not something extraneous, applied on, like the enamel which added outlines. Indeed, the distinction between the real Gothic glass so coloured in the "pot" and some of the later "stained glass," which was only plain glass with scenes painted on it, was emphasized by the artisan's insisting on calling the true stained glass, that coloured in the crucible, "pot metal." The rich colour of the stained glass we see in our great and beloved cathedrals was of the essence of the glass, born with it.

The design was also primarily achieved by arranging in vivid juxtaposition the vividly hued pieces of glass. As they were truly coloured at their source, so truly the design was born of them.

The painter, however, did perform one or two services besides adding the details, outlines and some shading. His brownish-black lines sometimes subdued too rich colours; and it took figures out of the completely flat and added at least the suggestion of perspective.

The painter's work finished, the glass was turned over to the kilns for firing so that the freshly applied enamel would approach in permanence the inner staining. The different panel groups were placed in trays; and when they were removed from the fire and cooled, they were brought back to the glaziers' half of the great designing table. There the panels were made solid by soldering the pieces with ribbons or tapes of lead, and by puttying or cementing any little crevices that might be left after the soldering. With infinite care always they puttied against the rains and storms of the ages.

The Romanesque windowmen had been glazier rather than artist minded. The mechanical contrivances, the lead ribbons they introduced, had been placed simply where convenience dictated. But with the incoming of the Gothic, these lead ribbons served an aesthetic purpose as well. They still bound the pieces of glass together, but now they were utilized in the design itself. They were placed at points where they would both solder the glass and also act as outlines for the medallions or little scenes. And these or the metal armature arms might stand for the trunk of the Tree of Knowledge of Good and Evil, the mast of a ship on Galilee, the upright of Christ's cross or the curve of His body as He lay asleep in the storm. Here was a functionalism in miniature which matched that in large of the structure of the cathedral.

These adroit early Gothic artists also observed a helpful optical effect of the leads. Even more than the painter's enamel lines, the ribbons prevented too great a diffusion of the often dazzlingly brilliant colour, and the consequent muddying of the design. Even as they bound the pieces of glass together they, as it were, bound the colour in.

As they got even farther out of the purely glazier into the artistic stage of windowmaking, the Gothic designers contrived to make even the iron armature a factor in the design. They did not cast it in the same old form every time. Each was an individual problem; and they made it to fit the specific mechanical requirements of the window they were working on. And the arms of the armature—to which were attached the insoldered copper wires of the panels—were cast not in any conventional pattern but in lines, curved or straight, that would enable them to take part, like the leads, in the actual composition of the window under way. So skilled were the artisans in their arrangement, so circumambient and alive was the rich colouring that never did binding leads or iron armature arms, not even the later crossing saddle bars, cut up the composition. These mechanical helps did not, in the best windows, stand out. They actually merged in the whole lovely ensemble.

So the bishop could watch a favourite window of his going through all these processes from day to day inside the heated, acrid shed with its glowing forges, white-hot seas, gesticulating workers and distorted doubles on the wall. It delighted his heart to see a Saint Denis or Saint Peter come into being—in sections—with a robe of red, standing on green glass grass, under a blue glass sky, with a yellow halo, a white book, and brownish-pink face and hands. Then he could see him being carried out—still in sections— and up the ladder to the scaffold platform by the great window opening and there attached for the ages, by little copper wires, to the arms of the huge inset iron armature. And he would climb up himself on the ladders, outside or within, at sunset when there was a double glory in the panes and hold converse with Saint Paul and Saint Peter and Saint Denis transfigured there. Until it was too dark to see, he would study all the little heartwarming scenes and sacred stories made up of mechanical things, the chemicals and metals of the earth, but casting on the Notre Dame choir a splendour that seemed of Heaven.

Many changes in design and colour would come in the various epochs of stained glass. There were: the Romanesque, which was really the glazier's era; the Early Gothic, when the glazier began to be exalted into the artist; the Middle Gothic, when he became the supreme composite artist; the Late Gothic, when he went decorative and altogether too much so; and the Post Gothic, when he lost his soul and became a mere enamelling hack. Through all these we must never lose sight of the two salient characteristics of the great glass. The first was that this magnificent feature was due to the Gothic construction which substituted walls that were light, seemingly fragile but eternal and very lofty, for the old low, thick walls of the Romanesque and so could turn over much of the wall space to glass.

The second truth was that in the truly Gothic glass the colour was its ingrained character, its very soul, and in itself contributed to the design. When the Post Gothic—and some of our Victorian designers in our last century churches painted plain clear glass and called it stained—they lost light, since enamel is apt to flake off and lets distracting light through. And also they lost the very soul attached to stained glass when it is born. As one cannot cork up a Caucasian into the true Othello he cannot enamel glass into the glorious things that bring Heaven and tears to the eye, exaltation and joy to the heart.

The Early Gothic windows were almost always made up of little scenes. When once in a while they experimented with large figures, these covered a third of the glass and they usually were placed in the triforium or high in the transept wall where they felt the beautiful smaller medallions would lose their effect. The typical twelfth-century window was composed of these little medallions, square, circular or quadrefoil, framing the little sets. The detail, though colourful and charming, was of the scantiest. A stalk represented a garden, an arch a palace. If there was any story sequence it was developed across or down the window. Between each bright little scene was some fine harmonious patterning, and the ensemble was framed in a decorative border. And the whole background was of crimsons and blues which in certain lights seemed even more brilliant and intense than the hues of the little serial stories.

Saint Bernard, the conscientious and great but austere, frowned on colour. He had his designers evolve a black and white or greyish white patterning to cover his windows entire in his great Cistercian abbey chain. This *grisaille*, though bits of it were used by later schools, was but rarely employed by the twelfth-century men.

And the later "white" never appeared. Fifteenth-century designers used "white" and a silvery wash to add a silvery look to their panes; but the earlier and greater designers disdained it. One would have said that these first Notre Dame designers rioted in those twelfth-century crimsons and particularly the blues which were rarely afterwards equalled and never surpassed, were it not for their superb control of taste and leads. You can see an especially beautiful example down at Chartres in the window appropriately called "Our Lady of the Beautiful Glass." The brilliance of those early hues made the first fragment of Notre Dame, the sanctuary choir, fairly glow, but those bright panes vanished with the fire of the next century to be replaced by glass of that time which had its own unique loveliness. The glory of the twelfth was the charm and composition of the little scenes and the rare quality of the blues and crimsons. It seemed as though the glass of that age was tinctured with the blood of Christ and shot through with the hope expressed by that heavenly blue.

In the thirteenth century they went in for the larger figures, before only tentatively tried. There were fewer now of the little scenes. These were usually relegated to the border. Scenes more elaborate than those with heroic figures covered more panes of glass than heretofore. Their use of the armature arms and of the lead ribbons was more skillful. Also they invented the "traceried window," by dividing a great window expanse with slender stone bars as in English mullioned windows. You can still see some fine traceried windows in Chartres and high in the Notre Dame transept walls under the great south and north rose. In these the delicate stone bars divide and do not blur, nay, even unite the hues and panels and component designs of these great round rainbows. If the blue of the twelfth century was never matched, the thirteenth achieved a divine violet. It was really an overtone. Though emeralds, yellows, browns, carnations might appear, the prevailing crimsons and blues were placed in such adroit juxtaposition that their interplaying refractions produced the most entrancing purples and violets that were the great characteristics of thirteenth-century glass. Unforgettable examples you will find in Amiens and Chartres, the Saint Denis north rose, at Bourges and the Tours choir, and in perhaps the most priceless jewel of all, the little sister of Notre Dame, Sainte Chapelle. There, with the great expanse of glass, they seem to have turned the whole stone shell into a heavenly garden of violets clambering up on delicately hued trellises. And one does not need to go further than our own Notre Dame. He can just stand in the crossing and look down the nave at the west rose in which much thirteenth-century glass survives, or up at the great north rose with its lovely blues, purples, and mauves.

One can perhaps overlook the later improvements, which were often degradations, of the glass and with which we at the building of Notre Dame have so little to do. The complete secret of the great glass of those centuries was to be lost, though part of it would be discovered again when modern designers would stop all senseless stippling and use of *grisaille* and white and especially the violating painting and enamelling of glass, and get back to the heart of the matter. And this was that stained glass must *be stained,* that the richness of the old glass was primarily in its own heart, in the colour with which it was born, and the skillful placing of all the hues in striking relationships.

Another part of the secret was that the mediaeval glass gained much of its beauty through its very shortcomings. Through its flaws it became flawless. The very naïveté of foreshortening, the early lack of perspective, the odd turn of a neck on a haloed saint's body, added an adorable artlessness to an amazing artistic skill and integrity. And there was marvellous ingenuity that was both mechanical and aesthetic, in their use of binding leads and armature arms as lines in the design.

But that is not all. The heart-warming, matchless loveliness of the twelfth- and thirteenth-century glass comes in part from the very inequalities of it, from manufacturing mistakes, from the use of pieces of glass which modern efficiency would reject but which not only blend in but lend additional beauty. These imperfections contribute to the whole perfection: The difference in intensity of hue in pieces of glass out of the same crucible. The chemical impurities—greater then than now. The frequent fogs, streaks, cloudinesses, and the very bubbles in the panes. The usually deplored, unforgiveable soft particles which, when pitted by time and weather, let in lights supposed to be treacherous and ruinous but which add beauty. And even the black cobwebs and lichens that took root in the bright panes.

It was very often the things which ordinarily would have been considered drawbacks that combined to make the Early Gothic's window's ineffable loveliness. They formed new depths, made new intensities, added variety, created an infinite number of new shades and tones, shot the whole window full of lights, multiplied the interplaying refractions. And they brought, with the new high lights, more richly complementing shadows and a fresh brilliance and lustre, a deeper mystery and meaning to the whole. As though by some uncanny magic, they turned the window into a miraculous, gorgeous maze for the eye and yet never confused its fascinating, enchanting design. So accident, turned to magnificent account, and the very primitiveness of device, with infinite pains and ingenuity and love and the true artistic spirit placed these windows of a naïve believing age beyond the matching by artists with all the tools, sophistication and accretion of knowledge of the ages.

When Bishop Maurice de Sulli stood on the scaffold, high over the kindling red forges, the sheds and tents of these vivid personalities, his stained glass workers, and saw his windows, panel by panel, being attached to the iron armatures of his choir, that bright glass symbolized for him something precious: Christ's kingdom and His Church. As the glorious Gothic window was through its very imperfections made perfect, so the Church made up of fragment souls of all forms and sizes and colours and with flaws and faults innumerable was bound into a perfect and glorious whole and immortally illuminated by His love shining through.

XXX

Ancient Saint Etienne Church comes alive again. . . . The Tent of the Master-of-Works. . . . The Gargoyle-Maker and the Wife of the Designer of the Our Lady's Window. . . . The Great Wood Model of Notre Dame. . . . The Six Spires that never went up. . . . The Fire of the Four Thieves that consolidated the Gothic. . . . Bishop de Sulli bequeathes a Lead Roof. . . . The Secret of the Gothic. . . . The Long Trail to the Pointed Arch and the Search for a Method of Construction of a Higher, Lighter, Better Illuminated and More Beautiful Church. . . . The Utility, Beauty, Functionalism and the Perfection of the Anatomy of the Gothic Cathedral.

1196-1218 A.D.

ACH MORNING FOR YEARS BISHOP MAURICE DE SULLI WOULD rise to the matutinal chorus of the chisels in the cathedral *chantier* and the antiphon of the tools in the hills at work on the city wall. His devotions and little excuse for a breakfast over, he would often go out from the bishop's palace, which was in the rear of Saint Etienne and also against the island wall, and take the crenelled walk on top of the wall, gazing Psalmist-fashion at the hills and then at the rising nave of his cathedral. Dear as that was to him, he had not lost his affection for Saint Etienne, which had always been called "the Old Church" even when Childebert's Notre Dame was up, and had now seen eight centuries pass, most of them filled with service. Its old window eyes, so long blank and dim with the grime and cobweb cataracts of the ages, had been brightly alive ever since old Notre Dame had gone down. It seemed to have taken a new lease of life just before it was to pass on forever. As those eyes sparkled with a new light, its voice, the old great bell, rang with a new vigour. It was a going church once more, celebrating mass and all the offices. There were other chapels, Saints Nicholas, Jean, Michel, the one falsely called Denis' prison, and quite a crowd of them on the island, but Saint Etienne was the pro-cathedral while the cathedral was abuilding and for the last years of its grand old life. In passing, the old man would often place his hand affectionately on its apse which also served as a turret for the city wall. It had indeed served God well.

He would make his way then to the great tent which stood at the foot of the wall, stained from the storms of many years. That old tent was to stay there for three-quarters of a century all told— from the time of the beginning of the excavating to the finishing of the towers. And either that or a canvas successor or a later rough one of unpainted wood was there when the work on the transept started in 1257. Not in any palace of a beautifully furnished architect's office like those of today but in the Nazareth of a humble old tent was conceived and matured the beauty that is the cathedral's.

Such was the office of the master-of-works of Notre Dame and the cathedral *chambre aux traits* or designing and draughting room. And here as well as in the temporary chapter room in old Saint Etienne and in the bishop's palace were settled matters of feuds, labour and wages. The chief architect, the master-of-works, did not attend to the last; he himself received his stipend; and the paymaster was a canon of the chapter. Occasionally there was a little trouble about wages, in times of depression that went with the Crusades, two of which, the Third and Fourth, came in the reign of Philippe Auguste, before the towers were up. But for most of the period of the cathedral's construction, there was a fine feeling due to the religious fervour and the hand-in-glove relationship of the communes and a wise king.

Still, there were always domestic matters, festival inebrieties and knifing affrays, such as that we shall relate, of the gargoyle maker and the designer of a beautiful madonna window, for some of these stonecutter-sculptors were almost as gusty as the glass men who followed the craft started by the Egyptians. There was one stonecutter who was given to alternate spates of passion and spells of sullenness and who looked as though he had come from his own hand, so greatly did he resemble one of the gargoyles he turned out. He was trying to force himself on the wife of the designer of the madonna window. Though one really did not need any model for the lovely form which he limned with his gown crimsons and blues and carnation and brown outline pigment for the face, he swore sometimes that his wife was the model. She was pure and lovely; and it was a question which, wife or madonna window, was the designer's chief delight.

Though she had resented the gargoyle maker's uncouth advances she did not inform her husband, fearing lest he should have murder on his hands, and so near a cathedral. But at last the rumours running through the artisans' tents around the cathedral works and in other quarters where the men were housed came to the designer's ears. So the madonna maker went to kill the maker of gargoyles in the *chantier*. Now had it been brought to their attention, either the chapter or the guild which had high standards for conduct, would have settled the matter. But in the tumult and surprise of the attack, the fellow-workers of the culprit, gathering around him not through any love for such a disagreeable rascal but through the primitive desire to defend one of their own craft from an attack by one of another, prevented the designer from getting his revenge.

He then visited the poison of his wrath on the innocent wife. The gargoyle maker disappeared for a time, but it seemed as if his sullenness and evil disposition had been transferred into the stained glass man. His fellows working at the crucibles, in the banked ashes, with all the sacks of materials, or at the designing tables, were able to do nothing with him. He kept to his dark moods and would not touch stylus or glass, lead or oxide, or miniver brush. Then one night he seized a hammer, and in a sudden mad fit shattered the chief panels of the lovely, almost-finished Our Lady window.

Now the ugly gargoyle maker could not stay away from the city torches and the forge fires of the cathedral—or perhaps it was from the bright eyes of the coveted wife. And the designer came upon the thieving man who looked so like his own work as he crept back in the dark to his old haunts in the cathedral precincts. And there, back of the bishop's palace by the island's upstream end where the nineteenth-century Morgue of Paris would be, the madonna maker threw the sculptor of gargoyles into the Seine.

It was then he swore—and all the men in the settlement of tents and huts, up on the ladders, high in the scaffolding, at the forges, on the carts and barges, and their women, believed him—that Our Lady herself appeared and waved toward the drowning man. Repentant, the stained glass maker leaped into the river and bore his enemy to the shore, near the spot where Julien le Pauvre, the ferryman, had landed the Christ he did not at first recognize. So the breach between husband and wife was healed and the Our Lady window bloomed with its rich crimsons, flowerlike yellows, refreshing greens, and heavenly blues, more beautifully than had the window he had shattered.

The stained tent, the *chambre aux traits*, of Notre Dame was for the Ile de France and cities beyond its borders a place of pilgrimage. Within, among the inkpots, quills, designing tables and ground plans and elevations on parchment yellowed and smudged with many thumb-prints, was the object of the pilgrimage. It resembled the later houselike shrines for relics, for it was a *molle* or model of wood, the cathedral in miniature. On it were visible all the details of the cathedral in scale. One could see features in advance of their incorporation outside. Others one could look at, in miniature in wood, and then go outdoors and see them magnified many times and embodied in the stone flesh of the cathedral. Or one could take in the whole finished ensemble of the *molle,* then go outdoors and in fancy add to the mass of the cathedral which was already constructed the rest of it—with upper galleries and colonnades, *flèche* and angels they had seen foreshadowed on the model; raise it even higher toward Heaven.

It was fascinating, that model. It would be priceless could it be found today. Among the pilgrims who had stood before it—and there were as many as ever circled through ambulatory to pay honour to a saint or in modern times to visit a Noel crèche in the apse—were kings, prime ministers, archbishops, cardinals, legates from Rome. Building bishops, guests of Maurice de Sulli, from Sens, Laon, Senlis, who were also putting up cathedrals, had examined it with admiration, piety and curiosity, also with an eye for ideas, borrowing some and repaying in kind—and then there would appear changes on the *molle.* A Bishop de Sulli, no kin of the bishop of Paris, made quite a visit in the bishop's palace and the tent, getting ideas too, but adding to them, for he would give to his smaller but beautifully glazed cathedral of Bourges five great portals instead of three.

Crusaders returning from the Third Crusade, which was in part consecrated and in part commercial, and from the Fourth, in which the politics sadly overbalanced the piety, would come into the tent, lean and brown and fit or white and wounded, with red crosses on the surcoats over their chain mail or with armour doffed for civilian mantles. And they would point out resemblances between features on the model and things they had seen in the East, exclaiming particularly over the rich colour in the glass of the windows outside. If they but infrequently gave practicable ideas, the net result of their testimony combined with that of returning bishops was some remodelling of the *molle.*

Ploughboys from the Grenelle grain fields, shepherds like those who had long ago come into a cave stable, would be admitted into the tent to see the cradle of the cathedral. Often, too, there appeared some one of Philippe's queens, who paid the little cathedral their homage if they gave no architectural notions. They were a curious three, Philippe Auguste having been as unlucky in love apparently as he had been fortunate in matters of state and war. The first was the little slip of a thing, Isabella, whom his conduct —inspired not by cruelty *per se,* but by reasons of state—had forced to walk barefoot through the streets. At nineteen she died in childbirth. The second was Ingebourg of Denmark who so well symbolized her cold north on the critical wedding night that in the morning he had said good morrow to her, as he thought, for good. The third, Agnes, the Church would not let him keep, naturally under the circumstances, and he took back the cold blonde Dane in name only, for he kept her in prison for quite a period. So it was only at intervals that these three queens would visit the old tent and toss at the puzzled bishop and master-of-works their questions, which might be prettily put but showed no mechanical bent or engineering understanding.

One great abbot, Robert de Thorigny, made the trip to that tent all the way from Brittany, to see if this cathedral could possibly match the marvel the Benedictines put up on Mont Saint Michel off the Breton shore. He stood a long time before the half-finished nave and the choir, and then before the *molle*.

"It is very beautiful," he said, awed, to his host, Bishop de Sulli. "And I venture to say that if you do carry this plan out, if when erected the rest of the cathedral turns out like what you have already up and also here, *in parvo*, in this model, there will be nothing in the whole world to equal it in splendour."

The most frequent visitor to the tent was the old bishop himself. With powder on his soutane, debris on his old black hat, he would often stick his head in the tent and remain there to study the *molle* and to discuss changes and building problems with the master-of-works, from the hour when the stars first glimmered in the pale twilight blue until they were swallowed up by the onrush of the gold of the sun rising over the Seine. For in the year 1196 he had a premonition that after all he who had started the great enterprise would be the Moses, not the Joshua of the cathedral. Only from the Nebo of the island wall, he was sure now, would he gaze into the Promised Land of the finished towers and many-ton bells and forest of timbers and the cross on high of the completed Notre Dame. And, if resigned, it made him also at times a little wistfully melancholy. And he would gaze long into the heart of that *molle*.

So many changes he had seen come and go in it. If there were features that appeared there long in advance of their reproduction in the body of the cathedral, there were others that appeared in the wood which because of change in style or policy, would never be cut in stone. The most striking instance was that of the high spires. They were complete and graceful then in the wood, one each for the twin towers and the transepts, and a great sky-scaling one for the central crossing. We are sure of what they would have looked like when actually up, for Viollet-le-Duc, who fancied the idea, gave us a carefully arrived at sketch of them in the days of his repairing of Notre Dame, cut short when the Germans besieged Paris. He entered service and with the rest dined first on horse, then zoo, finally rat meat, and not always even on these in the Franco-Prussian War.

These lofty and beautiful needles would have been a sensational thing in Christendom; but Notre Dame would not have been our Notre Dame. The façade, the great west front as it is now, is not overshadowed. The beautiful relationship of the fine horizontal bands of king row and colonnades with the splendid rose and the broad vaulted windows between to the four upsweeping vertical buttresses, the feeling of graciousness, of infinite serenity given by the whole, have not now been spoiled by overstriving. As it stands this mother of cathedrals seems anchored to earth, yet its eye-inviting lines lead up toward Heaven without assaulting it by any such gigantic galaxy of spires. The thirteenth and the fourteenth centuries were well advised when they failed to put them up. The gifted Viollet-le-Duc was wise like them when he stopped with putting the heads on the guillotined kings in the façade row, restoring the gargoyles to the upper stories, mending the saints, repairing the great bruised roses and other like healing things for Notre Dame. To have gone on with those spires after seven centuries would have been to commit the boastful sin of Babel.

And there were features which the bishop did not see either in *molle* or cathedral proper, but which later were incorporated. The *molle* too began with round windows in the choir. It would take that curious fire, not of the two but of the four thieves, to put them there. In 1218 that would come when a quartette of precious vagabonds (like Villon's own, of a later century, who robbed the Church of Navarre) made a burglarious entry into the cathedral and started that before alluded-to but never-described conflagration. Construction, of course, was still going on and they, eluding the night watchman, climbed the scaffolding to the forest of timbers over the nave vaulting and crept along to the vaulted ceiling over the choir. From an aperture they dropped a rope with a noose to the high altar to snare the exposed sacred vessels. But they knocked some candles over, the tapestries or altar cloth caught fire and the whole choir was gutted. The one fragment of his planned cathedral which de Sulli had seen completed was transformed—with the exception of those pillars at the ambulatory turns—into pure Gothic. By a strange coincidence, a fire purged Sens and made her too Gothically "whole."

Well the Bishop remembered the delight with which after a season of work the *chambre aux traits* had turned out a new *molle*. The very first morning he had seen it on the table with the heavy trusses, he had looked through the model's open and unglazed windows, absolutely entranced. Though the choir had been left as it had been for the time, all the nave windows and all the vaulting, all the portals of the west front and the two great side windows there had been given pointed arches. It seemed to him as though the whole of that miniature cathedral had been lifted up, such an extraordinary effect had been produced by the incorporation of none but pointed arches in the whole nave body. As he had glanced down at those phalanxes of arches, seeming even in that miniature to be marching toward him, he had had the feeling of one suddenly coming on a breath-taking, a heavenly view from some mountaintop. And though he and the whole chapter were familiar with the tentative Gothic of Saint Denis, he rushed over and dragged them all out, then the king and the queen, to see the magical transformation. Where before had been the settled feeling, the reliability, the wise-seeming serenity of the old Roman arch there was now the excitement, the uplift, the climb, the aspiration of the Gothic arch. The Indian builder had said, "The pointed arch never sleeps." It is infinitely more true of the broken one. Restless, striving as it is, it produces dreams of Heaven.

The premonition of Maurice de Sulli, bishop of Paris, was not vain. After 1196 they did not see in *chantier* or choir the sturdy walk of the fields, the broad powerful peasant features with the great dark eyes burning out of them. The old leader never lived to get over into the Promised Land of his cathedral. He was not even buried in it, but in a cemetery across the river.

Even in death he was helpful to the cathedral of which he had been prime mover. When they opened his will they found a provision for the lead roof he had wanted for his choir. It had not yet replaced the canvas or temporary wood roof; the funds of the picturesque mass tag day had been devoted to the hurrying on—if the term can be applied to a process that took so many years—of the nave. The bequest was a hundred pounds—more than the king had spent on an entire new roof for old Notre Dame, and this was only for the choir. He had been generous to his love. In purchasing power that hundred was equal to fifty times that sum today.

The little model had been a gauge of the cathedral's progress and a log of the great Gothic tide. It is perhaps wise now to look a trifle more closely into the secret of the Gothic, though very swiftly, if we want to see swinging down that nave the king's bloody, battered, bannered army from Bouvines Battle—it is just around the corner. Stirring will be that march but equally fascinating, even to those professing themselves of little mechanical understanding, should be a swift review of the march of the pointed arch. There is not only history but sheer poetry in it.

For that key to the Gothic was not only a symbol in architecture but one of other and very great things that were happening then to men. The very word Gothic, invented later by an obtuse Raphael, connotes much more than a style of building more handsome and elevated and inspiring than any ever conceived and the longest building boom in history. Like the steam engine later, it was tied up with the whole progress of the race.

Other races have had their high towers. Babel thrust hers up in insensate ambition. The hanging gardens of Babylon, the pyramids, were reared to parade the pride not of nations but of kings, the Roman landmarks to feed both. The Greek temple was admirably devoted to Reason, the skyscraper to Enterprise. The Gothic men in a vast mass achievement raised their cathedral for the use of all men, the rich and the poor, and to a very personal God.

The Gothic came in gradually. We have seen its birth at Saint Denis. We should, for a moment, glance back over the long trail. If a line could have been threaded through all the first broken arches in the world, it would have formed a cat's-cradle design covering many countries. One was used long ago in an Assyrian drain. In little Oise churches near Paris, it was tried out to solve difficult passage problems. Cluniac men constructed a porch with it in the Crusaders' church at Vézelay. Saint Denis, as we know, brought it into multiple life. But if the pointed arch was the discovery of one man, its first effective wholesale use can be credited to the French, particularly to geniuses in its heart, the Ile de France.

This is not surprising to any realizing *the creativeness of a people who have done so many things first, even if their foes, borrowing their inventions, have applied them better en masse*. Theirs, for a few examples, were the first soap, bathtub, coulter plough, piston, piston-and-cylinder engine, bayonet, manufactured pencil and paper, rayon, photograph, photofilm, double exposure, parachute, balloon flight, automobile that went, gas engine, heavier-than-air flight—yes, in an aeroplane that flew a decade before the Wrights, and machine gun in a plane. And theirs too, were the first development of barometers, sane surgery, practical tourniquets, electromagnetism, the earliest analysis of what fire truly is, chemical affinities, the pioneer blueprint of evolution, of the use of mechanized divisions, though in a book, and the first marvellous forays into the kingdom of germs. Hundreds of other first steps in science, education, general knowledge and art instantly spring to mind, so many of them achieved like most of the above when tools, processes, laboratories and books were infinitely fewer than now. The names of these pioneers are not for this but for another journey to the Seine, in another year when we may see Napoleon busily handing out little ribbons to as great a galaxy of geniuses as was ever gathered together. The point here is that it was natural that a race of so constructively fertile an imagination should have been the first to realize the possibilities of the broken arch so long in gestation. As God made out of the rib of man the complex and beautiful entity woman so these builders of Paris and the Ile de France caused to spring out of the arch rib the complex and beautiful world of the Gothic.

Now this pointed arch, in combination with the Romanesque vaulting, which we will glance at swiftly, was the secret of the Gothic. This combination formed a new solution of the weight and roof problem which is what all architecture in essence is. As the master-of-works of Notre Dame told the three queens and the visiting bishops, Notre Dame did not begin down on the ground as they thought it did but in the air, with its roof.

The first man near Eden tied saplings together for walls and roof. The Dordogne man put one stone on two, the Nile man one palm beam over two, and so arrived at the first post-and-lintel, or when multiplied, the column-and-lintel construction for the temple. The bamboo shoots he saw flowering he copied at his column tops for the first decorated capitals. The Greek split the lintel into the famous three all learn in school—architrave, frieze, and cornice —and added finesse, fluting his columns and bowing them out for perspective. His temple was exquisite but built on a rock shelf, a one-storey affair, a pocket-size cathedral.

Rome, with wealth of slaves and material, went in for size, huge monoliths, the heaviest of walls, colonnades and domes on high. She kept in the main to the column and lintel construction but borrowed the round arch from Etruria and her colonies, calling it her own. Already the Armenians in building up had projected their inner bricks one over the other, cantilever fashion, so narrowing in an arch to the top. Rome was the first great builder to use the arch extensively. But no matter how majestic the results, it almost seemed as though these heavyweight champions of builders succeeded chiefly through main strength and awkwardness. In vaulting over spaces they placed for centering or temporary support huge trusses, heavy planks on these, covered the planks with courses of two foot bricks, slewed in on the bricks many layers of their famous concrete. The Byzantine builders, while devising new decorative tricks, structurally copied Rome. They multiplied domes and half domes and further complicated the weight and roof problem. Men still must rely on huge pillars, heavy walls and masses of concrete.

The western designers of Romanesque churches, all of which had main characteristics in common, though they might show prominent regional variations, foreswore domes and monoliths and were less interested in sheer strength and height. Borrowing basilica features, they moulded these, added to them and turned out the building all think of as the typical church of the West until the Gothic came in, and in many places even after that. The Gothic men took over portals, clerestorey, transepts, apse, vertical buttresses, later chapel ring, and the nave-aisle-choir-gallery plan, then lightened and brightened the whole and raised the magically transformed church nearer Heaven.

But the Romanesque men had helped in the solution of the weight and roof problem with their transepts and vertical buttresses in the wall bays, also by experimenting in vaulting. They were particularly adept where the Romans had been fumbling, in the groining, where half barrel vaults met at the crossing of nave and transepts, and at all vaulted passage curves and ambulatory turns. Handling of the variously shaped, usually elliptical planes in such places requires great skill; their treatment is particularly difficult where the intersecting vaults are of different diameters. The Romanesque groining was much smoother in appearance and stronger than that of Roman halls, but still it looked heavy. There was but one thing that could transform it. Everyone in France was searching for it. It was something that had been discovered and lost more than once, that had been tried out and been discarded. The late Romanesque men at Pavia, Pisa, particularly those at Caen, had all almost stumbled on it again when they experimented with diagonal arches. As we noted at the dedication of Saint Denis, the Caen men conceived, if they did not give birth to the Gothic. When Suger pointed the arches up in his choir vault bays, the long search was over.

But there would have been no search, had there been no need. The new style is always born of necessity. All France had been shouting for vaster halls. The kings wanted larger audiences for proclamations, crusade sermons, the communes for their propaganda; and the clergy longed for greater congregations for their masses and *Te Deums*. How great may be guessed from the figure set first—eight thousand for Notre Dame in Paris—which was actually increased on its completion to ten thousand when the triforium galleries were thrown open.

To enclose in the old way such vast auditorium spaces as were now demanded would require more labour, stone and carts than were at the disposal of the builders of the Ile de France. The people had begun to consider their churches too low, thick and dark. Their walls had been siege-thick not only for support but for defense in disordered times. Conflagrations resulting from carelessness and from Norman fiery arrows had destroyed many wooden church roofs. They had begun to add more permanent ones of lead and stone in Romanesque times; and that had called for more weight and even thicker walls. A construction as strong as the old, yet lighter, was needed for permanent and fireproof roofing.

In spite of all the candles and the improvement in stained glass, the Romanesque naves, even of such beautiful churches as Saint Trophime at Arles and Notre Dame of Poitiers, did not have the light for which people longed in this age that was itself a spring-time. To get the increased light they would have had to build higher and to pierce their walls with more windows and so would have dangerously weakened the walls. These would have bulged and buckled. The old enemy, weight, would have conquered. For more height, light, audience space, better roofing, the old Romanesque would not do. But given new life it would serve. Its men had ably handled the groining and had done much to develop the ogive (the diagonal rib). The broken arch gave that life and resilience to the mother Romanesque. This Gothic feature, with the flying buttress and the help of the old features, solved the old roof-and-wall, the eternal weight problem. Where the Greeks had gracefully com-promised with gravity and the Romans had ostentatiously fought it, the ingenious Gothic builder tamed and used it for his own purposes.

The broken arch was stronger than the old Roman arch that had seemed so impregnable. At the same time it was more malle-able. It could be raised or lowered; its angle could be changed, its sides set at different angles. It could solve any intersection or aisle turn, make discordant vault sections symmetrical. This was a joy to the architect. The principle of perfect balance could be applied throughout. The frame of arch ribs was set up first. They sprang across space, in power and grace, from "springers" or solid take-offs in the pillar tops. Since the angles of the pointed arches could be changed, while the diagonals stayed semi-circular, as we saw at Saint Denis, all the arch summits down the long nave were in beautiful alignment.

On each strong elastic frame, the web or vaulting fabric was set, and direct. For support a few thin planks, soon withdrawn, would do. For the wedge-shaped stones, the *voussoirs*, fitted into and interlocked with each other. The Romans and Romanesque men had applied the passive resistance of their dead walls and inert pillars and abutments to the active thrust down and out of vault and roof and integers above. To this active thrust the Gothic builder opposed the very active resistance of all his very lively but integrated pointed arches and their allies; and here was all the difference in the world. Every stone in the vault was by weight and counterweight, thrust and counterthrust shot home and locked in. The whole structure aloft and all around was full of potential dynamite. Every unit had been ready to kick out and explode.

What the Gothic builders had done was to gather up all these stone rebels and out of disunity to create eternal union. Each stone, contrary striving, helped to support others in place as interlocked wrestlers uphold their opponents.

The gigantic pressure of Notre Dame's metal roof, towers, flèche, dormers, the timbers below, the ceiling and all the stones up aloft with their combined tendency to kick out, would have settled down crushingly on the old piers, walls and vertical buttresses. Now the devastating force is held in, controlled every inch of the vaulted way, and is beautifully distributed through arch, light pillar to the foundations, or channelled off sideways through aisles and flying buttresses into the earth outside. Yet the combined weight of all these arch frames and the component stones in lofty Notre Dame is only a part of what the tonnage of a much lower church, old style, would have been. It was light, elastic, and as man goes, eternal.

If one goes by the chair with the back charred from the Commune of 1871, where the skull-capped gardien has tickets for the Notre Dame treasury and all its relics, coronation robes and jewels, and around by the great side wall of the choir with its serial stories of man in wood carvings, he can observe how great was the amenability of the pointed arch. It would slant, bend, stand up or lie down at the builder's bidding. He could actually distort planes at will and make possible and pleasing a combination of surfaces that seemed geometrically impossible. This Bishop de Sulli's men did in the early finished ambulatory at the turns. In Roman hands, the many planes coming together at these junctures would have shown up as weak and awkward. The Notre Dame men made smooth ensembles of these variously shaped planes. They are visual delights and at the same time nerve ganglia of great strength.

The succession of circling arches in these rounded ambulatories, through which pilgrims once passed singing and cardinals and archbishops march in sacred feastday processions still, are a constant delight. The arched vistas of the aisles stretching past the gold and vermilion plaque to the British soldiers and by many saints' side chapels are grey and cool with an immemorial look, and ever seem to call down on the gazer the peace of past ages.

But the greatest uplift comes to one who stands, as Bishop de Sulli who never entered his Promised Land could not do, in the crossing near the lovely Our Lady of Paris, south, and the white Jeanne d'Arc on the west, and lifts his eyes, first to the two great transept roses and then to the upper ranges of the stone forest above. There on high ranges one sees the series of bays or vaulted sections, each containing its set of archribs and stone-composed planes and each spanning a tremendous space and doing it lightly.

The clerestorey windows thrust their pointed tops up between the lower side planes of these bays. The arches spring from pillar tops at the sides of these windows and curve toward the summits of the bays, the diagonals meeting in the centre of its bay, there to be knotted with a stone flower. If one goes to the portal or the west organ loft he sees long ranges of pillar tops, of window heads, of bays, and dominating all, the ranks of arches marching—for the Gothic arch is ever on the move—in an awe-inspiring procession from the purple and crimson rose window west over the organ loft to the great bay of eight planes at the sanctuary's end, above the high white altar and its guarding angels.

There are two features which, as you sit there, you should especially note. The first is the series of nave pillars that seem light for their burden, which they can carry only through this Gothic scheme. Their capitals look as though Bishop de Sulli's master-of-works started out to make them Romanesque like those at the ambulatory turns. However they are not inharmonious but very gracious there; and they are particularly appropriate in the great cathedral that started out old style and wound up so gloriously in the new, showing others the way.

And there are the two tremendous piers at the entrance to the nave. They are the only truly massive objects in the whole pile and uphold the organ loft and the mighty towers. Each is fifty feet around and is made of "drums," or solid slices of stone. Yet with their cluster outlines they are as graceful as the most delicate pillars and show what the Gothic men could do when they chose, making even such colossal factors seem gracious and light with all their strength.

One salient and superb characteristic of this God-given new style is everywhere evident, and that is that the skeleton, the anatomical workings of the cathedral, are not as they were in the old imperial Roman structures, concealed or elaborately dressed over. All stand out in the open, unabashed, even exulting in their functional perfection and the beauty of their naked grace. Everywhere joyously uncovered are vault joints and hips, roof vertebrae, apse coccyx, archribs, flying buttress feet. The cathedral's body should be a delight to the sculptor as well as to an architect, indeed to everyone with a spark of poetry in his soul. It has a body perfect in form, function, articulation. Even without its chapel ring— which serves a purpose too—its corona, its glorious windows, it would be breath-takingly beautiful for its admirable fitness for its objective, its resilience, integrity, its purity and simplicity through its perfect union of all complexities and its sheer beauty of line.

And nowhere in this architectural exposure is there an overdone, overweighty unit to be seen. Everything is lightness combined with strength. Even when you are amazed by the size of those piers, the flying buttresses, they never appear obtrusive. The cloak of grace seems to have been thrown over their obviously necessary power. The flying buttresses might appear as excrescent as scaffolding had not their tremendous objective been displayed with such sincerity. It was a daring conception to reveal these very evident shorers-up so boldly. It was a triumph to make them seem as indispensable to the cathedral's personality as they are to its staying up. And they are very beautiful as well as impressive, those ranks of mighty stone dragons or winged stone horses seen from the cathedral gardens, the Archbishop's bridge or the quais up the Seine.

As we stand on those quais and get those inspiring long-range exterior views from different angles upstream or sit entranced and worshipful within, we should ever keep in mind the fact that all these features, even those which seem designed for mere ornament, are structural factors, born of necessity. The gargoyles carry their messages of humour, grotesquerie, and moral warning, also carry off rainwater, thus obviating the need of visible leaders or downpipes which might corrode and disintegrate the walls. This architectural frankness again is admirable. The handsome exterior moulding also prevents water from dripping down, staining and pocking the Parisian limestone—though it must be said that this stone wears very well and has the peculiar quality of hardening with time.

The vertical buttresses add an impressive effect. They mark on the outside the inner division of the aisles and the bays. They also frame the stained glass windows set in the bays and give scale to the whole edifice by stressing to the eye the length and breadth and height of the cathedral. Nothing has been forgotten. Yet all this is a lovely, if designed, by-product. Primarily the buttresses are mighty columns designed to bear their share of that weight-thrust and burden.

It is so with many other familiar features. The apse is rounded out into beauty with a chapel, but it permits masses, baptisms, weddings, requiems, to go on simultaneously and throngs of pilgrims to circle through the ambulatory. We have noted the double purpose the transept serves. The superb galleries of the triforium allowed many a girl to catch a sight of the ill-starred but beautiful Mary Queen of Scots, Louise de la Vallière and Marie Antoinette, many a boy to see Duguesclin, Bayard, Condé, Napoleon. The spacious galleries also furnish a fascinating second-storey circuit of the cathedral. You can also, if you get official permission, cross an invisible little bridge past the traceried bars of the rose window. On feast days when the galleries are open you can see en route the old library and some of the musty rooms where the priests slept and with which Victor Hugo's fancy took such liberties. Those galleries also offer—from a point just over the high altar—the most fascinating view you can get anywhere of the western rose window, a stilled celestial kaleidoscope at the vaulted tunnel's west end, above the great west organ.

A very striking and original instance of the union of utility and beauty, the beauty being born of the utility through the most expert architectural midwifery, you will find in the rows of pinnacles on the nave side walls. Looking up from the lilacs in the presbytery gardens you will see little houses and pinnacles atop the buttresses all the way around. These are highly decorative and wholly delightful, but they are there because some mason or master-of-works found that a buttress slightly weighted at the top is infinitely stronger than it would be without that trifling addition of weight. So they turned these little extra burdens, these allies, into artistic adornment.

But the characteristic that Bishop de Sulli marvelled at was that the walls which for thousands of years had been walls were walls no longer. No more than skin and muscle can be considered the support for human ribs, spine, thigh bones, could these new walls be counted on to support as did walls of old the tremendous weight of vault and roof. These new walls seemed now nothing more than a connecting tegument between the true supports, arch, vault plane, *voussoir*, pillar and buttress, all the bones of the great Gothic skeleton. With those alone, without a wall, the cathedral would have stood for generations. The wall had been discharged from the rôle it had filled for ages as the primary support, the great upholder. Indeed, so numerous now were the windows, it almost seemed to the old bishop as though the walls had been transformed into a framing for the bright glass.

XXXI

The Oriflamme of France and the German Gold Eagle. . . . King Philippe defeats the Germans at Bouvines and marches his Bloody, Battered, Bannered Army through the Nave of Notre Dame. . . . The Bishop's Statue goes up in the South Portal. . . . Colour in the Mediaeval Cathedral Statuary. . . . Little Serial Stories in Stone. . . . The Great Last Judgment. . . . Symbolism in Stained Glass Windows and in Sculpture. . . . Foliage that is patterned after the Flowers in the Fair Fields of France

1214=1239 A.D.

WHEN IN THE YEAR 1214, THE FARM FIELDS AROUND THE outskirts of Paris were yellow with the July harvest, the Parisians were draping the pillars and tribunes of the nave of Notre Dame and the house fronts around the square with bright lilied banners and seas of oriental cendal and silk. The island was preparing to celebrate a truly great victory. The cathedral whose body was now in its main features complete, except for towers, transepts, chevet and the first belfry (which would stand up for many years until it was replaced with the high *flèche*), was ready for a *Te Deum*.

Over toward the sea, in the Flemish marshes, Philippe Auguste, who held his throne through most of the years of the cathedral's building—from 1180 until 1223—had won a conclusive and consolidating victory for France. This was over the great coalition of dark, perfidious John of England, many Dutch nobles and Flanders counts, some of the rebel French knights who were fighting for England because of Eleanor's dowry, and the German Emperor. Riders had come, exhausted, their horses almost foundered, over the north bridge of Paris with the battle news.

Near Lille, Philippe of France with the oriflamme, the German Emperor Otto in gold armour with a gold eagle and black dragon on his standard, who was in command of the allies, had engaged by a river. For the times, their armies were large, Philippe's numbering 7,000 cavalry and 30,000 foot, the coalition's 6,500 knights and some say 40,000, others 70,000 infantry. Philippe had been surprised with his army half on one side of the river half on the other, he himself—it was a very hot day, the courier said—with armour off in the shade and dipping a knob of peasant's bread in wine when the coalition horse under Otto attacked.

There followed one of those gallant rear-guard fights which brighten the sometimes dark pages of French history, like that of the Gauls at Alesia, the Old Guard at Waterloo. Vastly out-numbered, the covering squadrons of French knights and pikemen held off the allies under Otto until King Philippe came up with his two extraordinary lieutenants—Brother Guerin of the militant re-ligious order of the Knights of the Hospital, the Richelieu of his time, and another Philippe, the fighting bishop of Beauvais.

This battle of the little Flemish river was an earlier miracle of the Marne. The battle swayed uncertainly for a long time but in the end England and the German Empire at her mightiest, the German Emperor in his greatest display, were overthrown with all their allies. Once again France was free. No wonder they swathed Paris in silk, strewed their flowers and joyously tumbled the bells about in the fifty churches of the city, although the great *bourdons* had not yet gone up on Notre Dame. Another courier who had come on a foaming horse over the bridge related that King Philippe Auguste had narrowly escaped death. His horse falling, he had gone down fighting under a group of struggling knifing knights and yet had survived. Then the German Emperor himself was beset. Gold eagle, gold dragon, gold armour and all, he had run away shrieking for help, and had never stopped until he reached Valen-ciennes.

From the battlefield it was a festival all down the highway to Paris. Peasants had thrown down their scythes and flails and had come running to the sides of the road joyously to greet the con-querors. Many, singing and shouting, had followed in the wake of the marching armies toward Paris. The Parisians, hearing of their approach, went out into the fields and came back laden with branches and flowers. These they strewed on the north bridge, on the street before the palace, and all the way to the cathedral. Others they threw under the hoofs of the horses of the incoming con-querors: tall Philippe Auguste who rode unhelmeted, head up, and ruddy face smiling; the fighting bishop of Beauvais; and Philippe's right arm, Brother Guerin of the Hospitallers, with the black cross centering the red mantle over his grey armour.

For a week all Paris was joyous except for the few arch prisoners whom Philippe in the custom of the time publicly hanged, by corners where wine flowed free to take away the bad taste left by the sight of men kicking and jerking. The city with its white and coloured hangings seemed like a gigantic mercer's bazaar. Torches flamed all night. People danced in the streets. No Paris housewife dusted or university student looked in a book for a week.

For an hour, however, the army was subdued and humble, when it came into the finished nave with the windows all a fresh glory. Then, battered, bruised, bloodstained, with their banners, they marched around the ambulatory singing songs of thanksgiving, voices, spurs, arms, armour ringing out thrillingly together.

It had not been long before this that they had placed the statue of Maurice de Sulli up over a doorway. If he had been alive, the modest old man would never have allowed it up there with all the great men and saints. The vigourous tribe of stonecutters, whom he had gathered together, like the stained glass workers early in the operations, had started carving the statues of saints, angels and devils long before the niches and pedestals were ready for them. The whole enterprise was handled in this systematic way. Men worked at many different tasks in the cathedral simultaneously; statues, stained glass, pillars, piers, "forest" timbers being made at the same time. Some veterans who loved the old man must have watched him on his daily visits to the *chantier* and surreptitiously made this little stone portrait of him. Now, strangely, there were three bishops de Sulli, none of them kin to one another: a bishop of Bourges; our Maurice; and now a Eudes de Sulli, bishop of Paris, not a one-time farmboy like Maurice but a patrician. It was he who had this statue of his predecessor put up in the tympanum of the Saint Anne doorway with the King Louis the Seventh and angels, and with her in whose name this glorious cathedral was built.

Now few of us have a correct idea of mediaeval statuary. We think of these old statues as grey and quaint with one perhaps here and there, like the fair God of Amiens and the lovely hand-less Madonna on the Notre Dame north transept, as very beautiful. But the mediaeval painter turned the stone images into dazzling figures that would go well with the vivid story told in the rich glass. The heroes and saints the mediaeval sculptor wrought were not only individual but gorgeous costumed personages. Gold haloes and crowns adorned these statues. Lilies, swords, scrolls, sceptres, in gold or gay hues, were in their hands. Their blue and crimson robes stood out in a great glory against the gold leaf backgrounds of pediment and tympanum whose brightness was never allowed to dim. For these mediaeval folk were as unafraid of colour as they were of sentiment and belief in miracles. They tried, as best they could with earthly means—their stone, glass and pigment—to make their saints and heroes bright and gay and shining to fit the heaven in which they believed.

We should remember this when we go into the grey but noble

porches of Notre Dame and all the cathedrals, and in imagination reinvest them with the augmented magnificence of their brilliant colour. For the "little folk" of mediaeval days to enter church porch and aisles and nave was to come to a joyous and gorgeous carnival—a holy carnival for them.

It was a great event when the Saint Anne portal—the southern one in the façade by the Seine—with the bishop's statue, was opened early in the thirteenth century. A portal was a most important unit of a great cathedral. The Romanesque had developed the impressiveness of the deep recession and its intricate interweavings of stone figures, but the new Gothic portal was grander still. The sculptured figures showed now a greater individuality and artistry. The design in which all the little scenes blended attractively was even more complicated yet adroitly handled. And to the whole was added the aspiration of the noble Gothic arch. The portal had become one of the most splendid features of the cathedral.

It does not matter when we look at the cathedral today that the larger statuary is not, every bit of it, of the original workmanship. As one faces the west front, he sees a Christ standing by the Judgment portal, the Virgin on her door, four imposing figures in niches in the huge vertical buttresses between the portals—Saint Etienne, the Church, the Synagogue, and Saint Denis; twenty-eight kings in the row above; the Virgin, Child and two angels in front of the west rose; Adam and Eve on either side. All these large statues of the façade (with the beautiful Stephen on the south transept portal) are only about eighty years old.

In a way we should not mourn these changes for they came from two more of the innumerable great events that drenched, dyed deep, all Notre Dame with history. It was the French Revolution that destroyed the originals. It was the notable reconstruction by Viollet-le-Duc, one of the architectural geniuses of the ages, that set up those substitutes, all recreated in the spirit of their predecessors and with a new loveliness. The gargoyles aloft are half new, half ancient. The exquisite handless Madonna of the west transept and the fourteenth century Our Lady of Paris by the chancel, come down to us from the early days. That great noble west front, piers, balconies, buttresses, colonnades, towers, is itself, thank God, original; fortunately, also, almost all the little sculptured scenes within, those carved in 1351 on the wood wall of the sanctuary, the majority of those wreathed in and around the three portals and the doors of the transepts, and the curious little chain around the apse of the cathedral. The whole cathedral itself is original except for a few details such as the *flèche* and the treasury, and also for individual stones which have been put in here and there, parallelling the renewal of the wasted cells of the human body. And though the three great rose windows have some replaced pieces, their glorious light comes down to us through countless years.

Fascinating little serials, idylls, love stories, comics, frame the portals. On the central pier which splits the two doors of the Virgin's portal is her lovely figure with her feet symbolically on the serpent's head. In the three tiers of the great tympanum over her head are three exquisitely conceived and executed scenes. In the lower tier stand three of her royal ancestors, three kings and three prophets who foretold her coming, with admirable details of sceptres, hoods, papyrus rolls. In the middle tier she is being raised from her carved bed on a beautiful curve of shroud by two lifelike angels against an excellently composed group of her friends, the disciples. In the top she receives a crown from the hands of her dear Son. In the recessed framing of the portal (the archivolture) is an intricate collection of little scenes and an infinity of small figures. Each of these, through feature, pose or prop, has been made individual and all are engaged in a fascinating variety of duties—domestic, industrial, clerical, diabolic or angelic. In spite of their multiplicity, they line with perfect harmony the deeply-cut, receding sides of the archway, mounting higher up in ranks curved around the tympanum to the archway top.

The greatest portal, one which people come long distances to see, is the middle one, the great Last Judgment Door. On the central pier or post which separates the two great swinging doors here, is a Christ with book and fingers raised in blessing, and almost as lovely as the famous Beau Dieu of Amiens. On the lower archway sides flanking the doors are two platoons of disciples. Through a sculptor's curious mistake, Paul is included among them instead of the Matthias who took Judas' place. Below them are the Virtues and Vices. On the doorposts stand little images of the Wise and Foolish Virgins. Crowded in the upper sides of the doorway, curving toward the archway top and framing the tympanum, is a great mediaeval Tussaud Museum of kings, patriarchs, martyrs, obscene devils, beasts, wild horsemen, including the Four of the Apocalypse, and all manner of folk from both Heaven and Hell. But—a quaint little touch—in the two arch lanes immediately bordering the pointed tympanum panel, little haloed angels bend over, as though in balcony rows with hands and elbows on the rails, watching the great Last Judgment scene.

In the top pointed tympanum tier is an enthroned Christ dispensing justice—unfortunately not so tender as the One below. Two angels, one with cross, one with cup, and a kneeling Mary and John attend Him. In the middle panel a stately Saint Michael guards those about to be rewarded with bliss. A Satan that is one of the ultimate horrors of the fancy, with two repellent devil lieutenants, herds the damned in chains.

One would not think the chisel could cut into the stone such a tumult of striving as there is in the tier below, among the dead as they burst forth with an uncanny rhythm of movement from under clod and coffin lid at the last trump, into a resurrection so animated it almost brings life itself into the stone.

South, on the west front, is the oldest portal dedicated to Saint Anne, mother of Mary, though oddly Saint Marcel of Paris occupies the central pier here. The story of Anne and of Mary's father is told in the stone in serial fashion. It jumps all about the doorway from lintel to the base to the canopy above Marcel's head and back to the tympanum again. To begin with, in the tympanum's third panel up above, Joachim takes his wife Anne to the temple. A severe priest abuses them for their sterility. Joachim with a staff and a pack on his back goes off in disgrace. At the base of the doorway, Joachim hears the excellent news that he is about to become a father. Way up in the canopy corner Anne clasps her hands in rejoicing too. Then up in the tympanum again is the happy sequel: Mary, a grown woman now, has suitors. The favoured one, Joseph, comes to call on a horse in a brooched cloak. There he is betrothed to her. In the panel above is the lovely sequel: Our Lady, an exquisite Christ in a manger crib, most life-like donkeys and horses, and the kings. One can imagine that the sculptors enjoyed their work.

At the very top of this Saint Anne portal is the enthroned Virgin with an angel at either hand. Back of one is King Louis the Seventh, back of the other Bishop de Sulli himself with his very lifelike features, so like our own Cardinal Verdier's. Back of him is a little hooded clerk apparently taking dictation. The folds of their gowns, like those of the angels', are exquisitely done, and the bishop has a fine crook like that with which he long ago traced out the cathedral lines.

The ironwork on these doors is very beautiful, almost like lace-work, and very ancient. It was a nice little memorial touch to transfer it from old Saint Etienne to this new portal of Notre Dame.

Down the sides of Notre Dame other fascinating stories have been told in this great picture book of the poor we call the cathedral. In the south transept portal, an eager young Stephen preaches before an animated crowd of listeners, the angered doctors waiting to trap him—you can almost hear their conspiring. A young mother looks up at him as she nurses her babe. In the middle tier is the sad little picture of his being stoned and, as the Bible says, his last "falling asleep."

The north transept portal is more melodramatic. Saint Theophilus, like Faust, sells his soul to the Devil, but is rescued by Our Lady who holds a sword at the Devil's heart. In the third tier is a most delicately done infancy of Christ with sheep and ass nuzzling the Babe, and His being presented in the temple. Herod's soldiers, in mediaeval chain mail, start their slaughter of the Innocents; and Joseph in a curious pot hat like the modern German helmet, leads Mother and Child on the flight into Egypt. On the central pier is the Madonna who has lost her hands and Child, one of the loveliest statues in all the world. Over the famous Porte Rouge, the little red door leading to the choir, is the Virgin's coronation scene with Saint Louis and his queen anachronistically on hand to see it.

Extending toward the rear from this door, in the cathedral base and under the choir windows, is another little enchanting serial of the Virgin's life.

A curious mediaeval symbolism was represented in the statues and carvings within and without this and all the other cathedrals. For example, the faithful dog was a sign of the indomitable Saint Bernard and Saint Roche; the dove for Remi of Rheims, who wrote the story of the dove that brought the oil to the Clovis coronation. This bird was also the symbol for Ambrose of the great hymns and for Gregory the Great. The ass stood for John Chrysostom, also for Saints Germain and Marcel of Paris; the doe for Giles and Leu; the pig for suffering Anthony; the lowly rat for poor Gertrude; the cock for Landry; the stag for hunting Hubert; and the ox for that great theologian Thomas Aquinas. The fish was an ancient sign of Christ because the first letters of its Greek equivalent, *icthus*, were the first letters of the words of the phrase "Jesus Christ, Son of God, Saviour." The vine, the pelican, the lamb and the shepherd, of course, were used for Him also.

Even numbers were considered symbolical. I, because of its very integrity, stood for the Image of God; II for the Twin Nature of Christ; III for the Trinity; IV the Cardinal Virtues; V the Wounds of Christ; VI the Days of Creation; VII was mystically unique and sacred *per se;* VIII represented the Resurrection and the Beatitudes; IX the Angelic Hierarchy and the Gifts of the Holy Spirit; X the Commandments; XI was the emblem of Sin; XII the Disciples, the Tribes, the Minor Prophets, the Articles of Faith and the Credo. These numbers would be worked in and around every cathedral.

Just as under the great Gothic impulse the master builders shook off the old yoke of Rome, the round arch that had prevailed for ages, for the new Gothic arch, so the sculptors now shook off the chains of the classic acanthus and laurel which had appeared so often on pillar tops and which had freshness and significance in a past age but had now lost both.

The artists of Notre Dame and the cathedrals in the cities roundabout now went out into the fair fields of France for their models. It was an eloquent indication of the naturalness and joyousness in this springtide of the Gothic that they brought into their decoration not the old motifs but the things they saw on their kitchen tables being prepared for the pot, those that made lovely the wildwood or beautified their cottage walls. Very familiar things —the wild rose, violet, meadow lily, humble cabbage, parsley, fennel, thyme, the apple, pear and plum—sometimes their very trellises—the oak and beech trees, were wrought with the needle in the hangings, with the chisel on the pillar capitals, the niche borders and the doors. The stained glass designers also used them for their decorative borders and for the patterning between the scenes in the bright windows.

And artists, in their happy childlike way, not only drew on Nature's graceful vegetable forms for their models but on the barnyard as well. Often with the lordly lion, the faithful domestic horse, the ass, ox, steer and dog went into embroidered cloth, chiselled stone and coloured panes. No one, remembering Bethlehem, could object to this. They paid honour to whom honour was due when, on the façade of Laon cathedral, they set up a delegation of stone oxen, for oxen had done a great deal for the cathedral in hauling in its stone. With this refreshing if naïve approach to art, it was natural that demonology should be represented too. If they depicted the flowers, fruits, trees and animals they saw by day, it was to be expected that they would put in some of the queer beings their fancies summoned up at night. A grim mediaeval humour, as much as fearfulness, went into their shaping of the tailed fiends with cauldrons, flames, all the impedimenta of Hell which we have just seen on some of the cathedral portals. Not only shudders but riotous laughter accompanied the chisels that cut the gargoyles which spat out rain water and those dreadful but knowing chimaeras who are so fetchingly posed high on Notre Dame, and eternally gaze from these aerial heights out over the Seine, the massed city roofs and the hills.

In keeping with their return from the old classic ways to the freshness of the world all about them, their happy delineation of all its forms and the colour they used with such an abashed abandon, was the increased naturalness in the modelling of their human figures. Their saints and Bible heroes were no longer mere types as they had often been in Romanesque days. With the chisel, they were now given features, poses, characteristics that made them serene, confidence inspiring and heroic looking. Their villains and devils were excellent examples of the results of sin. All were individual and alive. As for the chief figure of all, the Romanesque sculptors had set the Christ up in majesty but in what might without irreverence be called the awfulness of Godhead. A new feeling, not unallied with the naturalness we have noticed, moved the artist now. Not as a victorious figure so much as a piteous one, did the twelfth- and thirteenth-century men portray Him. Sometimes, it is true, He did reign in their grand Judgment doors with His scales and grand sovereignty. More often he was stretched upon the Cross, mortally hurt and dying, One Who would appeal to the compassion of all, Who would stir all but the unfeeling with a melting gratitude that He had endured so much for them. Between the artists of the twelfth and thirteenth centuries and those that followed there was a great and significant difference. In the Gothic spring after the long Dark Ages' sleep men revelled in the newly aroused life, the sap, the bud. On their stones, in their glass, these men of the Early Gothic age left leaf and flower in the bud. Often by this little sign you can tell a portal's or a window's age. By the time the Notre Dame builders had turned another corner of time and come into the thirteenth century the stems and stalks had grown longer, the foliage and flowers had unfolded. At last, in the fifteenth, the foliage and verdure of the stone very often assumed an autumn-like, almost withered or at least a sharp about-to-be-frosted look. Its autumn then was the Gothic approaching, not its death, but the end of its development. But when its winter came its beauty had been frozen immortally for us.

XXXII

*Saint Louis Brings the Pieces of the True Cross and Crown of
Thorns in a Glittering Procession to the High Altar. . . . Tide-
Marks of the Gothic on Notre Dame. . . . Historic Changes in
After Years. . . . Celebrated and Picturesque Personages who
pass through the Portals of Notre Dame.*

1239 A.D.—With a Look Forward

BY 1218, AFTER ITS GLORIOUS HISTORY, OLD SAINT ETIENNE'S
had gone down. Five years later the great twin towers of
Notre Dame were up. By 1239, with so much done, Louis
the Ninth, who was considered the most just, the ideal ruler, the
King Arthur of the Middle Ages, thought it high time to provide
it with a relic. None but the most sacred in all the world would do
—a piece of the True Cross, if possible a bit of the Crown of
Thorns.

He had been searching in a very practical and logical and
legalistic way for these holy gifts. His scholars and wise men had
long been in the East examining into the genuineness of the piece
of the True Cross a Mohammedan sultan had offered for sale. This
was the fragment allotted to Sancta Sophia after the discovery of
the True Cross by Saint Helena. It had thence been carried off
by the Persians and later returned by Heraclius. Documents attest-
ing to these vicissitudes and original letters and pamphlets of
bishops around Saint Helena's time seemed to prove to Saint Louis'
scholars the truth of the sultan's claim. The existence of the Crown
of Thorns was not confirmed by so many famous men, though
early writers told of seeing it in a Mount Sion church. And Baldwin II of Constantinople presented Saint Louis with some thorns.

It was a magnificent procession that brought the priceless treasures to Notre Dame. Saint Louis had his nobles and crusaders wear
their usual fine mantles and shining mail while he himself, as a
symbol of the homage of an earthly to a heavenly King, walked
humbly clad and barefoot, behind the relics in a gold shrine.
There were not only candles and incense, jewelled cross and a
gorgeously vested delegation of the clergy to greet this procession,
but for the first time in the history of Notre Dame, the great
brazen-tongued bells rang out a welcome over the Seine.

Those relics were to stay in the cathedral for a few years until Saint Louis erected for them the most beautiful of all reliquaries, that miracle of glass, the Sainte Chapelle. Then, later, these relics of Our Lady's Son were returned to the cathedral, not to be taken out again except during times of danger such as the French Revolution, when they were sent for safety to the Bibliothèque Nationale.

Some fragments are kept in the treasury and are exposed on rare occasions to the reverent gaze of attending thousands. In the nineteenth century, that restoring genius, Viollet-le-Duc, took a bit of each and placed them in the gilt ball of the beautiful new *flèche* or spire which he erected high on the ridge pole of Notre Dame, where the original central belfry stood at one time.

Notre Dame, then, was tower-capped and finished, for most practical purposes, by 1235—in seventy-two years from the first excavating. It was now completely Gothic except for one or two features like the pillars at the ambulatory turns and the gracious and light ones of the nave, which have something of a Romanesque look and yet fit in so well with the prevailing Gothic in this grand transitional cathedral. About twenty years before Saint Louis' entry, the change to the new style had become final and definite. Masters-of-works exchanged visits from time to time, and we have seen how the bishops who were building cathedrals in other cities traded construction ideas when visiting the famous *molle*. About 1209 the younger cathedral of Chartres, or its bishop or architect, apparently influenced the authorities of Notre Dame. This and the fire of the four thieves in 1218, necessitating reconstruction, forced the final shift. In this period they changed the high clerestorey windows which only had single lights to large and lofty ones with double lights. You can still see the sole survivor of the original windows high in the north clerestorey wall not far from the organ loft. Soon they took down the first crude flying buttresses that had upheld Bishop de Sulli's beloved choir and started the great dragon troops that still amaze the world. Fortunately they never changed the galleries. They did not surrender them wholly to glass as they did in Chartres. The Notre Dame galleries were unique and noble in appearance and added fifteen hundred to the audience figure of nine thousand for nave and aisles.

On the exterior is an eloquent sign of this final capitulation of the Romanesque to the Gothic, in the tympanum of Saint Anne's door just above the figure of Bishop de Sulli. In the pointed panel capping this doorway are two distinct arch lines. The smaller and slightly lower one is round and Roman; the higher and outer one is pointed and Gothic. In the first quarter of the century they had changed to the new style and pointed its tympanum up. Those

two masonry arch lines in the grey tympanum of the old portal
are like two tide lines left in the sand. The lower and inner one
marked the high tide of the Romanesque, the higher one the
glorious flood of the Gothic.

Jean de Chelles in 1257 put the great doors and porch and
statuary on the beautiful southern—Saint Etienne's—portal and
later began work on the north door. De Montreuil and Pierre de
Chelles finished his work and Jean Ravy rounded out the apse
with chevet chapels about 1330. Ravy and Le Bouteille carved the
panels of Christ's life on the choir enclosure.

Soon the Porte Rouge was cut through into the choir so that
the canons might pass through from their cloister quarters for the
just-after-midnight office of matins. Now it is used by the choir
boys when they come in from their school on the Rue Massillon.
As final touches, the chapels were added to the ambulatories of the
choir as the thirteenth century ended.

A few other changes came with the years. The great Last Judgment Door is famous throughout France not only for its beauty
but because it is considered the heart of France, and the distances
from Paris to all parts of the land are measured from this door.
Yet Soufflot, the Pantheon architect, had to go and butcher it.
From the relief you can detect the place where, in the eighteenth
century, he cut out of the tympanum an arched hollow, simply to
allow the gilded canopies of the feastday processions to be carried
through without being lowered. He sliced through the magnificent
sculpture as high as the throned Christ's feet. When they filled
this false archway up, a century later, they restored the sculpture
to its former glory.

In 1700-04 the *hic jacets* of the dead were pried up from the
historic tombs in the floor, for prelates and high personages in the
Middle Ages were often buried under the pavings and pilgrims
walked over their horizontal headstones, as they still do today in
Senlis Cathedral. Undoubtedly some royal dust was displaced in
the process, perhaps even the very bones of old Bishop Saint Marcel,
whose remains had been transferred during an early stage of the
building.

It was that grand monarch and master of the ornate, Louis the
Fourteenth, who did this so that he might substitute for the ancient
and sacred pavement the then more fashionable tile. They also tried
their dubious improvements on the sanctuary, placing statues of
Louis the Thirteenth and Louis the Fourteenth incongruously
behind the high altar, changing that too—a mistake amply made
up for by the invaluable Viollet-le-Duc, who installed the beautiful
one at which they celebrate the mass today. In this same century,
so unhappy for Notre Dame, they tore down the mediaeval rood

screen or jube with its cross and saints and replaced it with one much lower—an alteration which, however, did permit the congregation to see more clearly the ceremonies in the choir.

The bell tower, which stood above the crossing from 1198 until 1225, was replaced by a *flèche*. The winds bent this one badly; in 1788 it was rebuilt; the Revolutionaries tore it down; and Viollet-le-Duc put up the present very handsome one.

In the seventeenth century the thirteen-ton bell of the south tower was recast. It still rings out on state occasions but the two north tower bells are always silent.

Up until 1741 all the host of windows of Notre Dame, about six hundred in actual count, bore the original, lovely, old stained glass. At that time the chapter serving Notre Dame wanted a clear white ray to fall on the white altar, and so robbed the chancel windows of their rich panes and substituted clear glass. And in the clerestorey an ambitious designer replaced the matchless early glass with his own inferior brand. Happily, in the nineteenth century, Maréchale redid all the chancel glass very satisfactorily. The window restoration of Viollet-le-Duc in the choir and chapels is especially beautiful. The amazing and versatile Viollet took the utmost pains both with major features and small details. Through all the many years of the restoration—during part of which Lassus worked with him—he superintended his sculptors in the ancient *chantier* back of the choir and gathered together the best stained glass workers of Europe in an *atelier* which, like the old canvas one of the first master-of-works, lay alongside the cathedral, and in another workshop over on Boulevard Henri-Quatre. There was not a fragment of glass which escaped his inspection. He came near rivalling the old hues. He wanted the choir and chapel windows to be of the finest quality, and all the little pieces with which he repaired the three ancient thirteenth-century rose windows to be worthy of a place in their magnificent glass.

It was in this period, too, before he took his place with the red-trousered French infantrymen on the Paris walls to fight the Germans, who apparently loved to destroy beauty as much as he did to create it, that he discovered several interesting things about the cathedral for us. Among these were the plans for the great assembly of spires, the gallery bends and the fact that while the walls of Notre Dame were of the Parisian limestone which hardens with age, the foundations were of granite of which there was very little in the Seine valley.

Some time after the Gothic age two landmark statues of Notre Dame disappeared. One was a mounted figure of Philip the Fair in full armour, as he once rode presumptuously into the nave, which had stood near Saint Pierre's chapel, the other an eighteen-foot

Saint Christopher in whose huge hands unfortunate girls often placed foundlings.

Above the vaulting extends the maze of timbers called the "forest." In little roof cells bordering this, roofers, leadsmiths and other workers lived while the cathedral was building and later during repairs. In 1710 Cardinal Noailles, finding too much rot and too many worms at work up there, had the tremendous acreage of beams and rafters replaced. Undisturbed during the following centuries, these have gathered a nine-inch layer of dust.

The cathedral setting, of course, was changed with the transfer by Napoleon the Third of the ancient Hôtel Dieu from the south to the north side of the square. Lawns, trees, flowers and the great riding Charlemagne took its place. The Communes of 1871, so different from their mediaeval brethren who built churches instead of destroying them, tried to burn Notre Dame and did succeed in burning down the long Bishop's Palace, the one built by Soufflot to succeed the mediaeval home of Bishop de Sulli. In its place one sees now the presbytery, home of the auxiliary bishop (the main episcopal palace is on the Rue Barbey-le-Jouy), its garden and lilacs. On part of its site and that of old Saint Etienne's now are the richly handsome sacristy and treasury wing built by Viollet-le-Duc and a close from which one frequently hears the shouts of the choir boys playing the young Napoleon's favourite game of prisoner's base. Along the river extend ivied guarding walls, gravelled paths and beds of fuchsias, snapdragon, lady's-slippers, salvia, chrysanthemums and other flowers in season, tended by old gardeners who have heard the shells of three invasions scream over Paris.

There were some tricks about Notre Dame. Just as the Greeks bowed out the temple columns for perspective, the master-of-works bent his galleries a little. He gave the façade three recessions for greater effectiveness. Also there are some peculiarities. The façade itself leans west up to the king row, then assumes the perpendicular. Inside, the north triforium gallery has a slight curve concave to the nave; the south gallery has one convex. The great interior piers under the towers are one and a half feet off the perpendicular in eighty feet, but revert to the vertical in their upper portions. Whether these divergencies were accidental or, as some claim, designed, they, like the imperfections in all beautiful handwork—which the cathedral is—have been knit into seeming symmetry. They give the cathedral life.

If you stand by the central Last Judgment Door and look toward the altar, you will see that the centre aisle of the nave is a little off axis. Perhaps the whole building was deflected to escape Saint Etienne's apse or a cloister building. Still, in the belief that Notre apse for halo

Dame was deliberately built off axis to indicate the bend of Christ's head on the Cross, there is the same appeal that there is for many in the rest of the supposed architectural symbolism: the chevet with the raying-out chapels is the Crown of Thorns; the altar, Christ's head; the transepts, His arms outstretched on the Cross that is the cathedral; the nave, the column of His legs; the west doors, His nailed feet; the little red door, the wound in His side; the open space at the crossing, the royal titling on the Cross over His head; the great white altar cloth, His winding sheet. So beautiful is all this symbolism that one is almost led into complete acceptance; indeed some would go so far as piously to endow every utile and mechanical part of the cathedral with a symbolic origin. But most of this symbolism is after the fact for, as over and over we have seen, the form of the cathedral, its every important feature, sprang out of a need simply and directly met. Still perhaps it is just one more proof of the many-sidedness of this great House of God that these imaginative parallels spring out of it as naturally as leaf and bud and flower spring out of the forest which that nave, that vault, so resemble.

Perhaps these fancies are, after all, as important as the facts which some insist upon: that the cathedral length is 430 feet, its width at the nave and aisles 124, from north to south transept tips 170, the height of the vault 108, the towers 223; that there are regularly 2400 chairs in the nave—2000 more can be comfortably placed in the aisles—the whole cathedral holding over all 10,500 standing and seated; that two night police and two police dogs with an electric protector system even now guard the pile to save the holy relics, coronation robes and sacred vessels from such thieves as centuries ago climbed up into the "forest" and set the choir on fire; or that in the big organ west are 6,584 pipes, 5 keyboards, 96 stops and 28 pedals. It was across those keys that, a few years ago, the organist, Viernes, fell dead while playing.

In the great pile there are many fascinating crypts and corners and nooks which one discovers on more intimate acquaintance with Notre Dame. Yet to name them all would only confuse the stranger or one who has made but a few visits to the cathedral. By the little chancel organ used for choir practice, low masses and canonical offices, under a red carpet is a little stairway leading down into the crypt. In its gloom are buried 15 prelates, cardinals, archbishops, bishops—ranged in their coffins all around. Nearby in a cave is a collection of the bones of all the dead royalty and priesthood so rudely disturbed by Louis the Fourteenth. Archbishop Darboy who was shot in prison in 1871 by the Commune, Archbishop Affre who was shot on the Bastille barricade in 1848 while exhorting the people to peace, and Archbishop Sibour who was shot in Saint Etienne's, all have elaborate tombs in the ambulatory.

Dark circular stairs lead up to the galleries. In a cavern near one of them can be seen the huge haunch of an original buttress. There are little invisible foot-bridges that cross the rose panes from the choir galleries to those over the side aisles. From the tribunes over the altar are visible the dusty cardinal and archbishop's caps suspended by the thinnest of wires from the vault ceiling, ghostly souvenirs of the past.

From there too one can see birds flying through the upper vault ranges. Their passage from the outer world, through the bright cathedral out into the world again, reminds one of the Northumberland noble who, when missioners preached to them, advised his friends to try the new religion.

"Life," he said, "is like the swallow flying through a warm and lighted hall, from the dark cold into the dark cold.

"So this life of man comes into sight for a little while. We are ignorant of what shall follow or of what may have preceded. If this new doctrine offers anything more certain, I think we should follow it."

In the upper reaches are many little doors for the host of people who once lived in the place. Many of those working on the roof gained access to the raftered cells through the little dormers visible on the roof outside. Now only the watchmen sleep in the cathedral and an occasional priest who occupies a chamber above the sacristy, reached by another of those curious little winding stairways.

One could explore the place for weeks and come across new refuges, discover each day new people whom he has not met and yet who have been there for centuries.

There is an especially fascinating aerial settlement in and around the towers. Another infinitely varied diabolical and saintly community dwells up among the world of dormers, penthouses, pinnacles and lofty galleries which crowd but do not clutter the three clearly marked ascending storeys of Notre Dame.

One can make an almost continuous pilgrimage on these outdoor galleries and upper stone terraces and the various levels of these three storeys, which afford a never tiring spectacle of interesting personages and objects and magnificent views of the city and of the shining curves and the many bridges of the Seine.

Great processions we have seen entering those three great arched doors. There are countless others to come. Here in 1431 the picturesque Henry the Sixth of England, a boy, was presumptuously declared King of France, because of that old dowry matter. Jeanne d'Arc could not protest. They burned her in Rouen, but the victory she had already won and those to be won by her armies led by her spirit were soon to void this English claim forever. In 1560 lovely Mary of Scotland was crowned Queen Consort of France, which honour, in the end, did not help her at all. In 1638 Louis the Thirteenth with picturesque pageantry made his coronation vows here. In 1687 the funeral oration of the brilliant Condé was preached by Bossuet, the most eloquent bishop of his time. In 1779 Louis the Sixteenth and his Queen, Marie Antoinette, had the square strewn with branches and flowers for a great mass marriage. One hundred poor girls in white, to each of whom he had allotted a *dot*, came in a body through Saint Anne's door, while through the Virgin's door came the hundred young grooms with orange blossoms. The wax seals of all their marriage contracts the King stamped with a fleur-de-lis on the hilt of his sword.

The Revolution brought the sacrilegious and drunken Feast of Reason. It was after this that the lovely fourteenth-century Madonna by the chancel was saved from the refuse pile on which the mob had thrown her. Her rescuer was the patriotic Le Nôtre, who did so much for lovers of the beautiful by hiding innumerable works of art, in whole or in fragments, which the *sans-culottes* had discarded or hacked to pieces. Originally Our Lady of Paris came from the little church of Saint Aignan around the bend of the Rue Chanoinesse. The beautiful blue of her gown and her gold lilies restored, she was returned to her niche where she has reigned ever since as Notre Dame de Paris.

The imposing yet *nouveau riche* coronation of that genius Napoleon, all too ebullient that day, came in 1804. Although he opened the churches after the Revolution, he made an almost profane riot of the affair. The pure beauty of the nave was hidden with imperial standards; special boxes were built all around for the spectators; the Pope was insulted; and tremendous plumed hats and epaulets, women's jewels and daring imperial gowns instead of sacred vestments filled the choir. Later, in 1810, he was married to Marie Louise. In 1853, his poor imperial imitation, Napoleon the Third, was married to Eugénie. Nothing could have been more imposing than the funeral of Marshal Foch, the little man who saved France and Paris and Notre Dame from the Germans. Alas, only for his generation! . . .

But hark, there are the sounds of people gathering before Notre Dame, of trumpets, of drums! A drama, which is a fragment of the great one, is being played out in the square. In the Middle Ages the famous folk and the little people of Paris saw it. They are playing it for us again. . . .

XXXIII

In the Square Before Notre Dame.

The Twentieth Century

THEY ARE PLAYING TONIGHT THE SACRED STORY OF THE LIFE and death of Him in the form of whose cross the cathedral was built, out before its doors, under the stars and plane trees in the open of the square. The borders are still the same—Hôtel Dieu north, prefecture and barracks west, riding Charlemagne and river south. But for the week of the play the emperor has vanished under a high tower. They have locked him up as though in a stable. Vanished too are the stones of the square under a great wood stand which starts from in front of the cathedral and slopes up far across the square to the west. And now, as night descends on the cathedral and the surrounding roofs, over the four bridges which lead into the square from every ward and suburb of the city, from the four corners of the earth the people throng. Their feet sound a vast military tattoo, as they mount the tiers until the last comers stand on a level with the prefecture roof and out against the stars.

Down this long ramp they gaze on a stage at the foot of the stand, also of extraordinary size. It extends parallel with the famous façade for the full width of the cathedral. The grey-black painted Palestine hills, the Gethsemane wood olive trees rise to about half the height of the three arched doors of the cathedral so that they blot out half of the stone population in the deep recesses. All of the sets for the principal scenes, from the opening to Calvary, are there all at once. The scene in action is spotlighted; those idle are left in the shadow. And at the wings rise two colonnaded palace rooms, each with a gold throne. The one left, over against Saint Anne's door, is for Caiaphas, the one right, over against the Virgin's portal, for Pilate. And still a little beyond these wings so that they extend the stage a little farther out than the cathedral's corner buttresses are two towers. The one right stands for Hell and has a lid opening in its side and worked by powerful chains so that it displays a fearsome pit with cauldron and squadrons of horrendous devils. On top, too, is a turret where a cardinal-red Satan may sweep his cloak with a magnificent gesture and hurl challenges, he the Prince of Darkness, at the Prince of Peace. The tower left is a

477

heaven with a little platform where any moment with his stunning lightning-flash of sword Saint Michael may appear, and built with transparencies and jewel-spots so that when lighted from behind it shines like a magnified stained glass window lifted out of the cathedral. And these little theatrical tricks of one Arnould de Gréban of fourteen hundred and twenty-one and Villon's and Joan's time, relived here for the night, need alarm no one at all of the thousands in that stand or on the surrounding roofs looking down. Nor will those batteries of light on the Hôtel Dieu roof, those in the tower south that boxes in high Charlemagne, nor any of the other modern devices, in the end take away from the drama's intrinsic majesty. The Archbishop, looking out from behind the curtains of the presbytery windows, will see to that.

There is a space—the usual roadway, now closed to all traffic by hosts of caped *agents de police*—between the stage and the cathedral and sufficient for Roman soldiers and heralds and ballerinas to move about and for the stagehands to lift high on the wood hills the three crosses, the centre one with its divine-human burden. In the side streets by the cathedral's north wall are the ranked shiny bays from the Garde Républicaine stables, mounts for the night for Roman soldiers. Dancers with angel wings or horns from every academy in the city limber up before the long-beard prophets on the great doors. By the piers cluster devils, flame-clad facsimiles of the sculptured ones peering over the stone galleries. Apostles from all the theatres from the Odéon to the Porte Saint Martin stride up and down murmuring their lines. Gay-clad clowns and tumblers liven the darkness of the flying buttresses. And from all the sisters of Notre Dame, from giant Saint Eustache and Sulpice down to little Saint Merri the choristers go through the Red Door. Up to the organ loft under the west rose they climb, carrying very tiny lights, for no matter how bright the stage the cathedral must be kept dark until the great climax.

And the Archbishop, as he looks out from behind the palace curtains, is hoping that some souls on those crowded upmounting tiers may be brought home by the central thread of this central drama of the world being played here tonight. Also he has the not too unworthy and commercial thought of all those francs there represented. They may do much toward keeping the cathedral still beautiful.

So three great and distinct companies there he sees: those on the seats uprising to barracks and stars; the gay, lively company of the cast in doublet, hose, horns, wings, armour; and that still congregation in niche, gallery and under stone coffin lid. And as the heralds mount their borrowed Garde Républicaine steeds to ride on, it occurs to him that those three great companies are not after all so distinct, that in fears, ambitions, fevers, desires they are as alike as peas in a pod. With the clothes pod changed, say a straw hat for a helmet, a bandeau for a halo, trousers for a prophet's robe, the mediaeval folk the cast represent and who once frolicked and died in this square might go up on those seats to watch the saints and prophets come down on the stage to play their parts; the auditors from the four corners of the earth go up in those niches, those towers, yes to struggle under those coffin lids. No, no one would ever be the wiser. Of course, it took a little technique to be a dancer, actor, singer, priest, prophet or, he supposed, devil. But the principle was the same. Through the centuries of change there had been no change after all.

But now, before all the ranked skeptics and believers, ride in the brilliantly tabarded heralds. From their old-fashioned long-tubed trumpets they send the shattering notes forth as once the bells sent the notes of lauds, complines and angelus flying over roofs and river and hills. And at once the great company of mediaeval folk rushes from cathedral door and the side streets up on the stage until the whole length of it from Pilate's gold throne to that of Caiaphas is a saffron, emerald, scarlet, amethyst, silver, purple, russet, turquoise, vermilion kaleidoscope, a tumbling sea of colour.

This mad mass dance then ceasing, the clowns come on seeming inconsistent, naïvely anachronistic, in a sacred story. But wait while those clowns cheat an old woman with a hen from which they extract two dozen Easter eggs in a minute. Wait again while a quack, a jumping jack in ludicrous sugarloaf hat and tortuous green, pulls a tooth from a yokel who sends his roars after those dying trumpet notes to the hills. Wait once more while a whirling squadron of vermilion devils rushes out from a lidded hell, dancing with forward-darting motions of knee and hands that suggest striking adders' tongues or thrusting daggers. Wonderful are those rhythms; wonderful were those, too, of mountebank and clown. Wonderful are those of the twelve who now come on. Those rhythms have pulled the attention of the crowd into the vortex of the matter. Even in cathedrals, great mysteries and passion plays must there be concessions, and Arnould de Gréban of Joan's time, Raphael's and Villon's was but holding his crowd, as prelates long ago saw and this latterday director and the Archbishop recognize this very night. And anyway it pays—and for a very good purpose. The crowd after this prelude ceases stirring. A hush, as though something tangible were laid down from the sky and stars on plane trees and roof and crowd, falls on those tiers as the main action starts with the incoming twelve.

Fine upstanding men they are, bearded—all but John—of good

stature and presence with spacious gestures and stride. And their commanding dignity and compelling rhythm is designed, the physical expression here of an integrity within, an inner power that comes from the Judean hills, the Galilean Sea, from the Christ waiting now behind the stage and under the tympanum of the Last Judgment Door.

Peter, heaviest-bearded of the twelve, his very stride smoking with the choler and impulsiveness of him, is in the van with a youthful blond and gentle John close by. A dark Judas lurks, obliquely apart from the rest, like an evil shadow. Through the whole play this power of pantomime asserts itself so that even if there were no fine resonance of the French tongue ringing in that square this fifteenth-century version of an old, old story would be a beautiful thing to see. A complete symphony it would be of many rhythms. Never do these cloy, never blur; each flows graciously into the following. From the first herald's flourish of trumpet to lips, the clown's palming of eggs, through Satan's wild sweep of his flame cloak to the little arc-like gestures of the Four Marys, the pointing finger of Christ or the all inclusive circle of His arms as He promises them the many mansions, that onward sweep of story as expressed in gesture alone is unforgettable.

But the speech gives the beautiful pantomime skeleton flesh and blood. At the very start, after the mediaeval prelude is over, the onward march of the tale is evident with the entry of the twelve. No cardinals or kings ever more grandly entered a stage. But that entrance, the nobly radiating gesture and majestic stride, is all but symbol after all. In an instant they flash to the vast crowd, some of whom cannot hear, that this is a heroic band. The farthest off, the highest up, can at once see that these humble men from tax books, fishing tackle and thole-pins will in time overthrow empires and kings, change the whole map and complexion of a world.

But that First Actor now is on. Robed in white, blond, too, and with pointed beard, He is yet no calendar saint. Rather the Beau Dieu of the old sculptors given life. That rhythm fairly sings now, though with tempo delicately changed, as He talks with a Mary whose blue, black and white robes have all the sculpturesque curves the old artists loved, those curves of immemorial things, of the sower, harvester and scythe, of the mother taking up her child in the crook of her arm. It is fortunate, perhaps, for the eye that the directors have now switched with Gréban from the first mediaeval costumes to those we affectionately associate with Bethlehem and the Jordan. And by that river most tenderly now the two portray that extraordinary relationship which lifted out of the drama would itself make a great drama, that tie between a mother and a son who is both God and man. With an infinite pathos it is realized, though batteries of light assail them now, batteries right, from the Hôtel Dieu roof, batteries left, from those high wood towers. Yet they stand the assault in the impregnable beauty not, superb as their art is, of themselves but of what they represent. Nor do these mechanical devices nor the service men irreverently smoking cigarettes as they work lights, amplifiers, radio, carillon or ropes disturb the play. That crowd upsloping to the horizon stars is reverently hushed. For the beauty of the scene is not of the skin, not even of Time. It goes ages deep.

And now in the waits or accompanying the action mysteriously there come Gregorian chants seemingly out of nowhere until one by guess locates them up by the beautiful rail over the twenty-eight kings on the cathedral façade, behind and just under the great western rose. And now suddenly the panes are lighted from behind and the whole window, so long dark, is transubstantiated into glory. And as the singing goes on, one almost does not know which is the loveliness of tone, which of glass, so heavenly is the magic and so do the two beauties melt into each other.

And as the Gregorian phrases, ages old, continue to float out from the grey walls and the bright panes over the heads of the twenty-eight kings, the painted wood Jerusalem hills and the square, there seems now no conflict at all between these ancient things of this night and the modern manifestations below—of electric button and switch, programme vendors, of caped police drawn up on the bridges against possible communist disturbances. Even the cathedral bells, not the great clamouring bourdons but the gentle, talkative little chimes which sound as they have for centuries the quarter hours all through the play tonight, seem to link up the centuries together. And that parade of the populace shouting hosannas which makes now a long silhouette of silvered palms on the wooded heights built over against the cathedral is not a pageant out of far-off Jerusalem but out of our own Paris today.

But the tumult and shouting is over, the tragedy at hand. Unforgettably cut out of the darkness is that long table now. All the rest of the stage has been blotted out so that the strong reds, blues and yellows of the apostles' robes, the white of a blond winning Christ and the twelve silver goblets on the board stand clear against the black background. And never were there more beautiful motions than those He makes with His hands as He first washes the apostles' feet, then parts the bread and with one and the same motion hands the portions right and left. The very apotheosis of pantomime, of sublime choreography, is there, used and glowingly interpreted all in a noble way, in what, the heart says, must truly have been His real words and accents. When He points to Heaven you believe Heaven is there. And as He takes John to His breast, you feel that that love is not something on that stage down there simulated but the historic love of Christ for John, that is, the love of God for Man for whom John stands but as proxy.

No trappings of Hell, no vermilion Satans, no stained glass heavens, no angels with silver swords can obscure or blur the sublimity, the heart-breaking pathos of the drama. The might, the majesty, the eternal drive of the central theme and story shear through these mediaeval concessions to the mob as through so much flimsy. It is evidence of the vitality of this tale of that life of thirty-three years and of eternity. The eight centuries of this great pile against which that life tonight is being played out is but a humanly comprehensible fraction and symbol of that eternity. Which is why, perhaps, it was built.

And a more striking symbol it is, this piteous minute, because the flesh which houses that life seems so frail and broken against the seeming invulnerability of the cathedral walls which it will outlast. For they have taken Him and buffeted Him, almost crushed Him, in fact, between the mob and proud officialdom—a scarlet Caiaphas enthroned on the left, a brooding troubled Pilate right. It seems to have satisfied the old playwright when he robed Christ and the Twelve in the manner of their time, for he has costumed this pair in the furred robes and hats with tippets of his own day. But no more than the earlier melodrama does this inconsistency make farcical the story. It is but an anachronism which accentuates the eternal freshness of the play and its eternal contemporaneousness, since people insisted so on seeing in it something that profoundly affected and was of their own time.

Between the pair then, that scarlet whited sepulchre of a Caiaphas and a half-believing half-fearful Pilate letting his opportunity forever go, Christ is bandied back and forth to the jeers of the mob. They are scourging Him now. It is as well, perhaps, that the lashing is concealed by the ring of soldiers. But you know that those lashes land. The upraised arms and bent backs in the ring keep such good time with the arms and backs of the scourgers. Rapid are the arcs they describe. Fearful are the rhythms now. You can see arcs like those among the crowding sinners and saints up on the cathedral walls. But they are stilled. That agitation below though governed by the director in tempest tempo now is tremendous. Those arcs flow so terribly into each other. And never since Time began was there composite curse and mass jeer like that which is hurled up now.

The whole stage is still bright with the lights of the Roman palace, the gold of the high thrones, the gleam of armour and lances, and the rosy heart of the little thorn fire where Peter denies his Friend. And in those lights Christ the conqueror, the one we were yesterday told pointed the way to victory over death, seems now such a broken thing. He bends to one side almost falling. The soldiers have given a mock twist to the crown of thorns. With it his head and beard are dishevelled. For a horrible moment the disorder even the blood running down seem ludicrous not tragic. His hands are tied, too, into a helplessness that appears absurd— an effect the soldiers wanted, to please the howling mob. It howls— not with delight. But still the lances, lowered to the horizontal in a long line, keep them back from tearing Him in pieces. If He is to be torn in pieces, it is for Rome to do that. The whole figure now seems so weak, as the reed, thrust mockingly between the thongs of the bound hands like some carnival sceptre, points up at an angle as absurd as the tilt of the thorn crown. If ever the Christ and the Christianity for which that cathedral there stands seem a failure, it is now. If such was the effect the mob and Caiaphas wanted, they succeeded. If such was the effect the play-wright, Arnould de Gréban, of fourteen hundred and Mans and Rouen, aimed at, he hit the mark. But the artistry is neither his nor director's. It is implicit in the tale.

Never before, even when by that painted Gethsemane tree he bent over to waken the careless Twelve in his hour of need or when Judas gave Him that traitor's kiss, did He seem so pathetic as now. Then, in His strength he appeared superb. Now He is the broken reed. This ludicrousness is the very nadir of the story. The humiliation has never before been so understood by most of the audience. And many of that unstirring twenty thousand watch with hearts in their throats, so great is their actual fear that the failure may not be mere stage play but real.

But only for a moment, for now the long-tubed brass trumpets of the heralds sound again. Startlingly the notes bound back from Hôtel Dieu and prefecture roofs to the walls of the cathedral. And now, not on the stage itself but by way of a concealed entrance that leads up into the great stand, the Roman soldiers appear in the very midst of the audience and ride their sleek bays down the long ramp toward the stage. A powerful cavalcade for the one pathetic figure who staggers, almost falls, under the weight of His own cross.

And again the rhythm, halting now with His broken march, like all the magnificent rhythms of this night, has nothing of the artificial in it. It seems as though that God Who knows something of rhythm, having set worlds whirling in their courses and taught the morning stars to dance, would have had the story told, the drama played this way.

And now behind the wood hills that rise halfway up the great

Judgment Door men unseen with pulleys raise the two thieves, then the central cross with its precious weight.

Its shadow falls full across those stone folk chained by the Devil, the saved whom the stone Christ signals on to glory. The upright itself is clearly shadowed on the tympanum gilt. And the anguished cry of *"Eloi, Eloi, lama sabachthani?"* breaks on that square, that river, the surrounding hills. For a moment it seems as though all the agonies of those who ever suffered in the fourteen hundred years of the hospital here were combined in that cry. With it the very heart of the universe seems to crack, and that crack is made visible with the lightning and thunder and darkness into which the whole world is plunged.

And then this universal cry of despair is turned into triumph by the final "Into thy hands I commend my spirit." So His head falls aslant on the upright, just under the twenty-eight kings of whom He is King. And with its drooping the lights shine behind the glorious rose, which makes a great halo for the still head.

So out in the historic square they played the beautiful drama whose high scene and its sacrifice have been relived in the sanctuary heart of the cathedral for eight hundred years. And as the Archbishop let fall the curtains and the throng disappeared back over the bridges into all the wards of Paris, the four corners of the world, the stagehands lowered the cross and the Christ. The effect for the few loving ones who still loitered in front of the stage was as though, just as He was lowered, the doors, the great cathedral itself took Him unto itself, His own now not rejecting Him.

And never, as those windows shone above, had the Cathedral seemed so glowingly alive. Eight hundred years old? The very bells above, the great bourdons now were ringing out its vitality.

The Cathedral is a magnificent gesture; the noblest, perhaps, ever made by man, upflung in pride in himself, entreaty to the unknown, in fear and delight, and arrested forever against the sky. Forever, unless man and his chemicals and violence destroy it. Even then there will remain the universal gesture of which the Cathedral is shadow, of Him with arms outstretched upon the Cross for all against the sky of the world.

Index of Names

A

Abbaye-aux-Hommes, Caen, 395
Abbo, abbot of St. Germain-des-Prés, 292 et seq.
Abelard, Peter, 4, 80, 175, 261, 329, 356 et seq., 391
Abraham, 46, 82, 91, 92, 267
Abruzzi, 223
Acre, 345
Actium, battle of, 37
Adamnan, St., 134
Adela, second wife of Louis VII of France, 424
Aegean Sea, 73, 77, 96, 98
Aetius, Roman general, 196-9, 270
Affre, archbishop of Paris, 474
Agendicum. See Sens
Agincourt, battle of, 393
Agnes de Méranie, wife of Philippe Auguste, 449
Agrippa, King, 78, 79
Aigulfe, Abbot, 232
Aix-la-Chapelle, 278, 281, 289
Alaric I, Visigoth king, 189, 197
Alaric II, Visigoth king, 204, 273
Albigenses, 325
Alcuin, 176, 282, 284
Alemanni, 201, 277
Alesia, battle of, 28 et seq., 138, 145, 461
Alexander, bishop of Alexandria, 149, 151, 172
Alexander the Great, Pope, 118
Alexander III, Pope, 410-12
Alexandria, Egypt, early see of, 246, 254, 434
Alfred the Great, king of England, 280, 302, 331
Algeria, 271
Alps, 20, 22, 204, 235
Ambiani, 29
Amboise, chateau of, 201
Ambrose, St., 103, 120-1, 127, 130, 160, 163, 172 et seq., 180, 223, 239, 258, 261, 466
Amiens, 29, 333, 335
Amiens, cathedral of (Notre Dame), 2, 3, 7, 401, 403, 404, 410, 442
Amorica, 258

Amos the Prophet, 56
Andrew, St., 96, 105
Angers, city of, 201
Angilbert, St., 282
Anjou, 393, 424
Anne, St., mother of Our Lady, 47, 87, 136, 137, 290, 462, 463, 465, 471, 476, 477
Anselm of Canterbury, 365
Anselm of Laon, 360, 367
Anthony, St., desert father, 218, 224, 225, 315, 321, 466
Antioch, 122, 151, 152, 246, 254
Antonia Fort, 83
Apostles, church of the, in Paris, 208, 212
Apostles' Creed, 127, 129, 152 et seq.
Apostolic Constitutions, 112, 122-3
Aquitaine. See Eleanor of Aquitaine
Arabs, 270, 340 et seq., 396
Aramaic language, 82
Argenteuil, 376, 379, 380, 382
Arianism, 164, 177, 178, 183, 189, 208
Aristotle, 82, 180, 186, 261, 361, 363, 378
Arius, 149 et seq., 172, 173, 182
Arles, 144, 157, 258, 319, 455
Armenians, 453
Arminius, Germanic chief, 183
Arras, 424
Artois, 424
Assyrians, 91
Astrolabe, son of Abelard and Heloise, 374, 384
Athanasius, St., 48, 96, 149, 151, 163, 172, 223
Athena, Greek goddess, 113
Athens, 106, 113, 280
Attila, king of the Huns, 189 et seq., 262, 319, 343
Augustine, St., bishop of Hippo, 103, 112, 172 et seq., 214, 221, 223, 227, 259, 283, 313, 323, 365, 378
Augustine of Canterbury, St., 146, 231, 258
Augustinian monks, 182, 186
Augustus Caesar, 37, 39, 40, 49-50, 73, 172
Aurelian, Roman emperor, 106
Ausonius of Bordeaux, poet, 145, 320